Adolescence, Adolescents

Barbara Schneider Fuhrmann
Virginia Commonwealth University

Photographs and Illustrations by Gary L. Waynick

 **Little, Brown and Company**
Boston   Toronto

Library of Congress Cataloging-in-Publication Data

Fuhrmann, Barbara Schneider, 1940–
    Adolescence, adolescents.

    Includes index.
        1. Adolescent psychology.   2. Adolescence.
I. Title.
BF724.F8   1985   155.5   85-18049
ISBN 0-316-29564-7

Library of Congress Catalog Card No. 85-18049

ISBN 0-316-29564-7

9 8 7 6 5 4 3

MV

Published simultaneously in Canada by Little, Brown and Company (Canada) Limited

Printed in the United States of America

Credits and Acknowledgments

From *The Disappearance of Childhood* by Neil Postman. Copyright © 1982 by Neil Postman. Reprinted by permission of Delacorte Press.

From Thomas J. Cottle, *Children in Jail* (Boston: Beacon Press, 1977). © 1977 by Thomas J. Cottle.

From David Elkind, *The Hurried Child,* © 1981, Addison-Wesley, Reading, Massachusetts. Pgs. 17, 28, 29, 55 & xiii. Reprinted with permission.

From *Family Therapy Techniques* by Salvador Minuchin and Harold C. Fishman. Copyright © 1981 by the President and Fellows of Harvard College. Reprinted by permission of Harvard University Press.

From J. E. Cooper, J. Holman, and V. A. Braithwaite, "Self-Esteem and Family Cohesion: The Child's Perspective and Adjustment," *Journal of Marriage and the Family* 45, no. 1 (1983):155. Copyrighted 1983 by the National Council on Family Relations, 1910 West County Road B, Suite 147, St. Paul, Minnesota 55113. Reprinted by permission of the publishers and authors.

continued on page 556

Preface

A course in adolescent development should be designed to meet the needs of the students who enroll in it. Because those needs are likely to be diverse, such a course, and the book that provides its foundation, face a considerable challenge. Some students, primarily those who are majoring in the social sciences, will be interested in the actual phenomenon of adolescence, especially as it relates to other life stages, and will be attentive to the theory and research concerning adolescence. Others will be taking the course as part of their curricula in teacher education, social work, family life, nursing, public policy, pediatrics, or criminal justice; they will be interested not so much in the stage of development known as adolescence, but in the individuals we call adolescents. Consequently, the course must emphasize both themes: the scientific study of adolescence and the person-oriented understanding of adolescents.

The title of this text, *Adolescence, Adolescents,* was selected to convey these dual themes: the integration of theory and research concerning *adolescence* as a stage of development on the one hand, and concern for the individuals we know as *adolescents* on the other hand. The book is designed to be theoretical and experiential, academically sound and practical. The reader will find not merely an encyclopedic compendium of research studies, but also a survey of the most useful theories and findings concerning adolescence, tied together with an overriding consideration for the content's meaningfulness to readers who seek to understand both themselves and the young people with whom they are, or will be, interacting.

The premise of this book is that adolescence is not an isolated period, but rather a normal part of lifelong development. Adolescents are seen as individuals experiencing new ways of thinking and being, and dealing with the developmental changes of adolescence in various ways. Their heredity and their environments have inter-acted profoundly and dynamically to produce unique individuals who are coping with physiological, cognitive, emotional, and social changes. Our dual goal is to achieve an understanding of the changes of adolescence that apply to all young people in all times and all places, and to develop a concomitant appreciation of the impact that modern American society exerts on the adolescence experienced by today's youth. This text will prepare students to apply both developmental theory and environmental awareness to understanding adolescents and will enable them to reason about the meaning of adolescent behavior in their own experiences.

The first section of the book addresses the contexts of adolescence — those social environments that influence growth and make the experiences of one adolescent different from those of another. Included in Part I are the historical context of adolescence, the societal context, the family context, the peer context, and the school context. The range of topics is broad, and the coverage includes not only theory but also such real-life issues as the impact of stress, the significance of family roles and expectations, the need for peers against whom to measure oneself, the effects of the high school experience, and the role of the computer in the lives of adolescents.

Equipped with an understanding of the critical significance of the contexts in which an adolescent grows, we move on to the developmental aspects of adolescence that are common to all adolescents. Part II addresses normal, healthy aspects of adolescent development — those profound changes that occur as a result of matura-tion. Included here are physiological, sexual, cognitive, social/emotional, moral, and career development. In this section you will find comprehensive coverage of the most widely accepted and useful theories of development, together with the impli-cations of these theories for understanding and working constructively with adoles-cents in all settings. Topics include the effects of early *vs.* late maturation, current attitudes toward health and nutrition, adolescent attitudes toward a variety of sexual practices, the reasons adolescents avoid the use of contraceptives, the school's role in sexual stereotyping, cognitive development and creativity, learning styles, the rea-sons for adolescent egocentrism, the role of religion and morality, and young peo-ple's ''fear of failure'' and ''fear of success'' attitudes.

Although the emphasis throughout the text is on normal, healthy adolescent development, Part III addresses the issues facing the approximately 20 percent of the adolescent population who experience serious problems. Topics include behavioral disorders (we offer an extensive discussion of anorexia and bulimia), juvenile delin-quency, and drug use and abuse. Both the possible reasons for disturbed behavior and current attempts to treat troubled adolescents and their families are explored.

While this book has been divided into three distinct sections detailing different aspects of adolescence, we must emphasize that the sections do not necessarily stand in isolation from one another. The contexts of adolescence (Part I) are seen as vital to understanding differences in development (Part II), and both context and develop-ment are crucial to understanding the differences between healthy and unhealthy behavior (Part III). Therefore, the chapters are designed to be read in the sequence presented. Ample cross-references and a comprehensive index make it easy to locate topics and concepts. Photographs and illustrations provide immediate graphic reinforcement, and each was selected specifically to illustrate an important concept. After studying this book, you should have a thorough and useful understanding of the complexities of adolescent development.

An undertaking of this magnitude is never a completely individual task, even though a single author's name appears on the title page. I am indeed indebted to a number of people whose assistance and support have been most valuable: to Bill Bost and Chuck Ruch, who supported me both emotionally and with the time to devote to the project; to Gary Waynick, who so carefully and creatively designed and produced the illustrations and photographs; to Mylan Jaixen, who challenged me to begin and supported all my endeavors; and to the conscientious and helpful reviewers whose ideas contributed substantially to the quality of the finished product: Stephen A. Anderson, The University of Connecticut; Robert Bornstein, Miami University; Sheldon S. Brown, North Shore Community College; Milton K. Davis, Portland State University; Robert W. Enright, University of Wisconsin-Madison; Harold D. Grotevant, The University of Texas at Austin; and Elizabeth S. Henry, Old Dominion University. And to my many friends and students who read and responded to various portions of the text, thank you all.

Finally, I dedicate this book to David and to the memory of Tutu. They have taught me the meaning of love.

Barbara Fuhrmann

Brief Contents

Contents

Chapter 9. Personality Development

I

The Context of Adolescence

Each of us grows up in a specific social and cultural context, a context that has a highly significant impact on our experience and on the way in which we grow. Although there are many things we have in common, our different cultural experiences make us unique from one another. Thus although you and a person your age in China share common developmental characteristics, your life experiences are probably different, with resulting differences in your behaviors, attitudes, and thoughts.

The United States of the last quarter of the twentieth century has experienced rapid technological and cultural changes, which have had a tremendous impact on the lives of adolescents. In Section I we will detail and explore the contexts of adolescence, including Chapter 1: A Historical Perspective; Chapter 2: A Societal Perspective; Chapter 3: A Familial Perspective; Chapter 4: The Peer Context; and Chapter 5: The School Context. We will look at the way society, the family, peers, and the school influence the lives and experiences of adolescents.

1

A Historical Perspective

THE MYTHS OF ADOLESCENCE

Adolescence, probably more than any other period of human life, is subject to stereotypes and myths, commonly believed but not borne out in reality. Yet our perceptions of the people we call "adolescents" are colored by these myths and stereotypes. In popular literature and conversation, adolescence is frequently characterized as only a transitional stage, a period between childhood and adulthood that is necessarily stressful but will end with happy adjustment in adulthood. The stage is seen to create unavoidable problems between adolescents and their parents, who are all too frequently advised to wait the period out and all will be better. A closely related myth is that all adolescents are alike, influenced by the all-powerful "peer group" and diametrically opposed to the attitudes, opinions, and values of the adult world. Each of these views has been demonstrated to be false but nevertheless holds powerful sway in general opinion. Let's look at each separately before exploring possible reasons for them and finally developing a more realistic portrait of modern adolescents in the United States.

"Adolescence Is a Transitional Stage"

More than a transition. Virtually every definition of adolescence includes the word *transition,* thereby highlighting the bridge between childhood and adulthood, and emphasizing the preceding and following stages rather than adolescence itself. But adolescence isn't only a bridge; it is a highly important, meaningful time in its

Adolescence is more than a bridge between childhood and adulthood.

own right, and we do adolescents a disservice when we think of them as either large children or incomplete adults rather than intensely feeling and thinking human beings.

Real needs. In addition to the disservice we do in not considering adolescents as fully formed people, thinking of adolescence as only a transition leads to behavior on our part that could actually be dangerous. We tend to treat adolescence as a period of craziness that will eventually pass, and we therefore fail to attend to the very real needs of many adolescents. Minimizing the significance of adolescent behavior can be a dire mistake.

Every stage a transition. Finally, we tend to label adolescence as a transitional time without realizing that it is no more transitional than any other life stage. A toddler, for example, is in transition between infancy and childhood, just as a fifty-year-old may be in transition from parenthood to grandparenthood. Every life stage brings new challenges and new opportunities, and every one can be thought of as transitional. We negate adolescents' experience when we choose to single out the adolescent years as the only transitional ones.

Challenges of adolescence. Each stage of development, including adolescence, poses challenges that an individual must master in order to move to the next stage successfully. Havighurst (72) called these **developmental tasks,** and we will discuss them in greater detail later in this chapter. A developmental task is

> a task which arises at or about a certain period in the life of an individual, successful achievement of which leads to his happiness and to success with later tasks, while failure leads to unhappiness in the individual, disapproval by the society, and difficulty with later tasks. (Havighurst, 72, p. 2)

But adolescents also must deal with the here-and-now tasks of everyday living, which Adler (32) called ''life tasks,'' encompassing the areas of life that demand attention and must be dealt with throughout life: love and sex, work and school, friends and community (society), self, and the meaning of life (the existential tasks). Adolescence is a time not only to master the tasks that will assure a satisfactory adulthood, but also to deal with the here-and-now of the life tasks as they interplay in daily existence. ''*They* [adolescents] don't feel transitional. They feel very real right here and now, and it is in the here and now that we must address their needs'' (Lipsitz, 79, p. 5).

''Adolescence Is Necessarily Tumultuous''

Beginning with the nineteenth century, professional literature, popular literature, and general folklore have stressed the necessary turmoil of the adolescent years. Many writers have blithely assumed that adolescence is innately stressful, even though current research does not support such an assumption. In the view of adolescence as necessarily tumultuous, adolescents are considered to be normally pathological in their affect and behavior, which are characterized by overwhelming, uncontrollable, and chaotic emotions.

Basis of myth. The professional view of adolescence as tumultuous stems from the writings of G. Stanley Hall (04), who hypothesized that as the adolescent's body and its hormones were experiencing chaotic upheaval, so too the adolescent psyche was in chaos. Writers since then, even as recently as the 1960s, continued to describe adolescence as inherently stressful (Blos, 62, 67); and the 1980 edition of the *Diagnostic and Statistical Manual of Mental Disorders,* the manual that classifies mental pathology, describes adolescent turmoil as part of normal development (p. 66).

Challenges to myth. Margaret Mead (28) may have been the first to note that adolescence is not universally stressful when she studied the adolescent transitions in Samoa, which she viewed as continuous, pleasant, and cooperative. Although Mead's findings have been severely criticized (Freeman, 83), numerous researchers have investigated the extent of adolescent turmoil, and generally conclude that stress and anxiety are no more a part of normal adolescence than of any other stage of development. Stinchcombe (64) cited the research of Westley and Elkin, who found that among young people in Montreal, those who expected the promises of adolescence to be fulfilled behaved with conformity and harmony; those who doubted the promises exhibited disharmony and rebellion. He used this finding as the basis for his own work in studying the extent of rebellion and alienation in high school and found that rebellious behaviors, including delinquency, are most common among those who do not expect to gain future status from conformity in high school. For example, a person who anticipates discrimination in employment opportunities is likely to be resentful and hostile; one who expects a fair shake is not. From this perspective, only those who feel outside the mainstream are likely to experience a tumultuous adolescence.

The greatest challenge to the stressful conception of adolescence has come from the continuing work of Offer and his colleagues (75, 81), who have studied hundreds of normal adolescents and found that although the adolescent years require some readjustments, turbulence is not universal, nor is it even present in more than about 20 percent of the population (Offer, 81). The danger of characterizing adolescence as normally pathological results in our not expecting cooperative, harmonious behavior from the majority of adolescents, and, even more dangerously, in our dismissing the severity of the disturbances of the minority by calling adolescence a stage of turbulence.

Offer (75, 81) found that normal (white, black, hispanic; not pathological, not delinquent) adolescents reported no intense emotional discomfort, did not dislike their parents or their values, and did not feel rebellious against society. Norman (81), who surveyed thousands of adolescents, concurred. Although early adolescents (middle school) experience some difficulty in controlling their impulses, middle adolescents (high school) and older adolescents (post-high-school) have found suitable outlets for their emotional energy. Turmoil doesn't occur when transitions are gradual, and the "association between turmoil and adolescence has been overextended" (Offer, 75, p. 185). The research methodologies of both Offer and Norman have been criticized, but their findings have nevertheless had a significant impact on our perceptions of the extent of adolescent turmoil.

Persistence of myth. Why, then, has the perception of a tumultuous adolescence in the United States persisted? In addition to the influence of early theories of adolescence (which we will discuss shortly) and of the portrait painted of adolescents in literature (Spacks, 81), Offer (81) points to the mental health profession. Most of our data concerning adolescent behavior and attitudes has been drawn from the population of adolescents in psychological treatment. Case studies, in-depth interviews, and research studies have been conducted most often with an *abnormal* rather than a normal population, adolescents who are experiencing significant behavioral or emotional problems. Such adolescents are most accessible to researchers, but they do not fairly represent the large majority who do not display such problems. To test the perceptions of mental health professionals, Offer (81) asked a group of such professionals to complete the Offer Self-Image Questionnaire (the instrument he used to survey adolescent attitudes about themselves) as *they thought healthy adolescents would complete it.* Seven out of ten professionals described adolescents as significantly more disturbed than the normal adolescents in Offer's survey viewed themselves. These professionals even saw more problems with normal adolescents than disturbed and delinquent adolescents reported about themselves!

Most adolescents adjust to the changes of this period of their lives with good coping mechanisms. Some do better than others, just as some adults do better than others in coping with life's challenges. Adolescence is no more stressful, no more tumultuous, no more anxiety-ridden than any other period of life, and it is time we recognized this fact. Only when we recognize it can we possibly interact with adolescents in the growth-enhancing ways that will foster healthy, harmonious development.

"There Is an Unavoidable Generation Gap"

As children mature, their intellectual capacity increases; their bodies become more adultlike; they shift much of the focus of their lives away from their families; they develop their own identities and value systems; they become increasingly independent; and they may question the behavior, attitudes, and opinions of their elders. These phenomena are perfectly normal, necessary aspects of achieving adulthood, but adults are sometimes unprepared for the changes and therefore have "created a 'generation gap' by systematically distorting the adolescent question" (Offer, 81, p. 129).

Conflict between generations. The term *generation gap* was originally coined by Margaret Mead to describe the tension that exists between the members of the parent generation and the members of the adolescent generation as whole units and not between the parents and children in individual family units. Nevertheless, because current usage implies conflict within families as well as between generations, we will use the term to apply to both kinds of tension and misunderstanding.

Theories that emphasize the turmoil of adolescence imply, if they do not state directly, that the turmoil also leads to inevitable conflict between adults and teenagers. Researchers, especially during the relatively turbulent decade of the 1960s, sometimes themselves assumed such conflict (Elder, 80). It was assumed that each new generation believed that the previous one had failed in its efforts to create a humanitarian society and that the task of saving humanity therefore fell to them (Feuer, 69). There is, however, little evidence to support the existence of an unavoidable generation gap (Conger, 71; Friesen, 72; Petroni, 72; Elder, 80; Offer, 75, 81).

Continuity between generations. There is certainly a widening of experiences during adolescence that brings young people into contact with ideas and behaviors that they did not experience at home. The wider world, including the peer group, will affect the adolescent's thoughts and attitudes. The adolescent is no longer influenced only by parents, and some differences of opinion may well arise. But

Generation gap

research has demonstrated that "strong ties to peers do not necessarily imply weak ties to parents" (Elder, 80, p. 18). Most adolescents share the values of their parents, especially in the areas of religion, morality, and political ideology, even though more transient values, like dress and taste in music or leisure-time activities, may be quite different (Offer, 75).

In addition, areas most affected by rapid change create conflict between the younger and older generations. Specifically, in our time, sexual behavior and illegal drug use appear to be controversial, both between generations and within families.

Conger (71) reported on the results of several large surveys into the attitudes and beliefs of teenagers and their parents and found that the perceptions of differences, even by the teens and parents themselves, were significantly greater than the differences themselves — both adolescents and their parents perceived nonexistent differences. Petroni (72) concurred, finding that "presumed differences are more apparent than real" (p. 232), and hypothesized that the generation gap is an assumption of significant differences used to provide a reason for some lack of understanding between the generations. Conger (71), for example, found adolescents to be more liberal in their attitudes than their parents; perhaps this difference becomes generalized into the assumption that the two generations are unable to get along with each other.

Friesen (72) investigated the effects of three social forces on the views of adolescents: the peer group, the social class, and significant adults in the cultural group (such as parents and teachers), and found that adults who share the same cultural background were the most influential. Most adolescents adopt the value orientations of their parents.

The evidence is overwhelming. The generation gap is more myth than reality, and adult perceptions of adolescents as diametrically opposed to their values bear little resemblance to reality. Adolescents may adopt fads of dress, music, speech, and leisure-time activities; they are likely to question adult values; and they may have difficulty talking with parents, especially about sexual issues (Hass, 79); but we do them a major disservice when we interpret these behaviors as a rejection of important parental values.

"All Adolescents Are Alike"

Closely related to the myth of a generation gap is the myth that all adolescents are alike — "that they out there, the teenagers, are a homogeneous group. This leads to a dangerous mental set in which we assume the inevitability of a generation gap, because they are they and we are we" (Lipsitz, 79, p. 4). The overemphasis on troubled behavior and the influence of the peer group has led us to believe falsely that adolescents are somehow molded into a single group that thinks and acts together. Nothing is farther from the truth, and you need simply to recall your own experiences as an adolescent to verify this. In terms of physical, cognitive, psychological, moral, and social development, there is no group that displays more variability than do adolescents. Adding to our misperception of the homogeneity of adolescents is the fact that until recently virtually all empirical research with adolescents was conducted with adolescent males. We have simply assumed that the development of males and females is identical and are only now beginning to realize, primarily through the work of Gilligan (82), that girls differ developmentally from boys more than just physically. Instead of homogeneity, individual variability could well be the theme of adolescence (Gallatin, 76).

No group displays more variability than do adolescents.

Why the Myths?

The myths developed from biased data and mistaken perceptions. The early reliance of researchers on clinical data as a basis for generalization about all adolescents has contributed to our misperceptions of normal adolescents (Offer, 75, 81; Norman, 81). Furthermore, "Adolescence . . . is the world's most perfect projective device for adults. Adults' own fears and urges may interfere with their ability to correctly perceive what teenagers are really like" (Offer, 81, p. 121). As adolescents grow up, they are likely to threaten adults, especially their parents, who may be reminded of their own unfulfilled dreams, the possibility of losing influence over their children, and the possibility that their children may surpass them in accomplishments. These fears, added to the misinformation that has been generated by innaccurate theories and warnings in the popular media concerning the difficulties inherent in the adolescent years, combine to create the myths of adolescence.

A Nonmythical, Working Definition of Adolescence

When we speak of adolescents, we assume that everyone understands whom we are talking about; but a clear, universally understood definition of adolescence has not yet been developed. Adolescence as we now know it has neither a clear beginning nor a clear end. If we look only at biology, we generally identify the beginning of adolescence with **puberty**, the development of primary and secondary sexual characteristics, but even these cannot be pinpointed with any real accuracy. For girls, the first menstruation usually marks puberty; but, as we shall see later, this is not the first of the pubertal changes. For boys the changes may be even more subtle. But biology alone does not account for adolescence; cognitive, social, and psychological changes occur, and definitions of adolescence based on these changes would differ from one based only on biological ones. We might also use age as a defining characteristic of adolescence, but we all know from experience that two thirteen-year-olds can be vastly different in the rate and onset of adolescent changes. Grade in school has been used; in fact, our educational system seems to be based on the assumption that early adolescents go to middle or junior high schools, middle adolescents go to high schools, and late adolescents are in post-high-school training programs, colleges, or entry-level jobs.

In some societies and at one time in our history, adolescence was short if it existed at all. Entry into adulthood came with adult physique and child-bearing capacity; but in our increasingly technological society, physical adulthood alone is insufficient to assure societal contribution, and we have found it necessary to delay entry into adulthood until individuals are educated sufficiently to contribute. We have become geared to paper credentials and have thus delayed the onset of full adult responsibilities, including economic ones. In this society, physical maturity is reached in the middle teen years; social and legal responsibility is varied, with virtually all legal rights obtained by the age of 21; but at 21 many young people are still not economically responsible for themselves. Ironically, because of the lengthy educational process, our brightest young people are those who become full-fledged adults last. Those who leave school earlier also take on adult responsibilities earlier.

For a comprehensive definition of adolescence, we need a physiological perspective, a social perspective, a psychological perspective, and even a historical perspective. Your adolescence was similar in biological ways to everyone else's, but just as yours was culturally different from that of an Australian aborigine, it was psychologically different from that of your brother, and it was historically different from that of your great-grandparents. All these factors must be taken into account, for any single concept is severely limited.

For purposes of this book, then, we will say that adolescence extends from the onset of puberty (at about 10 or 11 in girls, 12 or 13 in boys) to the assumption of full adult responsibilities: physical, social, legal, and economic (usually about 21, but as early as 18 and as late as the mid-twenties or even thirties). Our emphasis will be primarily on students in middle schools and high schools, with some attention to post-high-school youth. Adolescence is "an open-ended period in which individual character development defines the nature of the period" (Offer, 75, p. 180), with social, cultural, and historical factors exerting significant influence over the nature of that development.

A BRIEF HISTORY OF CHILDHOOD AND ADOLESCENCE

The Development of Childhood

Having grown up in an era that has been described as "child-centered," in which it is virtually impossible to read all that has been written about childhood and adolescence, it may seem strange to read here that neither childhood nor adolescence has always existed in the way that they do today. Certainly, babies have always been born, and they have grown into adults, but they have not universally been set apart from adults nor thought of as qualitatively different from adults.

Early societies. The early Greeks and Romans paid scant attention to children; they were, of course, vitally interested in education, but in an education that pertained primarily to youth who had obtained the ability to reason and who could learn the self-determination necessary to achieve full-fledged maturity. Little fanfare was accorded to younger children.

With the Middle Ages, interest in education was lost, and in an era in which there was no literacy, no concept of education, and no idea of shame, childhood simply did not exist (Postman, 82). In the Middle Ages, a very high infant mortality rate probably contributed to weak emotional attachments between parents and children; after all, who would risk becoming attached to an infant who was likely to die? During medieval times childhood was clearly not important. No records of birth or age were kept; no children appeared in artwork prior to the twelfth century, and from the twelfth to the sixteenth centuries, children in art were portrayed simply as miniature adults. The differences in shape and proportion apparently went unrecognized, and children were dressed no differently than adults (Aries, 62). Also, up until the thirteenth century, parents resolved problems with their children by sending them off to monasteries, nunneries, or foster homes, or by selling them into servitude (de Mause, 74).

The birth of childhood. Childhood began to be important as a separate stage of development during the Reformation and Renaissance, when, instead of miniature adults, children were perceived as *potential* adults, in need of both protection and education (Aries, 62; de Mause, 74; Postman, 82). In the sixteenth century, Postman (82) contends, the popularization of the printing press and the development of social literacy may have "created a new definition of adulthood *based on reading competence,* and, correspondingly, a new conception of childhood *based on reading incompetence*" (p. 18). Although he was merely speculating, Postman (82) argues that with the arrival of large volumes of printed materials, there began to be some skills needed in order for children to gain access to the secrets of adulthood. Without reading skills, the books, maps, contracts, and deeds of the adult world were inaccessible. The idea of childhood thus came into existence, and even the dress and features of children in paintings began to be distinct from those of adults. By the end of the sixteenth century, children had distinct clothing and language and unique names, and were introduced to formal schooling. Books on pediatrics had arrived on the scene, and topics including sex, violence, illness, and death became taboo subjects for children's ears. Children were separated from adults both in their unique institutions and in the concepts that were deemed appropriate for them.

Parental responsibility. In 1693 John Locke wrote *Some Thoughts Concerning Education,* which placed responsibility on parents and teachers for what became written on the *tabula rasa* (empty slate) of the mind. With this responsibility arose the sense of parental guilt that made nurturing children a priority. Then, in the eighteenth century, Jean-Jacques Rousseau wrote *Emile* and clearly established in society's mind the idea that the child is important as an individual who sees, feels, and thinks qualitatively differently from adults, and that a child's intellectual and emotional life is important in its own right, and not only for its value to future adulthood.

Focus on childhood. Although the concept of childhood had its roots in Aristotle and Rousseau, it did not become a social fact until the sixteenth century. In the seventeenth and eighteenth centuries, parents began to try to understand their children, and in the nineteenth and twentieth centuries an interest arose in children as unique persons. In the mid-twentieth century, another new perspective developed, that of the helping relationship, in which acceptance and unconditional respect, as well as parental love, began to be granted to children (de Mause, 74). The twentieth century has also seen a dramatic rise in the importance of schooling and an emphasis on childhood that has made it an important economic stage; consumer items for children are big business, as are the social and legal worlds of children. Never before has society been so child-oriented.

The Invention of Adolescence

Adolescence is an even more recent phenomenon than is childhood. It is clearly a twentieth-century invention that arose out of society's economic need to delay entry into adulthood. Tribal cultures and agrarian societies did not need adolescence, and either entry into adulthood was marked ceremoniously with clear rites of passage or the transition was so gradual as not to be noticed.

Before adolescence. Many primitive cultures celebrate entry into adulthood with puberty rites, which may involve physical ordeal or mutilation (circumcision for boys, clitoridectomy for girls, scarification for either sex), extrusion from the parental household, symbolic clothing, and ceremonies that may go on for days (Cohen, 64; Lincoln, 81). Before the puberty rite, the individual is a child; after it he or she is a fully accepted adult, with the new status being clear both to the individual and the community. In other societies, adult status is granted gradually, as soon as an individual is capable of adult tasks. Among the Cheyennes, for example, children's contributions to the welfare of the family were accepted and rewarded, and children slowly attained adult status as they were increasingly capable of adult tasks (Hoebel, 60).

> In our own history, one can picture the typical agrarian extended family of the mid-19th century. As soon as they were able, children were given meaningful and appropriate tasks, tasks which contributed to the family's welfare and which were rewarded accordingly. As children became increasingly capable, their tasks changed, so that by the time their bodies matured to adulthood, they were also sociologically capable of adulthood. Although our great-grandparents did not experience the formal puberty rites practiced by some tribal cultures, their passage from child to adult was noted by a change in the clothing they wore. The transition from short to long pants was a clear indication that a boy had become a man, and his acquaintances treated him accordingly. (Fuhrmann, 83, p. 209)

Today, long pants no longer make an adult, and we have an extended, open-ended period known as adolescence, during which young people may experience several rites of passage (such as confirmation or bar or bas mitzvah), but do not attain adult status through them. They then create their own rites of passage by embracing symbols of adulthood — dress, smoking, drinking, sexual behavior — but still do not attain the rights of adults.

The invention of adolescence. Historical events of the last 150 years created the need for the invention of adolescence. Kett (77) identified three historical periods in the development of the concept of adolescence. In the Early Republic (1790–1840), the migration from the farms to the cities began, and with it came greater educational opportunities, more career choices, the advent of work apprenticeships, and the use of children as servants. In the Approaching Age of Adolescence (1840–

1900), the economic gap between the middle and lower classes became apparent; the urban industrial society created the problem of large numbers of individuals who were physically mature but socially and educationally immature; and children became an economic liability rather than the economic asset they had been in an agrarian economy. During this period three significant social movements contributed to the invention of adolescence: child-labor legislation, compulsory schooling, and the juvenile justice system. This period was followed by the Period of Adolescence (1900–present), in which adolescence is considered a second stage of childhood, a social condition, and a social fact (Bakan, 71).

The social movements identified as contributing directly to the idea of adolescence bear closer examination. All three, child-labor legislation, compulsory schooling, and the juvenile justice system, had publicly humanitarian motives and benefited children, but all had unforeseen economic, political, and social consequences as well (Bakan, 71; Shephard, 75; Kett, 77).

Child-labor legislation. With the Industrial Revolution came the need for cheap labor, and a "reign of terror" on children (Postman, 82, p. 54) ensued. In 1832, 40 percent of the factory workers in New England were children (Bakan, 71); since then the regulation of child labor has been a continually controversial issue. Whereas child-labor legislation is designed to protect children from harmful, even abusive working situations, the same legislation has effectively barred many youths from the hands-on experiences that could equip them to become productive citizens. Our society speaks conflictingly about work: on the one hand we extoll the virtues of work and the harm of idleness, but we effectively keep adolescents out of the economic mainstream, with an incredibly high teen unemployment rate as a result. Child-labor legislation contributes to the concept of adolescence by keeping young people out of the workforce.

Compulsory schooling. The increasing industrialization of the turn of the century demanded ever-increasing skill from its workers, and industry, labor, and parents who were tired of slaving in factories sought to extend schooling. Children not only needed to be trained for more complex forms of work, but they also needed to be kept off the streets, and compulsory schooling was the result. In 1890, one in 18 youths, aged 14 to 17, was in school; by 1920 the proportion had jumped to one in three; and by the 1950s it had become four out of five (Elder, 80). The social consequences of compulsory schooling have been enormous: there has been an increase in the segregation of adolescents from both adults and younger children with an attendant rise in the significance of the peer group; there has been an increase in the social inequality resulting from differing levels of access to school rewards and life opportunities; significant functions that once were attended to in the home have been shifted to the schools (child care, socialization, and career preparation, for example); and the power of the state over the lives of children has been increased tremendously. The school district, not parents, determines whether an individual will even attend school, what school and what program that student will attend, and even, to some degree, what his or her chances for future success will be. The school both opens and closes many of life's doors, and compulsory schooling has contributed greatly to the existence of a prolonged adolescence in our society.

prolonged adolescence in our society.

Juvenile justice. By 1900 more than one third of the population of the United States had migrated to the cities, and with urbanization came a rise in crimes against property as well as a problem with unsupervised children in the streets. In 1875 came the first call for the state to stand *in loco parentis* (in place of parents) (Bakan, 71), and the idea of a justice system different from that for adults was born. The Illinois Juvenile Court Act, passed in 1899, was the result of the reform movement led by Jane Addams and others, generally middle-class women, who were also responsible for the child-labor and compulsory-attendance laws (Shephard, 75).

Although the juvenile justice system was established to protect children from the punishment philosophy of the adult courts and to treat children as a wise parent would, some historians have argued that it (as well as the other two reforms) was really a result of a paternalistic attitude on the part of middle-class reformers who were attempting to alter the inappropriate behavior of low-income immigrant children (Shephard, 75). Regardless of the motives, the idea spread rapidly, and by 1925 all but two states had juvenile courts. The differential treatment of children and adolescents further separated adolescents from adults, and although it removed the young from the rigidities of the adult system, it also suspended fundamental human rights. In juvenile courts, until very recently, the consideration of due process was not obligatory, and only in the juvenile system can an individual be detained even if no law has been broken (Shephard, 75).

Following the invention of adolescence, G. Stanley Hall (1904) popularized the concept with the publication of his monumental two-volume work, *Adolescence: Its Psychology and Its Relations to Physiology, Anthropology, Sociology, Sex, Crime, Religion, and Education.* Since then theorists, educators, researchers, and media personnel have contributed to its entrenchment in the American scene through lectures, books, films, magazine articles, TV documentaries, movies, and research studies. And adolescence today is not like it has been in previous decades. History and social occurrences indeed affect our experience and behavior.

Adolescence: 1900–Now

1900–1930. At the turn of the century, adolescents faced far fewer decisions than they do today. Most took on responsibilities much like those of their parents; they established economic independence, left home, married, and had families, in that order, but today a young person frequently leaves home and marries before establishing economic independence (Elder, 80). Parents may have exerted significantly more control over their children in preindustrial times, for children remained centered in the home for much longer. But with industrialization, the home lost some of its influence over adolescents, and by the 1920s the significance of the peer group began to be noticed, especially in the permissiveness that characterized the "Roaring Twenties" (Kett, 77). Along with permissiveness came a rise in juvenile delinquency, which was viewed as a response to the rapid change brought on by urbanization, immigration, and the resultant loss of familial and social controls (Elder, 80).

1930–1950. Although the historical events of the 1930s (the Great Depression) and the 1940s (World War II) were quite different from each other, their effects on adolescents were consistent. Both served to eliminate the hedonism of the 1920s and emphasize serious economic and political concerns (Kett, 77). Both also intensified class distinctions, with the affluent prolonging adolescence by remaining in school and the less affluent leaving school for work or military service (Elder, 80). During the 1930s and 1940s school size began to increase, and students began being segregated into age groups through the rise of junior high schools. It was a time of seriousness, hard work, and increasing interaction with peers. Following World War II, child psychology entered its "boom" period, both in terms of research and in terms of the popularization of that research through "how-to" books and articles for parents. Children and adolescents began being central in the lives of families, who expended much energy in learning to understand them (Elkind, 81).

1950s. Those of us who experienced adolescence in the 1950s were known as the "silent generation." We lived in a time of peace, affluence, and unbridled optimism for the future (Kett, 77). The role of formal education was expanding, as was the influence of youth groups and peer groups. We were pampered with social legislation, TV, and the promise of college; and a great deal of attention to the influence of the peer group began to appear in the professional and popular literature of the time (Elder, 80). We were indulged, even spoiled, for our parents were likely to fear repressing us through too much discipline (Elkind, 81). We were relatively free, optimistic, and generally enjoyed the good life. The time was one of relative normalcy.

1960s. In the 1960s the babies that were born in the post-war baby boom entered college (Americans aged 14 to 24 increased 52 percent between 1960 and 1970) (Elder, 80), creating more college students than ever before, and social emphasis began to be placed on *youth* rather than on younger adolescents. Youth can be viewed as yet another social invention, in response to the increasing need to delay entry into adulthood (Elder, 80). Racial awareness and the civil rights movement grew, especially on college campuses; and social protest, political protest, the Vietnam War, and the violence of the 1968 Democratic Convention in Chicago, along with increased drug use and sexual permissiveness, made the 1960s a time of the greatest activism among young people. Young people became extremely visible, yet also only marginally attached to the mainstream of society, and delinquency was seen as an adaptation to the disparity of the American dream of the 1950s and the constraints of social position that became evident in the 1960s. The 1960s were also a time of renewed interest by parents and educators in "achievement," for the launch of Sputnik in 1957 had put America on notice. The spoiled children of the 1950s began to be the stressed children of the 1960s (Elkind, 81). The 1960s were a time of rebellion.

1970–now. The 1970s were marked by conflicting events and movements. Whereas the adolescents of the seventies were children of the stress of the 1960s, they also experienced an era in which hard work and material interests replaced the social protest of the preceding decade. Emphasis was placed on the decline of the traditional family, with lower family cohesion and satisfaction reported (Offer, 81) and an increase in experimentation with alternative lifestyles. But there was also a corresponding increase in pressure from the family to achieve and grow up fast: "the behavior, language, attitudes, and desires — even the physical appearance — of adults and children are becoming increasingly indistinguishable" (Postman, 82, p. 4). In the 1980s, the pressures continue.

THEORIES EMPHASIZING DISCONTINUITY IN ADOLESCENCE

With an understanding of the social and historical conditions that influence the creation of modern adolescence, it is now time to turn our attention to the various theories of adolescence that have shaped our thinking about the people we call adolescents. A theory is a conceptualization of the world built upon observation, insight, experience, research, and reason. A theory involves both inductive reasoning, in which observation informs generalizations, and deductive reasoning, in which particulars are extracted from accepted principles. In order to be meaningful, a theory should be clear, consistent, and above all testable.

Theories concerning adolescence have developed in a number of different disciplines, most notably biology, psychology, sociology, and anthropology. They can also be divided into theories that hypothesize turmoil as a normal adolescent phenomenon and those that do not. Although we have already noted that the turmoil theory has not been borne out by empirical evidence, it is both interesting and an aid to understanding to review the highly influential theories that shaped the expectation that adolescence is innately stressful and anxious.

Turmoil theory, which posits a necessary and significant emotional disruption in adolescence, can be traced to the romantic writers of the eighteenth and nineteenth centuries, who seemed to enjoy writing about emotional disequilibrium, turmoil, mood swings, unpredictability, unhappiness, and conflict with parents.

Biological Theory

Hall. G. Stanley Hall (04) originally trained as a theologian and philosopher but became fascinated with physiological psychology and used current biological speculation to apply the principles of evolution to human development (Ross, 72). His theory is fascinating but extremely difficult to test with scientific methods. It was, however, the first major treatise on adolescence and as such was very powerful in its influence. Hall derived his theory from the work of Ernst Haeckel, a nineteenth-century biologist, who had applied the theory of evolution to prenatal development, positing that **ontogeny** (the sequence of growth in an individual organism) recapitulates **phylogeny** (the sequence of development of an organism's ancestors during evolution). That is, the experiential history of the race becomes a part of the genetic constitution of the individual, and each individual passes through the stages that repeat the history of humanity (Beller, 68). In embryonic development, the fetus passes through all the stages that the human race passed through during its evolution, beginning as a single-celled creature and moving through the stage of being a gill-breathing swimmer in early embryonic development to a human being with arms, legs, and all the equipment necessary for further human development. Hall applied the theory to postnatal development, identifying infancy as a reenactment of prehistoric stages of human development; childhood as a reenactment of a cave-dwelling culture, in which interaction is based in issues of power and authority; preadolescence as a reenactment of tribal cultures; adolescence as a reenactment of the transitional period between savagery and civilization; and late adolescence as a reenactment of the beginning of modern civilization (Gallatin, 76).

From Hall's point of view, adolescents could be viewed as a cross between savages and civilized peoples, with primitive and humane impulses in constant conflict, and he called adolescence a time of *sturm und drang,* or storm and stress. Though the theory itself is now interesting primarily for its historical significance, Hall did correctly observe that males and females develop differently, that adolescence is the most important time for developing a sense of individuality, and that adolescents are capable of reasoning, of complex emotional expression, and of appreciating beauty (Gallatin, 76).

Gesell. Arnold Gesell (49), a biologist, theorized that growth is laid down in the genes and always develops in a sequence of progression followed by partial regression, a kind of "three steps forward, two backward" philosophy in which what is learned at one stage has to be integrated in the next. He saw adolescents as alternating between integration and balance on the one hand and tension and moodiness on the other and thus contributed another voice to the turmoil theories of adolescence.

Zeller. Disharmony in adolescence was also predicted by Zeller (51), a biologist who postulated a relationship between changes in the constitution of the body and changes in the psychological functions. The incredible bodily and hormonal changes of adolescence are reflected, therefore, in psychological disharmony as well, resulting in a critical attitude, nervousness, anxiety, and impulsivity (Beller, 68).

These biological views of adolescence imply that all adolescents will progress through highly predictable, inevitable sequences of behavior related directly to their changing physiology. Thus they contribute to the myth that stress and turmoil are an unavoidable aspect of adolescent behavior.

Psychological Theory

The Freuds. Sigmund Freud (43) proposed a complex theory of human development based on instinctual drives. In adolescence, the basic drives of sex and aggression are reawakened following the relatively quiet years of childhood, and the young person is faced with tremendous conflict between desires and societal "rules." (We will discuss Freudian theory more completely in Chapter 9, Psychological Development.) Freud's daughter, Anna Freud (46, 58), extended her father's interest in adolescence and emphasized the internalized conflict between sexual impulses (id) and guilt (superego) as the primary characteristic of adolescence. Hers is the most extreme of all the turmoil theories (Offer, 81), for she describes a continual battle between the impulses and conscience, with neither ever winning successfully. The adolescent who gives in to the sexual impulses may frantically search for new love objects, engage in promiscuous behavior, and experience flighty and meaningless relationships. An adolescent who succeeds in repressing the impulses may repress all pleasures and become ascetic and emotionless. The task is to develop an appropriate balance (ego) between satisfaction and self-control in sexuality.

Sullivan. Sullivan (53a, b) was trained by Freud but later rejected the Freudian notion that sexuality is the basic motive in life while continuing to recognize the importance of sexuality as it relates to other needs. Rather, he suggested, we are driven by a need to overcome basic feelings of anxiety that probably developed in infancy when our parents disapproved of our childish interest and pleasure in our genitals. Because our parents' approval was so important, we denied those early sexual impulses. In adolescence, however, the sexual impulses are reawakened by the action of the hormonal changes of puberty. There ensues a clash between the need to satisfy sexual drives and the need to be free of the anxiety resulting from disapproval. Furthermore, the adolescent is aware that he or she is supposed, eventually, to form an intimate attachment and to find sexual pleasure, but this expectation is in opposition to the concept of sex as the source of anxiety. Finally, stereotypes about the other sex leave the adolescent anxious about how to relate to them. Male adolescents deal with the conflict between lust and intimacy by classifying girls as either "good" (marriageable) or "bad" (fun to be sexual with). Thus a major task of male adolescence is to learn that girls can be both good and sexual. The difficulty of the task contributes to the stress of adolescence (Sullivan, 53a, 53b).

Sociological Theory

Lewin. Lewin (39), a social scientist, was interested in the effects of the environment and its expectations on behavior. As he saw it, behavior is a function of the interaction between the characteristics of an individual (sex, age, intelligence, talents) and the environment (family, neighborhood, school). In adolescence, both the individual and the environment change dramatically, and stress is the result. The individual must cope with a multitude of physical changes, and with a host of new expectations. In addition, the adolescent is accepted neither as a child nor as an adult, and therefore occupies a unique and stressful position as a "marginal man," with neither childish behaviors and expectations nor adult behaviors and expectations being consistently applied. The environment is inconsistent in its demands: it wants adolescents to be "responsible" (adult), but also "obedient" (child). Both childish behaviors (dependency, silliness) and adult behaviors (smoking, drinking, sex) are taboo, and adolescents experience tremendous conflict as a result of these discrepancies in expectations. And this conflict coincides with their experience of rapid and unpredictable physical and emotional changes. As a result of their conflicts, they may attempt clarity by developing extreme views on subjects about which they know little.

All the theories mentioned here, whether they originate from a biological, psychological, or sociological perspective, are similar in their description of adolescence as a time of great discontinuity. What was appropriate as children is no longer appropriate, and there are no guidelines for how adolescents should manage their new bodies, new thoughts, new emotions, new impulses, and new desires.

THEORIES EMPHASIZING CONTINUITY IN ADOLESCENCE

Anthropological Theory

Mead. Since anthropology involves the study of the similarities and differences among cultural groups and questions the universality of any single pattern of development, it is not surprising that it was an anthropologist who first challenged the turmoil theories. In *Growing Up in Samoa* (1928), Margaret Mead publicized the fact that in Samoa adolescence poses no conflicts or stresses. She observed, for example, that there were no rituals surrounding the onset of menstruation and no sexual taboos. Cultural expectations for behavior and emotionality were no different for adolescents than for children or adults. As a result, Mead saw that growing up was continuous, with no surprises and no conflict. (These views have been challenged, most recently by Freeman [83], who claims that Mead's methods and observations were biased and that the Samoa that he studied gave a surface impression of calm that masks a society that experiences no less turmoil than more highly developed ones.)

Benedict. Benedict (54), in studying the varieties of experiences among different cultures, noted that our society, unlike some others, actually emphasizes the contrasts between children and adults. Whereas children are expected to be nonresponsible, obedient, and sexless, adults are expected to be responsible, to command obedience, and to be sexual. We thus teach our children discontinuity in several important areas, and do not provide the supports necessary for effective transition from one state to another. She contrasts these discontinuities with behaviors that are continuous, such as eating three meals a day or wearing clothing. As soon as they are able, children in our society learn to eat three meals a day and to wear clothing for the purpose of modesty. As they grow older and become adults, they need make no transitions, for eating three meals and wearing clothes are expected of adults as well as of children. In these two examples, they need not unlearn anything they have previously learned.

Although Benedict would argue that continuity in all aspects of behavior makes for the smoothest adolescence, she also notes that some societies that do expect different behaviors for children and adults nevertheless smooth the transitions by establishing very specific age-graded groups, with ceremonious graduation from one to the next. What is appropriate in one group is not appropriate in another, but everyone knows who is in each group, and the expectations are clear and consistent within each group. With such public graduations from group to group, nonconflicted behavior is quite possible at each stage; it is even possible to be homosexual in one stage and heterosexual in the next. Consistently knowing what's expected makes the difference (Benedict, 54).

Psychosocial Theory

Bandura. From the perspective of a social scientist, Bandura (64) links stress in adolescence with poor socialization resulting from parent-child relationships that are based only on the exercise of power. According to Bandura (64), stable, loving families that grant children appropriate rights and responsibilities foster adolescents who are well socialized: conventional and conforming. On the other hand, families in which there is a great deal of conflict, characterized by fights and arguments, foster aggressive, hostile, volatile adolescents. Adolescence is stormy only if families make it so.

Spranger. Spranger (55), a psychologist, offered what Gallatin (76) termed an **individual variability** theory. Spranger believed that people are so individual and unique that no single theory can explain behavior. Adolescence is not necessarily stressful, though it may be so. Spranger identified three basic patterns of growth in adolescence: stormy, calm, and dynamic. For some, storm and stress indeed characterize development, and adolescence is painful. For others, it is continuous and peaceful. And for yet others, both storm and calm are present. These dynamic young people experience crises, but overcome them by participating in their own development (Gallatin, 76).

Offer. Spranger's conceptualization of development is remarkably similar to the findings of Offer (75), whose research with adolescent boys reveals three patterns of growth that remain stable throughout childhood and adolescence. Apparently, the psychological system of development is established early, and coping strategies remain consistent throughout life. Approximately 23 percent of his sample of 73 normal adolescent males experienced **continuous growth**; 33 percent experienced **surgent growth**; 20 percent experienced **tumultuous growth**; and the remainder displayed a combination of continuous and surgent patterns. (Whether these patterns apply to girls has not been tested.)

The continuous growth subjects had good genetic and environmental backgrounds; stable families who encouraged independence, respect, trust, and affection; and good relationships with peers and adults. They were purposeful, self-assured, aware of their feelings, able to cope with trauma, and able to integrate and use experiences to further their own growth.

The surgent growth subjects, the largest of the three groups, grew in developmental spurts, sometimes mastering tasks well, other times getting stuck. They exhibited cycles of progression and regression, and their self-esteem and coping skills wavered. They had experienced more family problems, sometimes were in conflict with their parents, and developed many skills somewhat later than their continuous growth peers. Their overall adjustment was good, but they tended to suppress emotions.

Only the tumultuous growth subjects demonstrated considerable inner turmoil, behavioral problems, consistent self-doubts, parental conflict, and psychological pain. They tended to come from the lower socioeconomic groups, had strong but conflicted family ties, were unsuccessful academically, and had not developed good communication skills. These are the 20 percent of the population about whom we should be most concerned, for they are likely to carry their conflicts into adulthood (Offer, 75).

Developmental Theory

Both the continuity and the changes inherent in human development are addressed by those who consider themselves to be developmentalists. From a developmental point of view, life consists of a sequence of invariant stages, each qualitatively different from the others. There is a logical relationship between the stages, and characteristics within any one stage can be generalized to the entire population in that stage. The approach of the chapters in Part II of this book, ''Individual Development and Common Issues of Development,'' is developmental. Here we will discuss the developmental tasks of Havighurst (72), which have already been introduced, with only a brief introduction to the theories of Erikson, Piaget, and Kohlberg, which will be developed fully in later chapters.

Havighurst. According to Havighurst (72, p. 1) each individual ''learns his way through life.'' We learn to walk, skip, and run; and we learn to become parents and raise children, with each task being best learned at a specific time during development.

> The tasks the individual must learn — *the developmental tasks of life* — are those things that constitute healthy and satisfactory growth in our society. They are the things a person must learn if he is to be judged and to judge himself to be a reasonably happy and successful person. *A developmental task is a task which arises at or about a certain period in the life of the individual, successful achievement of which leads to his happiness and to success with later tasks, while failure leads to unhappiness in the individual, disapproval by the society, and difficulty with later tasks.* (Havighurst, 72, p. 2)

Timing is important, for there are critical periods during which the individual is most sensitive to learning particular tasks, and learning is therefore easier. "When the body is ripe, and society requires, and the self is ready to achieve a certain task, the teachable moment has come" (Havighurst, 72, p. 7). This does not mean that if a task is not learned at the critical time, it cannot be learned later, but rather that the later learning is likely to be more difficult. Healthy relationships with members of both sexes, for example, are learned in adolescence. The young person who does not develop these friendships then will have great difficulty learning them later, and in fact may never be as well accomplished in relating to both men and women as if he or she had learned at the proper time.

Implicit in the quotation "When the body is ripe, and society requires, and the self is ready" are the three sources of developmental tasks. Physical maturation is necessary, especially for tasks like walking and sexual activity; the cultural pressures of society create the need for some tasks, especially tasks like reading and social responsibility; and personal values and aspirations play a role, especially for tasks like choosing an occupation or a life philosophy. Most tasks require a combination of all three sources, with considerable cultural diversity in some. The most universal tasks rely most significantly on physical maturation; virtually every healthy individual, regardless of culture or historical time period, learns to walk. Others are more variable, as we will see when we look more closely at the tasks Havighurst proposed; and we might add some that have arisen in the past decade. Finally, some tasks recur throughout development; getting along with others and being socially responsible are required at all stages from childhood on.

Havighurst's six stages and the developmental tasks appropriate to each are outlined in Table 1.1. We will look more specifically at the tasks of adolescence, as outlined in the third column of Table 1.1.

1. *Achieving new and more mature relations with age mates of both sexes.* With the sexual changes of puberty, adolescents must develop new ways of interacting with one another, with gender playing a new and different role. Adolescents must learn to look at girls as female peers and boys as male peers, and must learn ways of working together harmoniously. Success with this task means good social adjustment throughout life.

2. *Achieving a masculine or feminine social role.* Fifty years ago this task was clearer than it is today. Roles are being defined more broadly, and adolescents need to examine the variety of roles possible in order to make informed choices.

3. *Accepting one's physique and using the body effectively.* Young people must learn about their bodies and the changes that are occurring, learn to accept the bodies they have, and learn to use them in healthy and effective ways.

4. *Achieving emotional independence from parents and other adults.* The rapid social change of our modern postindustrial society is making this task more complicated than it once was. The increased dependence forced by an extended adolescence, combined with pressures to achieve and grow up fast, create conflicting situations for young people and their parents, who need to understand the probable effects of extended dependence.

Table 1.1
Havighurst's Developmental Tasks

Infancy/Early Childhood	Middle Childhood	Adolescence	Early Adulthood	Middle Age	Later Maturity
1. Learning to walk	1. Learning physical skills necessary for ordinary games	1. Achieving new and more mature relations with age mates of both sexes	1. Selecting a mate	1. Assisting teenaged children to become responsible and happy adults	1. Adjusting to decreasing physical strength and health
2. Learning to take solid food	2. Building wholesome attitudes toward oneself	2. Achieving a masculine or feminine social role	2. Learning to live with a marriage partner	2. Achieving adult social and civic responsibility	2. Adjusting to retirement and reduced income
3. Learning to talk	3. Learning to get along with age-mates	3. Accepting one's physique and using the body effectively	3. Starting a family	3. Reaching and maintaining satisfactory performance in one's occupational career	3. Adjusting to the death of a spouse
4. Learning to control the elimination of body wastes	4. Learning appropriate masculine or feminine social roles	4. Achieving emotional independence from parents and other adults	4. Rearing children	4. Developing adult leisure-time activities	4. Establishing an explicit affiliation with one's age group
5. Learning sex differences and sexual modesty	5. Learning fundamental skills in reading, writing, and calculating	5. Preparing for marriage and family life	5. Managing a home	5. Relating oneself to one's spouse as a person	5. Adopting and adapting social roles in a flexible way
6. Forming concepts and learning language to describe social and physical reality	6. Developing concepts necessary for everyday living	6. Preparing for an economic career	6. Getting started in an occupation	6. Accepting and adjusting to the physiological changes of middle age	6. Establishing satisfactory physical living arrangements
7. Getting ready to read	7. Developing conscience, morality, and a scale of values	7. Acquiring a set of values and an ethical system as a guide to behavior — developing an ideology	7. Taking on civic responsibility	7. Adjusting to aging parents	
	8. Achieving personal independence	8. Desiring and achieving socially responsible behavior	8. Finding a congenial social group		
	9. Developing attitudes toward social groups and institutions				

Body acceptance

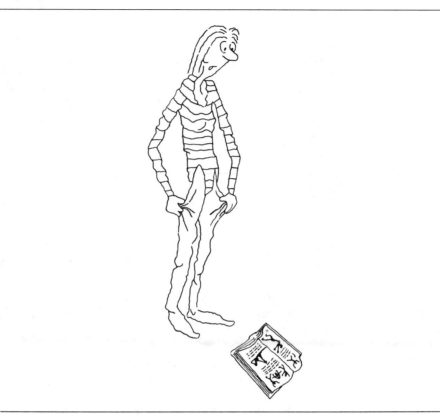

5. *Preparing for marriage and family life.* Implicit in this task is the assumption that most will marry and raise families. While it is true that most people, even in the 1980s and 1990s, are likely to do so, there are more single adults in the United States today than at any time in history; perhaps it is time to change the wording of this task to "exploring alternative adult lifestyles, and making tentative choices concerning the role of marriage and family in adulthood."

6. *Preparing for an economic career.* During the adolescent years career and vocational education and guidance should play an important role in preparing young people to become productive citizens.

7. *Acquiring a set of values and an ethical system as a guide to behavior — developing an ideology.* Chapter 10 will deal with this highly important task of developing a philosophy of life.

8. *Desiring and achieving socially responsible behavior.* The individual's responsibility to the community is developed in adolescence.

According to Havighurst, if these eight tasks of adolescence are achieved successfully, the tasks of adulthood will be made easier, and it is likely that adulthood will be successful as well.

Erikson. Perhaps the most comprehensive developmental theory of all is that of Erikson, whose psychosocial theory includes aspects from virtually all the other theories. Erikson (59) identified eight "Ages of Man," from infancy through old age, each characterized by a task that he called a "normative crisis," a central conflict that must be resolved successfully in preparation for future stages. We will discuss Erikson's theory in considerable detail in Chapter 9. For introductory purposes, it suffices to note that in this theory adolescence may be more or less conflict-ridden. Individual variability depends on the successful resolution of earlier tasks. If an individual has difficulty, for example, with the task of infancy — developing a healthy trust in the world — that lack of basic trust will make achievement of all future tasks difficult. An adolescent who experiences extreme conflict in the basic task of adolescence — achieving the sense of individuality known as *identity* — is likely to have had difficulty with earlier tasks, and may have a problematic adulthood as well.

Piaget; Kohlberg. Jean Piaget (discussed thoroughly in Chapter 8) used a developmental approach to the study of cognitive development and discovered that children at different stages of development think in qualitatively different ways, with each stage, of course, building on the previous one. Lawrence Kohlberg (Chapter 10) identified specific, sequential stages of moral reasoning, with people at different stages of moral development using very different arguments to defend their moral choices.

Developmental approaches to the study of human behavior have become popular because they meet the needs of sound theory. Those selected for discussion both here and in later chapters were built on observation, research, and reason. They are clear, consistent, and testable, and have provided us with a conceptualization of human development that is clearly helpful in understanding and working with both individuals and groups.

TODAY'S ADOLESCENTS

Empirical evidence gathered from adolescents themselves contradicts the pervasive myths that adolescence is necessarily stressful, that adolescents and their parents are doomed to travel a collision course during the teen years, and that all adolescents are alike. Two researchers, Offer (75, 81), and Norman (81), have provided us with the most comprehensive data concerning how adolescents themselves report their adolescent experiences, and although the two researchers used very different methods, their findings are remarkably consistent. Most adolescents cope well and move into adulthood relatively smoothly.

Offer's Findings

In 1975, Offer published the findings of his longitudinal research with normal male high school students. He first interviewed 73 14-year-old boys, and followed 61 of them until they were 22-year-olds. Psychological tests, teachers' ratings, parents' ratings, self-ratings, and interviews revealed the data on which the observations of the three patterns of growth — continuous, surgent, and tumultuous — were drawn. You will remember, too, that he found that only about 20 percent of the sample experienced a tumultuous pattern, and that the remainder displayed relatively healthy coping skills and satisfaction with their lives. Offer has continued and extended his investigations into the concerns, feelings, wishes, and fantasies of adolescents themselves, and in 1981 published the results of widespread investigation with normal, middle-class adolescent males and females in several different countries in the 1960s and again in the late 1970s and 1980. He found that, in direct contrast with turmoil theory, adolescents who are not scathed by external crises tend to "mirror in their adulthood their parents' behavior, affective range, and cognitive processes" (Offer, 81, p. 129). They are, in fact, "confident, happy, and self-satisfied" (Offer, 81, p. 83).

OSIQ. To study adolescents' perceptions of themselves, Offer used the Offer Self-Image Questionnaire (OSIQ), which had been demonstrated to tap into multiple areas of experience and to provide valid self-descriptions by the subjects. The OSIQ consists of 130 items that measure: (1) the psychological self, consisting of impulse control, emotional tone, and body and self-image; (2) the social self, consisting of social relationships, morals, and vocational-educational goals; (3) the sexual self; (4) the family self; and (5) the coping self, consisting of mastery of the external world, psychopathology, and superior adjustment. In addition to being administered in the early 1960s and again in the late 1970s and 1980 to normal teenagers in the U.S. and several other countries (primarily in Western Europe), it was also used with juvenile delinquents and psychiatric patients for comparative purposes. His findings follow, by area of testing.

Psychological self. Normal young people in the United States and in the several other countries studied enjoy life, are generally happy, and feel self-confident, relaxed, in control, strong, and healthy. Girls are more negative about their bodies than boys. Most adolescents reported some anxiety, but the anxiety is situationally induced and not pervasive. For example, anxiety around taking tests or going on a blind date would be reported, not a generalized, unaccounted-for anxiety. Adolescents generally relate to their parents in positive ways, but increasing autonomy is important and provides the context for parent-teen conflict when it occurs. The normal subjects reported decidedly better psychological self-images than did their delinquent and disturbed peers.

Social self. Normal subjects generally reported high values and positive social relationships, including work values, but there were some differences found between the 1960s and the 1970s samples, which we will discuss shortly.

Sexual self. In contrast to popular notions about sexual anxiety in adolescents, the samples studied were not afraid of their sexuality, which they found to be generally pleasurable. Males were more open to sexual feelings than females, but there were no differences either from one culture to another or from one decade to another.

Familial self. In all normal samples, families were found to be harmonious and well-functioning. There was, however, a marked difference between the normal and the disturbed and delinquent groups. Both the disturbed and the delinquent groups reported very bad feelings toward their parents, and both felt outside the structure of the family. The implications of this finding for understanding the origins of disturbance and delinquency are enormous.

Coping self. In contrast to the deviant groups, who saw themselves as coping poorly, normal adolescents across cultures felt competent to resolve daily problems without excessive pain or suffering.

That historical events contribute to adolescent experience was also demonstrated in this study. Although all normal adolescents reported positive self-images, the self-images of the late 1970s and 1980 sample were less positive than those of the 1960s sample. Those in the more recent sample had somewhat less self-confidence and were more easily hurt and less self-controlled. Their social self-images were most affected. Offer attributes the differences to historical events. Those who were adolescents in the early- to mid-1960s were children in the optimistic 1950s, but those who were adolescents in the late 1970s grew up in stressful times: civil rights demonstrations, Watergate, Viet Nam, and the like. They were the first children regularly to see world turmoil in living color on the nightly news, and although they have remained competent and confident, their self-images are not quite so optimistic as those of the previous generation. Family dynamics, relationships within and outside the family, cultural conditions, and historical situations affect each child and adolescent in complex ways.

Norman's Findings

Norman (81) wanted to survey as many adolescents as possible to discover their attitudes on a broad range of topics. He solicited written responses from high school students by publishing a questionnaire in high school magazines, conducted brief interviews with volunteers in shopping malls, and conducted in-depth interviews as well. In all, 160,000 young people were surveyed, with brief interviews conducted with 857 and in-depth interviews conducted with 100. Attitudes were gathered from young people regarding sex, drinking and drugs, school, friends, problems and fears, their parents' marriages, siblings, home rules and responsibilities, problem behavior, religion, race, the future, and the kind of advice they would give to parents. Although the methodology was not scientifically rigorous, the sheer number of responses is impressive. Norman's findings are consistent with those of Offer, which dispute the turmoil theories of adolescence. Many of the specific findings regarding particular topics will be discussed in the chapters pertaining to those topics. For our purposes here, the subjects' views of themselves (problems and fears), their most widely held values, their views on race and prejudice, and their views of the future will outline the portrait they present.

Happiness. That seven out of ten of the 160,000 respondents like themselves and that the single most common fear reported was the possibility of losing their parents bolsters our portrait of modern adolescents as generally happy both with themselves and in their families. When asked to select the number-one problem in their lives, the vast majority placed ''school'' at the top of the list. They tended to identify their own shortcomings (such as procrastination), be tough on themselves for them, and want to overcome these faults, but they did not present a picture filled with inner turmoil. The four most widely held values were: (1) to have convictions and to hold them; (2) to be reasonable and fair with others; (3) to be self-sufficient; and (4) to be friendly, honest, and realistic. These youth have grown up in the age of civil rights, and 64 percent reported having friends of another race, while 25 percent said they would date someone of another race. Many of them feel discriminated against because they are teens: 34 percent think the police don't treat teens of any race very well, and 26 percent think police treat white teens better than nonwhite teens.

Positive view of future. The relatively positive views these American adolescents have of the present hold for the future as well. They tend to focus on the ''good life,'' and believe that hard work will bring success. Brought up in an age of credit cards, these young people want a debt-free future. Ninety-two percent think that they will achieve what they want in life, with 77 percent reporting that they will get where they want to be by working hard. They want, in addition to success, to be loved, to be healthy, and to do work they really like, and seven of ten believe that girls as well as boys need to prepare for careers.

This current research into the attitudes and opinions of adolescents supports the observation that the majority are coping quite successfully, and we may be encouraged by that. However, the fact that they are handling the tasks well does not minimize the challenges of adolescence, which may be particularly great in these last decades of the twentieth century. In Chapter 2, ''The Societal Context,'' we will look at how modern technological change may be affecting the experience of adolescence.

A Cultural Perspective

Throughout this chapter, we have been emphasizing that the society, both in terms of the culture to which one belongs, and the historical period in which one exists, has a tremendous effect on the experience of adolescence. This book concentrates on modern North American adolescents, primarily those in the United States, and makes no attempt to generalize to other cultures.

Hypotheses. In fact, very little research into the experience of other cultures exists; yet we can hypothesize that because of societal variables, adolescence in some other cultures may be quite different from what it is here. For example, an adolescent living in war-torn Lebanon, where early military service and fighting in the streets are common, is unlikely to experience the extended adolescence of affluent America. Adolescents who spend their childhoods in Israel's kibbutz, where they may live away from their parents, are unlikely to experience the same independence issues, and those living in Communist and Socialist countries may not be faced with the educational and vocational choices so common here.

United States, China, and Israel. Boocock (74), in one of the few cross-cultural studies of adolescence, compared adolescents in the United States, China, and Israel. She found that both China and Israel, unlike the United States, expect and reward the meaningful participation of their youth in the lives of their societies, though they do so in very different ways. In China formal education is integrated with productive work, and Chinese youth occupy meaningful social and economic positions in the society from a very early age. In Israel, all youth regardless of their backgrounds share the common experience of serving in the army, which provides a testing ground for a host of skills and characteristics. Both countries offer considerably greater continuity from one life stage to another than does the United States.

Variations within the United States. Although there is not a great deal of research into the experience of adolescence in other countries compared with ours, cultural variations include much more than the country in which one lives. Nationality, race, social class, age group, sex, and religion are all areas of possible cultural variation (Havighurst, 76), and every American takes part in all these subcultures simultaneously. We need be sensitive to their effects. An upper-class white male of English ancestry, brought up in the Episcopal Church, the son of professional parents, experiences a different adolescence than does a working-class Mexican-American female, brought up in the Catholic Church, the daughter of immigrant farmers.

These two young people will experience adolescence in quite different environments, yet they also share the universal aspects of adolescence (Havighurst, 76; Table 1.1).

But even these universals, except perhaps for the biological changes, are subject to cultural influence. Sex-role differentiation, for example, occurs in all cultures but also varies according to cultural standards. In the United States it may be perfectly appropriate for girls to include the idea of a professional career in their concept of femininity; in more traditional societies, it is not. Eventually, all adolescents become relatively independent of their parents, but this varies from culture to culture as well. A former student of mine, a young Pakistani woman, was encouraged to study both in Europe and in the United States, yet when she reached what her parents considered the appropriate age for marriage, she was called home to marry the young man they had selected for her. In the United States she had been accustomed to making her own decisions independent of her parents, yet in this important area of her life her parents were unwilling to grant her the right to make a choice. The cultural clash became painfully personal. All adolescents eventually acquire an ideology as well, but the content of that ideology varies from culture to culture, as does the means by which the ideology is transmitted. In some cultures it is simply absorbed; in others it is made explicit and celebrated through ceremonies like confirmation or bar or bas mitzvah; in others it may be the result of study and introspection. Finally, everyone eventually achieves an identity, a sense of uniqueness and individuality, but the amount of effort and responsibility for the development of that self varies tremendously. My Pakistani student was granted the right to study where she chose, but her ultimate identity was carefully guarded by her parents.

SUMMARY

Adolescence is vulnerable to myths and stereotypes that paint it both inaccurately and unfairly. Throughout the past several centuries, literature, psychological theory, and common ''knowledge'' have portrayed adolescence as merely a transitional stage, highly stressful and laden with conflicts. Adolescents are all too often viewed as being in necessary conflict with both the adult world and their parents, and they are frequently categorized as being a homogeneous group, inevitably pitted against the rest of the world. None of these conceptions is borne out in reality.

Adolescence has been defined in various ways — physiologically, psychologically, chronologically, educationally — and for a comprehensive definition of adolescence, we need a number of perspectives. A working definition might be: Adolescence extends from the onset of puberty (at about 10 or 11 in girls, 12 or 13 in boys) to the assumption of full adult responsibilities, physical, social, legal, and economic (usually about 21, but as early as 18 and as late as the mid-twenties or thirties).

Adolescence, as a distinct social stage of development, is a relatively new phenomenon. Even childhood, in the sense that we view it today, developed slowly through the centuries. The early Greeks and Romans, as well as Europeans of the Middle Ages, accorded very little attention to childhood. It was only during the Reformation and Renaissance that children began to be perceived as ''potential'' rather than ''miniature'' adults. Then in the sixteenth, seventeenth, and eighteenth centuries childhood gained ever increasing importance, but it has only been in the twentieth century that we have become a ''child-centered'' society.

Although children have always grown into adulthood, adolescence as an ''idea'' or ''social fact'' can be attributed to three reform movements of the Industrial Revolution that served to separate children and adolescents from adults. These were child-labor legislation, compulsory schooling, and the juvenile justice system. Although all three were instituted with clearly humanitarian motives, they have had some unforeseen consequences in removing children and adolescents from the workplace and in denying them certain civil rights that are accorded to all adults.

The experience of adolescence is influenced by the historical events of the period. In the United States, adolescents in the 1920s experienced a new permissiveness; in the 1930s and 1940s the sobering events of a major depression and a world war were paramount, and adolescents may have been relatively more serious. The 1950s were a time of affluence and peace, with adolescents experiencing a sense of prosperity and hope for the future, but the social upheavals of the 1960s created a spirit of rebellion among the younger generation. The 1970s and 1980s seem to be characterized by paradoxes, with significant stress and pressure placing new demands on the coping powers of adolescents.

Theories of adolescence can be categorized into those that stress discontinuity (the "storm and stress" theories) and those that emphasize continuity. The early biological theories of Hall, Gesell, and Zeller, as well as the psychological theories of the Freuds and Sullivan and the sociological theory of Lewin, assume that all adolescents will experience a necessary and significant emotional as well as physical disruption in adolescence. Emotional disequilibrium, turmoil, mood swings, unpredictability, unhappiness, and inevitable conflict with parents are predicted by turmoil theory, whether it is based on biological, psychological, or sociological observations.

The continuity theories, on the other hand, emphasize the ways in which adolescents naturally evolve into adults without significant disruption or turmoil. The anthropological theories of Mead and Benedict, the psychosocial theories of Bandura, Spranger, and Offer, and the developmental theories of Havighurst, Erikson, Piaget, and Kohlberg emphasize the continuity of development. They do not overlook the changes that occur but document that the changes are not necessarily accompanied by stress.

Current empirical research supports the continuity theories of adolescence, with the developmental theories offering the richest explanations of human behavior at all developmental stages, including adolescence. Adolescence is stressful for about 20 percent of the population, the 20 percent who display emotional and behavioral disturbances severe enough to warrant professional intervention, but the remaining 80 percent, although they may experience periods of stress and turmoil, generally manage the tasks of adolescence with reasonable calm. In general, adolescents in the 1980s feel relatively good about themselves, relate reasonably well to their parents and other adults, value education and earned success, and hold convictions that would gain their parents' approval.

2

A Societal Perspective

I don't even know what people mean by adolescent. It seems to me people nowadays jump from being children to being adults.

You may not know that's what's happening, but it does. . .

I don't think I'm so special. Lots of kids I know, they feel all of a sudden they can't be kids anymore. . .

You can tell by looking at them too: their bodies aren't kids' bodies either. It's hard to guess people's age nowadays because everybody looks older; even if they don't, they act older. Everybody's acting one way or another. If you don't act you get lost; the world passes by without you. (Cottle, 79, p. 40)

The sixteen-year-old who made the preceding statement has commented on a unique, late-twentieth-century phenomenon: the blurring of the distinctions between childhood and adulthood, and a resultant confusion for adolescents that may well be a product of modern society. In Chapter 1 we traced the development of the concepts of childhood and adolescence through history; in this chapter we will explore the influence of modern, technological society on the experience of childhood and adolescence as it exists in the final decades of the twentieth century in the United States. We will examine the influence of society on human development and experience and look at some of the unique characteristics of what is now known as ''postindustrial society,'' along with the human effects of those characteristics. We will then specifically examine the pressures in society that may be blurring the lines between childhood and adulthood, pressures that are creating what one author has called ''hurried children,'' another the ''disappearance of childhood.'' Finally, we will consider the special impact that the computer may have in the lives of adolescents.

THE INFLUENCE OF SOCIETY

History

As we noted in Chapter 1, studying human development without considering the societal and historical factors surrounding it leads to a myopic vision of people. Historical events have a decided impact on the experiences of the people who live through them; and just as the relative calm and affluence of the 1920s led to a spirit of hedonism, the subsequent depression and world war created a more sobering view of the world and its people. We must not be guilty of overlooking the tremendous influence of social and economic conditions that influence individual development, especially in the last decades of the twentieth century, when change is more rapid and predictions less sure than at any previous time in history.

Changes in the economy. The economic world has changed dramatically. Any economy can be viewed as a mixture of agriculture (farming, mining, fishing, forestry), manufacturing, and services (trade, finance, health, recreation, government, education), and we can trace the major historical trends by focusing on the relative balance among these forces (Bell, 73). In preindustrial society, agriculture was the major form of economic activity. Society was dependent on raw labor power to extract primary resources from nature through such activities as farming, mining, fishing, and forestry. With the Industrial Revolution of the nineteenth century, manufacturing took over the prominent position that agriculture had held, and most people became involved in the production of goods. But the Industrial Revolution is now past; since about 1975, economists have described our society as postindustrial, a time of technological and social change that is moving us into a service-oriented society. People today and in the foreseeable future will be engaged primarily in the service occupations; agriculture and manufacturing are on the decline, and modern society requires a new and different kind of skill on the part of its citizenry, with tremendous implications for the lifestyle, education, and work of all involved (Bell, 73). Let's look at just one example of how technology has influenced development.

Revolution in communications. One hallmark of the postindustrial society is a revolution in communications. Information is processed and transmitted almost instantaneously, with a resultant explosion in both the amount of knowledge available and the speed with which it is communicated. Information doubles every five and one-half years (Cross, 84). Simultaneously, cultural change is more rapid today than ever before, and these two situations have made young people frequently better informed than their elders (Mead, 70). In times of slower cultural change, the older generation held the wisdom of the society, which they passed down to the younger generation as they saw fit. This is not so in a time of rapid change; young people are often exposed to more, sooner, than are their parents, and we are witnessing in postindustrial society the phenomenon of youth influencing societal standards. Mead (70) points to attitudes toward racism, sexuality, drug use, and popular music

Adolescents don't grow in isolation.

and art as areas in which this phenomenon is most obvious. And any parent who has tried to help an elementary school child with "computer literacy" homework is acutely aware that the child is gaining knowledge of which the parent never dreamed. In the last decades of the twentieth century, it may not be unlikely for a twenty-year-old to seem woefully old-fashioned to a fifteen-year-old!

Social Systems

Historical events are not the only social influences on the nature of development. Although there has been insufficient research into how various social systems within a particular time period interact to influence adolescent behavior and development, Bronfenbrenner (77) proposes that at least the following social systems need be considered when studying development:

1. Relationships with others. Adolescents do not grow in isolation; the nature and breadth of their relationships with others surely influences their attitudes and behaviors, but these relationships have been inadequately explored.

2. Physical settings. Although the nature of an individual's physical environment would appear to have an effect on development, the actual influence of physical environment (home, apartment, own room, and the like) has been the subject of very little research.

3. Changes in the adolescent's life. We assume, but do not have meaningful evidence, that changes (a new grade, new teachers, a new school, divorce in the family, a new job, an illness) in an adolescent's life significantly affect development. There has been some research into the effects of such stresses on adults, but little to date on adolescents.

4. Other cultural factors. We do not have adequate information on the influence on development of such factors as the nature of the work the parents do, the

effects of various health and welfare services, and law enforcement strategies. Again, logic would inform us that these societal factors are important; but we are not sure of the nature of their effects.

5. Socioeconomic factors. The effects of socioeconomic status are perhaps better known than the other factors mentioned here, at least in terms of the effects on the behaviors and attitudes of all people. What we do not know is if the effects are any different for adolescents than they are for children or adults; the research generally assumes no differences (Bronfenbrenner, 77). Socioeconomic status includes financial resources, occupational prestige, educational and occupational opportunities, and the power that such resources give to influence others. People are usually classified by their occupations into the upper class, which has inherited wealth and holds jobs of great prestige; the middle class, which generally includes most professional, managerial, and sales people; and the lower class, which includes blue-collar, unskilled, and semiskilled workers. The categories are obviously not always distinct, and we need be careful not to stereotype people as a result of the socioeconomic group to which they belong. Research has demonstrated, for example, that inadequate housing is positively associated with neglect, but that church and family influences can buffer the incidence of such neglect (Giovanni, 70). It is obviously prejudicial to assume that because a family is a victim of poverty and cannot provide adequate housing, their children are doomed to a life of neglect, even though the expectation of a life of poverty may well lead to one.

Socioeconomic influences. Given the caution against such stereotyping, it is nevertheless important to understand the potential influence of socioeconomic status on adolescent development. The United States espouses a philosophy of equal opportunity for all, but statistics belie the dream. The children of the wealthy themselves rise to positions of wealth. The "rags to riches" dream exists only in isolation; only four out of every 1000 children born into the bottom tenth (socioeconomically) of the population of the United States ever achieve incomes in the top tenth (Keniston, 77). The other 996 remain in the lower and middle classes.

The characteristics of the subculture of the lower class are well known. In addition to living in poverty, those in the lower class are powerless. Because they are poor and powerless, these people are also vulnerable and restricted in their choices. They have no prestige and are therefore snubbed by the rest of society. The middle and upper classes tend to judge them negatively because they do not adhere to middle-class standards, and the vicious cycle continues. Specifically, lower-class parents, who do not understand the middle-class value placed on self-sufficiency, do not systematically teach the skills of independence as do middle-class parents. They instead tend to be more authoritarian, to demand obedience, and thus to restrict the independence of their children (Jacob, 74).

Social class placement can affect not only opportunities, but self-esteem as well. Rosenberg (65), for example, found that high school juniors and seniors from the higher social classes exhibited higher self-esteem than those from the lower class.

The poverty of the lowest social classes is cumulative in its harmful effects. In exploring the meaning of poverty, Keniston (77) notes that, compared to middle-class children, children born to poverty have a two-thirds greater chance of dying in their first year; have five times as many unfilled cavities; are four times more likely to be in poor health, but only half as likely to have seen a physician in the previous year; are more likely to be in foster care; and are more likely to be in ineffective schools. Inadequate prenatal care leads to early malnutrition; poor living conditions lead to inadequate health care; the cumulative deprivations result in permanent physical, social, and mental handicaps. Poor children are, in Keniston's words (77, p. 33), ''systematically trained to fail.'' They are frequently blamed for their status, defined as no good, and labeled ''culturally deprived.'' The deck is stacked against the one-quarter to one-third of American children who suffer basic deprivations as a result of poverty, poverty being defined as being in a family whose income falls below half of the median income for families of similar size (Keniston, 77).

The nonwhite and the handicapped. Keniston (77) considers the poor to be among the excluded in this country. Also excluded, he finds, are nonwhite and handicapped children. Nonwhite children, for example, are four times more likely than white children to be poor; they have double the infant mortality rate and three times more nutritional deficiencies, and are disproportionately represented in social institutions such as foster care and detention centers. The one in 40 American children who suffers from a serious handicap is also excluded, labeled as defective, and frequently treated as if that child were to blame for being ''no good.'' Collectively, says Keniston (77), the poor, the nonwhite, and the handicapped do not enjoy the fruit of the espoused American value of freedom of choice and the pursuit of happiness. They are labeled, tracked, and systematically excluded; their families are blamed, and their futures effectively foreclosed. That they have been excluded from the American dream is clear to them, Keniston (77) says, and has led to the current emphasis in this country on ''rights'' for those left out. Movements such as the ''Poor People's March,'' handicapped rights, Chicano rights, and gay rights are all expressions by those excluded of their unwillingness to remain so.

Clearly, then, social factors affect development. The research may be spotty, with conjecture frequently replacing empirical evidence, but hypotheses are nevertheless made. Most are highly rational, based on studying social systems and behavioral trends, and offered in an attempt to make meaning from social situations. Such observations and hypotheses form the basis of the description of postindustrial society and its human effects that follows.

POSTINDUSTRIAL SOCIETY

A Description

We live in a time of extremely rapid technological and social change. As Keniston (77, pp. 49–50) describes:

Every aspect of the experience of children and parents in the United States today is radically affected by inventions that did not exist in the time of our grandparents. Our sophisticated technology delivers unimaginable benefits to today's families — from kidney dialysis machines to convenience foods, from the automobile to the pocket calculator, from no-iron children's clothing to the telephone.

Major societal changes.   Along with the benefits come inestimable costs in terms of unimagined physical effects, mental stresses, and cultural changes. In this technological society, the primacy of theoretical and technical competence has forced five major changes in the society (Bell, 73):

1. In the *economic sector,* we are moving from a goods-producing economy to a service economy; in addition, giant corporations rather than individuals set competition, quality, and price of goods and services, thereby manipulating the choices people can make.

2. In terms of *occupational distribution,* the technical and professional class is gaining preeminence.

3. In terms of *policy formulation,* those with theoretical knowledge are becoming most powerful.

4. Our entire *future orientation* is geared to the control and development of technology.

5. In terms of *decision making,* the power lies with the new "intellectual technology."

Together these changes strengthen the role of science and technology as basic cultural necessities. Scientists and economists become increasingly powerful, and advanced education becomes a necessity for meaningful involvement in society. As an example of the rising emphasis on extended schooling, Bell (73) points to the rise in the number of jobs that require at least some college: in 1940 there were 3.9 million such jobs; in 1964 the number had risen to 8.6 million; and by 1975 it had risen to 13.2 million. The trend continues, and so do the costs of advanced training, with even more potential for unequal distribution of wealth, power, and status. Postindustrial society, with its emphasis on technical competence and paper credentials, is likely to increase further the divisions between the "haves" and the "have-nots" of this society. The implications in terms of pressures on adolescents are enormous.

Effects on adolescents.   Adolescents today are exposed to considerably more, considerably earlier, than ever before.

Subjects that once were discussed only behind closed doors are now out in the open. Controversial issues are discussed in the media and in the classroom, and people who were once considered deviant are now on the lecture circuit. In sum, children are exposed to significantly more than their parents were, and at significantly earlier ages. Pre- and extra-marital sex, abortion, contraception, homosexuality, bisexuality, group marriage, open marriage, transsexualism, pollution, nuclear energy, fuel shortages, space exploration, diet, and drug use are concepts that average 14-year-olds have already been exposed to. (Fuhrmann, 83, p. 212)

Although adolescents have been exposed, we cannot assume they understand. Having and using a vocabulary is no indication of comprehension; yet if they are going to be productive members of this society, adolescents will have to learn to deal with both the technologies and the social consequences of them. Alternative lifestyles, frequent changes, and new technologies, filled with both promise and risk, are givens. It may well be that the only sure prediction is that tomorrow will not mirror today.

Benefits and Risks

The United States, established in an era of belief in the limitless potential of the land, developed an economy based on the assumption of abundance. Belief in the innate goodness of technological progress has led to the unchallenged supremacy of technology; we tend to want to believe that all progress is for the good of us all. As Keniston (65, 77) says, we have adopted the myth that technological progress is the safest and surest route to the good life. Belief in the myth leads us to disregard warnings of potential risk, yet those risks are often dire.

The delicate balance. With the new benefits come new dangers: we now worry about the pollutants left from numerous technological advances; we don't know the long term effects of exposure to radiation from nuclear energy sources; we consume more additives, salt, fat, and sugars as a result of the new convenience and fast-food diets that free us from long hours in the kitchen; we are exposed to noise, air pollution, anxiety, and tragic deaths because of fast, convenient means of travel. Although the benefits are obvious and numerous, we may be paying a heavy price for them. Our air and water are polluted; we may be destroying the ozone layer, with inestimable effects in terms of weather and radiation; we live with traffic problems, air quality indexes, and unknown quantities of personal information on computer files with the CIA. Computerized records lead to new privacy issues, including school records as well as those kept by banks and government agencies (Wiley, 82). As Bellak (75) points out, we have no control over the effects of technology, and massive governmental regulatory agencies like the Nuclear Regulatory Commission have control over what information about those effects will be released.

In addition to the risks that we know are associated with various new technological advances, there may be others that won't appear for another generation or more. We fall into the trap of extolling the immediate benefits and giving far too little attention to systematic evaluation, monitoring, and control (Keniston, 77).

what does technology do to us? why?

The risks associated with technology are not only the specific ones that result from particular technological advances. Social scientists are also concerned with the loss of esteem of that side of life that is not technological: relaxation, fun, emotion, family life, daydreaming, art, music, and literature all take a back seat to technology, and people who lack highly developed technological skills are devalued by the wider society as well (Keniston, 65).

Overload. In 1970, Toffler published *Future Shock,* in which he details the rapid societal changes that may cause maladjustment. Bellak (75, pp. 27–28) talks of information overload:

> We are forced to cope with an environment in which nothing stays the same for any appreciable length of time. We make too many technical advances too fast, and we get too much news to digest and make sense of. It all adds up to what is sometimes called an "information overload."

Klapp (82) uses a metaphor to describe overload. In the metaphor a person is seated at a table putting together a giant jigsaw puzzle, the pieces of which are pouring out of an overhead funnel at a furious pace. Not only is it impossible to keep up with the flow of the pieces, but many of the pieces do not even belong to the puzzle. The individual is inundated with both relevant and irrelevant facts, but has no time to ponder the meaning of the facts or to develop them into a comprehensible pattern. "Meaning formation," says Klapp, takes time, thought, discussion and debate. The speed of our flow of information results in a paradox: the more knowledge available, the less meaning we may be able to derive from it!

The unfortunate but necessary result of information overload, point out Bellak (75) and Klapp (82), is a tendency to put up emotional barriers to protect ourselves. The danger of putting up emotional barriers is the erection of permanent ones where we need them most, in our significant relationships with others. We may become superficial and alienated, and adolescents are particularly likely, with their newly developed intellectual capacities, either to feel overwhelmed with society's problems, or to give up on them in the despair of powerlessness.

> Scholars generally agree that there has been a crisis of meaning in modern times. Alienation, existential despair, absurdity, legitimation crisis, identity problem, anomie, sensate culture, counterculture, future shock, end of ideology, false consciousness, and social noise are some of the names by which the crisis has been identified. In a crisis of meaning, people find much that doesn't make sense, little that is basic or reliable to hang onto. (Klapp, 82, p. 56)

Of particular danger in an environment characterized by tremendous overload on the senses, combined with rules and regulations because of the overload, is the development of either aggression or apathy. Bellak (75) points to the aggression developed in some mice who are forced to live in overcrowded conditions, while others give up and let themselves be controlled. We might do well to ask ourselves how adolescents (granted that they are not mice), forced to live in technological society and at the same time forced to adhere to rules at home, at school, and in the community, can be helped to deal with the overload and the inherent conflict of values without becoming either aggressive or apathetic. That the majority do not is a tribute to their coping powers. As was pointed out in Chapter 1, the majority of adolescents seem to be managing modern stressors quite competently. This, however, should not lead us to a complacent attitude toward understanding the *potential* effects of those stressors.

The Future for Today's Adolescents

We have relatively comprehensive descriptions of today's society and its pressures, but we are not, say those who make social forecasts (Bell, 73; Madigan, 82), prepared for the continued changes. This country is still wedded, they say, to the idea of an industrial economy, powered by the so-called smokestack industries (such as steel, textiles, and autos), which have been declining in recent years. Our educational system is not keeping up either (see Chapter 5), and we are neither preparing children and adolescents for the future, nor retraining the hundreds of thousands of displaced industrial workers who no longer can find employment. Specifically, within the next few years, the following changes will occur (Madigan, 82):

1. Robotics and automation will increasingly replace industrial workers. Fewer and fewer skilled and semiskilled workers will be required to produce goods. The trades, as well as jobs in metals, textiles, the railroad, blast furnaces, and factories of all kinds, will continue to diminish, some of them being completely phased out. Displaced workers will not be replaced.

2. Because Americans believe in the promise of technology, it will continue to grow. Technology requires people with a solid basic education, with emphasis on science and math, preceding more specialized training.

3. Brain power will replace muscle power. The implication of this prediction is that those who haven't succeeded in an industrial economy will be even less likely to succeed in a technological one.

4. As a result of the emphasis on technical competence, it is possible that the American society could become even more polarized, with a strong and influential upper middle class making decisions for an increasingly stressed and frustrated lower class.

5. In addition to technical jobs, service jobs will flourish. People will need to be trained for retail work, food service, government, education, health services, finance, and real estate. All require training well beyond high school.

6. Technology has had a tremendous impact on the nature of family life, which we will discuss shortly. Tremendous changes are likely to continue.

Based on such social forecasts, the implications for adolescents are clear. To be productive citizens of the postindustrial society, they will need, in addition to the positive attitudes and values they already have, technical competence, advanced edu-

cation, and assistance in learning how to adapt to and manage change constructively. They need to understand, as do their parents and teachers, that traditional
expectations concerning the nature of work, family, and society as a whole no
longer hold, and they must be prepared for a future that we can't now predict with
any confidence. Adults, too, must develop these competencies, especially since they
will be responsible for teaching the new skills and understandings essential for
success.

THE INFLUENCE OF TELEVISION

The second half of the twentieth century might well go down in the history books
as the Age of Television. It can be argued that no social change has been so far-
reaching, with greater potential for impact on human life and development, than
the television set and its associated services: UHF, cable television, pay television,
videocassettes, videotex, home video games, and others that have burst upon the
scene between my writing and your reading of this book. The potential for even
greater options in the last fifteen years of the century are enormous, with technological advances and deregulation of television services creating new issues in government, questions about who owns broadcasts, issues concerning public and
private information systems, international issues, privacy issues, even employment
and politics as affected by television (Wiley, 82). Because of television, paper is no
longer the staple of the communications industry; TV has become responsible, as
Postman (82) points out, for the elimination of the need to learn to read to gain

Adolescents surround themselves with media.

access to adult secrets. . . . "The printing press created childhood and . . . the electronic media are 'disappearing it'" (Postman, 82, p. *xii*).

Viewing Habits

Television is the constant companion of children and adolescents; none of them today has known a time without television. In the late 1940s, 98 percent of United States' homes had radio. By 1958, 84 percent of them had television, and by 1972, 96 percent had it (Reynolds, 77). Television has become the electronic baby-sitter, with children between 2 and 5 years spending one-fourth of their waking time in front of the television set (Easterlin, 82). As Keniston (77) points out, the biggest difference between a human baby-sitter and the electronic one is the amount of control parents have over it: parents might well fire a human baby-sitter who constantly exposed their children to murder and sex and pushed sugared cereals on them; but they exert little, if any, influence over the electronic baby-sitter, which seems to play an increasingly significant role in child-rearing.

Amount and type of viewing. By the age of eighteen, the average adolescent has spent more time with television than in school or with her parents — about 11,000 hours in school as opposed to 15,000 hours of television (1970 White House Conference on Youth). There is consistent evidence that adolescents watch about three hours of television per day, with 29 percent watching more than that (Murray, 80). Television watching peaks in early adolescence, when comedies and adventure stories are preferred; older adolescents tend to add music programs but to reduce their total watching time slightly. Very few adolescents watch news, public affairs, or educational programming (Lyle, 72; Rubin, 77). And at this point we have no evidence of the impact of the movie and rock music channels that are currently available on cable, but much of the cable programming is directed to young audiences.

Potential impact. Since children and adolescents spend so much time watching TV, its potential for impact is enormous. Youth watch television for a number of reasons: for emotional release, to engage in fantasy, for information, to escape boredom, to have something to talk about with their friends, and as a measure by which to compare themselves (Murray, 80). That television is frequently youth-oriented can be verified by looking at the programming available. Adolescents and youth are frequently the subject of series and movies, and advertising is often directed to adolescent and youth audiences. If young people want an image with which to compare themselves, television provides it willingly.

On the positive side, television has the potential for enlarging the world of adolescents; they see and are exposed to more than ever before. If used properly, television can be a source of information, a stimulator of interests and curiosity, an effective teaching tool, a medium of entertainment, and a life enricher. Although McCabe (77) found evidence that positive social behavior could be influenced by adolescents watching sports shows edited to demonstrate positive social behavior, and Wynne (79) speculates that the television set may be bringing families back together again through common viewing activities, there is very little research into the benefits of television on adolescent development. Far more interest and research has been generated concerning its damaging effects, with sobering results.

Television, rightly or wrongly, has been accused of being responsible for all the ills of society, including the faults we perceive in adolescents. Television has been found to contribute to adolescent aggression (Comstock, 78; Liebert, 73; Lefkowitz, 72; Keniston, 77). Youth who watch significant amounts of television do so at the expense of reading, self-directed activities, visiting friends, and going to the movies; and there is a positive correlation between high television viewing and low intelligence, low socioeconomic class, and low self-esteem (Keniston, 77; Murray, 80). Although a positive correlation does not determine a cause-and-effect relationship, television is sometimes unfairly blamed for the other factors. (It is possible, for example, that people with lower intelligence choose television as their medium of entertainment, or that lower intelligence and television viewing are both related to some other factor.) But the fact that higher viewing time is associated with lower grades (Murray, 80) often leads to the unproven assumption that the grades are low *because* the viewing is high.

Additional concerns with television are that it is deceptively simple, with all problems worked out in 30, 60, or 90 minutes, leading young people to expect happy endings; that it teaches violence and sexual exploitation, provides an illusion of a free society, encourages stereotyping and racism, and diverts attention away from major world issues to fantasized side shows, with a soap opera star's exploits gaining more attention than international events (Real, 77). Finally, there has been considerable concern with the commercial advertising directed at children and youth. The United States is one of only three countries that allow commercials on shows designed for children (Kaye, 74), and much advertising in general is directed toward young people, with a not-at-all subtle message about what the "good life" entails: beauty, romance, wealth, and frequently alcohol. (About twenty years ago, cigarette advertising was banned from television because of its potential for encouraging smoking; at this writing, a controversy exists over the possibility of similar legislation to ban the advertising of alcohol because of its potential to encourage drinking. Young people are the concern of those who wish to ban the ads.)

Examples of Social Learning from Television

Social learning theory (Bandura, 64) posits that people learn attitudes and behaviors from imitating role models. The roles portrayed on television can be seen as a potentially significant influence on the attitudes and behaviors of adolescents. For this reason, many studies have been conducted to determine the images that television portrays. The several described below may be particularly important to adolescent development.

The family. The family, as it is portrayed on television, has been the subject of considerable recent research. Buerkel-Rothfuss (82), in a comprehensive empirical study of the influence of watching family programs on what children believe about families, found that those who watch shows in which affiliation is high among the television family members believe that real families are more affiliative than those who do not watch those shows. A second highly important finding was that positive interaction with parents encourages children to identify the differences between television and real families, thus reinforcing the belief of many that parental guidance can have an impact on what children learn from television.

Thomas (82) analyzed 97 episodes of family-oriented television series to test whether or not they disseminate the myth that "money can't buy happiness," and found that ". . . the data from our study indicate that, for the families portrayed on television, money clearly does not buy happiness and that, in fact, relative poverty does" (p. 186). To conduct the study, television families were classified as upper class (such as the Ewings of *Dallas*), upper middle class (such as the Lawrences of *Family*), the middle class (such as the Cunninghams of *Happy Days*), and the working class (such as the Evanses of *Good Times*). The family members were rated on measures of sympathy, cooperation, and interpersonal interactions. The researchers found that the upper class had the greatest percentage of "bad" characters and the worst interpersonal relations, while the working-class families resolved their problems cooperatively and invariably felt happy at the end of the show. They concluded that although TV overrepresents wealth and glamour, it also celebrates those who make it against tremendous odds.

Morality. Sutherland (82) notes that previous research into soap opera content is critical of soap operas for condoning immorality, yet that research merely tabulated the content, finding numerous examples of murder, child abuse, infidelity, illegitimacy, and incest, and did not examine the resolution of those problems in terms of their effects on people. Sutherland's research looked at the consequences to those who violated moral standards (primarily deceit, murder, and sex), and found that soap operas, although they present morally unacceptable behaviors, also punish the characters who engage in them. He concludes that the relationship between the content of soap operas and societal standards is complex, and that in general the soap operas do tend to present moral dilemmas, but they also uphold accepted mores by punishing the offenders. What these findings mean for adolescent behavior is far from clear but certainly intriguing.

Driving. For most adolescents, the attainment of a driver's license is a long-awaited symbol of adulthood, and Greenberg (83) hypothesized that driving behavior on television might have an effect on new drivers because of their openness to influence in a new and exciting activity. He therefore analyzed random samples of prime-time television from 1975 to 1980 for the extent of driving scenes, the context in which driving occurred, the driving acts shown, the consequences of irregular or dangerous driving, the character of the drivers, other driving behaviors (smoking, drinking, shooting, fighting), and use of seat belts. This research found that irregular driving acts, including quick braking, brakes squealing, tires screeching, speeding, and quick acceleration, occur more than seven times per hour on prime-time television, with very few instances of immediate legal penalties. People were endangered by driving almost once every hour, but relatively few deaths or injuries actually ensued. Both dangerous and irregular driving were engaged in most often by white male drivers under 30 years old, and only four of 719 drivers were seen buckling seat belts. None of five children in autos was restrained in any way. Based on the data collected, Greenberg (83, p. 54) concludes that:

> . . . the viewer who watches just one hour of prime-time fictional series programming each evening would see more than 2,700 irregular driving acts, more than 250 acts in which people are endangered, and about 30 deaths and 50 injuries due to auto accidents; only 15 cases of seat belt usage would be observed throughout the year, however.

Based on these findings, Greenberg (83) hypothesized that young people are likely to accept irregular driving by young males as normal, believe that speeding is not bad driving and will not result in legal penalties, regard seat belts as unnecessary, reject the serious consequences of irregular driving, and accept the roles of male driver and female passenger.

Sex roles. Finally, as we will discuss more fully in Chapter 7, the television images of men and women contribute significantly to the sex-role stereotyping so prevalent in American society. Women on television are most often portrayed in stereotypical roles; they are thin, young, attractive, passive, and concerned primarily with attracting and keeping men. Men, however, are most often portrayed as strong, aggressive, and competent, concerned primarily with achievement and only secondarily interested in women, whom they perceive as sexual objects.

These hypotheses, as well as others concerning the effects of various television role models on adolescents, need to be tested by ongoing and comprehensive research. Their implications, if they are accurate, are enormous.

THE BLURRING OF THE DISTINCTIONS BETWEEN CHILDREN AND ADULTS

Hurried Children: Disappearing Childhood?

Within a year of each other, two well-known and highly respected social scientists, David Elkind and Neil Postman, published books which comment on a late twentieth century phenomenon, the increasing similarities of behaviors and expectations for children and adults, the phenomenon alluded to in the quotation that opens this chapter. Elkind (81) calls the phenomenon *Hurried Children,* while Postman (82) refers to *The Disappearance of Childhood;* both are reacting to and describing the threat to

Children are hurried into adulthood.

the concept of childhood created by increased pressures on children to look and act like adults. The highest paid models are currently thirteen years old; the extent and type of child crime is increasingly similar to that of adults; children's games are becoming increasingly competitive, with professional trappings and expectations; there are no longer any secrets reserved for adults; children's dress and language no longer set them apart from adults; children travel unaccompanied all over the world; summer camps have lost their woodsy, leisure flavor in favor of pressure for skill development in athletics, computers, or artistic endeavors; and pressure for academic achievement begins even before kindergarten.

You will remember that Postman (82) ascribed the creation of childhood to the invention of the printing press, which created a clear distinction between those who could read and those who could not. With the electronic media, however, and especially through television, there was no longer any way to keep secrets from children, who are continually exposed to the same information and stimuli as are adults. There no longer, then, says Postman, is any distinction between childhood and adulthood, and childhood itself is in danger of again disappearing.

> Children are a group of people who do *not* know certain things that adults know. In the Middle Ages there were no children because there existed no means for adults to know exclusive information. In the Age of Gutenberg, such a means developed. In the Age of Television, it is dissolved. (Postman, 82, p. 85)

Elkind (81) concurs that childhood is endangered, but attributes the danger not only to television, which is one of the pressures children experience to hurry to adulthood, but also to pressures applied by parents and by schools; and he sees today's child as "the unwilling, unintended victim of overwhelming stress — the stress borne of rapid, bewildering social change and constantly rising expectations" (p. 3). Children today are pressured to achieve, succeed, please others, hurry and grow up; and they are threatened by the fear of failure, all of which create incredible stress and force them to take on adult roles before they are psychologically mature enough to deal with them. Rather than identifying children merely by the things they don't know, Elkind stresses that children have different needs than do adults, that they don't think or feel as adults do, and that it is psychologically dangerous to expect of them the same things we expect of adults. We are, he says, trying to hurry them into adulthood, but emotional maturity can't be hurried, and the result of the pressures to grow up fast results in troubled children: those failing in school; those involved in delinquency and drugs; those who are depressed and suicidal; those who experience somatic complaints (hypertension, ulcers, headaches); and those who are chronically unhappy. "These diseases and problems have long been recognized as stress related in adults, and it is time we looked at children and stress in the same light" (Elkind, 81, p. *xiii*). The sources of the stress are parents, schools, and the media. We'll examine each separately.

Pressure from parents. Parents, themselves stressed by the rapid societal changes of the second half of the twentieth century, feel afraid, insecure, and lonely. Because they are so stressed, they have little energy or enthusiasm for the demanding job of being parents, and, says Elkind (81, p. 28–29):

> Parents under stress see their children as symbols because it is the least demanding way to see them. A student, a skater, a tennis player, a confidant are clear-cut symbols, easy guides for what to think, to see, and how to behave. Symbols thus free the parent from the energy consuming task of knowing the child as a totality, a whole person.

Such symbols also serve the stressed parents as a screen on which they can project their own unfulfilled needs for success. The symbols Elkind identifies are the child as surrogate self, the child as status symbol, the child as partner, the child as conscience, and the child as therapist.

Dissatisfied parents are likely to live through their children, make them into surrogate selves, and thereby live out their dreams, especially on the athletic field. Children are thus hurried into expectations of top athletic performance at very early ages, even though child development specialists know that team competition is generally inappropriate for children prior to adolescence. Little League baseball, Pee Wee football, Tiny Tot soccer, and individual training and competition in tennis, gymnastics, and swimming are all taking on increasingly worklike rather than funlike trappings. It is clear to Elkind, as to Postman and others, that such early athletic competition fulfills the parents' needs rather than the child's. Children need to play their own games, with their own rules and nonrules, and not to engage in competitive sports which they neither understand nor even like, and in which only the best can succeed, while the vast majority learn nothing other than early failure.

When parents feel tenuous about their own status in their society, they are likely to use their children as status symbols. The right school, the right camp, the right clothing on their children all take on tremendous importance. Even nursery school attendance can become a mark of parental status; on a *60 Minutes* broadcast early in 1983 the topic was the competition in New York City for placing children into the "right" nursery schools, the few that were considered absolutely essential for getting into the "right" colleges: the correspondent interviewed a despondent father who was convinced that his three-year-old son had failed the interview! Affluent Americans apparently cannot stand to think of their children as average; in addition to going to the right schools, they are also pressured to perform academically; all too often, a *B* is perceived, by both students and parents, as tantamount to failure.

> There is no room today for the "late bloomers," the children who come into their own later in life rather than earlier. . . . Children have to achieve success early or they are regarded as losers. It has gone so far that many parents refuse to have their children repeat or be retained in kindergarten — despite all the evidence that this is the best possible time to retain a child. "But," the parents say, "How can we tell our friends that our son failed kindergarten?" (Elkind, 81, p. 17)

As a result of parents spending more time away from home, whether because of divorce or because both parents must work, children are often asked to be partners in home responsibilities at early ages. Having important responsibilities is not in itself harmful; in fact, *appropriate* responsibilities are essential to healthy development. It is when the responsibilities become inappropriate that they become overly stressful. Most six-year-olds are not old enough to come home and spend several hours alone before their parents arrive; most ten-year-olds are not ready to assume total responsibilities for several younger siblings, including getting them up, dressed, fed, and off to school on time; and adolescents should not be burdened with inappropriate decisions, like helping mother decide if she should quit her job or sue her exhusband for increased support money. Yet responsibilities like these are given to immature children and adolescents with increasing regularity as parents feel overwhelmed by the stresses placed on them.

A parent, particularly an insecure and frightened divorced parent, who is faced with making moral judgments about appropriate and inappropriate behavior, may ask a child to be her conscience. All too many parents, says Elkind, ask for the tacit approval of their children for behaviors that society does not condone. Children are supposed to accept a boyfriend's staying overnight with Mom, listen to one parent's condemnations of the other, or approve of a nontraditional living arrangement, but they are not supposed to condone or engage in such behavior for themselves. Indirect messages, especially about sexuality, get transmitted, and research has demonstrated that daughters of divorced mothers are more flirtatious and more sexually oriented than their peers from intact families (Heatherington, 78). Since divorced mothers are often dating, sexuality, from hand-holding to overt affection to overnight stays, is more overt, and the daughters apparently react by being more overt themselves.

Finally, stressed parents may ask that their children serve as <u>therapists</u>. Problems with anxiety, finances, loneliness, work, and love all become shared with the children, who are asked to listen and even to give advice that they cannot possibly have the wisdom to give. These problems are clearly beyond the capacity of children and adolescents to handle, and to burden them with such stressors puts them in situations of unresolvable conflict.

And parents are not the only ones pressuring children to grow up fast. Schools and the media are fully involved in the process too.

Pressure from schools. The technological society needs highly competent and skilled people to manage it, and the schools are held responsible for producing them. We will discuss the effects of schooling in detail in Chapter 5; here we will simply acknowledge those pressures from the schools to grow up fast.

Schools have become, says Elkind, "industrialized," with the emphasis placed on their products — the kids that leave them. As a result, management programs, accountability, and testing have become the watchwords of American schools, and children are labeled, expected to learn in assembly line and lock-step fashion, and not allowed to be slow bloomers. It is not difficult to find remedial reading programs in the first grade, and SAT prep courses in middle schools. Competition and high expectations are good for some students, but for those who can't keep up, early failure can be humiliating and may lead to loss of esteem and emotional disorders.

> Worse, students who fail to achieve are letting down their peers, their teachers, the principal, the superintendent, and the school board. This is a heavy burden for many children to bear and is a powerful pressure to achieve early and grow up fast. (Elkind, 81, p. 55)

Pressure from the media. I have already alluded to many of the pressures from the media to grow up fast. In the media there are no taboos; immediate gratification is the rule rather than the exception; young people are exposed to unrealistic standards of the "good life"; and much of what is portrayed on the media requires no thinking. In addition, young people on television are usually precocious: Gary Coleman deals in adultlike ways with adult subjects, and so do his television counterparts. We have already discussed the role of television in the lives of adolescents; here we will look specifically at those aspects of television and the movies that hurry children, and then will address music and printed media.

Since most movies now appear on television fairly soon after they appear in the theaters, it is not reasonable any longer to analyze the impact of movies separately from television. The two features of television and movies that account for pressure to grow up fast are the depiction of sex and of violence. Pearl (78) found provocative depiction of sexual relationships and violence in eight out of ten prime-time television programs. Sex, both explicit and subtle, is unavoidable, not only in the adult-rated movies, but even in commercials. Vaginal sprays, almost nude dancers, camera angles that focus on buttocks and breasts (even on exercise programs), kids portrayed in sexually provocative themes (*Pretty Baby, The Blue Lagoon, Little Darlings, Endless Love*); nothing is taboo. Elkind's concern is that children are exposed to sexual behavior before they "know the rules," and are likely to pick up a vocabulary that belies their lack of understanding. With exposure and vocabulary, they are too often forced into premature sexual behavior when they are too young to handle it (Postman, 82). And the warnings that television programs and movies contain adult language, adult materials, violence, and nudity probably only insure that adolescents watch. Parents exert very little control over their children's, especially their adolescents', viewing.

In terms of violence, the research is mixed, with some greater evidence of potential damage than of no damage (Goranson, 75; Pearl, 78; Murray, 80). Elkind (81) contends that modeling is not the issue in the television violence controversy, as some would believe; that is, normal children do not commit violent acts because they have seen those acts on television. The greater danger is in their emotional immaturity; even normal children see violence that they are not prepared to deal with, and no one helps them with it.

Television and the movies expose children to adult conflicts but do not require thinking or help children to comprehend what they see. This leads to pseudosophistication, expectations for early adult behaviors, and pressure to deal with things children are not prepared to understand. Once again, they are hurried.

Music appears to be a large part of adolescent life, and listening to music increases dramatically at adolescence (Avery, 79). Adolescents listen to music to relax, entertain themselves, avoid loneliness, and cope with anger and hurt (Avery, 79). From the origins of rock and roll in the United States and England in the 1950s, through the rockers, mods, and skinheads of the 1960s, to the punks and new waves of the 1970s and 1980s, rock music has been at least somewhat class-related, expressing resistance to the class-based social system that creates feelings of despair (Lull, 82). All too frequently, the music to which adolescents listen encourages unproductive behavior, especially those songs that glorify drug use, violence, and sexual and sadistic behavior (Key, 77; Shatin, 81). There appears to be some question as to whether adolescents actually listen to the lyrics, but the lyrics nevertheless are often graphically antisocial, and there is some evidence to support the belief that many messages may be subliminal (Key, 77). Regardless, adolescents spend a great deal of money on music and listen consistently. The image of the rather vacant teen walking down the street oblivious to all but a large and expensive portable stereo system is familiar to us all. The effects are not yet clearly understood, but Elkind at least fears that the escapism inherent in tuning out everything else is one more sign of the pressure to grow up too fast.

Just as movies, TV, and song lyrics abound with provocative themes and a new realism, so too do the books, newspapers, and magazines that teenagers read (Elkind, 81). Although newspapers are not highly read, both in newspapers and magazines adolescent males read sports while adolescent females turn to fashion and material published especially for teens (Avery, 79). And although the ''girlie'' magazines are supposedly kept behind the counter, their presence in junior high schools is well known by students and teachers alike. Once again, children are exposed to adult themes and conflicts at earlier and earlier ages.

Although certainly the media that surround adolescents are generally not pornographic, there may be some danger in the increasingly explicit sexuality of the media. Pornography is available to adolescents, yet there has been very little empirical evidence of its effects. Women have spoken out against it, but otherwise society has been relatively quiet (Zillmann, 82). Zillmann (82), believing that pornography must affect perceptions of sexuality and attitudes and behaviors concerning sex and gender, exposed 80 male and 80 female subjects (college students) to controlled amounts of filmed pornography, including no coercion or pain, but including fellatio, cunnilingus, coitus, and anal intercourse. The ''massive exposure'' group saw 48 minutes of film on six occasions for a total of four hours, 48 minutes over six weeks; the intermediate exposure group saw a total of two hours, 24 minutes; the nil group saw none. There were significant findings only for the massive exposure group, who, in comparison with the other two groups, lessened their views of pornography as offensive and lost compassion for women as rape victims and for women *per se*. In addition, the males became increasingly callous in their sexual attitudes toward women. Zillmann (82) concludes that it is not known now how exposure to pornography affects the sexual development of adolescents, but hypothesizes (p. 11):

> It is utterly unclear, for instance, how pornographic fare, with its common script of fellatio, cunnilingus, coition, anal penetration, and multiple partnership, influences and shapes the sexual expectations of young teens who are increasingly likely to be exposed to pornography prior to becoming sexually active.

Such exposure must, at minimum, contribute to the syndrome of hurried children.

Emotional and Behavioral Reactions to Stress

Stress takes its toll, though the effects of hurrying on children may not become evident until adolescence because it is not until adolescence that young people are capable of understanding or resenting the pressure they have been under (Elkind, 81). Hurried adolescents may be particularly prone to criticizing adults; they may become overly involved in sexual behavior, drug and alcohol use, and delinquency.

They are subject to stress-related diseases, vulnerable to the promise of easy answers offered by cults, and prone to suicide, which is the second leading cause of death during the teen years. They may experience free-floating anxiety, including restlessness, irritability, and inability to concentrate. They may display extremely competitive and aggressive behavior, or lose all enthusiasm for school or for the skill they were pushed into developing in childhood (such as the young tennis star who feels washed up in adolescence). They may display all forms of behavioral and emotional disturbances as well as somatic complaints and extreme reactions like anorexia nervosa (self-starvation) (Elkind, 81). They may, in addition, display what Seligman (75) termed "learned helplessness," a giving up resulting from repeated failure to successfully control important situations.

The results of stress will be discussed thoroughly in Chapters 12, 13, and 14.

The Response of the Law

Because the law reflects current cultural attitudes and standards and is the "codification of the culture," (Benedeck, 79) a brief look at how the law currently treats adolescents is instructive. The law today treats children and adolescents more and more like adults. The juvenile justice system, intended to separate legal proceedings for children from those of adults, contributed to the idea of adolescence; now it is increasingly erasing the lines in two distinct but identifiable ways: its treatment of the most serious youthful offenders, and its recognition of the rights of children and adolescents.

More severe treatment. Because adolescent crime involvement has changed from primarily misdemeanors against property to more and more felonies and personal harm (assault, rape, and murder) cases, adolescents, especially repeat offenders, are more and more often remanded to adult court and handed adult sentences rather than remaining under the protection of the juvenile system (Coakley, 81). In Richmond, Virginia, for example, the morning newspaper on one day in 1983 reported two separate convictions of seventeen-year-olds for murder; one was likely to receive the death sentence. Examples from the New York Police Department include a nine-year-old who robbed a bank at gunpoint, a ten-year-old arrested for the nineteenth time for purse-snatching, a fifteen-year-old suspected of murdering a policeman, a thirteen-year-old who killed two elderly women while purse-snatching, and a thirteen-year-old who confessed to over 200 felonies (Coakley, 81). Because of examples like these those adolescents who commit adult crimes are no longer treated like children in the courts. Both the crimes and society's reaction to them are examples of the blurring of the lines between childhood and adulthood.

Children's rights. The second area of the law as it deals with adolescents and children is the increasing recognition of children's rights. Foster (74) proposes eight moral rights of children, which should be supported by legal rights: (1) to be regarded as a person; (2) to receive parental love, affection, discipline, and guidance;

(3) to be supported, maintained, and educated to the best of personal ability; (4) to receive fair treatment from all in authority; (5) to earn and keep one's earnings, and to be emancipated when necessary; (6) to be free of legal disabilities; (7) to seek and obtain medical treatment and counseling; and (8) to receive special care, consideration, and protection in the administration of law and justice. Children and adolescents do not yet have these rights, but the trends in the law are in their direction. For example, the juvenile justice system, as practiced in most states well into the 1970s, did not grant due process considerations to children. Due process refers to the right to be present, be heard, argue in one's defense, and present evidence. Today, due process rights are emerging for children, but the issue becomes complicated when we consider the issue of a child in conflict with his or her parents (Benedeck, 79). The juvenile justice system also only began to appoint attorneys for children after the Supreme Court mandated that it do so in a decision rendered (*in re Gault* 387 U.S. 1, 1967) in a case in which a juvenile had been unfairly sentenced after being refused the right to a lawyer.

Treatment without parental consent. The single most problematic area of all is that of adolescents, especially females, obtaining medical and psychiatric treatment without their parents' knowledge (Sarri, 76; Benedeck, 79). When the treatment is for venereal disease, contraception, or abortion, the issue is particularly sticky, with arguments raging around adolescent rights versus parental rights. In 1982 and 1983 the U.S. Congress argued the so-called ''squeal rule,'' which would have demanded that clinics that receive federal monies report to parents that their daughters have sought contraceptive pills or devices. The battle was a hot one, with one side arguing that family communication would be enhanced by such disclosure, and the other side arguing that not only would family communication not be enhanced, but that many girls who might have sought contraceptives would not do so, but would merely remain sexually active without benefit of contraception. The law was struck down in court.

Trends in the law. Benedeck notes five trends in the area of adolescence and the law: (1) the adolescent is being seen as a person in her own right; (2) separate laws for adolescent females are being developed; (3) attorneys are being appointed for children; (4) due process rights are being extended to children; and (5) there is an increase in the collaboration between mental health professionals and the juvenile justice system in regard to the treatment of adolescents.

The crux of the problem, says Zimring (82), is that until recently the law recognized only a single age of maturity, with minors being considered in need of different laws and protections than adults. In the age of human rights movements, children (and adults who speak for them) are demanding equal rights. As a result, the laws concerning children and adolescents are being challenged. Zimring (82) argues, however, that although we need to treat children and adolescents like people, they are not yet adult. Because nothing magic happens on the eighteenth birthday, adolescents ought to be considered in training for adulthood, and our treatment of them ought to reflect our recognition of their *increasing* maturity without expecting them to display adult maturity. The result would be laws and public policies that reflect that there are wide developmental differences between early, middle, and late adolescents.

Prolonged Adolescence in the Midst of Hurrying

Our society hurries children to grow up, but when they reach physical maturity, an interesting paradox develops. We have already discussed the prolongation of adolescence that results from extended education and training, and it is certainly true that the social phenomenon of an extended adolescence allows for advanced education, raises expectations for personal success, and facilitates a happy ending to the career search, but it also creates conflicts. As early as high school, the double messages of "Be grown up" and "Remain a child" are evident. High school students have been pressured to dress and talk like adults, yet become frustrated because their maturity is thwarted by things like hall passes and lack of meaningful participation in decision making (Elkind, 81). They remain "marginal men" (Lewin, 39).

The prolonged adolescence has been found to have negative consequences for many students. Boredom, cynicism, disappointment, negative attitudes, prolonged emotional dependence, poor self-image, and poor progress have all been associated with prolonged student status (Goswick, 82; Finkelstein, 83). The paradox of a prolonged adolescence in the midst of hurrying remains unresolved.

The Special Role of the Computer

Our discussion of the impact of societal influences on the experience of adolescence cannot be completed without at least a preliminary discussion of the role of the computer in modern society. We as yet have only guesses about its effects on adolescents.

Computer literacy. There rages a current debate over the role of technological awareness and computer literacy in education, with the Sloan foundation going so far as to urge educators to rethink a new liberal arts that emphasizes math and technology (Marvin, 83). Postman (82) contends that the computer may have the capacity to reinstate the need for childhood, for just as television removed the necessity for the skill of reading to gain access to adulthood, the need to program a computer may be the new skill that separates children from adults. Paradoxically, children could end up being more computer literate than adults, who are more likely to resist the new technology.

But the controversy exists without a common understanding of what computers are and what skills are necessary for their mastery. Marvin (83) sent a comprehensive questionnaire to sixty professional computer network people. Among these, computers were conceived to be either tools or independent intelligences.

Children could end up being more computer literate than adults.

There was wide general agreement on levels of skill, but little agreement on what level of skill ought to determine literacy.

At the lowest level of skill are the nonusers; these people have daily contact with computers but are unaware that the microwave oven and supermarket checkout run on computers. Some of the experts believe that awareness was sufficient to constitute literacy. At the second level are casual end-users: these people are nonprogrammers who follow fixed procedures to accomplish specific tasks. I am writing this book in that fashion; I simply put in a word processing program and type in my manuscript. With the use of a guide I can then perform all the necessary editorial functions, but I have no idea how to program the computer I write on. It is between this and the next level of skill that the greatest debate concerning literacy occurs. Some experts believe end-user skills are sufficient; others define literacy as the ability to program computers. Next come programmers, who specify the procedures by which others solve problems, but who do not actually design programs. Design is reserved for the next two levels: hackers, who are chaotically creative; and wizards, who are the most talented and respected among designers, analysts, and computer scientists.

Marvin (83) points out that many people are learning end-user skills on the job, but that programming and design skills remain in the domain of the elite. He compares computer literacy to written literacy, and suggests that we are only in the opening days of the computer literacy movement.

Potential impact. We don't yet know even the basic language of computer literacy, and have not addressed the hard question of the likely impact computer literacy requirements will have on an already stratified society. Political issues, massive funding, revised educational requirements, retraining efforts, the availability of computers to the general public: all are forthcoming debates. With all its potential, the computer is likely to become, like the printing press and television, a force whose power we cannot anticipate.

> There is a sense in which all inventors are, to use Arthur Koestler's word, sleepwalkers. Or perhaps we might call them Frankensteins, and the entire process, the Frankenstein syndrome: One creates a machine for a particular and limited purpose. But once the machine is built, we discover — sometimes to our horror, usually to our discomfort, always to our surprise — that it has ideas of its own; that it is quite capable not only of changing our habits but, . . . of changing our habits of mind. (Postman, 82)

SUMMARY

The vast and rapid changes of our technological society are influencing the experience of adolescence in ways that we only partially realize. The industrial revolution is over; the technological revolution has begun.

With technology has come an emphasis on service occupations rather than agricultural or manufacturing ones. The communications industry, for example, is mushrooming, with new information replacing old information at a dizzying rate. Our young people are exposed to more, sooner, than at any time in history.

Adolescents are influenced by interpersonal relationships, physical environments, life changes, and cultural and socioeconomic factors. Of these, socioeconomic factors have been the most thoroughly researched, with social class placement influencing opportunities, values, attitudes, even self-esteem.

The technological society requires people with technological competence, the result of which may further separate the intellectual elite (upper middle class) from those who can't compete in an intellectual marketplace (lower class).

Technology's benefits are balanced by its inherent risks; stress is the result. One of these stresses is that which results from overload, which may force people to erect emotional barriers to protect themselves from too many demands on their attention and energy.

For adolescents to compete in the technological world, they will need technical competence, advanced education, and assistance in learning to adapt to change.

Television, perhaps more than any other single factor, has changed the lives and experiences of adolescents. Today's adolescents have grown up with television, and its potential for impact is significant. It can both enlarge their world and restrict their options. Its messages about families, values, sex, driving, and virtually every aspect of living are pervasive.

The stress of living in a technological world has led observers to comment on society's apparent need to hurry children to adulthood by denying them the joys of childhood. Children are hurried by their parents, who because of their own stress, demand that their children serve as status symbols, surrogates for their own unfulfilled dreams, confidants, and decision makers. Schools, with their emphasis on competition and management, hurry children too, as do the ever-present media, which have removed all taboos from the lives of children.

The law also is erasing the distinctions between children and adults through its increasingly severe treatment of the most serious offenses and its increased attention to the rights of children and adolescents.

Finally, though we know little about its effects on adolescent development, the advent of the computer in society will undoubtedly play a major role in the lives of adolescents, one which we cannot predict with any accuracy at this time.

3

A Family Perspective

THE ROLE OF THE FAMILY

Adam, Billy, and Carl were all born on the same day fifteen years ago, but their birthday is just about the only thing they have in common. Their respective families are constituted differently, and their parents engage in vastly different behaviors as they rear their children.

Adam is the oldest of three, and he is frequently called on to assume major responsibility for his ten-year-old sister and seven-year-old half-brother. His mother and stepfather, with whom he lives, work long hours and leave the children to care for themselves. Adam is required to do little, however, besides baby-sit. His parents are permissive, allowing him to do whatever he pleases and demanding little in the way of interaction. Adam spends as much time as he can with friends.

Billy has two older brothers (21 and 19) and two younger sisters (14 and 12). Both parents live at home, but they fight with each other frequently, especially over the all-too-meager supply of money. They demand obedience from their children, yell at them regularly, and sometimes resort to physical punishment. Both older brothers have left home, and Billy is now the recipient of most of his parents' hostility.

Carl has one older sister, now 18 and getting ready to leave for college. His parents have been divorced for eight years, but Carl has a good relationship with both parents, each of whom discusses with him both his concerns and interests and their reasons for expecting certain behaviors from him. Carl would be happier if his parents were together, but he knows that many problems were alleviated when they divorced, and he has accepted that fact. He appreciates that they have set reasonable standards and are willing to negotiate differences with him.

The family, it is clear, acts as the single most significant influence on the development of children and adolescents. Two definitions demonstrate the function and the power of the family:

The family unit, broadly speaking, is a unit of people who live together and share life's basic day-by-day functions. Throughout history, humanity has demonstrated need for such a core group, yet also has demonstrated need for each individual member to grow. These dual, sometimes contrasting, human needs create the paradoxes of the family unit, in which exist struggle for separateness and togetherness, differentness and sameness, protection and freedom, support and independence. (Dodson, 77, p. 3)

In human terms, joining up in order to "get along" usually means some sort of family group. The family is the natural context for both growth and healing. . . . The family is a natural group which over time has evolved patterns of interacting. These patterns make up the family structure, which governs the functioning of family members, delineating their range of behavior and facilitating their interaction. A viable form of family structure is needed to perform the family's essential tasks of supporting individuation while providing a sense of belonging. (Minuchin, 81, p. 11)

The family provides protection to the growing child and also shapes that child's behavior both within and outside the family unit. The family provides the child's primary source of nurturance and of learning, yet is rendered the conflicting task of protecting while also encouraging increasing autonomy. Adolescents, who are not yet ready to be completely independent yet are not as dependent as they once were, are likely to provide a source of confusion both for themselves and their parents. How well they are assisted toward the autonomy of adulthood is the subject of this chapter.

Healthy families are frequently compared to a symphony (Satir, 72; Alexander, 82), in which individual notes combine to form melodies and themes in harmony with one another, with the resultant piece being far more powerful and meaningful than a simple addition of the notes. Unhealthy families are discordant rather than harmonious.

In this chapter we will first examine the various functions performed by the family, especially the important function of assisting adolescents to become autonomous while remaining emotionally involved in the family. We will then look at how the developmental needs of adolescents and their parents frequently interact, with particular sensitivity to the changing nature of their concerns and the transformation in their interactions. We will examine the effects on adolescent development of various styles of parenting. We will then look at the many different family structures, including such aspects of structure as intact (both parents in the home), single-parent, and "reconstituted" or step-families, as well as birth order, family size, and spacing between children. Finally, we will discuss the relatively new emphasis in the mental health profession of treating the family as an interactive system responsible for the behavior and feelings of each of its members, with the resultant upsurge of interest in family education, counseling, and therapy.

Adolescents view their families as the most important institution in their lives (Jessop, 81); as students of adolescence we need to be aware of the vast impact of whoever constitutes the family, changing as it is in these last decades of the twentieth century, of how adolescents and their families interact, and of the family processes that contribute to adolescent development.

Healthy Family Described

Before attempting to distinguish the characteristics of healthy and unhealthy families, a caution is in order. In this, as in all other descriptions, we are necessarily relying on generalizations concerning what seems to be most often true, in this case, what is most often true for middle-class American families. As generalizations, our descriptions are not universal, nor are they predictive; some families may function very adaptively even though they do not fit our description of healthy families. Generalizations, then, describe only a likelihood, never a certainty, and must be read with this caution in mind.

Family functions. All families provide some sense of belonging, provide role models for their children, and teach communication skills (Olson, 80). Healthy families make a place for each individual without suffocation; respect the change in roles that occurs as children mature; and teach interaction skills that serve each individual well both within and outside the family. Family members have their biological and emotional needs met; feel loving and loved; respect themselves, one another, and the family as a unit; and evolve a system of interaction that assists each individual in achieving full potential (Dodson, 77).

Characteristics. Florence Kaslow, editor of the *Journal of Marital and Family Therapy*, characterizes healthy families as being creative, vital, and open. She identifies characteristics that make them unique, different both from more ordinary families, which function adequately but not optimally, and completely dysfunctional families, which are either completely chaotic or so enmeshed as to not be able to provide the support for individual autonomy that each of us requires (Booker, 81).

The healthiest families share clear structures and authority; have clear and straightforward communication, including effective negotiating skills; respect freedom and privacy; afford children age-appropriate decision-making influence; support increasing autonomy and independence while providing emotional support; and look forward to the day when the children are fully independent. Unhealthy families provide inappropriate amounts of support (too much or too little); have faulty communication and decision-making patterns, ineffective controls, and little respect; and may produce what family therapists refer to as a "symptom bearer" (Dodson, 77), an individual who signals the pain in the family by malfunctioning — acting out, running away, or becoming emotionally ill. We will look more closely at the phenomenon of the dysfunctional family a little later in this chapter.

We will first examine the development of autonomy, family interactions, and parenting styles, and the effects of various family structures on adolescent development.

The Development of Autonomy

Tara, a seventeen-year-old high school senior, expresses a common concern (Reinhart, 83, pp. 136–137):

> It seems like my mother keeps forgetting that I'm not five years old! She doesn't listen to me, and she doesn't seem to think I can handle things on my own. (Do you know how degrading it is to be asked whether you've turned off the stove? Or to be constantly nagged about homework?)
>
> I eventually do get my work done; my average never suffers. If only she'd let me trust myself, I'd be happier.

The transformation from helpless infant to independent adult occurs largely through parent-child interactions that facilitate the development of increasing autonomy; healthy parenting demands the relinquishment of control and the encouragement of independent decision making, while maintaining close interpersonal relationships within the family. This process is at the heart of family interactions and comes to a head during adolescence (Ausubel, 77). Adolescents develop autonomy through making independent decisions, first about relatively minor aspects of life like clothing, later about money, careers, values, and lifestyle decisions.

Executive autonomy. Ausubel (77) identifies two kinds of autonomy. **Executive autonomy** involves the ability to do for oneself — age-appropriate tasks and the chores of daily living. Although this executive or behavioral autonomy gradually develops throughout childhood, it increases markedly at adolescence, when young people can be expected not only to care for themselves, but to contribute to the care of the family through appropriate chores. Atwater (83) points out that adolescents may often appear inconsistent in their executive autonomy, being completely autonomous in things they wish to do (caring for a car, for example), but highly dependent in those they choose not to do (keeping a room clean, for example).

Volitional autonomy. The second type of autonomy, **volitional autonomy,** involves relationships and the ability to make independent decisions. Adolescents gradually shift their emotional allegiance, learning to rely on their own judgment rather than that of their parents. For a time, the shift may be away from parents and toward peers, but eventually, this volitional or emotional autonomy becomes independent of both parents and peers. Even while peer attachments are increasing, the parent-child relationship need not suffer, especially if parents understand that their adolescents need to widen their spheres of influence and judgment (Kandel, 72). Volitional autonomy is more difficult to achieve than executive autonomy, and many adults suffer from not having achieved the confidence necessary to be emotionally independent. They rely too heavily on the judgment of others and are especially vulnerable to criticism or rejection.

Family influence. The development of autonomy, whether executive or volitional, depends on the quality of the dependency relationship in <u>childhood</u>. Those who experience high degrees of warmth and love, without being suffocated, develop lasting self-worth and are capable of developing age-appropriate autonomy as they mature. Both those who are overprotected and those who are not loved develop dependent behaviors, feel incompetent, and are hampered in the development of autonomy (Adler, 63; Ausubel, 77). At adolescence, all children break away; parents who are successful and feel satisfied with themselves are more willing to let their adolescents go, modify earlier parenting and discipline strategies, and support independent decision making within reasonable limits. The development of independence also depends on the opportunity to disagree and thus to support ones' opinions. Parents need to help their adolescents develop autonomy through the experience of handling conflict, even when the conflict is with them. Because girls have been socialized to be more compliant than boys, they especially need positive support for independence and the experience of handling conflicts (Newman, 78).

Most parents do allow increasing participation by their adolescents in family decision making. Steinberg (78) found that in family discussions, the more physically mature an adolescent male, the more assertive he was allowed to be, and concluded that the more adultlike stature of the boy stimulated his parents to expect more adultlike interactions from him. By the time adolescents graduate from high school, they have usually developed an autonomy of action and of judgment so that reliance on both parents and peers has diminished. Kandel (72) found that late adolescents who have developed executive and volitional autonomy feel close to their parents, enjoy activities with them, ask them for advice, want to be like them, and experience only infrequent conflict with them. Grotevant (85) found that adolescents' capacity for autonomy is linked to their experiences within their families: <u>families that encourage independent decision making within a context of relatedness within family relationships help their adolescents to develop psychological competence *and* healthy parent-child relationships.</u> When handled well, the development of autonomy does not result in the rejection of parental influence, but rather in the adolescent's seeking parental input before making an independent decision. Such adolescents then leave home gracefully: they make their own decisions, do things for themselves, and feel mature, using parental influence wisely but not exclusively (Moore, 83).

Variations in Adolescent Autonomy

Although it is clear that autonomy is developed primarily through the interactions within individual families, there are nevertheless some generalizations about the development of autonomy that apply to societal expectations that may be broader than individual families. For example, there are empirically documented differences in autonomy between college students who go away to college and those who stay at home and commute, differences between males and females, and cross-cultural differences.

College attendance. Sullivan (80) and Kimmel (80) both addressed the differences between college students who board at college and those who commute from home. Those who board make a more complete break with their families, but report more affection for their parents, better communication with their parents, greater satisfaction with their families, and more independence. Going away to college apparently facilitates independence while simultaneously strengthening emotional bonds. Sullivan (80) cautions, however, that other factors may intervene, since the boarders have higher SAT scores and tend to go to four-year rather than two-year colleges.

Sex differences. Douvan (66) points out that males achieve emotional autonomy significantly sooner than do females and attributes the differences to socialization. Girls are reinforced for dependence; they are more dependent as children and remain more dependent throughout adulthood. Only 25 percent of eighteen-year-old females in an extensive study (albeit one published in 1966 and based on data collected in the 1950s) said that their parents expected them to become autonomous; the other 75 percent apparently felt trained to move their dependence from their parents to a husband. Martin (75), however, found that girls are not necessarily more dependent in situations outside their small circle of friends, and that parental modeling is more important. Girls whose parents expect self-reliance, maturity, and achievement are more independent and achievement-oriented than their peers whose parents have no such expectations. The societal stereotype of the dependent female may well be changing, but only if parents recognize the need for autonomy in their adolescent girls as well as their adolescent boys.

Cultural differences. Cultural mores also influence the development of autonomy. Americans tend to encourage relatively early independence, at least in comparison, say, with Indians, who encourage a long dependence and even continue to reserve the right to make their children's marital decisions (Sundberg, 69). Danish adolescents, however, are more autonomous than their American counterparts (Kandel, 69). Danish parents are more democratic in their child-rearing practices, have fewer rules, and are more likely to discuss the rules with their children; and their children are more likely to feel independent, free to disagree with their parents, and free to talk with their parents about their problems. As a result, Danish adolescents exercise greater self-control than do American adolescents. Kandel's research provides empirical support for the importance of open communication and negotiation within reasonable limits.

In a comparison of French and American adolescents, Wylie (65) found that although French adolescents are more dependent while living at home, they make a cleaner break from their parents when they do leave home. Americans, on the other hand, make more tenuous breaks and are likely to return home, for help with finances, assistance in the purchase of major items, and, a little later, baby-sitting. And the 1980 census reported that about 18 million adult children in the United States actually live at home with their parents (Peterson, 82), and most of these have returned after having been on their own for varying amounts of time. Most return for financial security, but many seem to find the relationship mutually rewarding, and some make the arrangement permanent. Issues of autonomy and independence must be carefully worked out in such circumstances.

THE INTERACTION OF ADOLESCENTS AND ADULTS

> To look at a family from the long view is to see it as an organism evolving over time. Two individual "cells" join, forming a multibodied entity like the colony animal. This entity moves through stages of aging that affect each body individually, until the two progenitor cells decay and die, while others start the life cycle anew.
>
> Like all living organisms, the family system has a tendency toward both maintenance and evolution. Demands for change may activate counterdeviation mechanisms, but the system evolves toward increasing complexity. Although the family can fluctuate only within a given range, it has an amazing capacity to adapt and change while maintaining continuity. (Minuchin, 81, p. 21)

Two Changing Systems

The family obviously evolves and changes over time, and the individuals within it change as well. Yet very little attention has been paid, until relatively recently, to the changes of adulthood (Vaillant, 77; Levinson, 78), and even less attention to how the developmental tasks of one stage interact with those of another. We are interested specifically in the changes of adolescence and the concomitant changes of middle age, the age occupied by most parents of adolescents. Although the empirical evidence is slim, "it is likely that transformations in familial relations at adolescence are influenced by social and intraindividual changes in parents who are approaching, or are experiencing, important changes in their own life trajectories" (Hill, 80a, p. 34).

Parent-child interaction occurs between two dynamic systems; to ignore one, as sociologists and psychologists who study adolescents have generally done (Hartup, 79b; Smith, 76), is to deny half the total system. Adolescence has its own unique tasks; so does middle age. The interactions between adolescents and their parents can be viewed from the changes each is experiencing physically, intellectually, emotionally, and socially.

Physical changes. In terms of their bodies, adolescents are experiencing the greatest changes of their lives. They are becoming adult, and with emerging adulthood is a significant increase in size, strength, and stature. Concomitantly, middle-aged adults are beginning to tire more easily, notice the gray hairs and the facial lines, and be aware of the tendency to gain weight. Adolescents are developing adult sexuality

The family provides a variety of influences on the adolescent.

and becoming increasingly attractive, while their middle-aged parents may be perceiving a diminishing sexuality and attractiveness.

Intellectual changes. Intellectually, adolescents are expanding their worlds, developing new cognitive capabilities, and beginning to question and test the once-unquestioned beliefs and values of their elders. They are looking to the future and its multitude of potentialities just as their parents are beginning to be concerned with the passage of time and to be aware of how little time is left to them. They may feel some urgency to make whatever contributions they are going to make before it is too late.

Emotional changes. Emotionally, adolescents may be developing some self-consciousness and an increased sensitivity to criticism, while their parents are experiencing some loss of control over their family and their future. Both are adjusting to new identities — adolescents to their emerging adulthood, middle-aged adults to new roles in relation to their children.

Social changes. Socially, adolescents are considering future careers and lifestyle options at the same time that their parents are realizing that they have probably reached a plateau in their careers and are not likely to achieve the dreams they once had. Adolescents are adjusting to newly developed needs for privacy, autonomy, independence, and peer interaction at the same time that their parents are adjusting to aging parents (with the potential of becoming parents to their own parents to compensate for declining strength and health), their children leaving home, the loss of friends to sudden deaths, and new roles for themselves. Finally, adolescents are moving from an age group that is not highly regarded (adolescence) to the most highly regarded age group (young adult, the subject of most movies, television shows, and advertisements depicting the ''beautiful people''), while their parents are moving from a highly regarded group (adult) to a significantly less highly regarded one (middle and old age).

Resulting interactions. Vaillant (77) identifies the forties as a time of introspection, with some personal discomfort and a shaky self-image, a description that is remarkably similar to that often used to describe adolescents; and Hill (80) speaks of an ''ironic complementarity'' between the concerns of adolescents and their parents due to developmental changes in each. It has also been documented that marital relationships tend to hit an all-time low when children are in early adolescence (N.B. Miller, 76). That there may be some difficulty in interaction between these two groups is not surprising, but the potential for healthy interaction is not to be denied. There may be a temporary disequilibrium as adolescents move from dependence to independence, some ambivalence about emerging sexuality, increased expectations for mature behavior, questioning of adult authority and decisions, the possibility of jealousy, a conflict between letting go and hanging on, and a shift in roles, with greater potential for mutual respect, mutual interaction and decision making, shared interests, shared responsibilities, and improved adult-adult communication.

Clearly, the changing interactions are complex, with potential for both conflict and increased mutuality. Parents and children socialize one another; just as the child is affected by parental situations and interactions, parents regulate and change their lives to accommodate their children's changing needs. As Minuchin (81) points out in the quotation that opens this discussion, the family system is flexible within certain limits, yet it has a tremendous capacity to adapt to changes while maintaining a sense of stability and sameness. Parents and adolescents may, within the differences and inevitable conflicts, nevertheless develop mutual respect and understanding. The healthy family system reaches out, doesn't expect perfect understanding, and changes its interactions to fit emerging needs.

Resocialization. Of particular interest is the family's capability to adapt to the increasing influence of adolescents. Baranowski (78) and Sussman (77) refer to the **resocialization** of parents, the turning of the tables that begins in adolescence, when children increase their attempts to change their parents' behavior, and ends when middle-aged children become the caretakers of their aging parents. Early in adolescence, children increase their assertive behavior in their first attempts to gain control. Parents often react by increasing their own assertiveness, but most realize that this only escalates conflict and so reduce their assertive reactions. After puberty, adolescents also decrease their attempts at asserting control, and a more egalitarian interaction pattern, which reduces family tension, is established (Steinberg, 78). Early adolescence, then, is seen as the time of the greatest potential for conflict. We will look at conflict in more depth a little later in this chapter.

The Role of Grandparents

Ever since the Industrial Revolution, nuclear rather than extended families have been the rule in this country. Multigenerational families are now rare, yet adolescents still report grandparents as the next most influential people after their own parents (Baranowski, 83).

Adolescents report grandparents as most influential, after their own parents.

Interaction. In a comprehensive review of the literature on grandparent-adolescent relationships, Baranowski (83) cites the factors that operate against grandparent-adolescent interaction, as well as those that encourage it. Operating against significant interaction are the facts that most grandparents don't live in the same household as their grandchildren, they are often separated geographically, many grandparents and their adult children have developed a hands-off policy concerning grandparents' influence, and most adolescents are less attached to the family than are their younger siblings. These factors seem to operate less in black families than in white, because black children have more contact with their grandparents, who are also more involved in childrearing and more likely to share a residence (Hays, 73).

On the other hand are the factors that facilitate grandparent-adolescent interaction: more adolescents today than ever before have living grandparents, who are generally healthier and better educated than previously; also, the fact that grandparents are removed from direct influence may actually serve to increase closeness. Grandparents, uninvolved in childrearing, are likely to be allowed to be indulgent and develop warm, close relationships with their grandchildren free from the necessity to discipline. "Thus, the factor that serves to limit grandparent-adolescent contact — the removal of grandparents from a position of dominance with obligation — increases the possibility for warmth and intimacy between generations" (Baranowski, 83, p. 577).

Relationship. The nature of the grandparent-adolescent relationship is generally defined by the parents, who serve as a bridge between the separated generations. Children are usually closer to their maternal grandparents, especially the maternal grandmother, probably because of continuing relationships between adult women and their mothers (Kahana, 70; Baranowski, 83). Interestingly, older adolescents are more involved with their grandparents than younger adolescents are. Early adolescents (aged 10 to 12) view their grandparents as playmates and gift givers; middle adolescents (aged 13 to 15) have least to do with grandparents; and older adolescents (aged 16 to 18) have a more balanced view, probably because of their increased maturity and more adult perspective. They tend to stay in close touch, appreciate their grandparents' personality and character traits, and to love, respect, and enjoy their grandparents (Robertson, 76; Baranowski, 83).

Importance. Baranowski (83) summarizes the potential impact of grandparents on adolescents:

1. Grandparents contribute to the adolescent's emerging sense of identity by providing continuity with the past and answers to the question "Where did I come from?" "Transmitting knowledge about cultural and familial roots may be the most important way grandparents can have an impact on adolescents' search for identity" (Baronowski, 83, p. 581).

2. Grandparents frequently improve the relationship between adolescents and their parents. They convey information about the parents, thus improving the ado-

lescents' understanding of them, and they also sometimes serve as conflict mediator, frequently providing the more impartial and casual view that facilitates resolution.

3. Grandparents provide a source for the development of realistic attitudes toward older people. It has been documented that adolescents who have close relationships with their grandparents have more positive attitudes and fewer negative stereotypes of the aged and the aging.

With the increase in stepfamilies and the accompanying increase in step-grandparents, new relationships must be forged and fostered. Because the phenomenon is still relatively new, no research has yet addressed these changing relationships and influences, yet they may be significant. The role of grandparents should not be overlooked in any study of the effects of the family on adolescent development.

Family Communication

As is evident from our preceding discussion, communication is the heart of family interactions and therefore the basis of development. When Satir talks of harmony and discordance in families, she is talking about communication, which includes all the verbal and nonverbal interactions from which children learn their value and role in the family. We have emphasized repeatedly that the family teaches communication skills and that the patterns of interaction determine what children learn about themselves. With developing autonomy in adolescence, communication patterns need to change to a more egalitarian sharing than was appropriate in childhood, and how well the family negotiates this change may well be the critical factor in how harmoniously family relationships are perceived. The quality of interactions provides a ready clue to the quality of interpersonal functioning.

Communication problems. Matteson (74) points out that problems in adult-adolescent communication do not begin in adolescence. Rather, poor parent-child communications during the earlier years ("Shut up!" "Do it now because I say so!") backfire in adolescence with adolescent hostility and rebellion. The onset of adolescence, with its increasing demands for reason and autonomy, generates some normal developmental stress, and unhealthy families respond with defensive communication patterns (Alexander, 73).

That some parents experience tremendous difficulty with the increasing maturity of their adolescents is seen in the communication patterns established with them. Instead of openly discussing issues and arriving at mutually agreed upon solutions, instead of spending time with their adolescents in leisure activities, these parents resort to snooping, interrogating, and blaming, all in a futile attempt to maintain control (Alexander, 82; Gordon, 70). These parents keep secrets from their children, model ineffective communication with each other as well as with their children, and are likely to be viewed by their adolescents as distant and ineffective (Norman, 81).

Dodson (77) describes examples of dysfunctional patterns of behavior and communication in families. For example, every family develops unspoken rules about who can talk to whom, and about what one may talk. In some families, this rule may be so dysfunctional that a child who wants Father to know something tells Mother, and Mother tells Father. It is easy to predict the quality of the relationship between that father and his child.

Healthy communication. Thomas Gordon (70) and William Glasser (69), the authors of *Parent Effectiveness Training* and *Schools without Failure* respectively, argue that open, honest, democratic communication and problem-solving skills are essential for healthy interaction between adults and adolescents. Both parties must learn to listen, express feelings, remain nonjudgmental, and solve problems in mutually enhancing ways. Instead of blaming and interrogating, which only put people on the defensive, we need to develop open and democratic relationships that serve to meet the needs of all involved. Both Gordon and Glasser have been severely criticized for offering what appear to be simple solutions to deep-seated problems in interaction, especially if adolescents have not yet developed the maturity to interact democratically, yet their specific recommendations for improving communications are clear, usable, and do facilitate positive interaction. They are not, however, a panacea and, especially in families that have a long history of dysfunctional interactions, are not likely to cause drastic change. In such families, including those that have already produced a hostile or even delinquent adolescent, nothing short of therapy is likely to have an impact.

In his surveys of adolescents, Norman (81) collected teenagers' advice to their parents, advice which encapsulates good communication:

1. Listen and understand.

2. Be upfront and honest.

3. Don't cop out when tough subjects come up.

4. Trust us and let us learn from our own mistakes.

5. Don't live in the past.

6. Discipline, don't dominate.

7. Compromise.

8. Show that you love, care, and will be there.

Conflict in Families

As we emphasized in Chapter 1, rebellion, turbulence, and rejection of parental values are not characteristic of adolescence. Basic values and behaviors are highly consistent between parents and their adolescents (Chand, 75). Norman (81), in a very large survey of adolescents, found that 83 percent can tell their parents how they think and feel (at least sometimes), 60 percent believe their parents listen and care; 67 percent say their parents respect their privacy; and most want parental advice on important decisions like careers. Gallup polls conducted in 1978 (79a, b) found that 91 percent of young adults (aged 18 to 24) are satisfied with their home lives through adolescence, and 95 percent of parents believe they get along well with their adolescent children. Parents clearly are influential in decisions involving basic values and the choice of a vocation, but less so when peer activity is involved, as in dress, appearance, and social customs (Brittain, 63).

Conflict. Differences, rather than representing a gap between generations, are primarily centered on: the relative minutiae of life (dress, hours of sleep, use of car, chores, dating); and social customs (including sexual habits and drug experimentation) (Block, 74; Kelley, 72). Adolescents and their parents may have very different tastes, but they usually agree where fundamental values are concerned (Coleman, 80). Where conflict exists it is usually related to a perceived lack of freedom, and with increasing freedom, conflict lessens (Kandel, 69). Often, conflict may arise because parental styles and expectations of responsibility have not kept pace with adolescent needs for autonomy, but once new rules are negotiated, conflict is minimized.

In summarizing the research on family conflict, Hill (80) notes that ordinary families, even though they engage in bickering and squabbling in early adolescence, nevertheless manage to engage in supportive and mutual communications. Only in troubled families do parents never learn that the authoritarian methods they used when their children were smaller are no longer effective. Instead of developing egalitarian interaction patterns, they either continue to demand or give up and allow any behavior. Neither approach facilitates adolescent development.

Rebellion. Although they are in the minority, some adolescents do rebel, and some rebel with a vengeance. Balswick (75) reports that 21 percent of males and 23 percent of females experience some rebelliousness during adolescence; rebelliousness is most often directed at excessive authority on the part of either parent (Martin, 75). More specifically, rebellion is associated with strong disagreements with parents concerning child-rearing practices, negative attitudes toward school, marital conflict and unhappiness, extremely restrictive homes, extremely permissive homes, and very large families, especially those dominated by an unhappy, authoritarian father (Chand, 75; Block, 74; Balswick, 75; Peterson, 75; Clemens, 79). Rebellion may be overt, as in the case of excessive argumentativeness, smoking, drinking, drug use, promiscuity, or delinquency; or more subtle, as in underachievement, carelessness, accidents, and sexual activity. How these behaviors result from faulty family interactions is eloquently described by Satir (foreword to Dodson, 77):

> . . . when family members are not making harmonious music, it is likely to be because some instruments have stopped playing, and therefore have no voice; some blare out only discords, which irritate; some just play loud and drown out the rest; some play out of tune, which frustrates; some will play only solo, and some only duets. . . . [it is not a problem] of bad instruments, but more of an education in understanding and using those instruments.

Although no one advocates conflict and rebellion as a healthy means of development, Skolnick (78) cites research that demonstrates that many mature and creative people had difficult adolescent years, and suggests that stress and conflict can produce psychological growth. Perhaps in our technological society, in which the potential for conflict between parents and adolescents is accelerated by rapid social change, this observation can serve as some comfort. There will be conflict in every family; how it is handled may be the key to healthy *vs.* unhealthy development.

Unbearable conflict — running away. In 1971 more than 500,000 adolescents ran away (Ambrosino, 71). In 1983, that figure had risen to 1,000,000, with 5000 being buried each year in unmarked graves because no one knows who they are and 500,000 (both male and female) under the age of fourteen turning to prostitution to survive (NBC Monitor, 83). These are the runaways, who leave what they perceive to be unbearable situations, and throwaways, whose parents kick them out because they no longer choose to deal with them, together comprising the "Hansel and Gretel" kids, whom no one wants and who have nowhere to go. They feel misunderstood, unloved, and often abused. For these young people, rebellion is insufficient; their only option is to leave, yet they are too young to be alone. They are the products of the most dysfunctional families of all. Yet, for some, perceptions may not be confirmed by reality. If they run because of a crisis in the family, they may well return home when they are assured that they are wanted. For this reason federally funded centers for runaways, runaway hotlines, and publicity surrounding the plight of runaways have developed. Many can and do return home, and when the return is accompanied by sincere efforts at communication and understanding, the return can be successful.

Clearly, adolescents are not ready to perform solo. They may not want their parents to perform with them, but they do need their support behind the stage. It is up to families to provide that support.

PARENTING STYLES

As the need for autonomy increases, parental responses in both attitude and behavior have a powerful shaping influence on how well adolescents learn to deal with their world. The classic research of Baumrind (71, 75, 78) has delineated three primary styles of parenting, the **authoritarian,** the **permissive,** and the **authoritative.** Each style approaches the issue of control in the family in a different way, and each has been demonstrated to have significant, predictable effects on adolescent feelings and behavior.

Ineffective Styles

Authoritarian parenting. Authoritarian parents believe that children should obey, unquestioningly, all commands from their parents. Such parents are dogmatic, demanding, controlling, forceful, and punitive. They do not discuss issues with their adolescents, nor do they offer explanations for their orders. They allow little expression of views by their children, and offer no opportunity for self-management (Elder, 62). Their behaviors have strongly negative effects on their children, who often become dependent and simultaneously rebellious. Their children are likely to have little confidence, poor self-concepts, and little ability to interact or initiate positively They may be extremely self-conscious (G. R. Adams, 82a) and are over-represented in delinquent and alienated groups. The repressiveness of an authoritarian home breeds nothing but problems.

Permissive parenting. The lack of involvement and control of an overly permissive home, in which few controls or demands are made and nothing is punished or expected, can also lead to problems. In this home, the adolescent is all-powerful, and there are no consequences for ignoring parental requests. Here too are bred the negative identities seen in delinquency and alienation, and adolescents from under-restrictive homes are likely to display immaturity, poor self-restraint, and an inability to assume leadership. Parents in overly permissive homes have abdicated their right to set the rules and determine the role of the children in the functioning of the family. In the overly permissive home, the children make the rules.

Permissive parents, as well as authoritarian parents, can be either warm and affectionate, or cold and hostile, with differing effects. Becker (64) sees hostile, controlling parents producing antagonistic children; warm, controlling parents creating overprotected, dependent children; hostile, permissive parents creating detached and resentful children; and warm, permissive parents producing more relatively healthy children, closest to those who come from democratic homes. Nevertheless, rebellious adolescents are likely to have come from either highly restrictive or highly permissive homes (Kandel, 72; Balswick, 75).

Without saying so directly, York (80) clearly implies, in a program entitled **Toughlove,** that out-of-control teenagers come from permissive or repressive homes. Toughlove is a self-help program for parents of out-of-control teens, and in the introduction, the authors identify the ''many parents in crisis'' as rich, poor, middle-income; educated, uneducated; white-collar workers, blue-collar workers; single, divorced, remarried; *permissive, repressive* (italics mine); sickly, healthy; open, private; black, white; rural, city, suburban. The program advocates reestablishing firm discipline, parental rights, structure, reason, and encouragement of autonomy, all characteristics of the **authoritative** home, which provides the healthy alternative to authoritarian and permissive homes.

The Alternative

Authoritative parenting. Whereas authoritarian parents demand control and permissive parents abdicate it, authoritative parents *earn* it. Authoritative parents use themselves as role models for their children. They invite participation, encourage discussion, use logic and supportive arguments, make their standards known and keep them consistent, value self-discipline, share decision making as appropriate to the age and competence of their children, and are warm and nurturing, but also maintain ultimate decision-making authority (Baumrind, 71, 75, 78). They, in short, encourage freedom within reasonable limits. Their children fare well (Enright, 80), for they cope better with a variety of problems (Henggeler, 79); feel close to their parents; are self-reliant, adaptable, and self-disciplined (Hamachek, 76); develop high levels of responsible autonomy (Elder, 62); and are self-disclosive, motivated, and feel good about themselves (Hill, 80). Authoritative (democratic) parents try to guide and show rather than order, and they set reasonable and negotiable limits. For example, the adolescent may be allowed to propose a curfew, provided that he always let his parents know where he is going, and always phones if he must be late. This is in contrast to the authoritarian parent, who would set a rigid curfew, and the permissive parent, who would set none. Authoritative parenting, characterized by warmth and moderate control, it seems, produces adolescents who are personally and interpersonally competent. In a comprehensive review of the research on parenting styles, Hill (80, p. 54) concludes:

> Given the literature on mechanics of socialization, we can suggest that authoritative parenting, as opposed to authoritarian or permissive parenting in early adolescence, ''works'' because authoritative parents more often are appropriate models for the kinds of psychosocial outcomes in question and because their acceptance of the child invites emulation. Owing to their greater warmth, they also may have greater reward value, thus making approval and its withdrawal more potent sanctions. Because authoritative parents may be less frustrating, they may less often induce emotional responses that could interfere with use of the more complex social-reasoning processes of which adolescents, more than children, are capable. Authoritative parents also may be more responsive to intraindividual change in their children at early adolescence than are authoritarian parents. They do seem to provide a secure base in the family for learning to deal with peers.

Socioeconomic Differences

Investigators who have studied child-rearing styles in different socioeconomic groups note consistent differences, especially between the middle and lower classes (Hill, 80; Kohn, 77; Gecas, 74; W. Simon, 72). All note that the lower class is significantly more authoritarian than the middle class. Kohn (77) attributes this difference to differences in the work of the parents. Lower-class occupations are most often simple, repetitive, concrete, and externally supervised. The work environment tends to value obedience and structure rather than self-control, and this expectation is passed on in the family, where physical punishment, little discussion, and little attention to long-term goals tend to create adolescents who also have few long-term goals and who respond to authoritarian parenting in the manner we already described. Middle-class occupations, on the other hand, involve self-discipline, discussion, negotiation, and autonomy far more than do lower-class occupations; and middle-class parents are more likely to use authoritative rather than authoritarian parenting styles. The support of authoritative parenting styles is therefore a middle-class value. It is probably safe to say that our discussion of adolescence, in total, provides support for middle-class values, just as the American society as a whole is a middle-class society. Unfortunately, those born into the lower-class are judged by middle-class standards and expected to perform accordingly.

Discipline

Not surprisingly, the findings of research into the effects of various forms of discipline (ways of gaining control) in the home are consistent with those concerning parenting styles. Discipline is, of course, one means by which parents socialize their children.

Hoffman (70, 80) identifies three primary methods of discipline: **power assertion, love withdrawal,** and **induction.**

Power assertion. Parents who use power assertion to discipline attempt to gain control of their adolescents by threatening and punishing, sometimes physically. When adolescents comply, they do so out of fear of reprisal, and although they may comply in the presence of their parents, they frequently defy their parents behind their backs. Adolescents who know only power assertion are likely to become hostile and respond only to external authority, without developing self-control (Hoffman, 80). Professionals agree that the use of power in discipline should be avoided because it arouses anger and fear while exposing adolescents to an angry, hostile model. Neapolitan (81) reports that a child who identifies with a parent who models and encourages aggression will also behave aggressively, and that children who are physically punished are generally more aggressive than those who are not. Children who are physically punished for being aggressive increase their aggressive behavior. Bryan (82) surveyed a college student sample for the prevalence of corporal punishment in their families, and found that 95 percent of college students report receiving corporal punishment at some time. Unfortunately, the extent of that punishment was not reported, so we can't be sure that the students were reporting regular or repeated punishments, or recalling only a few instances. Bryan (82) also reports a number of other studies that show that 77 percent of parents report using corporal punishment, which has been demonstrated to have long-term negative effects: lower grades, poorer self-concepts, negative social interactions, higher incidence of aggression, lack of friends, delinquency, and negative psychological states such as depression and anxiety. These findings are, of course, completely consistent with those of authoritarian parenting.

Love withdrawal. Love withdrawal is the direct, nonphysical expression of anger through such behaviors as not listening, turning away, and expressing negative feelings, even as severe as "I hate you." Implicit in love withdrawal is the threat of abandonment, and adolescents respond to the fear of being abandoned with a strong sense of inferiority, an equally strong need for approval, and high anxiety. Love withdrawal is little better than power assertion for developing autonomy and self-confidence.

Induction. Induction, like authoritative parenting, is the healthy alternative. Parents who use induction are authoritative; they reason with their adolescents, explain consequences, and behave themselves in a responsible and democratic fashion. The reasoning and negotiating lead to both behavioral and emotional autonomy, and even to advanced levels of moral reasoning. (See Chapter 10 for a description of moral reasoning.)

FAMILY STRUCTURES

Although vastly different from its historical predecessors, the modern American family is still called on to perform the functions of protecting and nurturing children and adolescents while simultaneously preparing them to become autonomous individuals. Family size, birth order, spacing of siblings, working mothers, divorce and remarriage, and the continual moving of America's affluent corporate families have all been studied for their effects on the development of children and adolescents. We will look at the findings concerning each of these variables.

Family Size

Kidwell (81) points out that both the power of parents over their children and the support they provide for them are affected by the number of children in the family, the birth order of the children, and the spacing between them. Overall, family size is decreasing (*Social Indicators,* Bureau of the Census, 1980), and although there are relatively clear advantages and disadvantages to both large and small families, on balance, small families have been found to have more beneficial effects on adolescent development than large families.

Large families. Large families (those with four or more children) have been found to be more authoritarian (Peterson, 75), to be more likely to experience conflict between adolescents and parents, to use physical force in discipline, and to have adolescents who identify with their peers rather than their parents and leave home earlier (Holtzman, 65). On the other hand, Swanson (72) cites the advantages of a large family as being the opportunity to learn the value of cooperation and the greater number of potential role models with whom to identify (especially if the parents are relatively weak or ineffective).

Small families. Small families (two children or less) seem to have more advantages than disadvantages. Rosenberg (64) cites the major disadvantages as being greater sibling rivalry, especially when adolescents are either the same sex or only a year or so apart. The advantages of small families have been demonstrated to include a greater likelihood of democratic parenting and less conflict between the generations, greater similarity of attitudes and interests between the generations and greater likelihood of children identifying with their parents (Douvan, 66), greater closeness between siblings (Bowerman, 74), greater parental attention (Trotter, 76), and greater self-confidence, more involvement in social activities, greater interest in educational plans, and higher achievement motivation (Douvan, 66). If family size were the only factor contributing to healthy development, the trend toward increasingly smaller families could only be heralded as beneficial for everyone. Unfortunately, size alone, as is clear from our earlier discussions of parent-adolescent interactions, is far too simplistic a factor to account for the health of the family.

Birth Order

As early as 1896, Francis Galton (Galton, 1896) discovered that an unrepresentatively large proportion of famous scientists were either only or first-born sons. He attributed this phenomenon to the opportunity afforded first borns through their inheritance of the family fortune, which freed them from financial responsibilities and allowed them to pursue scientific careers. Kidwell (81, pp. 317–318) offers a modern, sociopsychological explanation:

> The birth order of an individual — whether one is first or last, or somewhere in between — may make a significant difference not only in perceptions about family relationships but also in actual family behavior. This may be experienced in different parental expectations, in the ways parents evaluate their children as individuals, and/or in the amount of time in which they have to interact with them.

First borns. The empirical documentation concerning birth-order effects is considerably greater for first borns than for any other group, probably because there are, of course, more first borns at any one time than any other position, and the first-born phenomenon is least contaminated by other factors — spacing behind next oldest sibling, for example. Sutton-Smith (70), summarizing sibling studies, reports that first borns are more achievement-oriented, affiliative, and conforming than their later-born siblings. Belmont (73) studied the IQs of 400,000 males and found that first borns tended to have the highest intelligence, second borns the next highest, and so on. First borns of both sexes have the highest scores on the National Merit Qualifying Test (Breland, 78), but many also demonstrate greater anxiety than their later-born siblings (Rosenberg, 64). *Newsweek* magazine (69) reported that 21 of the first 23 astronauts were first borns or only children, and the two who were not were raised as if they were first borns due to wide spacing or the death of an older sibling. Why should first-born children display these obvious advantages? Probably because they receive greater parental attention, higher expectations, more reinforcement, more interaction and involvement, and more supervision (Kidwell,

"The birth order of an individual . . . may make a significant difference . . ."

81). As the oldest, they also are given the opportunity to teach their younger siblings and may therefore develop higher intelligence (Belmont, 73). They are the role models, surrogate parents, helpers, companions, and confidants of their parents, and carry strong influence over their younger siblings (Dreyfus, 76; Cicirelli, 77). Although like first borns in many ways, only children are somewhat different, too. Belmont (73) found them to be slightly less intelligent than first borns, perhaps because they do not have the opportunity to teach younger siblings, and Weller (74) attributes a lower level of marital happiness in adulthood to the only child's inability to accommodate the needs of others.

Later borns. Although there is less documentation concerning the characteristics of children born to later positions, both middle and last-born children have been studied. Middle children are often characterized as the "lost children," with a myth that middle children in three-child families are the most likely to experience difficulties because of being somewhat neglected in favor of older and younger siblings (Sutton-Smith, 70). On the other hand, Toman (70) suggests that middle children may achieve better socialization as adults because of the necessity to learn double or triple roles and thereby being better prepared for a greater variety of relationships as adults. Last-born children, the "babies" of families, have been found to be more relaxed and easy going, probably as a result of fewer pressures and expectations and the greater relaxation of their parents (Kidwell, 81).

Sibling relationships.   There is no question about the fact that sibling relationships are important. Although we cannot predict *how* siblings affect one another, research documents that siblings generally feel warm and positive about one another. Bowerman (74), for example, found that two thirds of a large sample of adolescents felt close to their siblings, that relatively few reported hostility or conflict, that most felt closer to older and same-sex siblings, and that closeness diminished from junior to senior high school. V. Adams (81), in studying sibling rivalry, concludes that rivalry is greatest when parents openly compare their children and when adolescents perceive favoritism (whether the parents engage in it or not), and that rivalry may be initiated by children vying for the attention and affection of their parents, even when the parents themselves do not show favoritism. The effects of siblings are complex, as we will examine in some greater detail in the next section on spacing, but their importance in the dynamics of the family should not be underestimated. It has been found, for example, that family therapy is considerably more effective when all siblings are involved (N. B. Miller, 76). When they are not, the changes that are begun in therapy may be inadvertently sabotaged by the continuation of old, dysfunctional patterns at home, including those that have been established between siblings.

Spacing.   Alfred Adler suggested several decades ago that birth order effects were subject to the spacing between siblings and that those effects were absent when the gap was great, strongest when the gap was small (Ansbacher, 56). Adler's theory was basically speculation, but his hypothesis was tested by Kidwell (81), who studied a sample of over 1700 adolescent males to determine the power and support of parenting in relation to the number of siblings, the spacing between siblings, the birth order of the respondents, and the sex of siblings. She concludes that family-size and birth-order literature may be inconsistent because spacing and sex are not considered, and that taken together, the factors studied form an immensely complex phenomenon. Her major findings are as follows:

1. Consistent with other family-size research, her studies show that having a large number of siblings seems to increase the adolescent's perceptions of punitiveness and decrease perceptions of support and reasonableness in the family.

2. Spacing is extremely important. As the spacing between siblings increases, the adolescent's perception of punitiveness decreases while the perception of support grows.

3. Parent-child relations are best when siblings are either very close in age (less than one year), or very widely spaced (four or more years). Wide spacing is associated with the best relationships; spacing of two or three years is associated with the least favorable relationships.

4. Middle-born males perceive greater punitiveness and less support than first- or last-borns, but this effect is diminished when wide spacing is a factor.

5. The sex of siblings is not important, except that adolescent males whose closest sibling is female perceive more parental punitiveness toward themselves.

These findings mean that we cannot study family size and birth-order apart from considerations of spacing. A first born with two siblings six and eight years younger is more like an only child than the oldest in a family of three, and the second child in this family is probably more like a first born than a middle child. And two fifteen-year-old boys, both of whom are middle children in families of three children, may have very different profiles based on the spacing between children. In one family, the fifteen-year-old may have siblings aged 20 and 10. By the time he was born, his older sibling was in school, and he was alone with his mother throughout his preschool years. Now he is the only one of the three in high school. In the second family, the fifteen-year-old has siblings aged 17 and 14. He too is the middle of three, but all three were home at the same time during his preschool years, and all are now adolescents. The implications for different experiences by these two fifteen-year-old middle children are enormous.

Working Mothers

Societal change. One of the most dramatic societal changes of the second half of the twentieth century is the astronomical increase in the number of mothers working for pay outside the home. In 1948 only 26 percent of married women with children worked outside the home, full or part time; today we are approaching 60 percent who work full time. This is the first time in history that the typical school child has a mother who works outside the home (Keniston, 77). For single mothers, of course, the number is even higher. Even mothers of preschool children are working in greater numbers: before World War II very few worked; now almost half do, with one third of the mothers of infants under one year old working (Easterlin, 82). Clearly, mothers are working not because they have given up the mythical ideal of the mother as keeper of the refuge, but because they have been pressured to by societal forces. Inflation and rising standards of living have made two incomes a necessity for many families; the rise in the number of service-oriented jobs has created new opportunities for women; the increasing divorce rate has forced single mothers into the marketplace for economic survival; and attitudes have changed to the point where women who do not work for pay are often seen as nonproductive. Child rearing is not, by societal standards, the virtuous and meaningful occupation it was once (Keniston, 77).

Although evidence from social science research shows that working mothers do not necessarily harm their children by their working, they nevertheless express considerable concern over whether their working is damaging.

Effects. There are, however, some clear effects of mothers working outside the home. A direct result of not having adults in the home is the likelihood that children will also spend more time away from home, and that their contact with other adults and children will be extended. Children and adolescents are therefore likely to be exposed to more, earlier, and to focus less of their attention in their families (Easterlin, 82). They also are more likely to spend unsupervised time, leaving home after their parents and arriving home before them. The phenomenon of "latchkey children" is a major concern of child-care workers and agencies. Whether such extended contacts with people outside the home are positive or negative is probably dependent on the nature of these contacts, and many of them probably are out of the immediate control of parents.

In addition to children spending more time away from home, mothers working outside the home have an impact on the relationships within the home. Roles and interactions are frequently renegotiated, with implications for the dynamics of the family. Each family, of course, negotiates them differently. In some, the mother simply does more; in addition to her work outside the home, she maintains the responsibility for the family just as was expected of her homemaking mother. The pressures on her are likely to be enormous. In other, more egalitarian homes, family responsibilities are more equitably divided.

Regardless of how the roles are negotiated, the mother's working contributes to the family's need to rely on people and institutions outside the family to perform what were once considered family functions. Imagine, for example, the increased complexity for the family when an emergency occurs. If a child is sick, does one parent stay home, or does the family have a neighbor or relative care for the child? What happens when the 14-year-old has to keep a regular appointment at the orthodontist, who is located ten miles from the school? Who cares for the children when the school system declares a snow day? Who intervenes when a child has trouble in school, and a conference is called for 2:00 P.M.? These are just a few of the hundreds of complications that modern families must work out, complications that didn't exist for the families that used to fit the stereotyped ideal of the mother at home whose most important responsibility was to minister to the needs of her family. Most of today's mothers must minister to the needs of their families by providing a regular paycheck.

Divorce

Marital dissolution, the birth of babies to single women, and "reconstituted" or "blended" families (the result of remarriages) are all increasingly common phenomena in our society. Cohabitation among unmarried couples increased eightfold between 1950 and 1970, and the proportion of first births to unmarried women doubled in the same time period, so that by 1970 over one million babies per year were being born to single mothers (Keniston, 77). Since 1900 the divorce rate has increased 700 percent, and about half of the children born in the 1970s will spend at least part of their childhood in a one-parent home (Keniston, 77). And most of those who live in a one-parent home will also have a stepparent, since the marriage rate is higher for divorced people than it is for the never-married. Although the result of these statistics for many children is the reduction of their natural parents in their lives, it also means that for those whose parents remarry, new networks of relationships are developed: stepparents, stepgrandparents, stepbrothers, and stepsisters, and a whole host of new aunts, uncles, and cousins. "Thus a complex situation is established of varied blood relationships and surnames, with little in the form of established societal norms to guide the structuring of these relationships'' (Easterlin, 82, p. 96). For most adolescents in the 1980s and 1990s, the traditional nuclear family, especially one in which the mother's sole responsibility is caretaker, is clearly a myth.

Rising divorce rate. In an effort to understand the changing dynamics of family life, it is useful to identify the societal pressures that have influenced the rising divorce rate in the United States. Many tasks that were once assigned to the family have been removed from it. Families no longer work and produce together; social institutions have assumed responsibility for education, care of the sick and elderly, and even religious training; the courts determine acceptable behavior; and children and adolescents no longer work and contribute to family productivity as in the past. The complex ties that at one time bound families together have dissolved, but at the same time, the impersonality of the technological society has created the expectation that marriage and family life will provide complete fulfillment. "Expectations of sharing, sexual compatibility, and temperamental harmony in marriage have risen as other family functions have diminished" (Keniston, 77, p. 17).

In the past, if marriage partners were less than satisfied emotionally, they still had many other bonds. "Furthermore, parents by and large had less elevated expectations about finding complete emotional, sexual, and interpersonal fulfillment in marriage. . . . A happy, long marriage was, then as now, a blessing and a joy; but an unhappy marriage was more likely to be accepted as simply a part of life" (Keniston, 77, p. 20).

That expectations for intimacy in marriage increased between 1920 and 1977 was demonstrated in an interesting study by Brown (82), who studied the portrayal of family life in general interest magazine advertisements. "Since magazine advertisements tend to conform to rather than transform cultural values, they are useful as historical documents" (Brown, 82, p. 175). What he found was that although advertisements present a very "sterilized" image of family life (children never misbehave, for example), it was "exactly this sterilized image that can provide information on the values concerning family intimacy that were predominant at any given time" (Brown, 82, p. 176). In the more than fifty years studied, there was clear evidence that husband-wife intimacy, as measured by the decreasing physical distance between them, increased significantly. If we accept the premise that advertisements reflect current values and expectations, fulfillment in marriage has become an increasingly prevalent ideal in this century.

Combined with increased expectations for intimacy and emotional fulfillment in marriage are several other societal changes that have made divorce more acceptable than it once was. As already mentioned, outside agencies provide many of the functions that families once served. Closely related is the fact that because so many children's needs are met outside the family, children themselves are perhaps less a deterrent to divorce than they once were. As a result of knowing many children with divorced parents, children themselves may be less troubled by the divorce of their own parents. Indeed, a happily married colleague told me of an incident in which her daughter asked her when she and her daddy were getting divorced. My friend was surprised, unaware of any friction that she and her husband displayed, and asked the child why she thought they would be getting divorced. The child had simply assumed that that is what all parents do!

As noted, parents are less likely today to stay together because of the children. Lidz (68) is one of many who points to research that confirms the belief that a tension-filled home is more damaging to children than divorce. Although divorcing parents may feel some guilt over the possible damage of the divorce to their children, they seem now to believe that staying together for the sake of the children has even more potential for harm.

Finally, although it is unfair to say that the rise in the number of working women contributes directly to the rising divorce rate, the fact that women have gained at least some measure of economic independence gives them the potential to at least consider the possibility of being self-sufficient. In a time when most women were completely dependent on their husbands for financial support, divorce was a less likely option, and these women often stayed in troubled marriages because they perceived no alternative (Keniston, 77).

Effects of divorce. For years, the literature has been replete with the dire effects of divorce on children and adolescents, yet, as we shall document shortly, divorce, like other family circumstances, is not a simple culprit. Rather, the reactions of the family to the divorce and the interactions of the parents with their children are the significant factors in adolescent adjustment. It is interesting to note, however, the many findings of negative behavior that have been associated with divorce and father absence. Divorce has been linked to, sometimes even indicated as the cause of, delinquency (Bronfenbrenner, 67; Kalter, 77), psychological disturbance (Biller, 71; Morrison, 74; Kalter, 77; Offord, 79), hostility and acting out behavior (Hetherington, 72, 79; Kalter, 77; Norman, 81), lower self-esteem (Parish, 79, 80b), lower evaluations of their families (Parish, 79, 80b; Saucier, 83), early home leaving (Moore, 82), and poor self-restraint and social adjustment (Suedfeld, 67; Hetherington, 72, 78). Yet many of these same researchers caution that divorce *per se* may not be the causal factor in the poor adjustment, and conflicting evidence suggests that the negative effects are more likely to be due to lowered self-esteem and difficult parent-child interactions, which may both be triggered by the emotional stress of divorce. A divorcing family is usually a disorderly family: ''We would hypothesize that parental divorce . . . may be only the trigger variable: the true causal variables would be the socioeconomic and psychological conditions that would prevail in the family following the divorce'' (Saucier, 83).

Children of divorce may also be subjected to unfair expectations of negative behaviors resulting from the divorce. Santrock (78) and Cooper (83) both uncovered a negative bias by teachers toward children from single-parent homes. In the Santrock study, 30 teachers were asked to view a videotape of a boy playing, then rate him on eleven personality traits and predict his behavior. Half the teachers were told the boy was from an intact family, the other half that he was from a single-parent family. The teachers who thought the boy was from a single-parent family rated him more negatively on happiness, emotional adjustment, and ability to cope with stress, and predicted that his behavior would be more negative than did the teachers who believed he was from an intact family. Cooper (83) found that teachers were much more negative about the family relations of children in one-parent families than were the children themselves, and concluded that it is the child's perceptions that are crucial, not those of observers who may be projecting their own anxieties on the children of divorce.

Adolescent reactions. Reinhard (77), Norman (81), and McLoughlin (84), in their surveys of adolescents' reactions to their parents' divorce, found that the vast majority (75 percent and more) viewed the divorce as the correct action, highly preferable to staying together in a conflicted relationship. Most did not experience anger or loss of love, did not conceal the divorce from their peers, and did not report antisocial behavior. Virtually all adolescents today have come into contact with divorce, either in their own family or in that of a close friend, and they seem clear that divorce itself is not the cause of unhappiness and disturbance.

Marital conflict. Cooper (83) summarized her extensive review of the literature by noting that when children's perceptions of marital harmony are measured, research findings show that marital conflict, not divorce, is related to poor adjustment and low self-esteem. She therefore investigated the perceptions of 467 fifth and sixth graders of the closeness of their parents and siblings, and related these perceptions to the students' scores on self-esteem inventories. The young people were asked to identify which of five family types, represented by the diagrams in Figure 3.1, was most like their own. The children were told to add or remove circles depending on the number of parents and siblings in the home, and to identify which circle represented themselves. They then took self-esteem inventories, and the results were compared with the family types.

Study Figure 3.1, and note the five family types:

1. Two-parent cohesive family: Children who selected this type perceive close ties between themselves, both parents, and all siblings.

2. One-parent cohesive family: Children's perceptions are much like that of the two-parent cohesive family.

3. Isolated child: Child perceives self as isolated.

4. Divided family: Children perceive a division between the parents and can attach themselves to either the mother or the father.

5. Parent coalition: Children perceive a division, with one group formed by the parents and the other by the children.

Cooper hypothesized that the cohesive families (1 and 2) would be associated with high esteem, the isolated child (3) with low esteem, and the divided families (4 and 5) with intermediate levels of esteem, depending upon the degree of acceptance or

Figure 3.1
Diagrams Representing the Family Types: Ⓜ = Mother; Ⓕ = Father;
Ⓟ = Single Parent; ◯ = Children

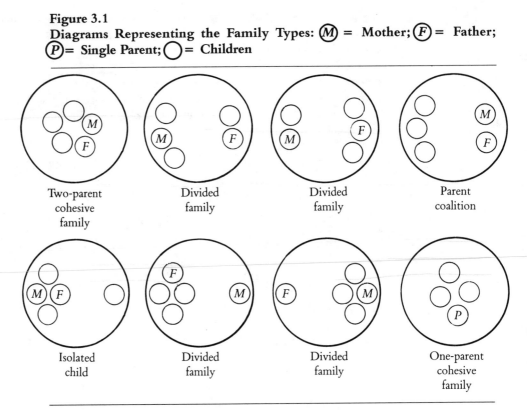

rejection the individual felt from significant people in the family. She found essentially what she expected to. Isolated children had the lowest esteem scores and the poorest social relationships. Highly cohesive homes, *whether one- or two-parent,* produced the highest esteem in their children. Where children perceive conflict, either between parents as in the divided family, or between parents and children, as in the coalition family, lower esteem can be expected. This important piece of empirical evidence lends considerable credence to the clinical and personal observations that a conflict-ridden home is considerably more damaging to adolescent development than a conflict-free, divorced home.

Broken homes are not the cause of broken lives. Rather, the quality of family life determines the psychological adjustment of all involved, including adolescents (Raschke, 79; Hetherington, 78). When matters of custody and support are mutually agreed upon, when the divorced parents are not fighting, and when adequate supports are available to both parents and children, divorce can be a positive solution to a potentially, if not actually, destructive relationship (Brandwein, 74). Yet divorce itself is virtually always traumatic. Wallerstein (74) notes that adolescents, in general, are less likely than younger children to internalize the divorce and feel guilt for it, and that the first year after the divorce is the most difficult for them, but that after the first year most adjust satisfactorily. Hetherington (78) describes the first

Many adolescent children and their divorced parents have warm, nurturing relationships.

two years as lonely and self-absorbed for the parents, but notes that after two years, the dysfunctional patterns disappear and more healthy relationships between parents and their children are formed. The speed and quality of the adjustment may also depend upon the quality of the support systems that are available; Luepnitz (79) found that adolescents adjust best by using institutional and social supports (such as counseling groups for children of divorce), by avoiding home and spending more time with friends, and by the self-determination to live their own lives and not be overwhelmed by the divorce.

Recently, Ganong (81) surveyed high school students from intact, single-parent, and "reconstituted" families on their attitudes toward marriage. Although he found some slight differences among the three groups, the attitudinal differences were very small, and not significant. He concludes, as do the vast majority of researchers today, that the structure of the family alone is insufficient to determine attitudes. Family processes, not structures, are the key.

Blended families. Since the vast majority of divorced parents remarry, there is a good chance that an adolescent from a divorced family will also be a member of a step, reconstituted, or blended family. The National Institute for Mental Health (78) states that 6.6 million young people live with a stepparent, and many of them live also with step- and half-siblings. Wilson (75) examined 68 different social and psychological factors from one national survey and 38 from another and concluded that remarriage can be either positive or negative for an adolescent depending on conditions not directly related to the marriage. As with intact families and single-parent families, blended families are no better or worse than the interactions of those involved. There are, however, some unique problems of stepfamilies that need to be acknowledged. Few clear roles exist for stepparents and stepchildren, and the development of trust and affection are not automatic. The marriage partners choose to be together presumably because they love each other, but there is no history of affection or understanding by which stepparents and stepchildren can claim a felt need to be together. Schlesinger (72) cites the three most difficult problems of stepparents to be adjusting to the habits and personalities of the stepchildren, disciplining the stepchildren, and gaining the acceptance of the stepchildren. The stepchildren, of course, experience the flip side of these: adjusting to the habits and personality of the stepparent, accepting the discipline of the stepparent, and gaining the acceptance of the stepparent. With only one parental model to follow, learning the patterns of a new parent is often difficult, and it is probably true that the adjustments of adolescence itself are not conducive to adjusting to a new parent as well. It should not be surprising, knowing what we do about styles of parenting, that the adjustment is apparently smoothest when problems can be discussed openly and frankly (Schlesinger, 72).

The relationship between stepsiblings is not so enjoyable as *The Brady Bunch* would like us to believe. Stepsiblings have as many problems to work out as their parents do, and as the stepchildren have to work out with their stepparents, but we must remember that stepsiblings generally have little choice in the matter and must learn to live intimately with previous strangers. Duberman (73) found that fewer than one quarter of adolescents with stepsiblings rate their relationship as excellent, with the remaining three quarters about equally divided between ratings of good and poor. These young people report getting along better when they live in the same house with their stepsiblings, or when the remarried parents have a child together. Perhaps both circumstances serve as daily reminders that the new marriage is a reality that must be dealt with as positively as possible. Its success depends upon the ability of all involved to develop healthy, nurturant patterns of interaction with one another.

Corporate Families

Modern America has produced a new phenomenon, the corporate family, which makes rather frequent major moves as the executive (almost always the father) moves up the corporate ladder. The U.S. Bureau of the Census (80b) reports that half of all families move once every five years, and it is likely that the vast majority of these can be classified as corporate families. The stresses of the moves on adolescents have only begun to be studied, but it is clear that such moves do not take the adolescent's needs into consideration, and they are likely to be highly stressful for all concerned. The family arrives at a new location and must change its living and working patterns while the father is simultaneously spending considerable time away from home in order to make his mark in the new job. Gullotta (81) found three different patterns of coping by the adolescents of corporate families to the moves: some simply comply, going along and seeming to cope well; some show quiet resistance through disappointing their parents, experimenting with disapproved behavior, and quarreling; others display intense anger and hostility through any number of overt acting-out mechanisms. Donohue (83) found that the number of moves an adolescent had experienced was not significant to the reaction, and that females cope better than males, presumably because they seem to have a larger repertoire of coping behaviors. They may also cope better because they have been socialized into greater compliance with parental dictates. However, once again, it is probably not the moving *per se* that causes particular reactions, but the family's patterns of interactions and negotiations that have prepared the adolescent for the lifestyle inherent in being a part of many large corporations and the societal supports provided for the family members. Many schools, for example, have instituted group counseling programs for new students. In these sessions, new students are oriented to the new school, assisted in becoming active in extracurricular activities, and encouraged to discuss any problems they are experiencing in the new environment. Just knowing other new students can often be the first step to feeling included. Without such groups, the new student may wrongly feel alone and that he or she therefore fits nowhere.

Given our discussion of the variety of family structures, it should be clear that there is no ideal family in modern American society. The functions that a family is designed to perform can be performed anywhere on the continuum of extremely successful to extremely unsuccessful by large families, small families; families with working mothers, families with homemaking mothers; intact, single-parent, and blended families; families that stay in one place, families that move. Each has its own stresses and its own strengths. If each family can recognize and deal with its particular stresses while building on its particular strengths, it is on the road to optimal functioning and meeting the developmental needs of all its members.

The Family Today

The changes in family structure and function that have developed in this century have considerable practical effects on the lives of children and adolescents. Parents, says Elkind (81), are the victims of rapid societal changes that have made them more afraid, more alone, and more professionally insecure. We are afraid, for example, because of increased threats of violence; alone because of isolation from family and friends; professionally insecure in a world of technological unemployment and unpredictable economic conditions. As a result of these stresses, parents are more likely than ever before to be more concerned with their own problems and less involved with their children. This self-absorption (dubbed the "Me Decade" by Tom Wolfe, 76), combined with the reduced presence of parents in the home, overall smaller family size, and the assumption of many child-care functions by agencies outside the family, has led to more child-care functions being performed outside the home than in it (Easterlin, 82). Adolescents today can be expected to have experienced a variety of care-takers and adult role models, with a potential for a corresponding decrease in the amount of control their parents have had over their lives.

With once-traditional family functions moving outside the family, a great deal of uncertainty has arisen. Never before, says Keniston (77), have parents been so unsure as to how to raise children, how to balance permissiveness and firmness, or what a "good" job of parenting is. The sense of having no sure guidelines is new, notwithstanding the voluminous expert advice offered in every bookstore and over the media. We are in a time of relying on experts and specialists to tell us what to do, how to do it, and when to do it.

The new function of parents, says Keniston (77), is an executive one; parents today manage the many services that provide for their children rather than supervising their children directly. Importantly, however, they do not have control over these services, but are subject to the opinions of professionals who assume that they know best what is appropriate for other people's children. The typical family today relies on friends, family, baby-sitters, camps, physicians, dentists, educational consultants, schools, teachers, tutors, coaches, ministers, child and youth workers, and youth-serving organizations to make the decisions and provide the guidance that once were assumed to be the responsibility of the family. We do not yet know the long-term effects of this remarkable transformation in the family.

FAMILY THERAPY

Rationale

Alexander (82, p. 10) succinctly states the rationale for family, rather than individual, therapy:

> A family is a group of individuals with unique histories, feelings, and needs and with specific ways of behaving in specific settings. But each member can be understood only in relation to each other member.

As we have been emphasizing throughout this chapter, the family provides the context for behavior, and if an adolescent is having difficulties severe enough to seek counseling or therapy, that difficulty can be conceived as a family, rather than as an individual, issue. Adler's family work was pioneering, but only recently has there been an incredible growth in interest in family work (Bowen, 66; Minuchin, 74, 81; Satir, 72, 83; Haley, 76, 80), which developed primarily as a result of continued observations that an individual who is removed from the family for treatment, and subsequently returns home after successful treatment, invariably reverts to the old, disturbed patterns. Also, when a disturbed child or adolescent is removed from a family, it is common to see another child begin to take on symptoms of disturbance. These observations led family therapists to view the disturbed individual as merely a symptom-bearer for a disturbed family, and they hypothesized that only by changing the nature of family interactions could the needs of all members be met. These eminent family therapists have developed a solid base in both the theory and the practice of family therapy, which focuses on <u>disordered communications and relationships within the family.</u>

Systems Theory

Family therapy employs **systems theory**, which emphasizes relationships rather than individuals. "The systems view says . . . that it is necessary to focus on the whole and to see parts only in the context of that whole" (Bavalas, 82, p. 101). Disturbed behavior is not the responsibility only of the individual who is acting out, but is a symptom of disturbed communicative behavior maintained in a social context. Alexander (82, p. 13) gives examples of how disturbed behavior serves a necessary function in a family:

> For example, squabbling with her teenage daughter characteristically results in mother's hysteria, which finally pulls the father out of his workshop and into a disciplinary role . . . one function of the argument is to force the father into contact . . . . if a worried mother constantly checks her daughter's pockets for dope or pills and the daughter reliably engages in extended arguments about the intrusion . . . one function of the interaction is to provide the mother with contact and a sense of having a mothering role.

The family, of course, is not aware of how their behavior serves these functions. In family therapy, the family characteristically engages with one another in exactly the ways they do at home. The therapist can see the disordered functioning and intervene to correct it at the moment it is occurring. Alexander (82, p. 16) describes the role of the therapist as well as further examples of dysfunctional relationships:

> . . . we view family members and their behaviors as a highly interdependent set of relationships. We first view individuals and the patterns of their interactions to see what they do to or with each other. In musical terms, we need to know the notes and the tune. Then we view the patterning of these sequences to understand family themes. From these themes, we then try to ascertain the function of maladaptive sequences for each family member in order to understand why each continues to participate in what most agree are unpleasant events. Sadly, in some families the father has an impact only when he comes home drunk; the son gets freedom only by running away; or the teenage daughter shows love for her mother only after the mother has lost an argument with the father.

Advantages

Obviously, if the entire family and its interactions are creating the symptom seen in the disturbed individual, the entire family needs to be in treatment. It is difficult to convince families of the need for everyone to be involved, since families have a great investment in seeing the problem as belonging to one individual (known in family therapy as the **identified patient** or **i.p.**). Yet the advantages to family counseling are clear:

1. The family members all have the opportunity to gain a clear understanding of one another.

2. Confronting the areas of conflict in the therapy sessions, members face the facts of the situation and are assisted in understanding how each family member contributes to the dynamics of the family.

3. Family members can become increasingly aware of how they are separate and how they come together (Dodson, 77).

4. The involvement of siblings provides a strong socializing agent. Siblings are usually not aware of how they unwittingly reinforce negative behaviors, and they can be helped to alter such interactions (Miller, 76).

5. All family members need to understand and to be involved if change is going to occur (Cicirelli, 77).

SUMMARY

If one factor can be isolated as the single most influential factor in adolescent development, that factor is clearly the family. The family unit, though changing drastically as a result of technological and sociological innovations, nevertheless is here to stay as the primary socializing agent. It provides protection to the growing child and simultaneously prepares the child for future maturity and independence. It provides a sense of belonging, models roles and adaptability, and teaches communication skills. In healthy families, the individuals work together to provide a harmonious symphony; in unhealthy ones, only discord results from their interactions.

Healthy families provide structure, appropriate authority, open communication systems, a place for negotiation, the development of independence, a place for the expression of emotions, and a basic set of values that give meaning and purpose to the life of the family.

Adolescents are faced with the task of developing autonomy, both executive (behavioral) and volitional (emotional), and their success with the task is dependent upon the interactions provided in the family, where proper amounts of warmth and encouragement facilitate its development. To develop autonomy, parents must alter their child-rearing practices to allow for increasingly mature participation by their adolescents. Although there are some sociological and cultural differences in the attainment of autonomy, all adolescents must achieve it if they are to lead successful, independent lives.

Although there will always be squabbles in families, the basic values of adolescents and their parents tend to be more similar than different. When different, it is usually a matter of degree rather than outright disagreement. Less agreement is found between adolescents and their parents on the less significant aspects of life, such as dress, hairstyles, or the use of leisure time. This is the stuff of adolescent-adult quarrels. Families need to understand that some conflict is inevitable; how they handle it is the key to healthy *vs.* unhealthy adjustment.

When conflict becomes unbearable, as in completely dysfunctional families, many adolescents either take to or are thrown into the streets. The situation concerning runaway and throwaway adolescents in this country has become one of national concern.

With relationships in the family forming the basis for adolescent development, it is essential to understand the interactions between the developmental tasks of adolescence and the developmental tasks of middle age, the age of most of their parents. There is tremendous potential in these interactions for both misunderstanding and improved adult-adult communications. And the relationships adolescents have with their grandparents should not be overlooked, as most older adolescents report that their grandparents are second in influence only to their parents.

Parent-adolescent communications form the basis of parenting styles. It has been clearly demonstrated that authoritative parenting, characterized by discussion, explanation, negotiation, and ultimate parental responsibility, contributes significantly to the development of healthy autonomy and responsibility in adolescents. Poor adjustment is associated with both authoritarian parenting, in which parents threaten and punish, and permissive parenting, in which parents abdicate their authority and the adolescents gain control. Effective discipline, too, is characterized by induction, in which reasoning and explanation predominate. Negative characteristics in adolescents are associated with both power assertion and love withdrawal as disciplinary measures.

Although considerable research has been conducted to ascertain the effects of various family structures, neither family size, birth order, spacing, working mothers, divorce, blended families, or corporate families by themselves can be causally linked to negative behaviors in adolescence. The impact of the family on adolescent development is far too complex for such simplistic explanations. Rather, the interactions of the family determine the health of the family and the subsequent healthy adjustment of adolescents. Each of the situations mentioned provides its unique stresses, and each may contribute to the anxiety and low esteem of its members, but it is their way of dealing with the stress, not the stress itself, which contributes to development. The quality, not the form, of the family determines the psychological characteristics of the adolescents in it.

Because it is clear that the relationship patterns in the family contribute so significantly to adolescent development, family therapy for families that include a disturbed or acting-out adolescent has become extremely popular. The family provides the context for adolescent development, and all members of the family contribute to that context, so all ought to be involved in treatment. According to family therapists, the symptom-bearer is only that: a symptom of family dysfunction that can be remedied only by including the entire family in seeing, understanding, and remedying their faulty interactions.

4

The Peer Context

Increasing autonomy in adolescence is necessarily accompanied by increasing interaction with peers, who progressively assume increasing importance in influencing attitudes and behaviors. Because as adolescents mature they spend more and more time with peers, adults frequently fear that peers and peer groups will assume controlling power over their children. We will see in this chapter that such a fear has no basis in fact. Nevertheless, literature, music, and folklore lament the waning power of parents. Note the following example attributed to Mark Twain:

> When I was seven my father knew everything; when I was fourteen my father knew nothing; but when I was twenty-one I was amazed how much the old man had learned in those seven years.

In this chapter we will examine the influence of peers on adolescent development.

It is in relation to adolescence that the term **peer** or **peer group** is most often raised, almost as if it is *only* during adolescence that peers are important. A moment's reflection, however, is sufficient to clarify the observation that peer influence is significant at virtually all ages, from early childhood through old age. Peers may influence us differently at different ages, and it may sometimes seem, especially to parents, that adolescents are particularly susceptible. But these same parents may be succumbing to peer influence merely by focusing on ''what the neighbors will think'' of their adolescents' behavior — just as they have been measuring their worth for years by comparing themselves to their peers (''keeping up with the Joneses'').

The concept of peer influence applies to people of all ages; in this chapter we will examine its influence during adolescence. We will begin by addressing the issue of the relative strength of peer and parent influences as the nature of peer interaction changes, the functions performed by peers in adolescent development, and the nature of conformity to peer standards in adolescence. We will then trace the development of peer groups in adolescence, with specific attention to the changing nature of friendship from early to late adolescence, standards for status and popularity, the problems of social isolates, and the changing nature of peer groups as adolescents mature.

Given the fact that most adolescents belong to a variety of peer groups, a controversy over the existence of a youth subculture has arisen. We will examine and attempt to clarify the controversy by defining it, looking at it from a historical perspective, and examining the evidence for the existence of a subculture or subcultures in the high schools of the 1980s.

As adolescents mature and their friendship patterns change, dating becomes an important aspect of social interaction. We will discuss dating, its social functions, how it develops, and the potential effects of various dating patterns, up to and including early marriage. Finally, consistent with our emphasis throughout this chapter as well as throughout the book on healthy development, we will focus on the positive potential that peers have on one another, and will look specifically at how peer tutoring and counseling are used to foster healthy development.

THE POWER OF THE PEER GROUP

The Changing Nature of Peer Interactions

In 1961, Riesman expressed a widespread fear of the power of the peer group by attributing to it the power of a jury (61, pp. 70–71):

> . . . if adults are the judge, these peers are the jury, and as in America, the judge is hemmed in by rules which give the jury a power it has in no other common-law land, so the American peer-group, too, cannot be matched for power throughout the middle-class world.

Though severely criticized by researchers who have documented that adolescents are not influenced by the peer group to the exclusion of parental and societal values, Riesman sounded a common concern of parents over a perceived loss of control over their adolescent children. We saw in Chapter 3 that as children mature and develop necessary autonomy, influence on their behavior shifts from parents in elementary school, to peers in middle and high school, to an independence of influence and reliance on self in the late high school and college years. Peer influence appears to gain in strength up to the ninth grade, whereafter it declines (Douvan, 66; Kandel, 72). By late adolescence, young people are surer of their own values, capable of autonomous judgment, and do not have to rely on either their parents or their peers (Josselson, 80). They have arrived at the point of mature acceptance noted by Mark Twain in the introduction to this chapter. Note, however, that the influence merely shifts, in varying degrees for various individuals, and is never the exclusive domain of any group or individual.

The increasing peer attachments in adolescence do not have to occur at the expense of parental attachments, especially if the parent-child relationship has been one of high quality (Kandel, 72) and if the individual adolescent has, throughout childhood, developed positive self-esteem (Costanzo, 70). Increasing peer influence does not necessarily undermine parental influence, nor are adolescents influenced in an either-or manner (Bronfenbrenner, 70). Parents and peers both influence adolescent attitudes and behaviors, often in a complementary fashion.

Offer (75) points out that many parents nevertheless seem to want to believe that the adolescent peer group is likely to have a stronger influence on their children than their own peers have on themselves. He attributes this phenomenon to the likelihood that these parents have not adequately dealt with the issue of the necessarily increasing autonomy and need for separation from them of their children and to the possibility that parents are using the peer group as a target for their own dissatisfaction with their children.

There is no doubt that the peer group takes on more importance in adolescence than it did in childhood, but the nature of its influence need not have the onerously negative cast so often popularly attributed to it.

The Relative Influence of Parents and Peers

Increasing peer interaction. Throughout Chapter 3 we emphasized the strong determining factor of family interactions in adolescent development. The influence is clearer in the younger child, if only because of the greater proportion of waking hours spent with the family. In adolescence the influence is less clear, especially since with increasing age, decreasing amounts of time are spent with parents. Condry (74) notes that young adolescents spend twice as much time with their peers as they do with their parents on weekends (their most concentrated free time). Furthermore, Czikszentmikalyi (77) found not only that teenagers have three times more interactions with their peers than they do with adults, but also that they are happier and more relaxed with their peers than they are with adults. (Interestingly, the feelings of greatest happiness and relaxation with peers were true for all age groups, with the exception of mothers and their infants, a finding that confirms our previous observation of the importance of the peer group for people of all ages.)

Parent and peer values. The increase in time spent with peers does not, however, mean that adolescents are engaged in activities or developing attitudes that are in contrast to those of their parents. Conger (77) and Offer (75) both point out that an adolescent's friends usually come from the same social environment — the same neighborhood, the same ethnic and cultural heritage, the same socioeconomic status. The peer group therefore tends to reflect the values of the parental culture. Any single adolescent is likely to choose friends who are more like his or her parents than like culturally diverse peer groups of the same age.

Numerous researchers have investigated the realms of influence of parents *vs.* peers and have reiterated the findings we reported in the previous chapter: basic attitudes and values are reflective of parental attitudes and values and are highly resistant to peer influence. Parental characteristics are stronger predictors of peer group involvement than peer characteristics (Smith, 76). For example, de Vaus (83) documents that parents are significantly more important than peers in the realm of religion. Curtis (75) surveyed 9000 adolescents in grades 7 through 12 and found that at all ages parental advice is valued over that of peers, especially for the middle class. The lower class, it seems, values parental advice, but not so strongly, apparently because lower-class youth see their parents as less socially influential. Young (79) asked students in grades 5, 7, 9, and 12 to whom they would turn for advice on moral situations (problems of right and wrong behavior), factual knowledge, and social issues (friendship and social behavior). Consistent with other findings concerning the value adolescents place on adult opinion, these students turned overwhelmingly to parents and other adults for advice in moral decision-making situations and for factual knowledge, while turning to peers for advice on social issues.

Blyth (82) found consistent results in asking 3000 students in grades 7 to 10 to list the significant people in their lives. He found that 40 percent of the significant others were adults; parents were listed consistently throughout all grade levels; other-sex friends gained in importance with increasing age: and same- and other-sex peers (nonrelated) were consistently listed. Males tended to have slightly fewer (about five) significant same-age friends than females (about seven), and both males and females generally chose friends who came from the same neighborhood, school, and grade.

Peer influence. Barring unforeseen influences and poor parent-child relationships, adolescents and their peers reflect the cultural characteristics, values, and attitudes of their neighborhood and school. Peers tend to influence matters of taste, dress, speech, and social behavior, but they do not change basic family values. Though parents and peers occupy somewhat separate spheres of influence, their influences act more often in combination than they do in opposition. Furthermore, the members of a particular adolescent peer group are most similar to one another in terms of their behavior and activity, less so in terms of values. Kandel (78) found that among 2000 best-friend pairs in high school, the greatest similarity occurred in activities; religion, post-high-school plans, and closeness to parents were relatively unimportant determiners of friendships. That activities rather than basic values form the basis of friendships is not surprising since adolescents are only beginning to form their values, especially since we have already seen that basic cultural values tend to be shared within peer groups.

Peer standards also vary from community to community and from school to school. Even within a relatively homogeneous community, peer standards may vary in two different schools. Of major concern to many parents is the value placed by the students themselves on academic achievement. More than a few families have either moved to a different school district or put their children into highly competitive private schools in the hopes that they would conform to the prevailing achievement-oriented attitudes of the students in that school.

Even delinquency may be linked to parental teaching rather than to the influence of peers. Offer (75) interviewed fathers of delinquent sons and writes of a father who denied understanding the motivations behind his son's delinquency: "In an interesting interview, one father told the researchers that he did not know why his son stole cars. He had told the boy that if he ever needed money, he should take only the batteries!" (Offer, 75, p. 189). Adolescents may vary from their parents' attitudes and values only in degree.

Authoritative, interactive parenting has been demonstrated to contribute to the development of autonomy and therefore to resistance to negative peer influence. But when the family fails to provide appropriate guidance, adolescents may turn to peers to fulfill their needs. We will discuss conformity to peers a little later in this section of the chapter. Slavish conformity and strong susceptibility to peer influence *in matters of values* can be considered deviant and the result of poor parent-child interaction. But all adolescents, like all adults, are subject to peer influence. Belonging to a group is an important aspect of healthy development, and adolescents are clearly able to seek assistance from both parents and peers, depending on whose help is more appropriate in any given situation (Larson, 80).

The peer group can therefore be viewed as auxiliary to the family, a link between the emotional dependence of childhood and the emotional independence of adulthood. Offer (75, p. 187) summarizes the varying influences of the peer group, depending on individual needs:

> The character of the person and the situation together will determine the extent to which peer group reinforcement forms a necessary or a voluntary part of the individual's life. A crisis situation or transitional stage such as adolescence can bring one individual closer to his family, while creating for another the need to have peer support, or for still another the need to isolate himself. A noncrisis situation, the problems of everyday living, may be responded to through peer conformism for individuals who will, when a crisis arises, ignore peer pressures to assert themselves in more individualistic patterns. Thus, generalizations are difficult to formulate. Among adolescents and young adults, certain individuals, whether those in turmoil or those experiencing less conflict, may turn to their peers as necessary supports in a time of transition. Such youth may be those for whom the peer group will have a continuing and special importance for the resolution of problems throughout life.

The Functions of Peers

Context for learning. The peer group provides the context through which adolescents move from the immature dependency of childhood to the mature relationships of adulthood. In the peer group adolescents experience their first adultlike one-to-one and group relationships, through which they learn interpersonal and social skills. They learn what to expect from friends; develop their own unique identities through comparing themselves with peers; compare their values and beliefs with those of others; try on and test out a variety of roles and behaviors; learn skills of leadership and followership; learn the joy of inclusion and the pain of rejection; gain social and emotional support and learn to support and understand others; learn how to manage heterosexual relationships; and establish self-concepts in relation to their friends. In short, the peer group, through its intrinsic reward system of acceptance and rejection, socializes adolescents into developing the behaviors and attitudes that will secure them a place in their world both now as adolescents and in the future as adults. It also serves the adolescent as a basis for developing moral judgments. Norman (81), for example, found that adolescents are tough critics of one another's behavior and attitudes, with their judgments falling along socially acceptable lines.

Psychological support. Without satisfactory peer relationships in childhood and adolescence, adults are severely handicapped both personally and socially. Roff (72), for example, found that poor peer relations in childhood are linked with neurotic and psychotic behavior in adolescence and adulthood, as well as to a significantly greater tendency to drop out of school. The literature on psychological maladjustment is replete with reports of similar findings.

Peer Pressure and the Nature of Conformity

The term **peer pressure** is bandied about as if there were a common understanding of its meaning. The concept also provides an easy and therefore compelling explanation for adolescent behaviors that are contrary to adult preferences, but empirical evidence concerning the extent of peer pressure is sparse. It simply has not been studied to the degree that would secure its place in current psychological literature. There is no doubt that a peer group sets standards for behavior, but the rigidity of the standards and the extent of pressure to conform to them is not at all clear.

Conformity. Rather than continue to explain the similarity in behavior among adolescents as the result of peer pressure, we can better understand individual behavior by studying **conformity,** the tendency to accept and go along with the standards established by the peer group. As with the importance of peers, conformity is a necessary aspect of mature social interaction. We all conform; the nature and extent of that conformity provides a fertile ground for investigation. Parents and teachers want adolescents to conform, and so does the peer group. When the expectations of parents and peers are consistent, there is no problem. It is only when the expectations conflict that adults raise fearful cries about the power of peer pressure. As Dunphy (80, p. 191) explains:

> There is also evidence that where conflict occurs between parent and peer expectations, the adolescent is more likely to side strongly with his peers in

cases where the choices relate to areas in which social values are changing rapidly and where immediate consequences are anticipated.

For example, Kandel (78, 80b) found friends to be very similar in their use of marijuana, an area of behavior in which values have changed rapidly, in which adolescents expect little understanding from parents, and which has immediate as well as potential long-range consequences.

Variations in conformity. Conformity to peer expectations in adolescence varies tremendously depending on a number of factors: the age and maturity of the adolescent, including the ability to think for herself; the type of conformity expected (toward positive or negative behavior, for example); the quality of family relationships and the resulting self-esteem of the adolescent; and the sex of the individual. We will look at each of these separately.

The literature on conformity is replete with findings that early adolescents are most likely to be influenced by the judgments of others (Costanzo, 70; Coleman, 80a). Ages 12 and 13 appear to be the most vulnerable years for boys, with girls' conformity peaking slightly earlier (Costanzo, 70). Teenagers' own reports of delinquent behavior show such behavior to peak in the ninth grade (Hirschi, 69), with all conformity declining throughout the high school years. As we will see in Chapters 8 through 11, the young adolescent is only beginning to develop new cognitive, social, emotional, and moral skills, and is therefore less well equipped than older adolescents to make her own judgments. Early adolescents are beginning to examine the previously unquestioned tenets of their parents, but haven't yet developed their own standards. They want to be accepted, and the peer group's expectations become the compelling means of belonging. With increasing cognitive and emotional maturity, they will be better able to judge the relative merits of those expectations and to exercise the self-confidence that allows them to resist group pressure.

Types of conformity. Conformity, as we noted earlier, is not always negative. Berndt (79) studied prosocial, neutral, and antisocial conformity by presenting children and adolescents (grades 3, 6, 9, 11, and 12) with hypothetical dilemmas that included peer expectations for a particular behavior. A **prosocial** action, for example, might be helping someone even when you don't want to; a **neutral** action might be going to a restaurant you really don't like because a friend wants you to go with him; an **antisocial** action might be doing something delinquent, like soaping windows on Halloween because your friends are. Berndt (79) found that the greatest conformity existed in prosocial and neutral situations, that sixth graders were most likely to engage in prosocial behavior, and that antisocial conformity peaked in the ninth grate (consistent with Hirschi's findings of self-reported delinquent behavior). Once past the ninth grade, all conformity against personal wishes declined.

Conformity and family relationships. One of the strongest and most consistent findings concerning conformity is its relationship to family interactions. Time and again, evidence links high peer conformity to poor parent-child relationships (Costanzo, 70; Iacovetta, 75; Devereaux, 70; Condry, 74; Sherif, 64). Extremely authoritarian or permissive parenting, antagonism, rejection, and poor communication at home are linked with adolescents' attraction for peers just as they are linked with adolescents' negative self-concepts and less-than-adequate emotional adjustment. The deprivation and lack of belonging at home leads to a poor sense of self and a slavish conformity to peer standards in an effort to be accepted (Marcia, 80). It is this orientation *to* peers, not pressure *from* peers, that predisposes peer-oriented youth to peer influence and may result in more deviant behavior, including drug use and precocious sexual behavior (Owuamanam, 83).

Conformity and sex. Finally, as noted earlier, girls seem to feel more pressure to conform than do boys, although there is some evidence that with increasing attention to the negative effects of sex-role stereotyping, this may be beginning to change (Bem, 75a; Sistrunk, 71). Girls, who have been socialized to base their expectations on relationships rather than on personal achievements, are apparently taught to be more susceptible to the influence of the judgments of their peers than are boys.

Brown (82) asked almost 300 college students to analyze the peer pressure they felt in high school and found that peer pressure was strongly sex-stereotyped, with girls experiencing significantly stronger pressure to conform to dress and grooming standards, standards for social activity, and pressure to smoke cigarettes. Boys experience both less intense and different pressures, specifically toward traditionally macho behaviors like having intercourse and using drugs and alcohol.

Conformity, then, like peer pressure, is not a simple concept, but is dependent upon a variety of factors. The most important variables contributing to conformity are age and maturity, the nature of the expectation, and the quality of family life. Only by considering all these variables can we begin to understand the degree and kind of peer conformity exhibited by any single adolescent.

THE DEVELOPMENT OF PEER GROUPS

Young adolescents begin to move out from the family into the wider social context of adulthood through friends, first individually, then in increasingly larger peer groups. Friendships in adolescence are based on social similarities (Duck, 75), and friends are vitally important to teenagers. Norman (81) reports that 82 percent of teenagers continue to see their friends even if their parents disapprove of them and that the majority of teenagers would never tell on a friend unless it was a clear case of life and death. This trust in one another is the essential quality of friendship. Friendships provide the means of sharing personal issues, including both troubles and joys, without fear of betrayal (Parlee, 79; Roll, 79). Friendships provide stability and emotional support and depend more on quality of interaction than quantity or frequency, though adolescents clearly spend most of their chosen time with their friends (Shapiro, 77; Parlee, 79).

The Changing Nature of Friendships

In what is probably the most extensive study of adolescent friendships, Douvan (66) interviewed 2000 adolescents and found that friendship patterns change with age in early, middle, and late adolescence, and that friendships between girls differ from those between boys. We will look at the same-sex friendship patterns of boys and of girls at each stage of adolescence.

Early adolescence (ages 11 to 13). Both boys and girls define their friends as people with whom to *do* something. Their friendships are based on shared activities, and they want friends who are easy to get along with. A friend is likely to be described as ''someone who lives next door and does things with me'' (Duck, 75). Boys are more likely than girls to define a *group* of boys as friends; girls more likely to name one best friend (Douvan, 66).

Friendships are based on shared activities.

Middle adolescence (ages 14 to 16). Friendships become more relationship-oriented rather than activity-oriented, especially for girls. Psychological inferences increase (Barenboim, 77, 81), considerably more time is spent with friends than with family, and there is an increase in the emotional investment in peers. In middle adolescence the difference between boys' and girls' friendships becomes dramatic, as boys tend to continue the activity-orientation of early adolescence while girls develop considerably more sensitivity to issues of trust and emotional intensity (Douvan, 66; Coleman, 80a; Duck, 75; Barenboim, 77, 81; Hill, 80a). Girls, in short, become considerably more capable of intimacy and are eager to share feelings and affection; they are also more attuned to rejection and exclusion, more anxious about friendships, and more likely to be involved in on-again, off-again same-sex friendships. During middle adolescence, disclosure to peers is greater than that to parents, and greater to same-sex than to other-sex friends (Hill, 80). Whereas girls expect friends not to reveal their secrets, boys expect their friends not to tattle on their behavior (Douvan, 66).

Late adolescence (ages 17 and over). With increasing cognitive and emotional maturity, friendships in late adolescence become calmer and more stable, with greater appreciation for individual differences and the unique personality of the other. For girls, same-sex friendships become somewhat less intense, as emotions are directed more toward males (Douvan, 66). Douvan didn't interview late adolescent males, but predicted that their same-sex friendships would also become more stable, and that same-sex friendships for males would be less important than those for females, with males never achieving the emotional intensity of same-sex friendships so common to females. (It has been documented in the literature on adult development that males have significantly fewer and significantly less intense same-sex friendships than do females [Goldberg, 83].)

Although Douvan's research is about twenty years old, the findings in terms of patterns of same-sex friendships in adolescence remain consistent (Duck, 75; Barenboim, 77, 81; Hill, 80a), with some evidence that the sequence currently begins somewhat earlier (Bigelow, 75; Coleman, 80a). The earlier development of the sequence is completely consistent, of course, with Elkind's (81) and Postman's (82) observations of the pressures to grow up faster in modern American society.

Status and Popularity

Success in the adolescent world is most often defined in terms of popularity — the acceptance by peers and ease in making friends that enhance one's power in the peer group.

Criteria. A good deal of research into the criteria for popularity in adolescence demonstrates remarkably consistent findings. Physical attractiveness appears to be the first criterion (Hollingshead, 75; Cavior, 75), with adolescents showing remarkable consistency in their judgments of what physical attractiveness means. Beauty, it

Adolescents don't want to be too different.

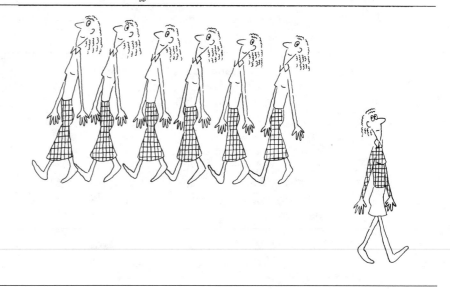

seems, is *not* in the eye of the beholder when it comes to adolescent popularity (Cavior, 75). Beyond the initial screen of physical attractiveness, skills and personal characteristics become important. For boys, being athletic contributes mightily to popularity (Coleman, 61; Eitzen, 75; Williams, 83; Weisfeld, 83), but not so for girls, who are more popular if they are social leaders (Williams, 83). Male athletes and female social leaders tend to have positive self-concepts, be well accepted, and be physically attractive (Weisfeld, 83). Money and material possessions (especially a car) have been linked to popularity (Snyder, 72), but more evidence has been amassed to link popularity to personality characteristics: self-acceptance and the ability to be alone some of the time (Jucha, 76; Coopersmith, 67; Kimble, 72; Hartup, 70; Larson, 78); being yourself; showing enthusiasm; caring for others; being friendly; conforming in speech, attitude, dress, and interests (Hartup, 70; Sebald, 81; Hollingshead, 75); and being an individual (Sebald, 81). One might wonder how an adolescent can be both conforming and an individual; apparently the expression of uniqueness by popular individuals takes place within the parameters of peer group standards. It is intriguing to be a little different, but not too different.

Although the general standards for popularity are widespread, it is also true that the criteria for popularity may vary somewhat from one school and community to another. The specific activities engaged in, for example, might be different, just as academic success is valued more highly in one school than another.

Academic success and popularity. Even in schools in which academic achievement is highly valued, it is seldom a criterion for popularity. Neither, however, is it a criterion for lack of popularity. Unpopular adolescents, like popular adolescents, may or may not be high achievers in the classroom. They are, however, likely to be nonconformers, too straight, too studious (Sebald, 81), conceited or cocky, unenthusiastic, uninterested in others, and uncaring about others' feelings (Hollingshead, 75; Sebald, 81). These students appear to lack the social skills that would equip them to make a more comfortable place for themselves in the world of their peers. They lack communication skills and may be suspicious of the outcome of any commitment they would make to friends (Conger, 77).

Loners

Description. Loners have few or no friends, either because they have been rejected (Horrocks, 67) or because they choose not to join (Palmer, 72). They may either prefer to be alone because they are easily embarrassed and therefore hesitant to make friendly overtures, or may actually be imprisoned in shyness and avoidance (Zimbardo, 74). Katz (68) found that one of three college-age youths either had not found or were not sure of having found a close and meaningful relationship with a same-sex peer, and Zimbardo (74) found that 82 percent of high school and college students perceived themselves as shy at some time in their lives, with 40 percent reporting current shyness and embarrassment around peers. Loneliness and shyness affect most of us at some time during adolescence, and more than a few experience considerable pain as a result. Dunphy (63) reports that 30 percent of adolescent boys and 20 percent of adolescent girls are loners, outside any social peer group. Moore (83) reports that loneliness is negatively related to self-reported attractiveness, likability, happiness, and self-satisfaction; and Goswick (82) found it related to alienation, lack of social facility, inferiority feelings, lack of acceptance, and lack of social integration. Although it is entirely normal for adolescents to experience some shyness and loneliness, most keep these feelings in perspective and eventually outgrow other than relatively infrequent episodes of them.

Social skill training. For the more severe social isolates, the ones who lack social skills and are therefore consistently isolated and lonely, as well as for those who simply want to improve their skills, training in social skills may be helpful. Numerous training programs, including assertiveness training and interpersonal skills training, have been used successfully with adolescents. In these programs, modeling, role playing, discussion, homework, and reinforcement are used to teach young people to communicate openly and spontaneously, speak up for themselves, and listen to and empathize with others (Hartup, 76).

Group Formation in Adolescence

Children, adolescents, and adults naturally tend to arrange themselves in groups. Within these groups they develop hierarchical positions, norms or standards for acceptable behavior, competition both within and between groups, and cohesiveness within the group (Sherif, 51, 61, 66).

Many adolescents feel alone.

Compared with children's groups, adolescent peer groups tend to be larger, more heterogeneous, more formalized (especially those sanctioned by the school or the church), and increasingly heterosexual, and they develop according to a clear and predictable pattern that moves from individual friendships to same-sex cliques of ten or fewer to larger crowds made up of several cliques, to smaller groups of heterosexual couples (Mussen, 74; Dunphy, 63, 80). Figure 4.1 details the development of groups in adolescence.

Pre-crowd. As noted in Figure 4.1, Stage 1 of group development in adolescence, the pre-crowd stage, is made up of relatively isolated unisex cliques. Youngsters are attracted to one another based on interests, personalities, and neighborhoods, and maintain friendships through spontaneous interaction and activity. Cliques are "home" for young adolescents, providing them with cohesion and belonging. They provide advice and feedback on newly developing social skills. Although adolescents deny that their cliques have leaders, they often identify various cliques by the name of an individual (such as "Cathy's crowd"), without whom the clique is not considered gathered (Dunphy, 80).

Figure 4.1
Stages of Group Development in Adolescence (Dunphy, 80, p. 183)

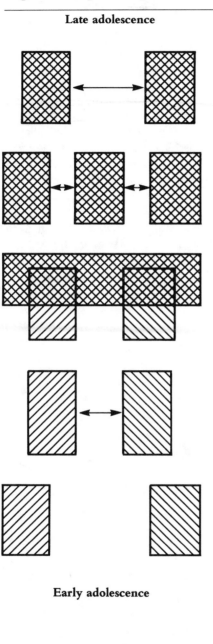

Late adolescence

Stage 5: Beginning of crowd disintegration. Loosely associated groups of couples.

Stage 4: The fully developed crowd. Heterosexual cliques in close association.

Stage 3: The crowd in structural transition. Unisexual cliques with upper status members forming a heterosexual clique.

Stage 2: The beginning of the crowd. Unisexual cliques in group-to-group interaction.

Stage 1: Pre-crowd stage. Isolated unisexual cliques.

Early adolescence

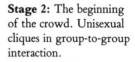

Boys   Girls

Boys and girls

Larkin (79) views the clique as the building block of adolescent social life. It ranges in size from three to ten members, and when it grows beyond that number, it splits. Cliques meet one another at larger, less personal gatherings, known as crowds.

Beginning crowd. In Stage 2 (generally occurring in junior high school) several cliques, some comprised of boys, others of girls, join to form a crowd. The crowd generally meets on the weekends, and individuals try out their developing social skills in the larger group. After a crowd activity (a dance, for example), adolescents return again to their separate cliques, where they debrief the latest crowd activity and prepare for the next one (Coleman, 80a). In their cliques, adolescents reflect on past events, plan future ones, and talk about the other sex and the adults (parents, teachers) in their lives. They hang out together, attend athletic events, and may become involved in activities that are not socially sanctioned (experimenting with drinking and drugs, for example) (Sherif, 64).

Transition. Stage 3 (high school) is a transitional stage in which the most popular members of the cliques within a crowd begin dating. Mixed-sex cliques then develop, with members maintaining membership in both their same-sex and the new mixed-sex cliques.

Fully developed crowd. In Stage 4 (late high school), the majority are dating, and a larger crowd develops as mixed-sex cliques join together. The structure becomes

Individuals try to fit into various groups.

considerably looser than it was in junior high, as noted by Sarah, a student, in an interview with Larkin (79, p. 88):

> Sarah: Our group started in the beginning of the year.
>
> Larkin: This is the group of people I met out in the back?
>
> S: Yeah, uh-huh. And it has grown and split. And each of those groups has grown and split. So we're now quadruple the size, but in more individual groups. We've sort of narrowed ourselves down. It's like choosing — you start out with a big bunch of things and selecting, and then getting all you select together and refining it even more, so you can really be with the people you really want to be with.
>
> L: Does the original group have any common interests? Does the whole group which has quadrupled get together, or is it relatively fragmented into a clique structure?
>
> S: Well, it's not really a clique structure. It's not nearly as bad as junior high was. [In] junior high the groups were so tight, you couldn't even go past without feeling nervous. When you see a group of kids [in junior high] in the hall, you try to go the other way. Not because they would harm you in any way — you just felt, "This is their group. I shouldn't be walking by them."
>
> L: You felt a boundary.
>
> S: Yeah, you definitely felt strong boundaries: really strong boundaries. But here it's much looser. I mean twelfth graders mix in with eleventh and tenth graders, which was never done in junior high. Ninth, eighth, and seventh graders were absolutely divided.
>
> I think it's a lot better here. It's not so tight that you feel uncomfortable when you go into somebody else's group if you know someone there. You know, there are floaters — people who go around to just any particular group they feel like that particular day. And, you just go in and you start talking and it doesn't matter. Nobody really cares. I think that's really good. It's quite an improvement over junior high.

Disintegration.   Finally, in Stage 5, the crowd begins to disintegrate as members graduate from high school and enter into steady dating, engagement, and marriage.

IS THERE A YOUTH SUBCULTURE?

The Controversy

There has raged for years a major controversy over whether or not the peer groups of adolescence form a separate subculture within society. Coleman (80a) argues that youth do, in fact, develop sufficiently different systems of values, beliefs, and behavioral standards to warrant consideration as a unique culture, a group subject primarily to its own standards and not to those of the wider culture. Dunphy (80) argues that no adult attempts to control the youth culture have succeeded, not even in the highly controlled cultures of the U.S.S.R. and China, where despite such attempts, youth have remained largely independent of the wider societal values.

Berger (63) and Offer (75) represent those who disagree. They argue that while adolescents do share common tastes, especially in dress, speech, activities, and behaviors subject to sociological change, their underlying values and ideologies have been demonstrated to be consistent with those of their parents, who represent the values of the broader culture.

Adolescent peer groups are clearly differentiated in identifiable ways, and they obviously provide young people with a bridge from family to the wider adult world, but we would agree with Berger and Offer that the differences are more superficial than deep, more cosmetic than enduring. The peer group, even into young adulthood, may provide a kind of haven from adulthood, but it nevertheless tends to mirror society's values. It has been demonstrated that the peer group, along with the family, quite satisfactorily socializes adolescents to assume adult responsibility.

A possible exception to the argument that adolescent peer groups do not form a separate subculture of society is the existence of the delinquent gang, which more clearly defies broader values and standards. The gang is usually found in urban, working-class areas. It is usually a male group, with females loosely attached, but not integral, to it. It is larger and better organized than a clique, ranges over a clearly delineated territory, which it considers its turf and which it fights to protect. It engages in illegal activity, determines members' status through their fighting ability, and seems to be in revolt against all socially sanctioned institutions — family, school, church, and the legal system (Dunphy, 80).

A further example of a youth subculture, relevant in the 1960s and 1970s, might be the hippie culture, whose values and ideals apart from their appearance were clearly different from those of their parents.

Groups in Schools

Whether or not you consider adolescent peer groups to comprise a youth subculture, it is clear both through empirical research and common observation that every high school contains a number of distinct groups as well as a large number of students who belong to no group at all. Groups form along social-class and ethnic lines, reflecting the larger society. Even in schools that have been desegregated and that serve a varied population only the more formal groups (school-sponsored clubs and teams) tend to have any semblance of cross-sectional membership. Cliques and crowds remain socially and ethnically homogeneous (Kandel, 78).

Normals, jocks, motorheads, and freaks. Leona (78) investigated the groups in one large high school and found that most students were considered normals, not belonging to a specific group. The remainder were divided among the jocks, the motorheads, and the freaks.

The jocks' (all males) lives revolved around sports. They tended to make average to above-average grades, wore sneakers and sweaters, called one another by surnames or nicknames, and were clean-cut, friendly, and self-confident. The motorheads' (all males) lives revolved around cars. They made below average grades, were rude to teachers, hung out together, "owned" a particular table in the school cafeteria, and wore clothes dirtied by working on their cars. The freaks' (males and females) lives centered on drugs. They had long hair, "owned" their own place in the cafeteria, and were so unconcerned about school that they frequently skipped.

Jocks, rah-rahs, politicos, intellectuals, freaks, greasers, grinds, blacks — and the majority. Larkin (79) did an extensive sociological study over five months in a comprehensive high school in 1976, with similar, though considerably more detailed, findings. Of 2000 students, only about 300 could be clearly placed in one of seven identifiable groups. The remainder, the silent majority, were middle-class, attended school regularly, were involved in various interest groups off and on campus, and had friends like themselves. This majority was aware of, but relatively untouched by, the seven fragmented groups: the jocks and rah-rahs, the politicos, the intellectuals, the freaks, the greasers, the grinds, and the blacks.

Together, the jocks and rah-rahs, politicos, and intellectuals (about 100 to 150 students in all) comprised the elite of the school. The jocks and rah-rahs were clearly the socially elite; the politicos the governing elite who ran the student government, assumed leadership positions, and interceded with the school administration; and the intellectuals the academic elite. The freaks (30 to 50 students) were hedonistic: they smoked marijuana daily, cut classes, and were generally ambivalent toward school. The greasers (30 to 50 students), a throwback to the fifties, were delinquent and near-delinquent, smoked marijuana and drank relatively openly, and were also ambivalent, if not hostile, about school. The blacks (about 30 students) tended to remain together except in organized activities, where they participated fully. The grinds, a very small group of math wizards, spent their time in the math lab.

Each of these identified groups, except the politicos, occupied a specific territory in the school, where they congregated when not in class. The politicos were active throughout the school and therefore could not be located in one spot. The jocks could usually be found in and near the gym, the intellectuals in the theater and library, the grinds in the math lab, the freaks in a second floor lounge and on the edge of the playing fields, the greasers behind the auto shops, and the blacks on the first floor stairs.

Not every school has these same groups, of course, but virtually all have identifiable groups of some kind. The majority of the students, however, tend not to be identified with so clearly defined a group.

Symbols of Adolescent Society

Clothing and hair styles. Although the arguments against a separate adolescent subculture are convincing, all adolescent groups nevertheless adopt symbols of their uniqueness. Clothing and hair styles, especially, vary from group to group and over time. One group may wear cowboy boots while another wears loafers; and jewelry, hair, and clothing styles vary yearly. Many of these styles also become adopted by the older generation; when they do, adolescents usually adopt new ones as a way of again expressing their uniqueness.

Automobiles. Regardless of change, two symbols of adolescence seem to remain consistently important: automobiles and speech patterns. To adolescents, the car represents personal independence, maturity, geographical mobility, and a wider range of social contacts (Dunphy, 80). Owning a car is a status symbol, with the type of car adding to the status in identifiable ways. With some variation in taste from year to year, sports and other powerful cars remain at the top of the hierarchy. Four-wheel-drive vehicles, trucks, vans, and well kept classics vary in popularity from group to group and year to year.

But driving is not only a status symbol. Shlechter (83) found that driving has a positive impact on teenagers' behavior and experience. Compared with nondrivers, drivers are more socially competent and responsible and more responsible in work-related situations, probably because they need to earn money with which to maintain their cars. Shlechter (83) concludes that driving contributes significantly to the developmental task of "achieving new and more responsible relationships with age mates of both sexes" (Havighurst, 72). (It could be, however, that it is the responsibly-behaving adolescents who are allowed to drive earlier than their less-responsible peers.)

Speech patterns. Nelson (75) comments on the importance of language in the socialization process of adolescents. Language helps adolescents to view themselves as distinct and separate from adults. Leona (78) found that the three groups discussed earlier (jocks, motorheads, and freaks) each had its distinct jargon based in its major identity. The jocks used terms and nicknames from athletics, the motorheads from cars, and the freaks from drugs. The speech of each group was heavily peppered with appropriate slang terms. Nelson (75) asked about 2000 adolescents to list slang terms, and found gender-related differences that reflected gender-interest differences. Boys used more slang terms for cars, motorbikes, and money, while girls listed more for clothes, styles, appearance, unpopular people, and boys. Slang was also more frequently used for negative than for positive connotations. Although slang terminology changes too rapidly to look critically at current slang, an early 1980s version is that of "valley talk," which originated in California but quickly spread across the country, wherever there was a high school or a shopping mall. Note Figure 4.2 to see how well you *parlez-vous* Valley.

Figure 4.2
Valley Talk: *Parlez-vous* Valley?

Awesome — Nice, you know, like really totally nice.

Bagged-out — Someone whose clothes are old and not in style or anything and they don't match, which is totally untogether.

Bag Your Face — A real put-down, cause like bagging something is throwing it away, see.

Bag Z's — Like, sleeping, you know?

Bail — When you skip school and your friends ask you where you were, it's cool to go, "Like, I bailed, man." Or when you leave a party you go, "Let's bail."

Barf City — Come on, you know, like, yuck.

Beige — For sure boring.

Blow Me Away — Freaking out, except more like, OK, like a dude who's a mega babe asks you if you want to meet him at the beach tomorrow and you like blown away 'cause you thought he'd already have a girlfriend, like, wo.

Book It — OK, if you're in a hurry, you go "Wo, like I gotta book it."

Chill Out — Calm down.

Clearly — Totally or maximum, or like really.

Completely — Like clearly.

Double-Bagger — Someone who looks skanky or grody, like they're so ugly you need two bags, one for them and one for you.

Excellent — What dudes say instead of mega-major-maximum-brilliant, they just go "Excellent, man."

Forget You — Like, no way!

For Sure — Um, what's the other word for that? Definitely, or sometimes just yes.

Fox — A dude or a chick who's a super-mondo-cool-maximum babe and a half.

Go — You know, I go to her, "OK, if you're so smart, how come you don't even know who Norma Kamali is?" and she goes, "Oh, huh."

Gnarly — OK, if you wanted to go to a totally hot concert with a super babe and your mom said you had to stay home and wait for the guy to come fix the hot tub 'cause she had an acupuncture appointment — that would be, like, gnarly.

Gross Me Out — Like being freaked out, only more like barf city.

Hyper — How you get around a dude who's a total babe and you would like freak out if he asked you to go anywhere, especially if he's got an awesome car, like a 'Vette, I mean, you get too, like you talk too much and giggle and stuff and he probably thinks you're a double-bagger anyway. Then you're hyper.

I Can't Handle It — When something is too gross or awesome like maybe a total fox asks you do you want to go to this party, it's like too much, you know?

Later — Instead of good-bye, you go, "Later," cool, huh?

Like — What you say when you're like, um, attaching one word to another, in a, like, sentence.

Major — Major cool is clearly the best.

Mega — Totally only even more total than totally — like megagross.

Mondo — Mondo cool max, OK, a new dress from Fashion Conspiracy is mondo-cool max, or like totally, like we did a mondo mac-out.

Oh — A word you use with "like."

Ooh, Base — What you say when someone totally puts down someone else real good, you go, "OOOOH, BASE!"

A Real Babe — A totally cute dude. Or a super cute chick, if you're a dude.

Really Fine — Like the opposite of totally nauseating.

Seeyabye — When you bail, you go, "OK, seeyabye."

Totally — To the max.

To the Max — Totally.

Tubular — If you were a hippie or something, you'd say it was cosmic except nobody says that anymore and tubular sounds more cool, like awesome.

UVs — OK, that stands for ultraviolet rays, like when you're soaking up the UV's you're getting a tan. Tans are totally important.

Wicked — Real good.

Wo — Like if you're impressed, you go, "Wo, man, like cruisemobile, huh," or something.

From "The Valley Girls' Guide to Life" by Mimi Pond. Copyright © 1982 by Mimi Pond. Published by arrangement with Dell Trade Paperbacks, Dell Publishing Co., Inc.

DATING

A Brief History of Dating

As cliques of boys and cliques of girls join, the highest status members of the cliques begin dating one another; they first form heterosexual cliques and then develop into a small crowd or group of couples. After a certain time, couples become engaged, marry, and eventually produce a new generation of children. Such is the current practice of young people in the United States, but it has not always been so. Only in this century has dating been under the complete control of adolescents and served a number of developmental functions in addition to mate selection.

In colonial times and up until the twentieth century, courtship in the United States resembled that in more traditional and regulated societies. Courtship was serious — object: marriage. Parents regulated courtship, with only seriously marriageable young men being allowed to court their daughters. Girls had little or no choice; they were to marry early and well. As a result they experienced only a very few, very brief courtships (Kett, 77). American courtships were never so regulated as those in some Asian countries, in which a prospective bride and groom may not meet prior to the wedding, but they were far more controlled than the youth-controlled, often casual relationships so common today.

During World War I, dating replaced courtship. It may be highly relevant that along with the liberalized attitudes of the Industrial Revolution and the increased freedom of women resulting from World War I, the advent of dating was also coincident in time with the rise in use of the automobile as a common form of transportation (Dornbusch, 81). The convenience of the automobile and the new freedoms afforded young people allowed them to grow away from their families, and they soon rebelled against traditional courtship customs and near arranged marriages. Dating began as a new form of social learning and social expression.

Functions of Modern Dating Practices

Unlike courtship, dating serves a number of important functions prior to and in addition to mate selection. For adolescents, as well as for increasing numbers of dating adults, dating is a form of recreation that allows people to enjoy not only a leisure activity but each other's company as well. For adolescents it is also a means of socialization in which young people learn the social and interpersonal skills that will allow them to interact meaningfully with one another throughout their lives. They also learn about sexuality and intimacy (see Chapter 7 for a detailed discussion of adolescent sexuality), and through their dates establish status in their peer groups (Skipper, 66; S. L. Hansen, 80). Girls tend to bring a person-centered orientation to dating, while boys bring a body-centered orientation, and within the dating context, both learn to integrate intimacy and sexuality (Hill, 80a).

Adjustment. That dating contributes to overall adjustment has been substantiated in the research of Lipton (80) and Himadi (80). Lipton (80) found that dating adjustment tends to reflect overall adjustment, with the infrequent college-age daters having significantly more difficulty initiating conversations compared with their peers who date more. Himadi (80) investigated the question, "Do men and women who do not date much also have difficulty in same-sex relationships?" Of 3000 undergraduates, the 24 who dated the most were compared with the 24 who dated the least. For men, dating adjustment reflected overall adjustment, with the most frequent daters also having the best same-sex relationships. For women, however, the relationship did not hold. Those who dated most had positive same-sex relationships, but those who dated least also had positive same-sex relationships. Once again, the observation that relationships of all kinds are more important to women than to men was confirmed. Women have female friends whether or not they have male friends. Men, however, are not likely to have close male friends unless they also have close female friends.

Socialization. Dating serves important socialization purposes, and those who do not date skillfully may be at a loss in later relationships. McGovern (75) tested three programs designed to increase adolescent males' dating skills. All three programs used a dating manual, a female confederate with whom to practice, and group discussion. Two also added behavioral rehearsal. Although the two programs that included behavioral rehearsal were the most successful, subjects in all three groups improved significantly over a control group that was not trained. Since dating is comprised of a constellation of social skills that can be learned, many high school and college counselors are offering such training to adolescents who want to improve their dating skills.

Dating Patterns

Age. Dating begins not at a particular age, nor when an adolescent reaches a particular level of maturity, but whenever members of the clique to which the adolescent belongs begin to date (Dornbusch, 81). This may be as early as age 11 or as late as 16 or more; approximately one fourth of teens begin at 13, one half between 14 and 16, and the other fourth at 16 or later (S. L. Hansen, 77; Place, 75), with girls generally beginning to date slightly earlier than boys. Although there seems to be no optimum age to begin dating, it has been found that dating too early (11 for example) is associated with immaturity, with limited same-sex friendships, and with superficiality in interpersonal skills. Those who begin too early usually don't develop the interpersonal skills necessary for marriage (Place, 75).

Number of partners. In addition to age of first dating, the number of dating partners has also been investigated. About a third of adolescents date just one person at a time, with another third dating two or more simultaneously, and the remaining third dating so infrequently as to not fit into either of the other categories. The number of partners increases as students advance through college (S. L. Hansen, 77; Place, 75), and Kephart (77) estimates that the average college student has eight romantic relationships before marrying.

Stages. Dating progresses through identifiable stages. Early dating is often group dating, in which several girls and several boys meet at a prearranged place. There may or may not be matching up at the rendezvous point, and issues such as who pays or who takes the initiative are avoided. Then individual dating begins. Herold (74) notes three stages through which individual dating develops: filtering, in which the focus is on physical appearance; narrowing, in which the focus is on social sophistication and personality; and finally, evaluating, in which the focus is on deeper psychological traits. Whereas physical attractiveness is high on the list of reasons for first dates, and remains a significant factor in the total number of dates an individual has in a year (Bersheid, 71), it clearly is not the reason for continuing to date an individual beyond the filtering stage. Early in the dating sequence, adolescents go to movies and parties, which are the top choices for first dates; later dates become less entertainment-oriented, with more dating occurring informally and consisting of driving around or staying at home in addition to continuing to go to parties. There are no apparent differences between the dating activities of black and white students (Gaylin, 78; Dickinson, 75).

Although it is clear that dating serves important socialization functions for adolescents, too much dating may not contribute to psychological development. Vockell (72) found those who date the most limit other activities to the extent that their broader social involvement and academic achievement suffer significantly.

Going steady. Over the past quarter century or more, about 30 percent of adolescents at any one time are going steady, with both advantageous and disadvantageous outcomes. Parents tend to be neutral or to approve of going steady (Gallup, 78), and through the steady relationship adolescents develop feelings of acceptance and security, learn to balance intimacy and sexuality, and have an opportunity to develop the skills of negotiation and conflict resolution. On the other hand, adolescents with low self-esteem have been found to be more likely than their higher-esteem peers to go steady (Klemer, 71), and going steady removes the adolescent from other activities, limits her exposure to the other sex, is more likely to include sexual involvement, and may lead to early marriage. Going steady may be a compensation for insecurity and has been associated with less studying and lower grades (Larson, 76).

Going steady may have disadvantages, but so too can the opposite: extensive multiple dating without involvement. Adolescents who date many different partners may experience only shallow, repetitive relationships that offer no opportunity for growth. The assumption that one can merely shop around to find the perfect mate, rather than build a relationship through prolonged interactions, may contribute to the continuation of shallow relationships throughout adulthood as well.

Early marriage. Having discussed the societal pressures that make marriage difficult in modern society, and having noted the difficulties imposed on families, especially children, by problematic marriage and divorce, it becomes obvious that young marriages, occurring when the marriage partners are relatively immature, are doomed to even greater problems than more mature marriages. Yet the 1980 Census reports that about one third of all marriages are early, with at least one partner under the age of twenty, and in most of these marriages, the woman is already pregnant. The partners involved in these marriages tend to come from the lower socioeconomic class and to be less intelligent than those who wait to marry, and it is no wonder that they are more likely to end their marriages with divorce. For white females, aged 14 to 17 at marriage, the divorce rate is three and a half times that of 20- to 24-year-olds, with those aged 19 to 20 at the time of marriage having a divorce rate two and a half times that of 20- to 24-year-olds (Bumpass, 72).

Although some few teen marriages may work in that the couple stays together (DeLissovoy, 73), it is abundantly clear that the societal cards are stacked against teens who marry and have children early. The technological society requires advanced education and training and a sophisticated, mature personality. Teenagers simply have not lived long enough to gain the maturity that society and marriage require of them.

USING THE POWER OF PEERS

Socialization Training

As we have seen, peers do not generally replace parents as the major agent of adolescent socialization, yet they clearly reinforce, consciously or unconsciously, one another's attitudes and behaviors (Charlesworth, 73; Solomon, 73). Psychological findings reiterate that we tend to perform similarly to those with whom we associate, whether in school, at work, or socially. Peer influence in adolescence, for example, has been found to be important to the smoking behavior of teens and to the psychological adjustment of adolescent patients on a medical ward of a hospital (Honig, 82). The positive power of peers is capitalized on in programs of peer tutoring and peer counseling, as well as in literature written expressly for teens. Figure 4.3, for example, is taken from a book written especially for adolescents entitled *If You Don't Know Where You're Going, You'll Probably Wind Up Somewhere Else*. Note how the authors attempt to sensitize youth to the influence of their peers and the ways in which they can use that influence to enhance their own lives.

Peer Tutoring

History. Peers have been used as effective instructional agents since the early 1800s (Endsley, 80; Strain, 81), when Joseph Lancaster founded a school for working-class children in London. Because he had many children and few financial resources, he devised a system of peer-instruction that was so successful as to have an international impact (Gerber, 81). In his monitorial system, one teacher was responsible for a hierarchy of children who tutored one another. The system was highly organized, used behavior management techniques, and depended on clear behavioral objectives (Gerber, 81). Although the use of peer tutors waned early in the twentieth century, it was revived with the compensatory education movement of the 1960s, and by

Figure 4.3
Your Friends (Campbell, 1974)

Along with your co-workers, your friends are going to be an important factor in your life, especially in what you will accomplish and the choices you will have open to you.

Parents are always worried about the kinds of friends their children have, and sometimes the children feel over-protected. But what the parents know now, and what you will eventually learn, is that hardly anything influences our lives as much as the people we associate with. There are many reasons for this, but one of the most important is that we continually use other people for models; that is, we use them as guides for our own actions, and close friends prove to be some of our most powerful models.

Consequently, look around you. The general kind of life that you are going to have will probably be similar to the life that your friends are living, partially because you will, consciously or unconsciously, model your life after theirs. If your friends are too young to have a definite life-style, then look at the parents of your friends. They offer the best prediction of the kind of life that you will be living in a few years. The prediction is far from perfect, but it is the best one you can make now.

No matter what group you choose to associate with over the next several years, you will become more like the members of that group in your attitudes, actions, and opinions. (They will become more like you, too; the influence works in both directions.) A specific example: A student who is majoring, say, in art who moves into a dormitory dominated by people majoring in another subject, say, science, will tend to change his attitudes in the scientific direction. He may even change his major to science. If he lives in the dorm for a long time, he will likely develop more positive feelings toward science than will art students who only associate with other art students. Over time, the minority tends to change to become like the majority. The changes are not necessarily large and are by no means certain, but the general tendency is there, and it will happen to you, too. Over the years you are going to change to become more like the majority of your friends, and they will change to become more like you.

Again, an important implication is that you had better choose your friends fairly carefully because this is one way of controlling your own behavior. By putting yourself in close contact with people whom you would like to be like, you are apt to change in ways that will please you.

Conversely, if you associate with people with problems, you are likely to find yourself with problems, too. If your friends are a bunch of losers, if they are always in trouble with the law, if they are fat and out of shape, if they never have any money, if they are frequently drunk, or smoke a lot, or use hard drugs, if they constantly have trouble in school, if they waste hours each day watching television, if they try to solve most of their problems by "being tough," then you are likely to slide into those same patterns. Through these kinds of friends you can pick up a significant number of liabilities and very few assets. The ancient adage "Birds of a feather flock together" is well supported by psychological research.

Fortunately, the other side of the coin is also true. If your friends are talented, if they get good grades, if they are thoughtful toward others, if they are good athletes and keep their bodies in shape, if they handle alcohol, tobacco, and other drugs reasonably, if they are happy, if they are involved in healthy pursuits such as singing, dancing, athletics, environmental programs, scientific contests, useful hobbies, or good jobs, then you are more likely to become involved in the same activities.

Although these comments are oriented toward students, the same factors operate throughout life. Whether you are 17, 37, or 67, your friends are going to have a sizable impact on you, especially in establishing your attitudes and opinions. If you mainly socialize with Republicans, you are going to think more and more like a Republican; if you spend time with people who value exercise and good health, you are going to keep yourself in better health; if you spend time with people who travel, you will inevitably travel more; if you spend time with people who complain about their lot in life, you will likely be a complainer yourself; if you spend time with people who contribute in worthwhile ways to our society, you yourself are likely to contribute also.

These are only probabilistic statements; each of them should be prefaced with the phrase, "the chances are that . . . ," but the trends are fairly strong. Good friends can be wonderful assets; poor ones can set you back for years.

One other thing you should know about friends. The people who do best with friends are the people who need them least. If you need your friends as a crutch, if you constantly lean on other people and cannot stand upright on your own, if you take from friendships more than you give, you will not be a welcome addition to most circles. Regrettably, in this as in so many other areas, those who need friends the most will have the fewest.

1970, over 10,000 elementary schools in the United States were using peer tutoring in one form or another (Gerber, 81).

Effectiveness. Evidence concerning the effectiveness of peer tutoring is still relatively slim, but seems to confirm that when adults carefully set up, monitor, and evaluate peer-tutoring programs, they can be highly effective. Allen (76) found that low-achieving students, when placed in the role of tutor to younger children, improved their own reading scores considerably. The tutors, not only the children being tutored, benefited from the increased status and adult attention they received. In fact, the tutors benefited considerably more than the younger students who were tutored. Endsley (80) also argues for the benefits to the tutors: increased learning as well as improved self-concept, motivation, attitude, and social behavior. Furthermore, Endsley (80) argues, peer tutoring works: it is efficient and cost-effective and provides students with tutors who are close to their own experience and better able to communicate with children than the experts who may know their subjects so well that they assume too much in trying to communicate it to children. Tutors should be selected based on their dependability, understanding, and patience, with fifth and sixth graders making the best tutors for elementary children (Endsley, 80).

Peer tutors are effective, too, with their handicapped peers. Young (81) reviewed the literature on the use of normal peers to tutor handicapped children (mentally retarded, socially withdrawn, behaviorally disordered, multiply handicapped, and skill deficient), and found numerous reports of highly successful programs. The use of peers as tutors to slightly younger people, both normal and handicapped, should not be overlooked as a positive socialization activity for both the tutor and the tutored.

Peer Counseling

One step beyond peer tutoring is the concept of peer counseling, in which the power of peer models is used to help students cope with personal problems, survive school, and develop healthy attitudes and behaviors in all areas of life. The American School Counselor Association defines peer counseling as follows (ASCA, 78, p. 1).

> Peer counseling is defined as a variety of inter-personal helping behaviors assumed by non-professionals who undertake a helping role with others. Peer counseling includes one-to-one helping relationships, group leadership, discussion leadership, advisement, tutoring, and all activities of an interpersonal human-helping or assisting nature.

Peer counseling includes counseling; referral; tutoring; providing information about drugs, sex, and venereal disease; helping with school problems; helping with special education students; and assisting in all the guidance functions of the school (Sprinthall, 76; Reyes, 81; Hohmann, 82). It is based on the knowledge that young people listen more carefully to people who are most like themselves, in age, race, sex, and socioeconomic status. Peer counselors must be carefully selected and trained in the use of counseling skills, supervised by competent faculty leaders, and involved in the programs they are providing.

SUMMARY

Although peers develop increasing power over one another during the adolescent years, adult fears of the power of the peer group are generally unfounded. Peers tend to choose friends who are much like themselves in terms of culture and basic values, and the peer group therefore tends to reinforce rather than contradict the larger society. And peers are important, not only in adolescence, as some would have us believe, but at all ages. Peers do tend to influence matters of taste — dress, speech, social behavior — but parents tend to influence basic values.

Peers function for one another in a number of important ways; they provide the context for learning social and interpersonal skills and thereby promote healthy social and psychological development. Positive peer relationships in childhood and adolescence are important determiners of healthy adult adjustment.

Although peer pressure is an ambiguous concept, it is certainly true that peers behave similarly to one another. They may, in some cases, do so against their will, but more often they consensually agree that a particular behavior is appropriate. Conformity in adolescence varies tremendously, with early adolescents being most susceptible. Throughout the high school years, though, conformity declines, so that by the time students have graduated from high school, they are more likely to act out of personal convictions than any desire to be like their friends. The nature and extent of conformity depends upon age, maturity, the nature of the expectation, and the quality of family life.

The nature of friendships changes as adolescents mature. Early adolescent friendships are based in common activities, but eventually move into more psychological compatibility, especially for girls. Status and popularity in adolescence are determined by physical attractiveness for both sexes, ahtletic ability for boys, and social leadership for girls. Academic achievement is consistently found to be insignificant in determining status and popularity.

There are always some adolescents who remain outside the social world; they are the loners, who, because of poor social skills, feel lonely and rejected. That social skill training may be helpful to them has become important to many of the adults who are concerned with their adjustment.

In adolescence, friendships develop into single-sex cliques of ten or fewer; cliques of different sexes join to form heterosexual cliques and larger crowds, within which dating begins. Although students can often identify a number of unique groups within junior and senior high schools, these groups (with the possible exception of delinquent gangs) cannot be said to form a unique student subculture, but rather simply represent different aspects and values of the broader society. Their cars and speech, in addition to dress and hairstyles, may set them apart, but their basic values are essentially no different than those of the adults who raised them.

Just as peer relations serve important socialization functions for adolescents, so does dating. Adolescents do not begin dating according to an age or maturity timetable, but when their friends start dating. Through the dating they do, they learn important interpersonal skills and how to build positive relationships. Both multiple dating and steady dating have positive and negative aspects, and through both, adolescents mature into adults capable, it is hoped, of creating healthy marital and family relationships. In modern, technological society, marriage is problematic at best, and even more so for the 30 percent of married couples who marry when at least one partner is still a teenager.

Given the necessity of peer interaction and socialization, the positive power of peers needs to be capitalized on. All over the country, programs of peer tutoring and peer counseling are doing just that. The influence of peers can and should be used to promote healthy socialization and adjustment.

5

The School Context

American secondary schools are under attack. Liberals decry the lack of equal opportunity afforded poor and minority young people; conservatives call for more stringent requirements. American secondary schools have assumed vast responsibilities, but may be inadequately equipped to carry them out. Public education is often seen as both the cause and the cure of all society's ills.

Following a talk to a professional audience, Theodore Sizer, a well known and respected educator, was presented with the following comment from a long-time high school principal (Sizer, 83, p. 679):

> I certainly agree with you, Mr. Sizer, that we need to coach students more on their writing skills and that age-grading hurts as many kids as it helps. I know that trying to teach 175 different students each day is difficult. Most of what you said is very good, very nice. But let me tell you about my school. They sent me two kids this morning who read at the fourth-grade level. I've got to help them. We have 50 Cambodians who can't speak a word of English. My people have to help them. However, my staff is shrinking faster than the student body. I have almost no math or science teachers left who really know their subjects. The mayor makes promises to us but always reneges. No one seems to give a damn any more — parents, politicians, even teachers. Now, Mr. Sizer, your ideas are very nice, but they don't help me very much. I wish they did.

This besieged principal summarized some of the most often-heard criticisms of secondary education: students are leaving school ill-equipped with basic skills of reading and writing, not to mention the skills needed to secure and maintain employment; the rigid structure of schools is unresponsive to developmental and skill needs; teachers' loads are unrealistic. The social reality is also summarized: secondary schools are expected to remedy the failures of earlier educational efforts as well as to provide for the socialization and educational needs of an educationally and culturally diverse population with very little real support from policy-makers at the local, state, or national levels. The result, all too often, is apathy.

But schools also do some things right: the majority of adolescents today finish high school; standardized test scores are rising; many adolescents leave high school well prepared for further education or for the world of work; many find high school a reasonably pleasant place to be; and the high school provides for most an adequate background and socialization for becoming productive citizens.

Regardless, however, of whether secondary schooling is, on balance, more positive or more negative to developing adolescents, it is an almost universal environment for them. In this country, the experience of an average high-school sophomore in New Jersey is likely to be very similar to that of an average high-school

Secondary schools provide a universal environment for American adolescents.

sophomore in Colorado. We have developed a vast, standardized, relatively homogeneous experience for adolescents. It might even be said that the only truly common denominator for most American adolescents is the American secondary school.

In this chapter we will trace the development of secondary schools in the United States and detail the functions that secondary schools are expected to perform.

We will then examine the effects of various external factors (socioeconomic status, family, peers, gender) on the experience of adolescents in schools, as well as the effects of school on these same external factors.

We will attempt to paint a vivid picture of what goes on in secondary schools, and how what goes on is affected by the size, organization, curriculum, teaching, discipline, and overall climate in a school.

With the public hue and cry about declining standards for achievement, we will examine the issues of achievement, underachievement, and dropping out of school.

In the relatively recent past, the needs of young adolescents have been addressed by a movement to establish middle schools, which are supposed to be philosophically and psychologically different from their predecessors, junior high schools. We will discuss this movement and the reasons for treating younger adolescents differently than older ones in schools.

Finally, we will examine the current controversy over the role and function, as well as the success, of secondary schooling. We will detail the criticisms levied against schools and will examine the recommendations that have been made by several important commissions and educational scholars set up to identify the reforms that might make public secondary education more responsive to the needs society views it as fulfilling.

A BRIEF HISTORY OF AMERICAN HIGH SCHOOLS

The Phenomenal Growth of Secondary Education

In comparison with other countries, the single most unique feature of the American secondary school is its growth to an almost universal institution (James, 83). Table 5.1 details the growth of the American high school from 1890, when 6.7 percent of 14- to 17-year-olds were in school, to 1978, when 94.1 percent of them were.

The figures in this table are rather astonishing. Note that high-school enrollments increased almost 500 percent between 1890 and 1978, with the high-school graduation rate increasing about 2000 percent. Since 1970, the median years of schooling (meaning that half the population have fewer years of schooling, half more) have .topped the twelve generally required for high school graduation. According to the 1978 and 1980 census reports, 80 to 85 percent of the population of the United States now graduates from high school. This means that currently, in the United States, of every 100 18-year-olds, fewer than 20 will drop out of school

Table 5.1
The Growth of the American High School (James, 83, p. 401)

Year	High School Enrollments	14- to 17-Year-Olds in School (percentage)	17-Year-Olds Graduating from High School (percentage)	Median Years of Schooling in the United States
1890	359,949	6.7	3.5	—
1900	699,403	11.4	6.3	—
1910	1,115,398	15.4	8.6	—
1920	2,500,176	32.3	16.3	—
1930	4,804,255	51.4	28.8	—
1940	7,123,009	73.3	49.0	8.6
1950	6,453,009	76.8	57.4	9.3
1960	9,599,810	86.1	63.4	10.5
1970	14,418,301	92.7	75.6	12.2
1978	15,654,000	94.1	—	—

Adapted from *Digest of Education Statistics 1980* (Washington, D.C.: U.S. Government Printing Office, 1980), p.44; and from *Historical Statistics of the United States: From Colonial Times to 1970, Part I* (Washington, D.C.: U.S. Government Printing Office, 1975), pp. 379, 381.

before reaching their eighteenth birthday, about 40 will graduate and then go to work or into the military, and about 40 will go on to some form of higher education. About 20 of these will eventually graduate from college (U.S. Census, 1980c).

There is absolutely no question that many more students graduate from high school today than ever before in history and that the United States leads all other countries in its secondary school graduation rates.

With such a phenomenal growth in high-school attendance, facilities for educating all these adolescents had to develop as well. But the schools of the latter half of the twentieth century are vastly different from those of earlier times. As noted in Table 5.1, for example, the number of students in public high schools tripled between 1930 and 1970; the actual number of schools, however, remained essentially the same (Garbarino, 80). Growth has not been in the number of high schools, but in their size. The effects of increased school size will be discussed later. First, we will examine the functions of secondary education in the United States.

Functions of Secondary Education

Education and socialization. From colonial days, when secondary schools prepared a few carefully selected young men to further their education and to take their places as the elite in society, until today, schools have served two primary functions: education and socialization. But as the schools expanded to serve virtually everyone instead of the elite few, these functions expanded as well, to the degree that virtually all social problems have come to be viewed as within the domain of the secondary school.

Certification. As public secondary education expanded, it took on functions in addition to those of education and socialization. It became the certifying agency through which young people could learn trades and be certified as competent to perform in them, and it became a container by which young people were removed from the work force (Kett, 77).

Promise and control. Within these varied functions, schools have been seen as a means of individual progress, offering the promise of future success to the diligent (Hechinger, 75). But they also have been seen as the means of controlling an otherwise potentially unruly populace (Kett, 77; Nasaw, 79). These dual demands sometimes conflict, and whereas highly motivated and already compliant students may flourish in what they perceive to be an atmosphere of promise, those not so well motivated nor compliant may suffer in what they perceive to be an atmosphere of punishment and humiliation.

Current expectations. Today's schools are charged with ever-increasing responsibilities, as attested to by the comments of the veteran principal that open this chapter. They have the responsibility to transmit knowledge and develop academic competence in an extremely heterogeneous group of students, develop social skills and relationships, transmit cultural heritages, prepare the young for vocational and business roles upon leaving high school, develop personal attributes and moral character, prepare the young for all their future adult roles, and provide a kind of "holding tank" that keeps adolescents from participating in adult society.

The Current Picture

Current criticisms of schools highlight the Herculean task expected of them. Most common is the observation that public schools simply can't remedy the social and economic problems that are endemic to them. The comprehensive high school, designed to meet the needs of everyone, is criticized for having become an assembly-line system that denies adolescents access to adults, breeds frustration, creates failure, and is concerned only with conformity and order rather than intellectual curiosity and love of learning (Silberman, 70; Cottle, 71). Although most high school students are satisfied with their schools (Poole, 84), they see schools as places that value competition, obedience, and achievement, in that order; as places where students with few skills feel unwelcome and uncared-for; and as places where the predominant mode of instruction is the teacher lecture (Fetters, 76; Hamachek, 78; Nielsen, 82). We will examine these criticisms and current recommendations for reform at the end of this chapter.

The comprehensive high school has become an assembly line.

That the American populace is dissatisfied with public education is also demonstrated by the increase in private-school enrollments. And private schools are not the sole domain of the affluent and the white. Between 1978 and 1980, minority student enrollment in private schools rose 20 percent. In addition, almost one third of the youngsters in private school in 1980 came from homes in which the total income was less than $15,000 (Coleman, 81). Researchers, educators, legislators, and parents too are critical of public education. The remainder of this chapter will provide you with information concerning the problems, practices, and criticisms surrounding schools so that your contribution to the controversy may be an informed one.

THE EFFECTS OF AND ON SCHOOLING

Given the functions that have been ascribed to schools, how well do they do? Critics are ruthless, claiming that schools do little to raise intellectual levels, provide vocational skills, develop morality and good citizenship, or equalize opportunities for minorities, the poor, and women. Even now, there is little direct evidence that schools raise intellectual levels (Stipek, 81). Furthermore, it has been virtually impossible to separate the effects *of* schooling on such factors as socioeconomic status, family and peer interactions, and achievement motivation from the effects *of* these factors *on* academic achievement. Before looking at these factors in detail it is necessary to acknowledge that although the empirical evidence is sparse, we believe that schooling does have marked effects, but that these effects vary considerably depending on the environmental factors that influence them. Merritt (83), for example, demonstrated that college freshmen from integrated public high schools were more tolerant of differences than those from segregated private schools. Did the school affect these attitudes, or were the attitudes themselves the primary reason for the students attending the schools they did? It is perfectly reasonable to assume that the children of less tolerant parents were more likely to attend the segregated schools. To discuss the effects of schooling is to become involved in chicken-and-egg reasoning.

Socioeconomic Effects

Family background. Mosteller (72) reports the findings of a massive study of 4000 schools, undertaken in 1966 to determine the equality of educational opportunity:

1. The United States remains a segregated society, with 80 percent of white students attending schools that are 90 to 100 percent white.

2. Minorities learn less than whites, and the poor learn less than the middle class.

3. Minorities with internal locus of control (who believe they have control over their own lives) and positive self-esteem perform as well or better than their white counterparts.

4. School facilities (books, number and training of teachers, physical plant, and the like) are generally equal across localities and the country.

5. The single most important variable contributing to learning is the family background, most particularly its socioeconomic status.

Although these data are twenty years old, more recent writers like Keniston (77, p. 45) concur: "In short, the main factors that 'predict' where a child will eventually end up in the economic and social hierarchy are related to the accidents of birth — family income, parental education, race, and so on." Schools have had little more than a marginal effect on equal opportunity. Social class (and ability level, which is positively associated with social class) sort out youngsters who will drop out of school and who will go on to college (Havighurst, 72). Young people of the middle and upper classes are more than 15 times more likely to attain a college degree than those of the lower class (Bachman, 78). There appears to be no question that socioeconomic status is related to both educational aspiration and educational attainment and that family influences interact with socioeconomic status to produce the predictable effects.

It is important to note that socioeconomic status, not race, is the deciding factor. Black-white differences in achievement declined significantly during the 1970s, with disparities continuing to shrink as the total percentage of young people finishing high school increases. But blacks are still more likely to be socioeconomically disadvantaged. When the socioeconomic differences are controlled, the black-white differences melt away.

Reasons for socioeconomic effect. Why do the young of the lower class benefit less from school than the young of the middle and upper classes? The schools, holding the public trust, are middle-class institutions, run by middle-class administrators and teachers, and rooted in middle-class values (Boyle, 66). They are intrinsically more receptive to youngsters who come from a similar background and environment, one which views education as intrinsically rewarding and considers their young to be academically competent (O'Malley, 77). Lower-class youngsters are more likely to lack language skills, face financial difficulties, have inadequate health care and nutrition, lack encouragement from a family that does not share educational values, have few intellectual resources at home, have poorer self-concepts, and even have suffered from poor quality elementary education (Epstein, 81). The result of socioeconomic deprivation and discrimination is low achievement.

Once in school, lower-class youth are faced with middle-class expectations, middle-class textbooks that do not reflect their experiences, and middle-class teachers. Teacher behavior toward students of varying socioeconomic backgrounds has been studied extensively, with highly consistent results. In general, even though the protests of the 1960s and 1970s focused on the ability of middle-class teachers to educate lower-class youth, it has been found that middle-class teachers lack understanding of the life, needs, perceptions, and attitudes of lower-class youth (Gottlieb, 66), that they have lower expectations for them, and that they treat them with less tolerance, less affection, less feedback, less help, less attention, fewer evaluations but more criticism, and less encouragement (Clark, 65; Fetters, 76; McDaniel, 82) than middle-class students.

With the complexity of social class impinging on the outcomes of schooling for the underprivileged, many critics conclude that the schools simply cannot be expected to redress the social, economic, and racial inequalities of society, and that they should not be expected to (Mosteller, 72). Nevertheless, schools must deal with all youngsters, and to that end they need dedicated, sensitive teachers who have high expectations for their students and programs that touch the lives of poorer students and instill the self-confidence and internal locus of control so necessary for academic success. The poor mistrust the schools, as they mistrust a discriminatory society; to regain that trust is a massive undertaking. Some believe the schools are capable of doing it; some do not.

Family and Peer Effects

Parental aspirations. Intricately interwoven with the impact of socioeconomic status on achievement in secondary schools is the impact of family and of peers. As Keniston (77) notes, the strongest predictor of a child's future is the family's lifestyle and aspirations, which are usually reinforced in the peer group selected by the adolescent. Youngsters who perform least well in secondary school most often have parents with little formal education and no motivation for educational attainment for their children (Tyler, 83). And these families most often reside in the inner cities or in rural areas, where schools are criticized most severely for not equaling the achievements of suburban systems. Parent education and aspiration influence both achievement test results (Johnson, 75) and academic ambition (Stahmann, 73), especially when adolescents clearly identify with the parents (Shaw, 65).

Parental aspirations for their children may be an even more powerful indicator of adolescent achievement than socioeconomic status. Davies (81), for example, found that regardless of socioeconomic status, parental aspiration and encouragement not only raised their children's educational aspirations, but equaled academic ability as a predictor of their children's aspirations.

Given the strong influences of parents, what can schools be expected to do? The problem is a knotty one; if school people succumb to the idea that parental influences are all-powerful, they are likely to give up in despair on those students who come from homes that do not themselves value educational attainment. Yet the schools must also be realistic about their chances of influencing such students. Some schools attempt massive parent education and involvement campaigns; others rely on their relationships with individual students to influence them. There are no easy answers.

Peer influence. Peers, too, influence academic achievement, usually in ways that are consistent with parental aspirations. Weatherford (67) and Rigsby (72) found that moderate peer involvement was associated with positive academic achievement, while either too little or too much involvement hindered achievement. The greatest influence tends to occur about the ninth grade, as students are moving into the high school (Blyth, 81). Most schools, recognizing the strength of peer influence, attempt to harness it in constructive ways through offering school-sponsored activities designed to enhance the motivation to succeed.

Gender Effects

Males and females achieve differently and are engaged in different activities and learning environments in school.

Male-female differences. Although generally not different on measures of intelligence, males achieve higher in math and science, females in verbal and language activities (Maccoby, 74). Females earn higher grades until college, when males surpass them (Maccoby, 74). Within courses of study, agricultural, technical (metallurgy, engineering, police science), trade, and industrial courses are dominated by males, while home economics and office occupations are dominated by females. Of the brightest high school graduates who do not go to college, 75 to 90 percent are women (*Facts,* 71). In 1973, 57 percent of the males but only 8 percent of the females entering the University of California at Berkeley had had four years of math. Yet all but five of twenty majors offered had a prerequisite of calculus or statistics. The women seldom qualified for these majors, and were therefore crowded into the remaining five: the humanities, music, social work, elementary education, and guidance counseling (Tobias, 76). How are the schools dealing with sexual stereotyping? Are they combatting it or reinforcing it? Once again, answers are unclear.

Title IX. To combat sexual discrimination, Title IX of the 1972 Educational Amendments Act declared that:

> No person in the U.S. shall, on the basis of sex, be excluded from participation in, be denied the benefits of, or be subjected to discrimination under any educational program or activity receiving Federal financial assistance.

More specifically, Title IX applies to course offerings (general, physical education, and vocational education), counseling and the use of appraisal materials, treatment of students, athletics, financial assistance, and employment (Matthews, 77). Although there has been some controversy over the interpretation of specific aspects of the law, it is now clear that no one can be excluded from a class or a course of study based on sex, that no one can be excluded from school participation because of marriage or parenthood, and that in athletics, equal opportunities for participation must be provided for both sexes. Girls do not have to be included in contact sports (boxing, wrestling, rugby, ice hockey, football, basketball), but they must be offered the opportunity to participate on interscholastic and intramural teams in the same manner as are boys (Matthews, 77). Lockheed (78), in a discussion of the effects of Title IX, notes that it has not produced interscholastic athletic equity for girls, but that the enrollments of college women in engineering, medicine, law, and business doubled in the first five years following its enactment.

Subtle messages. Although outright discrimination based on sex is now banned in schools, school influences on female development are both more complex and more subtle than overt discrimination. Everyone in the school, including administrators, teachers, and the students themselves, has been subjected to the powerful sex-role stereotypes that have pervaded our society. The mores and attitudes of the family and peer group influence female development in school, as do the curriculum, books, tests, and the attitudes and behaviors of teachers and other adults in the school (Berkovitz, 79).

Teacher attitudes. In addition to the messages from home and from peers, teacher attitudes and expectations are a powerful influence on behavior. Significant findings concerning teacher behavior include the finding that teachers influence girls to expect less of themselves than boys do (Parsons, 82); that girls are not encouraged toward achievement-oriented courses by their teachers and counselors (Erickson, 77); that differential practices by the teacher toward boys and girls result in differential performance; that secondary teachers want males to be dominant, independent, and assertive, but females to be submissive, dependent, unassertive, emotional, and concerned about their appearance (Levy, 72); that schools are changing less rapidly than society, and that they have reinforced narrow stereotypes, particularly for females (Berkovitz, 79); and that schooling actually harms many females, creating a "young woman who is likely to emerge from the classroom with promise and potential schooled out" (Frazier, 73, p. 114).

School activities. Teacher expectations and behaviors are not the only reinforcers of sex-role stereotypes. School activities collude as well, as Sheehy (76, p. 64) notes:

> Boys learn basic skills and teamwork and competition on the sports fields, skills that later serve them in business and political organizations. They are also introduced to buddyism in the locker room. In activities approved for girls, there has been little practice with competing and even less opportunity for comradeship. Girls rarely find themselves in situations comparable to a football game or a military service in which the adventure involves great enough risk to demand interdependency.

Frazier (73) notes that schools emphasize the traditionally male team sports, but do little with those that emphasize more individual talents: skating, tennis, swimming, golf, skiing, and self-defense sports, a lack which is especially important for females as well as for those males who are not competitive in the team sports.

What schools can do. Secondary schools currently both combat sex-role stereotyping and reinforce it. Given the fact that stereotyping will probably never be eliminated, there are nevertheless a number of things that schools can do. Berkovitz (79), who notes that single-sex schools do a far better job than coeducational schools of helping females develop assertion and leadership skills, suggests that schools demand from girls assertiveness and autonomy; give them the opportunity and encouragement to succeed academically, athletically, and occupationally; and give them full knowledge of their anatomy, physiology, and function in an effort to reduce fear, neglect, and inferiority feelings.

Boys need the right to be expressive in some things; the opportunity to pursue their interests, whatever those interests may be, including the artistic and humanitarian concerns they choose to develop; and complete and accurate information concerning their anatomy, physiology, and function, in an effort to allay fears and misinformation.

WHAT GOES ON IN SCHOOLS

Although the effects of schools on the development of adolescents cannot be unequivocally determined, schools nevertheless do influence student behavior, both in school and later. We have noted that, in general, schools in the United States are remarkably uniform, yet there are differences that appear to affect adolescents in significant ways. These differences include the size and organization of the school; the curriculum, teachers, and teaching; the philosophy and practice of discipline; and the overall climate of the school.

School Size

Large schools vs. small schools. As the numbers of adolescents in school increased, so did the size of schools. Conant (59) argued for large, comprehensive high schools in order to serve the needs of the diverse population of students. Large schools could offer a wide variety of specialized courses and a place where young people from varying backgrounds could come together to interact in a democratic and equalitarian way. There is no question that large schools offer greater breadth and depth of course offerings, better prepared teachers, greater diversity of activities, and ''extras'' (such as counselors, artists, and specialists) that small schools cannot match (Gump, 66), but the overwhelming evidence from the research is that students in small schools are significantly more involved in school life and therefore benefit from greater skill development, higher esteem, increased confidence, greater accomplishments, and even more active participation in the adult community (Hanks, 78).

The research evidence indicates that as schools get larger, participation, enthusiasm, and responsibility decrease; individual students are less needed to carry out the school's activities. They, in Barker's (64) words, become ''redundant.'' Differences between large and small schools can be classified by degree of participation, degree and kind of satisfaction, and actual educational attainment.

Participation. Participation has been found to be anywhere from three to twenty times greater in small schools, with a greater proportion of students from small schools holding positions of responsibility, and a much greater expectation for participation by all students in small schools (Barker, 64; Gump, 66; Grabe, 81). For example, although a large school may offer more specialized music activities, a larger percentage of students in small schools actually take part in musical activities. So too with drama, sports, and other activities. In a large school no more than 15 percent of the members of a class are likely to participate in a drama production, whereas in a small school 85 percent are likely to be involved. Students in small schools feel a sense of belonging that leads to commitment and enthusiasm; large schools are more likely to contribute to alienation (Schmiedeck, 79). In large schools, students are more often spectators than participants in the various activities of the school, and actually participate in a significantly narrower range of activities than students in small schools (Barker, 64; Schoo, 70; Williams, 67).

Satisfaction. Since students in small schools participate to a greater extent than students in large schools, it is not surprising that they also get their satisfaction from that participation. Gump (66) found that student satisfaction overall was greater in small schools, with students reporting satisfaction from cooperating, being important, and learning by doing. In large schools, overall satisfaction was less, and satisfaction was gained not from doing, but from watching — a game, a pep rally, a play, or a debate. The large-school students feel a part of their school through vicarious rather than direct means.

Achievement. Finally, school size seems to contribute to achievement. Berkovitz (79) argues that large schools create communication problems, increase the numbers of alienated and depressed students, and harm both self-esteem and group identification. Gump (66) found that small schools have fewer socially and academically marginal students; those who might otherwise be on the fringes are encouraged to participate and are less often allowed to fall between the cracks. They also drop out of school far less often. Gump's finding is challenged by Grabe (81), who found that students in small schools who lack ability may become alienated as a result of the pressure to participate. Since they cannot remain anonymous, he argues, their self-esteem may suffer. Even with this conflicting evidence, students who are on the fringe are more likely to be noticed in small schools, which are more likely to deal with their problems. Garbarino (80) concurs that the lower the academic potential of students, the smaller a school must be to help them be successful. The increased costs of smaller schools may be a sound investment in increased school success and lowered delinquency rates.

Curriculum

The comprehensive high school was designed to provide an intellectually challenging academic program for the most capable students, vocational training for those who were likely to become involved in the trades, and a general curriculum inculcating democratic values for the least talented. We expect schools to teach the fundamentals, expose young people to the world's knowledge, socialize them, develop individual talents, and even civilize them when their parents fail to do so (Goodlad, 83). Currently in the United States, the college preparatory curriculum attracts about half of all high school students; the vocational program attracts about a fourth, though that percentage has been increasing; and the general curriculum holds the remaining fourth or fewer (Dearman, 79). The greatest problems are found in the general curriculum, for the least committed, least motivated students assemble there and that is where two thirds of all the dropouts originate (Combs, 68).

Tracking. Tracking students into one of the three curricula provides opportunities for individualizing to meet diverse student needs, but it also has been severely criticized for reinforcing cultural differences and actually contributing to rather than alleviating class distinctions. Schafer (72) compared over 1000 college-preparatory and non-college-preparatory students on academic achievement, participation, and dropout rates. The study controlled for differences in intelligence and family background and still found that 40 percent of the non-college-bound students were in the bottom fourth of the class, were less involved in school activities, and dropped out at four times the rate of the college-bound. The researcher concluded that being in the lower track contributes to resentment and hostility and erodes students' self-esteem, resulting in poor performance and participation.

Expectations. Class distinctions are maintained through differing expectations for behavior as well. You will recall that in Chapter 3 we noted that whereas lower-class families tend to control their children through external means, middle-class families tend to use reason and negotiation to help their children set their own standards for behavior. Mickelson (80) found that these parenting styles are reinforced in schools. The vocational and general tracks tend to emphasize supervision and following externally determined rules; the academic track, on the other hand, is more likely to emphasize internalizing norms and assuming personal responsibility for one's behavior.

Socialization. The comprehensive high school has been charged with increasing responsibility for socializing adolescents, for preparing them for all facets of adult life, and for meeting individual needs in terms of both background and learning style. Dearman (79), however, found that only one of three high schools offers career education, family life education, or sex education, and even fewer offer such courses as environmental studies, women's studies, ethnic studies, independent study, or credit by contract or by examination. The goal may be to be everything for everyone; the reality is that students are expected to fit into one of the three curricula and to benefit from it as it is traditionally designed.

Thinking skills. Secondary schooling ought to be designed to encourage cognitive development and the use of mature reasoning. Walberg (73) found that emphasis on higher-order cognitive skills (such as problem-solving, hypothesizing, and abstracting) actually decreases as students move into the upper grades, with the emphasis on memory and knowing the right answer increasing from the sixth through the tenth grade. Walberg studied the perceptions of students in grades six through twelve, with the following results:

- Sixth-graders were more often expected to put methods and ideas to use; restate ideas; find trends and consequences; and invent, design, compose, and create than were students in any other grade.
- Tenth-graders were expected to make the least use of higher-order thinking skills.
- The emphasis on memorizing and knowing the right answer increased steadily from sixth to tenth grade, then fell slightly.
- Along with the decrease in emphasis on higher-order thinking skills went an increase in concern for grades.
- As concern for grades increased, a number of other activities decreased; included were the opportunity to participate, active participation by students,

independent exploration and the initiation of new activities, and excitement and involvement in the school.

Norman (81), in her survey of over 160,000 adolescents, found that 60 percent study only to pass tests rather than to learn, and that 55 percent admit cheating to make better grades. The emphasis on grades may be having strongly negative side effects.

Goodlad (83, p. 468) conducted an in-depth study of 1106 classrooms, and noted that:

> . . . the form and substance of the curriculum appeared to call for and make appropriate only some ways of knowing and learning, not others. Students listened; they responded when called on to do so; they read short sections of textbooks; they wrote short responses to questions or chose from among alternative responses in quizzes. But they rarely planned or initiated anything, read or wrote anything of some length, or created their own products. And they scarcely ever speculated on meanings, discussed alternative interpretations, or engaged in projects calling for collaborative effort. Most of the time they listened or worked alone. The topics of the curriculum, it appears to me, were something to be acquired, not something to be explored, reckoned with, and converted into personal meaning and development.

Various movements of the 1980s continue to call for reform to meet these criticisms. The high school has been handed the task of meeting conflicting demands for excellence.

Teaching

Nielsen (82, p. *vii*), a teacher, comments on the challenge:

> How was I to react when Joe Romines called me "an old lop-eared heifer" because he was so frustrated practicing the short vowel sounds? What was I to do with sixteen year olds who read at a fourth-grade level and thought that "far" was what caused buildings to burn? What was I to say to the angry young man with cerebral palsy who told me to go to hell in front of the whole class? And what had I done right when Troy, a delinquent, still carried in his wallet a complimentary note that I had written his parents four years earlier?

Teachers are too often discouraged by low salaries, large classes, a lack of parental involvement, inadequate materials, insufficient student preparation and remediation, and youngsters who don't seem to value an education (Ryan, 80). Yet they have a profound impact on adolescents; they are capable of encouraging either achievement or underachievement, acceptable or unacceptable behavior, positive or negative attitudes (Nielsen, 82).

Rutter (79) conducted an extensive study of twelve schools that varied in size, physical space per student, availability of sports facilities, age of buildings, leadership style, and educational aims. The students in these schools were measured both on entry into and exit from school on a number of factors; verbal reasoning, parental occupation, behavior, attendance, success, delinquency. It was found that the particular school does make a difference, but that school size and physical facilities are not as important to the success of school as the **processes** of the school, especially in the classroom. The key factors overall were the degree of academic emphasis, the teacher's activities and lessons, the availability of incentives and rewards, the extent of responsibility afforded students, and the overall climate. More specifically, within the classroom, the quality of homework assignments, teacher expectations, the total teaching time on lessons and in interaction with the class, the rewards and incentives, the style of discipline in the classroom, the pleasantness of the environment, and the opportunity for students to feel responsible were found to be most important to encouraging student achievement and satisfaction.

Personal qualities. Both a teacher's personal qualities and competence affect learning. Personal qualities affect how well a teacher is received by students; unfortunately, those who are not liked by their students lose effectiveness — being a good teacher involves significantly more than knowledge. Successful teachers, according to Silberman (70), are energetic, self-confident, concerned, humanitarian, innovative, and not impressed with middle-class values. The best-liked teachers are warm, friendly, and emotionall involved with their students, while the least-liked are sarcastic, strict, moralistic, and dull (Jersild, 78). Whiteside (76) claims that the single most important teacher quality is self-confidence, because self-confidence frees teachers from the need to belittle or degrade others. Adolescents are often vocal about what they like and dislike in teachers: Norman (81) reports that 76 percent of teenagers say teachers play favorites; 71 percent think that the brighter students are favored; and 54 percent say their teachers don't care about student ideas and opinions. These same teenagers like teachers who are fair and don't pick on particular individuals; who know and are enthusiastic about their subject matter; who will help with both schoolwork and other problems; who like kids; who can keep order in the classroom; and who give little homework. It is only the last criterion with which the experts may disagree.

Environment. Beyond their personal characteristics, effective teachers are able to provide the appropriate environment for the particular aptitudes and learning styles of their students (Cronbach, 77). Aptitudes, learning styles, cultural background, and values all contribute to whether a student achieves best in a classroom that is structured or flexible, fast-paced or more slowly paced, directive or nondirective. Brophy (79), in a review of the literature, concludes that high-socioeconomic students of high ability work best when the teacher moves quickly, challenges students, and demands high-quality work. Lower-socioeconomic, lower-ability students, on the other hand, work best in a classroom that is warm, encouraging, slower-paced, friendly, and based on praise rather than criticism. The good teachers are those who recognize these important differences in the needs of the students and are able to adjust their teaching style accordingly.

Discipline

An article in *The New York Times* on August 23, 1981, was just one of many that cited concern with student discipline as the single most important problem facing the schools, and this concern is not a new one. In 1974 Congress called for an investigation of school violence in which 4000 schools were studied. It was found that acts of violence by students against both people and property rose steadily through the 1960s and 1970s, with a leveling off in the late 1970s. It was further found that adolescents are at greater risk of being victims of violence while they are in school than anywhere else, especially for youngsters aged 12 to 15. Estimates of the costs of this violence exceed $200 million per year (*Violent Schools,* 79). Schools have responded with a variety of disciplinary measures ranging from prevention to corporal punishment, and teachers sometimes spend more time controlling misbehavior than they do teaching skills (Brophy, 79).

The problem. Why the discipline problem? Nielsen (82) cites study after study that verifies that adolescents who behave badly are most often burdened with learning disabilities, a history of school failure, and inadequate reading, writing, and speaking skills. The disruptive behavior is a coverup for these deficiencies.

Some out-of-control adolescents are victims of emotional disturbances, but many more, argues Long (71), are victims of an impossibly frustrating environment that demands more of them than they can deliver. They are faced with adults who demean them, settings that are inappropriate for their needs, and too much conflict and challenge. They have not received significant affirmation from others in their lives, have low esteem, and are unable to believe that they can gain by adopting the standards expected by the school (Curwin, 80). They act out in order to save face. And traditional, middle-class methods of control don't work. These antiauthority students do not respond to threats of long-term consequences; they merely bolster their defenses with more hostility and destructive behavior.

Discipline styles. Schools, administrators, and teachers use the same discipline styles that parents do: authoritarian, democratic, and *laissez-faire.* Authoritarian schools attempt to control and dominate. Authoritative or democratic schools are directive but rational, encourage interaction, and promote both independence and self-discipline. *Laissez-faire* schools are passive, providing little or no direction (Baumrind, 72).

As might be expected, more authoritarian parents (most often of the lower socioeconomic class) tend to favor authoritarian discipline in the schools, while middle-class parents tend to support more democratic approaches (Hill, 78). Interestingly, and in keeping with the increase in disruptive behavior in middle and junior-high schools, junior-high parents of all classes tend to favor authoritarian control. But strictly authoritarian control is no more effective in schools than it is in families. Violence and disruptive behavior are less likely in schools when students consider the rules and controls reasonable, when students perceive that they have some control over their lives, when the rules are fairly and firmly administered, and when teachers and administrators are not too hostile or authoritarian (*Violent Schools,* 79).

Students, if they are not to cause discipline problems, need to have their deficiencies and needs diagnosed; they need to master basic skills; and they need an environment that fosters self-esteem. All too many classrooms and teachers are ill-equipped to provide these services, especially when the students' problems are exacerbated by a societal and family environment that is toxic rather than nurturing.

Climate

The school's size, organization, curriculum, teaching, and disciplinary philosophy all contribute to the overall climate of the school; this climate, more than any single other factor, influences students' perceptions (Aptekar, 83). In 1970, Silberman identified successful schools as ones in which:

- The atmosphere is warm, humane, free, supportive, kind, and gentle.
- Disruptive behavior is handled positively.
- Teachers believe that students of all classes can learn.
- Teachers hold themselves accountable for student failure.
- Parents are involved.
- Self-esteem is enhanced.

Student involvement. Most central to positive perceptions of school is the extent of student involvement. "If students feel involved in the decision-making process and perceive that decisions which affect them are not arbitrarily or capriciously made, they are more likely to be involved in school life" (Aptekar, 83, p. 346), and such students are therefore more likely to rate their school, their teachers, and their administrators more favorably, as well as to be more serious about their studies. Alschuler (73) links achievement and achievement motivation with student involvement in decision making and evaluation based on a desire to improve rather than merely to make judgments.

Other factors. Trickett (74) used a classroom environment scale to evaluate school climate, with findings similar to those of Aptekar and Alschuler. Students' satisfaction was linked to high participation, high affiliation with other students, innovative teaching, and clear and fair rules. Mosley (82) found that students in grades 7 through 12 were most satisfied and successful when the learning environment was relaxed, when adults were motivated and interested, when individualization was provided for, and when explanations were complete and clear.

Student perceptions. Unfortunately, most students do not perceive their schools in such positive lights. Most find school only "OK" (Norman, 81). In a study of

2000 male students and 2000 teachers, schools were seen to place their greatest emphasis on athletics and conformity, with academics running third, and socialization and cultural transmission a weak last (Johnston, 76). Only about one third of students think that their teachers are doing an adequate job: three fourths of college-bound students believe that they are not being adequately prepared, and 92 percent of non-college-bound students think they are not being prepared for the job market (Aptekar, 83).

Successful schools with positive learning environments apparently do exist, but the norm, the large, comprehensive high school, especially if it is in an inner city, seems to fall short of the goals society and its students hold for it.

ACHIEVEMENT, UNDERACHIEVEMENT, AND DROPPING OUT

Although more young people, both in actual numbers and in the proportion of all young people, finish high school today then at any time previously, there is widespread concern for the approximately 15 to 20 percent nationwide who drop out before graduation. Ours has become a nation that assumes the necessity for a high-school diploma, and the question as to whether or not everyone needs twelve years of formal schooling is seldom asked. We act as if we believe they do. In a time of increasing technological sophistication, productive work for those with little education and few skills becomes increasingly sparse. As a result, our secondary schools have become charged with keeping adolescents in school, where they at least have the opportunity for developing the skills that will be necessary to survival.

Actual dropout rates vary, with a national average somewhere between 15 percent (Bachman, 78) and 22 percent (Jones, 77b). In urban and rural, as opposed to suburban areas, the rates are higher; in New York City, for example, 50 percent of high school freshman do not stay long enough to graduate (*Phi Delta Kappan*, 80). Most of these youngsters have no physical or mental handicaps (Jones, 77b), and most show identifiable signs of underachievement early in elementary school. Lloyd (78) found that 60 to 70 percent of future dropouts could be accurately predicted in the third grade, when they already compare unfavorably in intelligence measures; grades; parental occupation, educational level, and marital status; and family size. And although dropouts have available to them an equivalency diploma, most do not get it (Dearman, 79).

Underachievement

Definition. Potential dropouts generally have average IQs but are approximately two years behind their peers in reading and math, have failed one or more years, and began scoring low on tests of achievement early in elementary school (Voss, 66). They are, in other words, underachievers. Underachievement is difficult to define any more precisely because it depends on our estimates of an individual's potential ability (Nielsen, 82). We therefore are left to our observations that a particular

Socioeconomic circumstances tip the balance of achievement and failure.

young person may not be using his talents as effectively as possible. We compare a student's actual performance with our best measures of his potential to determine if he is, in fact, achieving less than we might reasonably expect.

Causes. As has been emphasized throughout the previous chapters, socioeconomic deprivation, racial and ethnic discrimination, and poor family relationships create significant problems for children, problems that often display themselves in lack of achievement motivation and resultant school failure. Socioeconomic deprivation, you will recall, is associated with social inadequacy, low self-esteem, poor preparation for school, school failure, and delinquency (Maruyama, 81). Poor family relationships also are associated with delinquency, rebellion, test anxiety, and negative attitudes toward school (Bachman, 71). Both deprivation and dysfunctional families create emotional difficulties, which are often exacerbated by learning disabilities, delayed skill development, and middle-class schools and teachers, which often seem irrelevant (Voss, 66).

What do underachievers look like? They have been found to suffer from low self-esteem, faulty family and peer relationships, and adjustment problems (De

Leon, 70); to be impulsive, pleasure-seeking, selfish, uncooperative, defensive, resentful, and disorganized; and to have poor study habits (Gawronski, 65). Their parents are usually anxiety-ridden and unhappy (McCandless, 73), as well as hostile and disinterested (Gallatin, 75).

Locus of control. The concept of **locus of control** (Rotter, 71) has been used to encapsule what may be the single most important personality dynamic associated with underachievement (Phares, 76; Frieri, 80; Nielsen, 82). Locus of control refers to the individual's belief about who controls the future. Adolescents high in internal locus of control believe themselves responsible for their own success. If they do badly on a test, for example, such individuals are likely to blame themselves for not studying enough, for staying up too late, or for not paying attention in class. Adolescents high in external locus of control believe that the factors that control success are outside of themselves: an unfair test, a poor teacher, or bad luck, for example. Underachievers and disruptive students are most often very high externals; they blame factors outside of themselves, assume little responsibility for their failure, and are therefore prone to giving up. They develop what Seligman (75) called "learned helplessness," an attitude of "I can't do it, so why continue to try?"

The toll of underachievement on society is great, both in human misery and in terms of the financial costs to society as a whole. Underachievers are most likely to become dropouts, commit delinquent acts, vandalize property, marry young, and become teen parents and adult criminals (Nielsen, 82). They are likely to create misery both for themselves and others, and the financial toll is enormous. Welfare aid, incarceration, social services, unemployment, and property damage are expensive. For example, it costs about $1.3 billion per year to have teenagers repeat a grade (Edelman, 80), and whereas four years of college cost approximately $20,000 in 1982, four years of incarceration cost $50,000. The challenge to schools is to find ways to help adolescents develop their skills and raise their achievement, thereby reducing the human and financial toll that underachievement levies.

Dropouts

Profile. The profiles of dropouts are not much different from those of underachievers, for most dropouts are underachievers. That is, most dropouts are of average intelligence and could have finished high school if intelligence were the only factor contributing to success. Some young people, of course, drop out because they cannot, intellectually, stay, but these are the adolescents who drop out very early; those who make it to high school tend to have average IQ scores (Voss, 66). The single most significant factor in dropping out is socioeconomic status. Although the dropout rates vary considerably by ethnic group, with minorities dropping out significantly more often than whites, when socioeconomic status is controlled, there is no difference in the dropout rates by race (Bachman, 71). In other words, poor blacks drop out, but so do poor native Americans and poor whites.

Most significantly, as more young people overall are finishing high school, the decrease in the dropout rate for blacks is especially dramatic, with the decline being greatest among black males (Burton, 82).

Statistics concerning the dropout rate by socioeconomic class are highly consistent. Depending on where a school is located and what kind of statistics are used, somewhere between 25 and 50 percent of the lower class drops out, while only 5 to 10 percent of the upper class drops out (Bachman, 71; Dearman, 79).

Like underachievement, dropping out is predicted by academic failure, previous or current retention, and lack of interest. Half of those who drop out do so as ninth and tenth graders, when declining grades and increasing absences also become more prevalent (Ruby, 82). You will recall that ninth graders are also most susceptible to negative peer influences. Poor family relationships, a history of truancy, trouble with authority, peers not in school, and low family educational attainment all are related positively to dropping out (Alexander, 75; Howard, 78). About equal numbers of boys and girls drop out, but boys generally give lack of interest and a need to work as their reasons, while girls point to pregnancy, marriage, and illness as reasons for leaving school (Dearman, 79).

Locus of control. Like underachievers, dropouts score as externals on measures of locus of control. In comparison with school finishers, they are also lower in self-esteem, have more negative perceptions of themselves and others, are more impulsive, and complain of a greater number of bodily ailments (such as headache, nervousness, or insomnia) (Bachman, 71). In studying dropouts, Mackey (77) identified three facets of a recent dropout's life: **personal inadequacy** (lack of skill or ability to succeed), **guidelessness** (rejection of conventional norms for behavior), and **cultural estrangement** (rejection of traditional standards for success). The personal inadequacy was felt deeply in dropouts, who, Mackey (77) argues, need significant assistance to focus on and develop competence in order to deal with the world. Guidelessness results from the dropout's belief that conventional rules have failed him. He needs to learn to build goals to which he can become committed. Cultural estrangement results from the dropout's lack of commitment to cultural values. He needs to learn how he can work within the system and to make the system work for him.

The future for dropouts. Mackey's observations were based on the difficulties experienced by recent dropouts. Bachman (71), however, studied dropouts several years after they would have graduated from high school. In comparing those who finished with those who dropped out, he found fewer differences than expected. The dropouts were more likely to hold blue-collar jobs and more prejudicial attitudes toward others, but their job satisfaction and incomes were about the same as those of their peers who had completed high school. The dropouts had also become less external and had developed more positive self-esteem since they had dropped out. Because it appears that dropouts eventually do well vocationally, the problems associated with dropping out might more appropriately be attributed to the factors that caused the adolescent to drop out in the first place rather than to the dropping out itself. It can also be argued that the school ifself contributes to perceptions of inadequacy; once out of the frustrating school environment, the dropouts experienced vocational success and their esteem rose.

Preventing Underachievement and Dropping Out

Nielsen (82, p. 11) argues for preventing underachievement through building success:

> Adolescents generally establish self-confidence and self-satisaction as a consequence of success at school. Low self-concept scores often result from repeated academic, social, or physical failure. But self-esteem is *not* a prerequisite for academic, athletic, or social achievement; it is the *consequence* of success. We are doing youngsters a grave injustice by blaming their underachievement on a poor self-concept or by merely assuring them that they are unconditionally loved and accepted. The humane gesture is to teach youngsters specific ways to master the physical, academic, or social skills that create self-esteem.

Every school district in the country employs one or more of hundreds of varieties of dropout prevention programs in which adolescents in danger of failure and dropping out are enrolled. These range from discussions of school, family values, and dropping out (Howell, 82) to alternative learning environments that remove young people entirely from the daily life of the school. Virtually all, whether they say so in so many words or not, are designed to increase internal locus of control and success experiences. Alternative programs allow for diverse approaches to teaching and learning. They include work-study programs, career education, remediation, alternative environments, community-based education, and more extensive student involvement in the life of the classroom and school. Contact with appropriate adult role models, peer teaching, values clarification, and a variety of therapeutic approaches based in human relations training are employed. We will look at two in slightly more detail: reality therapy and a positive learning program.

Reality therapy. Reality therapy (Glasser, 65, 69) is based on the belief that school failure is the basis of both underachievement and disruptive behavior. In order to prevent underachievement, students must be involved in the life of the school and must learn to accept responsibility for their own behavior, thus increasing their control over their lives. Glasser focuses on present behavior, and asks youngsters to carefully respond to seven cardinal questions:

1. *What are you doing?* The emphasis here is on developing awareness of present behavior, without explanation or defensiveness. Students who are not doing

homework, for example, would be encouraged to acknowledge that they have chosen not to do it.

2. *How is your conduct helping you?* and

3. *How is your conduct helping others?* The teacher helps the youngsters to evaluate their behavior in terms of its outcomes for themselves and others. Glasser emphasized that it must be the student's decision to change, based on the student's awareness of his or her behavior and its effects.

4. *What can you do to remedy?* Teacher helps students brainstorm all possible alternatives.

5. *What plan can we agree to?* Teacher and student work together to develop an alternative that is simple, short, and success-oriented. Assuming that students who have been doing no homework acknowledge that it is doing them no good, they might be willing to consider a plan whereby they spend a half-hour each afternoon on the homework for one class, with access to the teacher for help when they need it.

6. *Are you willing to commit to the plan?* The student's commitment must be sealed, preferably in a written contract signed by both teacher and student. The contract should include an answer to the final of the seven questions:

7. *When can we talk again?*

Through this process, as well as through building schools based on providing children with success experiences rather than failure experiences throughout their school lives, Glasser believes that students can be assisted in developing "success identities" that will prevent the tragedy of underachievement and dropping out.

Positive learning program. Ruby (82), like Glasser, argues for the inclusion in schools of programs that build success, and describes a positive learning program (PLP) designed to improve academics, attendance, and attitude among ninth-grade students who have been identified at risk of retention. The program consisted of homeroom and study hall in PLP, with a heavy concentration of academic and social support from the PLP teachers. Otherwise, the students remained in their normal classes. With this concentration of attention and assistance, significant improvements in achievement were made, with attendance and behavior also improving over time. Whereas 70 percent of the subjects who were in PLP went on to graduate from high school, none of the control subjects, who did not receive PLP assistance, graduated.

Success rates from programs like PLP and reality therapy indicate that intervention can be effective, and that the earlier the intervention the better. We know that most potential dropouts can be identified in elementary school, that grades and behavior take a turn for the worse about the ninth grade, and that half of those who will drop out do so in the ninth and tenth grades. There seems to be little excuse for postponing attention to these students until they are in high school. Dropout prevention belongs in the elementary and middle schools.

THE MIDDLE SCHOOL MOVEMENT

Dr. William Bosher, the superintendent of a large suburban school system, frequently refers to the practice of assigning teachers to middle schools as based on three "Ps"; the reason, he says, that a teacher is assigned to a middle school is either **penal**, as a punishment for incompetence at the high school level; **pastoral**, as a last assignment for those nearing retirement; or **preparatory**, for new teachers who must prove at the middle school that they are competent to be moved to the high school. Although Dr. Bosher makes his remarks tongue-in-cheek, the humor itself underscores the problems of middle schools and middle-school teaching, problems that are foremost in the minds of educators who consider early adolescents to be clearly different from older adolescents and therefore in need of schools that address their unique developmental characteristics.

Middle Schools

Reaction against junior high schools. Middle schools, which now number approximately 10,000, began in the 1960s as a reaction to the failure of junior high schools to meet the developmental needs of that most diverse population: early adolescents. Junior high schools were modeled after high schools, with subject-centered classes, interscholastic athletics, and large, formal social activities. They had been designed primarily to relieve crowding in high schools, and secondarily to train young adolescents for the expectations of high school (Brazee, 82).

Lipsitz (introduction to Feeney, 80, pp. *i–ii*) describes the inappropriateness of traditional junior high schools:

> Historically, junior high schools have inherited their organizational structure and staff from senior high schools. Too often there is a serious lack of fit between the institutional structure and the needs of the young adolescents in attendance. Teachers and administrators are defeated daily by the inappropriateness of the school organization and by their inability — both because of lack of training and because of the demands of an ill-suited institution — to connect successfully with their students. They conclude, as do many others, that it is cruel and unusual punishment to have to teach in a junior high school *because of the nature of young adolescents.* Given their day-to-day crushing experiences in a predetermined learning environment, it has been hard for them to recognize how many of their daily defeats are caused by the constraints of the institution and not the inherent nature of the students.

Middle school or junior high? Today it is difficult to distinguish between middle schools and junior high schools. Organization patterns and grade configurations vary tremendously; some middle schools house grades 4 and 5, others 5 through 8, 6 through 8, or 7 and 8; junior highs may or may not include grade 9. Decisions about which grades to include are more often based on economic and space considerations than on adolescent needs. Buildings that once were called junior high schools may now be called middle schools, with little or no real change in philosophy, organization, or curriculum. Those involved in the middle school movement believe that middle schools should reflect the research findings that demonstrate that early adolescents are qualitatively different (physically, cognitively, emotionally) from both younger children and older adolescents (Brazee, 82). Nevertheless, observers argue that although grades have been refigured, little substantive change has occurred, and virtually nothing *within* the classroom has changed (Arnold, 82).

Separating early adolescents from children has had some effects on the experience and self-concepts of young adolescents. For example, a sixth grader in a 6 through 8 middle school has a very different experience than a sixth grader in a 1 through 6 elementary school. Furthermore, the experience may be different for boys than for girls. In one study (Blyth, 81), seventh graders in a K through 8 school had more positive self-concepts and felt better integrated into their school than did seventh graders in a 7 through 9 grade configuration, apparently because those in the second school were new to it as well as the youngest in it. But there are so many interacting variables (grade, age, sex, physical maturity, cognitive ability, maturity, and the like) that simple agreement about which grades to assign to the middle school wouldn't address the issue of how best to teach early adolescents.

Middle schools suffer from inadequate understanding of early adolescent development, of the nature of knowledge and how young people learn, and of the impact of organizational structure and the process of change (Arnold, 82).

The Needs of Young Adolescents

Middle schools, argues Lipsitz (introduction to Feeney, 80), must begin with the question "What is the nature of the young adolescent?" The school's job is to assist students in their development, and it cannot do so unless its organization, philosophy, curriculum, teaching, and activities are derived from adolescent needs.

The extreme variability between young adolescents and even within individual adolescents and the rapid changes of the early adolescent years may result in ambivalence and unpredictability. These changes are primarily physical (rapid but uneven growth; developing sexuality), cognitive (new kinds of thinking become possible), and emotional (greater autonomy, new self-consciousness). And the primary developmental changes allow for development in the moral and religious realm and in career awareness and exploration. To meet the needs of young adolescents, middle schools should build and refine physical competence, develop physical and sexual self-acceptance, develop cognitive capacities, invite questioning and challenging, build on increasing autonomy and independence, use the positive power of the peer group, address newly emerging issues of identity, and help young adolescents move from the dependence of childhood to the independence and responsibility of adulthood (Feeney, 80).

Innovative teaching strategies are better at meeting diverse student needs.

Characteristics of Good Middle Schools

To accomplish these goals, good middle schools espouse and demonstrate the following characteristics (Arnold, 82; Brazee, 82).

Active learning. Young adolescents need to move, both physically and cognitively. Lectures and seatwork demand passivity and are therefore inappropriate as the primary teaching strategy. Team teaching, interdisciplinary teaching, flexible scheduling, experiential learning, group projects, and other innovative teaching strategies better meet diverse student needs.

Exploration. There needs to be a wide choice of offerings, both for sampling purposes and for intense, high-interest activity. The exploratory component should not be isolated from the more standard curriculum, but must be integrated within it. Exploration and innovation need to be encouraged in English, math, social studies, and science as well as in music, physical education, and mini-courses.

Recognition and acceptance of differences. Age-grading doesn't work; middle schools should use measures of maturity and provide choice to students in assigning them to programs.

Advisor/advisee system. All students need time with empathetic adults to deal with school matters *and* personal matters. Providing such time within the school day should be a high priority in middle schools. Such advising can be group-based, thereby also using the power of the peer group and building interpersonal and group skills.

Skill-based learning. Developing skills, not learning content, should be the emphasis in middle school. A curriculum that is experience-based is more effective than one that is content-based.

Emphasis on participation. Young adolescents need to participate, not to compete or spectate. Popularity contests, interscholastic competition, and social competition are inappropriate at this age. Extracurricular activities should invite universal rather than selective participation.

The demands are great, and very few middle schools provide the kind of curriculum and atmosphere needed. Instead, most middle schools still rely on age grading, content-centered curricula, selective participation, passive learning of seemingly irrelevant facts, little group work, little attention to variability and individual differences, too little acknowledgment of physical needs, too little parent and community involvement, and no regard for personal growth — in short, they fail to understand the developmental needs of young adolescents and are unable to provide for them (Feeney, 80; Arnold, 82; Lipsitz, 83).

CURRENT CALLS FOR REFORM

Criticisms

American secondary education may be the most criticized institution in the country, one which, it seems, is fair game for a host of attackers, from legislators to professional educators to the public. In 1974 two thirds of American adults rated the schools in their community as excellent or good, but by 1981 only 47 percent rated them so (Williams, 81). James (83) notes that between 1982 and 1983 over three dozen studies of secondary education were conducted, and each provided its own set of recommendations for reform. The deficiencies cited, both by the "experts" and the public, revolved around declining achievement scores, inappropriate and irrelevant curricula, and poor-quality teaching. The ineffectiveness of the large high school in redressing social inequities, poor discipline, and poor parent-teacher relationships were also cited (Jencks, 75; Williams, 81). Underscoring all the criticisms was an awareness that changes can be made only when the public is willing to support public education, not only in spirit, but with the funding that is necessary to accomplish the reforms that are recommended. A popular poster summarized this awareness: "Wouldn't it be wonderful if Congress gave education all the money it needs, and they had to hold a bake sale to buy a bomber!"

Table 5.2
Decline in SAT Scores, 1960 to 1980

Year	Average Verbal	Average Quantitative
1960	477	498
1980	424	466
	−53 points	−32 points

Achievement. Although the trend has now been reversed (*Guidepost,* 84), scores on the Scholastic Aptitude Test (SAT) declined continuously between 1960 and 1980 (Table 5.2) (*Washington Post,* 80; *National College,* 82).

As indicated in Table 5.2, the average verbal score of college-bound seniors dropped 53 points over twenty years, while the average math score dropped 32 points. In 1984, however, scores were rising, with the average verbal score at 426 and the average quantitative score at 471 (*Guidepost,* 84). Girls and upper-class whites are the most skilled readers and writers (*Changes,* 79; *Three,* 81; *National Assessment,* 81). In math, performance has declined significantly for all races and socioeconomic groups and both sexes (*National Assessment,* 79), with the greatest declines by disadvantaged urban youth and girls, who apparently lose math skills at age 17 (*Changes,* 79; *Three,* 81).

Most troublesome of all is the lack of clarity concerning the reasons for the declines. Changes in the student population, lack of stimulation at home, changes in testing and tests, changes in television viewing, increased disruptions in the classroom, declining standards for achievement, decline in homework assignments, and poor teaching have all been blamed, with educational practices bearing the brunt of the criticisms (Fiske, 75). The curriculum and teaching are the clearest targets. We will outline the most widespread criticisms in these areas before detailing several specific reform recommendations of 1982 and 1983.

Curriculum. The curriculum is criticized for not addressing the needs of socially disparate groups, for not equalizing opportunity, for emphasizing frills like sex education and health instead of the basics, for not preparing students for the world of work, for emphasizing memorization and drill rather than problem-solving, for not being socially revelant (Coleman, 75; Jencks, 75; *Changes,* 79; Marsh, 80). Not only are achievement scores declining, but too many students perceive school as nothing more than a place to go, a place that emphasizes grade-getting rather than learning, a holding tank that deprives them of real responsibility and meaning (Coleman, 75). The schools have been charged with wide-ranging responsibilities; current criticisms suggest that perhaps we have expected too much.

Teachers. Teachers too are criticized. Eighty-five percent of the adults in the United States are in favor of teachers having to take the National Teacher's Examination (*Time*, 80). And teachers too are dissatisfied. The number of teachers with twenty years of experience dropped by half between 1965 and 1980; fewer college freshmen choose teaching than at any time in the last thirty years; 40 percent of current teachers would not again choose a teaching career; 40 percent plan to quit teaching before retirement; current teachers are intellectually less talented than ever before, as measured by achievement tests (*Time*, 80).

Why the perceived decline in the quality of teachers? The rewards are few. Teaching is the only profession in which there is virtually no chance for advancement; a veteran teacher and a beginner have identical responsibilities, and there is little difference in their pay as well. Teacher pay is notoriously low; teaching loads are high; nonteaching responsibilities are many; job security is diminishing; the bureaucracy is frequently repressive; the women's movement is offering better opportunities to the bright women who used to gravitate toward teaching; and society as a whole places little value on teaching, with teachers being granted little respect. There are few rewards — material, psychological, or social, in teaching (*Time*, 80; Hechinger, 81). In an extensive survey of American teachers, the Gallup Poll (Gallup, 84) found that teachers generally rank their schools and their colleagues favorably; and they report that low salaries are the major reason teachers leave the profession, and that lack of parental support (*not* lack of discipline) is the number-one problem they face.

Reform Suggestions

Dozens of reform studies tend to emphasize a return to simpler goals for high schools, with academic and skill competence being primary. Dissatisfaction and calls for reform have existed as long as have schools, and they are not likely to lessen in the future. In conservative economic and political times, greater emphasis is placed on the basics of education and the need for discipline in the schools. (James, 83, notes that the educational editorials of the 1950s could be printed, nearly verbatim, in the newspapers of the 1980s.) In more liberal times the emphasis is on the broader functions of schooling, most particularly on the needs of those who remain outside the mainstream of American society, the educationally, economically, and socially disadvantaged.

Whereas Sewall (82) calls for a redefinition of mission, Sizer (83) sees the problems in high schools as due primarily to the basic structure of the school: more than 1000 students fractionated by age and program track. The structure is astonishingly uniform across the country and so bureaucratized and rigid as to allow for no innovation. Sizer identifies the following problems:

1. Goals are too broad and too numerous.

2. Many students complete high school unprepared for life.

3. School productivity is low.

4. Attendance, not mastery, is rewarded with a diploma. There is little incentive for hard academic work.

5. Students are not expected to educate themselves. School is delivered to them.
6. Subject labels are ambiguous and misleading.
7. Teachers feed facts in order to cover the curriculum.
8. Daily activities are too numerous and too frantic. There is no logic to a student's day.
9. The academic reward system revolves around time. The quicker a student can do something, the better.
10. Segregation by social class is profound; racial and ethnic stereotyping result.
11. There are few connections between the school and the outside world.
12. Schools teach values, but they have not articulated them.
13. Heavy teacher loads make individualization impossible.
14. The teaching profession offers few advancement opportunities.
15. Teacher salaries and benefits are not competitive.
16. The system insults teachers' intelligence.
17. Public leaders say they are interested in education, but they do not provide the necessary resources.

To solve these problems, Sizer (83) recommends the following structural changes:

1. The school must adopt fewer, simpler goals.
2. Students who can't read and write must concentrate on those skills.
3. Higher-order thinking skills (reasoning, analyzing, imagining) must be stressed. New teaching formats and smaller loads are essential to this task.
4. Graduation should be determined by mastery, not by time in school.
5. Schools should emphasize learning to learn, not rote memorization.
6. The curriculum should be restructured to emphasize basic skills that cut across subjects.
7. The pace of high school should be slowed.
8. Age-grading should be ended. Teachers must learn to adapt to student learning styles.
9. Tracking must be resisted.
10. Out-of-school learning opportunities should be developed.
11. Teacher loads must be cut.
12. Teachers should be given control over their schedules and those of their students.
13. Teachers need far greater autonomy.

14. A career ladder should be developed in teaching. As teachers mature, they should take on increased responsibilities and be rewarded with increased compensation.

And Cross (84) summarizes the calls for reform by noting that schools must convince students that they are capable of learning, provide cognition skills, and put students in charge of their own learning.

A Nation at Risk

The single most discussed call for reform is a study and recommendations made by the National Commission on Excellence in Education, entitled *A Nation at Risk: The Imperative for Educational Reform* (1983). Strong language occurs not only in the title, but throughout the document. For example (p. 5):

> What was unimaginable a generation ago has begun to occur — others are matching and surpassing our educational attainments.
>
> If an unfriendly foreign power had attempted to impose on America the mediocre educational performance that exists today, we might well have viewed it as an act of war. As it stands, we have allowed this to happen to ourselves. We have even squandered the gains in student achievement made in the wake of the Sputnik challenge. Moreover, we have dismantled essential support systems which helped make those gains possible. We have, in effect, been committing an act of unthinking, unilateral educational disarmament.

The authors of the document use as indicators of the risk the decline in achievement we have already discussed, as well as the following:

- Twenty-three million American adults are functionally illiterate, including 13 percent of all seventeen-year-olds and 40 percent of minority seventeen-year-olds.
- Half of gifted adolescents are not achieving to the full extent of their capabilities.
- Seventeen-year-olds do not possess higher-order thinking skills.
- Remedial math in college is up 72 percent from 1975.
- Business and the military are spending billions of dollars on remedial education.

Based on its research, the Commission finds education to be guilty of ''weakness of purpose, confusion of vision, underuse of talent, and lack of leadership'' (p. 15). Specifically, it looked at content, standards and expectations, time, and teaching. Its findings follow.

Content. In comparison with the curriculum in 1964 through 1969, the curriculum in 1976 through 1981 became homogenized. Forty-two percent of students were found in the general track, with only a few choosing academic courses (31 percent took intermediate algebra, 13 percent took French I, 16 percent took geography, and 6 percent took calculus). Furthermore, general track students earn 25 percent of their credits in physical and health education, work experience outside school, remedial English and math, and personal service and developmental courses. The Commission recommended significantly upgraded graduation requirements.

Standards and expectations. While homework has decreased, grades have risen. The United States does not spend as much time on science and math as do other industrialized nations. Language, math, and science requirements are very low. Thirteen states allow 50 percent of credits to come from electives. "Minimum competency" too often becomes the maximum. One fifth of four-year public colleges must accept all high school graduates, regardless of achievement. Books have been watered down, and book expenditures by schools are down. The Commission recommended raising standards for academics and student conduct.

Time. American students spend less time in school and on schoolwork than students in many other nations. Time is used ineffectively, both in and outside the school room. Schools are not helping students develop study skills. The Commission recommended longer school days, a longer school year, and/or more efficient use of time in school.

Teaching. Too many teachers come from the bottom quarter of college graduates. Teacher education focuses too heavily on methods courses. Salaries are dismally low. Teachers are not involved in decisions that affect them. There are dangerous teacher shortages in math, science, special education, and languages. The Commission recommended higher standards, better salaries, eleven-month contracts, incentives, use of personnel from outside education, and greater involvement in decision making for teachers.

The recommendations, if they can be implemented, may indeed raise educational achievement. Unfortunately, *how* the recommendations are to be implemented is not addressed, nor are the problems that schools face in unmotivated, frustrated students who have not been able to achieve in the schools as they are. Perhaps all reform movements should heed Goodlad's (83, p. 466) observation:

> Committed to the factory model without feeling the need to validate it, our reflex response to school problems as citizens and educators is to increase pressure through mandates, testing requirements, new standards for college entrance, and the like. We rarely look at what lies between the input valve and the output spigot. To treat even something as simple as frozen water pipes in this manner would be to court disaster. The interactions of individuals and other elements in and around schools are far more complicated than the interaction of cold air with water pipes. Strategies for school improvement that ignore these interactions and the rationales governing them are unlikely to have more than minimal impact on the culture of schools.

The problems are, indeed, complex, and can be addressed only through a comprehensie evaluation of purpose and practice at all levels and, from a developmental point of view, must always use the needs of the students as the first basis for such an evaluation. There is little doubt that the schools will remain at the center of controversy and calls for reform, just as they have throughout their history, and that educational endeavors will continue to attempt to respond to the challenge. Schools will perhaps always be under seige.

SUMMARY

Secondary education in the United States has grown to the point where about 95 percent of adolescents aged 14 to 17 are in school, and 85 percent graduate. Schools grew in size as the nation began to demand that its young people get an education to be productive citizens in an economy that demanded trained skill, and to keep the young out of the marketplace whose needs were met with adult workers. Thus adolescents came to spend a major portion of their time in institutions designed for them and apart from others both younger and older than themselves.

Schools have always been subject to criticism and calls for reform, with the specifics of criticism varying with the political and economic mood of the country. In conservative times, the basics are called for; in more liberal times, the broader social responsibilities of schools are stressed.

As schools grew, they also took on additional functions. They are charged not only with educating the young, but with socializing them for adult citizenship, with certifying them for employment, and even with remedying the social and economic ills of the society at large. Their inability to meet varying and conflicting demands is frequently cited as the basis for criticisms levied against them. Although schools are charged with the responsibility of raising educational aspirations, it is clear that socioeconomic status and family interactions and aspirations have far greater effects on educational attainment than does the school itself. Schools are middle-class institutions that serve middle-class young people far better than they do those from the lower socioeconomic group. Schools also appear to have different effects on girls than they do on boys, most often reinforcing and sustaining the sex-role prescriptions of the larger society. Attempts to combat sex-role stereotyping certainly exist, but major change has yet to be demonstrated.

Various aspects of what goes on in schools effect educational and personal growth. School size, the curriculum, teaching, discipline, and overall climate are aspects which may vary from school to school, with observable differences in the results on students. It has been demonstrated that small schools encourage significantly more participation and responsibility than large schools, with students in small schools benefiting considerably both academically and personally. Most high schools have three curriculums, the academic, the vocational, and the general, with students in the general curriculum being those least motivated and least interested in school and most likely to be underachieving. These students are also most likely to be from the lower socioeconomic class. Furthermore, the high-school curriculum has been accused of not meeting adolescent needs, especially in promoting the vital critical thinking skills that adolescents are capable of. Teachers too are under attack, specifically for not providing individualized attention, clear and high expectations, and concern for their students. Good teachers have not only outstanding personal qualities, but highly developed teaching skills and the ability to tailor their teaching to their students' needs. Discipline varies from school to school as well, with the most effective discipline demanding student input and responsibility in a democratic and fair environment. Finally, effective schools have an overall climate that is warm, free, and supportive; involves parents; believes in students; and enhances the self-esteem of its students and staff.

All high schools are plagued with the problems of underachievement and dropping out. But underachievement and dropping out can be predicted as early as the third grade, indicating that intervention programs should not be reserved for secondary schools, when the problems may be too great to be remedied, and when the students have been defeated by frustration and failure. Underachievers and dropouts are overrepresented in minority and poor populations, again demonstrating that schools are geared to the middle class. Prevention programs must begin early and be focused on providing the reading and writing skills that cut across all content areas.

The needs of young adolescents are different from those of older adolescents, and have not been met in junior high schools, which adopted the structure of the high school. Thus a middle-school movement has been launched to develop schools that are designed to meet the unique physical, cognitive, emotional, and social needs of early adolescents. Yet in its infancy, this movement has yet to exert its influence in global ways.

Current criticisms of schools are based in declining levels of student achievement, inappropriate and irrelevant curricula, lack of meaningful goals, and poor teaching. Numerous recommendations for reform offer suggestions for remedying the ills, with the focus being on greater stress on academic and vocational skills, clearer focus, and improved benefits and working conditions for teachers. Unfortunately, none of the calls for reform offer suggestions for how to accomplish them, or for how to raise the level of financial support provided.

II

Individual Development, Healthy Responses, and Normal Issues of Adolescence

In Section I we explored the contexts in which adolescents mature. In Section II we change focus to the universal issues of development during adolescence. These include Chapter 6: Physical and Physiological Development; Chapter 7: Sexual Development; Chapter 8: Cognitive Development; Chapter 9: Personality Development; Chapter 10: Moral Development; and Chapter 11: Career Development. We will emphasize healthy development and normal developmental issues, and will explore in detail all facets of individual development, from physical growth and sexual development to the development of new thinking powers and the implications of such development for adolescent thought, feeling, and behavior.

6

Physical and
Physiological Development

Shortly after entering the eighth grade, Sally turned thirteen. That year she spent an inordinate amount of time in front of the mirror, which alternated between being her best friend and her worst enemy. Sally was already taller than most of her friends, a fact that sometimes gave her pride (another Brooke Shields?) and sometimes terrified her (would she always be a head taller than every boy she knew?). Sally knew, deep down, that she wasn't really ugly, but there sure were some alterations she would like to make if only she could. Long, straight blond hair, the kind that blows in the wind, would certainly be an improvement over the brown, mind-of-its-own stuff that she spent long hours trying to make over. And why, as long as she was destined to be tall, couldn't she have the long lean legs of a model instead of the ordinary, almost thick ones she had?

Perhaps you knew Sally. Perhaps you were Sally. Although the details were probably different, you most likely experienced similar concern with your body and what was happening to it. For you it might have begun as early as age eleven, or as late as age fifteen, and you might have been concerned with your weight rather than your height, with your nose rather than your hair, with your shoulders rather than your legs. You were normal.

With the advent of puberty come the most rapid and dramatic bodily changes since the first year of life. Quite obviously, the growth that occurs between birth and the first birthday is phenomenal, usually involving a weight gain of about 300 percent, sometimes more. But from the end of infancy until puberty, although a great deal of growth and change occurs, the changes are gradual. As such, they hardly are noticed except by the child's distant relatives, who never fail to remark on the extent of growth that has occurred since their last visit. Then at puberty (from

Adolescents wonder if they will ever approximate society's image of the acceptable body.

the Latin *pubertas,* meaning grown up), there is another dramatic alteration in the growth rate, including a rapid increase in body size, a significant change in the shape and composition of the body, rapid development of the reproductive organs, and development of the secondary sex characteristics that indicate that an individual has reached physical maturity. What further emphasizes the importance of these developments is the individual's very personal observation of and involvement in them. The actual rate of growth may have been greater during infancy, but infants don't watch that growth take place, comparing themselves to their peers, or wondering if they will ever approximate society's image of the acceptable body.

BODILY CHANGES

Skeletal Age

Puberty begins with the first evidence of sexual development and ends when the individual is fully capable of reproducing. All the changes involved take from one and one half to six years in girls and from two to five years in boys, with boys beginning their pubertal changes about two years later than girls. Obviously, maturational age varies widely, and chronological age is not a reliable indicator of maturational age. Two other measures are more accurate: **dental maturity** and **skeletal**

age. Dental maturity, the number of erupted teeth, is the easier to use, but skeletal age is the more accurate. As children mature, the cartilage hardens into mature bone, and the ends of the bones show the degree of ossification, which is measured by x-raying the hand and wrist. There is a strong relationship between skeletal age and physical maturity. Furthermore, when skeletal age rather than chronological age is used, the six-and-one-half-year span during which the first menstrual period may begin is reduced to only two and one half years (Tanner, 75). In other words, a girl is likely to get her first menstrual period between ages 11 and 17, but the girl who starts at age 11 is probably only two and one-half years less physically mature than the girl who starts at 17. Skeletal age findings are also consistent with the observation that girls begin (and end) puberty earlier than boys. Their skeletal system, as well as their nervous system, is more mature than that of boys throughout childhood, and their bones reach mature ossification several years before those of boys.

Glands and Hormones

Exactly what physical characteristics each of us displays as an adult is determined to a great extent by the genes we inherited from our parents. These genes carry the hereditary instructions that strongly influence height, general body composition, and specific physical features, as well as whether our own development into adults will begin relatively early or late in comparison to others. There is extreme variability in the age and the duration of puberty, and whether yours was early or late, short or long, was determined by a combination of environmental influences and your own internal clock. Much of it was under the control of the **hypothalamus,** located at the base of the brain, just above the pituitary gland.

Hypothalamus. Until fairly recently, the relationship among the functioning of the hypothalamus, the pituitary gland, and the gonads (ovaries in females and testes in males) was not clearly understood. It was thought that at puberty the hypothalamus stimulated the pituitary to stimulate the gonads to release the sex hormones for the first time. We now know that small amounts of sex hormones are circulating throughout the body from infancy. Puberty does not herald the first release of hormones, but rather a change in their intensity (Garrison, 76).

Pituitary gland. When the hypothalamus matures, it sends revised messages to the anterior part of the **pituitary gland** (Figure 6.1). The pituitary is an **endocrine** gland; it secretes its hormones directly into the blood stream. (**Exocrine** glands, like your sweat and salivary glands, have ducts to the outside of your body.) The endocrine glands play the vital role in adolescent development. Endocrine glands secrete **hormones,** substances that stimulate the activity of other tissues.

Sometimes referred to as the **master gland** because of the large number of hormones it secretes, the pituitary gland releases some hormones that act on all body tissues and some that act only on very specific tissues. **Growth hormone** is

Figure 6.1
Relationship of Hypothalamus, Pituitary, and Production of Hormones

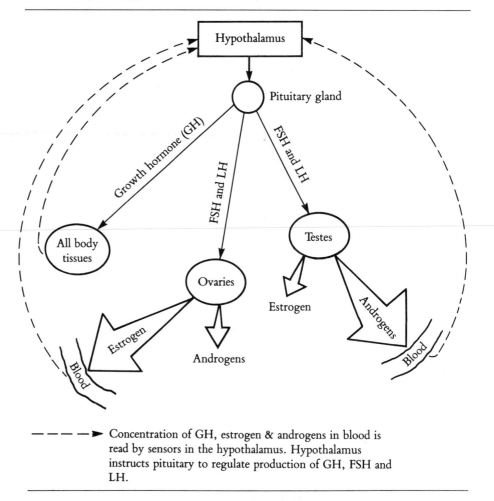

- - - - ▶ Concentration of GH, estrogen & androgens in blood is
read by sensors in the hypothalamus. Hypothalamus
instructs pituitary to regulate production of GH, FSH and
LH.

essential to the growth of all tissues. The **gonadotropic hormones** act specifically
on the gonads (sex glands) in both males and females. There are two gonadotropic
hormones: **FSH,** or **follicle-stimulating hormone,** encourages the growth of
eggs and sperm and stimulates the production of sex hormones; and **LH,** or **lutein-
izing hormone,** also causes the gonads to produce important sex hormones.

Gonads. The **gonads,** ovaries in females and testes in males, have two functions.
They are responsible for producing mature gametes (eggs in females and sperm in
males), and they secrete the hormones that are directly responsible for the bodily

changes of adolescence that make men different from women. The gonads produce the **androgens**, commonly referred to as male hormones, and **estrogen**, the female hormone. But it is not as simple as the ovaries producing estrogen and the testes producing androgens. Gonads produce both male and female hormones. Their concentration in the body determines whether an individual develops the secondary sexual characteristics of a man (such as beard, low voice, broad shoulders, and body hair) or those of a woman (such as breasts and wider hips). The androgens are necessary to the development of both sexes, as is estrogen.

Integration of glandular functions. All of the endocrine glands work more or less in conjunction with one another, but their integration is far from perfect, which explains why development during puberty is so variable, both in onset and in duration. The sequence of changes is relatively stable; hands and feet, for example, tend to reach adult size long before adult height and weight are reached, and before an individual is sexually mature. But one individual may wait five years between these events while another waits only two years. As J.M. Tanner (75, p. 513), a well-known British physician and researcher of adolescent growth notes:

> The basis of some children having loose and some tight linkages between pubertal events is not known. Probably the linkage reflects the degree of integration of various processes in the hypothalamus and the pituitary glands, for breast growth is controlled by one group of hormones, pubic hair growth by another, and the height spurt probably by a third.

Pubertal Growth Spurt

Timing. Among the monumental changes that occur during puberty is the rapid growth that may leave parents sighing in resignation when the almost-new shoes are suddenly too small or the pants that were bought just last month are too short. Just as in all other pubertal changes, there is tremendous variation in the timing of the growth spurt, with it beginning in boys between the chronological ages of 10.5 and 16 and ending between the ages of 13.5 and 17.5. It is thus possible for one fourteen-year-old boy to have completed his growth spurt while another boy born on the same day may not yet have begun his. In girls the growth spurt occurs approximately two years earlier. Therefore, it is entirely likely that in the eighth grade, when children are about 13 years old, the girls will be taller, heavier, and significantly more physically mature than the boys. You need only recall your own eighth-grade class to verify this observation. Although neither males nor females are completely finished growing by the time the spurt ends, they will have grown from two to five inches or more during this time, and they will also have developed maturity in both the primary sex organs (ovaries and uterus in females; testes, scrotum, and penis in males) and secondary sex characteristics. Girls, on the average, reach 98 percent of their adult height at 16.25 years, boys at 17.75 years (Tanner, 75).

One fourteen-year-old may complete his growth spurt while another has yet to begin.

Relationship to adult height. During the growth spurt, the velocity of growth about doubles, but the intensity or extent of the spurt itself is generally not indicative of eventual adult height. Adult height is more directly related to height before the growth spurt. Thus a short child is likely to be a short adult. But even this is not completely predictable, for, as Tanner found, about 30 percent of adult height is related to the magnitude of the growth spurt.

The growth spurt also complicates height differences, for the tall child is also likely to grow earlier than the short child, so the differences in height during the spurt itself are frequently extreme. Both the tall, early-maturing girl and the short, late-maturing boy are likely to feel out of place with their peers. All too frequently, adults, who have left the growth spurt far behind, are insensitive to the intensity of self-consciousness that pubertal youngsters experience, and tend to dismiss adolescent fears as something they will outgrow. Although they are likely to outgrow these fears, youngsters who are feeling out of place now are not comforted by assurances that they will catch up in a few years. Boys tend to worry about being too short, girls about being too tall. The earlier growth spurt experienced by the girls only intensifies the concern both sexes have for their ultimate height. It may be helpful for some youngsters to know that earlier maturers tend to be shorter adults than late maturers (Smart, 73). Apparently the secretion of sex hormones has an inhibiting effect on the pituitary's production of growth hormone, so as the level of sex hormones in the body increases, less body growth takes place.

Other changes. Several other important developments occur during the growth spurt. Weight increases, and although weight gain is generally consistent with gain in height, it may vary considerably. Weight gain results from increases in muscle, in the skeletal system, or in fat. Because of these different causes of weight gain, it by itself is not a reliable indicator of growth (Tanner, 61). In both males and females, the vocal chords thicken and lengthen, and the voice changes from that of a child to that of an adult. Both sexes experience the changes that result in a mature head and face: the forehead becomes higher and wider, the chin becomes more prominent, and the mouth widens and the lips fill out. Both males and females develop pubic and axillary hair. In summary, the growth spurt results in the body proportions, facial features, and primary and secondary sex characteristics of adults.

Sex dimorphism. **Dimorphism** refers to the development of two distinct forms of a species, in this case, male and female humans. Prior to puberty, there are few differences in the skeletal systems, respiratory systems, digestive systems, and body charactertistics of boys and girls. Little girls are just about as strong, muscular, and tall as little boys of the same age; they have about equal needs for oxygen and food; and except for the external genitalia, their bodies are quite similar. It is the effects of the sex hormones (androgens and some estrogen in the male and estrogen and some androgens in the female) that we see in the markedly different bodies of mature men and women. These hormone ratios affect the rate and amount of the growth of bone, muscle, and fat, and influence the development of the vocal cords and of body hair.

Boys develop larger muscles, larger skeletal systems, larger hearts and lungs, a higher systolic blood pressure, a lower resting heart rate, a greater oxygen carrying capacity in the blood due to a higher level of hemoglobin, and a higher basal metabolic rate (the rate at which the body burns energy) than girls. All these characteristics explain part of the boy's seemingly greater athletic ability, although activity level may be a contributing factor as well.

Girls too develop increased strength, musculature, respiratory function, and digestive function at puberty, but less dramatically so than boys. Whereas both females and males gain fat more slowly during puberty than before, girls' fat gain is relatively greater than boys', resulting in women having a higher percentage of body fat than men. This additional body fat in women contributes to the female's capacity for child bearing and breast feeding and to the relatively greater endurance that women display.

Primary and Secondary Sexual Characteristics

The growth spurt includes significant changes in both the primary sex organs and secondary sexual characteristics of both girls and boys, the timing of which is generally consistent with the timing of the other bodily changes. That is, a youngster whose skeleton matures early will also menstruate or shave early.

The primary sex organs of girls are the **vagina, vulva** (including the **labia majora, labia minora,** and **clitoris**), **uterus,** and **ovaries.** At puberty the vagina

Table 6.1
The Maturational Sequence

Girls	Boys
1. Initial breast development.	1. Beginning of testes and penis growth.
2. Straight, pigmented pubic hair.	2. Straight, pigmented pubic hair.
3. Maximum growth.	3. Early voice changes.
4. Kinky pubic hair.	4. First ejaculation.
5. Menarche.	5. Kinky pubic hair.
6. Axillary hair.	6. Maximum growth.
	7. Axillary hair.
	8. Marked voice changes.
	9. Beard.
	10. Indentation of temporal hair line.

increases in length and begins to produce an acid secretion: the vulva enlarge greatly and darken; the uterus doubles in length; and the ovaries increase in size and weight. These changes are associated with the **menarche**, or beginning of menstruation, which for many girls is the pivotal experience of puberty.

In boys the primary sex organs are the **testes, scrotum, penis,** and **prostate gland.** The testes increase two and a half times in length and eight and a half times in weight; the scrotum enlarges and changes color and texture; and mature sperm cells develop. The penis doubles in length and girth. (There is tremendous variation in adult penile size, which is unrelated to sexual functioning; nevertheless, adolescent boys frequently are concerned about the size of their penises and are likely to relate size to masculinity.) The prostrate gland increases in size and begins to secrete seminal fluid (semen) for carrying sperm. Only when the prostate matures is ejaculation possible.

The biological changes, both primary and secondary, of adolescence occur in a predictable sequence for both boys and girls. Table 6.1 outlines these changes. Notice that for girls, menarche comes quite late in the sequence. Girls have already completed most of their growth and development before the onset of the menses. For boys, first ejaculation precedes maximum growth, with the final voice changes and beard development following it. The development of the beard is among the last of the male changes and may continue on into the twenties.

The Secular Trend

Over the last 100 years a noticeable change in developmental patterns has occurred. Children are growing up faster; that is, they are taller and heavier at all ages than their ancestors, and they are experiencing the growth spurt earlier. Although there has also been a slight increase in adult height and weight, these are not so dramatic as the earlier maturation of children. Girls are now achieving adult height at 16 rather than 19, and boys at 18 rather than 24. Girls are experiencing their first menstrual period about three years earlier than females of the mid-nineteenth century (Tanner, 75). The trend, however, is slowing and seems to have stopped in many countries, the United States included (Tanner, 75).

Nutrition. Why are children growing up faster? Until very recently, better nutrition was advanced as the most plausible answer. This, of course, occurs only within the limits imposed by heredity. Good nutrition and other health habits are seen as facilitating the development inherent genetically in each individual. The genetic makeup of people is, of course, the reason why the secular trend is not likely to continue. Even though children may be maturing earlier, we will not see seven year olds becoming physiologically adult. We have reached the limits of our potential for earlier maturation.

Stimulation. Recently, Adams (81a) proposed an interesting alternative to the theory that the secular trend is due primarily to nutritional and medical factors. While acknowledging that better nutrition could account for a decrease in the number of young women having their first menstrual periods extremely late, he proposes that nutrition does not in and of itself account for an overall decline in the age of the onset of menstruation. Extrapolating from animal studies, Adams suggests that the increased stimulation and stress of living in an industrial society may be correlated with the secular trend of earlier maturation. Of particular interest is the hypothesis that the amount of infant handling, noise, crowding, and other stimulation factors could have an impact on human development. Such has been found in monkeys, rats, and other laboratory animals. Adams points out that stimulation can be both negative and positive (cuddling being positive and spanking negative, for example), and that there seem to be indications that there is an as-yet-undetermined optimum amount of stress. Both too much and too little are likely to have negative consequences. The stimulation-stress hypothesis has yet to be tested in humans, but it may provide an intriguing argument for the capability of humans to adapt to changing needs.

The irony of this earlier development is that it occurs in a society that simultaneously requires young people to wait to exercise their sexual maturity.

Early *vs.* Late Maturation

The onset and duration of puberty varies so greatly that two individuals of exactly the same age can easily look like they are several years apart in physical maturity. Furthermore, young adolescents are extremely self-conscious, and much of their self-image is determined by their image of their bodies. What, then, are the implications of relatively early or late maturation on the psychological adjustment of adolescents and on the expectations of themselves and others for their behavior? The classic research into the effects of early and late maturation, known as the California Growth Studies, investigated the relative effects of maturation among boys in the top 20 percent and bottom 20 percent of their sample of ninety (Jones, 50). Significant psychological differences, which are detailed in the following discussion, were found between these two groups. More recent research conducted by Lynn (59), Weatherly (75), Pomerantz (79), Hamachek (76), Smart (73), Peskin (72), and Runyan (80) support the earlier findings. The research also verifies that the timing of physical maturation has a significant effect on the self-concepts, behaviors, and happiness of both boys and girls, as well as on the expectations that parents, teachers, and their peers have for their behavior. The following discussion is based on the findings of all these researchers.

Although the effects are the most dramatic for those who develop either *very* early or *very* late, the timing of the development is important to all, even those who are only relatively ahead of or behind their friends. Because adolescents are conscious of their bodies and concerned with measuring up to peer standards, they are acutely conscious of relative differences and therefore are likely to think of themselves as taller or shorter, bigger or smaller, more or less developed than their most significant friends. Even if a boy is really quite near the statistical average in development, he will think of himself as big and strong if most of his friends are not as well developed or as small and weak if most of his friends are better developed. Once again, the perception is as important as the reality. Furthermore, some of the studies even indicate that the differences in self-image persist into adulthood, especially for boys. What, then, are these effects?

Early-maturing boys. The early-maturing boy is bigger, more muscular, taller, better coordinated, and more athletic than his later-maturing contemporaries. He is likely to dominate his friends, both in size and in leadership. He is likely to be more active in extracurricular activities, display more leadership characteristics, have earlier heterosexual interests, and be admired by both peers and adults. He is expected to act more maturely and is given more privileges and greater responsibilities. His advanced physical powers bring him prestige and success, and he is likely to maintain his psychological advantage into adulthood. Because his body comes close to the cultural ideal, he feels good about himself, and his esteem remains high. Also, the early-maturing boy is closer, developmentally, to the development of girls his own age. Remember that girls mature about two years earlier than boys, so the early-maturing boy is less likely to feel completely dominated by all the girls and many of the boys in his class. Obviously, early maturation is, for boys, filled with potential advantages, if he is successful in living up to expectations and in channeling his activities so as to earn status from his peers.

There are, however, a few disadvantages as well. The early-maturing boy may be shocked with the rapidity of the bodily changes he is experiencing and may become anxious about them, especially if he has not been adequately prepared. Although most boys look forward to the outward signs of maturity, being the first to have to shave could be an embarrassment. A further disadvantage for the early-maturing boy could be in the unrealistic expectations that adults have for him. If adults react to an early-maturing fifteen-year-old as if he were the eighteen-year-old that he appears to be, they might condemn his fifteen-year-old behavior as immature. He runs the risk of being expected to have the intellectual and emotional maturity of one considerably older than he. Early maturers also may be pushed into premature decisions about their identity, while later maturers have more time to adjust to change and to develop more flexible identities (Jones, 65; Peskin, 67).

Late-maturing boys. Late-maturing boys are left behind all the girls and most of the boys their age. They are likely to feel isolated, unattractive, awkward, and weak. The late maturer and the chubby boy are the most likely to develop negative bodily images and, consequently, negative self-images. In addition, the late-maturing boy must cope with the demands of high school while still looking like a child. Athletics, especially in a large school, are usually beyond him, as are relationships with girls his own age. Additionally, the late-maturing boy may wonder if he is ever going to mature, to be normal. Doubting his normality may also lead to doubting himself in more general ways. Psychologically, the difficulties experienced by late-maturing boys persist even into adulthood, long after the obvious physical differences between the early and late maturers have disappeared. All the researchers (Lynn, 59; Peskin, 72; Smart, 73; Weatherley, 75; Hamachek, 76; Pomerantz, 79; Runyan, 80) have noted that late-maturing boys have, in general, less healthy personality characteristics. They are more likely than early- or average-maturing boys to maintain adolescent conflicts beyond adolescence, seek a great deal of attention and affection from others, seek positions in which they can depend on and follow others, act out in rebellious rather than constructive ways, feel anxious and tense, abase themselves, delay adult commitments, and remain relatively unstable vocationally. This is not to imply that all boys on the late end of the normal continuum for maturity are doomed to develop unhealthy personalities, of course, but only that society's and the adolescent's ideal images create stereotypes that make it difficult for the late maturer, who does not fit the stereotype, to accept himself.

In an interesting followup to the California Growth Studies, which were conducted over a generation ago, Runyan (80) studied 45 adults who had participated in the California Growth Studies as adolescents to determine if the early and late maturers would recall their adolescence as less or more satisfying. These adults were asked to report levels of satisfaction with various periods in their lives. He found that the early-maturing boys, particularly those in the working class, recalled their adolescence as significantly more satisfying than did the late-maturing boys. Perhaps physique and physical maturity are even more significant among the working class than among the professional class.

Early-maturing girls. For girls, the data are less clear and considerably less dramatic. Early maturing is not perceived as an advantage, at least not during the early adolescent years themselves. The early-maturing girl is likely to feel embarrassed by her body, which is developed beyond those of most of her girl friends and all of the boys. She may be bigger than anyone else in her class and may feel uncomfortable in the body of a woman. A thirteen-year-old who looks eighteen is out of place in a classroom of thirteen-year-olds, and she is likely to be ostracized by her peers. She is also likely to be treated as a sex object by older boys, a circumstance she is not socially or emotionally prepared to handle. To exacerbate the situation, her parents and other adults may not trust her; seeing her so obviously sexually mature may raise suspicions about potential sexual behavior to accompany the physical development. However, she may show healthy integration and beneficial effects of early maturation not unlike those of the boys, including higher scores on intelligence and other age-related exams. Also, once they reach maturity, early-maturing girls are likely to have more healthy self-concepts than late-maturing girls. The evidence is obviously not consistent, with early maturers having both advantages and disadvantages. During early adolescence, however, the disadvantages appear to outweigh the advantages, and to the thirteen-year-old, it may seem like an eternity before she doesn't feel like a misfit.

Late-maturing girls. Late-maturing girls may also feel at some disadvantage in the early years of puberty and may be envious of their earlier-maturing peers, but they are generally on about the same level of development as the average maturing boys, so never feel too far out of place. They are not subject to the same sexual advances or adult criticism as early-maturing girls. Once they have matured, and look back on adolescence, they are likely to report satisfaction with adolescence to a greater extent than their early-maturing girlfriends.

One finding appears consistent: the timing of puberty is usually more significant for males than it is for females. Given the rigid physical role prescriptions that our society has developed for males, this finding is not surprising. The male stereotype prescribes strength and athletic ability as the *sine qua non* for males. Females, though also subject to societal stereotypes, have more options for acceptability.

For both girls and boys, the timing of puberty can heavily influence self-image. We know that adolescents incorporate society's views of early and late maturers, at least to some degree. They are then likely to attempt to live up to those ideals, and to become involved in self-fulfilling prophecies that might go something like the following, though the adolescents are not consciously thinking these things:

David, 15, early maturer:	I'm big, muscular, and athletic. You expect me to act responsibly, and because I've been successful in the past and you've rewarded me, I will live up to your expectations.
Sam, 16, late maturer:	I'm still small and continue to be pushed around. You expect me to act like a baby, and although I resent it, I'll show what a baby I can be. I'll be inconsistent, demanding, whiny, and slow. Just watch!

SOCIAL-EMOTIONAL DEVELOPMENT

Nature *vs.* Nurture

In the first part of this chapter, we focused on puberty, the physiological phenomenon accounting for the extensive changes in the bodies of adolescents. The changes themselves, though subject to some influence from the environment, are primarily genetic, with our size, shape, and body composition determined to a great extent by genes inherited from both parents, even though a particular trait may not have been present in either parent. It is certainly true, however, that environmental conditions (nutrition, disease, psychological stress, chemicals in the air, drugs ingested, bacteria, diet, exercise, and everything else our bodies experience) can affect human growth and development. The degree to which the environment affects growth has been the subject of a major controversy that has extended over many years. The **nature-nurture** controversy refers to the differences in opinion as to the relative effects of heredity vs. environment. To put it in vernacular terms, to what extent is each of us "a chip off the old block," or "the master of my fate"?

The early theories of human growth and development presented in the first chapter of this book can be classified as theories that supported either the idea that all behavior is determined by heredity (nature) or that behavior is purely, or at least primarily, determined by experiences (nurture). The theories we classified as biological, for example, support the nature side of the argument, while the sociological theories are primarily nurture-oriented. But in trying to decide which one influence was responsible, the early theorists were concentrating on the wrong question. Quite obviously, heredity and environment are not independent of one another. Every living organism grows up in an environment, and no two organisms experience exactly the same environment. Not even identical twins living in the same family experience exactly the same environment. One may become ill and be treated differently as a result; one may have different friends and teachers than the other; and unless they are unusually close, they probably spend a good deal of time away from each other. Thus even in a situation that provides the greatest consistency of environment, the two people do not experience the same environmental conditions. Each of us is a product then not only of heredity, but of environment too.

All behavior and development are the result of a unique interaction of biology and society. And every individual reacts in her own way. This is why human behavior is itself so varied, so complex, and frequently so unpredictable. If an individual is endowed with a remarkable genetic gift but does not develop it, it will not mature. There are many intellectually gifted individuals living ordinary, mentally unchallenging lives, and many of only ordinary intellectual capacities in positions of responsibility and leadership. It may be our genes that make each of us unique, and that in many ways put a limit on certain capabilities, but it is what we do or do not do with our uniqueness that makes us individuals.

Heredity is one obviously powerful influence in determining the characteristics of adolescents, but their *perceptions* of these hereditary traits determine both their attitudes and their behavior. In the remainder of this section we will study how perceptions, rather than facts, often account for the variation in adjustment that we see in normal and physically disabled adolescents, and how these perceptions are influenced by the society, the family, and the adolescent's peers.

Body Types and Idealized Norms

That adolescents are acutely aware of physical characteristics is attested to by the nicknames that develop during early adolescence. Recall the nicknames of your eighth-grade classmates. Chances are you knew people called Porky, Beanpole, Four-eyes, Hawk, Spider, or Blimp, names that may have been used as cruel jokes or as endearments, names about which their owners most surely had strong feelings.

Body types. Many of those nicknames were descriptive of the individual's **body type.** The most common way to classify body types is to use a comparison among **ectomorphs, mesomorphs,** and **endomorphs.** Ectomorphs are tall and thin, mesomorphs square and hard, and endomorphs soft and round (see the drawing of these types). Each of these body types has been stereotyped by our society, and each thus carries with it certain expectations for personality and character. The ectomorph, who is tall and very thin, may be called Ichabod or Bones, while the endomorph, who is short and fat, is likely to be called Chunkers or Fats. But a nickname is not all that is associated with body type. Descriptors like ''lean and mean'' or ''round and jolly'' carry behavioral expectations as well, expectations that may lead us to judge one another unfairly based on body type alone. Surely not all very thin people are mean nor all fat people jolly, and most fat adolescents are not happy people (Brenner, 78; Hendry, 78; Staffieri, 72).

Self-acceptance. Self-acceptance and self-esteem are very closely related to the individual's satisfaction with her physical self. This is more often true for females than for males, and of more significance in younger adolescents. Throughout adolescence, however, outer appearance, the individual's perception of that appearance, and inner self-image are closely correlated. Protinsky (80) found that the self-image becomes more stable from early (ages 9 through 11) to late (ages 17 and 18) adolescence and that self-consciousness increases from preadolescence to middle adolescence and then decreases as the individual reaches late adolescence. In other words, youngsters between the ages of 9 and 14 are likely to be acutely conscious of their bodies and physical characteristics and sensitive to criticism both from others and themselves; they change their opinions about themselves frequently. Middle and late adolescents (ages 15 through 18), though still very aware of their bodies, are less self-conscious and have more stable views of themselves. Self-consciousness is clearly related to cognitive development, as will be discussed in Chapter 8.

The most common way to classify body types is as ectomorphs, mesomorphs, and endomorphs.

Adolescents' awareness of physical types has been studied with highly consistent results. Boys invariably prefer the mesomorphic body type, a body type with which no negative nicknames are associated. The mesomorph is essentially the athletic build, and boys not only prefer it but also attach positive personality characteristics to it. Mesomorphs are perceived as strong, intelligent, popular, and happy (Lerner, 72). Boys between the ages of 13 and 15 who are physically tall, strong, and muscular are more satisfied with their bodies than are their peers who do not have a strong mesomorphic body component (Azcarate, 71). Girls prefer the mesomorphic and ectomorphic body types for themselves, and neither boys nor girls ever prefer the endomorph (Brenner, 78; Hendry, 78; Staffieri, 72). Thus we can see that athletic boys and athletic and thin girls are perceived more favorably by one another and by themselves than are very thin or fat boys and fat girls. Furthermore, most of us are not pure ectomorphs, mesomorphs, or endomorphs. We simply don't come in only three sizes, but rather are spread along a continuum. You may have the long, thin legs of an ectomorph combined with the broad shoulders of a mesomorph. Our parents probably weren't pure types either, and our genetic makeup is the result of a combination of inherited traits.

It is clear that younger adolescents are significantly more sensitive to their bodies, and less satisfied with them than are older adolescents. They are changing rapidly, and the changes may be so dramatic that the young person has little time to integrate them into a consistent concept of physical self. At the same time, the changes are not themselves synchronized, leaving some young adolescents wondering if they will ever be properly coordinated. But just as the body eventually settles down, so does satisfaction with the body. Clifford (80) found that older adolescents are relatively satisfied with their bodies, with females being significantly less satisfied than males. For both males and females, height, weight, and physique are of most significance in their satisfaction with their bodies. Lerner (76) found that girls are most concerned about their bust, ankles, hips, thighs, buttocks, stomach, face, and complexion, while boys are most concerned with profile, height, neck and shoulder width, face, overall appearance, and weight distribution. Boys equate attractiveness more with athletic build and strength, girls with physique and facial features. These findings have not changed over the last several decades, for essentially the same concerns were discovered by Douvan (57) when she asked youngsters what they most liked and disliked about themselves: younger adolescents in particular identified physical aspects of themselves, while older adolescents were more likely to include characteristics like intelligence, creativity, and skill in their lists.

Idealized norms. Because their bodies are changing so rapidly, young adolescents become fixated on physical appearance and physical development. At the same time they are moving away from depending on their families for support and nurturance and looking more toward their peers, who also are focusing on physical appearance. With peer expectations for conformity, and the media presenting stereotyped ideals of successful men and women based on physical attractiveness, deviations are not easily tolerated. Young adolescents are likely to feel out of place because they do not conform to the one standard for physical attractiveness. Never mind that no one else does either; they all are likely to be looking only at themselves and overlooking the slight deviations of their peers. In order to hide the perceived flaws, adolescents may support group standards of dress or behavior that seem totally irrational to their parents. It may be to hide perceived deviations that young adolescents are so willing to conform to the current dress fad, even having to have the right label on their clothes. By dressing and acting alike, perhaps adolescents are trying to negate the physical differences that they have not yet learned to accept and appreciate.

Phenomenology and Self-Perceptions

Phenomenology. The term **phenomenology,** as it is used in psychology, refers to the importance of an individual's perception of an event in influencing behavior, rather than the event itself (Combs, 71). Albert Ellis (79), a well-known theorist and therapist, designed his *A-B-C* theory to explain the significance of perceptions. In Ellis's conception, *A* refers to an activating event, *B* refers to the thoughts the individual has about that event, and *C* refers to the emotional reaction that results. For example, Tom, who is fifteen, is cut from the football team because he is not as strong nor as fast as some other boys (event *A*). Tom believes that not being on the team is the end of the world (thought at *B*). He therefore perceives himself as a failure (reaction at *C*), and he never again tries out for any athletic team, even though he had been a reasonably good tennis player. Tom's friend Andy, also fifteen, is cut from the team for the same reasons (event *A*). Andy decides that although he would have liked to have been on the team, not making it is not the end of the world (thought at *B*), and he is not a failure as an athlete as a result of this disappointment (reaction at *C*). Andy puts his effort into improving his high-jumping skill and in spring makes the track team. Tom has a negative image of himself as an athlete, Andy a positive one, yet Tom may in fact have the greater athletic potential. We can see, then, our perception of reality, rather than reality itself, often determines our behavior and our self-images.

Self-perceptions. Self-perceptions, of course, may be accurate or inaccurate. Obviously, they are never objective. An individual's perceptions are influenced by prior experiences, by family and peer judgments, and by the individual's awareness of faults that are unnoticed by all others. We may look at Sandy and see a normal, healthy, even pretty fourteen-year-old. But Sandy may once have been fat; she had to buy clothes for chubby girls, and was made extremely conscious of her size by cruel remarks from her peers and a weight-conscious mother and aunt. When she looks in the mirror, she may not see the attractive girl we see, but may see instead her old, chubby self. She still may think of herself as fat and unattractive, and she may behave accordingly, trying to hide herself under baggy clothes that make her look more careless than chubby, for example. In trying to hide her body, she may also isolate herself from her peers. Then, because she has isolated herself, she feels lonely and unattractive, reinforces the negative image she started with, and further withdraws. Because Sandy perceives herself negatively, she acts as if the negative image were true, and the self-defeating spiral continues.

Sources of self-perceptions. The perceptions that adolescents have of their bodies are derived from many sources. The mirror is only one source of self-perceptions; others include past emotional experiences, parents' attitudes toward the adolescents' bodies, peers' views, and the ideal, stereotyped body images portrayed by the media. These various influences can, of course, be both positive and negative, and positive body images are equally as strong as negative ones. Minahan (71) discovered that girls who perceive themselves as attractive are in fact happier, more sociable, and more likely to see themselves as successful than girls who perceive themselves as ordinary or unattractive. Our perceptions, regardless of their basis in fact, influence behavior and create a self-fulfilling prophesy that eventually reinforces the original perception.

Changing self-perceptions. If the self-image develops over years and is based on such a wide range of inputs, it may seem difficult to effect change in it. Counselors believe that the self-image can be changed and are committed to working over fairly extensive time periods to help individuals change their self-defeating images of themselves. It generally has not been thought possible to change self-images significantly either in brief periods of time or with groups of individuals, but Harris (80) found that it is possible to increase body satisfaction and self-image in groups of teenagers. Harris used body movement exercises combined with guided fantasies with a group of fifteen-year-olds twice weekly for just one month. Harris found that this group, when compared with a group that did not do the exercises and fantasies, were significantly more likely to hold positive views of themselves and of people in general and to be significantly happier with their bodies. Apparently it is quite possible to influence the body images of adolescents by direct intervention. The implications for these findings should assist teachers and other adults in designing programs to help adolescents focus on building positive images of their changing bodies.

HOW BEHAVIOR AFFECTS DEVELOPMENT

Given the strong influence of experience and societal attitudes, current attention to health and nutrition should have an effect on adolescents' concern for their health. The rise in consciousness concerning health, especially that concerning the role of nutrition and exercise, that has come about during the 1970s should have a positive influence on adolescent attitudes toward health and fitness. We know better than we ever have before that our habits and activities do influence our health and well-being. During the 1970s and continuing in the 1980s, the rise of popularity of health clubs, running groups, health-food stores, vitamin centers, and sports and athletic stores for everyone (not just the athlete) attest to the recognition that fitness is indeed everyone's business. Adolescents can't help but be affected by this new awareness.

Adolescents are, in fact, the healthiest people on earth. By adolescence, the childhood diseases are no longer a significant factor, strength and endurance are at their peak, and the declines associated with adulthood and aging have not yet begun. The two most common reasons for absence from school are upper-respiratory problems and injuries due to accidents, both of which are generally short-lived. But healthy as adolescents generally are, they can be influenced by proper attention to nutrition and exercise. We will examine each of these before going on to a discussion of the role of athletics in adolescent health and adjustment.

Nutrition

In the past 100 years, worldwide nutrition has improved considerably, so much so that the improvement has been advanced as the basis of the lowered age of maturation of adolescents known as the secular trend. Yet it is also true that many adolescents have inadequate diets, even in the midst of affluence (Dufty, 75; Rice, 81). Why might this be so, and what might concerned adults, as well as adolescents themselves, do to correct this deficiency?

Nutritional needs. During adolescence, nutritional needs increase dramatically. This increase is due to the rapid growth of all parts of the body, including the size of the stomach. The growth spurt itself demands additional nutriment over that required for the more gradual growth of childhood, and the mature body has greater need for nutrition to sustain its increased activity and endurance.

The rise in nutritional needs is both considerable and variable, with boys having a much greater quantitative nutritional need than girls. Boys have a higher basal metabolism and higher needs for the nutrients that build muscle. Girls, once they begin menstruating, have increased needs for iron and other vitamins to replace those lost through menstruation, but they do not need significantly greater amounts of food. Whereas boys and girls had about equal nutritional needs prior to puberty, by age 18 boys need up to twice the calories they needed at 12, whereas girls' caloric needs increase only slightly. By the end of adolescence, boys require about one-and-one-half times the calories required by girls the same age, and about twice the calories required by their mothers (Johnston, 48). This difference in caloric requirement sometimes comes as a shock to the parents of adolescent sons, who find it difficult to keep adequate food supplies in the house. The difference may also account for some of the difficulty adolescent girls experience in maintaining their desired weight. All their lives, they have been eating about the same quantities as their brothers and male friends, and the temptation is to continue to do so. The social life of adolescents often includes food, but if adolescent girls continue to consume the quantities and kinds of foods that their male friends consume, they are destined to gain.

Inadequate nutrition. Many adolescents have inadequate diets, especially insufficient calcium and vitamins (Rice, 81), insufficient iron in young women, and too much sugar and other additives (Charlton-Siefert, 80; Dufty, 75). Although the potential for good nutrition has increased, and although attention to health and nutrition has increased among many people, the United States still suffers from poor nutritional habits, and middle- and high-school cafeterias suffer from charges of inadequate nutritional offerings. Specifically, inadequate knowledge of good nutrition, habitual snacking, reliance on fast foods of poor nutritional quality, too few fresh vegetables and fruits, and habits like skipping breakfast or eating only a nonnutritional sweet for breakfast contribute to the problem. Girls have greater nutritional deficiencies than boys, probably because they are prone to fad diets, irregular eating, and loss of iron and other nutrients through menstruation.

In addition to not providing the nutrients needed for growth, strength, endurance, and general good health, poor nutrition has also been cited as a cause of depression. Apparently both the nutritional problem and the individual's unhappiness with the resulting overweight or underweight body are causes of the related depression (Kaplan, 80). Nutritional disorders will be discussed in Chapter 12.

Sugar. Of increasing concern over the past ten years has been the quantity of sugar consumed by Americans, especially children (Charlton-Siefert, 80; Dufty, 75). In the United States, the average man, woman, and child each consumes over 95 pounds of sugar per year, yet we know that sugar has an addictive quality, that it can cause judgment problems by those who are unknowingly allergic to it, and that is has been blamed for hyperactivity and behavior problems in children and adolescents (Dufty, 75). Dr. Lendon Smith, a popular media pediatrician, has brought the problem to the attention of the television audience, as has "60 Minutes," which presented a documentary on the subject in November 1977. There are innumerable examples of how removing sugar from a child's diet has decreased hyperactivity and problem behavior, increased attention and concentration, and improved attitude. Concerned parents have encouraged schools to evaluate their cafeteria offerings, develop sound nutrition education programs, and increase awareness of the dangers of massive quantities of junk food in the diets of children and adolescents. In one residential treatment center with which I am familiar, the adolescent residents are required to read *Sugar Blues* by William Dufty, and are not allowed any desserts or sugar snacks while on campus. The staff firmly believes that the removal of sugar from the diets of these delinquent and predelinquent adolescents has had an observable and positive impact on their behavior. Removal of all sugar from our diets is probably close to impossible, since it is included in so many common products, but it does seem clear that elimination of overt sweets — such as candy and pastries — is not only possible but extremely beneficial. Adolescents learn dietary habits at home, of course, and years of habit are difficult to alter. Perhaps with attention paid to nutrition education now, the next generation of children and adolescents will have fewer bad habits to break.

Exercise

Exercise and physical fitness have caught on in the United States. Along with increased awareness of nutritional needs has come increased interest in keeping fit, particularly among young and middle-aged adults. Perhaps nowhere is this movement more clear than in the development of health clubs and in the amazing interest in jogging and aerobic dancing for physical fitness. Physical activity has become fashionable for both men and women and has even spawned a new development in the clothing industry known as "active wear." The old gray sweats are no longer the symbol of an Olympian in training. Updated in expensive fabrics and a rainbow of colors, sweats are one more indication of sophistication and belonging.

Physical fitness. Physical fitness has strong implications not only for physical health, but for social and emotional adjustment as well. In a comprehensive review of the research in physical fitness, Folkins (81) found that physical fitness training

Physical activity has become fashionable.

leads to improved mood, self-concept, work behavior, and cognitive functioning both during and after physical stress. Guyot (81) found that children in grades 4 through 6 who scored above the seventieth percentile on a physical fitness test had significantly higher self-concept scores than children who scored below the fiftieth percentile. The very fit felt significantly better about themselves than the average and below average in fitness. This was especially true for the boys, whose self-concept scores also correlated with sports participation. The girls were more likely to have self-concept scores correlated with body build. Sjoberg (75) found that physically fit college men were significantly better at mental tasks involving a high information load, continuous concentration, switching of attention, and short-term memory than were the unfit. Finally, Jasnoski (81) found that physical fitness training was correlated with improved ability and confidence both in the physical area and in nonphysical areas like frustration tolerance. Exercise, especially running, is also being used in the treatment of depression and psychosomatic illnesses (those physical illnesses for which no organic cause can be found). Some of the positive effects of physical fitness come from improved circulatory and respiratory function, some from improved body image, and some from such additional factors as belonging to a group and enjoying the recreational aspects of such training.

Worthy of special note is the changing attitude toward women's fitness. It has been only about ten years since women have been paying attention to exercise and fitness, but the awareness has changed lives significantly. Whether they involve joining an all-women's health spa, exercising with tapes by Jane Fonda, jogging and running, or body building, women's exercise programs have become exceedingly popular. Many women become involved to trim down and shape up, and in the process find themselves feeling stronger, happier, and better able to tolerate frustration, and functioning more effectively. Women are only beginning to discover their physical potential and are having fun doing so. Even body building for women is no longer considered as bizarre as it was only a few years ago, for women and men have discovered that muscles on women do not turn women into men. Because high levels of the hormone **testosterone** are required for masculine muscle development, women need not worry about looking like Atlas. Women can be strong without being muscle-bound. The days of sitting and watching, of not participating in strenuous activity, are over. This development can only be a blessing in helping adolescents perceive health and fitness as measures of success and fulfillment, though we as yet have few statistics concerning the impact of the positive national attitude toward physical fitness on adolescents.

Athletics

Power, athletic skill, and endurance all increase dramatically during adolescence, for boys more than for girls, but increasingly for girls too. Because of this increased strength and endurance, new competence in athletics becomes possible, with boys and girls developing different competencies. Because of the significant difference in strength and musculature, coeducational athletics decrease following puberty.

Males. Athletics become central in the lives of many adolescent males, especially because of the heavy emphasis on athletics in high schools and, increasingly, in middle and junior high schools. The best athletes are, of course, the stars, but many more adolescents participate, whether by managing the teams or cheering them on in the spirit of the school. For males in this country, popularity has been found, again and again, to be correlated with athletic success, and athletes have the highest social status of all groups in the school. Even fitness among seventh- and eighth-grade boys has been found to be directly and significantly related to participation in youth sports. It is clear that male athletes enjoy prestige and esteem, and that their self-concepts and even their achievement in other areas can be attributed to athletic success.

Whether the emphasis on athletics in schools is positive for nonathletes, however, is debatable. Some seem to enjoy the supportive role; others resent their lack of participation. Team managers, cheerleaders, ticket sellers, and spectators who feel they belong probably benefit. Those who only feel more isolated do not. Male nonathletes may tend to be ignored.

Females. The formal athletic programs are also beginning to recognize girls' sports, especially basketball, field hockey, swimming, tennis, and gymnastics. That these programs still do not demand the attention or the resources that the boys' programs demand is a major cause of concern, especially among women physical educators. Numerous court cases throughout the country have demonstrated the inferior quality of girls' sports programs, and many school systems have responded favorably, at least in recognizing the legitimate place for girls' athletics in the school's extracurriculum.

An interesting note on girl's athletics concerns gymnastics; as gymnastics competition has developed, women's gymnastics have become almost a prepubertal sport. Many girls involved in world-class competition have begun to show evidence of breast development, but have probably not yet experienced the major growth spurt. For the most part, they have not added fatty tissue to hips, buttocks, and thighs. Following her winning of the gold medal in Olympic gymnastics, Nadia Komenic literally retired from the sport for several years. She was reportedly depressed about gaining weight and filling out as a woman. Are millions of young girls being trained to be over the hill at 14?

Interscholastic sports. The premium placed on high school interscholastic athletics has had both beneficial and questionable results. Whereas it is universally acknowledged that adolescents need healthy activity, there are a number of dangers inherent in relying on interscholastic athletics to provide it:

1. Only the best participate.
2. Those who most need exercise are left out.
3. Those who most need social acceptance are left out.
4. An unhealthy emphasis on competition for the sake of winning develops.
5. A ''farm team'' society has developed, with children involved in competitive athletics at very young ages.
6. Too much contact and sports emphasis is unhealthy for young adolescents, whose bones grow before their muscle, leaving the bone epiphyses (ends of long bones) relatively unprotected and vulnerable.
7. Too much emphasis on sports raises unrealistic hopes and expectations among high-school athletes. Only the very special high-school athlete will obtain a college scholarship or succeed as a professional athlete, yet every middle-school athlete dreams of such stardom.

Informal sports. Perhaps of greater consequence to overall fitness and health are the intramural and informal sports programs in and outside of schools. Here all can participate, regardless of athletic skill. Where the emphasis is on participation and fun, not on competition and winning at all costs, real involvement and all that acccompanies it can be available to every adolescent. Then the physical benefits of exercise and fitness go hand in hand with the social and emotional benefits of group participation and individual challenge. We need sane, all-involving programs with an emphasis on health. We need to help successful athletes keep their success in perspective, to introduce physical activities that continue throughout life, to provide honest but supportive feedback to adolescents as they engage in physical activity, and to provide activities in which everyone can participate. In this way we can provide the challenge and training desired by the athletically endowed while not ignoring the more ordinary adolescents.

PROBLEMS IN PHYSIOLOGICAL DEVELOPMENT

Although adolescents, in general, are very healthy, there exist both common and uncommon problems associated with physiological development and health. Before discussing specific conditions, it is necessary to discuss the implications of any physical disorder for the individual and to distinguish between a disability and a handicap.

The Meaning of a Disorder

Problems in physiological development are complex in both causes and consequences. A particular disorder may be completely genetic in origin (for example, being born without a leg), or it might be both genetic and psychological (such as asthma). Further, the consequences are physical, behavioral, and emotional. The meaning of any specific variation in physique or health to any particular adolescent can be determined only by understanding the individual, her family, and her social and educational environment. Clearly the psychological significance of the condition and not the condition itself is responsible for the adjustment of the individual.

> The psychological significance of the deprivation has to do in large measure with such matters as the threat of social isolation, the struggle for independence, acceptance of personal limitation, and so on — experiences with which many, if not all, human beings are conversant. (Wright, 60, p. 3)

Disability or handicap. As with all other aspects of human growth, medical conditions may be perceived in different ways by different individuals. This phenomenological view leads us to be able to distinguish a **disability** from a **handicap.** A disability is the loss of a normal function. It is a medical condition, with no *necessary* social implications. A handicap, however, implies loss of personal and social capabilities. The American Health Association defines handicap as follows:

> A child is considered to be handicapped if he cannot within limits play, learn, work or do things other children his age can do; if he is hindered in achieving his full physical, mental, and social potentialities. (in Travis, 76, p. 4)

The distinction, then, is that a disability is a physical or medical condition, while a handicap is the personal and social result of that disability and depends on the interaction of the person with the environment. A disability may result in any degree of handicap, and persons with the same disability may not be equally handicapped. Each disability can be judged only in terms of the demands of the situation and the attitude of the person with the disability toward herself.

As Wright (60) points out, the psychological aspects of a particular disability may actually be more of a handicap than the physical aspects. She refers to the ancient Chinese custom of binding a woman's feet, crippling her for life. This is certainly a physical disability but was not perceived as such by those who engaged in it because their particular situation and attitude saw the tiny feet as a mark of feminine beauty, and the women whose feet were thus altered were not required to walk long distances, run, or use their feet in other functional ways. The bound feet were not a handicap. On the other hand, a high-school athlete who aspires to the National Basketball Association may feel severely handicapped if he is only 5'6'' tall, even though the physical condition that is handicapping him is not a disability in the medical sense of the word. The questions then become, given the particular condition: How does the individual cope with the physical, emotional, and social connotations of the condition? What effect does the condition have on the individual's ability to get along in the world? What are the implications of the condition for the individual's interaction with others?

A word of semantic caution is also in order. There is a tendency to refer to people with disabilities as **disabled** or **handicapped**, implying that the disability is the single most important feature of their lives and personalities. But the disability is only one characteristic and should not be so singled out. It is important to remember that every individual with a disability also has numerous *abilities,* which are not overshadowed by the single disability. It is preferable, then, to refer to persons with disabilities or illnesses, rather than to disabled or ill persons. "It is precisely the perception of a person with a physical disability as a *physically disabled person* that has reduced all his life to the disability aspects of his physique" (Wright, 60, p. 8).

Family influence. Because our perceptions of ourselves are so heavily dependent on the perceptions of others, it is imperative to understand the contexts in which an illness or disability occurs. When we are discussing adolescents and children, the first context, of course, is the family. The involved child is, first and foremost, a child in a family, and the overt and subtle messages that the child receives in the family have lasting implications for her adjustment or lack of it. The impact of an illness or disability on the family can be enormous, in some cases requiring a total alteration in family goals and lifestyles. Even minor illnesses and injuries can be disruptive, especially in a family in which there is no adult free from responsibilities outside the home. As Travis (76) emphasizes throughout her book on chronic illness in children, the family response is the crucial factor in the child's adjustment. For children and adolescents with chronic illnesses or severe disabilities, the family must provide sufficient support and nurturance without becoming overprotective and thereby hindering the child from achieving the independence of which she is capable. This is a big task, and it has been found that those children who fail to become rehabilitated come from families in which disordered family dynamics, family alienation, or collapse by a concerned but overwhelmed family are a factor (Versluys, 80).

Reactions of others. Outside the family, children with illnesses and disabilities must cope with society, including both adults and peers. People who deviate from the norm in any way are subject to unusual reactions ranging from disgust, through pity, to support and understanding. There is, as Wright points out, a **disability stereotype,** which categorizes anyone with a physical or medical problem as "one who has suffered a great misfortune and whose life is consequently disturbed, distorted, and damaged forever" (Wright, 60, p. 17). Because of this stereotype, people with disabilities are looked down upon, devalued, and therefore either feared, pitied, or rejected. It is disconcerting for normal people to see those with illnesses or disabilities, and we tend either to stare or to look away; both reactions are hurtful to the recipients of the stares or rejection. This is not to imply that all reactions are negative, or that progress in acceptance of those who deviate from the norm is not being made. The mainstreaming efforts made by schools, with their attention to preparation of both teachers and schoolchildren to accept illnesses and disabilities, are significantly influencing attitudes (Frith, 81; Thompson, 81). It also has become common to find heartwarming feature stories in newspapers about adolescents who have demonstrated considerable care and understanding for a classmate with a disability or illness. In my own local newspaper I recall, within the past year, stories about youths raising money to buy a van for a classmate who became paralyzed, sponsoring a footrace to honor and raise money for the care of a classmate with leukemia, and buying a wheelchair for a classmate with spina bifida so that she could become more independent. These were not acts motivated by pity or rejection, but by the understanding that these students needed assistance to express their independence and capabilities.

Adolescent complications. Adolescence complicates the process of adjustment to an illness or disability. On one hand, adolescents have greater intellectual understanding and more alternatives for expression than do children, so should be more capable of coping than younger children, who do not have the cognitive capacity for understanding the condition and its implications. Adolescents also have not already established vocational identities, as have adults, so do not have to change their image of themselves in the world in the way that adults faced with an illness or disability must. On the other hand, the body and physique take on special significance in adolescence, and deviations from accepted standards are not easily tolerated. This makes acceptance of an illness or disability especially difficult for adolescents in general, especially if disturbances in growth and maturation are involved, or if the individual is likely to doubt her attractiveness or eventual desirability as a sexual partner. Adolescents are in a particularly vulnerable developmental position.

In addition to being concerned about their bodies and how they compare to their peers, adolescents are faced with a number of other developmental issues.

Primary among these is increasing independence from family. Anderson (79) found that adolescent adjustment to a chronic problem depended on the adolescent's attitude toward the problem, the maternal attitude toward the problem, the dependence of the adolescent on her mother, and the self-concept of the mother. Mothers who themselves have positive self-concepts and who encourage independence and mature acceptance of the adolescent's problem influence healthy acceptance, adjustment, and independence by the adolescent. Hung (78) found that youngsters with disabilities were more dependent than normal youngsters, and that those in special schools were more dependent than those in mainstreamed schools. These children perceived themselves as dependent, regardless of their need to be. Achievement of independence from parents poses a special challenge to adolescents with illnesses and disabilities and to the adults whose responsibility it is to assist them in this task.

Bryan (80), in her review of the literature concerning depressive reactions of adolescents to handicapping conditions, confirms the difficulties imposed on adolescents with medical problems. Adolescents with disabilities and illnesses may have to accept permanent differences from their peers; they may be unable to take part in recreational activities; and they may experience conflict and confusion about their attractiveness and sexuality. She also found, however, that adolescents with less visible or milder disabilities sometimes have more difficulty adjusting than do their more seriously afflicted peers. They apparently have higher expectations for themselves, so although the disability is milder, the discrepancy between ability and expectation is greater.

People with extremely serious illnesses and disabilities, on the other hand, have been known to perform remarkable feats. A television special in 1981 featured a group of severely disabled persons climbing a mountain. The group included persons who were sightless, deaf, severely diabetic, or had only one leg. They did, however, treat each individual in terms of what he or she could contribute to the expedition rather than in terms of the disability, and through cooperation, understanding, and encouragement, the group succeeded at a task that eludes most fully able individuals. These people, like the person who goes backpacking or completes marathon races in a wheelchair, do not consider themselves in terms of their disabilities, but rather in terms of their abilities.

In evaluating a particular condition, whether it be a common medical problem of adolescence or a more severe chronic illness or disability, we must look first at the individual, and ask questions concerning the physical limitations imposed by the condition, possible treatments, family perceptions, individual evaluations, and support systems available.

Common Problems

In addition to the upper respiratory ailments (colds, flu, bronchitis) and the injuries that account for the majority of school absences of adolescents, **psychosomatic complaints, acne, menstrual dysfunction,** and **weight problems** are significant health problems facing many adolescents (Zeller, 70).

Psychosomatic illnesses. Psychosomatic illnesses are all those illnesses involving a heavy interrelationship between the body and the emotions. As we are well aware, the mind and body are not discrete, and just as physical problems can have a lasting effect on how we feel, so too can our feelings, especially stress and anxiety, affect our bodies. Virtually all systems of the body can be involved. Some common adolescent disorders that have significant emotional involvement include acne, hives, arthritis, asthma, hay fever, migraine headaches, ulcers, colitis, menstrual disorders, obesity, and anxiety.

All these conditions are affected by stress. We can verify this involvement by noting the language we use to express the experience of stress: "butterflies in my stomach," "stomach in knots," "heart racing," "weak knees," "legs like jelly," "the weight of the world on my shoulders." We quite literally *feel* stress in our bodies, and it also takes it toll in the diseases outlined above. Adolescents are no less prone to them than are adults, and they need to realize that these diseases are not purely physical. Prevention can occur, at least to some degree, in learning to deal with life's stresses before they take their toll on our bodies. This is not to imply that there is not a very real physical component, or that these diseases are totally controllable through stress management. They are diseases, with heavy somatic involvement, for which a proclivity is frequently inherited. They can only be reduced, probably not eliminated, through psychological means.

Acne. Acne is the most common disorder of medical significance in adolescence (Zeller, 70). It is properly known as *acne vulgaris,* a skin disorder that involves inflamation and pimple formation, primarily on the face but frequently on the back and chest as well. Katchadourian (77) noted that 85 percent of adolescents have some acne at some time during adolescence, girls most often between 14 and 17, boys between 16 and 19. In a survey of 1254 high school students, 69 percent of the boys and 58 percent of the girls reported current concern with facial acne (Schachter, 71). Acne occurs when the sebaceous glands produce excess cellular debris and skin oil. The ducts become clogged, and sometimes painful pimples form. Acne seems to be related to the level of testosterone secreted, which is present in greater concentrations in males and therefore responsible for the higher prevalence of acne among males. Acne is treatable partly through diet, hygiene, and medication. Although it usually clears up by the end of adolescence, it can be a painful condition, both physically and psychologically. The students reporting acne in Schachter's study felt that people stared at them and that they did not get as many invitations or have as good a time in social situations as their nonaffected peers. Adolescents with acne should be referred to a physician, for modern treatments are effective in treating this potentially disfiguring condition.

Menstrual disorders. Virtually every adolescent female has experienced some menstrual dysfunction (Lerner, 80). Many know some degree of painful menstruation, properly known as **dysmenorrhea.** The cramps usually disappear after adolescence, but can be painful and disruptive enough to keep girls home from school and out of participatory activities. Dysmenorrhea results from both biological factors like hypersensitivity of the uteran lining and from psychological factors. **Amenorrhea,** or the failure to menstruate, can occur because of either physical or psychological problems: girls who become excessively thin fail to menstruate, as may those who are excessively worried (especially about menstruating). Some girls experience excessive bleeding, either regularly or occasionally, and as many as 60 percent experience the headache and anxiety known as **premenstrual tension** (Lerner, 80). That all these menstrual disorders (except the tension and emotional changes known as **premenstrual syndrome,** or **PMS**) tend to decrease following adolescence may be of little comfort to the young woman experiencing them. She should be advised that they are very responsive to medical treatment and referred to a gynecologist, who can treat her physical problem and help her to understand what is happening to her, thus allaying any fears she may have.

Weight problems. Many adolescents are unhappy with their weight, and significant numbers of them are overweight or underweight. Hendry (78) found that underweight adolescents were considered to be lacking in physical skills and social poise and were more likely to be withdrawn and to watch more television than adolescents of average weight. Underweight is perceived as more of a problem for boys, for whom athletic competence is especially important, than it is for girls, who tend to value the ectomorphic body build. Fashion models encourage thinness, as does the media: ''No woman can be too thin or too rich.'' (The excessive loss of weight known as anorexia nervosa will be discussed in Chapter 12.)

A more widespread problem of adolescence is that of overweight. Between 10 and 30 percent of adolescents are overweight to the point of being considered obese, with weights at least 20 percent above others of the same height, when that weight difference is due to fat, not muscle (Katchadourian, 75).

Overweight to the point of obesity is caused by a number of factors. Heredity accounts for some of it, but even in a family of fat people, heredity is not the only culprit. Fat families tend to have poor dietary habits, so poor eating habits are learned from infancy. Some obesity is a result of overeating to relieve stress or tension. Some is due to developmental disturbances. Some is the result of poor family relationships (Steele, 74); in a mother-child relationship based on extreme dependency, for example, the mother may overfeed the child in her attempt to maintain a dependency relationship. Some is due to inactivity or insufficient activity; obese children and adolescents exercise significantly less than their peers (Katchadourian, 75). Regardless of the causes, which are probably complex within any individual, obesity has been held responsible for a number of other problems, including cardiovascular disease, hypertension, joint disease, gynecological disorders, impaired social relationships, poor school performance, and inadequate emotional adjustment. Obese adolescents have problems with dependency, in that they are often passive and emotionally immature, and with sexual identity, being unprepared for the changes of puberty and unwilling to become involved in heterosexual activities. There is also a 28:1 probability that an obese teenager will become an obese adult (Zakus, 79).

As anyone who has tried to work with obese adolescents knows, treatment is extremely difficult. Treating diet alone seldom works, nor does merely encouraging exercise or setting up a reward system for small weight losses. The multicausal nature of obesity must be recognized and dealt with, including the emotional components of both obesity and weight loss. What is needed is an appropriate combination of behavioral counseling, nutrition education, monitoring of eating, exercise, problem solving, attention to self-concept issues, and even family education and involvement (Gormally, 81; Brandt, 80; Steele, 74).

Weight loss itself is often not a sufficient motivator to continue losing weight. In an interesting presentation of case studies, Steele (74) demonstrates the problem by showing how, when weight loss is not accompanied by the expected fantasies of sexual attractiveness and popularity, girls who lose weight become discouraged and are likely to give up.

Treatment of obesity is a complicated and painstaking process, and it should not be assumed that weight loss is an easy matter for anyone who is sufficiently motivated.

Chronic Illnesses

Extent. A **chronic illness** is a long-term, functionally disabling disease. Chronic illnesses have been considered, collectively, the nation's number-one health problem, a problem that is especially important because it is treated primarily within the family. Hospitalizations certainly occur, but only for traumatic episodes. The primary care is handled within the home and may have to continue for years, even a lifetime. Travis (76) estimates that the largest number of chronic illnesses occur in children between the ages of 10 and 16, and that 23 percent of children 17 and under suffer from one or more chronic conditions. Of 12- to 17-year-olds, one youth in five has one or more significant cardiovascular, neurological, musculoskeletal, or other physical abnormality. She further estimates that 20 to 40 percent of children with chronic conditions come from low-income families, and that less than half of these are medically treated for their conditions. Fifteen percent of 18-year-olds rejected by the Selective Service in 1965 were rejected because of chronic handicapping conditions, two thirds of which could have been corrected or prevented prior to the age of 15 (Travis, 76). Of the chronic diseases, asthma is the most prevalent among all children, with males being significantly more susceptible than females. Most children outgrow asthma by the time they reach adulthood, but they are likely to pass the susceptibility on to their children. Among whites, diabetes is the second most prevalent; among blacks, sickle cell anemia ranks second (Travis, 76). Obviously, chronic illness is of major concern to a sizable minority of adolescents.

Psychological aspects. Despite the large number of chronically ill adolescents, Zeltzer (80) found that they are basically psychologically healthy. Contrary to the popular notion of chronically ill adolescents as psychologically weak, he found that those with life-threatening or chronic diseases (renal, rheumatologic, or cardiac disease; cancer; cystic fibrosis; diabetes mellitus) do not demonstrate psychopathology, nor do they demonstrate increased anxiety or low self-esteem. Zeltzer compared 345 healthy with 168 chronically ill adolescents, and found that the healthy group perceived minor illnesses as of much greater impact than did the chronically or seriously ill. Thirty percent of the the healthy group reported current illness, primarily headaches, colds, sinus problems, and allergies, whereas the ill group tended to report their current status as free of illness. The healthy group also reported greater disruption in their lives from illnesses. He attributes this difference to perception; to the chronically ill, only major illness is considered a disruption. He concludes that chronically ill adolescents have developed flexible and highly adequate mechanisms for coping with disease. The diabetic and cardiac patients in his study actually reported less impact on their lives from illness than did some of the healthy adolescents. The rheumatoid and cancer patients, expectedly, reported more. The chronically and seriously ill have been well equipped to deal with occasional disruptions, and do not perceive them as major intrusions into their lives. Because the school enviroment is the normal one, and because these students should be assisted to live their lives as normally as possible, they should, Zeltzer concludes, be in school regardless of their disease. Being in school causes less disruption and stress than special placement or staying at home. This is true, he says, even for the most seriously ill: the cancer patients who may also be facing death. They have too much to cope with to take away the most normal peer environment possible.

Many chronically ill adolescents have been coping with their disease all their lives, but some face the onset of illness in adolescence. This onset, says Travis (76), always leads to depression. The adolescent who is suddenly faced with a change in body image, social role, and goals needs to mourn a major loss, loss of the old self, before hoping to develop a new self-image, and the depression is an appropriate mechanism for mourning.

Many chronic childhood illnesses tend to clear up by the end of adolescence. This is especially true of asthma, childhood arthritis, and childhood colitis. Even diabetes may take on a less significant role in the individual's life once adolescence has passed. Berlin (80) suggests that these diseases may be used as a means of covering up serious conflicts in the family that interfered with the child's development and allowed the child to remain dependent. The family could then focus on the child's illness and ignore its conflicts. This view is certainly consistent with the structural view of families presented in Chapter 3. This is not to suggest that the family consciously or maliciously makes an individual ill, only that the complexity of family dynamics may be responsible for much more than we had previously thought possible. If the family is so powerful an influence, it would also follow that it could be an equally strong influence in positive directions. We know this to be true; incredible misfortune can be borne with the help of a nurturing and understanding family.

That chronic and serious illnesses need not daunt the spirit is clearly evidenced by two outstanding television stars. Gary Coleman, star of television's "Diff'rent

Strokes," suffers from kidney disease and must cleanse his blood several times daily. The disease is responsible for the stunted growth that this adolescent uses to his advantage in playing children's roles. Geri Jewell, who suffers from cerebral palsy, has been waging a one-woman campaign to further the cause of acceptance of CP victims through her comedy act on stage and her appearances on television's "Facts of Life." Not only have these courageous young people refused to succumb to self-pity or dependence, they have actually used their affliction in ways that promote human understanding.

Disabilities

Physical disabilities. Wright (60) estimates that approximately two million children in the United States have physical disabilities. Unlike a chronic illness, a physical disability is almost always public. Whereas a child can hide diabetes to a greater or lesser degree, a child cannot hide a wheelchair. Curiosity, then, is a constant companion of the child with a physical disability. That the visibility of the disability is an important concern was verified by Steinhausen (81), who compared twelve-year-old physically disabled youngsters with twelve-year-old hemophiliacs on personality integration. He found that the physically disabled lacked emotional integration into their environments without conflict, while the hemophiliacs did not differ from controls on measures of integration.

In addition to the obvious physical disabilities, visual, speech, and hearing impairments deserve separate attention. These disabilities are often not so obvious at first glance, and normal people are frequently caught off guard when they realize that an individual whom they considered normal cannot interact in normal fashion. With these disabilities, human communication is frequently impaired, and the individual with the disability suffers a unique kind of isolation.

Visual impairments. Approximately 300,000 adolescents in the United States have **visual impairments,** and about half of these are blind. Blind people can learn to get along in the world quite independently and with the assistance of braille and voice-synthesized electronic equipment need be left out of very little. The difficulty lies with the rest of us who, not knowing how to interact with blind persons, either exaggerate our interaction or ignore the person. We must learn to take the lead offered by the individual; if help is in order, we should offer it; if it is not, we should not.

Speech defects. Approximately two million Americans suffer from **speech defects,** which can be the result of congenital defects like cleft palate and harelip, or of social-psychological problems resulting in stammering or stuttering. Speech defects are difficult to live with, for they make these individuals appear incoherent, and the public is likely to react to them as if they were stupid. The congenital anomalies are usually surgically correctible, and stammering and stuttering are highly responsive to therapy. The presence of audiologists and speech therapists in elementary schools has had a significant effect on the decreasing incidence of speech defects among adolescents.

Hearing impairments. Only recently have we begun to understand the profound implications of **hearing impairments,** disabilities that literally affect every aspect of an individual's growth and development. Some 700,000 adolescents in the United States have profound auditory loss, and 90 percent of them have had the loss since infancy. Deaf students consistently perform poorly academically and socially; they are immature, lack judgment, and are frequently difficult to discipline. Although they perform adequately on nonverbal tests of intelligence, their performance on academic and social tasks falls sadly below expectations. Why is this so? The reason lies in the difficulty deaf children have in incorporating language into their lives. Imagine what it would be like to have no language. You might learn to point at objects to make your wishes known, but you would not understand anything that does not have a concrete component. You could learn what a chair is, but how could you learn concepts like ''patience,'' ''consideration,'' ''planning,'' and all the other concepts that form our basis for reasoning with and understanding one another? The language of deaf students is concrete; they use nouns but almost never use adverbs (Liben, 78).

Further complicating the situation is the unfortunate observation that the parents of deaf children, unless they are deaf themselves, frequently do not learn sign language and therefore have very limited communication with their deaf children. These parents have no way of reasoning with their deaf children, and therefore tend to give in to their demands as if they were very young. The children grow up expecting every impulsive desire to be catered to by those around them; they remain immature and never learn to delay gratification or to be patient. Deaf children raised by deaf parents, by parents who learn and use sign, and in residential settings for deaf children do better both academically and socially than those raised in environments in which the primary mode of communication is verbal. Rules and reasons for rules must be communicated in appropriate and meaningful ways; if they are, the deaf are quite capable of developing mature behaviors and attitudes (Meadow, 75).

Acceptance of people with disabilities. What progress has been made in the acceptance of people with disabilities? Society is certainly changing for the better. Public access has been improved, and legislation (PL94-142, specifically) has guaranteed equal access to education for all students with disabilities. But attitudes change slowly, and people with disabilities are not relaxing their attention to the continual struggle to gain acceptance and equal treatment. It has been demonstrated repeatedly that teachers and students can change their attitudes toward disabled children through dissemination of information and exposure to individuals with disabilities (Frith, 81; Thompson, 81; O'Moore, 80), and that being in a mainstreamed class can positively affect the learning and socialization of students with disabilities (Thompson, 81; Haraguchi, 81).

SUMMARY

The most rapid and dramatic physical changes since the first year of life occur at puberty. Rapid growth is accompanied by development of the reproductive organs and secondary sex characteristics, and the young adolescent is required to adjust to what often seems to be an entirely new body.

Puberty begins with the first evidence of sexual development and ends when the individual is fully capable of reproduction, and may take from one and one-half to six years to complete.

At puberty the hypothalamus sends revised messages to the anterior pituitary, which secretes growth hormone and the gonadotropic hormones. Growth hormone stimulates general tissue growth, while the gonadotropic hormones encourage the development of the ovaries in females, the testes in males, and the secondary sex characteristics. Because the integration of glandular functions is not perfect, development during puberty is extremely variable.

The growth spurt results in increased height, maturity of primary and secondary sexual characteristics, weight gain, and the physical proportions and features of adults. Prior to puberty, there are few differences between males and females except for the external genitalia, but after puberty all systems of the body show the sex dimorphism that distinguishes males from females.

Puberty is occurring earlier today than it did 100 years ago, due to advances in nutrition and to the increased stimulation of modern society, but we have probably reached the limit of early maturation.

Very early or late maturation seems to have significant psychological effects, more so for boys than for girls. Whereas early-maturing boys tend to have a psychological advantage over late-maturing boys, early-maturing girls may be subjected to stresses that their late-maturing girlfriends escape. For both boys and girls, society's views of early and late maturers influence their self-images.

Physical and physiological changes at puberty strongly influence social and emotional development, with all behavior being the result of the unique interaction of biology and society. Societal norms concerning the acceptability of body types (ectomorph, mesomorph, and endomorph) strongly influence self-acceptance and self-esteem. Boys therefore invariably prefer the mesomorphic body type, while girls prefer the ectomorphic and mesomorphic types.

Adolescents' perceptions of reality rather than reality itself determine their behavior and self-images. Their perceptions come not only from the mirror, but from past experiences, parental attitudes, peer views, and the stereotyped images portrayed in the media. These perceptions strongly influence behavior.

But behavior can also affect development. Nutrition, exercise, and athletics all play important roles in the outcome of physical development. Inadequate nutrition is responsible for unhealthy growth, poor endurance, and general poor health as well as depression and behavior problems. Physical fitness and general exercise influence both physical and social adjustment, including cognitive and emotional functioning. Athletics, which are heavily emphasized (especially for boys) in middle and high schools, influence the adjustment of all adolescents, whether or not they participate. Whereas interscholastic sports benefit only the most athletically competent, more informal sports programs have the potential of benefiting all adolescents.

Although adolescents as a group are very healthy, both common and uncommon health problems exist. A particular disorder or problem may become a handicap to the individual depending on her perception of it, with the psychological aspects of the disability having the potential of being more of a handicap than the physical aspects. Family attitudes, the reactions of others, and adolescent development itself contribute to the individual's capacity to adjust to a physical or physiological problem.

The most common physical problems experienced by adolescents, other than respiratory infections and accidents, are psychosomatic illnesses, acne, menstrual dysfunctions, and weight problems. More serious are chronic illness and disabilities, including physical disabilities, visual impairments, speech defects, and hearing impairments. American society as a whole is taking giant strides in the acceptance of people with illnesses and disabilities, and it is the reponsibility of all adults to assist young people in learning to accept and understand those who are different as a result of physical and physiological problems.

7

Sexual Development

In 1904, G. Stanley Hall wrote eloquently of the conflicts involved in sexuality:

> As most closely related to this great pleromal sea of life, abounding stand in the higher plants and animals the sexual organs, which in ancient phallicism and in the modern love of flowers are objects of great esthetic interest and curiosity. In them and their function, life reaches its maximal intensity and performs its supreme function. The *vita sexualis* is normally a magnificent symphony, the rich and varied orchestration of which brings the individual into the closest rapport with the larger life of the great *Biologos,* and without which his life would be a mere film or shadow. As this vast subject looms up to the psychologist and he begins to catch glimpses of its long-neglected wealth and beauty overgrown with foul and noxious fungoids and haunted by all the evil spirits that curse human life; as he clearly sees to what a degree art, science, religion, the home, the school, and civilization itself suffer from this degradation; as he understands the all-conditioning importance of normality of primary acts and organs and the hitherto unsuspected range of qualities that are now coming to reveal themselves as secondary sexual both in their origin and in their present deeper relationship, he realizes that it is his preeminent prerogative and duty, from which it would be base cowardice to shrink, to sound a cry of warning in terms plain enough if possible to shock both quacks and prudes, who have, the one perverted, and the other obscured, the plain path of life for adolescence. (pp. 412–413)

Although much of what Hall proposed over three-quarters of a century ago has been called into question (see Chapter 1), he was certainly aware of a number of

Adolescents report being comfortable with their emerging sexuality.

points concerning human sexuality that now form the basis of our understanding. Sexuality includes much more than the development and function of the primary sex organs; it is "the style or way of enacting one's maleness or femaleness personally, interpersonally, and societally" (Morrison, 80, p. 214). It includes the entire range of human life and expression and is one of the primary motivators of many of our behaviors. It is sometimes thought of as the central issue of adolescence, in that sexual behavior itself separates children from adults, and one of the primary tasks of adolescence is to make the transition from nonsexual to sexual being. Children must, during adolescence, transform their "social roles and gender identity to incorporate sexual activity with others" (Hill, 80b, p. 5).

This transformation is, as Hall (04) so descriptively emphasizes, frequently problematic. Sexuality is both a "magnificent symphony" and a "degradation." Somehow, the beauty of sex has become "overgrown with foul and noxious fungoids" and "haunted by evil spirits," and "both quacks and prudes" have made the path to healthy sexuality rocky at best.

This is not to suggest that many adolescents, perhaps the majority of them, do not traverse the path successfully. Offer (81) found in a sample of 15,000 adolescents that the transition into sexuality was smoother than anticipated. These adolescents reported being, for the most part, comfortable with their emerging sexuality and with the sexual changes in their bodies.

Nevertheless, sexual development is frequently problematic as well. We all grew up with conflicting messages: "Sex is beautiful"/"Sex is dirty"; "Be proud of your body"/"Be modest"; "Prepare yourself for parenthood"/"Don't be sexual." Evidence of the difficulty many people experience with sexual development comes in the rising popularity of sex and marital therapy as a legitimate speciality in the mental-health field, the attention paid to such therapy in professional journals and conferences, and even the attention given it in the popular media.

In a way, it may seem arbitrary to separate this chapter on sexual development from the previous one on physiological development. After all, the primary sexual changes are biological. But sexual development is both narrower and broader than physiological development. It is narrower in the sense that the maturing of the sex organs is but one of the physiological changes of adolescence. It is considerably broader when we consider sexuality as underlying all human expression. Then sexual development cannot be discussed in isolation and must include the physiologic changes, sex-role development, development of sexual attitudes, sexual behaviors of adolescents, and sex education. We will discuss each of these and emphasize throughout the ways in which individuals experience the biological and social implications of their emerging sexuality.

DEVELOPING SEXUALITY

Gender Identity

Gender is the assignment of sex — male or female — to each individual. It is primarily genetically determined and is evidenced in the developing fetus within the first trimester of pregnancy. It is also influenced, however, by both hormones and social influences. Although we are aware of the sex of each newborn infant, the child does not establish an identity as a boy or girl until about age two. This identity is then strengthened by socialization, the messages the child receives about what is expected of each sex and what it means to be that sex.

Genetic contribution. Genetically, sex is determined by the gene contribution of the father. Every normal woman carries two X chromosomes; the child inherits one of them. Every normal man carries an X chromosome and a Y chromosome; the child inherits one of them. If the father's X chromosome is passed on, the child is a girl and has, like her mother, two X chromosomes. If the father's Y chromosome is passed on, the child is a boy and has, like his father, one X chromosome and one Y chromosome. But since nature isn't always perfect, mistakes can occur that create gender problems. Occasionally, a child will have too many or too few sex chromosomes: the XXY combination (Klinefelter's syndrome) produces a very feminine man, while an XYY combination produces an extremely masculine man, to the degree that impulse control is often difficult. An XO combination produces what might be called a partial woman (Turner's syndrome). Each of these conditions is really quite rare; the vast majority of us can be clearly classified as genetic men (XY) or genetic women (XX). Variations within each sex are determined by factors other than the sex chromosomes (Money, 72).

Hormonal contribution. **Hormones** (from the Greek "to excite") also influence gender development and identity. As we discussed in the previous chapter, the gonads produce male and female hormones, and the levels of each of these hormones in any one individual is partly responsible for the development of both primary and secondary sexual characteristics. The ratio of **estrogen** (from the Latin "frenzy") and the **androgens** is responsible for sex characteristics, the size and function of the reproductive organs, and sexual receptivity in both sexes. **Progesterone** (from the Latin "for carrying") prepares the uterus for pregnancy and maintains pregnancy; it also controls the length of the menstrual cycle. While pregnant, a woman no longer ovulates, and because progesterone inhibits the ovulation, it is also the primary ingredient in birth control pills. The pills fool the system into believing there is a pregnancy, and ovulation does not occur. Because the regulation of progesterone also regulates the menstrual cycle, birth control pills are sometimes used to regulate irregular cycles. You will remember from the previous chapter that testosterone, a male hormone, is implicated in the development of acne. But when androgen levels are proportionately reduced by female hormones, the acne frequently clears up. This is why birth control pills are also sometimes used in the treatment of acne among both girls and boys.

In males, **testosterone,** one of the androgens, is produced by the testes and is responsible for the secondary sexual characteristics of males: voice change, facial and body hair, and muscular and skeletal development; and for the development of other male sex organs: the seminal vesicles, prostate gland, epididymus, penis, and scrotum. The male hormones are also partially responsible for sexual excitement in both sexes.

Social contribution. The gender originally established at conception is usually reinforced by the family and broader society as soon as the sex of the child is known. This, of course, usually occurs in the delivery room with the announcement "It's a boy'' or ''It's a girl,'' but with modern medical technology, **amniocentesis** (a study of the cells of the uterine fluid surrounding the fetus) allows the determination of fetal sex long before birth. In either case, as soon as the sex is known, society reacts to the individual not only as a baby, but as a baby boy or baby girl.

These societal influences help to shape both gender identity and the development of sex roles. The child matures as a boy or girl, and then in adolescence, gender identity is confirmed by the hormonal changes. The hormonal changes also influence the objects of erotic love (Money, 72). According to Lidz (76) ''the choice of a love object of the opposite sex helps to settle residues of identifications with the parent of the opposite sex and desires for the physical attributes and social prerogatives of the other sex'' (p. 309).

The need to establish appropriate love objects in adolescence creates significant questions for all adolescents, especially since most adolescents have experienced at least some degree of homosexual play and feelings. We will discuss this issue thoroughly later in this chapter. Suffice it to say here that homosexuality is not now considered pathological, and that gender identity and homosexuality are different issues. Homosexuals usually have strong, appropriate gender identities: homosexuality is not a result of confused gender identity (American Psychiatric Association, 80).

Although gender assignment begins at birth and is continued throughout childhood, only at adolescence do the physical and sociological implications of that assignment become truly clear and meaningful. Children are allowed far greater flexibility in behavior than are adolescents and adults. Girls, especially, are allowed and even encouraged to act like boys, and many prepubescent girls express the desire to be boys. Whether this desire is a gender issue, however, is debatable. Even though Sigmund Freud advanced the hypothesis that little girls develop **penis envy** and a **castration complex,** it is more reasonable to consider little girls' wishes to be boys to be related to sex-role development than to gender identity. That is, girls do not wish to be boys because they want to be physiologically male; they merely want the perceived privileges that the male role affords.

Impact of Pubertal Change

In addition to reconciling themselves to the reality of an imperfect body, adolescents must also deal with significant differences in physiological functioning, differences that carry major psychological meaning as well.

Reactions to physical changes. In boys, spontaneous erections, first ejaculation, development of pubic and body hair, and voice changes can produce everything from delight to confusion to embarrassment to inordinate concern, the latter if the boy has not been prepared for the changes. Spontaneous erections occur throughout childhood, but once penis growth begins, they can be embarrassing. They can occur at any time, when the boy is dancing, swimming, or just sitting in class or in a movie. Because they are often unpredictable, they are cause for consternation, and the boy may feel that he has no control over his body. First ejaculations usually occur at night during sleep, and thus are known as "wet dreams" (or nocturnal emissions). They may or may not be accompanied by erotic dreams and may cause the boy to feel everything from pleasure to chagrin. Dreams may contain homosexual or incestuous elements, which though normal, may be disturbing. The parents' reaction to nocturnal emissions is especially important; all too frequently an embarrassed mother reacts negatively, accusing her son of either wetting the bed or masturbating, and creating fear, guilt, and shame, especially if the emission is accompanied by erotic fantasies. In a delightful book about puberty written for prepubertal and pubertal children, Mayle (75) deals sensitively with the topic of wet dreams by stating that the only thing wrong with wet dreams is that the boy is not awake to enjoy them! The development of pubic, axillary, and other body hair is usually of less significance to the boy than are spontaneous erections and ejaculations, but may also be a source of either pride or concern. Voice changes too can be the source of a variety of feelings, but most adults and adolescents treat the unpredictability of voice cracking in a relatively light manner and as a normal sign of impending maturity. Most adolescent boys are relieved when their voices have finally lowered sufficiently to be recognized as male on the telephone.

Except for the voice changes and spontaneous erections, which boys frequently feel are all too public, the majority of male adolescent changes are the topic of locker room concern rather than the classroom. A girl's changes are not so private, and her new body dimensions become the topic of attention for everyone, including her parents, family, peers, and even teachers. The first brassiere is a memorable occasion for almost all girls, sometimes a source of great pride, other times of shame. The early-maturing girl may want to hide her development, the late-maturing one to enhance it. And breast size is frequently a major concern. Those who are too big are no more or less embarrassed than those who are too small. Here again the reactions of parents and peers have a significant impact, and all too frequently that reaction is one of teasing. Whether the good-natured teasing of parents or the less-than-sensitive teasing of peers, teasing hurts all but the most confident and assured. In the midst of puberty, few young adolescents have that confidence.

Menarche. Of all the changes of puberty, perhaps none has the significance of menarche. Although almost all normal girls will have their first menstrual periods between the ages of 9 and 18, three fourths will have it by their thirteenth birthday. At this time, the major developmental changes in girls have already occurred (see Table 6.1), but the onset of menstruation is not an indicator of complete sexual maturity. It may be another year or more before the ovaries mature sufficiently to release eggs and the uterus is mature.

In describing the possibility that the amount of stimulation received by a child may affect its age of maturation, Adams (81a) identifies a number of factors that are associated with age of menarche. In addition to the obvious influence of heredity, most important seem to be factors associated with degree of stress: 1) children who

A girl's changes are not so private.

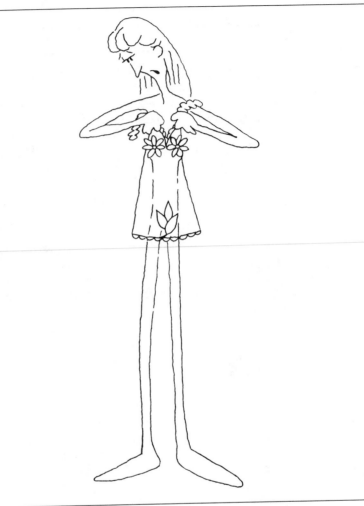

have no siblings have earlier menarches, perhaps because they receive more attention from parents, while first borns have later menarches, perhaps because as younger siblings are born, the younger children receive more attention than the first born; 2) urban girls, who are subject to greater stress, reach menarche earlier than rural girls; 3) earlier menarche is found among girls with physical problems, obese girls, girls whose fathers left home early, girls who are separated from their mothers at birth, and blond girls, each of whom apparently is subjected to greater stress than are other girls (Adams, 81a). Though the stress theory is still untested, it makes some sense in light of these findings. Additional factors frequently associated with earlier menarche include nutrition, race, climate, and season, but none of these are conclusive. Regardless of reason, however, we have already noted that menarche occurs for most girls by the age of thirteen and is virtually always a signal event in a girl's life.

Following a study of what females remember about menarche, Koff (82) concluded that the more knowledge a girl had prior to menarche, the more adequate she perceived that preparation to be; the older she was at the time of her first period, the more positively she remembered the experience. They note that good preparation is especially important for the early maturer, who is, of course, the least likely to be adequately prepared.

Numerous studies report that women frequently recall their first periods in neutral or negative ways (Bloch, 78; Morrison, 80). This is not surprising in a culture that uses the colloquial "the curse" to refer to menstrual periods. Some girls, though, if they are adequately prepared both physically and psychologically, welcome the menarche as a symbol of their evolving womanhood. Morrison (80), in her compilation of the recollections of 228 college students, noted that the onset of menstruation is unforgettable, that starting before being prepared is traumatic, that embarrassment is nearly universal, and that good preparation, particularly by the girl's mother, can make the menses an expected and natural event. She noted also the wide variety of attitudes women hold toward menstruation and emphasized the need for sensitive, accurate education.

Although it is clear that such information is necessary, and that the best source of a girl's information is her mother, Bloch (78) noted that only 26 percent of all mothers provide their daughters with information about the physiology of menstruation and its relationship to pregnancy; most simply tell the minimum and indicate where the sanitary supplies are kept. That such preparation is inadequate is obvious. Parents usually don't know how to greet the menstrual periods of their daughters. Morrison (80) found a variety of responses, from silence to congratulations. Neither of these alternatives is appropriate, however. The silence leaves the girl with unasked questions; and she doesn't deserve congratulations for something she didn't do. One of the worst reactions, in my opinion, is that of the often-heard "Now you're a woman." A thirteen-year-old is not a woman and shouldn't be expected to think or act like one. It would be far better for parents to simply note the event, talk with their daughter about the changes she is experiencing, assure her of their continuing support and affection, and make themselves available for discussion. Parents should not assume that the infamous fifth-grade movie has prepared her. She may know what a sanitary pad is, but she may not know how to use it or what to expect from the menstrual experience. Most girls also experience some dysmenorrhea (painful menstruation); they need to know that diet, exercise, and expectations all play a part in its severity (Morrison, 80).

The Psychology of Sex Differences

Maccoby (74) has provided the most extensive documentation on well-established psychological differences between the sexes. Whereas girls have greater verbal ability than boys, boys excel in visual-spatial and mathematical ability and are more aggressive than girls. Money (72) found boys to be more vigorous and more self-assertive, to prefer functional rather than ornamental clothing, to view the other sex more as a sex object than a romantic one. From longitudinal data on over 3000 adolescents, Douvan (66) found girls to be more compliant with parents, whereas boys were more competitive, especially over issues of independence. Maccoby (74), however, sounds a note of caution. Although some clear differences have been evidenced, the respective roles of biology and society can become clouded. Maccoby (74) warns that the following are unfounded beliefs about the differences between the sexes: girls are more social, more suggestible, more affected by heredity, more auditory, better at rote learning and repetitive tasks, lack achievement motivation, and have lower self-esteem. Parallel unfounded beliefs about boys are that they are more analytic, more visual, more affected by environment, and better at higher-order cognitive processing.

SEX-ROLE DEVELOPMENT

One of the major tasks of adolescence, as we have seen, is the development of healthy, appropriate gender identities, with confidence and pride in being men and women. But acceptance of and pride in being female or male does not mean having to accept stereotyped roles and rigid behavioral prescriptions. As Lidz (76, p. 317) points out, ''acceptance of being a woman is not the same as acceptance of the place and roles that have been given to women in society.'' The same statement should be made for men.

Roles and Stereotypes

Roles. It is useful to distinguish between **roles** and **stereotypes.** A role is a category of behaviors appropriate for a group of individuals. For example, one of my roles is that of a mother, another is of a college teacher. As a mother there are certain behaviors expected of me, such as seeing to the physical and emotional needs of my son. As a college teacher, other behaviors are expected, such as preparing syllabi and sitting on committees that guide academic matters. These are legitimate expectations, and I accept them because I accept the roles of mother and college teacher.

Stereotypes. Stereotypes, on the other hand, are behaviors (usually exaggerated) that are assumed to belong to a group, but which in fact are rigid, unfair rules based on irrational rather than rational expectations. A stereotypical mother expectation is that of the happy chief cook and bottle washer, merrily creating fantastic culinary delights and keeping her children spanking clean and always smiling. These expectations I do not accept, nor do I accept the stereotyped notion of the absent-minded professor, brilliant in a little piece of the world but totally inept in the daily chores of living. We are all subject to both appropriate sex-role expectations and inappropriate sex-role stereotypes. Distinguishing between the two is often difficult.

Sex-role stereotyping. Sex-role development and stereotypes became a major research focus during the decade of the seventies, spurred by the women's liberation movement and aided by increasing numbers of women in the workforce. In summarizing the literature of the seventies, Scanzoni (80) identified that sex-role stereotyping includes: the sexual stratification system that considers males to be superior to females; the gender-linked division of labor that has prescribed different careers and different jobs within the household based on gender; and the attitudes resulting from involvement in the stratification system and the gender-linked division of labor. He found, in general, that stereotyping is decreasing, more for women than for men, more for the better-educated than for the less-well-educated; that women are moving into higher status positions (in the ten years from 1972 to 1982, the number of female chief executives in two-year colleges rose from 16 to 73 [*Parade,* 83]); that there is more change outside of the home than there is within it; that decision making is becoming more open and consensual, even in working-class families; and that there is a greater overlap of interests between women and men than ever before. Scanzoni's review of the literature is optimistic, but we certainly are not free of sex-role stereotyping and must attend to the effects of such stereotyping on the ability of adolescents to develop healthy attitudes and expectations for themselves and others. Stereotypes limit current behavior, so that adolescent girls lead cheers while adolescent boys score points; they also limit future career choices, so that the bright verbal girl-child becomes the secretary for the surgeon who developed from the mischievous, nonacademic boy-child; and they even limit psychological and physical health, so that males, who learn to hold in emotions, die at younger ages and from different diseases than do women, who learn to express emotions.

A Historical Perspective

Early matriarchies. The sex-role prescriptions that are familiar to most of us are neither universal nor have they always been as they are now. There is considerable speculation and some evidence that very early societies may have been matriarchies, with women playing the predominant decision-making roles, probably because the women held the power of childbirth. In some ancient tribal communes, the women collectively raised the children, with the fathers not identified at all and all women sharing motherhood responsibilities. Then, between five and eight thousand years ago, the tribal lifestyle evolved into the agrarian, extended family lifestyle, in which large families, including several generations, shared the life and work of an agrarian economy (Ritvo, 76).

The agrarian lifestyle. It was in this style of living that the male as breadwinner role probably began. In the extended family, the oldest male was the source of all life, both literally and figuratively, and the family became important as the keeper of the land. Because there was never-ending work to do and a large family ensured prosperity, every new addition to the family was greeted as an economic and familial asset. With abundant progeny a necessity, women were pregnant much of the time, and nursing infants when they were not. In the early agrarian economies, fifteen or twenty pregnancies were not unusual for a woman, so women began to assume the duties associated with child rearing. Thus was born the domestic role, and women became responsible for hearth and home, while men became responsible as providers. Though the roles were becoming specialized, families nevertheless enjoyed unity of purpose and appreciation for the various contributions of each member, and even small children had valuable contributions to make to the life of the family (Wynne, 79). Perhaps, though, women were already becoming resentful of their roles, as witnessed by the popular rhyme, "Men work but from sun to sun; a woman's work is never done."

The Industrial Revolution. The Industrial Revolution created the need for a different family structure, and sex roles became even more specialized. Extended families were broken into small, nuclear families; communal child care and the family as a self-contained unit were no longer possible; and the family was maintained, not by cooperative effort, but by the male leaving home to seek employment while the female frequently remained at home to rear children and maintain the household. This is not to imply that large numbers of women did not leave home to work; they did (Kessler-Harris, 82). Both those who worked outside the home and those who worked in it nevertheless bore complete responsibility for the home. Specialization increased even further with industrial expansion, rapid travel, the development of mechanical aids for housework, and the decline in family size. The male's role increased in importance while the female's declined, and the sexual stratification system and gender-linked division of labor was born (Fuhrmann, 75; Berkovitz, 79). What was once a necessary and functional division of labor was reinforced by traditional interpretations of the Old Testament, which emphasized the moral necessity for separation of the roles and elevation of men. But in the technological age of modern America, rigid role prescriptions have proved unsatisfactory to produce the highly adaptable, flexible, and creative people that society needs.

Cultural variations. Note that although society needed to create different functions for men and women, the attendant expectations for behavior and dress are subject to extreme cultural variation. Margaret Mead (35) noted three peoples for whom behavioral prescriptions varied considerably from ours: among the Arapesh, both men and women were sensitive and nonaggressive; among the Mundugamor, both were ruthless and unpleasant; and among the Tchambuli, the women were dominant, the men emotional. Today, European men embrace one another, kiss, and cry openly; American men do not. Appropriate behaviors also change over time. The royalty of several centuries ago, both male and female, wore jewels, velvet, and furs; at the time of the founding of this country it was common for men to wear tights, jewels, ruffles, and powdered wigs. A man dressing like that today would be considered strange at best.

Influences on Sex-Role Development

Early messages. The learning of sex roles is clearly unavoidable, and the impact of both overt and more subtle messages cannot be underestimated. Even before birth, an active fetus is labeled male, a quiet fetus female (Denmark, 77). It continues in the delivery room, where males are described by medical personnel as sturdy, handsome, and tough while girls are described as dainty, delicate, sweet, and charming (S. L. Hansen, 80), and where girls are frequently wrapped in pink blankets and boys in blue. It continues throughout infancy and childhood. Parents react differently to boys than to girls, with boys getting greater attention in the first six months of life but being encouraged to be more independent by the time they are two (Fagot, 75). Strangers also react, as did the medical personnel in the delivery room, on the basis of an infant's sex. Since children do not establish a gender identity until about the age of two, it shouldn't matter whether an infant is male or female, but judging by adult reactions, it does.

Schooling. This early difference in socialization is clearly seen by the time children enter school, with boys being more inquisitive and independent, girls more quiet and content (National Education Association, 77), and is continued in the schools themselves. Within the elementary-school classroom, the traditionally feminine values of passivity, conformity, and quiet are reinforced by the mostly female teachers. Most elementary teachers are women, most administrators men, and the stereotype of the nurturing female and decision-making man are enhanced. These social realities, along with stereotyped textbooks, language, athletics, and activities further reinforce the ideas that women are passive waiters while men are active doers (Levy, 74). Although significant changes are being made to create nonsexist curricula and books, many schools still use the older materials, and the stereotyping continues (Federbush, 74; Showalter, 74). Further, nonsexist materials will not be sufficient to overcome human influences.

Media. The media contribute mightily as well. All you need do to verify that sexist roles are still being portrayed by that great American baby-sitter, the television set, is to keep track of the roles and activities engaged in by the principals in the advertisements on any day or evening. As was pointed out in Chapter 2, you will most likely see women still happily scrubbing the toilet while men relax after a hard day's work with their buddies and a couple of beers. It has become common knowledge that the greatest stereotyping still occurs during daytime television, when the "soaps" are literally supported by household products, and during weekend athletic events, when the beer commercials hold significant prominence. Children see adult women in the media being concerned with their bodies and their homes, all in the pursuit of happiness with a man, while they see men actively

Male roles hold the promise of adventure; those for women promise dullness.

managing their lives and careers. At home, at least in the traditional home, children see women performing the menial tasks of housekeeping, while they see men leaving home for who knows what exciting adventures. Without male models around, as is the case both in the traditional home and in the home with a female head of household, both boys and girls are likely to define maleness as "that which is not female" (Denmark, 77, p. 129), and boys may develop an extreme masculinity as a result of relying only on the highly stereotyped information presented by peers and in the media and by what is perceived as the opposite of femininity. Is it any wonder, then, that every elementary teacher can tell you that little girls read stories about boys, but little boys do not read stories about girls? Is it any wonder that girls frequently express a desire to be boys, but boys seldom express a desire to be girls? The roles assigned men hold the promise of adventure and excitement, those assigned women too often hold the promise of dullness.

Societal attitudes are especially significant in helping children learn both what it means to be male or female, and on how adolescents learn to develop male-female relationships (Morrison, 80), with the influence of mothers being particularly strong on the development of their daughters' sex-role attitudes (Smith, 82). Interestingly, it seems that girls may be raised with greater flexibility of role until adolescence, when the messages change and role expectations narrow to the traditionally feminine. Whereas there is no difference for males, who adopt a masculine role at all ages, females become increasingly stereotyped as they mature (Nicholson, 81). Once again, the society as a whole, with the family, peers, and school in particular, molds the developing adolescent's attitudes and relationships.

Traditional Stereotypes

Stereotypes are kind neither to males nor females, just as they are not to any group. Both the female and male stereotypes are limiting and injurious. We will examine both of these, and their effects, in detail.

The feminine stereotype.   **The Cinderella Syndrome** (Downing, 81) can be considered a euphemism for the feminine stereotype, which prescribes dependence, passivity, waiting, looking good, and not being too intelligent. The girl's life is not to be planned, for the lifestyle of her eventual husband, her knight in shining armor, will decide her future. All efforts are expended in attracting the right man and providing a home for him and "his" children. The prescriptions harden as children become adolescents. Rust (82) found that junior-high students labeled girls as friendly, weak, neat, careful, shy, gentle, graceful, easy to push around, nice, busy, obedient, fearful, and smart. Mokros (77) also found that seventh- and eighth-grade girls viewed intellectual achievement more positively than boys of the same age; however, by late adolescence, the boys viewed intellectual achievement more positively than did the girls. We might therefore expect that if Rust were to conduct the same study four years from now, "smart" would not longer be attributed to the girls. Morrison (80) found that girls actually do achieve better than boys until puberty, but their high achievement is usually attributed to their wanting to please others rather than to ambition. This view, of course, makes excellence difficult for women. Horner (72) based her **fear of success** theory on the extensive research she did with college students. Using an open-ended story technique, she discovered that predictions of academic success for women were accompanied by expectations of personal doom. She hypothesized that the expectation of negative social consequences accompanying academic and occupational success leads women to fear and even to deliberate underachievement. There are, however, conflicting findings concerning fear of success. Several researchers have found that both males and females displayed fear of success in gender-inappropriate situations. That is, both expect negative social consequences from success in traditionally inappropriate fields (Cherry, 78; Nash, 78; Peterson, 79; Bremer, 80).

From a sample of over 500 eleventh- and twelfth-grade girls, Aneshensel (80) found that these adolescent women saw highly stereotyped roles. They conformed to sociocultural expectations; they planned to marry and have children; and they believed men's and women's work to be different. One change from earlier research was that most of the girls expected to work after their children entered school. She also found that the earlier the intention to marry, the lower the occupational expectation of these women. And Humphrey (84) found that teenage girls are ready to live through others rather than on their own terms. They were less career-oriented than boys and did not see hobbies as integral to their lives.

Scanzoni (80) found that teenage nonvirgins report more traditional sex-role preferences than do virgins and concludes that the young women who are more "modern" may reject intercourse because they are more aware than the traditional women of the negative effect of pregnancy and early childbearing on educational and career opportunities. The more feminine women may consider sexual activity a necessary means to gain male attention and approval. Adler (81) concurred, noting that traditional feminine sex-role acceptance is related to ineffective contraceptive protection. The traditionally feminine girl doesn't plan ahead and leaves all decision making to her male partner. (The reasons for lack of contraceptive use will be discussed more fully later in this chapter.)

That the sex-role prescriptions are carried out in behavior and that the home plays a most salient role in the sex-role socialization process was demonstrated by Cogle (82), who studied the amount of time teenagers spent in various household chores, by sex. Predictably, girls spent their time in shopping, food preparation, housecleaning, and dishwashing, while boys provided maintenance assistance and some help with food preparation. Apparently, men may sometimes use the kitchen, but the outdoors is their bailiwick.

The effects of stereotyping may be insidious. Lack of career and life planning, lack of contraceptive protection, succumbing to the wishes of others, and general passivity all occur for female adolescents. But the worst effects come later. Once a woman has had a child or two, she may become relegated to the shelf and spend an uneventful, unfulfilling life waiting for her family to grow and leave her behind. With no skills, no achievements, and virtually no interests, the older stereotypical female is useless baggage in a society that values competence and independence in men and beauty and charm in women. Females of all ages report more physical and psychological problems, and Nicholson (81) found that femininity was significantly related to the number of problems reported. The pressures to comform to the feminine stereotype are strong, and those who succumb find themselves unhappy, lonely, and fearful.

This is not to imply that all aspects of the feminine stereotype are negative. Emotional closeness, nurturance, understanding, and care are positive qualities that ought to be nurtured in all people, boys as well as girls. It is the absence of these from the male stereotype that makes it so devastating to the healthy development of men.

The male stereotype. The **Great American Male Stereotype** (GAMS) demands achievement, competition, success, power, virility, aggression, and action. Boys are socialized to be responsible for solving life's problems. But these messages are given to little boys in schools that value passivity and good manners. Little boys in the elementary years are beset with contradictions. They are expected to be active and mischievous, but also to be good. Further, as we discussed in the previous chapter, girls mature earlier than boys and achieve more in school during the elementary school years. Little boys experience extremely high expectations for success in all areas, and often crumble under the pressure. Given the stress, it shouldn't be surprising that school records reveal that the overwhelming majority of learning and behavior problems in school belong to boys. It may be no wonder that most delinquent acts by both children and adults are committed by men, men who have failed to live up to GAMS, but for whom the taunt "sissy" is so appalling that delinquency is preferred. The stereotype certainly isn't the cause of delinquency or behavior problems, but Coleman (81) pointed out that during adolescence, boys must learn how to be men, to like themselves, to understand sexuality, and to develop relationships. The last of these may be the most difficult for the stereotypical male, who has not been socialized to value relationships.

That adolescents accept the masculine stereotype has been demonstrated in numerous recent studies (Maccoby, 74; Rust, 82; Emmerich, 82; Coleman, 81), as well as in older ones. The studies by Rust and Emmerich, however, also show some promise of a change. Rust found that both males and females in junior high school rated positive nonstereotyped traits as feminine, indicating some identification of feminine as positive. Emmerich, in surveying 1251 high school students, found that academic learning was not sex typed; that careers as doctors, scientists, mathematicians, artists, and musicians were not sex typed; and that the brighter an adolescent was, the less likely he was to hold stereotypical views.

Fortunately, there are alternatives to traditional stereotypes for men as well as for women. At one time, adolescent males could choose between the image of John Wayne, who was rough, tough, silent, and uncomfortable around women; or that of James Bond, adventurous, sexy, romantic, but not emotionally involved — a womanizer. Now there is also the image of Dustin Hoffman, assertive and successful, but emotional and nurturing as well, a combination of the best of the traditional male and female stereotypes.

Androgyny. Psychological androgyny (from *andro,* male, and *gyne,* female) refers to the individual's capacity for both activity and passivity, strength and nurturance, emotionality and rationality, leadership and followership. The literature generated during the seventies argues that psychological androgyny is the most healthy sex role, and that it is equally healthy for men and women. Although much of the androgyny research has been criticized because it *assumes* that positive mental health is the result of flexibility in sex role behaviors and cognitive processes, the concept of androgyny continues to generate interest and continuing research (Lenney, 79; Wilson, 80). Androgyny is not unisex, but a healthy appreciation for the psychological complexity that contributes to adaptive lifestyles. In an androgynous society,

Now there is an image of an emotional, nurturing male.

women would be encouraged to think and to assert themselves, men to feel and express themselves, with neither posing a threat to the other. Recent scientific study of androgyny has been voluminous, with most studies demonstrating that androgyny is indeed a healthy psychological state. Bem (75), Erdwins (80), and Small (80) found that androgynous and masculine individuals possess the greatest degree of the attributes of ego strength, positive coping mechanisms, emotional integration, and communication skills. Miller (81) found evidence of a positive relationship between masculine values and math ability and between feminine values and verbal ability for both sexes. Hinrichsen (81) found androgynous individuals of both sexes to have more positive self-concepts and more positive overall psychological health, and Paul (80) found black eighth graders with masculine and androgynous sex roles to have higher self-concepts; these youngsters exhibited higher intimacy, internality, and acceptance of black identity than did their more traditional peers.

Not all the research supports androgyny, however. For example, Spence (78) and Whitley (83) found that high masculinity was associated with high self-esteem in both sexes, and Baumrind (82) found traditionally sex typed parents to produce more competent children.

Although the literature is inconsistent, it has more often been found that masculine and androgynous individuals have better self-concepts and overall psychological health (Wynne, 79). It becomes interesting to look at the effects of androgynous or cross-typed roles on each of the sexes separately. Lamke (82) studied high school students and found not only that the androgynous students of both sexes displayed higher self-esteem, but that masculinity is a predictor of high esteem in females, while femininity is a predictor of high esteem in males. Wells (80) noted that these cross-sex values are likely to predict high esteem because they add to the repertoire of behaviors for each sex. She noted that it is not high femininity that causes low esteem among girls, nor high masculinity in boys, but rather the absence of the other values. High-femininity scores for boys tended to be associated with nurturance, while high-masculinity scores for girls were associated with assertiveness. She concluded that girls need not give up femininity, nor boys masculinity, but that both should be socialized to appreciate the positive values generally assigned to the other sex. Both assertiveness and tenderness are necessary in a world that requires all its citizens to be active in both career and family roles. Good decision makers who also nurture the next generation are vital to the health of all society.

SEXUAL ATTITUDES

A Brief History of Sexual Attitudes

We are in the midst, we are told, of a sexual revolution, a revolution of both practice and attitude. It is important, however, to distinguish between attitude and practice, for although attitudes most certainly influence practice, and although behavior can significantly alter existing attitudes, the two are not the same. I, for example, may hold an attitude of acceptance of the behavior of others while not condoning the same behavior for myself; I also can be guilty of behaving in a way that I would not accept as a principle of behavior for everyone. For this reason we will discuss sexual attitudes before discussing sexual behaviors.

Early attitudes. In his critical examination of how the postindustrial era is creating demands on children that they no longer be children, protected from the secrets of adulthood, Postman (82) summarized the history of sexual attitudes from the middle ages to the present time. In the middle ages, he said, "The idea of concealing sexual drives was alien to adults, and the idea of sheltering children from sexual secrets, unknown" (p. 17). Not only did adults have no reluctance to discuss sexual matters or to behave sexually in the presence of their children, but they also engaged in playing with the sexual organs of children as an amusement, and without negative connotations. As Postman noted, "Today that tradition will get you up to thirty years in prison" (p. 17). It was about the end of the sixteenth century before any separation of children from adults occurred, and with the separation, children came to be identified as qualitatively different from adults; they were to be protected from the secrets of adulthood, secrets about sex, illness, death, violence, money, and even certain aspects of the language. (Adult language, as modern movie raters describe, it that not suitable for the ears of children.) It was about this same time that artists began to depict children as proportionally different from, rather than merely smaller than, adults. With this separation of childhood as a distinct stage of development came the concept of indecency, which had not existed previously. This concept created the possibility of indecent books, obscene language, and pornography; taboos began to develop.

Juhasz (76) traced sexual attitudes beginning with the Old Testament, in which the values of male dominance, the double standard in sexuality, and rules against incest and perversion can be found. In the Talmud, marriage and procreation are valued. The early Greeks and Cretes valued monogamy, sexual enjoyment, and the double standard, including prostitution. The Romans saw the bearing of children as the rationale for marriage. With Christianity came the notion of sex equalling sin. Intercourse was seen as a necessary evil, and all children were therefore born in sin. Women were frequently thought of as wicked and as rightfully belonging to men. With the Protestant reformation in the fifteenth century came the recognition of sexual needs, approval of intercourse within marriage, and the legitimacy of divorce on grounds of impotence or frigidity. By the nineteenth century, "the ostrich approach toward sex and the double standard for sexual behavior had set their indelible stamp on Western culture" (Juhasz, 76, p. 454). The ostrich approach refers to the denial that sexual behavior occurs outside of marriage. Most people over the age of thirty, and many younger, know at least one couple who conceived a child before marriage, but who pretended, as did their families and friends, that the bride was a virgin and that the child was conceived on the honeymoon and born prematurely. The ostrich approach and the double standard for sexual behavior, which allows sexual activity before marriage for males but not for females, are still with us but are less prevalent in modern thinking than they once were.

The twentieth century. The twentieth century has heralded significant and all-encompassing changes in the ways in which people live their lives, and sexual attitudes are changing as well. We will examine the current attitudes, particularly of adolescents, a little later; first we need to specify the changes that have had important impacts on our views of sexuality.

Early in this century, Sigmund Freud revolutionized thinking about sex. He explained sex in natural terms and as a natural instinct, described the individual as being sexual from infancy, saw early sexual behavior as important to overall social development, and legitimized talking about sex. Societal changes of the twentieth century include greater contact among diverse groups of people, a lessening of the importance of the homemaker role, a significantly greater time lag between reproductive capability and marriage, and the information explosion that has inundated every home. Rapid change has created inconsistency, and competing pressures have resulted. Today's adolescents are exposed to divorce, trial marriage, cohabitation, homosexuality, traditional marriage, surrogate parenting, artificial insemination, explicitly sexual language, literature, movies, and advertisements, and all of these on the living-room television set.

It is ironic, in a culture that gives tacit approval to overt sexuality, that there is a conflict over sexuality among adolescents. Yet there is, as we shall see. As Woodman (80) noted, the sexual idea held by adults is still that of youth abstaining from sexual activity and essentially not needing to consider issues of sexuality. Despite the obvious loosening of interpretations of obscenity and the unavoidable emphasis on sex in the media, adolescents are still expected not only to refrain from sexual behavior but not to worry about sexual matters. This discrepancy deserves attention.

Development of Sexual Attitudes

Children and adolescents learn their sexual atittudes in complex ways. Much of this learning goes on despite what might be called a ''conspiracy of silence'' by many adults concerning sex. Hass (79) found in surveying 625 adolescents that difficulties in communication about sex exist between adults and children, between sexual partners, and between same-sex peers. The vast majority of us are uncomfortable talking about sex, and therefore tend to keep our thoughts and feelings to ourselves. He found very little open discussion of sexual anxieties, sexual expectations, and feelings concerning sex.

Clayton (80) found three sources of sexual attitudes: 1) the overall prevalence of the attitude in the home and among the adolescents' peers; 2) the timing of entry into sexual behaviors; and 3) the choice of specific reference groups to aid in sexual decision making.

Family. When mystery and silence are prevalent, adolescents beset with questions about their normalcy find answers not in accurate and sensitive information, but in myths and misinformation from both home and peers. Because of the reticence to discuss sexual issues, sex takes on the connotation of being dirty and is associated with guilt. These negative judgments may leave the child believing that anything sexual is wrong, and once sexual fantasies or play begin, the child feels guilty and unworthy, but the behavior usually persists anyway, often with greater secrecy. In this way parents teach the attitude that sex is dirty, an attitude that continues to have a residual negative impact on adult perspectives (Morrison, 80).

Attitudes develop from incomplete and unclear messages, both overtly spoken and more subtly conveyed through behaviors, especially those concerning touching and nudity. These mostly familial behaviors teach children how to talk about sex, how to express caring, and how to behave in intimate relationships (Gagnon, 78). Darling (82) found that parental messages are considerably more straightforward for males, more complex for females. He found that the greater the talk between parents and children, the lower the rate of teenage sexual behavior. The subtle negative messages conveyed by those who were reluctant to talk were associated with earlier and more frequent sexual behavior among teens. Males and females reported hearing essentially the same double messages, but the order of their importance was different for girls than for boys, with girls receiving the more negative messages (Table 7.1).

Table 7.1
Parental Messages to Girls and Boys (The lower the number, the more often the message was heard.)

Girls' Ranking	Boys' Ranking	Parental Messages
1	1	Pregnancy before marriage is terrible.
2	4	No nice person has sex before marriage.
3	3	Petting leads to intercourse.
4	2	Sex is a good way to express love.

Media. The media presents sexuality as a tantalizing sweet, with song lyrics, movies, and television shows extolling all aspects of sexuality. And the reference group has its own standards and attitudes, which are difficult to resist during the peer-group-important years of adolescence. That young adolescents are confused by the conflicting messages may be expressed in their attention to sexual humor, which they are beginning to outgrow by the end of adolescence (Prerost, 80).

The conflicting attitudes concerning sex, undergirded by primarily negative parental messages, make attaining open, expressive sexual attitudes difficult. As Hall noted eighty years ago, the "magnificent symphony" is overgrown with "noxious fungoids." In far less elegant language, it is difficult for sex to change from dirty to beautiful between the altar and the marriage bed.

Current Attitudes

Attitude research. The sexual changes of adolescence are so great that sexuality often preoccupies adolescents, but until recently most research into sexual attitudes has focused on adults, college students, and unwed mothers (Juhasz, 76). Research into the attitudes and behaviors of adolescents under the age of eighteen is difficult to conduct because of the reluctance of parents and school administrators to grant the required permission for such research. Thus a bias sets in, and only the children of the most liberal parents are likely to be included in the research. Hass (79) visited a number of school administrators to explain that he wanted to survey the sexual attitudes, feelings, and practices of high-school students, and although all the administrators with whom he spoke agreed that the study should be done and that both the teens and their parents would benefit from the information, none of them would allow him to come into the school to talk with students about the project and enlist volunteers, even though the volunteers would still have to obtain parental permission to take part in the study. Research with high-school and junior-high-school students therefore must be done on a voluntary, out-of-school basis, with the resultant potential for biased samples.

Most studies indicate a general increase in sexual permissiveness among all populations, a narrowing of the differences in attitude among racial and ethnic groups, and a declining double standard for sexual behavior, with the double standard declining especially during the college years (Clayton, 80; Bell, 70; Ferrell, 77; Long-Laws, 77; Glenn, 79; Singh, 80).

Because Hass's (79) study of over 600 high-school-age students is the most extensive and comprehensive to date, we will use it, supplemented with other corresponding studies, as the basis of our discussion. Table 7.2 summarizes Hass's findings, both for attitudes and behaviors, for all males, all females, 15- and 16-year-old males, 15- and 16-year-old females, 17- and 18-year-old males, and 17- and 18-year-old females. We will be referring to Table 7.2 throughout this and the next sections of this chapter.

Hass asked all the students in his sample to rank in order six activities in terms of their importance in their lives. The rankings were not different for older and younger girls, so are reported together; boys, however, had slightly different rank orders as they got older, and the boys' rankings differed from the girls', with the older boys' rankings being more like the girls' rankings than the younger boys'. For girls, friendships with the same sex were most important, while same-sex friendships, though they became more important for older boys, did not rank first with either group of boys. This finding is consistent with the explanation offered by Hill (80b), who noted that prepubertal friendships of both sexes are based on common activities, but that after puberty the same-sex friendships of girls become more emotion-laden and based more on mutual sharing, whereas those of boys tend to remain based on companionship rather than personality. Morrison (80) found that boys focus first on sex and only later on relationships; girls, however, focus first on relationships and only secondarily on sex. All the adolescents in this sample rated doing well in school and having friendships as more important than athletics, being romantically involved, and having sex; and only the younger boys considered having sex as more important than athletics or being romantically involved. For girls, especially, sexual expression was unimportant without romantic involvement (68 percent of the girls and 41 percent of the boys indicated that sexual activity was acceptable only in a caring, committed relationship). For boys, the importance of having a steady girlfriend declined with age, as 51 percent of the 15- and 16-year-olds and 48 percent of the 17- and 18-year-olds preferred having one steady. For girls, the percentages were 57 percent for the 15- and 16-year-olds, and 66 percent for the 17- and 18-year-olds. As teens get older, apparently, the girls increasingly want commitment; the boys increasingly want to explore more than one option. And teens believe that their feelings for one another are those of love: 82 percent of all boys and of older girls report having been in love at least once.

Table 7.2

Sexual Attitudes and Behaviors of Males and Females, 15 through 18 Years of Age

	All males (n = 307)	All females (n = 318)	Males aged 15 – 16	Females aged 15 – 16	Males aged 17 – 18	Females aged 17 – 18
Rank order of importance of activities:						
Doing well in school	—	2	1	—	1	—
Friendships with same sex	—	1	3	—	2	—
Friendships with other sex	—	3	2	—	3	—
Having sex	—	6	5	—	6	—
Athletics	—	5	4	—	5	—
Being romantically involved	—	4	6	—	4	—
Have sexual fantasies	—	—	87%	80%	84%	73%
Casualness of sex: Approve of sexual contact only with romantic involvement	41%	68%	—	—	—	—
Dating preferences						
One steady girl- or boyfriend	—	—	51%	57%	48%	66%
Several girl- or boyfriends	—	—	49%	43%	52%	34%
Love: Have been in love	—	—	82%	76%	82%	82%
Saying no: Percentage of "yes" responses to, "Have there been times when you have had sexual contact when you didn't feel like it?"	43%	—	—	65%	—	48%

Table 7.2 (continued)

	All males (n = 307)	All females (n = 318)	Males aged 15 – 16	Females aged 15 – 16	Males aged 17 – 18	Females aged 17 – 18
Petting						
Approve of boy touching girl's breasts	98%	—	—	69%	—	91%
Experienced	90%	91%	—	—	—	—
Approve of touching partner's genitals	—	—	93%	79%	98%	83%
Experienced	77%	78%	—	—	—	—
Oral sex						
Approve of girl kissing boy's penis	—	—	90%	67%	94%	72%
Approve of boy kissing girl's vagina	—	—	87%	69%	93%	76%
Experienced	55%	59%	—	—	—	—
Intercourse						
Approve	83%	—	—	54%	—	64%
Experienced	—	—	43%	31%	56%	44%
Masturbation						
Approve	—	—	76%	70%	85%	72%
Experienced	—	—	75%	52%	80%	59%
Marriage						
Want to marry	71%	79%	—	—	—	—
Do not want to marry	6%	3%	—	—	—	—
Not sure	23%	18%	—	—	—	—
Girl should be a virgin	—	—	13%	21%	17%	26%
Boy should be a virgin	—	—	8%	15%	9%	17%
Girl should have experience	—	—	55%	52%	55%	53%
Boy should have experience	—	—	65%	59%	59%	64%
Homosexuality						
Have had at least one experience	14%	11%	—	—	—	—
Approve of two females	—	—	77%	76%	80%	71%
Approve of two males	—	—	67%	77%	76%	69%
Might involve self	14%	20%	—	—	—	—
Pornography						
Experience with books and magazines	99%	91%	—	—	—	—
Experience with movies	58%	42%	—	—	—	—
Parent communication						
Think parents know about teen's sexual behavior	28%	25%	—	—	—	—
Tell parents everything	9%	11%	—	—	—	—
Tell parents nothing	26%	23%	—	—	—	—
Tell parents what they think their parents approve of	20%	15%	—	—	—	—

The double standard. Responses to the question "Have there been times when you have had sexual contact when you didn't feel like it?" indicate that a double standard for sexual behavior still exists, but that it may be decreasing as youths mature. Only 43 percent of all boys answered yes to this question, while 65 percent of the younger girls and 48 percent of the older girls answered yes. Unfortunately, "sexual contact" was not defined, so it is likely that different individuals answered the question differently, some thinking of an unwanted kiss, others thinking of more.

Petting. Concerning petting, 98 percent of all boys approved of a boy touching a girl's breasts, with 69 percent of younger girls and 91 percent of older girls expressing approval. Petting below the waist, that is, touching a partner's genitals, was approved by 93 percent of younger boys, 98 percent of older boys, 79 percent of younger girls, and 83 percent of older girls. An interesting discrepancy in these findings is that, among the younger girls, below-the-waist petting was approved of more often than above-the-waist petting. Even so, the majority of teens approve of petting, and the approval increases with age.

Oral sex. This study clearly indicates that teenagers consider oral sex as less significant than intercourse, and therefore part of only a very committed relationship. In our culture, oral sex is not completely accepted, and most of the teenagers responding to this survey reported an initial uneasiness with it. That so many nevertheless approve of it may be an indication of the relaxing of societal sanctions against it, and perhaps, among those who wish to avoid the danger of pregnancy, of the realization that oral stimulation can be a substitute for intercourse.

Intercourse. In Hass's study, 83 percent of all boys, 54 percent of younger girls, and 64 percent of older girls approved of intercourse. In comparing these figures with those for approval of sexual contact only with romantic involvement, we see that only about half of the boys who approve of intercourse require a romantic involvement, whereas all of the girls do. This again points to the existence of a double standard in attitudes toward sexuality. Girls focus on involvement; boys are more likely to focus on girls. Studies of college students reveal some differences, with the major difference being the increased emotional involvement of males. According to Kallen (82), males and females now share about the same attitudes concerning coitus: it is considered appropriate in a love relationship. The data concerning incidence of premarital sexual intercourse bear out this attitudinal finding.

Masturbation. Probably no sexual activity is so fraught with myth and negative connotations as masturbation, because children normally engage in masturbation during the preschool years, and many carry it on throughout childhood. Early in this century, G. Stanley Hall (04) devoted a full twenty pages to a discussion of the evils of and remedies for masturbation, which he described as "one of the very saddest of all the aspects of human weakness and sin" (p. 432). We now know, of course, that masturbation is natural, pleasurable, and not harmful. It causes no diseases or deformities, is not a sign of psychological weakness, and does not diminish sexual expression with a partner. But even when enlightened, many parents are concerned when their children masturbate and send the subtle negative messages that convey that the child is doing something wrong. In Hass's study, fewer younger boys approved of masturbation than of intercourse, but the older boys and girls approved of it more than of intercourse. Perhaps these data reflect that the younger boys are closest to the negative sanctions imposed during childhood. Boys receive more sanctions than girls concerning masturbation, and the younger boys in this sample have not yet matured beyond them.

Marriage. Only 6 percent of the boys and 3 percent of the girls in Hass's sample definitely do not want to marry. This is consistent with the findings of a survey of 9000 students from the most elite colleges in the the country (*Parade,* 83), in which 94 percent indicated that they wanted to marry. Dreyer (75) found that two thirds of youth still hold traditional views of marriage, but that one third are interested in exploring alternatives. Whereas marriage was once considered a means to an end, the end being sexual expression, children, and legal sanction, marriage is increasingly being seen as the end itself. That is, the ideals of personal growth, mutual sharing, and intimacy are seen as attainable through marriage, and marriage is no longer viewed as the prerequisite necessary to attain other life goals. Dreyer noted that college students increasingly demonstrate the values of love, autonomy, and family, but the recent study identified in *Parade* revealed that only 87 percent of the elite college students want children. And for those who do, men intend to take significant responsibility for the rearing of children. Perhaps the double standard in sex roles is decreasing along with the double standard for sexual behavior.

Homosexuality. Given the historically negative attitudes toward homosexual activity and given that adolescents have frequently been found to be especially hostile toward homosexuality, the approval given for homosexual acts between consenting partners found in the Hass study is surprising. The American Psychiatric Association removed homosexuality from inclusion in its list of pathologies only in 1974. Adolescents, who are developing a sense of themselves sexually, are often confused by feelings of attraction toward members of the same sex. Further, many children have engaged in childhood sex play with members of the same sex, and the adolescent may perceive this play as having been sexual, even though childhood sex play is not so much sexual as simply exploratory. Frightened parents may have placed negative labels on this play and issued dire warnings about its consequences. Furthermore, a sizable minority of young adolescents, 14 percent of the boys and 11 percent of the girls in the Hass study, reported having had at least one homosexual encounter. With the lack of acceptance of homosexuality in high schools (Woodman, 80) we might expect adolescents to be highly disapproving of homosexual encounters. Perhaps because the survey used in the Hass study posed the question in reference to an *act,* rather than to *persons,* the respondents were more accepting. The question was phrased, "I believe it is okay for two girls (boys) to have sex together if they want to" (p. 143), not "It is okay for a person to be homosexual." A visit to any junior high or high school will likely confirm the generally negative attitude toward homosexuals: appellations like "fag," "fairy," "queer," "homo," and "lesbo" are used indiscriminately, and the connotation is always negative. Yet many adolescents question their sexuality, so while they continue to use derogatory terms to describe people, they may be relatively more accepting of occasional behavior. Hass found that even those who agreed with the experience statement nevertheless responded to an open-ended question concerning homosexuality in strongly condemning ways, labeling homosexual behavior perverted. Perhaps they are willing to let others do as they please, but still see the people who engage in it regularly as sick. That 20 percent of all the girls and 14 percent of all the boys indicated that they might involve themselves in a homosexual encounter indicates their recognition of attraction to members of the same sex and acknowledges some personal thought about being involved. The issue is a complex one for many adolescents, and that conflicting attitudes exist simultaneously is merely an indication of that complexity.

SEXUAL BEHAVIOR

From Nonsexual to Sexual

Earlier sexuality. One of the tasks of adolescence can be thought of as developing from a nonsexual child to a sexual adult. As the data that we will examine shortly reveal, there is no doubt that sexual activity begins earlier and is more widespread among modern adolescents than it ever has been before. Elkind (81) pointed out the societal factors that have contributed to enhanced sexual activity: rapid changes in social values; the women's liberation movement; the exploding divorce rate and the concomitant dating activity of parents, which creates more overt sexuality; the decline of parental and institutional authority; and a sense of fatalism that makes virtually anything permissible because "we're all going to die anyway once the bombs start to fall." Hetherington (78) documented the increased sexual orientation of the daughters of divorced women, and both Morrison (80) and Hass (79) demonstrated that pressure from the media, peers, and even parents influences girls to date and become sexually involved before they want to and without enjoying it. There is also a clear association between the onset of sexual activity and the onset of other exploratory activities associated with being more grown up, such as smoking, drinking, and drug use, activities labeled by Jessor (77) as "transition behaviors," which "rather than being isolated events, probably represent a syndrome of activities oriented toward accession to a developmentally later status" (p. 206).

Although the trend is toward increased earlier sexual behavior, Story (82) noted that college students in 1980 had generally experienced a smaller variety of sexual activities than had students in 1974. For example, the reported incidence of adult homosexual experiences, group sex, and sex with an animal were down, but reports of masturbation, premarital sex with someone other than an intended marriage partner, and oral sex increased. These findings are consistent with those of Hass, who found an increase in intercourse in a caring relationship and an increase in heavy petting, including oral sex.

Childhood sexuality. It is useful to consider how sexual behavior begins. Depending on whether or not we consider childhood sex play to be *sexual* influences our thinking. Freud, of course, thought that infants are innately sexual and that experiences involving the genitals are sexual. More modern thinking differs, and although it is certain that the genitals are pleasurably sensitive from infancy, most child-development specialists consider childhood sex play and experimentation as essentially nonsexual; that is, it is pleasurable but not directed toward a love object or hormonally influenced.

Sexual stimulation clearly begins with self-exploration, and first orgasm is often accidental. Parental reaction to such sex experimentation influences the child's perception of it; all too often, it is perceived as dirty and unnatural, and the seeds of guilt are planted. Self-stimulation and sex play with playmates of the other sex are motivated by curiosity and pleasure and generally involve looking and touching (''Let's play doctor''; ''I'll show you mine if you show me yours''). Fifty-two percent of males and 37 percent of females in Morrison's (80) sample reported sex play with same-sex friends; 34 percent of the males and 37 percent of the females reported it with other-sex friends. And sometimes appearances are deceiving: one mother in her sample reported seeing her preschool-aged-son astride a neighbor girl, both writhing and laughing. She calmly asked them what they were doing, and they answered, ''Playing motorcycle!'' Imagine their confusion had they been reprimanded for being dirty.

Hormonal influence. Before puberty then, sexual behavior is pleasurable and erotic because the genitals are extremely sensitive, but children have no hormonally driven urges toward sexuality. In adolescence, however, sexual drives result from hormones and cannot be suppressed (Lidz, 76). The hormones increase the erogenous sensitivity of the mature sex organs in preparation for procreation, and adolescents may sometimes feel that their sex drives are virtually uncontrollable. The first sexual feelings are often directed toward those who are closest, especially family members, and the adolescent may feel guilty as a result (Lidz, 76). Remember that nocturnal emissions are often accompanied by erotic dreams, often homosexual or incestuous ones. These intense feelings are normal but may seem strange and frightening, and the adolescents don't often talk about them, primarily because they are accompanied by guilt. They thus remain intensely personal, and no one can help in their management. Morrison (80) noted that fantasies and crushes often precede real male-female relationships and that these crushes are often on someone, of either sex, who is older. Male junior-high-school teachers frequently report large numbers of young adolescent females who are quite public about their crushes on them. Fantasies and sexual arousal differ for the two sexes, boys being aroused by the literal and visual and girls by the more imaginative (Morrison, 80); girls are also likely to have more romantic fantasies than boys (Hass, 79) — "Sexual fantasies are, by far, the most common erotic phenomenon" (p. 112).

Adolescent tasks. With the end of puberty, the individual is reproductively mature, with all the drives toward sexuality and sexual behavior of an adult. But in our society, adolescence "involves the discrepancy between sexual maturation with the drive toward procreation and the physical, emotional, and social unpreparedness for commitment to intimacy and for caring for a new generation" (Lidz, 76, p. 307). Another of the tasks of adolescence is developing the commitment, and this is done in a slow process that generally proceeds from the monosexual prepubertal groups; to males and females mingling in a public place (the "hangout"); to smaller mixed parties at which junior-high-aged students begin to pair off and begin a self-centered exploration of the other sex, sometimes in the dark; to double dating; and finally to individual dating. Through this process, the individual usually becomes more secure, begins to concentrate on the other rather than only on himself, develops first affection, and finally develops the intimacy of psychological maturity (Lidz, 76).

Heterosexual experience. Somewhere in the process of developing relationships, heterosexual activity begins, with the sequence being embracing, kissing, light caressing, petting, heavy petting, and finally intercourse. As we noted earlier, oral sex may be considered as either less intimate or more intimate than intercourse. Although the ideal process would be to learn about sex through leisurely exploration free of pressure, such is not usually the case (Morrison, 80). The first significant sexual experience invariably includes an emotional reaction, which may range from fear to pleasure, and could include virtually any emotion.

Peer influence is powerful; generally, individual adolescents will do what their closest reference group is doing or will act as if they are. And sexual behavior is a constant topic of adolescent talk, whether the highly exaggerated locker-room stories of boys or the "reputation-protecting" of the girls:

> Those first few clumsy attempts at kissing and touching left me embarrassed and somewhat afraid of boys because of the sudden passion that sometimes seemed to overwhelm them. I was afraid of myself for feeling that passion too. I learned from my friends at school that "nice girls" didn't let the boys go too far. A quiz on sexual experiences that, as I recall, came from Ann Landers, was circulated at one time. We girls all took the quiz and rated ourselves on a scale from nuns to nymphomaniacs. Of course no one wanted to be at either end of the scale; we had to "protect our reputations." (Morrison, 80, p. 81)

Sexual decision making. "The onset of puberty, sexual attractions, and entrance into the adolescent peer culture generally force most teens into the sorts of male-female decision-making they never before experienced" (Scanzoni, 80, p. 748). How much actual, planned decision making goes on between adolescents is questionable and has not been adequately researched. Given the general conspiracy of silence about sex, the anxiousness of most adolescents as they approach sex, and the reluctance to appear unsophisticated, it is probably safe to assume that very little thoughtful, consensual decision making occurs. Rather, the passions of the moment are either allowed to take their course or nipped at some point by one of the partners, usually the female.

Juhasz (75, p. 344) presented a model of sexual decision making that involves six issues (Figure 7.1).

Figure 7.1
A Model for Sexual Decision Making

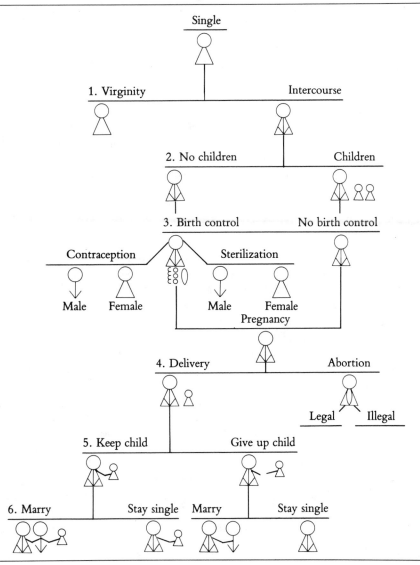

The model focuses primarily on the decisions made by the female in the relationship. At Step 1 the decision is between virginity and nonvirginity. If the decision is to remain a virgin, there are no further decisions at that time, except for defining what level of sexual activity is acceptable short of intercourse. But once a girl opts for intercourse, a series of decisions must be faced. At Step 2 she decides (or fails to decide, as is often the case) whether or not to have children. If she does not want children now, she *should* opt for birth control, or else she leaves herself open to pregnancy. If she and her partner choose birth control (Step 3), they must decide on a method. If birth control has not been used, pregnancy may result. At Step 4 the pregnant female (and the father) must decide whether to deliver the child or not, and if not, how to abort the pregnancy. If the child is delivered, Step 5 involves keeping it or giving it up. In either case, the last decision at Step 6 is to marry or stay single. Juhasz pointed out that the decision at step 6 might have been the first decision, but in light of the prevalence of premarital sexual activity, decided that the first decision does not concern marriage, but rather whether to have sexual intercourse. The marriage decision could come at any point in the decision-making process. Notice that each decision necessarily leads to the next, except the decision not to have intercourse, in which case the same decision is faced repeatedly until it is made in favor of intercourse; then the others follow. That most adolescents do not engage in planned decision making is borne out by the statistics concerning teen pregnancy, which we will discuss later in this chapter.

Current Adolescent Practices

Because of its extensive survey of high-school-aged adolescents, we will use Hass's (79) study (Table 7.2), with supporting documentation of other recent empirical studies, as the basis of our discussion of the extent of masturbation, petting, oral sex, intercourse, orgasm, and homosexuality among adolescents.

Masturbation. The vast majority of both males and females in the Hass study approved of masturbation, with 75 percent of young males, 80 percent of older males, 52 percent of younger females, and 59 percent of older females reporting using masturbation for sexual gratification. Coleman (81) reported somewhat lower figures, and stated that 58 percent of 13- to 18-year-old males masturbate. Morrison (80) found that three quarters of the males and half of the females in her sample who masturbated accompanied the masturbation with sexual fantasies and cites some of the benefits of masturbation: it aids in learning about one's body; it releases sexual tension without intercourse; and it helps adolescents learn privately about their sexual responses. Lidz (76) pointed out that psychiatrists now consider the absence of masturbation among adolescent boys to be a cause for concern, in that it may indicate repression of sexual urges. What a remarkable change from the view espoused by G. Stanley Hall! But the practice is still not talked about openly, especially in families, and adults are not generally aware of how to deal with the masturbatory activity of children and adolescents. Morrison (80) suggested that adults must neither give unlimited license, for public masturbation has dire social consequences, nor create harmful attitudes. It is therefore advisable for adults to help young people understand that masturbation is normal but should be conducted in private, and that it is not the only means of satisfaction.

Petting. The Hass (79) study revealed that over 90 percent of all adolescents (aged 15 through 18) engaged in petting above the waist, with over three quarters also engaged in petting below the waist and with boys and girls about equally experienced, and he labeled petting the primary focus of heterosexual activity among high-school-aged students. Clayton's (80) review of the literature supported Hass's findings: petting behavior is now similar for males and females, whereas boys used to be more heavily involved; and as students get older, the incidence of heterosexual activity beyond petting increases.

Oral sex. As we noted earlier, the approval of oral sex is widespread, but fewer adolescents have experienced it than approve of it. In Hass's sample, slightly more girls (59 percent) than boys (55 percent) reported having taken part in oral sex. Morrison (80) found more reports of oral sex as preceding intercourse; a number of women in her sample considered themselves virgins as long as there was no penetration, and oral sex allowed them to maintain their virginity.

Intercourse. Premarital intercourse is the most frequently and extensively studied sexual behavior, with most studies focusing on the extent of premarital coitus and the age of onset of coital activity. In Hass's study, 43 percent of younger boys (aged 15 and 16) and 56 percent of older boys (aged 17 and 18) had had intercourse; the corresponding figures for girls were 31 percent and 44 percent, respectively. Postman (82) reported that coital activity among teenaged females increased 30 percent between 1971 and 1976, with 55 percent of 19-year-olds having had intercourse. Jessor (75) reported the incidence of coitus among high-school students in the tenth, eleventh, and twelfth grades: in grade ten 21 percent of the males and 26 percent of the females were nonvirgins; at the eleventh grade the corresponding figure for males was 28 percent and for females 40 percent; in the twelfth grade the figures were 33 percent of the males and 55 percent of the females. Jessor (73) hypothesized that females engage in intercourse at earlier ages than males because they date older males, develop earlier, and/or are influenced by changing sex roles. Zelnick (77) compared the incidence of premarital intercourse among 15- to 19-year-old females, by race, in 1971 and again in 1976. For whites, the incidence rose from 21 percent to 31 percent; for blacks it rose from 51 percent to 63 percent; and the average age of first intercourse declined by four months, from 16.6 to 16.2. Clayton (80) reported that among college freshmen, 51 percent of the females and 46 percent of the males had had intercourse, with the corresponding rates for seniors being 85 percent for females and 82 percent for males. Obviously, adolescents and young adults are increasingly sexually active, yet all the reasearchers who studied numbers of partners or attitude toward intercourse noted that, for most adolescents, coital activity occurs within a caring relationship (Hass, 79; Morrison, 80; Scanzoni, 80). First intercourse is often disastrous, with insecurity, possessiveness, jealousy, and egocentricity mitigating against a mutually sharing experience (Coleman, 81), but when it occurs within a caring and thoughtful relationship, it could be pleasurable and mutually positive (Hass, 79). He also found, however, that teenagers experience performance anxiety just as adults do. Most were concerned about being acceptable and making their partner happy. The lack of communication between partners contributed to the level of uncertainty about their performance. Boys are likely, in comparison with girls, to be younger at first coitus, have intercourse with a pickup or casual date, not plan or discuss intercourse, enjoy it more, talk about it more, tell their parents, engage in intercourse more often, have more partners before marriage, and have less guilt (Lerner, 80). Girls are more likely to have both their first and all subsequent coital activity in the confines of a committed relationship.

A number of researchers have looked into the relationship of sexual activity and self-esteem, especially for girls. All concur that coital activity is related to low self-esteem for younger adolescents, but to high self-esteem for older youth (Scanzoni, 80; W. B. Miller, 76a; Chilman, 78; Herold, 79). All also concur that among the younger girls, traditional sex-role stereotypes contribute to increased coital activity, while among college women nontraditional sex roles are related to coital activity. At the younger ages, among girls with traditional views of sex roles and low esteem, femininity is probably equated with attention and approval from males, and intercourse serves as proof that the girl is attractive and desirable. Among older young women, high esteem and nontraditional views provide an independence and assurance that allow for assertiveness and liberation, and coital activity is seen as one means of expression. As we will discuss further a little later, it is also the young sexually active females who fail to use contraceptives; this too is apparently related to their esteem and to their views of the roles of the sexes, as well as to a lack of accurate information and planning skills.

Orgasm. Although the topic of female orgasm has been extensively studied and researched, very little investigation into the extent of orgasm among female adolescents has been done. Both Hass (79) and Morrison (80) begin to address the question. Both report that young women do have orgasms (Hass's study reporting 42 percent), but that frequently girls are not sure whether or not they have had them, and that masturbation is a more frequent source of orgasm than is intercourse. This, of course, is because of the anatomy of the female genitalia; the clitoris is the most sensitive of the female sexual organs, yet it is not necessarily stimulated during coitus. The fact that many women do not discover orgasms until adulthood may have nothing to do with an increased sexuality *per se,* but an increased freedom to explore sexuality without guilt and embarrassment, coupled, perhaps, with greater confidence and patience on the part of the woman's partner.

Homosexuality. Studies of homosexual behavior and of homosexuality (and the two should not be equated, for many heterosexuals have engaged in one or more incidents of homosexual behavior) among adolescents are scant, probably because adolescence is still a time of experimenting, and most homosexuals do not declare themselves gay until adulthood, when they are more sure of their identities. The well-known Kinsey research of sexual practices in the 1940s revealed that more than 60 percent of all men had engaged in some homosexual activity before the age of 16, but much of this might be called prepubertal sex play rather than homosexual encounter. Hass's (79) study found that 14 percent of the boys and 11 percent of the girls had had at least one homosexual experience. Woodman (80) provided the most comprehensive discussion of homosexual activity and homosexuality among adolescents. She, as well as others (Juhasz, 76), emphasized that homosexual experimentation in adolescence is normal and not an indicator of future homosexual identity. She concluded that (p. 79):

1. Homosexual and heterosexual experimentation is not unusual among young people.
2. The fact that a young person finds pleasure in a homosexual act is not necessarily an indication of homosexuality.
3. The type of sexual activity actually engaged in should not be seen as confirmation of sexual orientation.
4. Adolescence is a time for discovering more about oneself sexually as well as in many other ways. There is no need to establish one's identity or to accept a label used by others unless the person feels that it fits with the self-image.

Since approximately 10 percent of the adult population eventually establish a homosexual identity (Woodman, 80; Silverstein, 77), we can assume that about that percentage of the adolescent population is seriously questioning their sexual orientation, or have already decided that they are gay. Woodman (80) noted that approximately 15 percent of gay men knew they were gay by age 14, with 75 to 80 percent knowing by 19. Women make that decision later, with only 57 percent knowing by 19. (Society is also more tolerant of homosexual women than of homosexual men; women are not accused, for example, of being potential child molesters). She suggested that many deny a homosexual preference until adulthood because of the lack of support provided for adolescents who are questioning their sexual identity. The effects of negative stereotypes of homosexuals are devastating to adolescents, who are under strong pressures to conform and have nowhere to turn for accurate, sensitive information and support. Furthermore, the homosexual adolescent has no social outlets, as do gay adults, and other adolescents may actually be afraid of the homosexual because of their own tenuous identity as sexual beings. (That a large number of people are actually afraid of homosexuals is evidenced by the fairly recently coined term **homophobic** to refer to such people.) Nevertheless, there appears to be an increase in the number of gay teenagers within school settings (Woodman, 80), while the helping professionals seem judgmental rather than helpful in the minds of the youths who would benefit from their help.

Consequences of Sexual Behavior

As we have noted throughout this chapter, the entrance into sexuality is universally confusing, sometimes frightening, and sometimes enjoyable. Adolescents vary tremendously in their emotional reactions to their own sexual behavior; but all evidence clearly indicates that the transition to sexuality is made smoother by adequate, nonjudgmental sex information coupled with a positive self-esteem and a genuine caring for the sexual partner. The greater the understanding and commitment on the part of adolescents, the more likely they are to develop responsible and healthy sexual attitudes and practices.

As we have seen, sexual decision making involves consideration of contraceptive use and pregnancy. A third consequence of sexual activity is venereal disease. We will address each of these separately.

Contraceptive use. Adolescents are notoriously poor contraceptive users (Zelnik, 72, 77, 79; Smith, 82; Scanzoni, 80; Urberg, 82). Only about 30 percent of sexually active adolescent females report always using contraception; two out of three report using none on last intercourse; and among contraceptive users, only about half use a reliable method (such as the pill or an IUD). Most use unreliable methods such as withdrawal (Zelnik, 79). Of those who never use contraception, approximately 58 percent will become pregnant; among those who sometimes use it, 42 percent will become pregnant, though the most recent studies are beginning to show that contraceptive use is increasing (Zelnik, 72, 77, 79). Both males and females agree that contraception should be the responsibility of both partners, but their behaviors are not consistent with this belief: actions bear out that for brief encounters, the male is considered to be responsible by being supplied with condoms; in long-term relationships, the female is considered to be responsible, preferably for a noninterfering method like the pill. Furthermore, the less traditional a girl is, "the more likely she is to *negotiate* for the kinds of contraceptive behaviors that will enhance her own interest" (Scanzoni, 80, p. 751).

Why do adolescents fail to use contraceptives in such alarming numbers? The answer to this question is complex, and is related to developmental variables. Urberg (82) presented a well-conceived theoretical model, documented with empirical research, which specified five competencies necessary for effective contraceptive use: 1) problem recognition; 2) motivation; 3) generation of alternatives; 4) decision making; and 5) implementation. We will examine each of these competencies.

1. *Problem recognition:* The person must realize that pregnancy is a likely result of unprotected coitus. The first aspect of this competency is knowledge. The adolescent must know that intercourse is likely to lead to pregnancy. Many young adolescents still are surprised at conceptions, thinking that it was the wrong time of the month, or that kids can't get pregnant, or for any other of a host of myths and misinformation (Smith, 82). Hass (79) noted that as late as 1973 one third of all adolescents believed that a girl wouldn't get pregnant if she didn't *want* a baby. In addition to knowledge, the adolescent must possess

the cognitive skills involved in understanding long-term consequences and planning for the future. Sexually active adolescents must also accept the reality of their activity. Many who are sexually active but who see sexuality as unacceptable may feel so guilty that they actually deny their activity (Urberg, 82; Smith, 82). Guilt, apparently, is more effective in preventing contraceptive use than it is in preventing intercourse.

2. *Motivation:* The motivation for contraceptive use involves the adolescent's sense of vulnerability, locus of control, and value of pregnancy. To be adequately motivated to use contraceptives, the individual or couple must feel vulnerable to pregnancy; unfortunately, all too many adolescents live under the illusion that "it won't happen to me." (See the discussion of the "personal fable" in Chapter 9.) They must also recognize that they have control over their bodies and what happens to them, and they must place a negative value on pregnancy, a value that is influenced by the age, social class, marital status, and ethnic group to which the adolescent belongs. Many young adolescents do not see early pregnancy as a hindrance to them.

3. *Generation of alternatives:* The younger the adolescents, the less likely they are to know of all the alternatives for contraceptives. Many apparently equate birth control with the pill; if they do not have pills, they use nothing.

4. *Decision making:* Clearly, cognitive skills affect decision-making ability. The adolescent must be able to weigh the costs and benefits of contraception and of various types of contraception, as well as to incorporate and evaluate the attitudinal components involved in the decision to use contraceptives. Such considerations as cost, necessity for physician visit or parental knowledge, convenience, messiness, and the perceptions both of the couple and of others need be taken into account.

5. *Implementation:* Finally, there are personal and social barriers to the successful implementation of contraceptive measures, barriers that are too great for many adolescents. There are legal restrictions, financial restrictions, and the necessity to overcome embarrassment, talk with the sexual partner, and think in terms of both means and ends.

The decision making involving contraceptive use is obviously complex, involving knowledge, skills, motivation, access, sex-role socialization, and issues of control (Adler, 81; Morrison, 80; Schneider, 82; Cretkovich, 78). The higher the self-esteem, the less traditional the sex role, the greater the knowledge and cognitive skills, the higher the motivation for not being pregnant, and the more available the contraceptive device, the more likely the adolescent is to use it. That many young adolescents do not have all these competencies is attested to by the high incidence of unprotected coital activity among them.

Does the availability of contraceptives influence the incidence of coitus? Apparently not. All the researchers referred to above, plus extensive research by Planned Parenthood, concluded that contraceptive information and availability do not increase sexual activity. Most teens who seek contraceptive information and advice do so after they become sexually active, not before. Contraceptive information is more likely to affect pregnancy rates than coital rates. Torres (78) reported that among sexually active females under the age of 17 using the services of a physician in a birth-control clinic, 55 percent said that their parents knew they were active and using contraceptives. Of the remaining 45 percent, only 4 percent said they would stop having sex rather then tell their parents. Thirty-two percent would use either an over-the-counter product or nothing. Only 9 percent were willing to tell their parents and continue coming to the clinic.

Pregnancy. Teen pregnancy is the topic of voluminous research, all of which documents the extent of both pregnancy and birth among the teen population. Each year, 10 percent of teenaged females, over a million in all, become pregnant; they give birth to over 600,000 babies (Roosa, 82; Elkind, 81; Postman, 82), and the 15- to 17-year-old age group is the only one for which the birth rate increased between 1966 and 1975 (Postman, 82; Stickle, 75). Eighty percent of the teenaged mothers are under 16, and 60 percent of these will have another baby while still of school age (Stickle, 75). Furthermore, more of the babies born to teen-aged mothers will be born and raised out of wedlock; marriage is no longer the almost automatic solution to an unplanned pregnancy that it once was, and the races are becoming more alike in their behavior. Most teenaged pregnant girls, both black and white, *are not* marrying and *are* keeping their babies (Simkins, 84).

Pregnancy poses a unique problem for adolescents, whose development from girlhood to womanhood is interrupted by motherhood (Schneider, 82). It also poses problems for the children of these young mothers. Most research shows that children born to adolescent mothers are more likely to have physical, social, behavioral, and intellectual problems; that teens have more problem pregnancies, more premature babies, and more babies with low birth weights; and that young mothers and their children are more likely to find themselves on the welfare rolls than are other mothers and their children (Schneider, 82; Roosa, 82). Roosa (82), however, raised a challenge to the statistics concerning developmental deficits of infants due to the young age of their mothers. The observed deficits may be more a result of inadequate prenatal care than of the age of the mother *per se.*

Why do teens get pregnant? Given the complexity of the decision-making process concerning contraceptive use, teens get pregnant for a variety of reasons, including the poor decision-making skills already discussed. But some teens get pregnant intentionally. Schneider (82) first refuted the "old-wive's-tale" theories — the "bad seed" theory that said the girl was just born bad, the "wrong side of the tracks" theory that blamed her geographical location and social status, the "over-sexed" theory that blamed her inordinate sexual appetite, and the "mental retardation" theory that blamed her stupidity. He then suggested, from a psychological viewpoint, that the pregnant adolescent may be trying to satisfy an underlying wish for a strong identification with her mother, with whom she does not enjoy a good relationship and from whom it is time to separate. This need leads her to seek attention and affection from men, to act out against her mother, and to want a baby to fill the void she feels. Adler (81) suggested that the teen mother is attempting to replace a perceived loss, perhaps of her mother, and is likely to become pregnant during a time of stress. Other motivations include the wish to establish an identity as an adult, to feel a sense of adequacy ("Look at what I can do"), or simply to do what is expected. The influence of socioeconomic status is pervasive, not only on the rate of pregnancy, but also on pre- and postnatal care, effect on the development of the mother, and likelihood of subsequent pregnancies.

Most teen pregnancies are unwanted, and virtually all are unplanned. When the girl finds she is pregnant she is faced with new decisions, none of which is painless (Adler, 81). Abortion, forced marriage, adoption, or keeping the child as a single parent all involve major physical and emotional costs. Frequently, however, the decision is made on the basis of pleasing others rather than on the effect of the decision on the mother, father, and child (Adler, 81).

The effects of teenage parenthood may or may not include disruption of educational plans and career aspirations. Whereas research indicates that young parents do not have high educational and career attainments, the differences are most likely due to preexisting conditions and not to the fact of the parenthood itself. That is, those who are likely to be teenaged parents are not likely to have high educational or career aspirations to begin with, so although early pregnancy may, indeed, curtail the plans of some adolescents, it likely has no effect on the plans of most (Haggstrom, 81).

Because the female bears the children, we have focused our discussion of the effect of pregnancy on her. There are consequences, however, for the male as well. A boy may be faced with financial responsibility (for abortion or for the child), a forced marriage, curtailment of education or career choices, accusation of rape, accusation of statutory rape, and accusation of paternity (Lerner, 80).

Venereal disease. Venereal (from *Venus,* the goddess of love) diseases include trichomoniasis, herpes simplex #2, vaginal thrush, crabs, prostatitus, gonorrhea, and syphilis. Although the syphilis rate in the United States is down, the gonorrhea rate has reached epidemic proportions, especially among adolescents. Between 1956 and 1979, the number of 10- to 14-year-olds with gonorrhea increased from 17.7 to 50.5 per 100,000. The corresponding rate for 15- to 19-year-olds went from 415.7 to 1211 per 100,000 (Postman, 82), and the World Health Organization ranks gonorrhea as the most prevalent communicable disease after the common cold. There is, however, very little concern among young people concerning venereal diseases. Strother (83) reported a study that showed that although 75 percent of the women and 93 percent of men in a college sample were sexually active, and over half had more than one sexual partner, almost none indicated an interest in information about venereal disease. The prevailing attitude seems to be one of seeking treatment if necessary, but not being concerned prior to contraction. This attitude could be dangerous both physically and psychologically, and to both the current and future generations, especially because gonorrhea is often asymptomatic and therefore never treated. The condom provides the only partially effective preventative; the increased popularity of the pill among adolescents and the corresponding decrease in the use of condoms may be partially responsible for the increase in gonorrhea.

Of increasing importance in the 1980s is herpes simplex #2, a condition that is easily transmitted and, as of this writing, has no cure. The disease is contagious only when lesions are present, but afflicted individuals are subject to eruptions of lesions throughout their lives.

SEX EDUCATION

The Controversy

A controversy over sex education has been raging for almost 100 years. G. Stanley Hall (1904), in the quotation that begins this chapter, noted the psychologist's responsibility to clarify "the plain path of life for adolescence" that had been obscured by both "quacks and prudes." His concern was to correct misinformation, a concern which continued through the 1950s; in the 1960s thoughts concerning sex education expanded to include not only information about reproduction, pregnancy, and venereal disease, but human sexuality in its broader sense, including sexual adjustment. Through all of this, some parents have objected, as have some religious and political groups, to sex education being included in the curriculum at all. These groups hold that sex education belongs in the home and/or in the churches, where parents have control over the values espoused. That sex education belongs in the home is inarguable; it *is* in the home and is demonstrated through all the interactions parents have with each other and with their children. The problem in the argument that sex education belongs in the home lies in the widespread lack of attention given to sex education by parents, the discomfort of many adults to discuss sexual matters, and the highly judgmental attitude all too many parents have toward normal sexual expression and curiosity by their children (Morrison, 80; Zelnik, 79; Hass, 79). Yet parents frequently refuse their children permission to take part in voluntary sex education classes, including seeing the infamous movie in the fifth or sixth grade, and they provide no opportunity for their children to ask questions and discuss sexual matters. It seems that sex education belongs in the schools by default, as a result of parents and churches not providing the kind of sex education that would allow schools to remain uninvolved in providing assistance in this most personal area of development.

Regardless of the controversy, we need to find ways to help adolescents deal sensitively and respectfully with both the facts and the issues of sexuality. Only if young people are adequately prepared with accurate information and sound decision-making skills can they hope to resist coercion and make informed, respectful decisions. If the setting of the home and church do not provide an atmosphere conducive to such learning, the school must fill the void. Research supports the observation that sex education programs yield positive gains, and that these gains remain over time (Klein, 84).

Current Status

Inadequate attention. It is widely recognized that current efforts in sex education are woefully inadequate (Hass, 79; Morrison, 80; Zelnik, 72, 77, 79): parents don't talk about themselves as sexual beings; many parents convey the attitude that sex is bad or dirty and thereby create feelings of guilt and confusion for their children; reproductive facts are learned too late; knowledge about reproduction and contraception has not kept up with the increase in sexual activity among adolescents; the emotional impact of intimacy is virtually never discussed, either between adults and adolescents or among adolescents themselves; girls learn little to nothing about boys, and vice versa; controversial but universal topics like sexual anxieties, sexual expectations, and feelings and values are usually excluded from discussion; current sex education, both in the home and the school, focuses on reproductive functioning. Adolescents have usually been introduced to the anatomy of their own sex, and perhaps to the anatomy of the other, with girls' information focused on menstruation. Sexuality itself, if referred to at all, is frequently couched in vague abstractions that mean little or nothing to the developing adolescent. In short, the most important questions concerning adolescents are usually not addressed.

Some of the reason for the inadequate attention to sex education lies, of course, in adult discomfort with their own sexuality. Some of it lies in the conflict of values between groups, and some of it lies in the fear that knowledge about sex will lead adolescents to increased experimentation and sexual activity. This last fear should be put to rest. It is safe to state unequivocally that formal sex education does not lead to increased sexual behavior (Darabi, 82; Philliber, 82; Morrison, 80; Mehl, 77; Zelnik, 72, 77, 79; Juhasz, 76). Formal sex education has been demonstrated to lead to significant gains in factual knowledge; an increase in the *intention* to use birth control; an actual increase in the use of birth control among previously active adolescents; a greater acceptance of other people; a decrease of fear and doubt; an increase in self-understanding; an increase in problem-solving and decision-making skills; and an increase in communication about sex and sexuality among adolescents; but not to a change in personal behavior.

Guidelines for sex education. There is now widespread agreement among experts that sound sex-education practices, whether the informal ones of the home or the more formal ones of the church and school, should provide information, understanding, and reassurance. Sex education ought to begin early and be appropriately responsive to the developmental level of the children involved, answering their questions on the level of their interest and understanding. Formal sex education ought to be group-oriented, with same-sex groups for early adolescents and mixed groups for older adolescents. Information alone is insufficient; sex education must allow for articulation of values and should include materials that help adolescents understand and feel. (See Evonne McMillan's description of an activity she used to help adolescents *feel*, to a small degree, the responsibility of parenthood, at the end of this chapter.) Adults must realize that even good information can be distorted; it is therefore necessary to check to see that the information has been appropriately understood and internalized. Morrison (80, pp. 56–57) provided the following guidelines concerning the appropriateness of information for various age levels:

Two to Seven Years Old

- Anatomical gender similarities and differences: ''Why does he have a penis when I don't?''
- Names of all body parts including genitals; scientific terms, special family or ethnic terms, and terms used by peers for genitals might all be appropriate.
- Discussion with the child about the matter of deriving pleasure from touching one's genitals — masturbating.
- How babies are conceived.

Five Years Up

- Information picked up from inadequate sources (such as a TV news report of a rape and murder victim) can be dealt with in conversation.
- Vocabulary — accurate definitions for terms heard and parental interpretations.

Seven to Twelve Years Old

- Personal development, changing body, and new emotions.
- Information about the development of the opposite sex.
- Timing should be related to the individual's development. When a girl's breasts begin to develop, even though at seven or eight years, she should have information on menstruation.

Twelve Years and Up

- Arousal — same and opposite sex.
- Premarital sex when ready to date.
- Contraception.
- Venereal disease.
- Sex and relationship.
- Homosexuality.

In addition, sex education encompasses interpersonal relationships, dating, preparation for family living, attitudes, and the like. Perhaps education for living is a more appropriate container than sex education alone.

Recollections of a Sex-Educator's Experiment: Evonne McMillan

I had been teaching a course called "Sexuality and Self" to students aged 15–19 and was about to cover a unit on pregnancy and parenting. At the end of one of the classes, I asked the students how many of them intended to become parents some day. All of them raised their hands. Then I asked if they would like to have an opportunity to become parents in this class. I told them that I had a way for them to observe first-hand the development of a fetus and to accept responsibility for its well-being. Just as they were beginning to believe that I had gone completely "bonkers" I explained that I meant for each of them to become the parent of a chicken!

I had first gotten the idea for the "Chick Project" when I was raising some chickens of my own. While incubating the eggs and observing the first signs of life by "candling" the eggs, it occurred to me, "What a wonderful way to demonstrate the development of a fetus to my sex education students!" I knew that the early physiological development of a chicken is very similar to that of a human and that similar projects had been done in classrooms before, especially with elementary students. But I doubted that such a detached intellectual exercise would accomplish what I wanted to with these very sophisticated students, who were nearing the age of parenting themselves. I wanted to involve them emotionally in the study in some way — to give them a sense of the responsibility and the risk associated with parenting. So, I devised a way for each student to "role play" a pregnancy, by accepting personal responsibility for the development of his/her own egg.

First, I asked the class as a whole to make the decision whether or not to do the project, with the understanding that the whole class would either participate or not participate: no exceptions. After much discussion about the pros and cons of parenthood, of forced pregnancy and of the boys' possible role in the project, they all agreed to participate. They decided that the boys (roughly 1/3 of the class) would become "mothers" just like the girls, with no partnerships or sideline parenting allowed.

The next week I entered the class with a carton of fertilized eggs in each hand and cheerfully announced, "I have wonderful news! You're all pregnant!" You would have thought that we had never discussed it, the way some of them reacted. I got all kinds of reasons why they couldn't do it now — they didn't have the time, or it wasn't convenient, or they weren't ready for the responsibility. Having resolved to make the project as close to real-life as possible, I explained that most pregnancies are unplanned and that their reactions were not unusual for newly expectant parents; however, *no one* would be allowed to back out of the deal. They were pregnant, and they would just have to deal with it.

After letting this reality sink in, I encouraged them to discuss their feelings about being pregnant, as well as their options for managing their pregnancies. A few were really excited and wanted to know all the details of caring for their "babies." Others were not as keen on the idea, but felt committed to the project. Only one student, a girl, was adamantly opposed and wanted out of the pregnancy. This gave us the perfect opportunity to discuss her only other option: abortion.

I told her that this was, as in real-life, the only way to become "unpregnant." However, she would have to make that choice herself, before the end of the class, and would have to effect the abortion herself, by cracking the egg open and flushing it down the toilet. While she pondered this possible solution, two other girls pleaded with her to carry her pregnancy, with their help, and to allow them to adopt the "baby" upon birth.

She struggled with the decision during the whole class, interrupting at times to ask me questions regarding the care required for her chick, and finally announced that she would not abort. It was a very emotional moment for everyone, and I was thankful that it happened.

In the meantime, the rest of us had been discussing the various levels of responsibility that one might take for the chick. The highest level was to devise a method of incubating it at home, and provide for it to be turned four times a day. Only one student, Suzy, took on this much responsibility, saying that she could count on her family to help out, while she was in school.

Three of the students decided to form a team for the care of their chicks. This required them to participate in turning the eggs at least once a day, and taking turns for the nights and weekends.

The remainder of the group (12 in all) created a schedule in which they had to participate only every three days. They felt that this level of involvement compared with

Recollections of a Sex-Educator's Experiment (continued)

that of many human parents, who are minimally involved in prenatal care. They were responsible for checking on the eggs only seven times during the pregnancy, or about as often as a human expectant mother would visit the obstetrician. Each egg was marked with the student's initials and placed in the incubators, and we began counting the days.

In addition to candling the eggs during the incubation period, we spent our class time discussing the biological, social and psychological aspects of human pregnancies. We viewed films on childbirth, discussed different methods such as Lamaze and Leboyer, and explored all the alternatives of human parenting. The students continued their usual practice of writing letters to me after class, keeping me posted on the effectiveness of the presentations and on their feelings about the "big event" coming up.

The results of the project were even better than I had hoped for. I was pleasantly surprised that the students took the project so seriously and really used it as an opportunity to experiment with their feelings about becoming parents. It became clear to me that I was giving them a vehicle to explore a very natural curiosity about their ability to be parents, in a socially acceptable and short-term way. The letters they wrote after that first class were my first indication of just how effective a teaching tool I had hit upon:

> What a great idea about the chickens! I've been having thoughts (for the first *real* time) about actually ever experiencing motherhood. This will be a wonderful way to see if I'm capable without my parents having a fit! *Suzy*

> I am looking forward to being a father. I think the process of caring for my chicken will teach me something about what it is actually like to be a parent. This type of early exposure to the pros and cons of being a responsible parent could become very helpful if I become, unexpectedly, a father to a human child. *Mark*

> I feel a little bit like I want to abort this chicken because the responsibility, even though it's a small amount, is there. But I feel morally wrong about that. I'm also finding that the more I think about being responsible for a baby the more I like it. I'm afraid of doing something wrong or having an egg

that doesn't hatch. But I also like this and it will be a good experience because I'd sort of like to have a baby even though I know it's not realistic at this time in my life. I'm glad we're doing this. I'm attached to my baby already. *Anne*

> I feel that hatching a chicken is having most of the good parts of being an expectant mother without morning sickness and the scaryness of the responsibility of someone else's life for 18 years. I wonder what color he/she will be? I hope she makes it! *Marie*

> I am excited about becoming a mama chicken. It sounds more "fun" to me right now than responsibility. There's none of the social put-downs when you're 17 and pregnant. But I still try to pretend that this is really it. I don't want to abort because I'd like to have something that is dependant on me, and makes me feel needed. I have a hamster at home and it's like a little baby to me. Maybe I'll have stronger feelings towards the chicken, since I saw it grow *before* it was born. I can't wait until I can see it move or hear it living. I'm a mother . . . *Astrid*

As the class pregnancies progressed, I saw more examples of normal feelings of expectant parents:

> I'm very excited about seeing my baby chick, and I feel very important to my chick because I'm like the chick's heart — it's up to me weather *(sic)*the chick lives or not — weather (it) survives when it's born. *Teresa*

> (I feel) expectant, fullfilled, pregnant . . . semi-excited, curious about what my two chicks will look like . . . protective of my child. *Jon*

> To me I feel as though I am really having a baby in a way. If I were having one I would have to take care of myself the way I am taking care of my eggs, and that is something I'm really happy about — having twins. When I really have a child or children I want to have twins. *Eileen*

> P.S. I hate my egg. *Wendy*

The most rewarding day for me and certainly for most

Recollections of a Sex-Educator's Experiment (continued)

of the students was the day of the birthing. I was shocked by the intensity of their reactions. Students hovered over the open incubators, paced the floor and demanded explanations from me as to what was happening to their eggs. They were surprised and distressed over the time involved in the hatching, and expressed concern that their babies might be deformed or stillborn. They kept a steady watch over the event, covering for each other when they had classes. One boy, who had shown little interest in his egg prior to this, refused to leave even for classes, and could only be coaxed away for a moment under the ruse that his other prized possession, his car, had been hit on the street. As the birthings went on into the evening, one young man took all of the remaining eggs home to give them the necessary supervision.

A few days after all the eggs had hatched (with the exception of the casualties) and the new parents had had an opportunity to spend some time with their babies, we met again to share our reactions and feelings about the project. Again, I was amazed to see the parallels with real human pregnancies. There was unmitigated joy and pride in the babies, even reluctance to let others handle them. There was also sadness for the lost babies — one young man said that he would hesitate trying parenting again; another, the girl who had considered abortion, felt that she was being punished when her egg did not hatch. Another girl expressed her sense of loss, and even held a funeral at home for her chick. Of course, there were also several who appeared relatively indifferent to the new chicks.

In short, I felt that the project had been a tremendous success, and it reaffirmed my belief that students learn best when they are personally invested in a learning activity, especially in an area which has so much significance for them.

SUMMARY

The development of adult sexuality is one of the most significant aspects of adolescence. It includes not only the ability to reproduce, but the solidification of gender identity, the psychological reactions of the individual to sexual changes, the development of sex roles and sex-role behavior, and the development of both sexual attitudes and behaviors.

Gender identity is the assignment of sex (male or female) to each person. Genetics, hormones, and society all play important roles in gender identity. Gender assignment begins before birth and continues throughout childhood, but the physical and social implications of that assignment are not truly clear until adolescence.

The physical changes of puberty are accompanied by significant psychological reactions. Boys learn to deal with spontaneous erections, first ejaculation, the development of pubic and body hair, and voice changes. Girls learn to accept the development of breasts and buttocks, body hair, and the complications of menstruation. The onset of menstruation can be a particularly frightening and confusing event if a girl is not properly prepared for it.

In addition to the physical and physiological differences between boys and girls, psychological differences exist as well. The best-documented differences are those of cognition: boys excel in mathematical and visual-spatial ability while girls excel in verbal ability. Although there are other differences that have been documented (aggressiveness, for example), these are not so clearly sexually related. Most of the differences observed can be accounted for by social learning rather than inherent differences.

It is useful to differentiate between roles and stereotypes and to note that many sex differences are actually the result of stereotyping that has occurred over hundreds of years. Girls have been stereotyped by families, schools, media, and society as a whole as passive, nurturant, and submissive, while boys have been stereotyped as aggressive, rational, and dominant. As is generally true of stereotypes, these expectations are neither true nor fair, and both sexes suffer as a result of them. Both the traditional female and the traditional male can be viewed as rigid and inflexible, with each benefiting from some of the positive psychological characteristics of the other.

Sexual attitudes among adolescents tend to be somewhat more liberal than those of previous generations. Their attitudes are learned primarily from their families and from the media, both of which are translated through peers. Although differences in attitudes are narrowing, a sexual double standard still exists, with boys being allowed greater freedom in matters of sexuality than girls. The double standard appears to decrease somewhat as adolescents get older. The most current research evidences that adolescents tend to approve of most sexual behavior, at least in the context of a caring relationship.

Along with increasing permissiveness, adolescents in general are engaging in sexual behavior at earlier ages. Sexual decision making is one of the tasks adolescents must face. Fewer adolescents actually engage in all sexual behaviors than approve of them. Sexual behavior appears to be related to self-esteem, with the youngest sexually active adolescents displaying lower esteem than older sexually active adolescents. The younger the adolescent engaged in sexual behavior, the more likely it is that the youngster is using his or her sexuality as a means of obtaining needed affection.

The consequences of sexual behavior (contraceptive use, pregnancy, and venereal disease) are of major concern. Adolescents are notoriously poor contraceptive users for a variety of reasons. Teen pregnancy is on the rise, with the majority of teen mothers choosing to keep and raise their babies rather than aborting or giving them up for adoption. The prevention of pregnancy and venereal disease is a major health concern of the 1980s.

There has been a continuing controversy over sex education, with more conservative groups advocating that sex education should be handled only in the home and church. Yet children and adolescents are frequently ill-informed by their families and churches, and schools and other agencies have taken up sex education by default. Careful and sensitive sex education is designed to help children and adolescents deal with all aspects of their emerging sexuality.

8

Cognitive Development

Anna was the child of whom every parent dreams. She walked at ten months, spoke coherent sentences before she was two, and read at four. She was curious, learned easily, showed artistic talent, and sailed through school with consistent praise from teachers. At seventeen, she is a high-school senior with grand plans. She scored over 1400 on the SAT; has been accepted as an early admittee at a prestigious college, with a sizable scholarship; and is already looking ahead to law school. Her parents feel blessed and thankful, aware that Anna has been more pleasure than pain and an easy child to raise. She always did what they expected of her.

Mike, however, presents a different picture. A healthy and active baby, Mike walked and talked late. He was difficult to toilet train and showed little interest in the many books his mother continued to buy for him. He played hard but quickly lost interest in the counting and letter recognition tasks that were a part of his nursery school. School has been less than joyful for Mike, except on the playground. He trudges along, and although now, at sixteen, he says he wants to go to college, his achievement tests and grades place him below average for all students his age. He dutifully opens his books each evening, but the assignments frequently seem incomprehensible, and he looks with wonder at classmates for whom it all seems so easy. His teachers say he is not working up to potential and tell him to work harder. He doesn't understand what they mean; after all, he reads the assignments and writes answers to the questions. He is, he thinks, doing what he is supposed to do. It sometimes feels downright pointless.

And then there is Casey. Numbers have always fascinated her, ever since she started counting the big pop-it beads that were in her playpen. Casey, now fourteen, is a math whiz, but she hates the math class, where everything is too easy, and she can't take anything more advanced until she moves up to the senior high school next year. So she waits, and in the meantime, merely struggles by in English and social studies classes, where her talents are more ordinary. She doesn't understand why she can't spend all her time in math and science, why she has to bother with history and English, and why she has to put up with stupid and boring math assignments. Casey is unhappy and is making trouble for herself with her negative attitude and mediocre performance. She is absolutely positive that high school will be different; she will be recognized for the math genius she is, and her teachers will finally appreciate her.

The differences among Anna, Mike, and Casey are enormous, and although they involve all aspects of development, may be viewed as primarily cognitive in nature. That is, the differences among them can be viewed in terms of how their minds function. Investigation into the functioning of the mind is relatively new, even in psychology. **Cognitive psychology**, as a distinct branch of professional interest, is only about thirty years old, even though interest in testing mental abilities has been prevalent since the turn of the century. In this chapter we will examine the concept of both intelligence, or *how much* one knows or is capable of doing in relation to others of the same age, and cognition, or *how* an individual thinks. Both intelligence, which is essentially a quantitative (how much) concept, and cognition, which is a qualitative (how) one, are concerned with knowledge, the acquisition of knowledge, differences between individuals, and developmental differences, or differences as they relate to age. They are different in that people who study intelligence are primarily concerned with differences between individuals and among groups of individuals (the **psychometric approach**), whereas those who study cognition are primarily concerned with differences within the same individual, that is, how thought processes change as a result of maturation (the **developmental approach**). Both groups are interested in the roles played by heredity and environment in the development of intellectual functioning, and both note the significant changes in thinking that occur at adolescence. In addition to these two approaches to the study of the mind, we will discuss the individual differences in ways of learning known as learning styles, and we will note the unique situations of exceptional learners, especially the learning disabled, the gifted, and the creative.

In cognitive psychology as well as in other areas, the nature-nurture controversy continues to challenge those who study people. Obviously, as in all other forms of development, both heredity and environment have significant impact on the quantity and quality of cognition. It is clear, for example, that some mental structures and abilities are genetic, but to what extent, or how nature and nurture interact in any one individual, is far from certain. The psychometric approach generally places more emphasis on the influence of heredity than does the developmental approach, but both recognize the interactive nature of heredity and environment. Elkind (74) summarized the relationship of nature and nurture by pointing out that mental structures or abilities are probably laid down in the genes, but that the environment serves as nourishment for their growth. Environment is certainly influential in determining the content of all thought: for example, which language or languages individuals learn, the particular perspective concerning values or con-

Table 8.1

Psychometric *vs.* Development Approach to Study of Intelligence and Cognition

Psychometric Approach	Developmental Approach
Intelligence is randomly distributed in the population and is determined primarily by heredity. We inherit the quantity and nature of our intelligence.	Genetic factors operate to give cognitive development a definite sequence. We inherit the manner in which our intellect develops.
The contributions of nature and nurture to intelligence are measurable, with nature contributing more than nurture to overall intelligence.	Nature and nurture interact dynamically. We inherit the developmental processes, but the environmental interacts with these processes in varying ways to produce specific abilities.
Intellectual development is a statistical concept, and there is a quantitative increase in mental ability associated with increasing age. A 16-year-old knows *more* than a 10-year-old.	Cognitive development involves the growth of new mental structures, new ways of thinking. A 16-year-old not only knows more than a 10-year-old but actually thinks *differently* than a 10-year-old.
Intelligence (ability) can be measured statistically and is especially useful in predicting school success.	Cognitive development can be studied clinically and is especially important in diagnosing learning problems.

cepts that they acquire, and the cultural aspects of their approach to the world. Genetic ability, however, may determine the upper limit of the mind's functioning, though we as yet may not know exactly what anyone's upper limit is.

Before examining the psychometric approach and the developmental approach to intelligence and cognition in detail, it is useful to summarize their major differences. Table 8.1 does just that. Note that both approaches appreciate the interactive relationship between heredity and environment, but that the psychometric approach places value on measuring the relative weight of each in contributing to individual differences in the population, while the developmental approach doesn't separate their influences. The psychometric approach views intelligence as a fairly static, measurable set of abilities, while the developmental approach emphasizes qualitative differences in thought processes based on maturation and environmental influences. The two approaches should not be thought of as opposed to each other, however, for both are useful and can be seen complementing each other. Each approach studies a different aspect of intelligence or cognition, and each contributes mightily to our still relatively meager understanding of just how the mind functions. The psychometric approach allows us to compare intellectual abilities of individuals and groups and to predict success in school-related tasks. The developmental approach offers us an explanation of how people think and the opportunity to diagnose developmental differences. Both are valuable to our total understanding.

THE QUANTITATIVE APPROACH

Intelligence

Definitions. Although there is no one universally acceptable definition of that which is measured by intelligence tests, most researchers conceive of intelligence as the relative ability to perform various mental functions, including reasoning, understanding, remembering, applying concepts, and manipulating figures. Intelligence is just one component of cognitive function. Along with intelligence, cognitive development and academic achievement also contribute to overall cognitive functioning.

Although intelligence is considered to be an **aptitude,** that is, an innate capability or set of capabilities, it is difficult to measure apart from learned content and therefore is subject to various environmental influences to some degree. Throughout history, such attributes as curiosity, memory, interest, reasoning skills, problem-solving skills, attention span, and even motor coordination have been recognized as aspects of what is commonly referred to as human intelligence, and all of these are tapped in modern methods of assessing intelligence. But not everyone is satisfied with the concept of intelligence as a constellation of abilities. Although we do not yet have it, Wu (80) is convinced that we need a general definition of intelligence instead, one that would represent the coordination of all mental characteristics and the flexibility involved in their interactions. Nevertheless, what is measured is what we can measure; we will examine the components included in current thinking about intelligence a little later in this chapter. First, we shall take a brief look at the history of concepts of intelligence and intelligence testing.

History of intelligence testing. Hundreds of years ago, Plato and Aristotle noted distinctions between rational and emotional aspects of human behavior, and Cicero coined the term "intelligentia" to refer to cognitive abilities (Eysenck, 81). But it wasn't until the early twentieth century that anyone attempted to measure intelligence. At about the same time, Charles Spearman in England, Alfred Binet in France, and Hermann Ebbinghaus in Germany developed the first intelligence tests, based on the assumption that intelligence was distributed normally among all people and that it would be useful to identify those who possessed average, above-average, and below-average intelligence, especially to predict success in school. In the United States, Louis Terman of Stanford University collaborated with Binet, and developed the Stanford-Binet in 1916. This test, which serves as the benchmark of intelligence testing, exemplifies the global-intelligence approach to intelligence testing. Wechsler (58), in contrast, developed the WISC (Wechsler Intelligence Scale for Children) and the WAIS (Wechsler Adult Intelligence Scale) to measure twelve different mental functions grouped into two overall categories, verbal intelligence and performance intelligence. The Wechsler scales allow the tester to pinpoint relative areas of strength and weakness rather than global intelligence alone and thus provide significantly more information than does the Binet test. Knowing that an adolescent has superior visual-motor coordination but less than average vocabulary is more instructive than knowing that her overall intelligence is average.

Components of intelligence. Although each individual intelligence test measures somewhat different mental activities and products, there is general agreement as to the kinds of mental activities that contribute to overall intelligence.

The Wechsler (58) model, widely understood because it is the basis of the WISC and WAIS, conceptualizes global intelligence as composed of verbal and performance components. Within the verbal component are information, comprehension, arithmetic, similarities, vocabulary, and digit span. Within the performance component are picture completion, picture arrangement, block design, object assembly, coding, and images. The relative strengths and weaknesses of the individual on the subscales are combined to form overall intelligence. In addition, the examiner observes the behavior of the testee and notes such emotional variables as persistence, care, and attention in the testing situation.

The I.Q.

Definition. The I.Q. or **intelligence quotient** is a number, derived from performance on a specific test, that determines an individual's relative standing in relation to all other people of the same age taking the same test. With a score of 100 representing the absolute mean or average, any score over 100 indicates performance above average, and any score under 100 indicates performance below average, but each I.Q. test has a different area of allowable variability or potential error, so any one I.Q. measure should never be taken as an absolute indication of constant ability. Any I.Q. measure is only one score on one test taken at one particular time and is subject to variation. Figure 8.1 depicts the distribution of I.Q. scores in the general

Figure 8.1
Distribution of I.Q. Giving Rough Indication of the Meaning of Scores

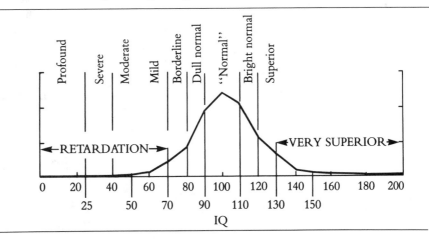

population. Note that all scores between 90 and 110 are considered normal or average, and that approximately two thirds of the population is included between the scores of 80 and 120, or within the range of dull normal, normal, and bright normal.

Heritability. There seems to be little question that the I.Q. becomes increasingly stable from birth to age 18, and that at about 18 an individual's maximum I.Q. score is reached and maintained. There is also little argument that a variety of factors influence I.Q. measures, including anxiety, motivation, cultural biases in the test, and the physical conditions of testing (including distractions, comfort, and lighting), but there is considerable controversy over the more socially sensitive issues of the heritability of I.Q., especially as it might or might not relate to racial, social, and class differences in I.Q. scores.

Arguments for the heritability of I.Q. are most often based on studies of fraternal and identical twins, which clearly demonstrate that identical twins, who share identical genetic constitutions, are more similar to each other than are fraternal twins, who do not share exactly the same genes. From such twin studies, Eysenck (53, 79, 81), as well as others, concluded that intelligence is most likely to be between 70 and 85 percent dependent on genetic inheritance. The heritability argument also notes that I.Q. tends to be similar in families; that the closer the biological relationship, the more similar the I.Q. is likely to be; and that children of different socioeconomic groups have different average I.Q.'s. This last observation, that people from different groups, including racial and socioeconomic groups, have different average I.Q.'s, is an especially controversial issue. Those arguing for heritability tend to argue that one group is genetically more intelligent than another (Jensen, 73), while those arguing for environmental bases of intelligence regard the differences as due to biased testing rather than innate differences (Eysenck, 81).

For example, on I.Q. measures, Jewish people consistently score higher than all other groups, Asian people score next highest, non-Jewish Caucasians rank next, and Blacks next. From a strictly hereditary viewpoint (Jensen, 73), these data would be interpreted to mean that Jews are genetically superior in terms of intelligence; from an environmental or interactional viewpoint (Eysenck, 81), the reasons for the differences would be found in such factors as the artifacts of the test and testing conditions, cultural learning, education, nutrition, discrimination, deprivation, and bias. That differences in test results by various cultural groups exist is fact; the reasons for the differences are open to a variety of interpretations (Eysenck, 81; Page, 79; Jensen, 73).

Another area of interest in intelligence testing is that of the differences between the sexes. Although there are virtually no differences between males and females in overall measures of intelligence, there are some notable differences that occur at adolescence and some long-term differences in terms of specific intellectual abilities. Overall, men are better at spatial tasks: tasks requiring the ability to organize, visualize, and perform quantitative functions. Women are better at verbal tasks: talking, articulating, writing, spelling (Maccoby, 74; Eysenck, 81; Denno, 82;

Wormack, 80). Furthermore, males show more variability in I.Q. scores; that is, they have more very high and very low scores than do females. Interestingly, however, most studies do not show these differences until puberty, and during adolescence, males' scores tend to rise slightly while females' scores decline slightly (Campbell, 76; Denno, 82). Although there are clear differences in cognitive functioning between males and females, their overall intelligence is no different (Maccoby, 74), and the differences between them may be as much a result of differences in socialization as of innate differences.

Although differences among racial and ethnic groups and between males and females are clearly demonstrated, it is necessary to interpret these findings with a word of caution. The differences are frequently quite small, often so small as not to reach statistical significance, and therefore should never be used to indicate the ability of either an individual or a group. The differences should never be used as an indicator of innate superiority or inferiority.

Uses and Misuses of Intelligence Measures

Expectations. Just as we do not have clear scientific evidence concerning the reasons for group differences, neither do we know beyond any reasonable doubt how much influence the expectations of significant adults have on the performance of young people. It has been demonstrated that teacher expectations significantly affect achievement. For example, Rosenthal (68), in *Pygmalion in the Classroom,* reported that in an experiment in an elementary school, 20 percent of the children in a class were randomly selected and labeled as likely to achieve great gains during the year. Eight months later they had, even though they had been randomly picked and there was no evidence on which to make the predictions. Apparently the prophesy of high achievement provided to their teachers became a self-fulling one. Because teachers expected them to achieve, they did. There is no compelling evidence to suggest that the same is not true for measures of intelligence.

Norm referencing. Measures of intelligence are norm referenced; that is, they provide a rough comparison with all others of the same age on the same test. Each score represents only a comparison with other people and does not measure a person's performance against some established criteria for success. By definition, half the population taking a norm referenced test will fall below the mean, but that in itself does not mean the individual will not be successful. These tests do not in themselves provide sufficient information for individual decision making; they neither provide information concerning how the mind processes information, nor do they measure problem-solving skills and social competence. Although intelligence has been found to be related to these qualities, there is no scientific evidence to suggest a direct causal relationship, and we do not know why the relationship exists. For all these reasons, intelligence test results should be used cautiously, and should never be used to predict success in life, which depends on much more than a high score on an intelligence test (Holowinsky, 80; Eysenck, 81; Rosenthal, 80).

Guidelines. Based on this evidence, it is safe to provide the following uses and misuses for intelligence tests. Intelligence tests can be used to:

1. Compare large groups of young people with one another.
2. Compare any group of young people with all other people of the same age.
3. Provide a general indicator, to be correlated with other information, of scholastic aptitude and potential school success.

Intelligence tests should not be used to:

1. Predict individual ability or intelligence.
2. Demonstrate achievement over time.
3. Compare one individual with another.
4. Provide the sole criterion for placement in academic programs.
5. Label individuals.

Conclusions

Conclusions concerning intelligence, from the psychometric point of view, can be summarized as follows:

1. Intellectual abilities can be described.
2. Intellectual abilities can be measured but not with complete accuracy.
3. Measurable intelligence is a product of the interaction of several components.
4. Intelligence has a strong genetic basis.
5. Intelligence is influenced by environmental factors.
6. Measured differences exist among racial, cultural, and socioeconomic groups.
7. Measured differences exist between the sexes.
8. These measured differences may be due to a variety of factors.
9. Further research is needed better to assess the components of intelligence as well as the degree of influence of the various factors contributing to it (Eysenck, 79).
10. Intelligence tests have appropriate and inappropriate uses. Care should be taken to use them appropriately.

PIAGET'S DEVELOPMENTAL APPROACH

Jean Piaget

Jean Piaget, the single most influential theorist in the field of intellectual development, was born in 1896 in Switzerland. His early interest was in biology; he published his first biological paper at the age of 10, and earned his Ph.D. degree at the age of 21. In addition to his fascination with biology, he became intrigued with

epistemology, the philosophy of knowledge and how people know what they know. These two compelling interests led him to the clinical study of children and to the combination of biology and philosophy into his study of how the mind works, which he called **genetic epistemology,** and which, according to Gardner (80), "probes the origins of intellectual structures in children, the evolution of knowledge within specific scientific disciplines, and the parallels that may obtain between these two developmental trajectories" (p. *xxi*).

Background. Piaget worked with Binet in France, but he was much more interested in children's incorrect answers to test items than he was in their correct ones, because the incorrect answers gave better clues as to how the children arrived at their responses. His experiences with children in France led him to become interested, not in the content of the children's thinking as the psychometricians were but in the process of that thinking. He believed that those who were interested in testing intelligence were emphasizing differences between groups rather than looking for the commonalities underlying human thought, and he therefore rejected the standardized test as the way to study intelligence. Instead of searching for a definition of intelligence, he wanted to know how thinking matures from the intelligence characteristic of infancy to that characteristic of adulthood. He therefore developed a clinical method of investigation in which he interacted with individual children, frequently his own, and noted the changes that occurred in their thinking when presented with certain kinds of problems. He studied both normal and abnormal children and supplemented his investigations with reading in philosophy, especially logic (Furth, 70; Ginsberg, 79).

Contributions. Piaget saw mental growth "as an extension of biological growth and as governed by the same principles and laws" (Elkind, 74, p. 129). He looked for the commonalities in development and the processes involved in thinking. His discoveries, which are contained in over 100 articles and 40 books and which focus primarily on the identification of distinct and observable stages of development, revolutionized our thinking about intelligence and thought to the degree that no other theorist has had an impact close to his. In this section we will examine in some detail the basic concepts of Piagetian thinking, the stages of childhood and adolescent development, and the research that both supports and questions the universality of the process he uncovered. These concepts do not contradict the psychometric approach to intelligence, but complement it; both the quantitative approach and the qualitative one contribute to our overall understanding of the content and process of intelligent thought.

Intelligence, as Seen by Piaget

An activity. Whereas the psychometricians view intelligence as a capacity for knowing, Piagetians view it as an activity, the structure of which is laid down in genetics and which is triggered by the active involvement of the learner. Piaget was a **constructivist,** which means that he believed that each of us must actually construct all our knowledge; we do not merely incorporate the already developed knowledge of the world but recreate it in all its complexity. Intelligence involves the adaptation of inherent biological structures, interaction of the individual and the environment, and the maturation of new structures to facilitate the development of new ways of thinking. Furth (70) defined the Piagetian concept of intelligence as ''the totality of available structures within a given organism at a given period of its development'' (p. 19). Furth (70) further differentiated between general knowledge or intelligence, which is the capacity to learn, and specific knowledge or intelligence, which encompasses the particular information that one knows. The activity of intelligence is thought, and whereas intelligence is a function of development that can be described by stages, learning is the acquisition of specific information. Piaget was interested in the former rather than the latter.

Mental structures. Elkind (74) compared the development of intellectual structures to the development of computers:

> The several generations of computers can be likened to the several stages in the development of intelligence. Just as the hardware of the computer determines its memory and speed, so the mental structures at any given level of development determine the limits of the child's learning. Likewise, just as the number of programs run on a computer leaves its speed and memory unaltered, so does the number of problems a child has solved or the number of concepts attained not change his problem-solving or concept-learning capacities. Furthermore, just as we can, with elaborate programming, get the computer to do things it was not intended to do, so we can with specialized training get children to learn things which seem beyond their ken. Such training does not, however, change their capacity to learn any more than an ingenious computer program alters the speed or memory of the computer. (p. 134)

For example, many young children memorize the sounds that make up the Pledge of Allegiance, but they are unable to make meaning from those sounds until they have developed the mental structures that make understanding a concept like allegiance possible. The memorizing does not alter their capacity to understand.

At any particular stage of development, then, the child is capable of certain functions, the purpose of which is either to understand its perceptions or to invent new ones. At all levels, from infancy on, intelligence operates to make sense of the world, and as the child matures, her mental structures develop to allow her to act on the world in qualitatively different ways. The intelligence of the child, then, is not merely less than that of the adult but qualitatively different from it.

Basic Piagetian Concepts

Before studying the stages of development discovered by Piaget, it is useful to clarify the basic concepts that undergird his work. Throughout his writing Piaget emphasized the ways the mind adapted incoming information to its current capabilities for understanding, how it adapted itself as new capabilities emerged, and the continual interaction of the mind and environment in dynamic development. As Elkind (74) pointed out, the processes involved are **adaptation** (through **assimilation** and **accommodation**) and **equilibration**.

Assimilation and accommodation. Adaptation of the mind and the environment to each other occurs through the complementary processes of assimilation and accommodation, which are the two modes of incorporating incoming information. When we use the process of assimilation we transform incoming information to fit into our already existing forms of knowledge. In writing this chapter, I developed an outline and had a concept of the material that would be included. Then, when researching the field, I easily assimilated all the information that I found that fit readily into my outline. But when I found something that didn't fit into my preconceived outline, I had to choose between ignoring that bit of information and accommodating my outline to allow for its inclusion. In those instances in which the material was important to the chapter, I had to change my existing outline (my existing form of knowledge) in order to accommodate that which challenged my original structure.

Equilibration. Assimilation and accommodation are reciprocal and complementary processes, which together account for cognitive growth and learning. They are regulated by the higher-order process known as equilibration, the continual balancing act between assimilation and accommodation that allows us to use both productively. Equilibration helps to explain the development from one stage to a higher-order one. ''Mental growth can thus be seen as a progressive series of attempted assimilations, necessary accommodations, and new equilibrated assimilations at a higher level'' (Elkind, 74, p. 8).

Stage Development

Piaget's theory of cognitive development is one of the stage theories, the general characteristics of which we discussed in Chapter 1. Before examining Piaget's stages in detail, let's review stage development as it applies to this theory in particular. Piaget (69) outlined the following as general characteristics of his theory of development:

1. The sequence of the stages is constant and universal. Everyone progresses through the stages in exactly the same order, although intelligence and training may account for some variation in the age at which a stage is reached. Furthermore, movement is always one stage at a time.
2. Each stage is distinguishable from the others by the unique mental operations that characterize it. These operations can be observed in all the mental activities of the individual, whether solving problems or at play.

3. Each new stage develops from the preceding one, which it integrates into itself, "and prepares for the subsequent one, into which it is sooner or later itself integrated" (Piaget, 69, p. 153). As the individual matures, the next stage of reasoning becomes increasingly attractive, and the cognitive maturation allows the individual to be challenged by slightly more sophisticated thinking rather than overwhelmed by that which is too advanced to begin to comprehend.

4. Physical maturation plays an important but limited role in the development of new stages, with accelerations and delays in development being attributed to differences in heredity, environment, and experience. Development is a product of the continual interaction of maturation and experience. Thus the ages that Piaget ascribed to different stages are only averages, yet "mental growth is inseparable from physical growth: the maturation of the nervous and endocrine systems, in particular, continues until the age of sixteen" (Piaget, 69, p. *vii*). It is not coincidence that accounts for the adult stage of reasoning being met in middle adolescence, for physiological development sets limits to what can be learned at each preceding stage of development.

5. Movement from stage to stage is dependent on four factors: the maturation of the nervous and endocrine systems; exercise of cognitive functions in one stage that prepare the mind for movement to the next stage; social experiences; and the equilibration between assimilation and accommodation. For movement from one stage to another, then, the mind must be physiologically ready, experientially ready, socially ready, and challenged to move on to the next higher form of reasoning.

Childhood Stages

Prior to adolescence, Piaget found, children progress through three distinct stages of mental development, each characterized by certain mental operations that eventually evolve into those of the next higher stage. The childhood stages are the **sensorimotor** (birth to about two years), the **preoperational** (about two to seven years), and the **concrete operational** (about seven to twelve years, though sometimes extending well into adolescence, and sometimes never developing further).

Sensorimotor stage. The intelligence of infancy is called sensorimotor because it is apparent only in action; the infant does not "think" other than **sensing** (seeing, hearing, touching, smelling) in the immediate moment and **doing,** or acting on its perceptions. During these first two years of life, children's intelligence progresses from responding only to their own sense of comfort and discomfort to being able to reconstruct in their minds objects that are no longer present to their senses. With the end of the sensorimotor period comes the beginning of true thinking because for the first time children are capable of expanding their thought beyond the immediate and present and remembering images that are not sensorily available.

Preoperational stage. Between the ages of two and seven or eight the child is in the preoperational stage, which is characterized by the gradual acquisition and sophistication of the ability to symbolize. During this period the child develops symbolic play (a pointed finger represents a gun), the ability to imitate animals or other people, the acquisition of language, and the capacity to form mental images and represent them through drawing. In this stage the child neither separates symbol and object nor distinguishes between fantasy and reality. This latter characteristic is what makes fairy tales, Santa Claus, and night terrors real, even in the face of conflicting evidence.

One of the hallmarks of this stage is also the inability to create notions of conservation. For example, a preoperational child can be shown a glass of water. If you then pour the water into another glass that is taller and thinner than the original glass and ask the child which glass contains more water, the child will say that the taller glass does. This will occur again and again, even if you continue to pour the same amount of water from one glass to the other. In Piagetian terms, the child has not yet developed the notion of conservation of matter (that the amount of water does not change) and responds purely on the basis of which glass *appears* to have more water; that is, taller equals more.

Concrete operational stage. Piaget (69) described the stage of concrete operations, from age seven to age twelve or beyond, as "a transition from subjective centering in all areas to a decentering that is at once cognitive, social, and moral" (p. 128). Concrete operations allow children to form mental operations, to do in their heads what they previously could only do through physical manipulation. Concrete operations allow children to form inversions of things and to understand concepts like reciprocity; that is, children can mentally reconstruct images, reverse situations, and predict the outcomes of such reconstructions and reversions. All these mental operations are applied to things, not to abstractions, but they allow children to reason about those things. Children can do thought problems and mentally manipulate objects into a variety of possible classifications and relationships. As a result of concrete operations, children can take the point of view of another, judge truth and falsity, and reason from rules to instances; these characteristics make them oriented to reality (no longer believing in Santa), and capable of working cooperatively, engaging in organized play, and benefiting from formal instruction (Elkind, 74).

Formal Operations

Just as development from preoperational to concrete operational thinking is marked by movement from fantasy to reality, development from concrete operational to formal operational thinking is marked by movement from reality to possibility. In adolescence, young people have the opportunity to develop hypothetical reasoning skills, increased use of logic, and abstract thinking, marked by the ability to think about thought itself. They are capable of reasoning about contrary-to-fact propositions (for example, reasoning from the point of view of someone with whom they disagree), imagining ideal futures, and understanding the subtleties of metaphor and political cartoons.

Characteristics. Ginsberg (79) identified five fundamental characteristics of formal operational thought:

1. Reality is secondary to possibility; the ability to reason about alternative futures allows formal operational adolescents to imagine what might occur in the future if specific events occur in the present.
2. A combinatorial system develops; the formal operational thinker is capable of imagining all possible combinations of factors in any variety and number.
3. Thinking becomes increasingly flexible; the formal operational thinker can deal with events and factors from a variety of perspectives and is not likely to be confused by unanticipated outcomes.
4. The formal operational thinker tends to become involved in theoretical matters and develops grandiose plans to reorganize society, sometimes to the extent of losing touch and patience with the real world.
5. The formal operational thinker is capable of developing feelings toward ideals and concepts instead of only toward people.

An example. This new capacity for hypothesizing and dealing with propositions can be seen in the approach formal operational thinkers take to the pendulum problem that Piaget used as one test of formal operational thinking. In this experiment the subject is presented with the variables relating to the action of a pendulum — the weight at the end of the pendulum, the length of the pendulum, the force of release of the pendulum, and the height from which the pendulum begins swinging — and is asked to determine which of the four variables determines the speed at which the pendulum swings.

A concrete operational thinker presented with a variety of weights, a variety of lengths, and a variety of heights from which to drop the pendulum is likely to assume that weight is the controlling factor, so will try several different weights. Even after discovering that the second weight does not alter the speed, a concrete operational thinker is likely to have difficulty eliminating weight as a factor and might then vary both height and weight, or randomly vary all four factors, and eventually find some reason to support the assumption that weight is the significant variable. Or, she might try a number of different alternatives and may even discover the correct answer but will do so by trial and error rather than by logical hypothesizing.

In contrast to this method, the formal operational thinker uses a logical propositional method that "consists in dissociating factors according to previously stated hypotheses and in varying them experimentally, one by one, while neutralizing all the others, or in combining them in various ways" (Piaget, 70, p. 51). When

Piaget used a pendulum problem as a test of formal operational thinking.

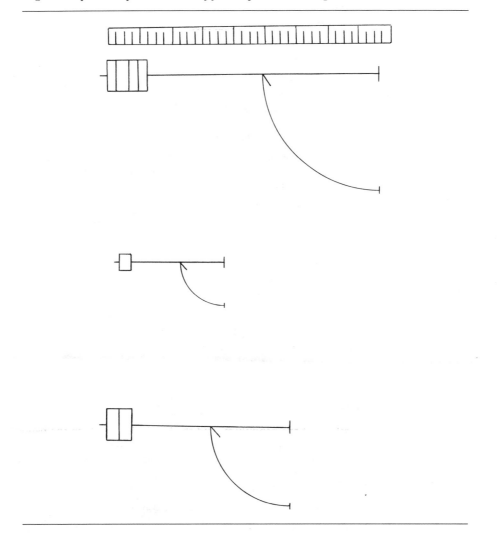

presented with the pendulum problem, the formal operational thinker may also hypothesize that weight is the controlling variable, and so first vary the weight while holding the length, force, and height constant. If a change of weight does not alter the speed, as it will not, she then rules out the original hypothesis, forms a new one, and varies that factor while holding the others constant. If the speed is affected, she has found the answer. If not, there is another variable to try. The answer is found efficiently. This experiment clearly identifies the fundamental properties of formal operational thought: the adolescent is able to derive a proposition from several variables, hypothesize the possible effect of the variables on one another, and combine and separate the variables in a logical and efficient manner (Gallagher, 76).

The results of these new capabilities in adolescence are seen in the adolescent's ability to reason, be introspective, and deal with the future as a reality. We will discuss the social and emotional consequences of these possibilities a little later. We first must address the attainment of formal operations and the variations in that attainment that appear in adolescents and adults.

Attainment. Like the attainment of the other stages of cognitive development, formal operations depend on neurological and hormonal readiness, individual opportunity to use mental operations in experimental situations, a social environment that encourages development, and the equilibration factor, or felt inadequacy of old mental operations to deal with new problems. But it has been noted that not all people attain formal operations. Schooling apparently has a much greater effect on the development of formal operations than on the development of concrete operations, which are attained by all but the profoundly retarded. Neimark (75), however, found that socioeconomic status has no known effect, sex is not a factor, I.Q. higher than a minimal level is apparently not a factor, and education is a factor only where profound differences in education occur. Although Piaget generally set early adolescence as the time of capability for attaining formal operations, more recent research supports the finding that formal operations develop throughout adolescence and that students who remain in high school become increasingly competent in formal operational tasks as they progress through the high school grades (Treagust, 82).

Beyond Piaget. Psychometricians and cognitive psychologists have criticized Piaget's work because it does not lend itself to standardized measures and because there may be some inconsistencies in the model and in the research data supporting it. There is also a considerable controversy between those who would like to develop a valid and reliable method of assessing attainment of cognitive stages and those who see no value in such tests. Roberge (82) developed and validated a test of formal operations. The FORT (Formal Operational Reasoning Test) tests for the subject's ability to form combinations, to use propositional logic, and to determine proportionality. If such a test is used to diagnose developmental problems, which can then be remediated through direct teaching, and not used merely to label and classify groups or individuals, the objections to such a test would be satisfactorily addressed. It was also found by Eysenck (79) that tests of attainment of Piagetian stages give similar results to those obtained by I.Q. tests; he therefore concluded that Piaget's work supports and is consistent with the work of the psychometricians.

Cognitive psychologists have embraced Piaget's findings and incorporated his theories but certainly are not satisfied that all questions concerning mental functioning are now answered. Riegel (73, 76), for example, has proposed a fifth stage of cognitive development, **dialectical operations,** which involve the individual's production of new problems and ability to alter the environment rather than the solution of old ones.

Variations in Development

Cross-cultural studies by Piaget and others (Piaget, 69, 70; Orbell, 81; de Fonseca, 80; Flavell, 77) have demonstrated that cognitive development through concrete operations is universal for all but the severely retarded, with some slight variation in time of onset dependent on environmental factors. These researchers have also demonstrated that formal operational thinking is present in virtually all cultures in all parts of the world, with considerable evidence of socioeconomic and educational factors facilitating development of formal operations. But it seems that, unlike concrete operations, formal operations are not universal; Keating (80) found that 37 percent of eleventh graders did not operate formally on physical science problems, and Murray (78) found that 25 percent of college students did not use formal operations on a problem in probability. If these educated young people did not use formal operations, we can only surmise at the vast numbers of less educated who do not use them.

Selective formal operations. The fact that large numbers of normal people do not achieve formal operations is accounted for in two primary ways (Ginsberg, 79): either a deprived social and educational environment does not encourage the development of formal operations, or many people use formal operations only in areas of particular interest for them. Piaget favored the latter interpretation. If it is true that we might be selective in our use of formal operations, with a lawyer using them in matters pertaining to the law and a mechanic using them in problems pertaining to engines, a great deal of variation would occur based on the results of one test. Most Piagetian experiments are concerned with problems in mathematics and science; these may discriminate against the individual who favors human and social issues. ''One cannot infer the lack of competence from a subject's failure at some conventional task which is inappropriate to his interests or culture'' (Ginsberg, 79, p. 202).

Flavell (77) referred to the phenomenon of individual's exhibiting formal operations selectively as ''ecological validity,'' and used the example of Kalahari Bushmen, who, although uneducated in the traditional sense, showed remarkable inferential and analytical skills when tracking animals, where they had to make inferences, hypothesize about probable animal behavior, test their hypotheses, and adapt their thinking to new discoveries. This theory also explains the adolescent who has tremendous difficulty in analyzing chemistry experiments but is highly adept at using foresight, judgment, and split-second analytical skills on the football field. The observation that many adolescents and adults fail to use formal operations may then be the result of inflexible testing rather than a true measure of capability.

Education and practice. Piaget believed that all adolescents are capable of formal operations, but that all do not use them in all situations. Elements like boredom, fatigue, and lack of interest mitigate against their use (Ginsberg, 79). Danner (77) also demonstrated the availability of formal operations in a study in which younger and older adolescents who did not demonstrate formal operations were coached in their use. The older adolescents quickly began to use the coached skills, but the younger ones did not, even after several coaching sessions. The researchers concluded that studies that assess formal operations without prompting may underestimate the competence of the subjects. Linn (81) also demonstrated that expectations influence formal thinking skills; when the subjects identified with the variable involved in a mental task, they used formal operational skills.

In summary, it seems reasonably clear that all normal and bright adolescents develop the capacity for formal operations, some earlier than others, that most of us are somewhat selective in our application of formal operations, that formal operational thinking is facilitated by appropriate education, and that our use of formal operations is affected by interest, practice, and motivation.

Implications for education. Piagetian concepts of cognitive development have been used as the basis for curriculum development, especially in elementary schools, where the focus is on the child rather than on the subjects to be learned. They have not, however, had much educational impact at the secondary level, where the content or subject becomes the focus of the curriculum. All too often, teachers and text writers assume that adolescents have attained formal operations and are therefore capable of learning through reading and lecture alone. More progressive programs at the middle- and high-school level recognize that many adolescents are still in concrete operations and need more experiential learning methods to develop the concepts associated with secondary-school subjects.

OTHER QUALITATIVE APPROACHES

Piaget's stage theory of cognitive growth is the most comprehensive and most widely known of the qualitative approaches to understanding the functioning of the human mind, but it is not the only one. The work of Epstein (78) and Toepfer (79) in studying the growth of the brain lends support to Piaget's observations, and the work of Klausmeier (78) offers a slightly different but complementary analysis of the qualitative changes in mental activity noted throughout the developmental period.

Brain Growth

Growth. Herman Epstein (78) studied the physiological growth of the brain and by so doing presented biological evidence of the neurological changes that allow for cognitive development. By eighteen months of age, the brain has all the brain cells it will ever have, but it is far from mature. Growth continues, in identifiable spurts

Figure 8.2
Brain Growth and Periodization

Piaget's Stages	AGE	Epstein's Stages
	0	
Sensorimotor	1	Brain growth/new structures possible
	2	Periodization/no new structures
	3	Brain growth/new structures possible
	4	
Preoperational	5	Periodization/no new structures
	6	
	7	Brain growth/new structures possible
	8	
	9	Periodization/no new structures
	10	
Concrete operational	11	Brain growth/new structures possible
	12	
	13	Periodization/no new structures
	14	
	15	Brain growth/new structures possible
	16	
Formal operational	17	
	18	

Adapted from Toepfer, Conrad F. "Brain Growth Periodization: A New Dogma." *Middle School Journal,* 1979, p. 3, 18–20.

associated with specific ages, by the increasing complexity of the nerve networks feeding the brain. This growth occurs in five distinct stages, between three and ten months, two and four years, six and eight years, ten and twelve years, and fourteen and sixteen years (Figure 8.2). Only during periods of growth are new mental operations possible, so only during these periods can the child move to the next higher stage of mental development.

Periodization. The periods of no growth — four to six years, eight to ten years, and twelve to fourteen years — are known as times of **periodization,** and during these times no new mental activities are possible. As Figure 8.2 demonstrates, the times of brain growth coincide with the times identified by Piaget as times of readiness to move to the next higher stage. Although Piaget was probably unaware of this brain growth research, it is likely that he would have welcomed biological evidence of the neurological readiness that he inferred as one of the factors contributing to cognitive development. Epstein and Toepfer both noted that no higher-order thinking skills can be initiated during times of periodization; therefore, if young adolescents have not attained formal operational thinking by the time they are twelve years old, they are not likely to attain it until they are at least fourteen. Since 95 percent of twelve-year-olds have not attained formal operations, Toepfer argued that middle schools should not be presenting students with formal operational tasks but should concentrate instead on refining concrete operational skills. (Refer back to Chapter 5 for a more detailed discussion of middle-school curricular issues.)

Problem Solving

Klausmeier (78) and his associates conducted an extensive longitudinal and cross-sectional study in which 400 adolescents were each tested three times over a number of years to assess their attainment of problem-solving skills. Through this study he

True problem solving emerges after the mastery of the concrete and identity levels.

demonstrated the validity of four propositions: 1) individuals attain four successively higher levels of the same concept in an invariant sequence; 2) individual attainment and use of these concepts vary somewhat; 3) the same individual will attain different levels for different concepts at different ages; and 4) higher-level understanding of concepts allows more efficiency in the mental skills of understanding relationships, understanding principles, and solving problems. With effective problem-solving skills the end point of Klausmeier's developmental scheme, the similarity of this to Piaget's theory is evident.

Klausmeier's research revealed that the higher-order skills of understanding principles, understanding taxonomic relationships, and true problem solving emerge only after the mastery of the concrete and identity levels. None of the adolescents in his study achieved these skills before high school, and a significant portion of them never did. He associated slow development with specific and preventable factors: a poor home and family situation; an inadequate curriculum; poor instruction; poor relations with teachers, parents, and school; absenteeism; lack of reading skills; low self-esteem; and low achievement motivation. Although he identified a cooperative relationship between the home and school as the single most important factor in facilitating mental growth, he unfortunately, though not surprisingly, offered no concrete methods of attaining such cooperation or of preventing the factors associated with slow development.

SOCIAL-EMOTIONAL EFFECTS OF COGNITIVE DEVELOPMENT

Egocentrism

Definition. The most fascinating concomitant of cognitive development is the phenomenon known as **egocentrism,** which ''would seem to be a useful starting point for any attempt to reconcile cognitive structure and the dynamics of personality'' (Elkind, 74, p. 95). The term egocentrism is often misunderstood; it is *not* synonymous with selfishness or self-centeredness but rather refers to the universal characteristic of being centered on an individual point of view and unable to see the views of others. A historical example serves to illustrate: at one time all people believed that the universe revolved around the earth, and it was inconceivable to them, based on their observations, that any other system was possible. When Copernicus advanced a conflicting theory, that the earth was merely a part of a universe that revolved around the sun, he was considered foolish at best, an obviously egocentric attitude.

Just as the people of Copernicus's time were cognitively unable to conceive of an alternative point of view, so too each of us is subject to egocentric views. This very human characteristic offers us a link between cognitive and affective theories, for it is the result of mental structures and operations and is seen in emotional and social situations as well as cognitive ones.

In general, growth involves a progression from egocentric to nonegocentric thought (Piaget, 70; Elkind, 74; Muuss, 82a,b; Wegner, 77). As we mature, we become increasingly sociocentric and develop ever increasing objectivity, reciprocity, and relativity. We discover illusions, learn that appearance and reality are not always equivalent, develop increased capacity for role taking and for seeing the world from other points of view, and learn that things exist in relation to other things. We move from total nondifferentiation of self from the world (infancy), to self-awareness (early childhood), to differentiating ourselves from others (childhood), and finally to understanding the concept of reciprocity (childhood and adolescence).

Relationship to cognitive development. This decentering process is never complete, nor does egocentrism manifest itself in exactly the same way at each stage of development. The mental structures and the operations that they allow create unique forms of egocentrism related to each stage of cognitive development, and just as each new stage of cognitive development incorporates within it the preceding stages, so too each new stage of egocentrism incorporates the earlier stages without being tied to them.

At the sensorimotor stage, egocentrism is seen in the child's inability to differentiate between an object and the sense impressions associated with that object. If the child doesn't see a ball, it doesn't exist for her. She also does not separate herself from her environment: she may cry when she scratches her face, but doesn't know that *she* caused the hurt.

At the preoperational stage, she fails to distinguish between words and their referents, between dreams and reality, or between her feelings and those she ascribes to others. She fully believes that her teddy bear has feelings, that the moon and stars can talk to her, and that Mickey Mouse is as real as Daddy. She cannot put herself into the position of another, and when she continues to pester her parents she does so because she is unable to fathom any view but her own. She is unable to coordinate her efforts with other children, and although they may play in the same vicinity, each child is playing alone, each following her own rules, talking only about herself, and unable to attend to the needs or wishes of others.

At the concrete operational level, she doesn't know the difference between what she thinks and what she perceives and is unable to distinguish between facts and opinions. She therefore appears to be stubbornly wedded to her ideas, which she perceives as fact, and is frequently willing to alter the facts to fit her assumptions. She develops "cognitive conceit" (Elkind, 74, p. 80), which leads her to believe that she is always right and that an adult who is found wanting in one area is likely to be wanting in all areas. She becomes a know-it-all.

Quite obviously, we who have grown beyond these childhood stages of development look with amusement upon them but may also be aware that, despite our continued growth, we sometimes revert to earlier modes of thinking. Superstitions, for example, are but an adult version of preoperational egocentrism, and who among us has *not* blamed a typewriter for our grammatical or spelling errors!

Adolescent egocentrism. With the availability of formal operations, the adolescent develops the characteristic egocentrism of adolescence: she is now capable of recognizing that other people have other thoughts, but she is likely to assume that their thoughts are just like hers; specifically, that everyone in her environment is as concerned with her, especially her appearance, as she is. She assumes that everyone is as aware of her flaws and as critical of her as she is, and she is therefore susceptible to a variety of behaviors that serve either to draw attention to her or to divert it from her: attention-getting behavior, conformity to the standards of the peer group, self-consciousness, self-criticism, fads in clothing and hairstyles, disrespect, risk-taking behavior, and the need for privacy from adults (Muuss, 82). Adolescent egocentrism also results in two identifiable phenomena of adolescence: the **personal fable** and the **imaginary audience** (Elkind, 74).

Personal fable. The personal fable results from overemphasis on personal experience and leads the adolescent to the belief that she is unique, not only realistically unique in that there is no one else quite like her, but *historically* unique in that no one has ever felt the same feelings, thought the same thoughts, or endured the same humiliations as she. Along with the sense of uniqueness, which results from introspection and manifests itself in adolescent poetry, diaries, and impatient expressions of ''You couldn't possibly understand!'' is a false sense of power and indestructibility, which manifests itself in foolish risk-taking behavior: flings with alcohol and drugs, unprotected intercourse, and accidents of all kinds based on the belief that ''It won't happen to me.''

Imaginary audience. Along with the personal fable is the imaginary audience, the belief that others are as concerned about the adolescent's appearance and behavior as she is. She fancies herself the focus of all attention, either admiring or critical depending on her own view of herself. She may develop extreme self-consciousness or even boorishness, along with the conformity and attention-getting or attention-avoiding behavior. The frequent short flings of adolescence may be accounted for here, in that each of the two young adolescents is so concerned with her or himself that each literally pays little to no attention to the other, with a resulting disaster as far as a companionate relationship is concerned.

The importance of the imaginary audience is most noticeable in early adolescence and more prevalent in girls than boys, though boys are certainly not protected from it (Elkind, 79). I know of one young adolescent boy who was so concerned that his new pants had the right label that he removed such a label from another article of clothing and sewed it into the inside of the waistband of the pants. Apparently his imaginary audience could even see inside his trousers!

Elkind (79) developed a scale to measure the prevalence of the imaginary audience, and it has been used with some interesting results. Anolik (81) found that delinquents express greater concern with the imaginary audience than nondelinquents, a finding which is interpreted to explain their heightened attention-getting behavior (Chandler, 73). He also found, contrary to Elkind's (79) finding, that males worry more than females about the imaginary audience. C. Peterson (82) found no evidence that the imaginary audience is a purely adolescent phenomenon, nor that it is associated only with the advent of formal operational thought, but that it did decrease with increasing age and heterosexual involvement for males. Common observation and personal experience would support the idea that it is not only an adolescent phenomenon: can you recall the last time you were out in public and noticed that something you were wearing was stained, torn, or inappropriate, and how you became so obsessed with the flaw that your interactions with others were significantly affected by it? You were likely the victim of your own imaginary audience; the flaw may not have been noticed by your colleagues. G. Adams (82a) studied the relationship of parental socialization styles and the prevalence of the imaginary audience and found that both perceived overprotection and perceived rejection by parents were associated with increased imaginary audience reports. Both apparently heightened the self-consciousness of adolescents.

Adolescent egocentrism results in the commonly observed behaviors of adolescents: self-criticism, time spent grooming, modesty, need for privacy, conformity, ease of embarrassment, and feelings of shame all increase in adolescence.

Egocentrism in adolescence is overcome through maturation and systematic training in social perspective taking — for example, role playing, theater production, and verbal exercises that require taking the point of view of another (Chandler, 73; Elkind, 74). Through these processes the adolescent gradually learns to differentiate between her own thoughts and feelings and those of others, and learns that others sometimes react differently than she does. This social perspective taking increases throughout adolescence, with older adolescents displaying significantly less egocentric behavior than young adolescents (Enright, 79, 80b).

Idealism

A closely related phenomenon of adolescence is idealism. "Adolescents cannot and will not understand why the rest of the world does not accept their idealistic solutions to social, economic, or sociological problems, and they may get angry and express unwillingness to accept reality" (Muuss, 82, p. 257). Idealism comes from the potential for thinking about all possibilities, untempered by actual experience. Adolescents conceive of ideal families, ideal schools, ideal religious institutions, and ideal societies, and may rebel against the imperfect ones they experience. They may become hypercritical, messianic, and impatient; they may identify with the weak and the underdog and may dedicate themselves (for a little while, anyway) to the latest ideal. Although this behavior is sometimes frustrating to adults who must listen to their passion, Menge (82) pointed out that "active imagination and the dreaming of ideals are not wasteful activities nor a function of past poets and writers, but can be a constructive part of everyone's life, making for the improvement of human functioning in a socially meaningful way" (p. 419). Indeed, without the idealism of youth, what social reforms would endure?

Learning Styles

If egocentrism provides one way of reconciling cognitive development with personality, learning styles provide another. In the past twenty years, the apparent personality differences that contribute to the unique preferences for ways of learning have been the topic of a variety of studies. These investigations have uncovered cognitive, emotional, physiological, environmental, and social components of learning style, and have combined several of these components into models of learning style.

The cognitive differences include preferences in ways of perceiving, forming concepts and retaining information; the affective factors include motivation, attention, and valuing; the physiological differences include preferences for hearing, seeing, or touching; and environmental differences refer to such things as social interaction and preferences for heat and light differences. These data have important implications for understanding the variety of cognitive behavior displayed by adolescents and offer us some insight as to why not all adolescents thrive in the same educational environments.

Field Independence and Field Dependence

Perceptual differences. Witkin (75, 77a,b) referred to specific and characteristic modes of cognitive functioning that occur throughout our intellectual activities pervasively and consistently. Each of us develops a typical approach to receiving information, forming concepts, retaining information, generating hypotheses, and solving problems. The most significant research into this area of functioning is that of Witkin (54, 75, 77a,b), who conducted extensive studies into the degree of influence of the surrounding environment on an individual's perceptions. He and his colleagues differentiated **field-dependent** and **field-independent** thinkers. Field dependents are heavily influenced by the background or context in which an item is embedded and are not competent at separating the component parts. Field independents perceive items more discretely and are readily able to separate the components. When listening to a piece of music, for example, field independents will be far more able to isolate the sound of individual instruments then field dependents, who will hear only the meld of sounds.

Information processing. In addition to differences in attending to stimuli, the field dependence-independence concept also describes characteristic modes of processing information. Field independents rely on internal cues, analyze wholes into parts, and work independently. Field dependents process the whole rather than the parts, rely on contextual cues, and are likely to consult with others. Cross (76) noted further differences between field independents and field dependents:

1. Whereas field dependents perceive the world as a whole and emphasize relationships, field independents tend to separate items and to approach the world analytically.

2. Field independents are less socialized than field dependents.

3. Field dependents are more influenced by authority and by peers.

4. Field dependents better remember social information.

5. Field independents refer more to themselves than to others, while field dependents refer more to others.

6. Field dependents prefer social occupations, while field independents prefer analytical occupations.

7. Field-dependent learners and teachers prefer discussion and democratic classrooms, while field independents prefer lectures and direct influence.

8. Field dependents are more affected by criticism than field independents.

9. Both field dependents and field independents prefer people like themselves; matching promotes acceptance.

Gallagher (76), in a review of the literature on cognitive style and formal operations, reported that field independents are more likely than field dependents to achieve formal operations, a finding that supports Witkin's contention that field independents are generally superior in traditional academic tasks. Flexer (80) also proposed a link between formal operations and field independence and suggested that cognitive style may be the source of variability in the performance of formal operational tasks, tests of which have been analytical in nature. Perhaps future research ought to seek to develop tests of formal operational thinking that tap into the skills of field-dependent learners rather than field-independent learners. The football star we discussed earlier may well be able to demonstrate formal operational skills when tested for them in the context of a social rather than an analytical approach.

Career choice. In addition to identifying the different skills of field dependents and field independents, the concept also is predictive of fields of study and occupation. Witkin (77a) surveyed over 1400 college students and found that knowledge of cognitive style predicted college major and eventual occupation. Field independents were more likely to major in mathematics and the sciences, areas in which independent endeavor is most important; while field dependents were more likely to choose education, social work, nursing, and personnel work, areas that emphasize social interaction.

The Dunn Model

Dunn (79) defined learning style as "the manner in which at least 18 different elements from five basic types of stimuli affect a person's ability to absorb and retain. The combination and variations among these elements suggest that few people learn in exactly the same way, just as few people think exactly alike" (p. 41).

The stimuli and elements included are: (1) environmental stimuli (preferences for different levels of sound, light, temperature, and different kinds of furniture, as well as preferences for hearing, seeing, reading, manipulating, and moving); (2) emotional stimuli (degree of motivation, persistence, responsibility, and structure); (3) sociological stimuli (preferences for working with colleagues, alone, with one partner, and preferences for authority and supervision); and (4) cognitive stimuli (field independence *vs.* dependence, a global *vs.* an analytical approach, and a tendency toward reflective *vs.* impulsive decision making). Although an extensive analysis of these many components is beyond the scope of this book, it is nevertheless important to be aware of the vast number of individual differences that contribute to learning.

Just as most of our tests of intelligence seem to rely on the qualities associated with field dependence, so too do most middle-school and junior-high and high-school programs emphasize only some components of learning style. Most high-school teachers, for example, rely on lecture and reading. Unfortunately, students whose styles differ from the one acceptable one end up being labeled either slow or uncooperative or both. Attention to these components of learning style are not adequately addressed in this country's secondary schools.

Hemispherality

The dual brain.   Another aspect of learning style and cognitive functioning that has become increasingly studied in recent years is the functioning of the two halves of the human brain. The human brain is divided into two essentially similar hemispheres, each resembling half of a walnut. Although the two halves look alike, they do not function alike. Brain researchers have known for 150 years that brain dominance is related to handedness, for example, and that language and language-related activities are usually controlled by the left hemisphere. They have known this from studying people who suffer brain injuries; if the left brain is affected, so is the right side of the body and most language functions (Edwards, 79).

The two halves of the brain both perceive the world differently and respond differently; that we are not aware of the different functioning is due to the nerve network (corpus callosum) that connects the two halves and allows impulses to travel between them (Edwards, 79).

Our dual brain allows us to think and respond both rationally and intuitively, verbally and nonverbally. You are using both sides of your brain when you carefully weigh the alternatives in an election, and then vote on your gut instinct as to which person is the better candidate, or when you listen to a speaker and recognize that her words make a great deal of sense but find yourself intuitively feeling untrusting of her. The right brain is the intuitive side, the left the logical side. Edwards (79) presented the two modes of functioning as in Table 8.2.

Even the style of the lettering in Table 8.2 representing the left and right modes is indicative of the difference in style of the two halves of the brain. The left brain verbalizes, abstracts, counts, reads, writes, does math, plans sequentially, uses logic, and thinks rationally. The right brain innovates, is creative and aesthetic, appreciates

Table 8.2
A Comparison of Left-Mode and Right-Mode Characteristics

L—MODE	**R**—MODE
Verbal: Using words to name, describe, define.	*Nonverbal:* Awareness of things, but minimal connection with words.
Analytic: Figuring things out step-by-step and part-by-part.	*Synthetic:* Putting things together to form wholes.
Symbolic: Using a symbol to *stand for* something. For example, the drawn form ⊙ stands for *eye,* the sign + stands for the process of addition.	*Concrete:* Relating to things as they are, at the present moment.
Abstract: Taking out a small bit of information and using it to represent the whole thing.	*Analogic:* Seeing likenesses between things; understanding metaphoric relationships.
Temporal: Keeping track of time, sequencing one thing after another. Doing first things first, second things second, etc.	*Nontemporal:* Without a sense of time.
Rational: Drawing conclusions based on *reason* and *facts.*	*Nonrational:* Not requiring a basis of reason or facts; willingness to suspend judgment.
Digital: Using numbers as in counting.	*Spatial:* Seeing where things are in relation to other things, and how parts go together to form a whole.
Logical: Drawing conclusions based on logic: one thing following another in logical order — for example, a mathematical theorem or a well-stated argument.	*Intuitive:* Making leaps of insight, often based on incomplete patterns, hunches, feelings, or visual images.
Linear: Thinking in terms of linked ideas, one thought directly following another, often leading to a convergent conclusion.	*Holistic:* Seeing whole things all at once; perceiving the overall patterns and structures, often leading to divergent conclusions.

From B. Edwards, 1979, p. 40.

how parts make up wholes, understands metaphors, dreams, and uses intuition and insight (Edwards, 79; Reynolds, 78; McCallum, 79; Torrance, 80; Gowan, 79).

The right half of the brain is not under good verbal control; we don't reason with it, and we can't sequence, rationalize, categorize, or name with it. Because it is not verbal, it was once thought to be subordinate to the more verbal, rational left brain, but researchers are now believing that neither half is superior to the other. They are merely different, and both are valuable to human functioning.

Although the two halves of the brain look alike, they don't function alike.

Educational response. Unfortunately, just as secondary schools tend to ignore all learning styles that do not depend on reading and listening skills in the context of an authoritarian relationship, so too do schools emphasize the activities of the left brain and either ignore those of the right brain or allow them only in the context of the arts curriculum. Schools, curriculum, and teaching are sequenced, verbal, numerical, analytical, and scheduled — all left-brain functions. The right brain is harder to work with, for to do so means involvement in imagination, alternative perceptions, nonverbal knowing, intuition, and leaps of insights. "Ah-ha!" experiences do not lend themselves to grades, seats in rows, or language and math.

In elementary schools, both sides of the brain are valued; children are encouraged to dream and to count, to use body expression and to verbalize, to move and to sit quietly. But in secondary schools, the right-brain functions are valued far less; success in high school is defined by left-brain success. The adolescent who functions better in a holistic, intuitive, nonverbal, and nonsequential manner is likely either to suppress that functioning, to succeed in spite of demands to be logical and rational, or to feel incapable of functioning as she is "supposed" to. In very few schools would her talents be recognized and nurtured to any great extent. And the student who is already a competent left-brain functioner is likely never to learn the pleasures of right-brain activity. Yet we know that both halves of the brain can be taught (Reynolds, 78; Edwards, 79; McCallum, 79). Would that our schools conscientiously nurtured both halves, making individuals better able to use both important modes of functioning and to use all of their brains all of the time!

EXCEPTIONALITIES

Although special education includes emotional disorders, retardation, learning disabilities, and gifted and talented, emotional disorders are not primarily cognitive, so will not be discussed here. Retardation is defined by impaired intellectual functioning, but need not be examined in detail. Generally speaking, all but the most severely retarded adolescents achieve concrete operations, and virtually none achieve formal operations; their capacities can be understood in terms of the Piagetian tasks associated with concrete operations. Exceptional cognitive development will therefore be discussed in terms of learning disabilities, giftedness, and creativity: aspects of development that may be seen in any secondary classroom.

Learning Disabilities

Definition and diagnosis. An adolescent with a learning disability is neither retarded nor emotionally disturbed, though she may be labeled as either or both. A learning-disabled individual is "a person who has average or above average intelligence, but who is impeded in the processes of learning by a neurologically based syndrome characterized by sensory and motor dysperceptions" (Chesler, 80, pp. 6–7). These dysperceptions may be visual, auditory, kinesthetic, social, or any combination thereof. Public Law 91-230, dated April 13, 1970, defined L.D. children as follows:

> Children with special learning disabilities exhibit a disorder in one or more of the basic psychological processes involved in understanding or using spoken or written language. These may be manifested in disorders of listening, thinking, talking, reading, writing, spelling, or arithmetic. They include conditions which have been referred to as perceptual handicaps, brain injuries, minimal brain dysfunction, dyslexia, developmental aphasia. They do not include learning problems which are due primarily to visual, hearing, or motor handicaps, to mental retardation, emotional disturbance, or to environmental disadvantage. (U.S. Statutes at Large, Vol. 84, p. 177)

Estimates concerning the number of learning disabled vary considerably, but tend to cluster around the 10 percent figure, with at least 10 percent of these being severe enough to require special education. Learning-disabled youngsters experience a developmental lag; their nuerological functioning is retarded and they require more time than others to accomplish cognitive tasks (S. Smith, 81). They frequently display difficulty in abstract thinking, speech and writing problems, conceptual lags, hyperactivity, distractibility, inability to sustain attention, poor organizational skills, a lack of resourcefulness, inability to pick out significant information, difficulty with time relationships, extreme difficulty with sequencing, directional confusion, mixed dominance, poor oral reading, poor spelling, poor handwriting, and trouble getting ideas onto paper (Lehtinen-Rogan, 71; Stevens, 80). The frustration of the classroom often leads to behavior problems and feelings of stupidity, and performance always lags behind potential. These are the students whom teachers describe as underachievers, not working up to potential. They are told to pay attention, work harder, quit fooling around; yet these behaviors are seldom under their conscious control. At the root of the problem is neurological disorganization:

> Separating out is at the root of the learning disabled child's problem. Because of the lag in his neural development, he is bombarded by too many sensations at once. Because of his immaturity, he reacts to too much with too much body and mind. He doesn't discriminate. . . . It's not just that he doesn't pay attention; he pays too much attention to too many things. (S. Smith, 81, pp. 11–12, 13)

Expression in adolescence. Learning-disabled children are usually diagnosed in the primary grades, when lags in reading and writing become evident, and most attention is paid to them in the elementary years. By the time they reach adolescence, most still need special help and special understanding, but secondary teachers are generally not prepared for them. They may still have lags of from one to five years in gross motor development, sensorimotor development, perceptual skills, language development, and conceptual skills. They are notoriously poor spellers, show poor logical reasoning and abstract-thinking skills, and frequently display a high level of inconsistency in performance.

Learning-disabled adolescents might make *A*'s one day and *F*'s the next, in the same subject, being unable to alter their method of approach to allow for a different approach by the teacher. Their report cards are usually inconsistent, and teachers report inconsistent study habits and application. They do the same thing every day in every class; if it doesn't work they don't understand why not. Their performance doesn't match their ability.

Figure 8.3 details the performance of Randy on the WISC (Weschler Intelligence Scale for Children).

Note that Randy is fourteen years, six months old, and on the WISC he displayed average verbal I.Q., performance I.Q., and full-scale I.Q. These scores alone would lead us to believe that Randy has no learning problems, but is simply aver-

Figure 8.3
Randy, Age 14 Years, 6 Months — Performance on WISC

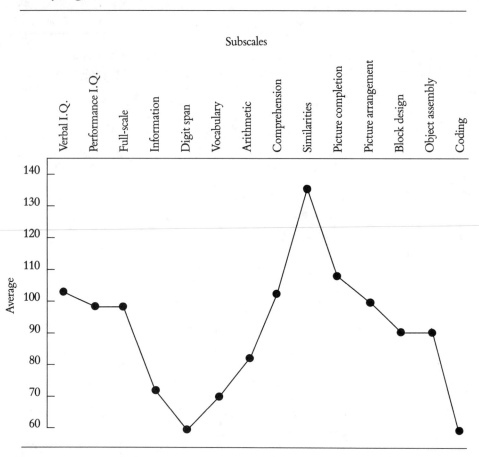

age. However, when we look at the various subscales, we see a great deal of variability. His grasp of general information and other more concrete tasks is well below average, comprehension and picture completion are average, and similarities (the task that requires abstract reasoning and higher-order thinking skills) is well *above* average. We therefore see a student who is *better* at formal reasoning than he is at concrete reasoning skills. It was also noted that his major weakness was in his inability to attend to concrete tasks. A reasonable conclusion, then, is that his *true* intelligence is probably significantly greater than the average scores shown on verbal, performance, and full-scale I.Q. measures. It is not hard to imagine the frustration that Randy and his parents and teachers must feel.

This very frustration, fueled by a history of failures, makes learning disabilities difficult to diagnose in adolescence. These students have failed repeatedly and have developed behavioral, motivational, interest, and even emotional problems that make them look little different from their emotionally disturbed peers. As a result, there is a high incidence of learning disabilities in delinquents, who are less mature, more involved in the imaginary audience of egocentrism, and needy of recognition. They may have given up on academics, feeling no control, and therefore are looking for control in other ways (Canino, 81).

Finally, learning-disabled adolescents lack good judgment. They make snap judgments, reach conclusions that don't follow from the facts, and fail to use problem-solving skills (Brutten, 73).

Quite obviously, learning-disabled adolescents are vulnerable. They are misunderstood, expected to behave more maturely than they are able, made to feel inadequate and stupid, and not helped to any great extent in the traditional secondary-school curriculum. They may compensate by developing an absorbing interest, by becoming aggressive or withdrawn, by denial, by developing somatic complaints, and by projecting their problems onto others.

Lucky are the L.D. adolescents who have skills or interests that compensate; lucky are the L.D. adolescents who were diagnosed and helped early, and who understand the kinds of problems they are likely to continue to face. Many mildly L.D. adolescents eventually catch up and become highly successful: the stories of Albert Einstein, who didn't talk until he was four; of Nelson Rockefeller, who had difficulty reading his speeches; and of others less famous are told to L.D. children along with large doses of tutoring and alternative ways of compensating for neurological lags.

Far too few adolescents who suffer with learning disabilities get such help, and virtually no help is given the mildly learning-disabled adolescent whose problems don't become obvious until the requirement for formal operational thinking develops in high school.

Giftedness

Definition. Gifted students are almost always defined by their high I.Q.'s, though some educators combine giftedness with creativity. For purposes of understanding cognitive functioning, however, it is useful to separate gifted from creative youngsters, even while recognizing considerable overlap between the categories.

Ginsberg (77) defined giftedness as consistent cognitive performance beyond the level normally expected for a given age, or with a measured I.Q. of 130 or more. Three out of 100 children have I.Q.'s of 130, one out of 1000 has an I.Q. of 150, one out of 10,000 an I.Q. of 160, and one out of 100,000 an I.Q. of 168 or more. These parameters define giftedness in general intellectual aptitude, but Kaufman

(76) also noted five additional categories of giftedness: specific academic aptitude (the math whiz who doesn't do well in other subjects); creativity (the innovative thinker who thinks of novel solutions and novel problems); leadership (the political student who makes only average grades); visual and performing arts (the artists and performers); and psychomotor dexterity (the athletes). Most school systems, however, refer to the gifted as the intellectually gifted; the others may be referred to as ''talented,'' thereby identifying the limits of their gifts.

Table 8.3
Some Learning Characteristics of Gifted Children

Characteristics	Concomitant Problems
1. Keen power of observation; naive receptivity; sense of the significant; willingness to examine the unusual	1. Possible gullibility
2. Power of abstraction, conceptualization, synthesis; interest in inductive learning and problem solving; pleasure in intellectual activity	2. Occasional resistance to direction; rejection or remission of detail
3. Interest in cause-effect relations, ability to see relationships, interest in applying concepts; love of truth	3. Difficulty in accepting the illogical
4. Liking for structure and order; liking for consistency, as in value systems, number systems, clocks, calendars	4. Invention of own systems, sometimes conflicting
5. Retentiveness	5. Dislike for routine and drill, need for early mastery of foundation skills
6. Verbal proficiency; large vocabulary; facility in expression; interest in reading; breadth of information in advanced areas	6. Need for specialized reading vocabulary early; parent resistance to reading; escape into verbalism
7. Questioning attitude, intellectual curiosity, inquisitive mind; intrinsic motivation	7. Lack of early home or school stimulation
8. Power of critical thinking; skepticism, evaluative testing; self-criticism and self-checking	8. Critical attitude toward others; discouragement from self-criticism

Characteristics. Gifted children usually read above grade level, have good memories and large vocabularies, long attention spans and complex ideas, and good judgment. They are well informed, curious, learn easily, understand relationships, and develop cognitive skills earlier than their peers (Kaufman, 76; Henderson, 82).

Related difficulties. But gifted youngsters are frequently hard to raise; they pose unique problems related to their gifts, as Seagoe's list in Table 8.3 details.

Characteristics	Concomitant Problems
9. Creativeness and inventiveness; liking for new ways of doing things; interest in creating, brainstorming, freewheeling	9. Rejection of the known; need to invent for oneself
10. Power of concentration; intense attention that excludes all else; long attention span	10. Resistance to interruption
11. Persistent, goal-directed behavior	11. Stubbornness
12. Sensitivity, intuitiveness, empathy for others; need for emotional support and a sympathetic attitude	12. Need for success and recognition; sensitivity to criticism; vulnerability to peer group rejection
13. High energy, alertness, eagerness; periods of intense voluntary effort preceding invention	13. Frustration with inactivity and absence of progress
14. Independence in work and study; preference for individualized work; self-reliance; need for freedom of movement and action	14. Parent and peer group pressures and nonconformity; problems of rejection and rebellion
15. Versatility and virtuosity; diversity of interests and abilities; many hobbies; proficiency in art forms such as music and drawing	15. Lack of homogeneity in group work; need for flexibility and individualization; need for help in exploring and developing interests; need to build basic competencies in major interests
16. Friendliness and outgoingness	16. Need for group relations in many types of groups; problems in developing social leadership

From May V. Seagoe, Professor of Education, University of California at Los Angeles, in *Delp,* 77, pp. 22–23.

At adolescence, the social and emotional needs of the gifted are no different from those of the more ordinary; these make gifted adolescents sometimes willing to repress their gifts in favor of peer-group acceptance (number 12 in Table 8.3), even more critical of others than more ordinary adolescents (number 8 in Table 8.3), and even greater susceptibility to rejection and rebellion (number 14 in Table 8.3).

Even though a gifted adolescent may be performing well above average, the gifted adolescent may for the first time experience less than unqualified success at a task. For this youngster, a *B* may be perceived as failure, and the emotional reaction may be intense. It is not surprising, for example, that the suicide rate for gifted adolescents tops that for all adolescents, and these young people, who frequently appear so successful and assured, may in fact experience their first failures as devastating.

Giftedness may be particularly burdensome for females. Prior to adolescence, girls outperform boys on all academic tasks, but at adolescence, stereotypes and the social acceptance of women subordinating themselves to men cause many gifted girls to play dumb so as to attract the boys; for the gifted female, the pressure to conform to societal expectations may create intense feelings of conflict, even the fear of success documented by Horner (see Chapter 7).

When recognized and properly nurtured, gifted youngsters offer potentials that most of us envy. They are highly curious and capable of high self-esteem, and generally, as they get older, become increasingly positive about both themselves and their environments (Henderson, 82). They frequently become the leaders and decision makers of the future and need to be both nurtured and challenged in a rich and understanding environment that views them as adolescents first and gifted adolescents second.

Special educators have paid less attention to the gifted than they have to other categories of exceptionalities, with the rationale that the retarded, learning disabled, and emotionally disturbed need the most help. After all, some reason, the gifted will make it anyway. And when resources have been allocated, they have all too often been used merely to add more work to the load of the gifted, who don't benefit from 100 math problems rather than 50. Educators of the gifted are arguing strongly for the development and establishment of new programs, programs that offer qualitatively different experiences that challenge development instead of make-work programs to keep the gifted busy and quiet.

Creativity

Definition. As already noted, many educators and researchers have identified links between giftedness and creativity, yet it is also true that many creative individuals are not gifted. Creativity is harder to define than giftedness, probably because giftedness is defined in traditionally left-brained ways, while creativity belongs to the realm of the right brain. Gardner (80) noted that "the height of creativity, as exemplified by the scientist or the artist, remains one of the most enigmatic issues facing any student of human psychology" (p. *xxxv*), and Hausman (79) identified

Creativity involves fluency, flexibility, originality, and elaboration.

the criteria for creativity as outcomes that are simultaneously unpredictable and valuable. Creativity is seen in divergent thinking, in redefinitions, in transformations (Guilford, 67), and in

> . . . becoming sensitive to or aware of problems, deficiencies, gaps in knowledge, missing elements, disharmonies and so on; bringing together available information; defining the difficulty or identifying the missing element; searching for solutions, making guesses or formulating hypotheses about the deficiencies, testing and retesting these hypotheses and modifying and restating them; perfecting them and finally communicating the results. (Torrance, 70, p. 22)

Creativity, as defined by Guilford and Torrance, involves four primary skills: fluency, flexibility, originality, and elaboration. Fluency is the capacity to produce many solutions for a given problem; a fluent person is able to imagine 100 uses for a given item, many of them completely original. Flexibility is the capacity to produce ideas that show movement from one level of thinking to another; for example, using a brick as a paper weight and as a way to hold down a pile of clothes displays fluency but not flexibility, while using it to throw at someone shows a different level or kind of thinking. Originality is the ability to produce unusual ideas, and elaboration is the ability to add details to a basic idea. Jariel (80) found these capacities to be significantly related to intelligence in high-school students, indicating that by this definition of creativity, giftedness and creativity are related.

Relationship to other factors. To the four abilities identified by Torrance and Guilford, Khatena (78) added the ability to synthesize and abstract, obtain closure, engage in emotional expression, be articulate, see movement and action in pictures, be expressive, use combinational logic, take an unusual perspective, use humor and imagery, and respond quickly and spontaneously. In his research, he found that high I.Q. does not always indicate high creativity, that students with high intelligence but low creativity are viewed as the best students by their teachers, and that students with both high intelligence and high creativity may provide the greatest frustrations to teachers, who frequently view such students as pains in the neck. High creativity is not a universally valued trait, especially in schools that emphasize order and conformity.

Wolf (81) reasoned that the presence of formal operational thinking skills should increase the potential for creative thinking, but that this potential is often not realized. Formal operational thinking may increase the potential for creative thought, but as we noted earlier, it also increases awareness of the need for peer approval, and the pressures to conform may be stronger than any inclinations toward creativity and nonconformity.

Newland (81) found left-handed adolescents to be more creative than right-handers, females more creative than males, and college students more creative than noncollege youth. But Tara (81) found that among young adolescents in India, boys were more creative than girls. This may, however, be a cultural rather than a true sexual difference, for Indian parents respond negatively to the nonconforming behavior of their daughters and give boys many more opportunities to explore their environments.

What is clear, however, is that creativity can be taught and learned, and that there is little evidence for its heritability (Torrance, in Khatena, 78). It is rather the result of experience. Parents are primarily responsible for inhibiting the creative endeavors of their children, especially when they punish such characteristics as curiosity and high energy. Hlavsa (80) and Edwards (79) demonstrated that creativity training in groups increases the levels of fluency, flexibility, originality, and the use of right-brain functions, and Khatena (78) argued that educational experiences help to develop creative potential.

Although creative people are necessarily nonconforming in many ways, they are not as a group poorly adjusted. Singh (81) found creative students to be well adjusted on three different measures of adjustment, and Rosenthal (80) found no differences in creativity between well-adjusted and problem students.

Creative adolescents do, however, experience some problems, for they must learn to deal with their uniqueness, a task that is made particularly difficult by the social demands of adolescence. They must learn to walk the fine line of expressing their creativity without alienating both their peers and adults, to maintain their nonconformity without becoming obnoxious. Khatena (78) found that "as adolescents grow older and become adults their creative activities in the world are likely to increase both in number and complexity" (p. 54). It seems evident that the adolescent need to conform may mask the creative potential of the adolescent population.

SUMMARY

The workings of the mind are the subject of this chapter. From the psychometric point of view, intelligence refers to how much an individual knows or is capable of doing. Intelligence is a set of capabilities that can be measured, both globally and in terms of various components that make up all that a person can do. Both large cultural groups and the sexes display some differences in intelligence, but how much is due to heredity and how much to social learning and test bias is difficult to determine. Intelligence measures are subject to training effects and to the expectations of the examiner and must therefore be used cautiously. Further research into the components of intelligence and the degree of influence of the many factors contributing to it continues to be needed.

Whereas the psychometricians are interested in measuring intelligence and in comparing large groups of people on measures of intelligence, the cognitive developmentalists are more concerned with how knowledge is acquired and how thought processes change as individuals mature. Most prominent among developmental theories is that of Jean Piaget, who looked for the commonalities in cognitive development and the processes involved in thinking. His findings do not contradict the findings of the psychometricians but complement them. Both the quantitative and the qualitative approaches to the study of the functioning of the mind contribute to our understanding of the content and process of adolescent thought.

Piaget viewed cognition as an activity, the structure of which is inherited and which develops in a predictable sequence throughout childhood and into adulthood. Each stage of development is marked by unique and identifiable mental structures that allow the individual certain characteristic cognitive functions. Development from one stage to another proceeds through the processes of assimilation, accommodation, and equilibration. The sequence of stages is constant and universal; physical maturation plays an important but limited role in the development of new stages, and development is the result of the interaction of maturation and experience. Adolescence is preceded by the childhood stages: the sensorimotor stage, the preoperational stage, and the concrete operational stage. Adolescents are usually at least partially, if not completely, in the stage of concrete operations, which are characterized by the ability to perform operations mentally that previously had to be physically manipulated. The concrete operational thinker can form inversions of things, understand concepts like reciprocity, reverse situations, and predict outcomes of concrete events, but applies these capabilities to things rather than to abstractions.

Adolescents, according to Piaget, are also ready to begin the final stage of cognitive development, the use of formal operations. They become capable of developing hypothetical reasoning skills, the use of logic, and abstract thinking, which may be characterized as the ability to think about thought itself. They become capable of thinking in terms of possibilities, manipulating combinations of factors to determine causes and outcomes, dealing with ideas from a variety of perspectives, becoming involved in theoretical matters, and developing feelings toward concepts as well as people. The attainment of formal operations, unlike that of the earlier stages, is not universal and is subject to teaching. Some of us develop the ability to use formal operations only in selected areas in which we have the greatest interest and motivation for thinking in complex ways. All too often, our secondary schools do not encourage and nurture the development of formal operational thinking, but either assume that all adolescents are capable of it or resort to encouraging only the lower-level thinking skills.

According to the research of Epstein, the brain grows in predictable spurts, and only during the times of brain growth is the development of new mental structures possible. These findings seem to indicate that during times of no growth, our schools would concentrate more effectively on developing breadth in the already-developed structures than on encouraging new ones.

Each stage of cognitive development is accompanied by unique forms of egocentrism, the tendency of each of us to focus on our own point of view to the exclusion of other views. In adolescence egocentrism is characterized by the personal fable and the imaginary audience. The personal fable leads the adolescent to believe that she is historically unique, that no one has ever felt the same feelings, thought the same thoughts, or experienced the same humiliations as she. Because she considers herself unique, she may also consider herself immortal and may take foolish risks. The imaginary audience is the belief that everyone else is as concerned with the adolescent's appearance as she is. She is on stage all the time, and may therefore become overly self-conscious, self-critical, and self-absorbed. Along with adolescent egocentrism, formal operational thinking also sometimes results in adolescent idealism, which results from the ability to think about all possibilities.

Although cognitive development proceeds in predictable stages, learning itself is characterized by a variety of learning styles. Some individuals are more field independent than field dependent; some react to different stimuli in different ways; and some seem to depend more on the style that characterizes left-brain or right-brain activity than the other. Unfortunately, most schools have not responded to the varieties of learning style that are prevalent in their students, but tend rather to assume that all youngsters learn in the same way and at the same time and rate.

Variations from the norm in cognitive functioning result in young people who are retarded, learning disabled, gifted, or creative. Retardation results in impaired functioning, and retarded children are relatively well served in schools. More difficulties accrue with learning disabled, gifted, and creative youngsters, for it is they who most often defy teacher expectations. Learning-disabled youngsters have sensory and motor dysperceptions, especially in using spoken or written language. Although at or above normal intelligence, they experience difficulty in school as a result of their language problems. Gifted youngsters are those with superior intelligence in one or more areas. Although they generally perform well in school, their social and emotional needs are no different than those of their more ordinary peers, and the difference between their cognitive and emotional development may cause temporary problems for them. Creative youngsters frequently find unique solutions to common problems, and although creativity sometimes accompanies giftedness, there is no necessary connection between the two. Creative youngsters are usually well adjusted but may experience some difficulty as a result of their tendency toward nonconformity. Most secondary schools are struggling to develop appropriate responses for exceptional adolescents.

9

Personality Development

To be somebody means:

. . . a feeling of self-worth and importance as a person in spite of imperfections.

As for myself, I know my strengths and I enjoy them. I know that I have weaknesses and I try to make them as little destructive as possible.

I know that I can't sing because I can't carry a tune. I don't deprecate myself because I can never be an opera singer.

I know I have unusual powers of concentration, and I enjoy that. It is very productive.

I know that I am not an athlete, and I don't blame myself for not keeping up in the pool or on the track, or whatever. I love to listen to good music, and I appreciate my sense of appreciation for good music. But it is an agony for me to play the piano. But I don't blame myself for not being able to perform musically.

I know I like many people, and I know I don't care for others. I am also aware that not everyone likes me. I cannot give and I cannot get total approval, and I come to terms with that. I know I am a human being and as such, I know that I will "goof" — hopefully not too frequently. I know that "goofs" can be learning processes.

I hope I make them so. (Bernhard, 75, pp. 10–11)

Yetta Bernhard has an identity, a sense of who she is, and she is comfortable with her strengths and accepting of her weaknesses. Her personality seems secure. What strengths do you have? How do you use and enjoy them?

What are your weaknesses? Can you accept them and make them "as little destructive as possible"?

In this chapter we will explore the dynamics of personality and its development, particularly as it is understood in the theory of Erik Erikson and the extension of that theory by James Marcia. Although the seeds of adult personality are sown in conception and nurtured throughout childhood, the physical and cognitive maturity of adolescence fosters their bloom. Only in adolescence do we have the maturity to identify those aspects of ourselves that we share with all people and those that make us unique and to use our awareness to make a place for ourselves in the world.

PERSONALITY

Ideas about Personality

Characteristics. We've all heard comments like "Susie's got a super personality," or "Joe has the personality of a fish," comments that lead us to believe that personality is composed of descriptive characteristics that an individual possesses. We may even believe that personality is quantifiable, as in the comment "Jack has absolutely *no* personality." But personality is not, in fact, a static constellation of characteristics, nor is it something that one person has more of than another person.

Popular notions of personality include descriptors of characteristics, often thought of in terms of continua ranging between opposites: reserved/outgoing, serious/happy, trusting/suspicious, tense/relaxed, or traditional/liberal; but psychologists do not limit their view of personality to public characteristics. They look beneath these outward signs of personality to the "underlying, relatively stable, psychological structures and processes that organize human experience and shape a person's actions and reactions to the environment" (Lazarus, 79, p. 1). Personality then becomes a theoretical inference that is made by observing external behaviors and listening to reports of individuals concerning what is going on inside them.

Process. Personality is developed through the complex interaction of genetic inheritance and social learning. We know, for example, that even newborn infants display differences in temperament and behavior and react differently from one another to the same environmental stimuli. In addition, each of us grows up in a unique environment, and our inherent characteristics and tendencies interact with these stimuli to develop unique characteristics, both behavioral and emotional.

Personality, when viewed as the interaction of physical, cognitive, and social development, can be seen as not just a constellation of characteristics nor a quantity of something, but a life-long process of differentiation that is shaped by previous life experiences and inheritances and continually influences subsequent development. This complexity does not allow for a simple definition of personality; Hayes's (82)

Susie's got a super personality, but Joe has the personality of a fish.

description, however, emphasizes the process by which personality develops in adolescence:

> [The] discovery of the self involves an examination of the self in relation to the society of which the emerging adolescent has recently become aware. Adolescent development can thus be described in its simplest form as a differentiation of the self from the nonself through social interaction. (p. 158)

Healthy Adolescent Personality

Individuation. If personality encompasses all the external, observable characteristics of an individual in interaction with his inner feelings, beliefs, and attitudes, and involves physical and cognitive development as well as psychological development, how do we determine whether an adolescent has a healthy, that is, constructive and productive personality? Since one of the tasks of psychological development is the separation of the self from the nonself, the individual's sense of uniqueness and connectedness to others is one criterion of evaluation. For adolescents especially, this task of **individuation,** the separation from parents and family, is an important one that we will discuss in considerable depth later in this chapter when we consider the works of Erik Erikson and James Marcia.

Tasks. Adolescents face very specific tasks in the development of healthy personalities. Juhasz (82) noted these:

> Adolescents are developmentally programmed (a) to seek unique identities, (b) to try to somehow make a difference, not just here and now, but from a wider social perspective in the future and in history and (c) to search for something to be faithful to — an ideal, an idea, a task, another. In addition, adolescents are capable cognitively of formal operational thought, of taking the historical perspective. They are able to deal with cause and effect, to consider past, present, and future relationships, and to think about those aspects of the historical past which are relevant today. (p. 444)

The adolescent must, in short, find a place in the world by identifying with appropriate and meaningful values from the past while simultaneously sculpting a unique personal identity. The adolescent who manages the task is said to have developed a healthy personality. Family, teachers, peers, and environmental circumstances all contribute by providing the social context in which individual development occurs.

Continual growth. In our society, the task has become a more formidable one than in any time previously. As we discussed in Chapter 2, the choices and rapid changes inherent in a technological society have made development less sure, less predictable, and far more problematic than ever before in history. The healthy personality must not only have been successful at integrating the values of the past with the demands of the present, but must develop a flexibility and continual readiness to learn the new things that are required for the future. The healthy personality continually develops; it assimilates new information, accommodates itself appropriately, and reaches new potentials. A person with a healthy personality is not always aware of his own growth, not invariably satisfied with himself or happy, and may not be particularly introspective about his development. "He simply feels and acts predominantly in tune with himself, his capacities, and his opportunities;

A sense of uniqueness and connectedness with others is part of a healthy personality.

and he has the inner means and finds the outer ways to recover from experiences which impair this feeling. He knows where he fits (or knowingly prefers not to fit) into present conditions and developments'' (Erikson, 80, p. 232).

The Relationship of Personality to Other Aspects of Development

Implicit in our discussion so far is the recognition that personality development encompasses all other forms of development. As we noted in Chapter 6, an individual's perception of his body and physical competence significantly affects his self-concept. So too do his cognitive abilities; his intelligence, and his perceptions of his cognitive competence, sexuality, and sex role; his role in the family and with peers; his moral beliefs and values; and his occupational and vocational experiences. All are intertwined, and none can be separated for any but academic purposes.

The development of cognitive capacities is clearly of great significance in the development of personality, especially in adolescence. As we noted in the previous chapter, the development of formal operations in adolescence allows the adolescent to abstract, hypothesize, weigh alternatives, consider consequences, and be introspective, all of which are important in the development of a healthy, consistent personality. Formal operations allow adolescents and adults to make meaningful choices and decisions from among the myriad of competing alternatives for assuming adult roles, understanding personal and interpersonal experiences, self-discovery and integration of the many dimensions of life (Hayes, 82). Bernstein (80) noted that the ability to abstract, along with greater ability to integrate and differentiate, contributes to awareness of personal motivation and the capacity to develop a comprehensive and complex self-system. With formal operations, adolescents can consider the possibilities of who they are, who they want to become, how they are seen by others, and how they value the various selves they identify within themselves. All of these contribute to the individual's sense of self, his personality, and the value he places on himself.

In the previous chapter, we discussed the possibility that some adolescents and adults may never develop formal operations. If this is true, we might speculate that those who do not probably develop personality characteristics and acquire various roles in life without the introspection that formal operations encourage. They may simply take on the aspects of society around them and be spared the questioning and self-searching that accompanies thoughtful and provocative consideration of the myriad alternatives available.

Self-Concept and Self-Esteem

Definition. In studies of self-concept and self-esteem, definitions vary and are highly imprecise. Even scales that are used to measure self-concept and self-esteem overlap. Two examples are the self-concept inventory (Sears, 64) and the self-esteem inventory (Coopersmith, 67), which measure approximately the same characteristics. Whereas some writers use the term *self-concept* to refer to a description of self-perceptions and the term *self-esteem* to refer to the individual's evaluation of all that he perceives himself to be (Gray-Little, 79), this distinction has not been clarified in the literature. Most often, the terms are used interchangeably (Shavelson, 76). We shall therefore use them interchangeably here to refer to an individual's basic concepts of himself, his thoughts and opinions about himself, his awareness of who and what he is, and his comparison of himself with others and with any ideals he has developed. Figure 9.1 details the numerous areas of behavior that contribute to specific and more global self-concept (Shavelson, 76, p. 413).

Our definition includes all of an individual's self-perceptions, whether they be physical, sexual, cognitive, moral, occupational, or have to do with skills, roles, competencies, appearances, motivations, goals, or emotions. The self-concept is derived from a variety of sources. Notice that much of the adolescent self-concept comes through the eyes of others. The self-concept or self-esteem then becomes an individual's evaluations of all that he perceives himself to be.

Figure 9.1
One Possible Representation of the Hierarchic Organization of Self-Concept

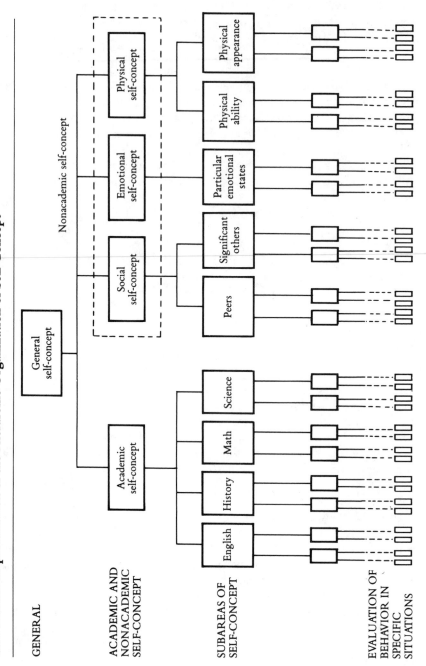

GENERAL

ACADEMIC AND
NONACADEMIC
SELF-CONCEPT

SUBAREAS OF
SELF-CONCEPT

EVALUATION OF
BEHAVIOR IN
SPECIFIC
SITUATIONS

***Global* vs. *temporary*.** Each of us has both a global self-esteem, our overall evaluation of ourselves, and temporary self-esteem, our more immediate evaluation of ourselves in the moment. For example, Janie, who is sixteen, has an overall positive self-concept; she sees herself as intelligent, competent, and consistent. She also may have temporary feelings of incompetence, as when she occasionally does badly on a test or does something silly in a social setting. Since her overall esteem is high, she can accept temporary self-evaluations of stupidity without lasting damage. If, however, her overall esteem were low, temporary mistakes would serve only to confirm her already low self-evaluation.

Self-esteem is truly a phenomenological creation, for it is developed only in the eyes and mind of the individual and may or may not be consistent with reality. If Janie were to develop an image of herself as stupid, even though she really is brighter than normal, she would be likely to act as if she really were stupid.

A generally positive self-esteem is essential for healthy personality development. Those with esteem problems not only fail to achieve their full potential, but also tend to be quite anxious and show the symptoms of anxiety: nervousness, headache, vulnerability to criticism, awkwardness, insecurity, withdrawal, acting out, even physical ailments (Offer, 77). Fortunately, as Offer (77, 82) discovered, most adolescents are relatively happy and have generally positive self-concepts. The normal concerns with acceptance and the searching that so often characterize adolescents are not indications of overall poor esteem. They are merely the external signs of the growing personality.

Bases of self-esteem. We learn to evaluate ourselves as a result of the totality of interactions and experiences we have had. Our society as a whole has placed certain values on particular characteristics and qualities. Our family has either accepted and valued us and taught us to do likewise or has devalued us and taught us to degrade ourselves. Our peers have created standards to be met and have let us know how well we measure up to them; and our achievement in school has given us a powerful measure of our competencies. A positive self-concept can only be developed in an environment that promotes both acceptance and realistic self-appraisal.

Factors that have an impact on self-esteem include family identifications and relationships and perceptions of socioeconomic status, race, nationality, and physical characteristics (Rosenberg, 65; Louden, 80; Gray-Little, 79). It doesn't matter if an individual is black or white, male or female, tall or short; what does matter is the evaluation of each characteristic by the individual.

For each of us, the overt and subtle teachings by our family and other significant adults about how they view us has a significant impact on our self-esteem (Shavelson, 76; Wilson, 78). For example, if minority children are taught that their race or culture is inferior, they develop a negative judgment about that race or culture (Wilson, 78); but if the important adults in their lives do not accept the negative images that a dominant society has of them, they develop a positive self-concept (Paul, 80). Louden (80) challenged the assumption that blacks internalize society's negative opinion of them. Both in his review of the literature and in his own research, he found that blacks and other minorities do not have lower self-esteem than whites. Although discrimination and prejudice most certainly affect an individual's life experience, they do not necessarily generate low self-esteem. As Louden (80, p. 31) says, "Given the structure of his immediate environment and his psychological coping mechanisms, the individual may quite readily evade the distasteful conclusion that he personally is unworthy."

Not accepting negative images is as important for girls as it is for minorities. As we discussed in Chapters 6 and 7, the sexual stereotypes of the past have had far-reaching effects, and girls tend to value themselves more for how they look than for what they can do. They also tend to differ in how they account for success, girls more often attributing success to luck while blaming themselves for failure and boys more often attributing success to their own efforts and failure to the situation. Also, as we noted in Chapter 8, very bright girls sometimes have trouble with self-esteem because the traditional expectations of women are in conflict with the expectations of the gifted. The gifted girl then has to negotiate her self-concept between opposing expectations and is at some danger of developing a negative self-image.

Stability of self-esteem. The stability of self-esteem has also been a fertile field for study. Montemayor (77) analyzed younger and older adolescents' responses to the question "Who are you?" into thirty different categories. This analysis confirmed that as they mature, adolescents apply different cognitive skills to their self-concepts as well as to external reality. The youngest group tended to respond to the question in completely concrete ways, answering with details of address, appearance, possessions, and play activities, while the older adolescents answered with far greater abstraction, like their beliefs, motivations, and interpersonal characteristics. Whereas the response, "I am a boy who lives in Seattle" was typical of the younger group, "I am a dreamer" was typical of the older group. In an extensive review of the research on self-esteem in adolescence, O'Malley (83) found that global self-esteem increases between the ages of 13 and 23, but that school-related experiences have mostly negative effects on self-esteem. The lowest self-esteem seems to be exhibited by 12- and 13-year-olds, who tend to be more self-conscious and have lower opinions of both themselves and others than any other age group (Simmons, 73; Elliot, 82; Protinsky, 80). We noted in Chapter 6 that young adolescents are faced with rapidly and unpredictably changing bodies, so some instability in self-concept might be expected. Simmons (73), however, suggested that the self-image difficulties may be more related to school experience than to body changes. She found that those entering junior high were significantly more upset than those remaining in an elementary school, even though both groups were the same age and in the same grade. It may have been the position as the youngest in the school or the change to a new school rather than the age that created image difficulties for these students. Furthermore, lack of success in school has a significant impact on self-esteem.

Global self-esteem reaches its lowest point in early adolescence and slowly increases throughout the teen years. Most older adolescents feel fairly good about themselves and perceive little change within themselves (Handel, 80). And those who feel comfortable with who they perceive themselves to be do not need to put up a false front or play games to cover their insecurities. Elliot (82) found that the need to fabricate decreased with increasing age, and that girls tended to fabricate longer than boys, probably because girls are more often taught to rely on approval from others while boys are more often taught to rely on personal achievement. Adolescents who fabricate are also more vulnerable to criticism and more self-conscious than those who do not and are more likely to find it difficult to express themselves in the real world. They therefore spend more time fantasizing than those who have higher self-esteem and do not need the world of fantasy to the same degree.

Finally, our discussion of the importance of self-esteem cannot be ended without acknowledging the negative stereotypes adolescents are subjected to just by virtue of being adolescents. The media as well as general adult conversation are consistently riddled with stereotyping of teenagers "that would be offensive to most were it in reference to race or religion. If such stereotyping is harmful to the self-concept of one group — e.g. blacks, Jews — why do we assume it is not to this subsection of our population, adolescents?" (Lipsitz, 80, p. 29). That most adolescents survive the period with relatively positive self-images is a tribute to their psychological strength.

THEORIES OF PERSONALITY

Three main schools of psychological theory have been developed to explain personality functioning, with many variations and adaptations of each also having been developed. A major portion of this chapter will be devoted to the extremely popular and useful psychosocial theory of Erik Erikson, which is an adaptation and extension of Freud's psychodynamic theory; but before discussing Erikson, it it useful to review the three major perspectives on human functioning. These are the **psychodynamic,** the **humanistic-existential,** and the **behavioral.**

Table 9.1 compares the psychodynamic, humanistic-existential, and behavioral approaches in terms of their differing assumptions about personality determinants, personality description or structure, personality dynamics or process, psychopathology, and personality change or psychotherapy. Please refer to this table as we discuss the three approaches.

Psychodynamic Theory

Id, ego, and superego. Sigmund Freud (43) was the father of the psychodynamic approach, also known as psychoanalysis. From the Freudian perspective, we are driven by complex biological instincts, unconscious forces that compel us to expend our energies in gaining pleasure and avoiding pain. The personality is composed of three interconnected processes, the **id,** the **ego,** and the **superego.** Behavior is the

Table 9.1
Three Approaches to Personality

	Psychodynamic	Humanistic-existential	Behavioral
Personality Determinants	Behavior is lawful and completely determined. Biological forces (e.g., sexual and aggressive instincts and an inherited, predetermined, developmental sequence) are heavily emphasized, though social forces also are important to shaping personality. Contemporary versions of this approach acknowledge a greater balance in the interplay of both biological and social determinants.	Free will, choice, and purpose actually allow the person to transcend instinctual and environmental forces. Emphasis is on biologically-rooted forces such as self-actualizing tendency and inherited "potentialities" rather than on tissue drives or deficits. But emergent self-concept is shaped mainly by social forces.	Behavior is lawful and completely determined. Environmental/social forces are the prime shapers of personality. Biological drives (e.g., hunger, thirst, sex) are downplayed: their importance, according to some adopting this approach, is that biological drive satisfaction, when associated with social stimuli, establishes influential social motives.
Personality Description (structure)	Id, ego, and superego comprise the structures of personality, along with various levels of the psyche (conscious, preconscious, and unconscious).	The major structure of personality is the self which consists of the individual's private images of what he or she is and would like to be.	Personality structure consists of a collection of habitual responses or learned behavior patterns. Emphasis is on respondent and operant behaviors, though recent approaches also stress "person variables" such as cognitive styles and strategies.
Personality Dynamics (process)	Tension-reduction ("pleasure-principle") and the interplay between the expression and inhibition of the life and death instincts constitute the main processes of personality.	"Force-for-growth" and tension-production are psychological processes of most importance, along with congruency between the self and experience. When incongruency exists, threat and anxiety result and lead to defensive reactions. A search for meaning and purpose also motivates much human behavior.	Environmental/behavior relationships are emphasized, along with "principles of learning" related to respondent and operant conditioning and modeling. Tension-reduction is a major motivational concept for some behavioral theorists, but largely irrelevant for others.

Personality Development	Growth is exhibited as a biological unfolding of stages or developmental landmarks. Successful resolution of these developmental landmarks leads to a more mature ego, while unsuccessful resolution may lead to character traits or to inadequate personality functioning.	The growth of a unique self-system which influences characteristic ways of acting, feeling, thinking, and perceiving is emphasized. Interactions between the person, with his or her need for positive regard, and significant others, who may freely or conditionally give positive regard, greatly affect the emergent self system.	There is no guiding concept of inherited and unfolding developmental stages or crises. Growth is a function of reinforcement and imitation. Schedules of reinforcement, stimulus generalization and discrimination, shaping, and social learning are key concepts which affect the production of habits and therefore create personality.
Psychopathology	Symptoms reflect underlying conflicts and defensive reactions to anxiety. Fixations and regression under stress result in inadequate (too weak or too strong) development of ego and superego.	Pathology reflects great incongruency between the self and experience, and a rigid, defensive support of a restrictive self-image. Anxiety threatens the person and if defenses fail altogether, total personality disorganization ("psychosis") results. A sense of purposelessness or meaninglessness may also lead to pathology.	Pathology is based on faulty learning. Symptoms are viewed as the problem to be treated, rather than as signs of pervasive underlying conflict or "disease."
Personality Change (psychotherapy)	Adult personality change is difficult but possible with a highly trained and objective therapist. Resolution of unconscious conflict through insight is the prime goal, along with the strengthening of ego functions. Techniques such as free association and the therapist's analysis of patient's resistances, dreams, and transference, help uncover the patient's past difficulties and illuminate their operation in the present.	Change is highly probable given the proper "atmosphere" of congruence, unconditional positive regard, and empathic understanding. Therapy emphasizes the "client's" perceptions of personal experiences, as well as his or her own innate tendencies and responsibility for healing and growth. Client is encouraged to discuss the "here-and-now," and to gain insight into his or her own functioning. Therapist facilitates growth (e.g., expanding awareness) by providing the proper atmosphere noted above and by reflecting and clarifying the client's feelings and meanings.	Behavior is highly malleable and under the control of environmental contingencies, and hence is readily capable of alteration. Behavior modification techniques emphasize the present, rather than the past, and concentrate on overt behaviors, though cognitive and emotional (covert) variables are often manipulated and changed too. Highly specialized techniques rely on numerous procedures such as extinction, positive reinforcement, desensitization, cognitive restructuring, and modeling. Because goal of therapy is to teach patient to unlearn problem behaviors and/or to learn more adaptive ones, insight into possible underlying and unconscious processes is irrelevant.

result of the relative interactions of these processes. The id is that part of personality with which an individual is born, the instinct to satisfy needs and be comfortable, which is expressed in the drives of sex and aggression. "The id never matures but remains the spoiled brat of personality" (Corey, 82, p. 10). The id is completely selfish and wants only to please itself. The ego is the thoughtful, managerial process of the personality. It has been compared to an executive or a traffic cop, who adopts a rational approach to planning and problem solving. The ego always makes sense. The superego is the conscience of the personality, the judge and disciplinarian continually striving for perfection and thereby being responsible for both pride and guilt. Both the ego and the superego develop as a result of maturation and socialization. In each individual, these three processes are in conflict, and behavior or personality is determined by the relative strength of each system. A person who is dominated by the impulses of the id is likely to be hedonistic, amoral, and selfish; one dominated by the ego is rational and emotionless; and one dominated by the superego is moralistic and authoritarian. Healthy personality results from an appropriate mix among the structures, so that an individual can be playful and fun-loving (id), thoughtful and efficient (ego), and develop a consistent value system and morality (superego). Overemphasis by any one system creates pathology.

Childhood psychosexual stages. From the psychodynamic perspective, personality develops through a universal set of psychosexual stages, so named because at each stage the individual's sexual impulses are met in specific ways. The success with which a person masters each stage determines the influence of that stage on adult personality. Freud's five stages emphasize the importance of early childhood in personality development.

The oral stage: birth to one year. In the first year of life, much of an infant's pleasure and gratification is achieved through the mouth. Sucking is erotically pleasurable, and also fulfills the infant's needs for nourishment. When the teeth develop, the infant also has the means for meeting aggressive needs. Negative characteristics in adolescence and adulthood resulting from problems in this developmental stage are greediness, insecurity, or hostility stemming from not getting enough food or love. Children whose needs for both physical comfort and love are met adequately do not later have such problems.

The anal stage: one to three years. The anal stage is so labeled because of the significance of the child's gaining control over the bowels during these years. Toilet training is often the child's first experience with discipline and parental demands, and the ways in which parents manage this significant training influences the child's attitudes toward body functions and often sets up a contest of wills between parent and child that may heighten during adolescence. Such adolescent and adult characteristics as compulsiveness, extreme orderliness or disorderliness, inappropriate expressions of anger and hostility, even hoarding, have their roots in difficulties first experienced during these years.

The phallic stage: three to five years. During these years, childhood masturbation becomes evident; children derive erotic pleasure from the stimulation of the genitals.

They do not desire adult sexual behavior but develop increased curiosity about sexual matters. Freud also believed that children of this age desire to possess the other-sexed parent (known as the Oedipal conflict after the Greek character who loved and married his mother), and that they inherently consider boys to be superior to girls because of the presence of the penis (penis envy). With the development of curiosity about their bodies and those of others also arises the potential for the development of guilt, especially when parents negatively judge the natural curiosity and pleasure-seeking common to preschool children. Feelings about sexuality are bred in these years, and Freud was aware of the great difficulty many adolescents and adults have with their sexuality. Repression, frigidity, insecurity, negative concepts of masculinity and femininity, and guilt are common, and they begin in the tender years before children ever begin school. Negative characteristics resulting from unsuccessful resolution of the phallic stage include self-centeredness, insecurity, and an extreme need to prove oneself in addition to problems with sexuality.

The latency stage: five to twelve years. These years are ones of relative calm. Instead of being focused on body parts, children become socialized and extend their energies into the world and other people. Freud did not elaborate the importance of this stage to adolescent and adult development, but, as we will see later, Erikson recognized gains and problems unrelated to the psychosexual concerns of Freud.

Adolescence. *The genital stage: twelve to adulthood.* Since this was the last stage identified by Freud, we can see that he viewed development as essentially complete with the completion of adolescence. During this stage, the concerns of the earlier stages interact with socialization skills, and adolescents are faced with the task of achieving mature sexual identities, which include interest in the other sex, identification of potential sex partners and mates, the capacity for intimacy, concern for others, and setting up of ideals and goals for life. Successful resolution of all the stages of development culminates in what Freud referred to as the capacities to love and to work, the two hallmarks of the mature adult.

Pubescent sexuality is manifested through the need to release sexual tension. Sexuality is awakened, and with it comes an increase in nervous excitement and anxiety, and the adolescent is particularly vulnerable to the development of psychological disturbances.

The increased sexual tension of adolescence requires that the young person seek appropriate love objects. During the previous latency period, the superego developed a barrier to incestuous desires, and the adolescent therefore seeks love objects that are separate from the family. The first of these is likely to be a mature adult of the other sex (for example, a teacher).

Humanistic-Existential Theory

Two of the major proponents of a humanistic-existential approach to personality are Carl Rogers (61) and Abraham Maslow (71). This approach to the study of personality emphasizes the importance of finding meaning in life. It takes a phenomeno-

Figure 9.2
Maslow's Hierarchy of Needs

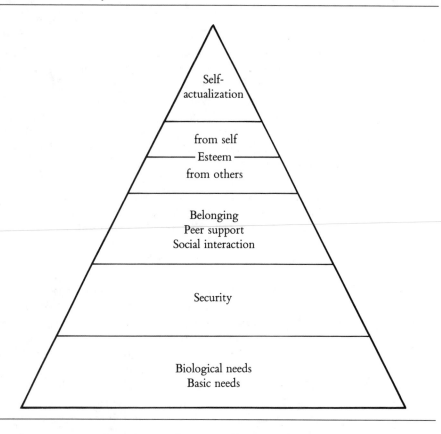

logical perspective and emphasizes freedom and responsibility in the development of innate human potentials. People have the capacity to develop in self-actualizing ways and reach their potentials if they are provided with a climate of empathy and positive regard. Rogers's (61) idea of the self-concept is central to this approach, for the self-concept literally determines all behavior.

In addition to a self-concept, we all also have an ideal self, a notion of who we would like to be. Congruence between the self and the ideal self is associated with healthy personality. Obviously, if my concept of myself is consistent with my concept of who I want to be, I will be at peace with myself and will not be spending energy in self-degradation rather than productive activity.

Abraham Maslow (71) identified a hierarchy of needs that we all must strive to meet (Figure 9.2). Only when lower-order needs are met are we free to meet the higher-order needs. At the lowest level are the biological needs: the needs for food, clothing, shelter, and elimination. When these needs are not being met, we are incapable of attending to higher needs. For example, if I am starving, I am not likely to be attentive to needs for love and affection, and I will choose food over companionship. But when my biological needs are met, I am free to develop my needs for security, social interaction, esteem from others, self-esteem, and finally self-actualization, the reaching of my positive human potentialities. Notice that in this scheme, I cannot develop self-esteem without first having received esteem from significant others. This is consistent with Rogers's observation that the healthy personality can develop only in an environment of unconditional positive acceptance, acceptance just for being alive. Unfortunately, the parents of adolescents often focus on their desire for the adolescents to be appropriately grown up. They tend, therefore, to emphasize what the adolescent does rather than valuing him simply because he is.

Behavioral Theory

Learned behavior. Whereas the psychodynamic view emphasizes instinctual drives that will be destructive if not harnessed, and the humanistic view emphasizes positive growth potential that is actualized in a supportive environment, the behavioral view of personality (Skinner, 71, Bandura, 74, Mischel, 76a) assumes no innate psychological characteristics. From a behavioral view, all behavior is learned, though the most recent behavioral writers also acknowledge the importance of the individual in directing that learning. In this view, personality is nothing more than a collection of responses that have been learned. We literally learn to be who we are as a result of the conditioning we have received as we have grown up. And because personality is learned, it can be unlearned; alterations are not only possible but predictable and controllable. The strictest behavioral view, then, would suggest that human beings are infinitely malleable, and that an individual's behavior as an adolescent can be directed into very different paths by the application of the principles of learning. Behavioral principles are, indeed, used extensively with children and adolescents, especially in treatment programs for delinquents and in programs that purport to train individuals with mental deficiencies. In a token economy, for example, adolescents earn tokens through behaving acceptably. They then can cash in their tokens for material goods or free time.

Cognitive theory. Another aspect of some behavioral views, sometimes identified as yet another major stream of psychology, is that of the cognitive theorists, who emphasize the power of individual thought in shaping personality and behavior. Albert Ellis (73), for example, believes that we control our behavior and our emotions by the rational and irrational thoughts with which we continually indoctrinate ourselves. From this view, people are seen as conditioning themselves to feel as they do, that it is not the external events that affect us but the thoughts we tell ourselves about those events. This obviously is a phenomenological view and may be seen as one bridge between the behaviorists and the humanists.

We used one example in Chapter 6. Another will clarify: suppose that two adolescents, Steve and Bill, both get turned down when they ask girls to accompany them to the prom. Steve is so discouraged by the rejection that he doesn't go, while Bill, though disappointed, picks himself up, asks someone else who accepts, and has a terrific time at the party. From the cognitive theorist's point of view, it was not the original rejection that determined the behavior of Steve and Bill but their thoughts about that rejection. Steve told himself it was terrible, that he was unworthy and would never get a date. Bill, however, felt disappointed, but told himself that it was too bad, that he was nevertheless attractive and worthy of a date, and that he would simply try again. The difference in their behavior is obvious.

As the science of psychology becomes more mature, the interaction and acceptance of various theories increases. At one time, the behaviorists, the humanists, and the psychoanalysts argued the merits of their approaches and discounted one another. Now, however, just as the nature *vs.* nurture controversy is being resolved in favor of an interactionist approach, so too the various approaches to personality are being integrated, with the most useful and applicable concepts from all fields dynamically interacting to enrich our understanding of the complexities of human behavior. Both the humanistic awareness of the importance of self-esteem and Erikson's adaptation of Freud's psychosexual stages to better represent the social influences on development have contributed immensely to our understanding of human personality and are especially relevant in our study of adolescent development.

THE PSYCHOSOCIAL THEORY OF ERIK ERIKSON

Few theorists have had the impact or been as widely accepted and acclaimed as has Erik Erikson. Erikson was born in Germany in 1902; originally a painter, he began tutoring children under the supervision of Freud in Vienna and eventually was trained as a psychoanalyst. The psychodynamic theory was the only one he studied, and he embraced it but was uncomfortable with the emphasis on pathology and the neglect of environment inherent in Freud's theory. He therefore changed the focus of analysis from pathology to normalcy and positive adaptation and developed an acute awareness of the role of society in that adaptation. His emphasis on the interaction of the individual and society is encompassed in his choices of the term **psychosocial** to describe his theory of normal development and the title *Childhood and Society* for one of his major works. Erikson believed that we are born with inherent structures that guide development, but that only in the context of unique historical and personal environments does our development unfold. He looked for the social sources of both individual and group strengths and was particularly interested in the reasons for difficulties between dominamt and subordinate groups. After moving to Boston in the early 1930s, he did anthropological fieldwork to study the problems of Indian tribes and advanced the notion that a subordinate group is likely to accept and adopt the negative stereotypes of them proferred by the dominant group. Through his emphasis on positive, adaptive development, his

A ground plan guides our personal growth.

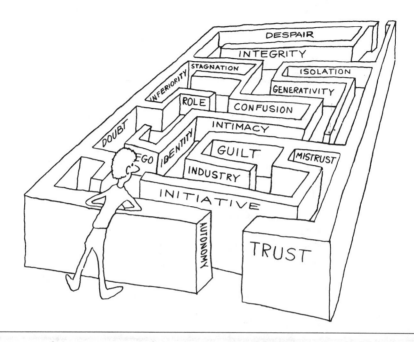

awareness of the importance of the social context of development, and his appreciation for ambiguity and change in development, Erikson added a humanistic dimension to the Freudian perspective.

The Epigenetic Principle

A stage theory. Erikson changed the focus of psychodynamic theory from an emphasis on the gratification of pleasure (id) to an emphasis on successful adaptation (ego). His theory is also known as ego psychology, which dramatizes his belief that the unconscious ego has the role of ensuring coherent behavior, unifying the various aspects of the individual, maintaining individuality within societal contexts, and, essentially, making sense. We are governed by inner laws of development, with stages of development emerging at predictable times. The **epigenetic principle** (*epi* meaning upon; *genesis* meaning emergence), in Erikson's (59) words, refers to the observation that "anything that grows has a *ground plan,* and . . . out of this ground plan the *parts* arise, each part having its *time* of special ascendancy, until all parts have arisen to form a *functioning whole*" (p. 52). Implicit in the epigenetic principle are the following:

1. We are born with a ground plan or blueprint that guides our psychological growth.

2. We are all regulated by the same inner laws of development.

3. The bases of all the stages of development exist in one form or another from birth, but a particular stage commands more immediacy at a particular time of development.

4. The stages of development are related to one another in a universal sequence.

5. The successful resolution of one stage contributes to the successful resolution of successive stages, with overall adjustment depending on proper development through the stages in proper order.

The theory emphasizes continuity of development, the mutual impact of all the stages, and the importance of developmental sequence (Morgan, 82).

Erikson expanded Freud's five stages to eight, for he believed that development doesn't stop with the end of adolescence. He therefore used Freud's five psychosexual stages, reanalyzed them from the growth-and-adaptation point of view, and added three adult stages. Instead of emphasizing the area of sexual gratification most obvious during each stage, Erikson saw the stages as representing the ego's attempts to mediate between inherent growth and environmental demands, which become ever wider as the child matures. In addition to being interwoven with Freud's psychosexual stages, Erikson's stages also encompass physical, motor, and cognitive development. As we have noted repeatedly, one aspect of development cannot be realistically isolated from others.

The normative crisis. Each stage holds both new potentials for development and new dangers, and the balance between the potentialities and dangers is highlighted by Erikson's term **normative crisis.** Each stage contains a normative crisis, which is merely a turning point, not a catastrophe. Each stage is seen as a conflict between opposing forces, the resolution of which prepares us for subsequent stages.

Table 9.2 summarizes the eight stages and notes the personality characteristics represented by success or failure at each stage. The eight crises also form the diagonal in Table 9.3. We will discuss the other aspects of this table later.

The Stages of Development

The first five of Erikson's stages are directly analogous to Freud's five stages, but Erikson expressed them in terms of the psychosocial conflicts that the child faces during each. Erikson then added three more stages and conflicts to describe adult development. Notice that the emphasis is still on childhood development, with five of eight stages occurring during the first quarter of life. Theorists and researchers since Erikson have noted that considerable development also occurs during adulthood and have therefore expanded the adult stages (Levinson, 78; Sheehy, 76). The stages, with their conflicts and potential contributions to adult personality, are described below; refer frequently to Table 9.2.

Trust vs. mistrust (birth to one year). During the first stage of development, which Freud labeled the oral stage, the infant's only psychosocial task is to develop a

Table 9.2
Erikson's Eight Ages of Ego Development

	Success Brings	Failure Brings
First Age: Early Infancy (birth to about one year; corollary to Freudian oral sensory stage)	Basic Trust: Result of affection and gratification of needs, mutual recognition.	Mistrust: Result of consistent abuse, neglect, deprivation of love; too early or harsh weaning, autistic isolation.
Second Age: Later Infancy (about ages one to three years; corollary to Freudian muscular anal stage)	Autonomy: Child views self as person in his own right apart from parents but still dependent.	Shame and Doubt: Feels inadequate, doubts self, curtails learning basic skills like walking, talking, wants to "hide" inadequacies.
Third Age: Early Childhood (about ages four to five years; corollary to Freudian genital loco-motor stage)	Initiative: Lively imagination, vigorous reality testing, imitates adults, anticipates roles.	Guilt: Lacks spontaneity, infantile jealousy, "castration complex," suspicious, evasive, role inhibition.
Fourth Age: Middle Childhood (about ages six to eleven years; corollary to Freudian latency stage)	Industry: Has sense of duty and accomplishment, develops scholastic and social competencies, undertakes real tasks, puts fantasy and play in better perspective, learns world of tools, task identification.	Inferiority: Poor work habits, avoids strong competition, feels doomed to mediocrity; lull before the storms of puberty, may conform as slavish behavior, sense of futility.
Fifth Age: Puberty and Adolescence (about ages twelve to twenty years)	Ego Identity: Temporal perspective, self-certain, role experimenter, apprenticeship, sexual polarization, leader-followership, ideological commitment.	Role confusion: Time confusion, self-conscious, role fixation, work paralysis, bisexual confusion, authority confusion, value confusion.
Sixth Age: Early adulthood	Intimacy: Capacity to commit self to others, "true genitability" now possible, *Lieben und Arbeiten* — "to love and to work"; "mutuality of genital orgasm."	Isolation: Avoids intimacy, "character problems," promiscuous behavior; repudiates, isolates, destroys seemingly dangerous forces.
Seventh Age: Middle Adulthood	Generativity: Productive and creative for self and others, parental pride and pleasure, mature, enriches life, establishes and guides next generation.	Stagnation: Egocentric, nonproductive, early invalidism, excessive self-love, personal impoverishment, self-indulgence.
Eighth Age: Late Adulthood	Integrity: Appreciates continuity of past, present, and future; acceptance of life cycle and life style; has learned to cooperate with inevitabilities of life, "state or quality of being complete, undivided, or unbroken; entirety" (Webster's Dictionary); "death loses its sting."	Despair: Time is too short; finds no meaning in human existence, has lost faith in self and others, wants second chance at life cycle with more advantages, no feeling of world order or spiritual sense, "fear of death."

Table 9.3
Erik Erikson's Psychosocial Theory of Development

	1	2	3	4	5	6	7	8
VIII								INTEGRITY vs. DESPAIR
VII							GENERATIVITY vs. STAGNATION	
VI						INTIMACY vs. ISOLATION		
V	Temporal Perspective vs. Time Confusion	Self-Certainty vs. Self-Consciousness	Role Experimentation vs. Role Fixation	Apprenticeship vs. Work Paralysis	IDENTITY vs. IDENTITY CONFUSION	Sexual Polarization vs. Bisexual Confusion	Leader- and Followership vs. Authority Confusion	Ideological Commitment vs. Confusion of Values
IV				INDUSTRY vs. INFERIORITY	Task Indentification vs. Sense of Futility			
III			INITIATIVE vs. GUILT		Anticipation of Roles vs. Role Inhibition			
II		AUTONOMY vs. SHAME, DOUBT			Will to Be Oneself vs. Self Doubt			
I	TRUST vs. MISTRUST				Mutual Recognition vs. Autistic Isolation			

The diagonal represents the eight conflicts associated with the eight stages of development. Vertical column 5 summarizes the contributions of each of the first five stages to the identity vs. identity confusion conflict. Horizontal row V identifies the recurrence of all eight conflicts in adolescence. (Erikson, 68, p. 94) sense of basic trust in the environment and himself. Erikson (68) labeled the sense of trust "the cornerstone of the vital personality" (p. 97). The infant comes into the world with only needs; if these needs, both the physiological ones for food and warmth and the psychological ones for love and nurturance, are reasonably well met, primarily by the parents, the baby will learn that the world is a relatively safe place to be and will therefore develop the necessary trust. However, the infant whose bodily needs are not met or who is deprived of sensitive care will develop basic mistrust and a consequent suspicion of both the world and himself that may lead to adult withdrawal and pessimism. Remember that we earlier said that the individual must develop an appropriate balance between the negative and positive poles of the conflict. This means, of course, that the infant should not learn to trust everything and everyone indiscriminately. He needs to learn to be realistically cautious within an overall sense of security and faith in the world. Successful resolution of the first stage of development contributes to later development of the capacity for having and giving faith and hope. An adult who experienced the conditions for trust during infancy greets the world with fundamental hope; one who did not greets the world with a sense of doom. (Note that Table 9.2 and items in vertical column 5 of Table 9.3 summarize the contribution of each of the first five stages to the adolescent conflict.)

Autonomy* vs. *shame and doubt (one to three years). Freud observed that bowel and bladder control are the hallmarks of achievement during these years, an achievement which Erikson labeled as **autonomy.** During this stage, the child develops self-control, will, and the beginnings of mutual interaction with his parents. Rapid gains in muscle control and capacity to verbalize give the child the promise of holding on and letting go (to objects as well as to stool and urine), walking, running, and making himself heard and understood. He can now exert power over both his own body and other people. The two-year-old's desire to "do it myself" and to say "no" to whatever an adult suggests are characteristic of the need to express an autonomous will.

The child with a healthy sense of trust whose parents do not attempt to overcontrol his body functions and movements will successfully negotiate this second crisis and develop a sense of rights and obligations, privileges and limitations. Overcontrol, however, leads to doubt and shame, which later may be expressed either in too much conscience or in flagrant disregard of social convention. A successful resolution of the crisis gives the individual the capacity to be loving and cooperative yet firm in dealing with others, whereas the overcontrolled child is likely to become hateful and anxious. The positive contribution of this stage of development to later childhood, adolescence, and adulthood is a healthy awareness of the ability to stand on one's own two feet within society's norms.

Initiative* vs. *guilt (three to five years). Corresponding with Freud's phallic stage is the development of curiosity and imagination. During the preschool years, children expand the area in which they move freely and develop language facility that allows them to question — sometimes incessantly. These two new phenomena allow the expansion of children's capacity to imagine, and they can begin to envision the things they will be able to do and be. Whereas Freud emphasized the emerging sexuality of this period, Erikson emphasized the capacity for children to intrude themselves into space and other people's lives and thoughts. If parents and others in the social world punish them for their intrusions, they develop overwhelming guilt and an overactive conscience that may lead to meek compliance and a perception of themselves as evil. Conflicts with parents over issues of right and wrong may also lead to the child's overcritical judgment of others, especially the parents, when they fail to live up to the ideal they demand. In later years, the child who manages this stage well is capable of imagining alternative futures; the one who does not is locked into either continuously trying to prove himself or in being hypercritical of everything concerning himself and others.

Industry vs. inferiority (five to twelve years). Freud didn't elaborate significantly on what he called the latency stage because he saw it as relatively unimportant in terms of personality development. He also saw it as a passive stage. Erikson, however, placed heavy emphasis on these active elementary-school years during which skill and competence are paramount.

School-aged children are eager to make things and to make things work and may be impatient with imperfection. Perhaps you remember working diligently at making something, only to destroy it because of a slight mistake. School-aged children are ready to share in planning and building, to watch and imitate, and for systematic instruction. The society of the school and beyond becomes immensely important, and teachers become very important people in fostering children's sense of competence. Far too many teachers emphasize what children can't do rather than what they can and thereby contribute not to a sense of competence but to a sense of failure and inferiority. Children who learn that they are skillful tend to take the sense of competence with them throughout their lives; those who learn failure early tend to carry the sense of inferiority throughout their lives. William Glasser's well-known book *Schools without Failure* (69) is based on the premise that success rather than failure contributes to healthy development. The potential contribution of this stage to healthy adolescent and adult personality is the awareness of skillfulness in managing life. Individuals with a healthy sense of their own competence are able realistically to appraise those things they can and cannot do and will enjoy pride in their accomplishments, recognition of their weaknesses, and a capacity to integrate them in such a way as to emphasize the strengths.

Identity vs. role confusion (twelve to eighteen years). Freud concentrated on the integration of the previous stages in adolescence to provide the basis for mature sexual identity. Erikson expanded Freud's concept considerably and saw adolescence as the most complex, dynamic, and significant stage of all. In the next section of this chapter, we will explore the adolescent identity crisis in depth; here we will provide only an overview.

The term **identity crisis** has become part of the vernacular and is usually misused to express frustration over the necessity to make a choice. From Erikson's point of view, the identity crisis is a process in which the individual achieves a sense of both continuity with all people and individual uniqueness, an ideology and commitment to values and to other people, a balance between the past and the future. Physical and cognitive development contribute significantly to identity development, for with an adult body and formal operations, the adolescent is equipped with the maturity to face significant personal questions and decisions. Adolescents develop a central perspective on themselves, the world, and what others think of them, and evolve an **identity**, which is not a set of traits or roles, but instead a "sense of psychosocial well-being. Its most obvious concomitants are a feeling of being at home in one's body, a sense of 'knowing where one is going,' and an inner assuredness of anticipated recognition from those who count" (Erikson, 68, p. 165). From all past identifications, adolescents merge unique and reasonably coherent senses of who they are. The crisis feels more serious and deep than the preceding ones because of the adolescent ability to be introspective and to make the commitments — to a career, lifestyle, ideology, other people. The earlier stages reappear and contribute. From stage one comes a sense of trust or a fear of commitment; from stage two comes duty and service or shame and shamelessness; from stage three comes ambition or apathy; and from stage four comes the willingness to commit to an occupation, or lack of such willingness. (See column 5 in Table 9.3.) The identity crisis is one of conflicting demands and roles offered by the society; parents, teachers, peers, other influential adults, and the media all compete for the commitments of youth. Adolescents who manage the stage successfully have a strong sense of their values and directions and are at peace with who they have become. Those who do not traverse the path successfully remain confused, sometimes isolated, frequently directionless; or they merely adopt, without analysis, the roles imposed upon them.

***Intimacy* vs. *isolation* (young adulthood).** The task of achieving intimacy is not only a sexual task, but one of mutuality, either in deep, committed friendships or in a loving sexual relationship. The main criterion for the achievement of intimacy is the successful resolution of the identity crisis, for "at any time in history, in order to lose one's identity, one must first have one" (Erikson, 64, p. 100). The idea of losing an identity refers to the ability to be so empathetic with another person that one's own needs and awareness of self are temporarily suspended. This can obviously occur only after individuals have succeeded in becoming comfortable with themselves and no longer suffer the pains of adolescent egocentrism. Those who have not achieved a solid sense of themselves will be unable to give in intimate relationships and may either withdraw from such demanding relationships or substitute formalized relationships or sexual encounters that lack true intimacy. With true intimacy, individuals include in their own identity those people and things that they truly love.

Table 9.4
Rosenthal's Items for Measuring Crisis Resolution

	Positive Items	Negative Items
Trust	I have few doubts about myself. Other people understand me. Things and people usually turn out well for me. I think the world and people in it are basically good. I'm as good as other people. I trust people.	I wish I had more self-control. I find the world a very confusing place. I worry about losing control of my feelings. I find that good things never last long. People are out to get me. I find myself expecting the worst to happen.
Autonomy	I am able to take things as they come. I know when to please myself and when to please others. I really believe in myself. I like to make my own choices. I can stand on my own two feet. I like my freedom and don't want to be tied down.	I can't make sense of my life. I can't make up my own mind about things. I'm never going to get on in this world. I am ashamed of myself. I don't feel confident in my judgment. I find it hard to make up my mind.
Initiative	I am able to be first with new ideas. I am an energetic person who does lots of things. I can stop myself doing things I shouldn't be doing. I cope very well. I like new adventures. I like finding out about new things or places.	I don't seem to have the ability that most others have got. I rely on other people to give me ideas. I think I must be basically bad. I feel guilty about many things. I find myself denying things even though they are true. I'm a follower rather than a leader.

Generativity **vs.** *stagnation (middle adulthood).* The word **generativity** refers to the need to care for the next generation, pass on something to the future, be needed, teach, and contribute, especially something of lasting value. It means "to generate in the most inclusive sense . . . children, products, ideas *and* works of art" (Erikson, 74, p. 122). If a sense of generativity is not achieved, boredom and stagnation result, and the individual may either feel totally impoverished or engage in self-indulgence as a substitute for altruistic concern for others. The contribution of this stage to the overall identity of the individual is a sense of knowing which of his contributions will survive him.

Integrity **vs.** *despair (old age).* The strength of this stage is in wisdom, the wisdom of accepting "one's one and only life cycle and of the people who have become significant to it as something that had to be and that, by necessity, permitted of no substitutions" (Erikson, 68, p. 139). When the seven previous stages have been negotiated successfully, elderly individuals look on their lives with wisdom and

Table 9.4
Rosenthal's Items for Measuring Crisis Resolution (continued)

	Positive Items	Negative Items
Industry	I'm a hard worker. I feel I am a useful person to have around. I'm trying hard to achieve my goals. I'm good at my work. I can't stand lazy people. I stick with things until they are finished.	I don't seem to be able to achieve my ambitions. I don't enjoy working. I waste a lot of my time messing about. I'm not much good at things that need brains or skill. I don't get things finished. I don't get much done.
Identity	I've got a clear idea of what I want to be. The important things in life are clear to me. I've got it together. I know what kind of person I am. I have a strong sense of what it means to be female/male. I like myself and am proud of what I stand for.	I change my opinion of myself a lot. I feel mixed up. I can't decide what I want to do with my life. I don't really know what I'm about. I find I have to keep up a front when I'm with people. I don't feel really involved.
Intimacy	I'm ready to get involved with a special person. I'm warm and friendly. It's important to me to be completely open with my friends. I care deeply for others. I have a close physical and emotional relationship with another person. I find it easy to make close friends.	I get embarrassed when someone begins to tell me personal things. I keep what I really think and feel to myself. I think it's crazy to get too involved with people. I'm basically a loner. I prefer not to show too much of myself to others. Being alone with other people makes me feel uncomfortable.

acceptance and are free of the lament that things should have been different. They value comradeship and look to the present while appreciating the joys and struggles of the past. Those who have not negotiated successfully feel instead the disgust and despair that life somehow dealt them a poor hand, and they worry about time being too short to be dealt another one. They are unhappy and make those around them unhappy too. Although I have no scientific evidence to support my observations, it seems that older people, more clearly than any other group, display the polarities of integrity and despair, being either all one or all the other. Some older people are filled with wisdom, content with their lives, and genuinely interested in other people; others are contemptuous of others, dissatisfied with their lives, and generally demanding and self-serving.

Relationships among the stages. When manifested, each stage of development contributes its own unique virtue to the human personality; infancy contributes faith, early childhood contributes will power, preschool age contributes purposefulness, school age contributes efficiency, adolescence contributes commitment, young adulthood contributes love, adulthood contributes responsibility, and old age contributes wisdom.

Although the stages are achieved in sequence and there is an optimum time for the development of each stage, people nevertheless move up and down the scale depending on environmental demands. An accidental crisis, for example, causes regression to earlier stages. Meet Al, a healthy nineteen-year-old, successful college student and good athlete majoring in physical education. He wants to work with children and adolescents and to coach in a middle or high school. He has a steady girlfriend, is considering marriage, and generally feels confident about himself, his aspirations, and his future. He, according to Erikson's scheme, is completing the identity crisis and experimenting with the stage of intimacy, just as he chronologically should be. While jogging along the shoulder of the road one day, Al is hit by a reckless driver, and his neck is broken. He finds himself in the hospital a paraplegic, paralyzed from the shoulders down, unable to walk, sit without braces, or control his bladder or bowels. He can move only his head and arms, and the prognosis is that no feeling or control will return to the affected parts. Though he is still nineteen, Al is likely to be concerned not with issues of intimacy and of the consequent giving of himself to another, but with issues of autonomy, centered around the question "What can I do for and by myself?" He will have to reestablish his autonomy, initiative, industry, and identity as a paraplegic before he can again enter the stage of intimacy. How well he renegotiates these stages will depend on how well he negotiated them the first time around.

Psychosocial stage inventory. Rosenthal (81) developed an instrument, the Erikson Psychosocial Stage Inventory (EPSI) to measure achievement of the first six of Erikson's stages. The items pertaining to each of the stages are listed in Table 9.4. An examination of these items will enhance your understanding of the self-perceptions that are a part of each stage of development. Notice that items are expressed both positively and negatively and scored accordingly.

IDENTITY IN ADOLESCENCE

Ego Identity

Characteristics. To achieve identity means to have a realistic self-concept that includes both physical and cognitive mastery of the environment and social recognition within society. Individuals with strong identities recognize both their continuity with others and their unique individuality. Identity achievement has many components and is achieved in relative stages or steps: although not universal, first probably comes physical identity, acceptance of the body and its capabilities; sexual identity follows; then social identity; vocational; moral; ideological; and finally psychological identity, which encompasses and expands on all the previous identities. Contributing to the achievement of a separate identity in adolescence are both physical maturation and cognitive development; adult bodies and adult minds are necessary for the awareness and introspection required to forge an ego identity. Erikson believed that the achievement of an identity in adolescence provides the strength to tolerate conflict and diversity, reconcile the contradictions that are so much a part of modern society, and weather adversity and recuperate from pain. Successful identity achievement, remember, does not exist apart from successful resolution of the earlier childhood conflicts; a basic sense of trust and hope in the world, an awareness of individual responsibility, a willingness to experiment, and a sense of competence are necessary prerequisites to the achievement of an ego identity.

Fidelity. Erikson believed that the hallmark of identity achievement is commitment to an idealogy, without which youth would suffer from confusion in values. The search for something and somebody to which to be true he called **fidelity.**

Adolescents *need* a commitment to an ideology, for it offers them a clear perspective on the future, a means of reconciling the inner world of ideals and the outer world of reality, opportunities for identifying with others and for experimenting with roles, a rationale for values, a clear world view, and even the opportunity to follow important leaders (Erikson, 68). But because they are experimenting, adolescents may also change their commitments frequently; it is not unusual for a high-school student to feel passionately committed to one set of ideals one week, only to change to an opposing set the following week, or be absolutely certain of his commitment to one girl one month and to another the next. Such changes are to be expected, for they are part of what Erikson termed the identity crisis, which takes place within a psychosocial **moratorium.**

The Moratorium

Definition. Erikson believed that in order for adolescents to develop fidelity, they must be offered a kind of way station between genital maturity and full adult responsibility, a postponement of the commitments we expect of adults.

> By psychosocial moratorium, then, we mean a delay of adult commitments, and yet it is not only a delay. It is a period that is characterized by a selective permissiveness on the part of society and of provocative playfulness on the part of youth, and yet it often leads to deep, if often transitory, commitment on the part of youth, and ends in a more or less ceremonial configuration of commitment on the part of society. (Erikson, 68, p. 157)

In many ways, society actually sanctions the moratorium by approving of youth taking time for academic life and for travel and by noting youthful pranks as pranks rather than delinquency.

During the moratorium, adolescents search for something to which to be true. They seek durability in the midst of the vast changes of society, and their search usually involves a desire for locomotion, for "going places" or "getting on with it." Erikson used the adolescent love affair with cars as a symbol of this desire for

The adolescent love affair with cars is symbolic of the desire for movement.

movement, especially fast movement. He also used adolescent dancing and movies as examples of the need for continual movement, continual stimulation.

Symptoms of confusion. More specifically, the conflict between identity and identity confusion that occurs during the moratorium contains seven parts or symptoms of confusion. These are related to the other conflicts of development and are included in Table 9.3, across the table at row V. Successful resolution of each contributes to a healthy achievement of ego identity, while unsuccessful resolution leads to identity confusion.

1. Temporal perspective *vs.* time confusion: related to the trust-mistrust conflict. During the moratorium adolescents need to develop a sense of time, coordinate the past with the future, develop the concept of a lifetime, and estimate accurately how long a task will take.

2. Self-certainty *vs.* self-consciousness: related to the autonomy-shame conflict. During the adolescent moratorium, a physical self-image, social relationships, and a sense of accomplishment contribute to a healthy identity.

3. Role experimentation *vs.* role fixation: related to the initiative *vs.* guilt conflict. Adolescents need to try on a variety of roles in order to develop the experience on which to make productive choices. Erikson saw the establishment of a career as a significant aspect of identity achievement.

4. Apprenticeship *vs.* work paralysis: related to the industry *vs.* inferiority conflict. School and work tasks provide adolescents with a sense of what they can do. Inferiority feelings prevent successful experimentation.

5. Sexual polarization *vs.* bisexual confusion: related to the intimacy *vs.* isolation conflict. Adolescents must learn what it means to be female or male and what role sexuality will play in their lives.

6. Leadership and followership *vs.* authority confusion: related to the generativity *vs.* stagnation conflict. In school, at work, in social situations, adolescents must learn to make choices among competing demands and must figure out to whom they choose to listen.

7. Ideological commitment *vs.* confusion of values: related to the integrity *vs.* despair conflict. Adolescents must search and make commitments.

Identity achievement. Only with the successful resolution of all seven aspects of identity is a true and lasting identity achieved. Research evidence supports the necessity of both the resolution of each preceding conflict at its appropriate time, and the recurrence of each in the aspects just discussed (Waterman, 82). In Erikson's (68) words:

> Young people must become whole people in their own right . . . Individually speaking, identity includes, but is more than, the sum of all the successive identifications of those earlier years when the child wanted to be, and often was forced to become, like the people he depended on. Identity is a unique product, which now meets a crisis to be solved only in new identification with age mates and with leader figures outside the family. The search for a new and yet reliable identity can perhaps best be seen in the persistent adolescent endeavor to define, overdefine, and redefine themselves and each other in often ruthless comparison, while a search for reliable alignments can be recognized in the restless testing of the newest in possibilities and the oldest in values. Where the resulting self-definition, for personal or collective reasons, becomes too difficult, a *sense of role confusion* results: the young person counterpoints rather than synthesizes his sexual, ethnic, occupational, and typology alternatives and is often driven to decide definitely and totally for one side or the other. (p. 87)

Identity Confusion

Definition. When identity achievement is too difficult, the individual experiences identity confusion (also called identity diffusion), ''a split of self images . . . a loss of centrality, a sense of dispersion and confusion, and a fear of dissolution'' (Erikson, 59, pp. 122–123). Confused adolescents have found the demands too great; they aren't ready for commitments, don't want to make occupational choices, and resist defining themselves. The normal adolescent issues of confusion of time perspectives, self-consciousness, transient ideals and commitments, feelings of incompetence, tendencies to identify with strong leaders, and some confusion regarding sex roles may become exaggerated, leading to such symptoms as poor work habits, an inability to concentrate, self-destructive preoccupation with one idea or activity, dropping out of school, staying out all night, withdrawal from social contacts, clannish behavior, intolerance for others, fixation with fads, sexual promiscuity, experimentation with bizarre behavior, even delinquency and retreat into psychopathology. In general, identity-confused adolescents are at odds with themselves and the world and feel like nobodies.

Examples. Two of the most famous literary characters that displayed identity confusion were Shakespeare's Hamlet and Holden Caulfield (from *Catcher in the Rye*, by J.D. Salinger). Both felt apathetic, found it difficult to commit themselves to the future, and adopted transient roles as substitutes for ego identities of their own. For identity-confused adolescents, the need is to find something enduring to which to commit themselves.

Negative identity. All adolescents need to make commitments, but the confused may be overzealous in their pursuit of an all-or-nothing commitment to a cult or a powerful leader who promises to save them from their problems. They may also choose a **negative identity**, such as delinquency or joining a group that is in direct opposition to the values of their parents or the wider society. Erikson saw such negative identity formation as a last-ditch effort at achieving mastery over something. For example, the young man who joins a motorcycle gang may be saying that at least here he is accepted by his peers, perhaps even admired, whereas in the community he came from he never knew acceptance or success.

When the choice is between being somebody bad and being nobody, the choice is usually in favor of *any* identity, even if it is a negative one by societal standards. In fact, Erikson even explained suicide as the desperate attempt to resolve the identity conflict; being dead is preferable to being nobody.

When delinquency and behavioral problems in adolescence are viewed as pitiful, destructive attempts to establish some identity, they are generally dealt with in more humane ways than when they are seen as signs of individual pathology. When viewed as identity issues, they become temporary manifestations of unresolved conflict and can be treated by identifying the specific conflicts that remain unresolved and structuring the environment to provide the adolescent with the support to work them through.

Technological change. The achievement of identity has been complicated and the conflict exacerbated by the technological society in which we live. Adolescents today have a greater challenge than any group before them, because "rapid technological change makes it impossible for any traditional way of being older to become so institutionalized that the younger generation can step right into it or, indeed, resist it in revolutionary fashion" (Erikson, 68, p. 38). Never before have there been so few models, so few sure paths. Adolescents who know how to pursue expanding opportunities and identify with emerging competencies and roles will be better equipped to manage new values, new ideologies, and new problems. It seems imperative that all adolescents be afforded technical expertise as the basis for their emerging identities. With technical competence and an understanding of history, today's youth will be able, as Erikson (68) said, to "renew and regenerate, to disavow what is rotten, to reform and rebel" (p. 258).

Race and Sex Differences

Erikson addressed the issue of identity achievement from a white male perspective, and noted that for minorities and for women the achievement of identity was complicated in identifiable ways.

Race. We noted earlier that the research on self-esteem documents that race, by itself, is not a causal factor in self-esteem, but that one's attitude toward one's race is highly significant. The danger to which all suppressed people have been subjected is the tendency to accept negative evaluations of themselves placed on them by the dominant group. Oppression of slaves in this country, for example, led to the acceptance by many slaves of the characteristics of docility, subservience, even stupidity, even though these characteristics were no more a part of their genetic inheritance than were any other set of personality characteristics (Wilson, 78). Erikson noted that blacks in this country have worked hard to regain positive identities, value their cultural heritage, and battle against the stereotypes that tend to hide latent self-esteem. Blacks today know that the battle is not yet completely won, but racial pride is continuing to advance the progress of individual identity achievement for young blacks. It is the responsibility of all of us who work with young people to encourage that pride.

Sex. Barbara Jordan, former Congresswoman from Texas, noted repeatedly in her public addresses that being female was a far greater barrier to public success and acceptance than was being black. Her experience might have been predicted by Erikson, who recognized that a woman is likely to have far greater difficulty with the achievement of a unique identity and societal acceptance of that identity if it deviates from the traditional than are males of any race.

Freud used the symbolism of "penis envy" and the "bleeding wound" left by the lack of a penis to explain the psychological difficulties he noted in his female patients. Erikson progressed far beyond this blatantly sexist symbolism but nevertheless explained psychological differences between the sexes as arising primarily from anatomical differences. He studied the play behavior of early adolescents (aged 11 to 13 years) by instructing them to create a movie scene. Girls tended to emphasize what he called "inner space," while boys emphasized "outer space." Girls put people and animals in static, peaceful positions within enclosures, where men and other animals frequently intruded on them, usually pleasurably. Boys, on the other hand, built their scenes outdoors and included towers, moving vehicles, and action scenes involving collapse and ruin. Because his training was based in psychoanalysis, Erikson related these differences to the anatomical differences of the reproductive organs, but he also noted that the children may well have learned these different approaches rather than having acquired them merely by their inheritance of maleness or femaleness. He suggested that although the sexes may be predisposed to differences in personality, each is capable of learning the characteristics of the other (Erikson, 68).

Because of the demands of traditional society, Erikson also suggested that women have a different route to the achievement of identity than do men. Whereas for men the path is clearly that of identity achievement followed by the achievement of intimacy, Erikson thought that for women the identity and intimacy tasks became fused. For a traditional woman, identity comes only after the choice of a mate, for her identity is dependent to a significant degree on that of the man she chooses to marry. O'Connell (76) found that traditional women tend to delay developing personal identities until their children are in school; nontraditional women develop them in the same manner and at the same time as men.

Erikson's discussion of the identity achievement issue for women has been severely criticized by feminist writers, who note that for the nontraditional women that modern society demands, such an alternative route to identity achievement is no longer satisfactory. With the necessity for virtually all women to work, declining fertility rates, increasing divorce rates and a corresponding increase of people living alone, women can no longer anticipate that the major effort of their adult lives will be the nurturance of husband and family. They cannot wait to establish an identity based solely on the expectation of being a wife and mother but must, in order to function successfully, attain unique identities as women before adding to their identities the roles of spouse and parent, just as men do. Erikson himself was influenced by these criticisms to revise his thinking concerning the role achievement of women.

Morgan (82) noted that for young women there still exist two competing sets of expectations, the traditional and the nontraditional, expectations that may create inevitable conflicts for modern adolescent women; and Stein (82) found that feminist women scored significantly higher on a measure of identity achievement than did traditional women. Both these researchers concur with the findings concerning adjustment that we noted in Chapter 7: acceptance of traditional sex roles and sex-role personality stereotypes does not equip today's adolescent women to achieve the personality constructs that are essential to healthy adjustment to society's demands. Just as we who work with young people must accept the challenge to encourage positive racial identities, so too must we encourage positive sexual identities. If women will be required to work outside the home, as we now know they will, the traditional role is no longer sufficient. We need to help adolescent females achieve personal competence and set occupational goals while also making decisions con-

Table 9.5
The Identity Statuses of James Marcia

	Crisis	Commitment
Foreclosure	O	X
Moratorium	X	?
Diffusion	X/O	O
Achievement	X	X

cerning the place raising a family will play in their lives. Carol Gilligan's (82a,b) work on the moral development of females, which is discussed in the following chapter, also helps to make sense out of the literature concerning sex differences in identity formation.

THE IDENTITY ACHIEVEMENT STATUSES OF JAMES MARCIA

The Task of Identity Formation

As we have seen, Erikson's concept of identity achievement refers to a process of struggle (crisis) leading to commitments, usually occuring during a period of psychosocial moratorium, a reprieve from adult responsibilities. In studying the task of identity achievement, James Marcia (66, 67, 70, 76, 80) developed a structured interview procedure to measure the extent of the crisis and of commitments in the areas of occupations, religion, and political ideology. He interviewed college students and developed four categories related to the extent of crisis and commitment (Table 9.5).

The Four Statuses

Each of the four identity statuses has been found to be quite consistent in terms of expected behaviors and personality characteristics. We'll look at each separately. The descriptions below are a compilation of the findings of Marcia (66, 67, and 80), Rowe (80), Donovan (75), Waterman (82), and Adams (82a).

Foreclosure. College students with **foreclosed** identities feel strong commitments but have not experienced the struggle of crisis. They have simply adopted their parents' values and identify strongly with their parents, with whom they have good relationships. They come from warm, supportive families that both control and encourage their children, and they tend to see their parents as supportive, possessive, intrusive, authoritarian, and caring. The young man who attends his father's *alma mater* and enters the same profession without exploring real alternatives is a classic example of a foreclosed identity status. Such students are often hard-working, talkative, constructive, dependent on parents and teachers, and relatively cautious. They have avoided the stress of crisis and feel comfortable in their views, which tend toward the authoritarian. Because their self-esteem is dependent on approval, they are vulnerable to criticism. They tend to set unrealistically high goals and are prone to adopting a facade when faced with conflicting demands. Although foreclosure avoids the moratorium and the true attainment of a unique identity, it can be adaptive, especially when there is little expectation of change or the need to be flexible. In our grandparents' days, for example, there may have been little need to explore alternatives, for the future was certain and roles secure. This was also true for women at one time in history. But today, with the technology of change ruling our society, the foreclosed identity is likely to be less adaptive than it once was, even though it remains less painful than the alternative of experiencing the confusion of crisis.

Moratorium. Students in the midst of a **moratorium** are acutely aware of the choices they must make but have made only tentative commitments, which may change daily. These students are usually actively applying formal operations to themselves and their studies and are actively searching for commitments. They are likely to be competent, autonomous, active, aware, avoidant of dependency, quick to disagree, competitive, sensitive, and sometimes hostile. Their self-esteem is strong and not subject to the evaluations of others. Their relations with their parents may be strained, for in their search they are likely to have rejected, at least temporarily, the parents' values and aspirations for their children. The family is likely to have been democratic and encouraged individuation, and once these adolescents move into the achievement status, their relations with their parents are likely to improve.

Diffusion. Ambivalence characterizes students in **identity diffusion.** They not only have made no commitments but aren't concerned about them. They have no interest in varying ideologies, don't care about the future, are committed to no values, and may appear suspicious, angry, fearful, and resistant. If diffusion does not abate and an identity develop, the diffused individual may either drift through life with no commitments and very poor work habits, or may resort to delinquency or even suicide. Family relationships are poor, self-esteem is low, and such adolescents are likely to wear a facade of bravado. The family may have been either overly permissive and indulgent or rejecting and neglecting; both styles lead to insecurity and acting out.

Achievement. Students who have weathered the crisis and **achieve an identity** have come to their own conclusions and feel good about themselves. Their sense of esteem is not vulnerable to criticism. They accept and feel in harmony with themselves and are calm, nurturant, mature, measured, tolerant, and active. They are truly independent of their parents and are likely to have established new, mature relationships with them, based on the individuation that they were encouraged to achieve by a democratically led family decision-making style. They use formal operations consistently, are able to understand and negotiate a variety of points of view on any subject, and can empathize with people who are vastly different from themselves (Waterman, 76, 77, 82).

Observations Concerning the Statuses

Research has demonstrated the following:

1. Family styles (authoritarian, democratic, or *laissez-faire*) have an important impact. Democratic parenting encourages the most positive development.

2. Choice is a vital ingredient in the achievement of identity (Waterman, 82; Bardwick, 79; Morgan, 82; Fannin, 79). The young person exposed to more alternatives is more likely to experience a crisis and be forced to choose from among competing demands. Students in completely homogeneous environments are more likely than those in heterogeneous environments to foreclose on identity issues.

3. Adult role models who themselves are successful in their lives encourage commitments because they offer alternative methods of coping with life's diversities.

4. Where the environment encourages questioning, crisis is more likely.

5. An individual who has been more successful in negotiating the earlier conflicts of childhood is more likely to work through the crisis to achieve an identity.

6. The achievement of formal operational thinking skills enhances the individual's likelihood of making strong, consistent commitments. Identity might be achieved without formal operational thinking, but both research and logic support the vital role it usually plays (Waterman, 82). ''. . . individuals in the identity achievement and moratorium statuses exhibit a better performance in formal operational thinking than those in the foreclosure and identity diffusion statuses when confronted with problems that reflect identity-related issues'' (Leadbetter, 81).

7. Curiosity and exploration enhance the achievement of identity.

8. Work experience may stimulate identity achievement.

9. Full-time college attendance stimulates the moratorium in that it legitimizes searching, role taking, consideration of alternatives, and exposure to a variety of viewpoints and lifestyles.

10. Identity is not achieved once and for all. Rather, the process is a continuing one, often throughout an individual's life.

Stability. The moratorium is the least stable of the statuses; it invariably leads to another status. In the vocational area, achievement and foreclosure are stable; in the area of political ideology, diffusion is the most stable. This means that political ideology, as we all are probably acutely aware, is the least consistent commitment for most people. Those who are most consistent in political ideology are those who hold no committed views and who tend not to care.

Any one of the statuses may evolve into the others (Waterman, 82). Diffusion is seen as the lowest status, with movement to foreclosure or moratorium representing progressive development. Second to diffusion is foreclosure, with movement to moratorium representing a progressive development and movement to diffusion representing a regressive development. From moratorium, movement to achievement is progress, while movement to diffusion is regression. Finally, any movement from achievement represents at least a temporary regression.

In the college years, then, most students progress from a foreclosure that is not unlike that of their childhoods through a moratorium and into an achieved identity, with some possibilities for diffusion or confusion along the way. The road is not smooth, and achievement is not assured, but the majority of college students do leave college with at least some semblance of a unique, personally defined and committed sense of who they are and what they believe in, apart from parents and family. Those who achieve a sense of identity in the college years also begin to work on the next task, that of intimacy. It is not merely coincidental that so many marriages take place shortly after college graduations.

Noncollege youth. The research concerning identity achievement comes from college populations, and with college students we are relatively clear about the course of identity development. Considerably less research has been done with working youth and with high-school age populations, yet these too need to be addressed. Is the achievement of identity a luxury afforded only to those who attend college?

We discussed earlier the role that college attendance plays in providing a sanctioned moratorium and exposure to a variety of alternatives; certainly the traditional college represents the ideal of a socially approved moratorium. Working youths, however, have not been granted such a moratorium. They tend, at younger ages than college youth, to assume adult resonsibilities: to work, marry, and raise a family. It has been hypothesized that they do not experience the identity crisis but are more likely than college youth to foreclose on an identity and adopt the lifestyles of their parents without considering alternatives. Morash (80), however, compared working-class and college youth and found that the working-class youth were more likely than the college youth to be in the status of achievement or of diffusion, while the college youth were more likely to be in moratorium or foreclosure. She found that the working-class youth experienced a different process of identity formation. Because they are not granted a long moratorium, they may experience a shorter, more concrete crisis, and make choices quickly and concretely. ''It is conceivable that working class youth go directly from a state of diffusion to a choice of occupation, experiencing a 'crisis' quite different from the discussion and exploration that has been assumed to occur in the moratorium phase'' (Morash, 80, p. 319). As long as these youth are not placed in positions that demand adaptability, their shortened version of identity development, which admittedly considerably resembles foreclosure, may be highly reliable and useful for them.

High-school students. Identity development is completed only in late adolescence, and Marcia's categories have been found to be too advanced for high-school students, who are only beginning the moratorium. Raphael (80) noted that living at home and being in high school are restrictive; most homes and schools do not provide significant support for real consideration of alternatives. He therefore revised Marcia's statuses to assess **openness to alternatives** and **presence of commitments** and generated the following categories by which to assess the identity development of high-school students:

- *The open status:* Adolescents in this category are aware of the presence of alternative futures and are interested in exploring them.
- *The closed status:* Adolescents in this category have made commitments and do not expect to be influenced by other possibilities.
- *The diffused status:* Adolescents in this category are not aware of alternatives, have little interest in exploration, and have made no commitments.

Although these categories are not so precise and elaborate as Marcia's, they do make sense in assessing younger adolescents, and may provide some insight into the possible paths that development may take for the individuals in each status.

PSYCHOLOGICAL EDUCATION

Just as our knowledge of sexual development should influence the way in which we educate adolescents concerning sexuality, so too should our knowledge of personality development inform the ways in which we interact with them. If we wish to promote the achievement of identity, enhance self-esteem, and help students develop their potentials, there are identifiable means that we can take to assist in their development, and it is my strong opinion that schools should take the lead in advancing individual development. We discussed in Chapter 5 the many pressures on school personnel and made recommendations for enhancing the educational environment. Here we will briefly discuss the purpose of **psychological education** and present two approaches that might be incorporated in any educational setting.

Definition

Psychological education (also known as affective or humanistic education) is predicated on the psychological knowledge that has formed the basis for this chapter. It arose in the late 1960s and early 1970s as a response to the strongly cognitive nature of schools, which, it was charged, were neglecting the more human aspects of their students' development. In short, individual needs and personal aspects of learning were missing from the curriculum, and it was the mission of those involved in the psychological education movement to reemphasize personal learning as well as content and skill learning.

> *Significant contact with pupils is most effectively established and maintained when the content and method of instruction have an affective basis.* That is, if educators are able to discover the feelings, fears, and wishes that move pupils emotionally, they can more effectively engage pupils from any background, whether by adapting traditional content and procedures or by developing new materials and techniques. (Weinstein, 70, p. 10)

One focus of psychological education is assisting students to examine their personal responses to life situations, consider alternatives, try out new behaviors, and make choices based on personal awareness. This focus, which is represented by the "Education of Self" (Weinstein, 76) curriculum described below, is clearly consistent with the description of identity development offered by Erikson and Marcia. It makes the individual's development the primary content of learning.

A second focus of psychological education is employing our knowledge of individual needs in designing appropriate alternative ways for students to learn more traditional content and skills. The use of Maslow's hierarchy of needs to assign writing assignments based on students' needs rather than on teacher expectations is described by Hill and Boone in *If Maslow Taught Writing* (82) and represents just one approach to innovative teaching based on psychological principles.

Education of the Self

Developed by Gerry Weinstein at the University of Massachusetts, "Ed of Self" (as it is affectionately called) is a college-level course in personal growth, based on psychological theory and designed to promote introspection, self-analysis, consideration of alternatives, risk-taking behavior, and cognitive integration. The goal is for students not merely to acquire self-understanding, but to do something constructive with that understanding, develop a scientific attitude toward personal development, and thus grow. In the course, students are faced with behavioral experiments or exercises that require that they attend to their ordinary responses. A warmup or getting-acquainted activity, for example, affords the opportunity for students to examine their thoughts, feelings, and behaviors in that situation. Following the experiment, students are asked to observe their reactions, look for their typical patterns of reaction, and determine the function of those patterns and learn to accept their purpose. For example, in the getting-acquainted example, a student might recognize that he typically hangs back until someone approaches him.

Though he feels awkward waiting, the payoff is avoiding possible rejection if he were to be the approacher. After analyzing his typical response behavior, he is asked to consider the consequences of this behavior, then to generate and allow alternatives for behavior, then to make evaluations, and finally to choose the behavior that he wants to be a part of his personal style. Thus his behavior in the situation comes under his conscious control rather than being spontaneous and uncontrolled. Although we used here a simple example of getting-acquainted behavior, more complex issues like sex roles and other aspects of identity development can also be examined in this systematic manner.

If Maslow Taught Writing

Although the content of "Ed of Self" is the students themselves, many teachers are uncomfortable with such directly psychological education, believing that it belongs in the realm of counselors and psychologists, not teachers whose job it is to teach history, math, or English. Ada Hill and Beth Boone, both high-school English teachers, felt frustrated in their attempts to teach writing skills to high-school students and, in their search for ways to motivate students, came upon the idea of identifying the needs that motivate students and adapting assignments to meet those needs. They used the hierarchy of needs developed by Maslow, which we described briefly in the section of this chapter on humanistic-existential theory, to describe the need levels of their students and developed assignments geared to meeting those needs. You will recall that the most basic needs must be met before higher-order needs can be addressed. (Look back to Figure 9.2.)

Hill and Boone recognized that many adolescents are motivated by needs for belonging to the peer group, and for those students they devised group writing projects that rewarded cooperative effort as well as writing skill. Peer critiques, group development of outlines, and editing of one another's work all fell into this category. For students motivated by the need for esteem from others, they devised ways of publishing good work and making public the accomplishments of these students. And to those motivated by self-actualization, they gave wide latitude in terms of the kinds and styles of assignments allowed. They never pigeonholed students into categories or told them the basis for the assignments but used observation and intuition to assess individual needs and then offered a number of writing assignments from which students could choose. Students invariably chose the assignment that best met their individual needs. As a result of attending to the motivational needs of the students, the authors reported that writing became an interesting, even enjoyable activity for virtually all their students, rather than the meaningless drudgery it had often been when everyone was required to do exactly the same assignment according to exactly the same requirements, those that motivated the teacher rather than the students themselves.

SUMMARY

The seeds of adult personality are sown in conception and nurtured throughout childhood, but the physical and cognitive maturity of adolescence fosters its bloom. Personality, which refers to the psychological structures and processes that shape human behavior, is developed through the complex interaction of genetics and social learning.

Although personality development encompasses all other forms of development, the cognitive maturity of adolescence is particularly significant. With cognitive maturity, adolescents are able to consider who they are, who they want to become, how they are seen by others, and how they value their perceptions of themselves. Their evaluations of themselves, both specifically and globally, form their self-concept or self-esteem. A generally positive self-concept is essential to healthy personality development, and low esteem is associated with low achievement, anxiety, insecurity, withdrawal, acting out, and even physical complaints. Because of the vast changes to which they must adjust, young adolescents tend to display relatively low esteem, but esteem tends to improve through adolescence and into young adulthood.

The three main approaches to the study of personality are the psychodynamic, the humanistic-existential, and the behavioral. From the psychodynamic point of view, personality results from the interactions of the id, ego, and superego. The id is the seeker of pleasure, the ego the manager, and the superego the conscience. All are necessary in appropriate balance. Personality develops through predictable psychosexual stages, each of which contributes specific characteristics to adult personality. In adolescence, the individual must deal with the reawakening of sexual impulses and tension and learn to direct them in appropriate ways.

From the humanistic-existential point of view, personality develops as needs are met or not met in the environment. An individual who is provided with basic biological needs and is raised in an environment that provides security, belongingness, and positive regard will develop a realistic and positive sense of self and will be able to achieve full potential. From this point of view, the environment, most especially the significant adults in a child's life, thwarts the development of a healthy personality by not valuing the child simply for being alive, but instead puts conditions on his acceptance.

Whereas the psychodynamic view emphasizes instinctual drives that must be harnessed, and the humanistic view emphasizes positive growth potential that must be actualized in a supportive environment, the behavioral view assumes no innate psychological characteristics. From the behavioral view, all behavior is learned. Personality is the result of all an individual has learned, and all can be unlearned in the same manner in which it was learned. From the behavioral view has evolved the cognitive view, which emphasizes that individual thought is a powerful force in the shaping of personality. As the science of psychology has matured, these various streams of theoretical thought are being integrated, with the most useful and applicable concepts from each interacting to enrich our understanding of human behavior. Erik Erikson's psychosocial theory of development is an adaptation of Freud's psychodynamic theory that better represents the social and humanistic influences on development.

Erikson emphasized the interaction of the individual and society and changed the focus of psychodynamic theory from the pathological to the normal. His epigenetic principle refers to the development of personality from an inherent groundplan, out of which parts arise at special times eventually to form a functioning whole. His stage theory parallels that of Freud, with each stage representing the ego's attempt to mediate between inherent growth and environmental demands. He saw in each stage a normative crisis, a turning point that is decided more or less positively, the resolution of which prepares the individual for subsequent stages. The crisis of adolescence, that of identity *vs.* role confusion, is the most complex of all, for it is during this time that the individual achieves a sense of both continuity and uniqueness, an ideology and commitment to values, and a balance between the past and the future. Adolescents who manage the stage successfully emerge with a strong sense of their values and directions and are at peace with who they have become. The achievement of identity in adolescence provides the strength to tolerate conflict and diversity, reconcile the contradictions of modern society, and weather adversity. The danger for those who do not develop a sense of who they are is role confusion, which leads to poor habits, inability to concentrate, self-destructive behavior, withdrawal, intolerance, promiscuity, and even delinquency and severe behavioral problems.

James Marcia identified four identity statuses in college youth and measured them based on the extent to which an individual was experiencing crisis (concern with the search for values and ideology) and commitment to a particular lifestyle and its attendant values. Those in foreclosure had made commitments, but without the experience of crisis; those in moratorium were actively searching and may or may not have made tentative commitments; those in diffusion had made no commitments and may or may not have felt in crisis; and those in achievement had experienced the crisis and made commitments as a result.

Identity achievement is not static but may continue and/or recur throughout life. Family interaction styles, the availability of choices, successful adult role models, success in the previous stages, formal operational thinking skills, curiosity, work experience, and college attendance all seem to facilitate healthy achievement of identity in late adolescence.

To promote personality development, psychological (humanistic, affective) education addresses the emotional aspects of learning. Students are encouraged to examine their lives, make choices, and increase their awareness of themselves and their worlds.

10

Moral Development

SHARON'S DILEMMA

Sharon and her best friend Jill walked into a department store to shop. As they browsed, Jill saw a blouse she really liked and told Sharon she wanted to try the blouse on. While Jill went to the dressing room, Sharon continued to shop.

Soon Jill came out of the dressing room wearing her coat. She caught Sharon's attention with her eyes and glanced down at the blouse under her coat. Without a word, Jill turned and walked out of the store.

Moments later the store security officer, salesclerk, and the store manager approached Sharon. "That's her, that's one of the girls. Check her bags," blurted the clerk. The security officer pointed to a sign over the door saying that the store reserved the right to inspect bags and packages. Sharon gave him her bag. "No blouse in here," he told the manager. "Then I know the other girl has it," the clerk said. "I saw them just as plain as anything. They were together on this." The security officer then asked the manager if he wanted to follow through on the case. "Absolutely," he insisted. "Shoplifting is getting to be a major expense in running a store like this. I can't let shoplifters off the hook and expect to run a successful business."

The security officer turned to Sharon. "What's the name of the girl you were with?" he asked. Sharon looked up at him silently. "Come on now; come clean," said the security officer. "If you don't tell us, you can be charged with the crime or with aiding the person who committed the crime." (Guidance Associates, 76)

Although you may never have been faced with the dilemma of choosing between your best friend and the authority of a security officer, you have certainly made

Moral development concerns the question of choices based on concepts of right and wrong, good and evil.

thousands of decisions based on your concepts of morality. These judgments and behaviors are the substance of our moral development.

As we discussed in depth in Chapter 2, our postindustrial society offers a world of choices, which have led to widespread alarm over apparently declining standards for moral conduct. The Watergate scandal and other examples of corruption in business and government, increasing sexual openness and experimentation, decreasing influence of traditional family values, and increasing drug use and youth crime have all contributed to increasing interest among psychologists and educators in the process of moral development, the question of how we learn to make choices based on concepts of right and wrong, good and evil, just and unjust.

In simpler societies, the development of morality was a relatively simple process, as was the development of an identity. Without choices, there is no conflict, and the values of the past are handed down without fanfare and without question, for there is only one set of acceptable beliefs and behaviors. But in an environment that both allows choice and offers no dependable answers, the development of a coherent, consistent philosophy of life becomes problematic at best. And for adolescents, who are developing new physical, cognitive, and psychological capacities that stimulate both questioning of established values and experimenting with new roles and behaviors, the search for an enduring commitment takes on a passion that sometimes confounds, even frightens, adults. The result has been an increasing emphasis by adults on understanding and influencing the moral development of children and adolescents.

In this chapter we will examine various theories of moral development, with particular emphasis on the moral development theory of Lawrence Kohlberg, which we will relate not only to other theories of moral development, but also to the theories of cognitive and psychological development we have already studied. We will also discuss the development and importance of religion in adolescence and will examine various approaches to moral, religious, and values education both in and outside of schools and churches. But first, what do we know about the attitudes toward morality held by modern adolescents?

VALUES AND MORALITY IN ADOLESCENCE

Current Attitudes

Thousands of research studies in recent years have examined the attitudes and values of adolescents with predictably contradictory results. Statistical and methodological problems abound in the research, with the result being a real inability to say with any confidence that adolescents today are any more or less moral in their thoughts and behaviors than any other group in any other period of history. Results from several well-designed and executed studies will serve as samples of the variety of findings available in the literature. Comeau (80) found that among high-school students who were asked to list ten characteristics in order of importance (honest, understanding, likeable, dependable, independent, intelligent, realistic, generous, attractive, and talented), students at all grade levels rated honest and understanding highest, attractive and talented lowest. Through the high-school years, honesty lost in importance, though it still ranked first, and attractiveness (for males) moved from sixth place in the ninth grade to tenth place in the twelfth (consistent with what we know about the decrease in egocentrism related to body image), and males ranked intelligence higher than did females (consistent with what we know about sex-role stereotyping throughout adolescence). This study would seem to indicate that adolescent values are no different than those espoused by a moral society. However, the high value placed on honesty is contradicted in studies by Schab (80), who compared adolescent responses concerning knowledge of and attitudes toward cheating in 1969 and 1979. He found that although both samples believed cheating to be highly prevalent (above 95 percent), more in 1979 reported willingness to let others copy their work, sign their parent's name, plagiarize, and believe that dishonesty might be necessary on the job. An interesting change from 1969 to 1979 was in their response to punishment for cheating. Both groups thought that failure should be the punishment, but the 1979 group felt that the teacher and student together should work out an appropriate punishment whereas the 1969 group felt it should be the teacher's prerogative to determine the punishment. According to these data, the more current group had learned to value collaborative rather than authoritarian decision making.

In an extensive analysis of the major concerns of adolescents associated with churches, Strommen (74) found that the two most prevalent issues were those of alienation (self-hatred, low esteem, lack of value orientation) and of identity achievement (joy, sense of worth, purposefulness). Though it seems ironic that the two most prevalent findings are diametrically opposed to each other, we can make sense of them when we think back to our understanding of the development of identity: those who have achieved an identity know themselves and their values; those who are in diffusion do not and therefore have no basis on which to make moral choices. Are adolescents today less moral than those of the past? We simply don't know, but the rapid changes and more open discussion and awareness that characterize modern society make moral issues a topic of intense interest.

Approaches to Moral Development

The general path of moral development is from an absolutism in moral judgments that clearly delineates right from wrong through a relativistic "anything is OK" attitude, to final arrival at personal commitments within an awareness of legitimate competing alternatives (Perry, 70). There are, however, varying theoretical explanations regarding how this development takes place. In the last chapter we explored the relative views of the psychoanalysts, behaviorists, and humanists, and in the chapter previous to that one we discussed cognitive developmental theory. Cognitive development, personality development, and moral development each address different, though closely related, facets of adolescent development (Lutwak, 84). Each of many theories includes an explanation of the development of morality, with the most prevalent approaches being the psychodynamic, behavioral, and cognitive.

Psychodynamic perspective. From the psychodynamic perspective, innate drives toward fulfillment of sexual and aggressive needs are controlled by the development of the superego, the conscience that balances instincts with learned controls. Throughout childhood, parental injunctions gradually become internalized, and guilt and conscience develop. Moral behavior is controlled by a highly developed superego, which emerges as the result of the anxiety associated with guilt for wrongful actions and thoughts.

Behavioral perspective. From the behavioral perspective, morality develops through modeling, imitation, and reinforcement. Children are neither moral nor immoral but develop as a result of their interaction with the environment, which provides the content of morality.

Cognitive perspective. That both conscience (the internalization of society's rules) and social learning play important roles in the development of morality is not debated, but neither alone provides a sufficient explanation of the development of moral thought and behavior. More sophisticated theories combine both the psychodynamic and behavioral approaches with our awareness, from Piaget, of the sequential development of cognitive capacities. The resultant theories offer comprehensive and complex descriptions of the qualitatively different reasons individuals use for making moral choices. The innate development of cognitive capacity combines with environmental stimuli to produce qualitatively different stages of moral development. Once again, the interaction of nature and nurture provides the most complete explanation of development.

Interactionist perspective. We know that as we mature, we gradually replace external behavioral controls with internal ones, so that we grow to act consistently and morally even in the absence of external control. Whereas small children may not go to bed until forced to by their parents, adolescents regulate their own bedtimes for their own best interests. So too with moral decisions: they learn to respect the property rights of others through punishment for taking what was not theirs, but now manage their behavior on the basis of personal honor. The differences among the psychoanalytic, behavioral, and cognitive views lie in their disagreement as to the relative importance of parental discipline, identification, and cognitive disequilibrium in the process of internalization (Hoffman, 64). The psychodynamic perspective emphasizes identification, the behavioral perspective emphasizes parental discipline, and the cognitive perspective emphasizes cognitive disequilibrium.

Regardless of emphasis, however, it seems clear that three major processes contribute in a collaborative manner to the internalization of values:

1. Children become aware of external judgments and act to alleviate negative evaluations.
2. Children develop a social perspective, an empathy that allows them to be aware of the consequences of their behavior on others.
3. They use their developing cognitive skills actively to process morally relevant information (Hoffman, 72).

Though using different terminology, other researchers have identified similar processes in the development of morality. Wilcox (79) noted that different theorists emphasized different aspects of moral development, some emphasizing the cognitive, others the social or environmental; and Juhasz (82) noted that regardless of theoretical approach, values are always acquired through a process of incorporating value-laden information into the cognitive structure, processing it, and finally acting on it.

Moral development, then, results from the complex interaction of parental values and behavior, experiences, cognitive development, active thought processing, and general environmental factors. The ultimate tests of one's values come in everyday questions, as eminent Harvard psychiatrist Robert Coles noted, like "How did I drive my car today?" (Booker, 83). Daily choices of behavior are made in these questions. For the adolescent, moral choices revolve around friendships, school, and leisure activities that comprise daily life.

THEORIES OF MORAL DEVELOPMENT

Though consistent with one another, the various theories of moral development differ in their assumptions about the nature of humanity, in their emphasis on cognitive *vs.* social aspects, in the specific behaviors studied, and in the comprehensiveness of their approaches. In the next section of this chapter we will study the theory of Lawrence Kohlberg, which has been most thoroughly researched and provides the most practical understanding of moral development for educational purposes; but before doing so, it is instructive to note the similarities and differences among other selected theories of moral development. We will compare those of Jean Piaget with those of Joseph Adelson.

Jean Piaget

Piaget (32) was most interested, of course, in the qualitative cognitive changes that occur as children mature. In conjunction with his studies of conservation and the creation of meaning, he also studied the moral development of children and noticed that as children mature, they move from a highly rigid interpretation of rules imposed by external authority to a considerably more flexible interpretation based on reciprocity and social considerations. Specifically, he studied four aspects of moral development: behavioral conformity to rules, verbalized notions about rules, more general moral attitudes, and conceptions of justice.

Rules. Behavioral conformity and verbalized notions about rules were studied in relation to the marble-playing behavior of children, and clear stages of development, parallel to the stages of cognitive development, were found (see Table 10.1). Preoperational children, he found, had no concept of rules; they played marbles individually, each doing whatever she pleased independently of playmates. In early concrete operations, the children began to imitate the behavior of others, each interpreting the rules in an egocentric fashion and behaving erratically and inconsistently. It was not until late concrete operations (ages 8 to 12) that children tried to conform to mutually agreed-upon rules, and not until the onset of formal operations that they fully understood complex rules and used them appropriately and fairly. During this time, the children became increasingly able to verbalize about the rules, moving

Table 10.1

Relationship Between Cognitive and Moral Development Theories of Jean Piaget

PIAGET: Cognitive Development	PIAGET: Moral Development
Sensorimotor period	No concept of rules
Preoperations	Obedience by punishment
Early concrete operations	Beginning of conformity to mutually agreed-upon rules
Well-developed concrete operations	Beginning of understanding of motivation
Early formal operations	Full understanding and appropriate use of rules
Well-developed formal operations	Full comprehension of justice

from an awareness of rules without compliance to them in the preoperational and early concrete operational stages to an ability to negotiate appropriate rules in adolescence.

Moral attitudes. Piaget studied the more general moral attitudes of children by asking their reactions to stories involving moral decisions and their attitudes toward lies. For younger children, a lie was wrong because it was punished; if not punished, it was not wrong. (This immature belief system is seen in some delinquent adolescents who consistently believe that they are punished for getting caught rather than for the offense itself.) For most older children, however, intention became important; an undetected lie was just as wrong as a detected one.

Justice. Piaget's excursions into the minds of children are particularly interesting in his findings concerning the development of ideas of justice. He asked children how severely someone should be punished for various offenses and found that the younger children relied only on the magnitude of the offense, without regard for motivation, to determine consequences. For example, a child who accidently broke two valuable vases should be punished much more severly than one who intentionally broke one nonvaluable vase. It is not until the age of nine or ten that the motivation behind the offensive act is considered in determining appropriate punishments.

These early findings of Piaget have been criticized for being overly simplistic, but they are generally accepted as valid and have formed the basis for other, more complex formulations. Piaget can be credited for being the first to document that early morality, based on constraint, absolute right and wrong, authority, and rigid punishment, gradually evolves into a morality of cooperation, equity, and justice based on motive and intent as well as behavior itself, and that this development is the result of both cognitive maturity and social interaction.

Joseph Adelson: The Development of Political Views

Bridge between cognitive and moral development. The extensive research Joseph Adelson and his associates (66, 71) conducted with adolescents in the United States, West Germany, and Great Britain provides a bridge between cognitive and moral development. Adelson was interested in charting the development of political thinking through adolescence and found that between the ages of 12 and 16 most adolescents move from being completely incapable of political discourse to being capable of complex political abstractions, including the beginnings of formulating a morally coherent view of the world. The changes occur, he found, in three areas: cognitive mode, attitude toward authoritarianism, and capacity for ideology. The links between cognitive and moral reasoning are obvious.

Because Adelson wanted to analyze adolescents' thinking apart from any societal contexts and learned opinions, he formulated an interview situation involving a potential utopia and asked his subjects to comment on specifics of how they would deal with social issues in that environment. The subjects (450 were interviewed) were asked to imagine that a thousand people had gone to an island in the Pacific to form a new society. They had to devise a government and a legal system and address all the problems of a society. They were asked to choose among various forms of government, state the purpose of government and of laws, comment on proposed laws (such as a requirement for annual medical exams), explore problems of public policy (such as how to deal with a dissenting religious group or an unenforceable law), and consider all the issues facing a society (such as the relationship between majority and minority rights and the nature of crime and justice).

The researchers found only insignificant differences between sexes, among the various cultures, and among a variety of socioeconomic groups and levels of intelligence, but they found highly significant differences between the younger and older adolescents. These differences, categorized by cognitive mode, authoritarian views, and capacity for ideology, are summarized in Table 10.2.

Cognition. From early to late adolescence, four aspects of cognitive processes changed: abstraction, time perspective, understanding of motivation, and modes of reasoning. These are, of course, completely consistent with Piaget's findings, for the late adolescents demonstrated formal operational thinking while the early adolescents demonstrated only concrete operations. For example, in response to the question "What is the purpose of laws?" young adolescents answered personally and concretely, saying such things as "so people don't get hurt," but older adolescents could articulate a sense of principle and community, answering with phrases like "to ensure safety and enforce governmental regulations." In terms of time perspective, young adolescents were locked into the present, being able to imagine only immediate rather than long-range outcomes, while older adolescents were able to make decisions based on an analysis of alternative futures resulting from current actions. Young adolescents also displayed no sense of appreciation for motivation. In response to a question concerning the reasons for recidivism, they responded with caveats about people being bad. It wasn't until late adolescence that an understand-

Table 10.2
Adolescent Cognitive Development: Growth of Political Thought

		Early Adolescent		Late Adolescent
Cognitive Mode	Abstraction	concrete experience personalization	→ →	abstraction/synthesis/generalization sense of community
	Time perspective	locked into present	→	sense of past, future, causality, alternative futures
	Understanding of Motivation	little sense of motivation or inner complexity	→	sense of complex motivation/ appreciation for human change
	Modes of Reasoning	use of conviction, intuition, loose associations, absolutism	→	acquisition of logic, hypothetico- deductive capacity, conditional mode
Authoritarianism		emphasis on control and constraint/absolutist morality	→	appreciation of democratic forms/ situation ethics/relativistic morality
Ideology		little or no grasp of principle	→	well-developed sense of principle

ing of the dynamics of imprisonment and the concepts of psychopathology and rehabilitation were expressed. Concerning modes of reasoning, early adolescents used only loose associations, personal convictions, and intuition as reasons for a law against cigarette smoking being hard to enforce. Older adolescents, however, were capable of using the hypotheses, logic, and conditional reasoning of formal operations.

Authoritarianism. The development of formal operations also contributed to the decline in authoritarian views during adolescence. When young adolescents were asked what to do about the law against cigarette smoking, they tended to respond by designing elaborate detection and punishment schemes. If punishment didn't work, they offered to punish harder. They conceived of the law as being absolute and did not offer the possibility of amendment or repeal. If it's a law, it must be enforced. Only in late adolescence was the absurdity of the law itself raised, along with an awareness of democratic process and an appreciation for moral relativism based on the needs of the situation. In summary, the young adolescent is overwhelmingly authoritarian, fails to appreciate democratic process, is insensitive to individual rights, and is harshly punitive. Adelson concluded that the two most dramatic developments of adolescence are the rapid increase in the ability to abstract and the rapid decline of authoritarianism. The two are obviously related.

Ideology. Finally, young adolescents, unable to manage abstractions, generalize, synthesize, and transcend the present, have little or no grasp of principle and are unable to form ideologies. Through adolescence they gradually acquire the cognitive capacities that allow them to move from political slogans to true appreciation of principled moral judgment and consistent philosophical reasoning.

Moral development, as we have seen in the theories of Piaget and Adelson, involves cognitive development. Although physical and sexual development may not be so obviously involved in moral reasoning and behavior, it is certainly true that adolescents' physical and sexual self-concepts are as intimately involved in their morality as are their cognitive and social capacities. All that we have discussed here contributes to the highly popular theory of moral development and moral education proposed and researched by Lawrence Kohlberg.

THE MORAL DEVELOPMENT THEORY OF LAWRENCE KOHLBERG

Relationship to Piaget

Over the past 25 years, Lawrence Kohlberg (69, 71a, 71b, 75, 77) has developed, researched, and refined the most popular of the moral development theories. A confirmed Piagetian, Kohlberg built on the cognitive and moral development work of Piaget by adding adolescent males to Piaget's research and thereby demonstrated that the achievement of formal operations was a **necessary but not a sufficient**

Adolescents gradually move from political slogans to appreciation of principled moral judgment.

condition for the development of mature moral reasoning. Expanding on Piaget, Kohlberg first offered his theory, which is a broad description of growth that involves cognitive stage, political ideology, ego stage, and moral judgment, in his doctoral dissertion in 1958. He has since devoted himself to researching the theory and to studying the implications of the theory for education and the encouragement of moral development. The popularity of the theory can be attributed not only to its sophisticaed simplicity and researchability, but to the context it provides for application and study in schools, prisons, and other social institutions. It is logical, meaningful, descriptive, and applicable.

The Theory

Like other theories we have discussed, Kohlberg's describes how individuals develop moral judgment; that is, how they decide which of conflicting values to choose and act on in a situation of moral conflict. It does not address the content of moral decisions, which are subject to cultural determination, nor does it extend to moral behavior, though it does suggest that moral judgment allows an individual the potential to act in a morally consistent manner. As in the other theories, both cognitive maturity and social experiences are recognized as vital ingredients in moral development.

Stage development. As in all stage development theories, Kohlberg's stages are structured wholes (individuals tend to act relatively consistently across content areas); they form an invariant sequence (people always tend to move gradually up the scale of stages and do not regress or skip stages); and they are hierarchical (each stage integrates and understands all those below it but also represents entirely new patterns of thought unavailable previously). Each stage is also ''better'' than those below it because it allows for more comprehensive and elaborate solutions, while handling conflicts more consistently. People advance their moral reasoning through experiencing cognitive disequilibrium resulting from intellectual development and through role taking, which provides for increasingly wide perspectives on the issues involved.

Moral dilemmas. In developing and testing his theory, Kohlberg presented children and adolescents with moral dilemmas, hypothetical situations in which values come into conflict with one another. In such situations, learned values are insufficient, and people must exercise judgment in order to choose between conflicting values to arrive at a just solution to the problem (Reimer, 77). The dilemma of Sharon that opens this chapter is one example. Sharon must choose between loyalty to her friend and deference to authority, including the law. But it is not the choice that determines an individual's level of moral judgment; rather, the reasons given for the choice provide the clues to moral maturity.

Kohlberg identified eleven moral issues that come into conflict in moral dilemmas, and his dilemmas are built around them. They are punishment, property, affiliation, authority, character, law, contract, truth, liberties, life, and sex. When two issues are in conflict, as affiliation and authority are in Sharon's dilemma, an individual uses moral reasoning, including standards, consequences, fairness, and conscience, along with social perspective, to support the choice (Wilcox, 79).

The most well-known and thoroughly researched dilemma is that of Heinz, who poses a conflict between property and life:

> In Europe, a woman was near death from a special kind of cancer. There was one drug that the doctor thought might save her. It was a form of radium that a druggist in the same town had recently discovered. The drug was expensive to make, but the druggist was charging ten times what the drug cost him to

make. He paid $200 for the radium and charged $2,000 for a small dose of the drug. The sick woman's husband, Heinz, went to everyone he knew to borrow the money, but he could only get together about $1,000, which is half of what it cost. He told the druggist that his wife was dying and asked him to sell it cheaper or let him pay later. But the druggist said, "No, I discovered the drug and I'm going to make money from it." So Heinz got desperate and broke into the man's store to steal the drug for his wife. (Porter, 72, pp. 11–12)

To determine level of moral reasoning, subjects are asked to explain why Heinz should or should not have stolen the drug, why his stealing was right or wrong, whether or not it is a husband's duty to steal for his wife and why, and whether or not the druggist had a right to charge what he did and why. The reasons are then classified into the six stages of moral reasoning. Yussen (77) noted that a major shortcoming of Kohlberg's original dilemmas is that they do not deal with issues that are important to adolescents. He had adolescents write their own dilemmas, and found that the most real dilemmas to them included issues involving interpersonal relations, physical safety, drugs, sex, civil rights, working, and stealing. Sharon's dilemma, which opens this chapter, is more real to adolescents than is Heinz's dilemma.

Kohlberg's work is not without its critics, whose concerns we will examine a little later, but it is nevertheless the most promising theory of moral development and moral education to date, with particular relevance to adolescent development.

The Stages of Moral Development

Kohlberg delineated six clearly differentiated and identifiable stages that he classified into three more general levels of development, each containing two specific stages. These are described below and are summarized in Table 10.3.

I. Preconventional level. At the preconventional level, the individual responds to personal concerns and acts to satisfy personal needs, either physical or hedonistic.

Stage 1: Punishment-obedience orientation. Individuals in the first stage of moral reasoning make judgments in terms of their physical consequences; they avoid punishment and defer to power merely to escape punishment.

Stage 2: Instrumental-relativist orientation. Individuals in the second stage of moral reasoning make judgments in order to satisfy their own needs. Though elements of sharing and reciprocity are seen, they are used only to accomplish personal gain, not out of loyalty or concern for others. "You scratch my back and I'll scratch yours" describes the reasoning of this stage.

II. Conventional level. At the conventional level, egocentric needs are replaced by the expectations of the group. Conformity, loyalty, and identification with the group form the bases for moral judgments.

Stage 3: Interpersonal concordance orientation. Also known as the "good boy, nice girl" orientation, good behavior at this stage is that of which others approve,

Table 10.3
Kohlberg's Stages of Moral Development

Levels of Moral Development	Stages of Moral Development
I. Preconventional	1. Punishment–obedience: "I'll do it to avoid punishment." 2. Instrumental–relativist: "I'll do it if you'll do something for me."
II. Conventional	3. Interpersonal–concordance: "I'll do it to be nice and to have you like me." 4. Law and order: "I'll do it because it's the law."
III. Postconventional	5. Social contract: "I'll do it because we've agreed it's best for everyone." 6. Universal–ethical: "I'll do it because it's universally right."

especially those in authority. For the first time, the intentions of an action are considered, and a person is judged positively for meaning well. Conformity to stereotypical expectations is common.

Stage 4: Law and order orientation. Duty, rules, maintenance of the social order and respect for authority form the bases for moral decisions at the fourth stage. What is right is what authority dictates.

III. Postconventional level. Also known as the principled or autonomous level, judgments in the two stages of the postconventional level are made on the basis of what is right even apart from authority. Only in postconventional morality is civil disobedience condoned.

Stage 5: Social contract orientation. At the fifth stage, individual rights supersede authority, and decisions are made on the basis of the greatest good for the greatest number. Moral relativism becomes possible, and rational consideration of alternatives, with an emphasis on consensus, becomes the basis for establishing social contracts. The U.S. Constitution is considered to be a Stage 5 document.

Stage 6: Universal ethical principle orientation. Because of its complexity, stage 6 is not included in the scoring protocol used to measure stage attainment. Conscience, developed through logic, comprehensiveness, and universality, provides the basis for moral judgments. Abstract principles like the Golden Rule form the basis for justice. At this stage, the guiding principle becomes what is best for a person regardless of the position in which she finds herself. For example, on choosing a position on the issue of capital punishment, the principled thinker would consider the views of the defendant in a capital murder case as well as the views of the victim.

As we can see, the preconventional levels are used by immature reasoners who seek only to satisfy their personal needs, without regard for others or for justice. The conventional levels, where most Americans are found, are used by people who are most concerned with the group and their place in it. The postconventional levels go beyond the group and therefore are usually not rewarded by society's systems of rewards and punishments; but reasoners in these stages are not so concerned with following the rules as they are with universal principles of justice.

Example. As we already noted, it is not the response to a dilemma that determines a person's level of moral reasoning, but the reasons for making that choice. Let's see how this might apply in Sharon's dilemma by imagining how an individual could use each stage to justify either choice.

Response: "Sharon should tell the authorities who Jill is and what she did."

- *Stage 1:* Because she'll be punished if she doesn't.
- *Stage 2:* Because they'll let her off the hook or maybe even reward her if she does.
- *Stage 3:* Because they'll think well of her if she does.
- *Stage 4:* Because it's the law and she has the duty to uphold it.
- *Stage 5:* Because we all have agreed that shoplifting is damaging to the public.
- *Stage 6:* Because she would want all shoplifters to be stopped, and she would feel the same way even if she were tempted to shoplift.

Response: "Sharon should not tell on her friend."

- *Stage 1:* Because Jill might tell on her for something she did earlier.
- *Stage 2:* Because Jill will reciprocate the favor later.
- *Stage 3:* Because Jill will continue to be her friend and she owes her that loyalty.
- *Stage 4:* Because the code of friendship demands it.
- *Stage 5:* Because she and her friends had agreed that each needed to uphold the rights of the others.
- *Stage 6:* Because the principle of honor demands that she sacrifice herself for her friend.

You might try to argue at each stage of reasoning for and against Heinz stealing the drug for his wife. What would the arguments look like?

Relationship to moral behavior. Finally, we must reiterate that Kohlberg's stages apply only to moral reasoning and do not address moral behavior except in an inferential way. The link between moral reasoning and moral behavior is tenuous at best. As Kohlberg (77) pointed out:

> The relationship between moral judgment and moral behavior is not fully defined. That is, moral judgment is a necessary but not sufficient condition for moral action. Other variables come into play such as emotion, and a general

sense of will, purpose or ego strength. Moral judgment is the only distinctive *moral* factor in moral behavior but not the only factor in such behavior. (p. 58)

Research Findings

In general, research supports Kohlberg's theory, with some criticisms and contradictory findings.

Sequential development. Lee (71), in studying almost 200 adolescent males, found that sequential development in both cognitive and moral reasoning was evident, and that formal operations were necessary for advanced levels of moral reasoning. Kuhn (76) found that although there is evidence of some short-term fluctuation, significant progressive change is noted over a year's interval. Rest (76, 78) found sequential development in all stages of moral reasoning over two- to four-year periods.

Cultural universality. Parikh (80) found support for Kohlberg's cross-cultural claims when he compared upper-middle-class Indians and upper-middle-class Americans on moral development and family environment factors. He also found that in both cultures, negotiation and discussion in parent-child relationships favored moral development. This is consistent with other studies (Chapter 3) of the effects of differing styles of discipline. Edwards (81) reviewed the cross-cultural research and found that as exposure to modern social institutions increases, so too does the level of moral reasoning. Snarey (82), in an extensive review of the cross-cultural research, found that stage development is invariant and universal, that stages 1 to 3 are found in all twenty-two cultures studied, and that social class, urban multicultural life, and formal schooling contribute to movement from stage 3 to stages 4 and 5. White (78) found cultural universality in longitudinal studies of 426 Bahamian adolescents, with no adolescent reasoning beyond stage 3.

Moral reasoning and moral behavior. Kohlberg and his colleagues, in any number of studies, have found evidence that most adolescents think in stages 2, 3, and 4, as do most adults; that stage 5 thinking rarely occurs before the age of 20; that intelligence, socioeconomic status, peer-group status, and role-taking opportunities contribute to moral development; and that conduct is at least partially independent of moral reasoning. He found, for example, that whereas 70 percent of preconventional thinkers cheated, 15 percent of principled thinkers also cheated; and he posited that situational, motivational, and emotional factors, as well as ego strength, accounted for the differences between moral reasoning and moral behavior (Kohlberg, 75). Haan (68, 78) found that moral arguments encourage the growth of moral reasoning and that moral action is based as much or more on interpersonal needs as on formal reasoning. Adolescents were more likely to behave according to peer-group standards than according to their formal reasoning skills. Krebs (77), in studying average (stage 3 and 4 reasoning) adults, found that the structure of subjects' moral reasoning correlated with their moral behavior, especially in everyday decisions.

Similar findings were advanced by Weiss (82), who found that 16-year-olds were consistent in their moral reasoning, but when faced with real dilemmas, reverted to behavior that seemed personally useful and did not apply moral reasoning skills. This finding would explain the phenomenon with which we all may be familiar: although we are capable of reasoning at high levels of moral development, some actions (obeying the speed limit, for example) are motivated not by high levels of judgment (the increased safety of staying within the limit) but by personally motivated wishes (to avoid getting a speeding ticket). Milgram (62, 63) found, in his famous studies on obedience, that legitimate authority is extremely difficult to defy and that the stages beyond the conventional are therefore seldom realized.

Process of development. Several recent researchers have verified the process by which moral development advances. Wilcox (79), Blackburne-Stover (82), and Walker (79, 80) all noted that development is intellectual and reconstructive, conflict in opinions and role-taking opportunities stimulate development, and moral reasoning is influenced by the operative level of morality in the environment. Kurdek (78) hypothesized that perspective taking may be the most important cognitive component of moral judgment and behavior. As we develop the capabilities of more advanced stages of moral reasoning, we apply them to decisions made in the past as well as those we make now and may forget the original arguments we used. Blackburne-Stover (82), for example, interviewed women choosing to abort an unwanted pregnancy and evaluated their moral judgments concerning the abortion. She then interviewed them again one year later and found that those who had made developmental gains used their new reasons for terminating their pregnancies rather than the ones they had previously used. This supports Kohlberg's contention that we tend to favor and use the highest level of reasoning of which we are capable, even though we understand the arguments of levels of reasoning below our own.

Criticisms. But not all the research supports Kohlberg's theory of development. Critics have attacked the universality of the stages (Allport, 63; Feather, 74; Witkin, 74; Stanton, 75, 80; Gibbs, 77) and various methodological problems (Weinrach, 74; Wonderly, 80).

Concerning the problem wih the universality of the stages, Kohlberg himself noted that stages 5 and 6 are not universal and that most adults reason at stages 3 and 4. Gibbs (77) concurred, noting that stages 5 and 6 are so rare as to make stages 3 and 4 mature in their own right; the principled level, he suggested, is beyond universal stage theory. Stanton (80) found considerable variation in the acceptance of cheating behavior across five countries and noted that cultural factors are apparently stronger than Kohlberg allowed. Haan (82) criticized Kohlberg's heavy emphasis on logic as well as the lack of universality of the upper stages and suggested that moral development is considerably more complex, involving socialization and affective considerations more than Kohlberg acknowledged. The stage development theory has been criticized, then, for its assumption that intellectual capacities determine the quality of morality; for its progressive and irreversible sequence, which doesn't account for regressions and lapses (Kuhn, 76; Rest, 78), for the lack of universality of the upper stages, for its stress on justice and duty rather than on more social considerations (more about this in a moment), and for its emphasis on reasoning rather than on behavior.

Methodologically, Kohlberg has been criticized for some subjectivity in scoring procedures, a lack of validation of some of his methods of research, and his use of a variety of instruments and scoring systems (Weinrach, 74; Wonderly, 80).

Regardless of the problems and criticisms, Kohlberg's theory remains the most popular, and Kohlberg himself has welcomed and responded to the issues. The theory continues to evolve, with contributions like those of Carol Gilligan, which we will discuss in the next section, offering even greater applicability to all populations.

Carol Gilligan's Reconceptualization

Carol Gilligan (77, 82a, 82b) is a colleague and fellow researcher of Kohlberg's at Harvard. Concerned that research with his scheme generally found that men ordinarily make level 4 judgments while women make level 3 judgments, and aware that all the stage researchers, including Freud, Erikson, Piaget, and Kohlberg, based their research on samples of men, Gilligan proposed that the omission of women from the research created a limitation that tended to evaluate female reasoning as not as well developed, if not actually deviant, in comparison to that of men. She chose to investigate the differences between the moral judgments of males and females and found that females of all ages respond differently, not less adequately. She therefore offered a reframing of developmental concepts to include the unique response patterns of females.

Gilligan observed Erikson's suggestion that women may need to establish an intimate relationship before developing a unique identity and developed the thesis that perhaps women's development and moral judgments reflect a different understanding of societal relationships, one that values social responsibility more than autonomous judgment. Women and men both wrestle with the relationship between rights and responsibilities, but women tend to respond in terms of relationships while men tend to respond in terms of rights. However, all the developmental theories, including Erikson's and Kohlberg's, place the attainment of individual rights and justice above the attainment of social responsibility, which in Kohlberg's conception is scored as stage 3 thinking because it is focused on helping others rather than on concepts of justice.

Gilligan's research demonstrates that the common thread in female thinking is the wish not to hurt others and the hope that ways can be found to solve conflicts without anyone being hurt. For example, Gilligan used the Heinz dilemma with children and preadolescents and compared the responses of the boys with those of the girls. Her results were fascinating. The boys invariably used logic and principles of justice in deciding whether or not Heinz should steal the drug. They resorted to what all good people would do and made responses in favor either of Heinz and his wife's right to life, or in favor of the druggist's right to his property. Girls, however, tended to reframe the question. Instead of answering the question "*Should* Heinz steal the drug?", girls answered the question "Should Heinz *steal* the drug?" In doing so, girls tended to frustrate the interviewer, for they offered that Heinz shouldn't steal the drug but he shouldn't let his wife die either. They then went on to devise alternative solutions, which saved the woman's life *and* respected the property rights of the druggist. Their answers couldn't be coded using Kohlberg's scoring procedures, so usually ended up being rated as stage 3 reasoning, even though they went far beyond what Kohlberg conceived as the "nice girl" orientation. In responding as they did, girls did not choose between life and property, but relied on relationships as the ultimate basis for solution. Their resourcefulness and creativity were not rewarded, nor even acknowledged, in the standard scoring protocol.

As a result of her research, Gilligan has reformulated Kohlberg's stages for female populations. In her scheme, individuals move from Level I, orientation to individual survival; through Level II, goodness as self-sacrifice; to Level III, the morality of nonviolence. In this highest stage, the emphasis on helping others and avoiding hurt forms the basis for all decision making. If Gilligan is right in her assessment of women's moral development, the hopes of the world for peace and understanding may well lie in the hands of women, or in men *and* women who have been socialized in ways that attend more fully to the importance of relationships in morality.

The Relationship of Moral Development to Other Aspects of Development

Having discussed cognitive, psychological, and moral development, it now becomes possible to relate these different aspects of development more directly. We have, of course, indicated throughout our discussion the interactive nature of these various elements and have continually emphasized how one contributes to the others. Table 10.4 demonstrates how cognitive, psychological, and moral development are related and how a wide variety of developmental levels can be normally expected in any group of adolescents. Moral development may be viewed as interactive with parallel levels of cognitive and psychological development.

Cognitive development. Numerous writers, including both Piaget and Kohlberg, have noted the influence of cognitive development on moral development, and all conclude that cognitive maturity is a necessary but not sufficient condition for the parallel level of moral maturity. As shown in Table 10.4, for example, concrete operations are a necessary but not sufficient condition for conventional levels of moral reasoning, and formal operations are a necessary but not sufficient condition for postconventional moral reasoning (Lee, 71; Windmiller, 76; Rowe, 80). With formal operations, the adolescent is able to hypothesize, and this ability clearly underlies the difference between conventional and principled moral reasoning. The ability to hypothesize frees the individual from stereotypical thinking, allows for the

Table 10.4
Relationships among Development Theories

Piaget: Cognition	Freud: Psychosexual	Erikson: Ego	Marcia: Identity	Kohlberg: Morality
Sensorimotor	Oral	Trust		
	Anal	Autonomy		Punishment
Preoperations	Phallic	Initiative		Instrumental
Concrete operations	Latency	Industry	Foreclosure	Interpersonal
			Diffusion	Law and order
Formal operations	Genital	Identity	Moratorium	Social contract
			Achievement	
		Intimacy		Universal ethical

Normal adolescent development may be found anywhere within bold lines.

awareness of alternatives, creates the potential for increased understanding through more varied perspectives, and affords the opportunity for reevaluation of all former beliefs and behaviors (Blackburne-Stover, 82). Cognitive maturity also allows for the experience of cognitive dissonance (Festinger, 62), a conflict that forces reevaluation. When we are faced with experiences that we do not understand, we are forced to accommodate our previous thinking to make sense of the new experience, and by so doing we build more complex means for integrating new experiences. For example, if you are faced with making a choice between two equally attractive alternatives, you will make a choice and then will construct additional reasons for that choice that make the chosen object considerably more attractive than the one not chosen. You have altered your original thinking to accommodate the choice. We use our cognitive abilities in similar ways to justify and accommodate increasingly sophisticated moral judgments.

Finally, the development of adolescent egocentrism may contribute to moral development. Windmiller (76) speculates that egocentric adolescents may be so concerned with personal issues that they may reject conventional morality in favor of more personal systems and may develop advanced levels of moral reasoning through the discussion of new ideas with peers.

Personality development. Whereas cognitive maturity clearly precedes moral maturity, personality and moral development are not causally related. Both, it seems, are dependent upon cognitive development. Windmiller (76) hypothesized that identity formation preceded and contributed to moral development, but Podd (72) and Rowe (80) found that identity achievement and moral development both follow the development of formal operations. Both researchers compared the level of moral reasoning with the identity-achievement statuses of Marcia and found that only those subjects who had achieved an identity according to Marcia's criteria had achieved postconventional morality. With some variation among the other identity-achievement statuses, general conclusions in both studies were that subjects in diffusion and foreclosure statuses were most likely to display conventional moral reasoning, and those in moratorium displayed high variability in identity achievement, possibly indicating a transitional stage. A higher identity status was related to a higher stage of moral reasoning and vice versa. Polovy (80) studied the relationship between level of moral reasoning and various personality characteristics and found that those subjects who preferred principled levels of moral reasoning also displayed high levels of numerous positive characteristics: dependability, rationality, creativity, intelligence, independence, acceptance of societal needs, and awareness of the need for change.

Although there has been little attention in the literature to the relationship between the psychosexual (Freud) or ego-development (Erikson) stages and moral-reasoning stages, it should be clear that, though probably not due to a causal relation, a child in the industry stage is not likely to go beyond conventional levels of moral reasoning, and that without a succesful resolution of the identity crisis, advanced levels of moral reasoning are highly unlikely. The developmental stages are usually consistent and parallel in any one individual, even though they are not linked in a cause-and-effect manner.

Social learning. There is no question that developmental maturity is not the only factor influencing moral reasoning. Social participation, family relationships, child-rearing practices, socioeconomic status, cultural expectations, previous experiences, school and church environments, and all other environmental situations also contribute to the level of moral reasoning and behavior attained by adolescents, as they fuel cognitive and identity development as well.

It has been demonstrated that parental methods of discipline contribute significantly to moral development, with methods that include the child's active thinking being the most beneficial. Hoffman (77), Saltzstein (78), and Eisikovits (82) all demonstrated the importance of disciplinary techniques that emphasize the consequences of the child's actions on other people rather than those that use simple authority and external punishment. Mischel (76b) emphasizes the importance of social learning and parental interaction styles and notes in particular how children's moral judgments reflect changes in their parents' methods of socialization. Usually, parents of younger children use more tangible consequences while those of older children are more likely to use reason. Adolescents who have experienced family environments that include discussion, clear standards, moral principles, warmth, and little threat have thus experienced an enhancement of the development to high levels of moral judgment and behavior, while those whose parents continue to use authoritarian methods remain at lower levels of moral reasoning. Families in which there is a great deal of turmoil, as in the loss of the father through divorce (Parish, 80) may depress moral-judgment levels because of the parental focus on anger, guilt, and rejection. Children who are raised in cultures that stress social conformity develop strong adherence to social conventions, as well as less differentiated personalities and greater field dependence (Witkin, 74). Finally, people raised in poor countries, where the needs are more likely to be on safety and security, express values that are more conventional and materially oriented than those who have been raised in affluence (Feather, 74). The same may be true between less and more affluent cultures within a single country, which would explain the apparently more conventional attitudes of those from the lower socioeconomic statuses within the United States.

RELIGIOUS DEVELOPMENT

Religion in Adolescence

Related to, yet different from moral development, is religious and spiritual development. The relationship of religion to other aspects of development — cognitive, psychological, biological — is relatively new as a subject of scientific study. Only recently, for example, have religious leaders begun to look at how adolescents' experience in all areas of development affects their ideas about and practices of religion and to use developmental knowledge in religious programming.

What we don't know. The most comprehensive review of the research into religion and adolescence was done recently by Farel (82), who discovered the following gaps in the literature:

1. We have very little information about how beliefs and values develop and how religious organizations influence religious development.
2. We know little about the emotional component of religious development.
3. We know little about how religious experiences affect development.
4. We don't know how religion enhances self-control, if it does at all.
5. We have no consensus on definitions used to describe religion.
6. There is very little current research and writing in adolescent religious development.
7. There has been little attention paid to a comparison of various denominations and their effects on adolescents.
8. There has not been much done in comparing religious and nonreligious youth.

Adolescents face questions about the role of religion in their lives.

9. We need more research into the relationship between the social context and religious development.

10. We need longitudinal studies of religious development throughout childhood and adolescence and into adulthood.

11. We are not clear how the overall trend in modern American society away from organized religion affects adolescents.

12. We are not certain of the relationship, if any, between religious faith and religious practice.

What we do know. What we do know is that adolescents face puzzling questions concerning religion and the role it plays in their lives, that religion can provide an orientation to values and a context for morality and that the quality of beliefs changes in a fashion that parallels cognitive development (Fowler, 76, 81).

We also know that religious practice varies widely among adolescents. In a survey of over 1000 adolescents (Princeton, 80), it was found that 87 percent of the subjects reported praying, 52 percent said grace, and 95 percent believed in God. Although these figures indicate widespread acceptance of religion, the same students also reported dissatisfaction with religion: 60 percent felt that religion was not very important in their lives, and 67 percent felt organized religion did not reach out to them personally. In another research sample of church-related youth, Strommen (74) found many to be satisfied with their religious identity, many despairing of their religious identity, and one in seven embodying a prejudice that allowed for no views but the most rigid and a strict nonacceptance of anyone who believed differently from themselves. This he saw as an immature moral development among some church-oriented youth. Davids (82), in studying Jewish college students, found no relationship between identification of a Jewish identity and extent of religious practices. He did find, however, that those who were more religious were also more traditional in their attitudes toward sex.

Even though the research into adolescents and religion is sparse, we can say that religious development is often a part of moral development for those for whom religion is significant. For some, it is a major basis for moral judgment; for others it is not. Adolescents will test their religious beliefs along with all the other beliefs they have learned throughout childhood, and family ties are often strained when dearly held family beliefs and practices are called into question by all-questioning adolescents.

Religious Development

Throughout history observers have noted two broad categories of believers: those for whom religion is an externalized response consisting of stereotyped prejudices and rigid and simplistic rules; and those for whom religion is an intrinisic, thoughtful, open, and complex commitment. For young children, religion must be of the former category, and for many adults, it remains so. But for some, religious development allows for the transformation of once-externalized beliefs and rules into internalized faith that provides a meaningful context for moral decision making. Those who make the transition do so by use of their increasingly complex cognitive capacities.

Cognitive contribution. Although there has not been an overwhelming volume of research into the process of religious development, that which has been done focuses on the relationship between religious and cognitive development (Elkind, 61, 62, 63; Farel, 82). ''Religious development during early adolescence shows the effects of increased cognitive capacity and at the same time reflects the new active personality that has come with physical development and heightened social awareness'' (Farel, 82). The adolescent needs for self-discovery and security come together in religious development, and the advent of formal operations allows for the search for meaning in the world.

Increased cognitive capacities allow adolescents, for example, to alter significantly their conceptions of God and religion. With the ability to hypothesize and think in abstractions, they become aware of and are able to deal with inconsistencies, as in the necessity to reconcile ideas of creation with ideas of evolution. They also can create a less personalized image of God and are likely to become more interested in ethics than dogma, moral behavior than ritual.

Goldman (64, 65) studied the application of intellectual abilities to religious stories and found that children below the age of nine perceived God (or nature) to intervene physically in human affairs; God would physically mete out punishment, for example. Children between nine and eleven still believed in divine intervention but saw it as being through divine or magical commands rather than being direct. Only with the advent of formal operational thinking could adolescents view religious stories as purely symbolic. In similar investigations, Wilcox (79) studied the development of the symbolic interpretation of the Last Supper and found developmental stages roughly equivalent to the levels of moral development already studied. At Stages 1 and 2, the Last Supper story was interpreted literally, with no symbolic meanings attached. At Stage 3, meaning (love) was attached to the ritual, but there was no understanding of the abstract concept apart from the story. At Stage 4, the meaning was separated from the story, with the story being seen as one channel for expression of the abstract concept. Finally, at Stage 5, all possible meanings were incorporated and understood completely apart from the story itself.

Faith. Fowler (81) conducted the most extensive and comprehensive continuing investigations of religious development. He believes that **faith**, which he defines as patterns of thinking that motivate behavior, is the basis of the struggle to find meaning in life. Faith is common to all people, regardless of religious heritage and tradition, and develops in a sequence of stages, much as does cognitive and moral development. Three of his six stages may be found in adolescence:

Stage 2: Mythical-literal faith (ages 6 to 11). The concrete operational child and adolescent respond to religion according to their cognitive patterns and therefore respond to religious stories and music in concrete, literal ways. They enjoy ritual and music, perceive God in human form, and ask no questions concerning the beliefs and rules of their religious heritage.

Stage 3: Synthetic-conventional faith (ages 12 to 18 and over). Formal operations are required for this stage of faith development. Individuals emphasize the congruence between their views and those of others and conceive of a less personalized God, but one who is something of a personal adviser and guide.

Stage 4: Individual-reflective faith (ages 18 and over). At this highest stage of the development of faith, individuals engage in critical self-reflection and examination of their beliefs and values, which lead to a truly individual perspective on issues of faith and religion. God is not viewed as a personal adviser but as an abstract concept embodying moral truths.

Social practices. With so little research into the development of religion, it is not surprising that there also has been little attention paid to the societal variables that contribute to religious beliefs and practices. Parker (80) investigated the relative effects of Hebrew school attendance, youth-group attendance, sex, and parental practices on the religious attitudes and behavior of Jewish teenagers and discovered that the only significant influences were home environment and parental practice. At least for this sample, the home was still the most important factor in the beliefs and behaviors of adolescents.

Adolescent needs. Given what we know about physical, emotional, social, cognitive, and moral development, and given the fact that for many youngsters the church may be second in influence only to the home, religious leaders need to be recognized for their potential influence on healthy adolescent development. Members of the clergy, for example, often have a unique relationship to families, being present at all the significant life events from birth to death and knowing family members in particularly intimate ways. Adolescents especially are likely to be struggling with reconciling religious beliefs with the messages of modern society and need guidance in thinking through the meaning of their faith as well as the meaning of their new perspectives in all areas of their lives. Religious institutions, at their best, might offer an accepting environment where questions about sexuality, morality, friendship, and all the vital concerns of emerging adolescents can be supported and encouraged. Goldman (65) identified five social-emotional needs that religion must not only address but satisfy if commitment is to be ensured:

1. *Security in freedom:* The religious institution must allow the adolescent to test values in an environment of respect and must not merely demand obedience to authority.

2. *Significance and status:* The religious institution must afford adolescents opportunities to earn respect through responsible activity within it.

3. *Idealism and altruism:* The religious institution is in a unique position to develop the values of idealism and altruism through offering meaningful community service activities.

4. *Love:* Both divine and sexual love must be discussed in an open and supportive manner.

5. *Meaning for life:* Discussions need to assist young people in reconciling the conflicts of science and religion and dealing with the changes of the postindustrial society.

In a similar vein, Farel (82) identified five elements essential to healthy adolescent development that religious communities can offer:

1. Support and guidance in the development of commitments.

2. Support for autonomy and questioning.

3. Opportunities to show competence and achievement.

4. A social peer group with similar concerns.
5. A "framework upon which emerging views of self and the world are developed and supported" (p. 9).

Cults

Characteristics. A unique phenomenon related to adolescent religion is the popularity of religious movements referred to as cults. It is a matter of history that new religious movements have invariably engendered fear and criticism (the Christians in Rome, Catholic immigrants in the United States) and that religious revivals have always accompanied times of economic and social unrest, but it is important to distinguish between religion and cults. Adams (83) identified the following as characteristics of cults, though not of religions:

1. Cults discourage independent thought through the use of brainwashing and other mind-control techniques.
2. Cults demand complete loyalty of their members, often including all their time and money.
3. Cults exclude the families of their members.
4. Cults engage in elaborate rituals, often including the manipulation of body functions (sleep, diet) to create mental fatigue and vulnerability.
5. Cults frequently deal in deception.
6. Cults use fear as a mechanism of control. Mental and physical coercion are common.

In addition to the characteristics that clearly distinguish cults from religions, Ellwood (73) noted the following characteristics of cults: a founder who offers the secret of happiness; use of mysticism and magic techniques; a band of highly committed followers; alienation from traditional religion; emphasis on healing; optimism, the promise of heaven on earth *now*; extensive group participation in rituals; initiation rites; and a demand for commitment in exchange for the promise of happiness.

Although Kaslow (82) pointed out that there are widely divergent data and conclusions concerning the effects of cult membership, it is clear from the above list of characteristics that cults do not contribute to the healthy development of adolescents. Instead of encouraging young people to use their newfound cognitive and psychological capabilities to construct meaningful lives, cults offer ready-made solutions that demand no thinking. Why, then, are they attractive to thousands of older adolescents?

Appeal. da Nobrega (80) sees in cults a kind of spiritual placebo, a promise of bliss that seems like an oasis in the desert to youth who are tired of struggling with issues of identity. Cults provide security, answers, comraderie, and an escape from the loneliness of identity diffusion. Downton (79) demonstrated through case studies of young people who had converted to cults the themes of loneliness, misery, and drugs. Dean (82) found the same themes several years later. Adolescent idealism, including the wish for peace in the world, combines with relationship problems, self-esteem issues, and endless questioning to make the struggle seem futile. Along comes a spiritual leader who promises easy, comfortable answers (not unlike the promise of a drug trip), and the appeal is overwhelming. All identity questions are answered, all loneliness, sadness, and alienation alleviated — romantically, ideally, even heroically. Dean (82) identified five specific situations and conditions that make youth vulnerable to the appeal of cults:

1. *Identity struggle:* Youth in the throes of identity diffusion are anxious, even miserable in their search. The cult offers relief.
2. *Idealism:* Like no other possibility, the cult offers the promise of making a heaven on earth by eradicating all of society's ills.
3. *Intellectual curiosity:* New ideas are intensely interesting to the adolescent who is only beginning to question old values.
4. *Disillusionment:* The inner anxiety resulting from academic competition, social isolation, lack of emotional support, and concern for the future make the calm of cult members irresistible.
5. *Traumatic experience:* The high emotional intensity of a death, a lost love, a major failure, or economic problems increases vulnerability to the promise of joy.

The promise of happiness, the warmth and acceptance by cult members, the indoctrination and expectation of conversion all make cult membership a highly successful means of relieving the responsibility of personal choices, and older adolescents are particularly susceptible. Hundreds of thousands (accurate figures are not possible to obtain) of older adolescents have left their families and friends to join the easy path (Balswick, 74; Rice, 76), and most of these are white, single, and middle class and were in school at least part time prior to joining the cult (Galanter, 79). For these young people, the identity crisis is resolved by joining the cult. That they will have to face the crisis again, either voluntarily as they mature and decide to leave the cult or involuntarily through the imposition of ''deprogramming'' techniques (Stoner, 77) that are bought by their desperate parents, is not a concern at the time of joining.

Cults are a substitute for psychological and moral growth, made attractive by a rootless, changing society that creates situations in which older adolescents find themselves alienated, lonely, and directionless. The pain of ordinary living is relieved by the promise of a charismatic leader.

MORAL, RELIGIOUS, AND VALUES EDUCATION

History of Moral Education

Just as with sex education, we often hear the cry that moral education belongs in the home and the church, and that the schools should be in the business of developing minds not morals. But, as we have seen, the separation of moral issues from intellectual ones is not possible. Not only is moral reasoning dependent on and intertwined with cognitive development, but the society of the school, as well as that of the home and church, provides the content of moral decision making. Schooling is, as Kohlberg (77) noted, a moral enterprise, whether we like it or not. In the nineteenth century, the famous *McGuffey's Readers* openly indoctrinated values along with reading, and although we have clearly eliminated such direct moral teaching from the curriculum, schools nevertheless provide the conditions in which moral decisions are made, and they espouse, by example, a set of clearly delineated values that children are expected to adopt without question. Schools are simply not morally neutral.

Hidden curriculum. Early in this century, John Dewey observed that the most important values are taught by the nature of the school itself, a phenomenon that Jackson (68) later termed the school's "hidden curriculum," referring in particular to the school's emphasis on obedience to authority. Toffler (80) refers to the "covert curriculum," which includes three "courses" — punctuality; obedience; and rote, repetitious work — courses that were necessary to prepare workers for the assembly line. And Piaget (32) condemned traditional school goals as "the preparation of pupils for competitive examinations rather than for life," and the school's determination "to shut the child up in work that is strictly individual," a practice he saw as "contrary to the most obvious requirements of intellectual and moral development" (p. 405). The same criticism is often heard today.

Citizenship education. Nelson (80) distinguished between moral education and citizenship education and argued that whereas the two have been considered complementary, if not identical, a careful examination reveals that they are more different than similar. He ascribed the term **citizenship education** to the latent function of the school, the hidden curriculum that emphasizes conformity to rules, docility, uncritical acceptance of authority and prescribed roles. Being a good citizen results in praise and even affects grades. When I was in elementary and junior high school in the late 1940s and early 1950s, we received two grades for every subject, an academic grade and a citizenship grade, and the two were considered equally important. I will never forget the day in ninth grade that I got an *A* in algebra but a *D* in citizenship in the same class, all because I had chosen to confront a fellow student (inappropriately as far as the teacher was concerned) who had been playing practical jokes behind the teacher's back. The message, even then, was clear: "Don't show annoyance or defend yourself; keep docile and passive, and ignore unfriendly distractions." The functions of citizenship education continue. Yet, as Nelson (80) pointed out, a school organization designed to "produce loyal and obedient citizens" may be in conflict with moral education, instruction designed to "encourage autonomous moral reasoning" (p. 257).

Moral education. Moral education, as opposed to citizenship education, evolved from the rigid indoctrination characteristic of *McGuffey's Readers* to a whole range of approaches designed to encourage intellectual and moral growth and lead to autonomous, principled reasoning (Carter, 84). The irony, however, is clear. Institutions that latently espouse the values of docility and conformity may be hard pressed to develop values that go beyond their own. Schools, which are pretty clearly Kohlbergian Stage 4 institutions that often resort to Stage 1 and 2 reasoning, must somehow aspire to develop individuals who reason at the more advanced stages. Teachers who ask moral questions (instead of moralizing) and who encourage divergent thinking must accept the risk of creating conflict, sometimes with the school itself.

Approaches to Moral Education

Wilcox (79) identified four responses of schools to the issue of moral education. All too common is the response that moral education should be left to the home, which, as we have seen, is little more than an ostrich approach to a significant issue. A second approach is that of teaching traditional values, the transmission of acceptable social morality, which, as we have seen, occurs in the hidden curriculum and in traditional education for citizenship, as well as in traditional religious education. This response, however, appears incomplete, because it does not encourage moral judgment beyond the conventional level. It also is limited to those few broad values on which everyone can agree, and therefore ignores the morally rich environments in which value conflicts are found. Third is the values-clarification approach, which is based in humanistic psychology and espouses the development of self-justified personal choices to help people discover and make commitments to values. We will discuss values clarification in more detail a little later. Finally, the developmental approach uses more developmental theory and the process of analysis and inquiry to help people move from lower to higher stages of cognitive and moral reasoning. Along with the use of moral dilemmas and classroom and school democracies that involve students in real issues, which we will discuss shortly, a few general observations concerning developmental moral education are useful.

Developmental moral education. Developmental moral education demands collaboration and cooperation in order to allow for comparison of ideas, consensual decision making, and the decentering of egocentrism that is essential to advanced levels of moral development. Teachers involved in developmental moral education must be competent in their understanding of developmental theory and its manifestations in student thinking, must be willing to challenge their own moral reasoning, must provide students with significant moral content, must help them deal with both the cognitive and emotional aspects of moral reasoning, must provide a supportive yet confrontive environment for moral discussions, must know how to encourage students to produce a variety of alternatives and to develop consequential thinking, and must be able to use a variety of methods and techniques and give up authoritarian control of the classroom. A moral educator, in other words, must be personally and professionally competent and must be willing to take the risks that moral education promises to provide.

In an extensive review of the literature concerning moral education, Mosher (77) identified the processes and activities most often found to be effective in developing students' moral reasoning. Moral dilemmas, opportunities for role taking, peer counseling, moral discussion involving students arguing from several different stages, experience in social service, experience in rule making and democratic governance, values-clarification exercises, and the study of ethics have all been found to be effective in promoting moral development. We will look at several of these in greater detail.

Values clarification. Based in the self-actualization theory of humanistic psychology, the values-clarification approach (Raths, 66; S. Simon, 72) posits that through a process of careful analysis of value choices, people grow to be more positive, purposeful, and enthusiastic in their values and behavior. According to Raths (66), ''Persons have experiences; they grow and learn. Out of experiences may come certain general guides to behavior. These guides tend to give direction to life and may be called values. Our values show what we tend to do with our limited time and energy'' (p. 27). Whereas traditional approaches to helping children develop values have included such indoctrination techniques as example setting, persuading, demanding, and appealing to conscience, the values-clarification approach argues that free inquiry and thoughtful analysis of the confusing array of modern values leads to more lasting, internalized, and committed ways of being in the world.

Values are formed, Raths and Simon say, through three general processes and seven more specific behaviors. To be lasting and meaningful, a value must be **chosen, cherished,** and **acted on.** More specifically, values need to be chosen freely from known alternatives with full awareness of the consequences of the choice; prized, cherished, and publicly affirmed; and acted on and made a pattern in our lives. Any value, belief, or behavior may be measured against these seven criteria; the more criteria it meets, the more it is likely to be a lasting and meaningful value in our lives. We can use these criteria to evaluate the strength and meaningfulness of adolescent behaviors. For example, Janie may go to church regularly and publicly affirm her belief in the religious teachings she grew up on, but if she has never actively chosen that behavior and those beliefs from known alternatives and considered the consequences of them, they are not likely to be as influential in her life as if she had more carefully thought them through. She may, at some future time,

To be meaningful, a value must be chosen, cherished, and acted on.

subject them to question and analysis; and the conclusions she reaches at that time, which will meet more of the criteria, are likely to be the more lasting ones.

Table 10.5 outlines the seven values-clarification criteria and presents you with an opportunity to evaluate several of your values. You might select three specific values you hold and write each above one of the columns. These should be as specific as possible; for example, the place you live, your current thoughts on abortion, or the career you envision for yourself. For each, read down the list of values criteria, and check whether or not you have used those criteria in consideration of your behaviors and beliefs. The more you can check, the more likely that item is truly of value to you.

In the classroom, values-clarification techniques take many forms. Any activity that requires students to make choices, verbalize the reasons for their choices, and

Table 10.5
Values Clarification

		Value #1:	Value #2:	Value #3:
Choosing	Chosen freely			
	Chosen from known alternatives			
	Chosen after considering the consequences			
Prizing	Prized and cherished			
	Publicly affirmed			
Acting	Acted on			
	Made a pattern in life			

act on their choices can be considered a values-clarification exercise. These range from listing "Twenty Things I Love to Do" and analyzing them according to categories like "alone or with people," "costs $5 every time I do it," and "how often I do it," to writing letters to the editor expressing views on current issues. Values-clarification activities, like other moral education designs, are clearly in the realm of affective education and would fit nicely in the "Education of the Self" model proposed by Weinstein (Chapter 9).

But values clarification need not be divorced from academic content. S. Simon (72) discusses what he calls "Three Level Teaching." At level one is the content, pure and simple. At level two are the concepts that can be derived from the content, and at level 3 are the personal applications of the content. Using the discovery of America by Christopher Columbus as an example, different questions would be asked at each of the three levels. At level one the teacher would ask, "Who discovered America? In what year? How many ships and men were involved?" At level two she would ask, "What conditions in the world contributed to the discovery of America? What is adventure? What characteristics contribute to the development of an adventurer?" And at level three she would ask "Would you have been likely to accept the challenge of sailing with Columbus? Why or why not? What qualities of Columbus do you find in yourself and those you know? How do you challenge the existing views of your society?" Again, we see that teaching this way encompasses and goes beyond the cognitive by attempting to help students use the information they are learning to grow personally as well. Through such teaching, adolescents gain both the historical perspective and the role-taking ability necessary for advanced stages of psychological and moral development.

Values clarification is not without its critics. Because it emphasizes the individual development of values, critics have accused it of allowing all values, even negative ones, as long as they are carefully chosen, prized, and acted on. The door is left open, they say, for a criminal to be acceptable. Simon would argue that if all the alternatives were known and the consequences to self and others truly considered, a potential criminal would not choose criminal behavior, but this response has not satisfied those who want the proponents of values clarification to say that some values are better than others. Because they are firmly in the camp of the humanists, Simon and his colleagues have refused to do so.

Values clarification has also been accused of consisting of nothing more than a bag of tricks, exercises that can be used by untrained teachers merely to fill time. That untrained and unskilled teachers can misuse values clarification is undebatable; however, unskilled teachers may misuse any number of valuable teaching experiences. The proponents of values clarification argue that a thorough understanding of and commitment to humanistic education, as well as specific training in values clarification itself, are essential for those who would use it.

Finally, the effects of values clarification have not been adequately documented. Lockwood (78), in a critical review of thirteen values-clarification studies, notes that although there seems to be some positive impact on classroom behavior and reading ability, no significant impacts on self-esteem, personal adjustment, or values have been demonstrated. Research continues.

Moral dilemmas. Kohlberg and others have found that moral dilemmas are useful in education as well as in research. Hypothetical dilemmas like those of Sharon and Heinz provide one avenue for learning, but so do real-life dilemmas culled from the daily experiences of students and dilemmas taken from the content of the curriculum, history and literature providing the most obvious examples. In a supportive environment, moral discussions expose students to higher levels of moral judgment, and thereby encourage moral development. Turiel (66) found that students tend to prefer a response one stage above their current level, even though their behavior may not be consistent with their judgment. The content of each dilemma is not the significant influence, but the process by which arguments for various actions are justified provides the meat of the discussion, with self-reflection and dialogue providing the basis for development (Paolitto, 77). Lockwood (78) reviewed twenty-two studies of the moral dilemma approach and found that the direct discussion method does have an impact on the development of moral reasoning, especially from stage 2 to stage 3, or from preconventional to conventional moral reasoning.

Any dilemma, be it hypothetical, real, historical, or literary, contains five elements: a conflict of values that has meaning for students, a central character who must make a choice, a choice between conflicting alternatives, a truly moral issue (one of the eleven identified by Kohlberg), and a ''should'' question. In building a moral discussion, the teacher first has students confront the dilemma, clarifying the circumstances and the problem. She then asks students individually to reflect on and establish a position, which is then shared and examined in a group discussion. In examining reasoning, students are told that to change their minds is a positive indicator of growth. They are therefore asked to evaluate and select other opinions and reasons that make better sense to them than their own. Finally, they are asked to state their conclusions about what the central character should do. In moral discussions, the teacher must be careful to allow for all opinions, remain non-judgmental, encourage dialogue, and encourage students to recognize attractive arguments that they may not have considered. Unlike a debate, the emphasis is on growth and change, so well-developed listening skills are essential for both teacher and students. The teacher needs to be open and self-aware and able to use daily experiences of students as the food for moral discussions (Lickona, 77). The more real the dilemma, the more meaningful to those partaking in the discussion.

Garrod (77) emphasized the possibilities that literature affords as a vehicle for moral education. *Huckleberry Finn* could be used in this way. Beginning with the issue as presented in literature, the teacher can move the discussion to broader moral issues, much as Simon uses three-level teaching.

Ladenburg (77) described how history also affords a rich supply of moral issues for discussion. The history teacher who is to move beyond the facts and concepts and into the realm of morality must consider history an active, living process and combine subject matter with the aims of developmental psychology. The teacher must also attend to complex historical and philosophical issues and develop units that achieve the complex objectives of teaching facts, concepts, and moral reasoning.

Religious education. Just as religious development can be included in the broader category of moral development, so too can religious education be considered one form of moral education. It has been accepted by virtually all religious educators (with the possible exception of fundamentalist denominations) that merely passing on a faith from generation to generation is dangerous, for as minds mature they are likely to confront and question. If such questioning is not accepted, it may take the form of rebellion rather than acceptance. Instead, religious education must account for and use developmental information to help young people mature. To do this, Farel (82, pp. 19–20) identified eight criteria for successful youth programs.

1. The program provides a comfortable setting in which young people can explore the bases of their religious faith.
2. The program connects religious traditions with varied opportunities for self-discovery and self-definition.
3. The program involves both young people and their parents to foster mutual understanding.
4. The program has clearly articulated rules that youth-group members appreciate and accept.
5. The program is guided by mature adults who are comfortable with young people and are willing to explore sensitive issues with them.

6. The program provides opportunities for young people to gain a sense of competence by performing meaningful tasks in their communities and congregations.

7. The program includes time for laughter, high spirits, and physical activity as well as contemplation and opportunities to be alone.

8. The program encourages mutual acceptance and friendship among the young people.

A more radical approach to religious education is that proposed by Warren (82), who, dissatisfied with the lack of attention paid to social politics, suggested that religious leaders have the obligation to help young people become aware of how they are manipulated by society and to become active agents of social change. He believes that the oppression by schools, the entertainment industry, and the economy as a whole needs to be examined, with the church taking an active role in politicizing youth.

"Just" communities. Scharf (77) noted that John Dewey was the first proponent of democratic schooling. As we noted earlier in our discussion of the hidden curriculum, the school organization is itself a powerful tool of teaching, yet few schools succeed in giving students real lessons in democracy. At best, efforts to achieve student governance are mere tokens. Most student councils seldom deal with issues more meaty than planning the Junior Prom. The issues involving morality are too often reserved for the secrecy of the administrative suite. Scharf (77) identified the dilemmas presented to those who would like to encourage democratic decision making by students: most high schools are too big to allow for meaningful participation; the division of the day makes any sense of community difficult at best; the competitive model conflicts with democratic goals; teachers are unwilling to give up power to students; democracy is very time-consuming; and students are often not mature enough to make good decisions.

Regardless of these impediments to participatory democracies in schools, experiments with "just" communities have been instituted by Kohlberg and his colleagues in both private and public high schools in several major Eastern cities. In these schools or schools-within-schools, the students participate with the faculty on a one-person, one-vote basis, and the body as a whole (usually referred to as the "town meeting") decides all issues of governance, including curricular issues, which must, of course, be consistent with board policies. From issues of how to meet state mandates in curriculum to making decisions concerning academic and behavioral problems, all students participate in a true democracy. (For a more comprehensive description of school-wide just communities, see Reimer, 83, pp. 236–257.)

A less extensive form of the just community can be instituted at the classroom level (Glasser, 69). In the class meeting, which involves the entire group, students develop rules for the group, discuss and solve classroom problems, and evaluate their progress in the class. In these discussions the teacher must be careful to be a discussion leader, but not to impose values and ideas.

Though time-consuming, inefficient, and difficult to maintain, student participation in democratic decision making, whether at the classroom or larger level, is a laudable goal of moral education, for only through experience can adolescents learn the collaborative decision-making process that is the basis of advanced stages of moral development.

SUMMARY

Each of us makes thousands of decisions about how to behave based on our concepts of right and wrong, good and bad. These are the moral choices by which we live our lives. Although the media tend to proclaim that moral standards are declining in our modern society, there is little evidence that today's adolescents are any more or less moral than those of the past.

Moral development is not separate from physical, cognitive, or personality development, but evolves in an interactive way and along parallel lines. Physical maturation, the onset of formal operations, and the adolescent search for identity all contribute to new ways of evaluating behavior. Moral development results from the complex interaction of parental values and behavior, experiences, cognitive development, active thought processing, and general environmental factors.

The major theorists of moral development all note the interconnectedness of cognitive, social, and moral development. Piaget noted that as children mature, they move from a highly rigid interpretation of rules imposed by an external authority to a considerably more flexible interpretation based on reciprocity and social considerations. They also develop an appreciation for motivation. Adelson bridged cognitive and moral development with his studies of the development of political thinking in adolescence. He found related changes in cognition, authoritarianism, and ideology.

The most popular theory of moral development is that of Lawrence Kohlberg, who built on the cognitive and moral development work of Piaget by adding adolescents to Piaget's research and demonstrating that the achievement of formal operations is a necessary but not sufficient condition for the development of mature moral reasoning and that mature moral reasoning is a necessary but not sufficient condition for mature moral behavior. His stage theory encompasses two stages each in the preconventional, conventional, and postconventional levels. At the preconventional level, individuals respond to satisfy personal needs; at the conventional level, they respond in order to conform to group standards; and at the postconventional level, they respond according to more universal moral principles. To test the level of moral reasoning of his subjects, Kohlberg uses moral dilemmas, hypothetical situations in which values come into conflict. The reasoning behind the choice forms the basis for understanding the moral development of the subject. Research tends to support Kohlberg's findings that moral development is sequential and universal across cultures, that most adolescents and adults reason at the conventional level, that moral behavior is not always consistent with moral reasoning, and that people tend to favor the highest level of reasoning that they understand. Gilligan added females to Kohlberg's research and advanced a theory that proposes that males and females favor different moral reasoning, with women emphasizing helping others rather than individual rights.

Religious development has not been as thoroughly studied as moral development. It is important nevertheless because adolescents have many questions concerning religion, and religion can provide an orientation to values. If religion is to become an internalized context for moral decisions rather than a set of externalized rules, adolescents must use their increased cognitive skills to develop a personal and meaningful faith.

Unlike religions, cults discourage independent thought, demand loyalty, exclude family members, deceive, and use fear to control. They may appeal to adolescents, however, because they provide security, simple answers, comraderie, and an escape from loneliness. They are a substitute for psychological and moral growth.

Because it is impossible to separate moral concerns from intellectual ones, the school is necessarily involved in moral education, both overtly and more subtly. The hidden curriculum is the values of the school itself.

Developmental moral education emphasizes questioning, comparing ideas, decision making, and role taking. Moral dilemmas, opportunities for role taking, peer counseling, moral discussions, experience in social service, experience in democratic governance, values clarification, and the study of ethics are the most commonly used techniques. Values-clarification techniques require that students make choices, proclaim the reasons for their choices, and act on their choices. They are designed to help students use cognitive information for personal development. Moral dilemmas and discussions encourage self-reflection and dialogue as the bases of moral development. Just communities provide experience in democratic governance, whether in the classroom or the entire school.

11

Career Development

Imagine a well-meaning but distant aunt coming to visit after an absence of a year or more. It is predictable that in her interactions with the thirteen-year-old in the family, the inevitable "My, how you've grown" will be followed shortly with the equally inevitable "And what do you want to be when you grow up?" The question, of course, refers specifically to the young adolescent's occupation, but the implications are far greater. "What do you want to be?" ultimately refers to the entire lifestyle of the individual, including not only a means of earning a living, but also the extent of that living; the friends chosen; leisure-time activities; marital and family lifestyle; work, political, and religious values — in short, an individual's entire outlook on life and its meaning.

Studs Terkel, on the title page of his highly popular book *Working* (74), quotes William Faulkner on the importance of work: "You can't eat for eight hours a day nor drink for eight hours a day nor make love for eight hours a day — all you can do for eight hours is work. Which is the reason why man makes himself and everybody else so miserable and unhappy." In *Working* Terkel presents the eloquent statements of over 100 working Americans on their work. Although he found many "miserable and unhappy" people, he also found joyous people who had found meaning and fulfillment in their work, whether that work was labor or management, highly paid or barely subsistent. He summarizes his findings:

> [This book] is about a search, too, for daily meaning as well as daily bread, for recognition as well as cash, for astonishment rather than torpor; in short, for a sort of life rather than a Monday through Friday sort of dying. Perhaps immortality, too, is a part of the quest. To be remembered was the wish, spoken and unspoken, of the heroes and heroines of this book. (p. *xi*)

In these interviews, Terkel truly demonstrates the significance of an individual's occupation, especially his perception of the meaning of that occupation to the meaning of his life.

The average worker spends more time working than in any other single activity, including that which is spent with a spouse and family, and an occupation provides the cornerstone of one's identity in a way that no other characteristic can. Yet we pay far too little attention to the role of work, especially in adolescence, and have, as a result, produced young people who lack the self-knowledge and the knowledge of the world of work that might equip them to find meaning in their work and in their lives.

In this chapter we will examine the career development of adolescents. To do so we will first explore the context for careers in the postindustrial society, then compare various theories of career development and its relationship to overall development. The social context of career choice, including racial, cultural, and sexual influences, will be examined. Finally, the role of career education and the influence of working on adolescents will be discussed.

THE CONTEXT FOR CAREERS

Only a very few people in this world are faced with the choice of working or not working. For virtually all of us work is a necessity, for without it we are unable to provide for our needs. But work is much more than a means of physical survival. As Renwick (78) discovered, when people from all walks of life were asked if they would continue working even if they had sufficient money to live comfortably, most said they would. Many of these might choose different work than they are currently doing, but we are a nation of workers, workers who define ourselves by the work we do. When asked "Who are you?" almost everyone answers with an occupation, "I'm a teacher; I'm a bricklayer; I'm an attorney." We choose from some 22,000 occupations, encompassing eight broad fields and about six levels of work (Jordaan, 79) to find that socially useful, personally meaningful activity in which we will spend more waking hours than any other.

What Is Work?

Definitions. A few definitions are in order: We will use the broad term **work** to refer to an individual's **career**, that sequence of work activities carried on throughout life. Any career involves **positions, jobs,** and **occupations.** A position involves the tasks done by a single worker (a particular typist's position includes typing memos and letters and proofreading); a job is the group of similar positions in a single organization (there may be fifteen typists' jobs in a business); an occupation is the group of similar jobs in various establishments. An individual's pattern of jobs makes up a career, which also includes nonwork or avocational activities designed to round out work roles and includes movement within the career (the typist may gain more training and become a secretary, which will change the position, the job, and the occupation).

Satisfaction. Some people make positive occupational commitments; some do not. Some people have realistic career objectives; some do not. Some people feel secure, satisfied, and successful with their careers; some do not. Those who create successful and satisfying careers for themselves find in their work something meaningful, feel that they have some control over their occupational lives, and are aware of the importance of career decision making in their lives (Jordaan, 79). Terkel (74) found that those who found satisfaction in their work were more likely than those who did not to find meaning beyond the paycheck and that those who found no real satisfaction were more likely to focus on issues of status. Thus the dissatisfied janitor becomes a building engineer, the dissatisfied garbage collector a sanitary engineer, the dissatisfied factory worker a factory mechanic, the dissatisfied sales representative an account executive.

Terkel also found overidentification with the job, a consuming passion that leaves room for nothing else: the dentist who, sitting in an expensive orchestra seat at a famous play, found himself studying the dental work of the actors. Terkel himself, while writing *Working*, became absorbed in the "work" of Marlon Brando playing in *Last Tango in Paris* rather than in the messages and effects of the film itself.

Our occupation provides our principal source of financial security, a means of satisfying personal and family needs, a source of status, dignity, and respect, an expression of attitudes and values, a source of social interaction, and a source of self-concept and identity. Occupations can literally determine individual lifestyles and social roles and are fundamental to how people feel about themselves. As Herr (79) points out,

> . . . virtually any analysis of human development indicates that access to work, particularly access in ways that maximize freedom of choice, is critical to the ability to move effectively from adolescence to adulthood. Such a concern has particular vitality in those nations with highly developed technology and great affluence . . . (p. 67)

Access to work, then, is critical to effective adulthood, and thus should be a major focus of adolescence.

History. Although modern cilivizations clearly recognize the tremendous importance of work to the self-concept and to the meaning of life, work has not always been so valued. Ancient civilizations generally viewed work as necessary drudgery, to be engaged in only by the less fortunate and to be avoided at all costs. Zytowski (72) points out, however, that literature advising youth in the selection of educational and vocational goals existed as early as the fifteenth century. This body of literature, which can be found in numerous languages, was evidently designed for the educated, for it assumed a broad base of learning and was mainly informational in nature.

Like so many other social reforms that accompanied the industrial revolution and thus date their beginnings at about the turn of the twentieth century, theories and practices in career development began in the late nineteenth century. In 1895, Frank Parsons, known as the father of vocational guidance, was advising under-privileged youth in Boston. He drew on the diagnostic procedures that were developed in the 1880s and 1890s and on the developing body of occupational information to help these youth to learn about themselves and the world of work and to combine this information to make an appropriate occupational choice. He reasoned that people need to understand themselves and their aptitudes, abilities, and interests, and that they need information concerning the requirements for success, the prospects for employment, and the requirements of different occupations. They then need the ability to integrate these two sets of facts. This was the beginning of what later came to be known as the "trait and factor" theory of career development.

The information that Parsons was looking for has proliferated in the last eighty years. We have complete and accurate information about careers both in print form and electronically, and we have comprehensive and precise tools for assessing intelligence, aptitudes, interests, and work characteristics. Yet we are also aware that simply matching people and jobs is not completely satisfactory. In the 1950s a number of theorists and researchers began to address the inadequacy of trait and factor matching and developed theories that integrate career development with physical, cognitive, psychological, and socioemotional development.

The Relationship of Career Development to Other Aspects of Development

Career development must be seen as one aspect of general human development, intimately related to all other aspects of growth. For each of us, physical attributes allow for some occupations and effectively screen us out from others; differing cognitive abilities and styles create different capacities and interests; social and emotional development, including attitudes, self-esteem, and identity issues contribute significantly to our perceptions of our place in the occupational world. Who we are physically, cognitively, socially, and emotionally provides the basis for who we become occupationally (Tiedeman, 63; Fannin, 79; Osipow, 83).

Cognitive functions even contribute to the development of interests and abilities (Barak, 81). During the course of a lifetime, an individual has a variety of experiences and engages in a number of activities. Those in which the individual is successful provide the basis for an anticipation of future success and for perception of abilities.

Of tremendous importance also is the social environment in which we find ourselves. Not only does the social environment contribute to overall development, but it opens and closes occupational doors as well, and its significance should not be underestimated. There are, of course, the famous few who have overcome tremendous social obstacles and attained success by individual determination alone, but the vast majority of us select fields for which we have appropriate social, emotional, and financial support. Parental expectations, home and community opportunities, and family activities influence the skills and interests that contribute to career development (Healy, 82).

Erik Erikson's theory of psychosocial development provides a meaningful framework within which to understand career development (Tiedeman, 63; Munley, 77; Zunker, 81). The individual's cognitive abilities develop, allowing for the differentiation of an identity and the attainment of psychosocial tasks. Career decisions are reached "through a systematic problem-solving pattern requiring the individual's total cognitive abilities, and combining both the uniqueness of the individual and the uniqueness of the world of work" (Zunker, 81, p. 18). As we mature, our environment widens and our interaction with society provides the basis for career development.

Specifically, Erikson's theory has made four major contributions to career development theory (Munley, 77):

1. It offers a comprehensive framework for career development that integrates vocationally relevant dimensions of growth into an overall theory.

2. It recognizes the importance of social factors and integrates them into the theoretical framework.

3. It contributes the important concept of **identity.** The selection of an occupation can be seen as a public declaration of the individual's identity. Through a vocation, the individual defines himself, says "This is who I am," and, it is to be hoped, resolves the identity crisis. Dolores Dante, a waitress, joyfully identifies with her job:

   I have to be a waitress. How else can I learn about people? How else does the world come to me? I can't go to everyone. So they have to come to me. Everyone wants to eat, everyone has hunger. And I serve them. If they've had a bad day, I nurse them, cajole them. Maybe with coffee I give them a little philosophy. They have cocktails, I give them political science. (Terkel, 74, p. 294)

4. It outlines the relationship between career development and general personality developoment, and allows for an understanding of how the resolution of earlier stages contributes to the resolution of the identity crisis in adolescence.

Each of Erikson's stages can be viewed in terms of its contribution to career development:

- **Trust:** Trust in self, others, and the meaning and value of work.
- **Autonomy:** Self-control, self-direction, the ability to make independent work-related choices.
- **Initiative:** Ambition, purpose, realistic appraisal of capabilities.
- **Industry:** Competency, productivity, the ability to make things work.

Theoretically, successful resolution of the earlier crises contributes to successful achievement of identity issues, including those related to vocations, and unsuccessful resolution is likely to result in career choice difficulties (Bordin, 63; Munley, 75). Munley (75) tested this theory with college students. He measured their resolution of Erikson's stages and their vocational maturity and found that students whose vocational maturity was high also demonstrated more successful resolution of Erikson's stages. Students experiencing identity diffusion and career-choice problems had been less successful in resolving the earlier crises.

Careers in the Postindustrial Society

Predictions. Before discussing specific theories of career development, it is necessary to have as clear an understanding as possible of both the work climate and the psychological climate faced by today's adolescents. We know and have discussed at some length (see Chapter 2), that the society of the last years of the twentieth century will continue to change. We do not know exactly what form these changes will take, but we can make some reasonable predictions. Figure 11.1 demonstrates the extent of projected growth in various occupations. Note that the only area of actual decline is that of farming; the current reduction in people needed to farm the land will continue to erode the agrarian lifestyle. Consistent with the increased use of technology to perform noncognitive functions, unskilled and semiskilled labor occupations will grow only slightly. The greatest growth will be in the clerical, professional, technical, and service occupations. Work specialization is increasing; management is needed; and the service occupations are becoming a major employer, replacing industry as the nation's leading employer. These projections and trends have tremendous implications for adolescents.

1. Growth opportunities (except clerical) are in fields requiring advanced education and training, but not necessarily a four-year liberal-arts degree.
2. The average educational attainment of the population will continue to rise.
3. Many of the most rapidly growing fields require technical rather than broad training. Vocational training, community college preparation, and technical training are likely to be more relevant than college education for many.
4. Because more people will have college degrees, the unemployment rates for college graduates may rise.
5. Because of the advanced training necessary, entry-level occupations will be filled by slightly older workers.
6. There will be little to no place for unskilled labor.
7. Both women and men will need to plan for lifetime careers.
8. The gap in earnings between college graduates and noncollege graduates may continue to narrow; a college degree may no longer be an assurance of overall higher lifetime earnings. (According to the 1980 U.S. Census, college gradu-

Figure 11.1
Projected Employment Growth (Herr, 79)

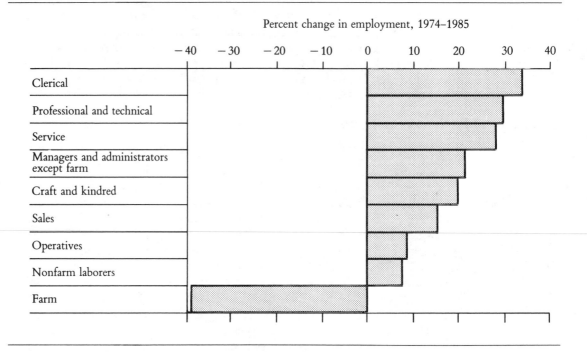

ates in 1970 earned 40 percent more than high-school graduates; in 1977 they earned only 24 percent more. The trend is likely to continue.)

9. Within colleges, the current emphasis on career preparation rather than the liberal arts is likely to continue.

10. The numbers of blacks, hispanics, and women attending college will continue to rise, as they have in the recent past (Dearman, 79).

11. Community-college enrollments will continue to rise. (Attendance at community colleges almost doubled between 1967 and 1977; Dearman, 79.)

12. Many college graduates will settle for jobs that do not require a college degree, contributing to the problem of overeducation in the United States.

13. Both the overeducated (unused college degree) and the undereducated (unskilled) are likely to be dissatisfied with their employment prospects. Sharon Atkins, an underemployed receptionist with a college degree, experiences dissatisfaction:

The machine dictates. This crummy little machine with buttons on it — you've got to be there to answer it. You can walk away from it and pretend you don't hear it, but it pulls you. You know you're not doing anything, not doing a hell of a lot for anyone. Your job doesn't mean anything. Because *you're* just a little machine. A monkey could do what I do. It's really unfair to ask someone to do that . . . .

I don't know what I'd like to do. That's what hurts the most. That's why I can't quit the job. I really don't know what talents I may have. And I don't know where to go to find out. I've been fostered so long by school and didn't have time to think about it. (Terkel, 74, pp. 30–31)

Preparation for career entry. Although the preceding predictions appear grim, career development need not be so. A positive sign is that extensive attention to career education at all levels, both in schools and out, has developed in the last fifteen years. If this trend continues, it can help young people open up their options, make realistic self- and occupational appraisals, and prepare themselves appropriately for the postindustrial society. Our schools cannot afford to emphasize college education only but must do a better job than they are currently doing of identifying and supporting alternative paths for training and development of the service and clerical workers needed in the modern world. We no longer can train people to make things but must instead concentrate on more people-oriented careers (service occupations, management, professions) that require preparation. It has always been true that the occupations that are physical, tedious, and require little thought are those that require the least preparation time, while those that are more interesting, more interactive, and demand some independent judgment require longer training (Srebalus, 82). In a society that does not need people for physical tasks, universal training becomes a necessity.

The increased demand for trained people combines with the incredible number of options available to make career choice a complex and sophisticated process. Our society allows great freedom of choice and provides thousands of alternatives from which to choose, but we have not done a satisfactory job, at least not yet, in preparing people to make those choices. Theoretically, adolescents today have the skills and power to make commitments and establish occupational identities, but we have not developed the personal planning and decision-making skills with which to make those choices. The problem is seen most dramatically in the work-entry problems faced by youth.

In an extensive review of the significant literature on the work entry problems of youth, Herr (79) found that a lack of job-seeking and retaining skills kept many from being employed, even though they had the work skills to do the job. Inadequate training, lack of information about occupational opportunities, lack of knowledge of the demands of the work world, poor work habits, an inability to fill out forms, and an inability to get along with other workers were all found to be prevalent among youth with work-entry problems. Self-knowledge, knowledge of alternatives, and good decision-making skills separate the successful from the unsuccessful.

How we might provide the necessary knowledge and skill is the subject of career education, which we will discuss later in this chapter.

The machine dictates . . . a monkey could do what I do.

THEORIES OF CAREER DEVELOPMENT

Career Development Theories

We have already seen that the work one does both results from and influences all other aspects of human development. In order to be able to make reasonably good generalizations and predictions concerning the relationships among all the factors involved, we need a comprehensive, useful theory of career development that is consistent with the theories of development already discussed in previous chapters. Elements of psychological theories need be present, but so too do sociological elements — social mores, cultural expectations, economic issues, experience. Currently, there is extensive interest in career development theory, and a number of different yet complementary theories are available. Unfortunately, because the development of career theory is relatively new, the research to document the theories is not as sophisticated as the theories themselves, and considerably more research needs to be done before any theory becomes universal. The research to date is also severely limited, for it has been conducted almost exclusively with middle-class, white, male populations. Data on minorities and women are sorely lacking in the literature (Tolbert, 80). Our discussion will therefore be more theoretical than research-based.

Career development theories, though numerous, have several important commonalities. They all assume that adequate psychological development is necessary for successful career development. Further, they rely on the necessity for self-knowledge. Therefore, certain levels of cognitive and psychological maturity are essential for healthy career development. The theories emphasize both career decisions themselves and the process of decision making, and they see career decisions as a function of the entire range of possible choices available to an individual. In making career decisions, people try to maximize gains and minimize losses, and they use whatever resources they are aware of to make effective choices. Career decisions are a function of awareness (of self and of the world of work), planning (extent of exploration and thought), commitment, and implementation (Harren, 79).

Central also to career-development theory is the concept of vocational maturity, which, while not referred to specifically in all the theories, is at least assumed to be of significance. Vocational maturity refers to the reasonable assumption of such characteristics as responsibility, realistic self-appraisal, appropriate planning skills, ability to use occupational and educational information, awareness of factors to be considered, and concern for good decision making (Jordaan, 79).

The theories are also intertwined with one another, even drawing on one another for concepts and support. They are therefore somewhat difficult to separate, but for discussion purposes, we will nevertheless separate them according to a logical paradigm. We have categorized the theories according to those based on **fulfilling needs,** those based on **personality types,** those based on **social learning,** and those based on **developmental theory.**

Need Theory

In Chapter 9 we discussed Maslow's theory of self-actualization, in which lower-order needs (food, shelter, security) must be fulfilled before higher-order needs (affection, esteem, self-actualization) come into play. This theory (Maslow, 54) is the basis for need satisfaction career theory and research, which postulate the direct relationship between life satisfaction and job satisfaction (Schmitt, 80).

According to need theory, individuals who are starving will take any job in order to feed themselves. Once biological needs are met, and once other, more emotionally satisfying opportunities become available, individuals are likely to look for work that satisfies more than their stomachs. "When career options are many, individuals emphasize expectancies regarding satisfaction and interest. When career options are few, personal skills and abilities, along with their implementation, are emphasized by individuals in their career decisions" (Osipow, 83, pp. 320–321). Thus career choice is affected by personally felt needs, which may change as individuals develop. What is satisfying at one time in life may not be so at another, simply because needs change. This phenomenon explains much of the career changing that occurs in midlife, when security needs are usually met and individuals are free to explore other, previously dormant, needs. A banker, for example, might become bored with paper and numbers and feel that his work is meaningless; a long-time dream of building his own house in the woods becomes a reality, and he finds new meaning in this work.

Though not a separate theory of needs, Herzberg (66) identified two groups of factors that contribute to how well an occupation meets needs. He called these **hygiene factors** (or dissatisfiers) and **motivators** (or satisfiers). The **hygiene factors** are job characteristics that are external to the job but must be reasonably satisfactory to prevent extreme dissatisfaction. They do not in themselves provide satisfaction. For example, such factors as salary, working conditions (such as hours and comfort), and the type of supervision employed are not sufficient for providing meaningful work, but they must be at least acceptable. **Motivators**, however, are intrinsic to the nature of the job and are the factors that provide real satisfaction and meaning. The nature of the work itself is one such motivator, as are the opportunities for advancement, recognition, and responsibility. For Hots Michaels, bar pianist, the rewards are great:

> . . . I hate to see it end. I'll dread the day it comes, because I enjoy the action. I enjoy people. If I were suddenly to inherit four million dollars, I guarantee you I'd be playin' piano, either here or at some other place. I can't explain why. I would miss the flow of people in and out. (Terkel, 74, p. 251)

In adolescence, occupational needs are usually of a very different nature than they are later in adulthood. The adolescent who works usually does so out of a need for spending money, a sense of independence, and an emerging sense of responsibility. Any job which fulfills these needs becomes satisfying. But the same adolescent should be made aware that other needs, especially those involving issues of identity and personal fulfillment, will become increasingly important, and that one's sense of identity may change. Thus an adolescent should be encouraged to explore long-term needs and interests and to develop accurate and comprehensive information about the kinds of satisfiers afforded by various occupations.

Theories Based on Personality Types

Closely related to theories of career development based on needs are theories of career development based on personality types. These include **trait and factor theory** and **psychodynamic theory**.

Trait and factor. As we mentioned earlier, trait and factor theory was the first of the career theories. It is a simple, straightforward matching of an individual's abilities and interests with the occupational opportunities available. An individual's personality is expressed in abilities, needs, interests, expectations, values, family, and environment. These traits can be profiled, as can the characteristics of alternative occupations. You are developing your personal profile when you take interest inventories like the Strong-Campbell or the Kuder. Your profile is then compared with that of various occupations, and a match is made. In traditional trait and factor theory, the problem is then solved. The difficulty with this approach is that it overlooks the changing nature of both interests and occupations and therefore neglects the dynamic interrelationships involved in growth. Trait and factor theory, though not inaccurate, is incomplete and has become absorbed into other developmental theories.

Psychodynamic. From a psychodynamic view (see Chapter 9 for a discussion of the psychodynamic theory of personality), to love and to work are the two main tasks of life. Freud saw work as maintaining a central role in the personality, for work could provide an outlet for unconscious motives and energy. This view is, of course, very closely related to that of need theory, for adult motivations develop through unmet childhood needs. The needs of early childhood are expressed in the adult occupation. For example, someone who became fixated at the oral-aggressive stage might become an expert at demolishing houses or writing scathing movie critiques, thereby expressing the hostility that was earlier repressed. According to psychodynamic career theory, work is enjoyable in that it allows the expression of taboo behavior (Brill, 49). Because these motivations are unconscious, so too is occupational selection; career education is therefore not useful in this theoretical conception (Herr, 79).

Social Learning Theory

As we have seen previously, social learning or behavioral theory places most, if not all, its emphasis on the influence of environmental factors as opposed to individual factors in development. In terms of career development, social learning theory posits: 1) that elements beyond the control of the individual exert major influence on career choice; and 2) that chance is a significant determiner of occupation. In social learning theory, ''the principal task confronting a person is the development of techniques to cope effectively with the environment'' (Osipow, 83, p. 10).

From a social-learning perspective, environmental circumstances are especially important in determining an individual's level of aspiration, with the most critical factors being familial ones. Accidents of birth like race, gender, order of birth and number of siblings, parents' occupational and social status, income, place of residence, early experiences, the interaction of parents and children, the availability of adult role models, and numerous other situational variables all have critical impact on vocational aspiration and choice. So does the school, for the type of school, the aspirations of friends, and the extent and kind of teacher influence all contribute to vocational aspiration. Ralph Werner broke out of his environment, but he clearly recalls its influence:

> In my neighborhood the kids grow up, they get married right after high school, and they work in the mills. Their whole life would revolve around one community and their certain set of friends. They would never get out and see what the world's like. It seemed terrible to me. (Terkel, 74, p. 453)

Ware (80) supports the social learning theory of career development. He measured the relative influence of four factors on college students' career development: social reinforcement or support from significant people; modeling by significant people in the chosen occupation; direct reinforcement or actual experience with a given occupation; and postive words and images associated with a chosen career. All four factors were found to be important, but direct reinforcement proved to be the single most influential factor. This research clearly supports the need for students to have direct experiences with careers in order to make well-informed choices.

A significant body of research has attempted to determine the relative effects of family versus friends on occupational choice, but no clear-cut answers have been found. What does seem clear, however, is that when parental expectations and peer expectations are consistent with each other, the influence is strongest. When parental and peer expectations vary, so do the vocational aspirations of the youth affected. Simpson (62) found that lower-class youth with middle-class friends tend to raise their aspirations, while middle-class youth with lower-class friends tend to lower theirs. He also found that when both parents and peers have high aspirations, youth are more strongly influenced by both than when both parents and peers have low aspirations.

Another body of research has sought to determine the relative effect of mothers and fathers on vocational aspirations, again with conflicting results. It is safe to say only that both parents exert considerable influence, depending on personal and familial factors that are too individual to detail. Some mothers exert more influence on some children, while some fathers exert more influence on other children. Louis Hayward, a washroom attendant, talks of an unrealized ambition influenced by his mother:

> I always wanted to be a writer. My mother was a writer. Sold a couple of short stories. I enjoy reading — thought I might enjoy writing. I thought a little of her talent might rub off on me. Apparently it didn't. Her desire rubbed off on me, though. (Terkel, 74, p. 110)

A particularly interesting body of research examines the effects of birth order and sibling relationships on occupational choice. You will remember from our discussion in Chapter 3 that birth order and spacing seem to be related to personality characteristics and motivation; these effects are also seen in vocational choice. Consistent with the characterization of first borns as achievers, Oberlander (70) found first borns to be disproportionately represented in careers involving supervision, direction, and control, and hypothesized that they had learned these characteristics by being expected to direct and control their younger siblings. Second borns, on the other hand, were disproportionately represented in careers involving sociable relationships. Sutton-Smith (64) found some interesting relationships between the sex of siblings and the sex-role stereotyping of vocations. Boys in families of all male children and girls in families of all female children were both highly likely to select strongly sex-stereotyped vocations consistent with their gender; that is, boys with only brothers were likely to choose traditionally masculine vocations, and girls with only sisters were likely to choose traditionally feminine vocations. Both boys and girls with other-sexed siblings chose more creative and expressive occupations.

Although it seems clear that environment is not the only determiner of vocational choice and development, it certainly is a significant one, for situational variables obviously hold tremendous influence over level of aspiration. They also clearly and effectively shut some occupational doors while opening others. The impact of family, community, and school factors has become a major focus of all current theories of career development.

Developmental Theories

Developmental theories of career development do not reject need-based theory, personality theory, or social learning theory, but rather include all of them and also emphasize lifetime development and change. They thus incorporate all the developmental theories we have discussed in earlier chapters of this book, though they may not refer to them specifically. It is important to recognize the influence on career development of physical development, cognitive development (especially the contribution of formal operational thinking to career choice), and personality development (especially the highly significant role played by the self-concept and the emerging identity).

Ginzberg. Ginzberg's (72) theory of career development views vocational decisions as attempts to meet current needs through available opportunities. The process of vocational choice remains open throughout life, and although decisions made in adolescence affect later decisions, life experiences also continue to influence occupational development. Ginzberg identified three basic stages of vocational development, the **fantasy period** (ages 0 to 11 years), the **tentative period** (ages 11 to 17 years), and the **realistic period** (ages 17 and up).

In the fantasy period, children imagine themselves in occupations based on their identifications with significant adults. Their choices are arbitrary and based on play activities. Because uniforms provide ready identification, children easily identify with police officers, fire fighters, and nurses, as well as with the superheroes, their parents, and other significant adults. They have not identified their own interests and aptitudes but rely solely on fantasy identification. If the fantasy period extends too long, say into the college years, for example, the individual is likely to change majors repeatedly because he has not made choices based on self-knowledge but is merely changing his identifications. Perhaps he first majored in business because his father wanted him to, then switched to biology because a favorite aunt was a doctor, and so on. Until he moves out of the fantasy stage, his choices will continue to be made arbitrarily.

In the tentative stage, adolescents consider subjective personal factors: interests, capacities, and values. Early in the period (ages 11 and 12 years), interests are paramount, and young adolescents select occupations based on what they like to do. Children of this age frequently select professional sports, race-car driving, and other activities that they view as great fun. The sole focus on interests is gradually replaced (around 12 to 14 years) by increased attention to capacities and aptitudes; and the things adolescents do well become the primary bases for their occupational choice. At about 15 or 16 adolescents begin to consider their values and look for occupations and activities that allow for the expression of those values. An interest in service to others is likely to arise at this time. Consistent also with the development of formal operational thinking, adolescents become more sensitive to the imminence of vocational commitment and finally, at about 17, begin to integrate interests, capacities, and values in a transition out of the tentative stage and into the realistic stage.

The realistic period is further divided into substages: exploration (ages 17 to 19); crystallization (ages 19 to 21); and specification (ages 21 and older). In the exploration substage, older adolescents find ways to implement choices made at the end of the tentative period. They then evaluate their experiences and the feedback they get in the realistic setting of the early college years or of entry-level jobs. Based on successes and failures during exploration, young adults move into crystallization, the emergence of a consistent vocational pattern. Finally, this pattern becomes a clear choice during specification.

Although Ginzberg attached approximate ages to each period of development, he also clearly recognized that the rate of development is dependent on a number of factors. The reality factor refers to the pressure of the environment to make a choice; affluence, for example, allows for considerable delay in making occupational commitments. The educational process, including both the kind and the length of training, also speeds up or delays development. The individual's own personal factors, such as emotional stability, the ability to compromise, the use of formal-operational cognitive processes, and the ability to delay gratification, contribute significantly to career development, as do individual values. If any of these personal factors do not develop during adolescence, mature career behavior will not occur, and the individual is likely to be occupationally dissatisfied and change jobs frequently, without ever gaining the self-knowledge and the knowledge of the world of work necessary for sound decison making.

Super. The single most comprehensive and influential theory of career development is that of Super (57, 74, 80). The theory thoroughly integrates personal and environmental factors based on the continued evolution and implementation of the self-concept. ''The basic theme is that the individual chooses occupations that will allow him to function in a role consistent with his self-concept and that the latter conception is a function of his developmental history'' (Herr, 79, p. 93). Individuals develop more clearly defined self-concepts as they mature, and simultaneously develop increasingly complex and accurate views of the occupational world. Career choice then becomes a function of the match between self-concept and the vocational concept allowed in the chosen career. The adequacy of the decision depends upon the adequacy of the match.

Super (57) built his theory on ten propositions about human development:

1. People differ in interests, abilities, and personalities.
2. People are qualified for a variety of occupations.
3. Every individual occupation requires a particular pattern of abilities, interests, and personality traits.
4. Vocational preferences and competence can change throughout the life span.
5. The process of change can be summarized in a series of life stages.
6. Career patterns are determined by socioeconomic class, mental abilities, and opportunities, as well as by personality charactertistics.
7. Career development is a function of biological maturation, reality testing, and the development of the self-concept.
8. The most significant factor in career development is the development and implementation of self-concept.
9. Career choice is often the result of compromise between individual and social factors and between the self-concept and reality.
10. Career satisfaction depends on the adequacy of outlets in the career for the individual's expression of abilities, interests, personality traits, and values.

Super identified five vocational life stages and defined vocational maturity as the ability to deal successfully with the vocational tasks appropriate to the life stage being experienced. Thus vocational maturity in one stage is different from vocational maturity in another stage, and even small children can be considered vocationally mature if they are dealing appropriately with the tasks at their stage of development. They become vocationally immature only if their vocational development does not keep pace with their chronological development. The five stages are **growth** (up to age 14), **exploration** (ages 15–25), **establishment** (ages 26–45), **maintenance** (ages 46–65), and **decline** (age 66 and over).

In the growth stage, children must develop an understanding both of the kinds of people they are and of the nature and meaning of work. The self-concept develops through identification with significant adults. Substages are similar to those of Ginzberg: fantasy dominates up until about 11 years, then interests become the major determiner of activities, and later abilities are given more weight in consideration of alternatives. During the growth stage, children should be encouraged to try a wide variety of experiences.

The tasks of the exploration stage (from 15 to 25 years) are to recognize and accept the need to make career decisions, obtain relevant occupational information, crystallize a career self-concept (including interests and abilities and an awareness of how they relate to career opportunities), identify appropriate fields and levels of work, and implement a vocational preference through securing the appropriate training and gaining entry into the occupation. Within the exploration stage are three identifiable substages:

- The **tentative** substage (ages 15 to 17) involves the consideration of needs, interests, capacities, values, and opportunities. Tentative choices are made and tried out in role play, discussion, course work, and early jobs. The adolescent begins to identify appropriate fields and levels of work.

- The **transition** substage (ages 18 to 21) involves increasing specification of choice and considerable attention to the reality factors. The individual is involved in specific training both through formal education and on-the-job experiences. The fit between the occupation and the self-concept is considered in the real context of school and work.

- The **trial** substage (ages 22 to 25) involves trying out the occupational choice as a potential life's work. Commitment is provisional, depending on the adequacy of the job for expression of the self-concept. The trial stage leads to commitment and establishment in the occupation.

After the crystallization, specification, and implementation of a vocational preference, individuals enter into the **establishment** stage of adulthood. If appropriate occupations have been found, individuals make a place for themselves in them, and rather than changing occupations completely, further changes are in positions, job, or employer. The two substages are **trial and stabilization** (ages 26 to 30) and **advancement** (ages 31 to 45). During adulthood, individuals gradually make a permanent place for themselves in an occupation, settle into it, become creative once security is established, and eventually acquire seniority and high-level status within the chosen field.

From age 46 to 65, the **maintenance** stage, people continue in already established patterns. The task is to preserve the achievements of the establishment stage. After retirement, in the **decline** stage, physical and mental powers decline. The individuals must develop new roles and new self-concepts as retired workers and find sources of satisfaction outside the occupation.

Super's theory is clearly a model designed for counselors and is not a valid scientific statement based on solid evidence. It has, however, generated considerable research, with most of the findings supporting the idea that occupational choice is one expression of self-concept. "The results of the research provide an impressive amount of empirical support for the general aspects of the theory proposed by Super" (Osipow, 83, p. 180). In another extensive review of the research, Herr (79) reached similar conclusions. Occupational choice is clearly an implementation of the self-concept, and self-identity is a necessary precursor to career commitment. College students with personally identified career goals achieve higher grades than those who have none, and even high-school students do better when they have a sense of the meaning of what they are learning and its relationship to their goals (Herr, 79). Problems in career choice can be seen as problems in the achievement of identity and the establishment of a clear self-concept (Osipow, 83; Herr, 79; Lunneborg, 75). Poorly defined self-concepts are directly related to occupational problems (Herr, 79), as are retarded rates of psychological development, inadequate emotional adjustment, and inaccurate self-appraisal (Osipow, 83). Career indecision may also be related to lack of achievement, for college students who are undecided about their majors tend to have lower grades, are less satisfied with college, and have fewer post-college plans than do those who have made at least a tentative commitment to a major (Lunneborg, 75).

Although the overwhelming research evidence supports the applicability of Super's theory to high-school and college-age students, younger adolescents may not have developed sufficiently consistent self-concepts to make self-concept the most significant factor in their vocational adjustment. Holland (81) tested 300 sixth graders on measures of career maturity, self-concept, socioeconomic status, race, sex, place of residence, and age. He found that socioeconomic status was the most useful indicator of career maturity in these sixth graders, and concluded that Super's theory may not be directly applicable to preadolescents. Nevertheless, Super's theory remains the single most influential theory of career development, primarily because of its comprehensive and integrative approach.

For children and younger adolescents, Gottfredson (81) offers an explanation of career and self-concept development that is entirely consistent with that of Super. He combines developmental and social systems views and sees self-concept development as the function of social class membership. Children react to their perceptions of prestige, sex type, and traits of people in various occupations, and develop self-concepts in four stages. From age 3 to 5, they are oriented to and identify with size and power; from age 6 to 8, sex role provides the major identification; from 9 to 13 they respond to social values; and only after the age of 14 do they become oriented to an internalized, unique self rather than to external perceptions. This framework would explain Holland's finding that vocational adjustment in sixth graders is related to socioeconomic status rather than to occupational self-concept.

THE INFLUENCE OF CULTURE AND SEX

Cultural Differences in Career Development

Any astute observer of American workers is aware that some careers are dominated by people of a particular group, with culture and sex presenting fairly obvious occupational distinctions. Blacks, for example, are disproportionately represented in professional football and basketball, white males in medicine and dentistry, women in teaching and social work. It is clear that these facts are related as much to the phenomena of socialization as they are to heredity. Geography, economics, social mobility, social resources, discrimination, educational availability, role models, and other situational variables confound issues of race, culture, and sex, making it mistakenly seem as if it is race or sex alone that creates the differences. That individual variables are strongly affected by setting, for example, is seen in the development of a good swimmer. A good swimmer who grows up in Miami has a significantly

Success experiences instill confidence and make achievement possible.

greater chance of becoming a scuba diver than does an equally good swimmer who grows up in the inner city of Philadelphia.

The research evidence to support the occupational effects of minority group membership is highly inconsistent (Osipow, 83). For members of all races, adult role models, as well as discrimination and poverty, are far more significant influences on occupational differences than is race or culture *per se.* Lack of access to educational and occupational opportunities, poor adult role models, and hostility resulting from low self-esteem, which itself is the result of poverty and lack of access, work to keep members of low socioeconomic groups from breaking out of the deadly spiral of failure and low aspiration (Herr, 79). These groups are less likely to achieve higher-order needs because they must struggle to satisfy basic survival needs. Their aspirations thus remain low, as does their ability to move up to the more psychologically fulfilling aspects of work.

This is not to say that upward mobility is not possible, for certainly many individuals have successfully raised their aspirations and attainments far beyond what their environmental circumstances might have predicted. As members of minority groups have recognized for some time, the channel for upward mobility of low socioeconomic groups is largely educational. It thus becomes imperative to help young people understand that their chances for occupational success, especially in the postindustrial technology, lie in staying in and succeeding in school. And school people must do everything in their power to create success experiences for the ''disadvantaged,'' success experiences that instill the confidence and self-esteem that make aspiration and achievement possible.

Sex Differences

Far more influential in career decisions that culture or race is sex. There are more sex differences than racial or cultural differences in educational and occupational values and goals, and sex has been found to be the single most important variable affecting work attitudes (Dole, 72).

Current predictions concerning the employment of women are that nine out of ten women will work full time for at least a significant portion of their lives. Economic necessity has forced even the mothers of young children into the labor market, and women are also encouraged to work because of the advent of labor-saving devices for housework, smaller families, legislation improving working womens' rights, the womens' movement itself, more varied lifestyles, increased day-care options, and the breakdown of the stereotypes of the past. Women have careers, yet our theories of career development have not included women. All the theories discussed were tested on predominantly white, middle-class, male populations, yet it is clear that the formation of an occupational identity is more complex for women than it is for men (Matthews, 64; Psathas, 69; Zytowski, 69; Dellas, 75; Fitzgerald, 80; Grotevant, 82a).

Female development. In Chapter 7 we traced the sex-role development of women and of men and noted that girls tend to have significantly lower needs for achievement than do boys, while they also have significantly higher needs for affiliation. The value placed on relationships was also noted over that for achievement in Chapters 8, 9, and 10. Career choices are affected too. Card (80) summarized the findings of a significant longitudinal study of 4035 participants in grade 9, who

Table 11.1
Representation of Men and Women in Various Professions

	Dentists	Physicians	Lawyers	Nurses	Elementary Teachers	Librarians
Percentage male	95	89	87	4	16	22
Percentage female	5	11	13	96	84	78

were subsequently followed one, five, and eleven years after they graduated from high school. In this study, women had higher high-school grades and scored higher on academic ability tests than did men. But by eleven years after graduation, the men were better educated and were earning more money. The greatest gains for the men were made in the period 5 to 11 years after high school graduation, leading the researchers to conclude that the main reason for the differences was the greater conflict, for women, between the roles of spouse/parent on the one hand and student/worker on the other. Harmon (81) followed 391 women six years after they entered college and found that 40 percent had given up on pursuing a college degree, 66 percent were married, and 50 percent planned to combine family and career. Seventy percent of the women were employed, mostly in social, medical, and clerical fields. They had not turned to nontraditional careers in any substantial numbers. The 1980 census (Table 11.1) also reflects that women are remaining in traditionally feminine occupations, even though these offer lower pay and less opportunity for advancement than nontraditional occupations. Weeks (84) found that high-school girls' sex-role attitudes were significantly related to the sex-role attitudes of their mothers.

Anne Bogan, an executive secretary, and Roberta Victor, a prostitute, have very different views on the role of women in society:

> *Anne:* I feel the wife of an executive would be a better wife if she had been a secretary first. As a secretary, you learn to adjust to the boss's moods. Many marriages would be happier if the wife would do that. (Terkel, 74, p. 56)

> *Roberta:* The overt hustling society is the microcosm of the rest of the society. The power relationships are the same and the games are the same. Only this one I was in control of. The greater one I wasn't. In the outside society, if I tried to be me, I wasn't in control of anything. As a bright, assertive woman, I had no power. As a cold, manipulative hustler, I had a lot. I know I was playing a role. Most women are taught to *become* what they act. All I did was act out the reality of American womanhood. (Terkel, 74, p. 65)

It is abundantly clear that the career development theories, like the male-based theories of psychological and moral development, do not adequately explain female development. Only women who display high levels of masculine traits are served by

Women in nontraditional careers display high self-esteem.

the theories. Wolfe (81), for example, found that Holland's personality types were valid only for women who make nontraditional occupational choices.

Choosing traditionally feminine occupations apparently creates considerable confusion for women because their choices are generally not consistent with their personality types. If this is true, it is no wonder that so many women working in traditionally feminine occupations report considerable dissatisfaction.

Even though girls have been shown to display higher academic aptitude than boys prior to adolescence, girls are very sparsely represented in careers requiring mathematical skills. A "math filter" seems to operate within the socialization process to teach girls that they are not supposed to like or to do well in math, but even among young women who have not been filtered out of math courses by their parents and teachers, many do not aspire to careers in math or science even when they are mathematically talented (Hollinger, 83). The few who do aspire to math and science careers rate themselves higher on traditionally masculine personality traits and have higher overall levels of achievement motivation and self-esteem.

Role conflict. High self-esteem and high achievement motivation are related to high occupational aspirations and to the achievement of identity, including occupational identity (Bedein, 78). Furthermore, as we noted in Chapter 7, women with high levels of achievement motivation display high levels of traditionally masculine traits, and they tend to place career values above other values (recreation, family life) (Marshall, 80). Women in professional and nontraditional careers display higher self-esteem and more internal locus of control than those choosing to work in the home or in traditional fields (Richardson, 75; Burlin, 76; Falkowski, 83). Herein lies the central issue of female career development. Women continue to wrestle with the conflict between career and family; men do not. For men, career and family are complementary; for women they are frequently conflictual. Clearly, every woman who chooses to be a mother is making a choice that will affect all her other choices. And we do not yet have a theory of career development that addresses the complexity of this issue.

Kassner (81) investigated current attitudes of college students toward two types of marriages, traditional and egalitarian, and found even further complications. The college men overwhelmingly indicated that they still prefer traditional marriages with sex-role divisions of labor, but the women indicated preferences for egalitarian marriages. The men saw marriage as facilitating their career development while the women saw marriage as hindering theirs. The dilemma persists.

Although the role conflict and the stress of fulfilling multiple full-time roles may be the central issue in the career development of women, other obstacles also prevent women from developing careers in the same way that men do. Sex-role socialization (Chapter 7) leads women to focus on marriage rather than a career and to ignore the necessity for career and life planning. Discrimination in hiring, pay, and promotion still exist. Sexist attitudes and stereotyping at home and in schools continue. Women are often caught in the no-win position of being expected to provide everything for everybody — to be wife, mother, homemaker, and career woman simultaneously, while also being a glamorous lover. The wonder-woman expectation is epitomized in a popular and long-running television perfume commercial: "I can bring home the bacon, fry it up in the pan, and never-never let him forget he's a man, 'cause I'm a woman, W O M A N!"

Hackett (81) explains how the socialization of women creates internal barriers that restrict their range of options (Figure 11.2). She postulates that low expectations for success are influenced by four sources of information: performance accomplishments, vicarious learning, emotional arousal, and verbal persuasion. These

Figure 11.2
A Model Depicting the Postulated Effects of Traditional Female Socialization on Career-Related Self-Efficacy Expectations

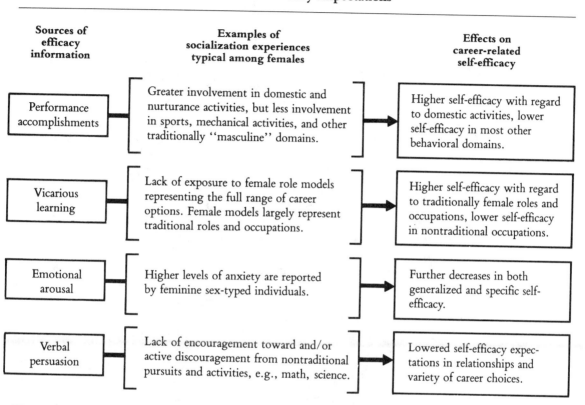

Sources of efficacy information	Examples of socialization experiences typical among females	Effects on career-related self-efficacy
Performance accomplishments	Greater involvement in domestic and nurturance activities, but less involvement in sports, mechanical activities, and other traditionally ''masculine'' domains.	Higher self-efficacy with regard to domestic activities, lower self-efficacy in most other behavioral domains.
Vicarious learning	Lack of exposure to female role models representing the full range of career options. Female models largely represent traditional roles and occupations.	Higher self-efficacy with regard to traditionally female roles and occupations, lower self-efficacy in nontraditional occupations.
Emotional arousal	Higher levels of anxiety are reported by feminine sex-typed individuals.	Further decreases in both generalized and specific self-efficacy.
Verbal persuasion	Lack of encouragement toward and/or active discouragement from nontraditional pursuits and activities, e.g., math, science.	Lowered self-efficacy expectations in relationships and variety of career choices.

sources of information lead to low expectations for success in nontraditional occupational fields and high expectations for success in domestic activities and traditionally feminine occupations.

Although there is clear evidence of changing attitudes toward women working, the socialization detailed by Hackett still affects adolescent choices. Women score significantly higher on measures of success avoidance than do men (Esposito, 77). Whereas males value status, luxury, and security, females value family, religion, and making a contribution (Lueptow, 80a). Females display considerably less confidence in achievement situations than do males (Lenney, 79). Barnett (75) asked 2500 adolescents to rate 24 jobs on prestige and then to indicate which they most and least liked. Whereas boys preferred high-prestige jobs, girls tended to identify the high-prestige jobs as those they least liked. Barnett concluded that girls have been taught not to aspire to high-prestige occupations. Fottler (80) surveyed over 2000 high-school seniors to ascertain sex differences in aspiration to managerial careers and found that very few girls aspire to management. The study concluded that girls were the victims of the socialization process, the absence of female role models in management, fear of success, limited self-confidence, low achievement motivation, and differential counseling for males and for females. That high school counselors perpetuate sex-role stereotypes was also found by Ahrons (76) and Donahue (77).

Grotevant (82a) notes that males and females apparently take different paths to the achievement of an occupational identity. Whereas boys tend toward an instrumental orientation, accept challenging tasks, and disregard negative evaluations from others, girls tend to value hard work and avoiding competition.

Evidence of change. Although the preceding research findings paint a rather bleak picture of the current status of female career development, there is some evidence that points to change. The percentage of young women expecting to spend their lives as full-time homemakers is decreasing (Turner, 72; Cherlin, 80; Falkowski, 83). Dunne (81) surveyed 1800 rural high-school students and found that in comparison with results obtained ten years previously, girls had higher educational and occupational aspirations. Their educational and occupational aspirations also compared favorably with those of the boys in the sample. Although Dunne cautioned that aspirations alone cannot predict actual attainment, there is convincing evidence that educational aspirations of females are being addressed. Between 1970 and 1975, the number of women attending college increased twice as much as the number of men, and the number of women attending graduate and professional schools increased 75 percent. The finding that the prospect of increasing numbers of women entering high-status professions does not result in a decline in the prestige or the desirability of those professions is heartening. It is now common knowledge that females outnumber males in overall college enrollments (Dearman, 79; Suchner, 79; White, 81; Crino, 83).

With this recent change in the educational aspirations of large numbers of women, it becomes interesting to study the influences that seem to affect increasing aspirations, and a number of researchers have begun just such studies. They seem to be particularly interested in the role of parents. Farmer (80) found that high achievement motivation was significantly correlated with the girl's perception of support for high achievement by her family, school, and community. Siegfried (81) found a significant relationship between high occupational aspiration and the girls' mothers' educational attainment. When a mother is highly educated, her daughter is increasingly likely to aspire to high-level careers. Weishaar (81) found that women entering college were more likely to be influenced by their fathers and other male role models, especially if their mothers were in traditional fields. Finally, Falkowski (83) found that young women who expect to be full-time homemakers are disproportionately represented by fathers and mothers with low occupational status. As we have noted repeatedly, the home environment is a most significant influence on educational and occupational aspirations.

Obviously, we need to address the career development of females directly, combat sex stereotyping, and encourage realistic occupational aspirations. Adoles-

Figure 11.3
A Woman's Life

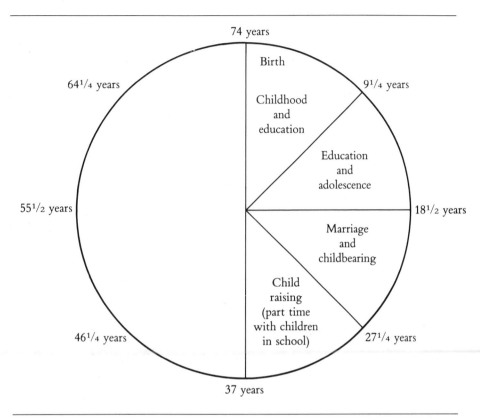

The blank half could be filled in with "vegetation," employment, political activity, community work, church or club work, etc., but should it not be filled with productivity and the utilization of talents, abilities, and interests? Do people stagnate if they don't continue to grow? What happens to a woman who hasn't worked in 20 years if she is suddenly widowed or divorced at age 43? Shouldn't the full-time homemaker's child-raising years be devoted part-time to continued education and preparation for the last half of her life? (Prepared by California Advisory Commission on the Status of Women, 1972)

cent females need to be assisted in discussing the effects of stereotyping; they need to see nontraditional role models and review and discuss the advantages and disadvantages of a variety of career options (Vincenzi, 77). Hansen (77) uses a graphic representation of a woman's life to emphasize the importance of career and life planning for young women (Figure 11.3). If you are a woman, how do you want to fill in the blank half? If you are a man, how would you want your wife to fill it in?

CAREER EDUCATION

The Need

Career education was introduced in this country in response to the problems observed among people entering and staying in the workforce. In general, problems of poor work attitudes, inadequate information concerning occupations and occupational expectations, poor decision-making skills, and the lack of meaningful relationships between school and work led to the awareness that we must provide people with survival skills as well as career awareness, career exploration, and career preparation (Herr, 79). The U.S. Office of Education hoped, through career education, to provide responses to the following identified needs (Hoyt, 74):

1. Too many high school students are deficient in basic academic skills.
2. Too many students find little meaning in the schools.
3. There is too little attention paid to those who are not going to college.
4. Education has not kept pace with societal change, resulting in large numbers of overeducated and undereducated youth. The overeducated are bored; the undereducated frustrated.
5. Too many students leave school without self-understanding or decision-making skills.
6. Girls are not encouraged to consider life-long careers.
7. The recurrent educational needs of adults are not being met.
8. The opportunities outside formal educational settings are not being used.
9. The public is not involved in making academic policy.
10. American education doesn't meet the needs of minority and disadvantaged youth.
11. There is too little attention to post-high-school education at the subbaccalaureate level. We focus too narrowly on college preparation.

Insufficient information. While it is acknowledged that students gain significant increases in their occupational knowledge and in their planning skills during high school (Westbrook, 73; Jepsen, 75; Herr, 76; Noeth, 78; Osipow, 83), it is also clear that high schools are not providing seniors with the occupational knowledge they need (Grotevant, 80; Redfering, 80). Redfering compared the incomes and job complexities of high-school dropouts and graduates with and without vocational training and found that vocational training was a far more potent influence on income and job complexity than was completion of high school. Grotevant surveyed high-school seniors concerning their first choice of occupation and then asked them how much education they would need for that occupation and how confident they were in their understanding of what was required. Table 11.2 details the results of the almost 3000 students who were confident that they had an accurate picture of what was required.

Table 11.2

Percentage of High School Seniors Who Were Undereducated, Appropriately Educated, or Overeducated for their Career Choice

	Undereducated	Appropriately Educated	Overeducated
Males	21.5%	47.4%	31.3%
Females	18.7%	55.3%	26.0%

As can be seen in Table 11.2, only about half of the seniors who claimed understanding of their occupational choices had appropriate information concerning the educational requirements of the occupation they had selected. The implications for job satisfaction are enormous, especially when we remember that these statistics apply only to those who expressed confidence in their knowledge of the requirements.

Poor decision making. In addition to insufficient and inaccurate educational and occupational information, problems in decision making complicate career choice considerably. Atwater (83) identified six factors that contribute to problems in decision making: lack of occupational information, accidental choices resulting from circumstance, indecision from too many alternatives, personal identity problems, lack of self-awareness, and lack of assessment skills. These combine to create real problems for many young people, problems which Herr (79, p. 19) describes in indecisive college students:

> . . .this tendency by so many college students to change courses of study and institutions or drop out entirely is at least partially caused by a lack of considered goals in the first place. Many persons think no further than gaining access to college. They have no real purpose to commit their energies to after matriculation, nor are they clear about ultimate career goals from which a considered choice of curriculum major could be related. These persons . . . experience identity crises, choice dilemmas, and information deficits, some of which could be reduced with adequate career guidance.

But it is not only high school graduates who need effective decision-making skills. As early as the ninth grade, students must make curriculum choices that will have lifelong implications. In entering high school, students must choose among academic, business, vocational, general, or even specialized (such as art or science) curricula, or even, in some cases, among high schools, decisions that clearly narrow later occupational options. They also must choose, during high school, whether or not to finish, and if they do, what electives to select, electives that can also open and close occupational doors. Then, at the end of high school, students must choose between work and further education or training. If they go to work, they must select and find a job, consider their occupational objectives, and make decisions about where to work, whether or not to marry, and so on. If they choose further training, they must decide among a four-year college, a community college, a technical institute, a company training program, the military, or an apprenticeship. Every choice has implications for later development.

Research. The need for career education in middle and high school is documented in numerous research studies, two of which we will highlight here. Healy (82) reported on Project Talent, which compared a total of 400,000 high school students in 1960 and 1970 and found no change in the intervening ten years on the realism of career choices, the appropriateness of career choices, or the consistency of those choices. Choices were found to be unrealistic and inappropriate and to change drastically within one year of leaving high school. The 1970 sample did become somewhat more realistic in their choices, and girls in 1970 were making a wider range of choices than those in 1960, but the choices were still found to be inappropriate to measured abilities.

The most influential longitudinal study of career development is the Career Pattern Study, which has followed some students for thirty years and has compared high-school seniors on several measures from 1955 through 1972. Jordaan (79) summarized the findings:

1. Ninth-grade boys lack planfulness, knowledge and use of resources, occupational information, and decision-making skills.
2. Twelfth graders were not much better prepared to make educational and occupational decisions than were ninth graders.
3. Seniors in 1972 were no more vocationally mature than seniors in 1955, although seniors in 1972 were more service-oriented than their earlier counterparts.
4. Two-thirds of seniors had no commitment or confidence in their decisions.
5. About half of the choices of seniors were not in keeping with their measured interests.
6. Over half of the choices of seniors were not in keeping with socioeconomic resources or abilities.
7. In general, high-school occupational choices were not realistic.

With such dismal evidence of occupational maturity, the need for career education and guidance can hardly be argued or ignored.

Career Education Defined

Hoyt (75, p. 304) defined career education as the composite of "activities and experiences through which individuals prepare themselves for and engage in work — paid or unpaid — during their lives." To be comprehensive, career education goes beyond the walls of the school to include the following (Tolbert, 80):

1. **Family life program:** To insure the positive influence of the home on children and to improve the care and motivation of young children. The role of parents in career education needs to be specifically addressed and supported.

2. **Career motivation program:** To develop positive attitudes toward and respect for work in children in grades K through 6.

3. **Career orientation program:** To increase awareness of career opportunities in children in grades 7 and 8.

4. **Career exploration program:** To provide first-hand experience for youngsters in grades 9 and 10.

5. **Career preparation program:** To provide vocational or preprofessional education for students in grades 11 and 12.

6. **Career training, retraining, and upgrading program:** To improve the attitudes and habits of youth and adults outside of school.

Career education assists people in developing life skills, personal worth, an appreciation for work and for commitment to society, and self-awareness (Beane, 79). Especially in the high technology of today, people need to be personally aware of their strengths, weaknesses, and preferences; they need the skills to use resources, weigh alternatives, make decisions, interact in meaningful ways, find and maintain employment, and understand the relationship between education and occupation (Herr, 79). Career education should address all these issues, as well as developing specific employability skills, including positive work-role identification and appropriate vocational goals (Oetting, 77; Srebalus, 82).

Seen in this way, career education is no less than life education, for career education provides the awareness, exploration, and preparation for the determination of an identity. Herr (79, p. 39) conceptualizes the elements of career education (related to the years in school) as pictured in Figure 11.4. Note that each element of career education on the left should, through the school years, result in the identity gain on the right.

School-based career education. Although more than one model of career education exists, we will focus on school-based career education, since it is in schools that most adolescents are exposed, to whatever degree they are, to the elements pictured in Figure 11.4. Sidney Marland (74), known as the father of career education, wanted to refocus American education so that every high-school graduate would be ready either for advanced education or for useful employment. Specifically, career education should

- Increase the relationship between schools and society as a whole.
- Relate the curricula of schools to the needs of persons to function in society.
- Provide opportunities for counseling, guidance, and career development for all children.
- Extend the concept of the education process into the area of employment and the community.
- Foster flexibility in attitudes, skills, and knowledge in order to enable persons to cope with accelerating change and obsolescence.
- Eliminate any distinction between education for vocational purposes and general or academic education. (Herr, 79, pp. 36–37).

Figure 11.4
Comprehensive Career Education

Comprehensive career education

	K	1	2	3	4	5	6	7	8	9	10	11	12	
Career awareness														Career identity
Self-awareness														Self-identity
Appreciations, attitudes														Self-social fulfillment
Decision-making skills														Career decisions
Economic awareness														Economic understandings
Skill awareness														Employment skills
Employability skills														Career placement
Educational awareness														Educational identity

Elements of career education

Element outcomes

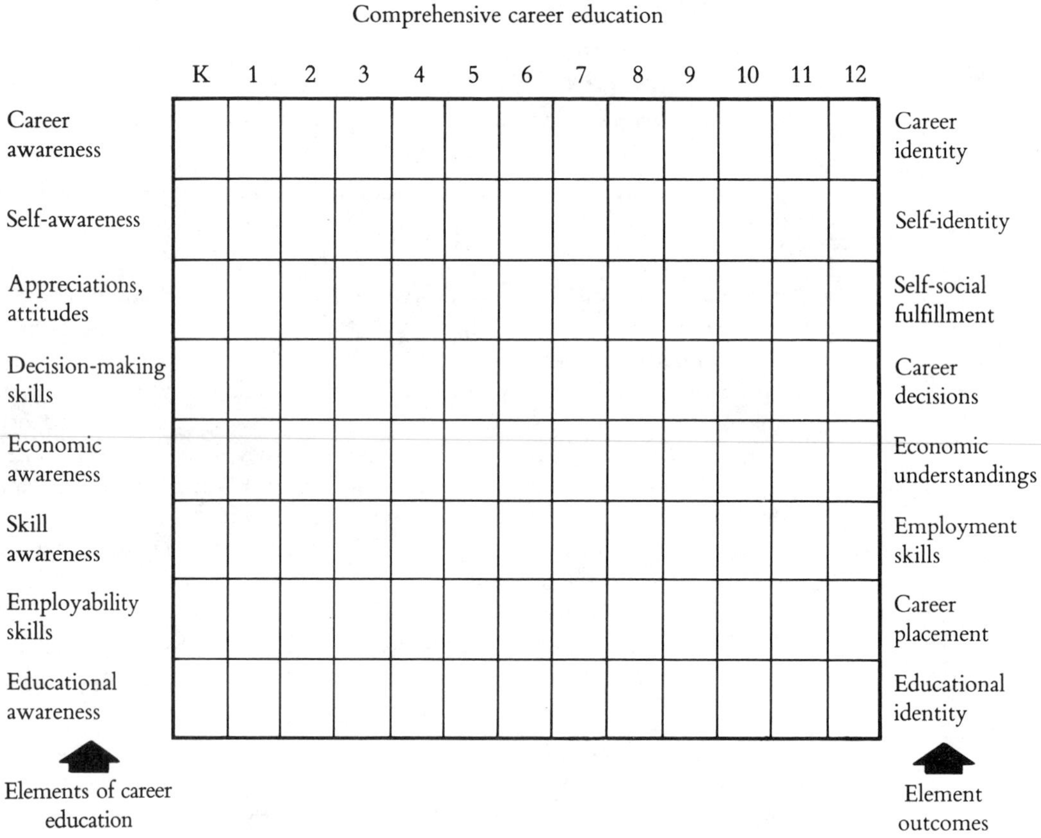

Although the goals of school-based career education are both comprehensive and laudable, the outcomes have been mixed (Herr, 79). Most of the effort has been at the elementary and junior-high levels, with most funding coming from local and state authorities. Although there is widespread support for career education among parents, teachers, and students, few comprehensive programs have developed, and there has been far too little effort focused on special populations. In the programs that have developed, career has too often been defined in a short-term manner, with little focus on long-term planning, decision-making processes, and lifestyle implications. Those programs that have been successful have high community involvement and have focused on process rather than outcome. They involve attention to self-concepts, are organized around life stages, and include planned and sequenced curricular materials (Srebalus, 82). In short, they increase self-awareness, awareness of the world of work, and reliable decision-making skills.

Alternatives to in-school programs. Although career education in schools can contribute to career maturity, schools probably cannot do it all. Perhaps most of what we learn about work and about ourselves as workers is learned through experience in the work setting. Yongue (81) compared the increase in career maturity of high-school juniors and seniors, half of whom participated in an intensive career-education class while the other half spent an equal amount of time visiting work sites, and found that the field-exposure group increased their career maturity while the classroom group did not. This learning-through-experience approach to career development is called **action learning** (Coleman, 74; Atwater, 83) and is generally of three types: work study, human services education, and volunteer work. In work study, students work for pay while earning academic credit. Cooperative education programs usually provide for a half day of school and a half day of work, all of which counts toward the high school diploma. Human services education (or internships) provide work experience for academic credit, but no pay. Youth usually work in people-serving professions or agencies (such as the Red Cross or mental health agencies). Volunteer work provides neither academic credit nor pay, but does provide real work experience. Almost as many 14- to 17-year-olds do volunteer work as work for pay (Eberly, 78), primarily in hospitals, social service agencies, schools, and libraries. Youth-serving agencies also can provide relevant work experience and career education.

Coleman (74) argues that more radical measures are in order. Legal restraints on adolescents, including compulsory school attendance, child-labor laws, occupational and trade-union regulations, and the legal minimum wage, all effectively bar young people from productive employment and keep them isolated. He suggests reviewing occupational restrictions, considering a dual minimum wage, radical changes in school structures, the alternation of full-time work or public service and school, the incorporation of youth into work organizations, and vouchers for youth to use for job training or education.

The idea of a dual minimum wage has been debated for a decade, and at this writing is contained in a bill (*H.R.* 285) that has been introduced in the House of Representatives. A subminimum wage of 75 to 85 percent of the adult minimum for those under nineteen would create, it is argued, 150,000 to 400,000 jobs for young people. Although some argue that the wage discriminates against young people, those who favor it believe that creating work opportunities and lowering the youth unemployment rate are more important than providing equal pay for equal work, at least in this circumstance.

Coleman argues that large, comprehensive high schools must be altered if youth are to develop career maturity in them. He argues for specialized high schools that focus on prevocational and preprofessional training, smaller schools and schools within schools in which students can take active and meaningful roles in decision making, giving students opportunities to serve as tutors to others, and restructuring the entire school philosophy better to serve youth.

Although cooperative education programs alternate school and work on a daily basis, Coleman argues that there should be opportunities for high-school youth to leave school for full-time work or for a year or two of public service (like VISTA or the Peace Corps) and return, with the work leave being selected for the achievement of specified, planned goals. The idea that the entire high-school experience must precede productive activity needs to be reconsidered. At the same time, work organizations should rethink their commitment to youth and provide structures that incorporate youth, perhaps by providing education within the work environment. Many companies provide regular, ongoing staff-development activities for employees. These might also be provided for school-age youth employed in the organization.

A truly revolutionary proposal is that of vouchers to be employed by youth. In our current educational structure, public money is provided to institutions of higher education, in effect subsidizing those who stay in school, while providing no support for those who do not. Coleman argues that we ought to subsidize individuals rather than schools and proposes doing so by providing vouchers to everyone.

> Such vouchers, perhaps equivalent in value to the average cost of education through four years of college, would be given to the young at age 16, to be used at their discretion for schooling and other skill acquisition at any subsequent time in their life. (Coleman, 74, pp. 169–170)

These proposals were made a decade ago, and except for cooperative education and the proposal of a subminimum wage, have not been implemented. Institutional change is notoriously slow, but if we are to educate young people for the technological world, we need to address the criticism that schools are not currently providing adequate career training. Unfortunately, we have not studied the potential effects of interrupting schooling, of part-time or full-time work, or of youth service programs, and have not seriously considered changing schools in any substantial ways. Research is sorely needed.

THE ROLE OF WORK IN THE LIVES OF ADOLESCENTS

The Effects of Working While in School

Although there is no doubt that work is a central aspect of human life and plays a significant role in each individual's sense of self, we know surprisingly little about the effects of working on adolescents who are in school. There is a real paucity of research into this important question, and what data do exist are contradictory. Work obviously contributes to career maturity and is assumed to be a positive influence on the development of responsibility. National commissions have called for

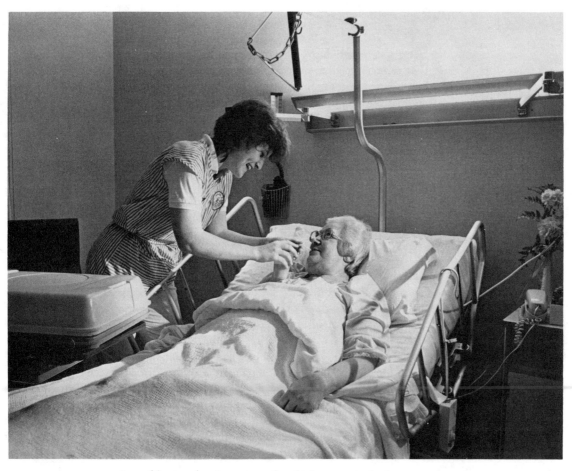

Successful career-education programs have high community involvement.

the early and deliberate integration of adolescents into the workforce, as Coleman's proposals detail, but we need considerably more research before we can state unequivocally just what kind of work and how much of it is developmentally healthy for adolescents. Cole (80) and Steinberg (82) have studied the effects of work on adolescents and found both beneficial and detrimental effects. Benefits include the development of a sense of personal responsibility, a means of testing abilities and interests, a way of being productive, the development of interpersonal skills, and the adolescents' ability to earn their own money. Work does not, however, develop a sense of duty to others. In addition, adolescents who work, especially those who work more than fourteen hours a week, tend to become cynical about work, spend less time on homework, are absent from school more often, do not participate in extracurricular activities, and spend less time with their families than adolescents who do not work or who work fewer than fourteen hours per week. Though surely some adolescents value their jobs, Terry Pickens, a fourteen-year-old newsboy, has become cynical:

> I don't see where being a newsboy and learning that people are pretty mean or that people don't have enough money to buy things with is gonna make you a better person or anything. If anything, it's gonna make a worse person out of you, 'cause you're not gonna like people that don't pay you. And you're not gonna like people who act like they're doing you a big favor paying you. Yeah, it sort of molds your character, but I don't think for the better. If anybody told me being a newsboy builds character, I'd know he was a liar. (Terkel, 74, p. *xliii*)

Since school is considered a full-time occupation, it makes logical sense that adolescents' work experiences should be limited, at least to the extent that they derive the maximum benefit from their school and school-related activities.

Youth Employment and Unemployment

We may not be sure of the effects of adolescent employment, but we do know that more adolescents are combining school and work than at any time in the last forty years, and that those who work do so for more hours (Cole, 80; Greenberger, 80). In 1940, only one out of every 25 boys and one out of every 100 girls combined work and school. Today one out of every four boys and one out of every six girls does so (Cole, 1980). For 16- and 17-year-olds the statistics are even higher: 43 percent of the boys and 37 percent of the girls work, with 20 percent of 14- and 15-year-olds working. It is estimated that 80 percent of high-school students will have had formal work experience by the time they graduate from high school (Greenberger, 80). With such large numbers of adolescents working while they are in high school, we must no longer postpone researching the effects of that work and using what we find to make policy that insures the benefits while eliminating the detriments.

Of extreme significance to adolescents who are no longer in school is the bleak picture of employment possibilities for youth between the ages of 16 and 24. Although the statistics vary from month to month, youth unemployment generally doubles that of the total community, with white teenage unemployment tripling that of adult males and black teenage unemployment exceeding the adult rate by anywhere from six to ten times (Herr, 79; Passmore, 83; U.S. Bureau of the Census, 80c). There is no question that discrimination — against youth, teenagers, and black teenagers in particular — is a major factor in youth unemployment, and that unemployment problems in adolescence may well contribute to helplessness, negative self-concepts, cynicism, hostility, and loss of all confidence (Brown, 80). In addition, youth unemployment is statistically related to motor-vehicle fatalities, mental-hospital admissions, narcotics violations, and all crimes (homicides, rape, assault, auto theft, prostitution; Brenner, 80). The personal and social costs are enormous, yet our society has done very little to combat youth unemployment other than to publicize the issue. Continued neglect may prove disastrous.

SUMMARY

Although work occupies more time in the life of the average adult than any other single activity, adolescents too often lack the self-knowledge and the knowledge of the world of work that might equip them to find meaning in their work and in their lives.

A career includes not only the pattern of jobs that a person engages in during a lifetime, but the avocational activities that person chooses to round out the work roles. Whether or not we find satisfaction in our careers depends on the meaning we attach to our work, which literally may determine our lifestyle, social role, and self-esteem. Career development is one aspect of general human development; who we are physically, cognitively, socially, and emotionally provides the basis for who we become occupationally.

In the postindustrial society of the last decades of the twentieth century, clerical, professional, technical, and service occupations will be in great demand. Most of these require advanced education and training, though not necessarily the traditional four-year liberal-arts degree. Those who are overeducated and undereducated are likely to be highly dissatisfied with their employment prospects. Career choice and career preparation are complex processes, and adolescents need considerable guidance in preparing for entry into the world of work.

A number of different, yet complementary theories of career development are available. These theories are primarily models designed for counselors, and, unfortunately, lack sound empirical data to support them. They are, nevertheless, useful in understanding the process of career development. Whether based in need fulfillment (Herzberg), personality types (trait and factor, psychodynamic), social learning, or general development (Ginzberg, Super), all the theories assume that adequate psychological development is necessary for successful career development. They all rely on the necessity for self-knowledge and knowledge of the world of work. They all emphasize both career decisions and the process of decision making, and they view career decisions as a function of the entire range of possible choices available to an individual.

Need theory posits that work is influenced by an individual's immediate needs, and that an individual's choices improve as the result of self-knowledge and awareness of the potential of a career choice to meet personal needs. Higher-order needs bring greater work satisfaction than lower-order needs, and needs change over time.

Personality theory posits than individuals seek work that satisfies their view of themselves as people.

From the perspective of social-learning theory, environmental circumstances, especially those within the family, determine an individual's level of aspiration. The impact of family, community, and school factors have become a major focus of all current theories of career development.

Developmental theories of career development include need-based theory, personality theory, and social-learning theory; they also emphasize lifetime development and change. From the point of view of Ginzberg, people progress through three basic stages of vocational development: the fantasy, tentative, and realistic periods.

Super integrated personal and environmental factors based on the continued evolution and implementation of the self-concept. Career choice is the result of the match between self-concept and the vocational concept of the chosen career. He identified five vocational life stages: growth, exploration, establishment, maintenance, and decline, which interact with personal and situational circumstances to determine occupational roles.

Race, culture, socioeconomic background, and sex all affect career development. Research supports the contention that of these factors, sex may be the most significant. The sex-role development of women and men strongly influences their career choices and their career maturity. Further, the career development theories are all based on the development of men. They may be valid for women only when women make nontraditional occupational choices. For females, the conflict between career and motherhood is significant, but no career-development theory addresses this issue. Though the picture of women's career development is currently inadequate, there are some signs of change. Women are aspiring to higher levels of education, but many adolescent girls are not addressing the issue of how they will spend the significant portion of their lives that will not be consumed with homemaking and child-rearing responsibilities.

The problems of poor work attitudes, inadequate information concerning occupations, poor decision-making skills, and a lack of meaningful relationships between school and work have led to an awareness of the need for career education, including career awareness, career exploration, and career preparation. Career education assists people in developing life skills, personal worth, an appreciation for work and commitment to society, self-awareness, and knowledge of careers. It is carried on both within and outside of schools. Although much attention has been directed toward developing comprehensive career-education programs, the movement is still too new to have a documented influence on work satisfaction in the adult population.

Many adolescents work while they are in school, with both beneficial and detrimental results. Many personal and work skills are developed, but the academic progress of an adolescent who spends too much time working may suffer. Care should be taken to help adolescents balance working with school responsibilities.

III

Problematic Responses to the Pressures of Adolescence

Some young people react to societal pressures and the new demands of adolescent development in unhealthy ways, and problem behavior results. These unhealthy responses include those discussed in Chapter 12, Behavioral Disorders; Chapter 13, Juvenile Delinquency; and Chapter 14, Drug Use and Abuse. Although most adolescents reach adulthood without serious problems, the minority who do experience them deserve our attention; we will therefore explore in depth these serious disturbances in functioning. Interestingly, these problems are often interrelated — that is, a delinquent may well be emotionally disturbed and/or abusing substances, and every behavior (problematic or not) can be viewed as an attempt to meet some personal need. We will therefore attempt to understand the possible reasons for problem behavior as well as to explore current attempts to treat troubled adolescents and their families.

12

Behavioral Disorders

Joe is sad because Marilee has dropped him for Jake, and he has even thought that maybe if he were dead, she would be sorry; but the thought is fleeting, and the sadness eventually dissipates. Carl, on the other hand, becomes seriously depressed when Kate leaves him, and he wanders alone through serious consideration of the value of his life, eventually deciding it's not worth the hassle. He shoots himself.

Janice is concerned about her weight, and she diets in order to lose the ten pounds she doesn't like. She is successful, feels good about her new image, and rewards herself with new clothes. Susan is also concerned about her weight, but when ten pounds have melted away, she still feels fat and continues to lose. She never reaches her elusive goal of being thin, and no matter how thin she gets, she still perceives herself to be fat. When she is down to about 80 pounds her parents become frightened and hospitalize her, where she continues to resist feeding. Susan is anorectic.

Earl is under a great deal of stress, which he deals with by plunging himself into his schoolwork and sports. Earl becomes productive. Steven, under similar stress, withdraws from everyone, eventually retreating into a world of fantasy that leaves him unable to care for himself. Steven becomes schizophrenic.

Defense mechanisms protect us from unbearable hurt. When the defense mechanism becomes excessive, out of control, we engage in disturbed behavior. Carl, Susan, and Steven can be called emotionally or behaviorally disturbed. Their reactions are outside of their rational control and seem to an objective observer to be excessive when viewed in light of the apparent stress. They, however, felt the stress to be unbearable, and each reacted in protective, though irrational, fashion.

A significant minority experience disturbances serious enough to require treatment.

In adolescence, new demands arise in the form of societal, familial, and educational expectations, and the adolescent is experiencing development physically, sexually, cognitively, emotionally, and morally. The demands and the development offer incredible opportunities for growth, but they may also make the adolescent particularly vulnerable, especially one who must also deal with deficits that have been left over from previous developmental problems. We have seen that most adolescents manage the stress reasonably well; but a significant minority, 10 to 15 percent at least, experience disturbances serious enough to require diagnostic evaluation or treatment (Feinstein, 79). Adolescent referrals to psychiatric and psychological services peak between the ages of 14 and 16 (Anthony, 70).

As we will see, problems generally do not arise in adolescence without warning. Individuals who are referred in adolescence generally present long histories of disturbance; it is in adolescence, however, that parents and teachers lose control and refer to outside agencies. In addition, with the developmental and societal demands placed on adolescents, disturbances take on both greater significance and different manifestations than they did in childhood. Whereas in childhood, spontaneous emotional outbursts and irrational thinking are quite normal and acceptable, they become problematic in adolescence and clearly deviant in adulthood. Thus behavior disorders are more difficult to differentiate in childhood and adolescence than they are in adulthood.

In this chapter we will try to distinguish between adaptive and maladaptive responses in adolescence and to examine the causes, degree, and kinds of disturbances of most concern during the adolescent period. We will look at the milder disturbances: psychosomatic disorders, hypochondria, anxiety, and school phobia; and at the more severe disorders: depression, suicide, and psychoses, as representatives of the complete list of diagnostic categories that are used for children and adolescents. In recent years there has been a significant increase in interest and attention to adolescent eating disorders, including obesity, anorexia, and bulimia. Finally, we will briefly discuss therapy with adolescents.

BEHAVIOR DISORDERS IN ADOLESCENCE

Adaptive *vs.* Maladaptive Responses

Degree and nature of response. The degree and the nature of response to the societal and developmental demands of adolescence is one determiner of whether a particular response is adaptive or maladaptive. For example, all adolescents experience periods of sadness, even transient depression, but most do not become seriously depressed. All experience mood swings, but most do not become schizophrenic. All are concerned, to one degree or another, with their bodies and their body images, but most do not starve themselves. All are likely to engage in pranks, but most do not become delinquent. All engage in risk-taking behavior and experimentation, but most do not endanger their lives through abuse of substances. All feel some degree of inadequacy, anxiety, loneliness, and self-consciousness, but most do not become disturbed (Reynolds, 76; Moore, 83a; Piazza, 83).

Those who *do* become disturbed are those who are extremely vulnerable, usually as a result of a combination of genetic predisposition and years of stress from unsatisfactory environmental circumstances. The most vulnerable adolescents are unable to control themselves; they are the seriously disturbed (Stott, 82). Others experience less severe disturbance. Reynolds (76) summarized a number of studies that classified adolescent disturbances into the mild–moderate disturbances and the moderate–severe disturbances.

Mild, moderate, and severe disorders. The mild-to-moderate category of disturbances includes those that may be seen quite widely in the population and can be helped with limited treatment, often by caring persons in the adolescent's life.

All adolescents experience sadness. But most do not become seriously depressed.

These include such conditions as shyness, overanxiety, lack of domestication, and low self-esteem. The disturbances in the moderate-to-severe category are those that are more likely to require therapy and even, in some cases, hospitalization or institutionalization for effective treatment. These include such conditions as schizophrenia, criminal behavior, and depression.

The categories of disturbance applied to adolescents are less clearly defined than are those applied to adults, primarily because adolescents have not yet solidified identities and personality patterns and are therefore more fluid and flexible in their responses than are adults. Reynolds (76) identified only five major categories of severe disturbance: schizophrenia, neurosis, acting out, confirmed criminal behavior, and depression. A quick perusal of a textbook in abnormal psychology will verify a much more sophisticated and particular classification of adult pathologies. Quay (79) argues that most emotional disturbances don't fit the adolescent population and proposes only three general categories of behavior disorders:

- **Anxious-withdrawn:** These adolescents are tense, shy, withdrawn, timid, depressed, sad, inferior, and sensitive. They may range from mildly withdrawn to totally isolated.

- **Immature:** These adolescents are unable to meet the developmental and societal demands placed upon them. They are sluggish, passive, and preoccupied.

- **Psychotic:** These are the most seriously disturbed. They are characterized by emotional bluntness, unresponsiveness, hypersensitivity, and avoidance. They cannot care for themselves, and they live in a world of their own making.

Symptoms. In schools, students with suspected disturbances are classified as either emotionally disturbed or behaviorally disordered. Symptoms of such disturbance are classified as disturbed relationships with others, physical manifestations, verbal manifestations, avoidant reactions, signs of restricted functioning, signs of fear and discouragement, signs of low self-concept, neurological characteristics, and characteristics of severely emotionally disturbed children (Lambie, 83). These are detailed in Table 12.1.

Regardless of the classification system used, it is clear that disturbed adolescents, like more normal ones, often defy classification. Symptoms may be mixed, with a particular adolescent displaying characteristics of several seemingly distinct disorders. Only about one-third of adolescent clients, for example, fit into only one cluster of disorders, and others have only one symptom or a pattern of symptoms that literally defy classification (Reynolds, 76). Furthermore, there is usually a relationship among problems: young people who act out are also likely to suffer from emotional disturbance, abuse alcohol and drugs, and display learning problems and underachievement. In any case, disturbance is a *relative* description. All experience some of the characteristics of disturbance at some time. We must be careful that we neither overemphasize normal emotionality nor ignore signs of trouble. The line is often a thin one.

Obviously, disturbance is a matter of degree. Any one of us is likely to identify a number of the symptoms, especially those identified as characteristics of severely emotionally disturbed children, that signals significant disturbances.

A more limited but highly useful list of symptoms of disturbance in adolescence is offered by the Center for Early Adolescence (82). Table 12.2 identifies eight signs of serious disturbance.

Causes of Disturbance

What causes an adolescent to withdraw, remain docile, run away, fight, act out sexually, abuse drugs or alcohol, or develop other aberrant behaviors and thoughts?

Table 12.1
Signs of Emotional Disturbance

A. Disturbed Relationships with Others
   1. Suspicious attitude toward people
   2. Jealousy
   3. Belittling efforts of others
   4. Lack of self-control
   5. Greediness
   6. Extreme selfishness
   7. Overaggressiveness
   8. Inability to abide by rules and regulations
   9. Negative reactions
   10. Defiance
   11. Quarrelsome attitude
   12. Excessive teasing and bullying of others
   13. Fringe memberships in all groups
   14. Lack of acceptance by others

B. Physical manifestations
   1. Quick fatigue
   2. Blinking with no eye irritation or visual problem
   3. Coughing when asked questions or reading, etc.
   4. Stuttering
   5. Frequent tears
   6. Nail biting
   7. Giggling
   8. Hair twisting
   9. Masturbating
   10. Thumb sucking
   11. Over-eating
   12. Extreme excitability
   13. Hyperactivity
   14. Showing off

C. Verbal manifestations
   1. Excessive lying
   2. Extreme boisterousness
   3. Bragging
   4. Overtalkativeness
   5. Excessively loud or high-pitched voice
   6. Rationalizing inadequacies
   7. Placing blame for inadequacies on others
   8. Blaming materials for lack of success
   9. Hesitations in speech

D. Avoidant reactions
   1. Purposely losing materials
   2. Habitual lateness
   3. Dawdling
   4. Truancy
   5. Absentmindedness
   6. Forgetfulness
   7. Extreme avoidance of reading
   8. General avoidant tactics
   9. Consistent failure to do assigned work

E. Signs of restricted functioning
   1. Lack of flexibility in behavior
   2. Confusion
   3. Inability to follow directions
   4. Lack of communication about family
   5. Lack of communication about past experience
   6. Lack of apparent interest in activities in the classroom
   7. Lack of curiosity
   8. Boredom
   9. Nonparticipant attitude
   10. Daydreaming
   11. Extreme shyness
   12. Excessively quiet voice
   13. Erratic performance on tests
   14. Erratic performance on daily work
   15. Restlessness
   16. Lack of attention
   17. Inability to concentrate
   18. Extreme distractibility
   19. Extremely limited energy
   20. Repeated use of modes of behavior that have proven unsuccessful
   21. Inability to sustain effort

F. Signs of fear and discouragement
   1. Excessive reaction to failure
   2. Constant need for reassurance
   3. Lack of confidence
   4. Shyness in use of new materials
   5. Withdrawal from new academic experiences
   6. Excessive worry
   7. Defeatist attitude
   8. Fearful reaction to reading
   9. Giving up
   10. Excessive requesting of help
   11. Overconscientiousness

Table 12.1 (continued)

12. Refusing to try
13. Excessive concern for food or desire for it
14. Excessive fear of tests

G. Signs of low concept of self
   1. Indecision
   2. Inability to act without specific direction
   3. Lack of self-reliance
   4. Inability to accept the fact of being wrong
   5. Minimizing accomplishments
   6. Excessive need for show of acceptance
   7. Inability to accept responsibility
   8. Over-acceptance of responsibility
   9. Satisfaction with inadequate performance
   10. Great insecurity about ideas
   11. Excessive desire to please adults
   12. Excessive self-consciousness
   13. Extreme sensitivity
   14. Compulsive desire to speed in work
   15. Excessive blaming of self for inadequacies

H. Neurological characteristics
   1. Poor coordination
   2. Awkward or uneven gait
   3. Poor balance
   4. Spatial confusion
   5. Minimal efficiency in learning

   6. Difficulty in motor coordination
   7. Speech difficulties
   8. Clumsiness
   9. Random motion

I. Characteristics of severely emotionally disturbed children
   1. Severe decompensation of personality (distortion and loss of contact with reality)
   2. Severe intellectual impairment and thought disorders
   3. Delusions and hallucinations
   4. Ambivalent, constricted and inappropriate emotional responses
   5. Withdrawal
   6. Regression
   7. Extremely bizarre behaviors
   8. Preoccupation with inner fantasies
   9. Emotional blunting
   10. Shallow or flat affect
   11. Obsessive desire for sameness
   12. Distortion of body image
   13. Severe language disturbances
   14. Obsession with space and motion (manifested by stereotyped motor behaviors)
   15. Spontaneous whirling and toe walking
   16. Avoidance of eye contact

Table 12.2
Signs of Serious Disturbance

1. The adolescent is withdrawn for long periods of time and shows no interest in others.

2. The adolescent has no friends of the same age and is not integrated into a peer group.

3. The adolescent is docile, never acts independently, never initiates activities.

4. The adolescent continually runs away from home or school.

5. The adolescent frequently gets into fights and physically abuses others.

6. The adolescent engages in indiscriminate sexual activity with a number of partners.

7. The adolescent is often drunk or under the influence of drugs.

8. The adolescent loses a dangerous amount of weight out of excessive concern for appearance.

A young person who exhibits these behaviors will not stop or change as a result of lectures, stricter rules, or punishment. Professional help may be necessary.

From: ''Living With 10- to 15-Year-Olds,'' A Planning Guide for a One-Day Conference. © 1982, The Center for Early Adolescence, Suite 223, Carr Mill Mall, Carrboro, NC 27510.

As we have seen throughout this text, biological, intellectual, and social factors work together in complex ways to affect adjustment, and they also interact to produce maladjustment.

Genetics. If we were to subscribe to a pure medical model of disturbance, we would explain behavior disorders as genetically determined illnesses, and we would treat them with mind-altering drugs, hospitalization, and so on. If, however, we were to subscribe to a pure sociocultural model, we would explain them as learned behavior that can be unlearned, and we would treat the disturbed individual quite differently. In reality, each individual is subject to both genetic predisposition and sociocultural influences, the most important of which is likely to be the family.

Stress. As we discussed in Chapter 2, adolescents in the 1980s are subject to a great deal of stress in a society that demands that they assume adult responsibilities and fulfill adult needs (Elkind, 81). Behavior disorders may be viewed as reactions to extreme stress, which is endemic to our technological society. Tyerman (83), for example, found that adolescents who were referred to a psychiatric clinic reported more stressful life events during the previous two years, as well as less satisfactory family support, than a matched group of nonreferred adolescents. Stressful events included changing to a new school, an injury or accident, a significant illness, punishment, suspension, trouble with the police, pregnancy, failure in school, a death in the family, personal losses, and significant changes in the family (such as divorce, remarriage, or a new sibling). The events reported were very similar to those used by Elkind (81) in the test he devised to measure adolescent stress. When these stresses occur in a family environment that provides neither cohesion nor support, the adolescent is likely to react with disturbed behavior.

Underachievement. Reynolds (76) found that underachievement in school is a frequent factor in behavior disturbances, but whether the disturbance lowers efficiency and causes the underachievement or the underachievement contributes to the disturbance is not clear. They probably interact in a circular fashion, spiraling the adolescent downward: disordered thinking lowers competence, which results in poor performance, reduced esteem, further failure, and so on. Earlier in childhood it may be easier to determine whether learning problems or behavior problems are the basis of disturbances, but by the time an individual reaches adolescence, the two are difficult to distinguish from each other.

Family dynamics. Paulson (80) found that virtually all adolescents displaying psychoses, anxiety disorders, and personality disorders suffer from a sense of alienation from others and that the alienation is related to faulty family dynamics, most often an ambivalent possessiveness and rejection by the mother with rejection and hostility by the father. Family members are frequently only loosely connected to one another.

That the family system contributes significantly to adjustment, and therefore to maladjustment, is clear. You will recall that in Chapter 3 we discussed how the family provides protection to growing children while also preparing them for maturity and independence. The family must help its adolescents to act independently without fear of retaliation or abandonment; those who fail to provide both the support and the autonomy tend to produce disturbances. Shulman (82) found that adolescents referred for psychiatric treatment came from one to two family types: families who prevent the adolescent from leaving the family system and families who push for premature independence. Those who discourage separation are likely to be overinvolved with their adolescents. They do not allow for disagreements but rather demand cohesiveness and agreement on all matters. These families tend to find fault with any friends the adolescent makes, impede the development of social relationships, and in many subtle and not-so-subtle ways tell their children how good life was when the children were small. The implicit message is to stay small and childlike. At the other end of the continuum are the families who can't wait for their children to grow up and leave home. They demand that their children demonstrate unreasonable control and lack of dependence.

> In summary, this study examines the family system of those families referring an adolescent for psychotherapy. These families were found to be characterized by a faulty family system which does not allow the adolescent to achieve a gradual and effective separation from the family. (Shulman, 82, p. 233)

What then causes behavior disorders? There may well be genetic predisposition to disturbance that makes one adolescent more vulnerable than another, even within the same family, but biology is certainly not a sufficient explanation. Both individual and family or interpersonal dynamics are involved (Feinstein, 79). At the risk of oversimplification, we may say that disturbances in thinking and behavior result when genetically and socially vulnerable adolescents are exposed to stressful life events as well as the developmental demands of adolescence and do not receive the emotional support from the family or other support systems that they need in order to cope. Such an adolescent may react in a maladjusted fashion.

MILDER DISORDERS

Any behavior disorder may range from mild to severe, and to identify one as mild and another as severe is obviously artificial. Anxiety, which we include as one of the milder disturbances, can become debilitating; and depression, which we include under the category of more severe disturbances, exists in milder forms in all of us. In general, however, included in this discussion of milder disturbances are those conditions that are either common to large numbers of adolescents or are treatable with intervention by school personnel, empathetic family and friends, or brief therapy. Under the category of more severe disturbances we will discuss conditions that are likely to require more long-term intervention by a psychotherapist, often in an institutional setting. It must be emphasized, however, that these categories are far from mutually exclusive.

Anxiety

Mild anxiety, experienced as apprehension and restlessness, is a common and perhaps even necessary human condition. Without some anxiety, few of us would achieve (Sarason, 75). Anxiety becomes a problem when it is either severe or chronic or when it is experienced as fearfulness and tension unrelated to specific and identifiable situations. Anxiety is differentiated from fear in that fear has a clear and obvious target whereas anxiety is diffuse, even mysterious: we may be *afraid* to give a speech in front of a large audience, but we are *anxious* when we experience fearfulness and tension in every social situation. Severe and chronic anxiety appear to increase between puberty and early adulthood (Chapman, 74). The anxious adolescent experiences fear *as if* something bad were about to happen. The fear is disproportionate to reality, and the individual is agitated and restless. Physical symptoms (upset stomach, sweaty palms, rapid pulse, headache, muscle tension, diarrhea, shortness of breath) and sleep disturbance are often associated with anxiety (Anthony, 70; Chapman, 74). In adolescence, anxiety may result from fear of separation from family, fear of contact with strangers in new social situations, unrealistic worry about the future, worry about the appropriateness of past behavior, doubts about identity development and independence, and fear of sexuality (Anthony, 70; Chapman, 74; American Psychiatric Association, 80). Quite clearly, the newly developing cognitive skills of adolescents allow for the development of anxiety, for the ability to be introspective and hypothetical allows for the development of worry and concern. The ability to worry, combined with the many new demands of adolescence, make adolescents highly vulnerable to anxiety. When their concerns get out of control, anxiety results.

When acute anxiety is unresolved, it may result in chronic anxiety, a state of tension that results in continued pain and other disorders: obsessive-compulsive behavior, psychosomatic illnesses, hypochondria, and even the more severe disturbances. Obsessive-compulsiveness results when highly anxious individuals try to control their anxiety through rigid thinking and behavior; they may become excessively concerned with orderliness, cleanliness, and perfection. Such behavior in adolescence is associated with parental expectations for perfection.

Psychosomatic Disorders

Common disorders. In Chapter 6 we discussed the common psychosomatic disorders of adolescents. In these conditions there is an actual physiological disturbance resulting from the complex interaction of medical, psychological, and social factors (Chapman, 74; Finch, 80). Disturbances in the gastrointestinal system, cardiovascular system, muscular system, central nervous system, skin, and respiratory system

Exercise affects the ways we deal with stress.

occur when constitutional predispositions combine with psychological stress and socially learned behavior patterns.

Causes. Each of us reacts differently. For example, Purcell (71) found that in some asthma patients, emotional factors are more important than in others, and those for whom emotional factors are more significant had more authoritarian and punitive parents than those for whom genetic factors were more important. Furthermore, whereas one person may react to anxiety with stomachache and diarrhea, another may develop severe headaches.

Our lifestyles contribute as well. The amount and type of exercise we get, our diet, smoking, and other behavioral patterns affect the ways in which we deal with stress and therefore have an impact on the potential somatic manifestations of that stress. It stands to reason, then, that in treating psychosomatic problems, all aspects of the problem — medical, psychological, and social — must be attended to. And with adolescents, the involvement of the family, which may produce much of the stress as well as providing a model for dealing with it, is crucial.

Hypochondria

Hypochondria, imaginary ill health and/or excessive concern with health and the body, is another common reaction to anxiety. Being concerned with health provides a reason for the anxiety and therefore seems to make it more manageable. Hypochondria is far more prevalent in adolescence than in childhood, for adolescents not only have the cognitive capacity to worry but also are quite naturally focused on their changing bodies and are concerned with their physical selves (Josselyn, 71; Weiner, 72). The hypochondriacal adolescent may use concern with health as a mask for concern with sexual attractiveness, may use ill health as an excuse for not participating in anxiety-producing events (parties, dances, athletic contests), or may transfer sexual guilt into a concern over venereal disease. Janie, for example, was an early developer. She was taller, heavier, and more sexually mature than her seventh-grade classmates when she began to develop chronic stomachaches. The pain kept her from trying out for the class play and from attending the boy-girl parties that took place every Friday night. When medical tests revealed no stomach abnormalities, the pain went away, but Janie soon developed headaches and fainting spells. Again, extensive medical tests revealed nothing unusual. Janie's illnesses, though real to her, were unfounded. The next year, when her friends' development caught up to hers, she no longer experienced them.

Whereas hypochondria may be the expression of anxiety, it is important to remember that concern with health may also be the result of ignorance, the signal of the beginning of real illness, or the result of family learning. If it is the result of ignorance, information will correct the problem. Symptoms should always be checked out medically before being considered hypochondriacal. And a bit of investigation into family patterns may reveal a family preoccupation with health and illness. In such families everyone has a litany of ailments to talk about, and family discussions themselves are frequently centered on health concerns. Ignorance, real illness, and family patterns should be ruled out before considering adolescent health concerns hypochondriacal.

School Phobia

One of the most common manifestations of overanxiousness is the extreme fear of school known as school phobia. The fear is clearly unrealistic and can be traced either to an aversive aspect of school (exams, peer problems, teacher problems) or to a problem in separating from parents (Kahn, 62; Reynolds, 76). School phobias generally first appear at age 7 or 8 and are more common in children than in adolescents. However, if the phobia remains unresolved, it tends to peak at 11 or 12 (Kahn, 62). Adolescents who are school phobic are likely to have long histories of dependency problems and, if allowed to stay at home, will likely isolate themselves more and more (Kahn, 62; Weiner, 70; Chapman, 74). School-phobic adolescents feel nauseous, have headaches and stomachaches, and get sick in class. They also worry about what is happening at home and want very much to be there. Unfortunately, parents often unwittingly collude by allowing such an adolescent to remain at home rather than dealing with the normal issues of autonomy and independence that are so prevalent in the school environment. Adolescents who experience school phobia need help in dealing with the developmental issues of adolescence, and their families need to learn how to provide emotional support for their separating from them. School-phobic adolescents must be emotionally supported while simultaneously confronted with their responsibilities as autonomous individuals.

MORE SEVERE DISORDERS

Whereas anxiety, psychosomatic complaints, and exaggerated concern with health are widespread in both adolescent and adult populations, the more severe disturbances of adolescence, such as depression, suicide, and psychoses, affect relatively few. As discussed in Chapter 1, Offer (81) found tumultuous growth in no more than 20 percent of the adolescent population. These adolescents are, however, of major concern, for without treatment they are unlikely to lead productive, fulfilling lives.

Depression

Extent. Depression and grief are normal, even adaptive, for both adolescents and adults. Depression, which occurs in 40 to 50 percent of adolescents (Albert, 75; Rutter, 76; Achenbach, 81), is a response to a loss such as a death, divorce, separation, or a move. It is adaptive in that it allows the body to slow down and recuperate following a loss (Coleman, 80b) and is experienced as sadness, grief, anxiety, loss of motivation, repetitive unpleasant thoughts, pessimism, even slowed motions. Depression, although it is usually transient and recurrent rather than chronic, *feels* irreversible and unending (Feinstein, 79).

Depression is common, even normal, and becomes prevalent in adolescence. Whereas only one in nine ten-year-olds report moodiness, misery, depression, and self-deprecation, 40 percent of adolescents between 14 and 15 do so, and depression is more common in adolescence than in adulthood (Rutter, 76). Depression is more common among females than males, with two to three times as many females reporting feelings of depression (Weiner, 80). Seligman (75) attributes depression to the learned helplessness of those in inferior social positions, who learn early that they have little control over what happens to them. If adolescent depression results from the perception that achieving separation and coping with the unknown is an overwhelming responsibility (Berlin, 79), the perceived helplessness of the depressed adolescent becomes understandable. Depression is more common in females because girls tend to internalize their problems, thereby experiencing depression, tension, and physical complaints, while boys tend to externalize theirs by acting out (Gove, 74; Weissman, 77). Sex-role learning is certainly implicated in these differences.

Masked depression. The incidence of depression in adolescence may well be higher than the previous statistics indicate. Because early adolescents are more inclined toward behavior than toward thinking, they are likely to mask their depression with troublesome behaviors (Langdell, 73; Weiner, 80; Ladame, 82; Emery, 83). Thus depression in adolescence may be seen in sadness, inability to concentrate, fatigue, insomnia, physical complaints, boredom, restlessness, abuse of alcohol and drugs, acting out, promiscuity, failure, running away, and even accident-proneness.

The case of "Sad Sandy" below illustrates a major depressive episode in a prepubertal child. Not only is Sandy feeling sad and bad, but his depression is also masked in behavior problems (stealing, disobedience, refusal to attend school):

> Sandy, a bright nine-year-old boy, was taken to the pediatric emergency room after his mother found him in the bathroom pressing a knife to his stomach. Examination revealed no more than a minor scratch. Upon questioning, the child told the psychiatric resident that he wanted to die because he didn't want to continue to live the way he did. When specifically questioned, he reported that he was feeling sad, bad, and angry most of the time, that he wasn't having any fun anymore, and that he felt very tired all the time. He had no difficulty falling asleep, but regularly woke up at about 3:00 A.M. and then again at 5:30 A.M. and couldn't fall asleep again. He also reported that he had heard a single voice talking to him, telling him to kill himself with a knife to his belly. He identified the voice as that of his grandfather, who had died four years previously from a stroke. He had been hearing such a voice for the last month.
>
> Sandy's mother corroborated his report from her observations and added that the onset was about six months ago and that he had gotten progressively worse. Four months ago he began to steal from her and became quite disobedient and had temper tantrums. During the last two weeks he had resisted going to school and cried all the way there. She also reported that he had been very preoccupied with the separation of his parents two years earlier, and felt it was all his fault. His teacher had reported to her that his attention span was rapidly decreasing and that he had withdrawn from friends and appeared quite sluggish. (Spitzer, 81, p. 285)

Symptoms. Acute depression in adolescence is a brief, severe reaction to an immediate and identifiable loss, and the chance of recovery is relatively assured. When depression becomes chronic, it becomes more significant and can often be traced to an early family loss from which the young person never fully recovered (Emery, 83). Symptoms of depression are only warning signals, for it is difficult to distinguish between the normal developmental ups and downs of adolescence, acute depression in response to a loss, and actual depressive illness or chronic depression, which is the result of earlier developmental deficits (Ladame, 82). The difference between normal grief and depression is mainly that the depressed person develops *unrealistically* negative feelings, self-image, and expectations (Reynolds, 76).

Severely depressed adolescents do not recover easily. In normal, acute depression, the individual experiences three phases of depression: protest (crying, denial), withdrawal (apathy, nonresponsiveness), and recovery (return to optimism). The more severely depressed get stuck in the withdrawal phase (Martin, 77). They lose contact with others, isolate themselves, continually tell themselves that they can't make it, and may even feel responsible for all problems, even natural disasters like floods and earthquakes. Their behavior becomes self-destructive (Coleman, 80b). The longer they engage in it, the more intense it becomes, and although they tend to maintain contact with reality, they avoid everyday problems and interactions. They overexaggerate their weaknesses and experience defeat after defeat as a result of their self-defeating behavior. Chronic depression is a vicious and paradoxical downward spiral (Beck, 67; Weiner, 70; Josselyn, 71; Easson, 77).

Causes. Like all other disorders, severe depression in adolescence is often related to a combination of life stresses and lack of family cohesion and support to deal with them (Friedrich, 82). Almost all chronically depressed adolescents report a significant and unretrievable loss occurring earlier in childhood, with self-deprecating thoughts and behaviors increasing throughout childhood and into adolescence (Weiner, 70). With the increased cognitive capacities of adolescents, depression may for the first time be experienced as an internal state, which may account for the increase in depressive responses by adolescents.

Treatment. Treatment of severe depression may require hospitalization, especially if the risk of suicide is high, or may be conducted on an outpatient basis, the latter being preferred because adolescents need to experience successes in the real world to overcome their exaggerated misperceptions of their own competence to effect happiness for themselves. As with the other disorders, family involvement is often crucial, for it is within the family that young people need to live and discover their potentials. Families and adolescents must be assisted in focusing on and developing the adolescents' competencies so as to affect a positive change in their self-perceptions.

Suicide

There is perhaps no topic that raises emotions more than does suicide, especially suicide by young people, who, it seems to others, have everything to live for. Suicide has a long history of conflicting attitudes surrounding it; some cultures so despised suicide that a suicide victim could not be given a funeral or burial place; at other times a suicide victim might be praised, especially if the life were given for a noble cause. Currently, in this country, the right to die is gaining favor, with suicide being seen by some people as individuals' right to control their own bodies. Many states have passed laws allowing living wills, by which an individual can require physicians to refrain from using life-support systems when it is clear that they alone are responsible for prolonging the individual's life.

But the right to die and the living will are generally not applied to adolescents. Even though literature is filled with adolescent suicide (Romeo and Juliet being perhaps the most famous), and we are inundated with death on the media and in the news, our culture responds to adolescent suicide with great alarm. It is seen, as one headline proclaims, as a national tragedy ("A Double Tragedy Adds to the National Tragedy of Teenagers Who Take Their Own Lives" *People Magazine,* June 27, 1983, p. 32).

Rates. The suicide rate for adolescents tripled between 1960 and 1975 (Holinger, 78; U.S. Census, 81). Suicide is now the second leading cause of death among adolescents, being topped only by accidents. And the number of suicides might be even higher, for there is no way for us to be sure how many accidents actually involve subintentional suicidal motivation (for example, crashing a car at 90 mph) or have been reported as accidents rather than suicides to protect the families.

Suicide is rare in childhood, but increases dramatically at age 15. One out of every 1000 adolescents will attempt suicide, with one of every 50 to 100 attempts being successful (Weiner, 80). There may be as many as 4000 successful adolescent suicides in any one year (D.F. Smith, 80). Males are three times as likely to kill themselves as are females, but females are more likely to try unsuccessfully.

That males are more successful when it comes to suicide is attributed to the fact that they are more likely to use active methods, such as shooting, that don't allow for rescue. Girls, on the other hand, are more likely to use passive methods, such as pills, that take longer to work and are more easily reversed (Holinger, 78; Resnick, 80; D.F. Smith, 80; Ladame, 82). Firearms and explosives are responsible for more completed suicides; pills and other poisons for attempted suicides. Some writers hypothesize that males more often truly want to die, while females more often want to be rescued (D.F. Smith, 80), but others contend that it is impossible to distinguish the motives of those who attempt suicide from those who succeed (Resnick, 80). In our culture, boys are introduced to firearms and explosives; girls generally are not. It is therefore more likely that this familiarity, along with the socialization that encourages boys to be active and girls to be passive, is responsible for the difference in method employed by girls and by boys, and not the motive behind the attempt.

Cultural differences in suicide have been reported. Frederick (78) reports that suicides among whites of all ages in the United States is 13.2 per 100,000. The corresponding rates for blacks is 6.1 per 100,000, and 21.6 per 100,000 for native Americans. Although the rate for whites is higher than that for blacks, D.F. Smith (80) reports that all minorities tend to kill themselves at younger ages than do whites, for whom the rate rises steadily up to age 60. Smith hypothesizes that minorities learn earlier that the world is hostile and that their dreams are not likely to be realized. The suicide rate for American Indians would support this hypothesis; they kill themselves five times more often than the national average, with most of the suicides occurring among adolescents and young adults. These young people find themselves in extremely frustrating social circumstances. Their race is demeaned; they are forced to leave home to go to school; they find that both the reservation and the wider world offer only a meager existence. They exemplify the conditions identified by McAnarney (79), who found that suicide rates are higher in cultures with: (1) loose family bonds; (2) less religion; (3) greater transition; (4) emphasis on achievement; and (5) suppression of aggression. Although McAnarney was comparing cultures within society, it is not difficult to identify these conditions as endemic to all of modern American society. Perhaps the rise in suicide among adolescents is a symptom of these characteristics on the wider societal level.

Precipitating events. On the more personal level, most adolescents at one time or another have suicidal thoughts. These are primarily transient and are not thought of as a final self-destruction but rather as an alternative solution to frustration (Ladame, 82). Adolescent suicide often appears to be situationally related — for example, precipitated by a breakup, fear of pregnancy, rejection, conflict, arrest, failure — but the immediate factor is not sufficient to trigger suicide. There is usually a long history of family instability (Weiner, 80), with the adolescent feeling alienated from the family with underlying hopelessless, unhappiness, and despair (Jacobs, 71). Distress has been going on for some time, with suicide rarely occurring without warning (D.F. Smith, 80). The vast majority of completed suicides are among young people who tried to communicate their despair and intentions during the three months prior to their deaths. Those who do it have usually talked about it.

History of problems. Some researchers identify depression as the basis for suicide (Weiner, 70; Jacobs, 71; Resnick, 80; D.F. Smith, 80), while others emphasize hopelessness (Kazdin, 83). But whatever the terminology used, it is clear that adolescents who resort to suicide have a history of problems within the family, an escalation of new problems in adolescence, and a dissolution of meaningful relationships to provide support for current conflicts (Jacobs, 71; Greulin, 80; Emery, 83). Suicidal adolescents feel alienated, isolated, alone, unable to cope. Their emotional needs have not been met at home, either through the loss of a parent or through parental detachment, tension, or conflict (Caine, 79), and they have not found meaningful, long-term attachments outside the home either. They are despairing, hopeless, and out of contact with important people. Ladame (82) argues that the potential suicide victim presents three identifiable characteristics: (1) chronic depressive illness, differentiated from the ups and downs of normal development; (2) signs of alienation, including estrangement from peers, family, and perhaps the loss of a meaningful relationship; (3) mounting anxiety and overwhelming distress within days of a potential suicide attempt.

> The suicidal act is a breakdown of the whole organization of the personality. . . . If we expect the adolescent's suicidal behaviour to improve and the long-term prognosis to be favourable something must change in his mind, his life style and his familial and social environment. (Ladame, 82, p. 364)

Table 12.3
Suicide among Adolescents: Early Warning Signs

Early Warning Signs

1. Direct suicide threats or comments such as "I wish I were dead." "My family would be better off without me." "I have nothing to live for."

2. A previous suicide attempt, no matter how minor. Four out of five people who commit suicide have made at least one previous attempt.

3. Preoccupation with death in music, art, and personal writing.

4. Loss of a family member, pet, or boy/girl friend through death, abandonment, break-up.

5. Family disruptions such as unemployment, serious illness, relocation, divorce.

6. Disturbances in sleeping and eating habits and in personal hygiene.

7. Declining grades and lack of interest in school or hobbies that had previously been important.

8. Drastic changes in behavior patterns, such as a quiet, shy person becoming extremely gregarious.

9. Pervasive sense of gloom, helplessness, and hopelessness.

10. Withdrawal from family members and friends and feelings of alienation from significant others.

11. Giving away prized possessions and otherwise "getting their affairs in order."

12. Series of "accidents" or impulsive, risk-taking behaviors. Drug or alcohol abuse, disregard for personal safety, taking dangerous dares.

As we discussed in Chapter 8, cognitive development in adolescence involves a unique form of egocentrism, with adolescents experiencing the personal fable, through which they imagine themselves to be both personally and historically unique ("No one has ever experienced this before"). When faced with situational problems after a lifetime of adjustment difficulties, they may feel that no one can possibly understand them and that no one has ever experienced such pain as they are experiencing. Their new cognitive maturity contributes to their sense of hopelessness, isolation, and despair, and may be the reason for the increase in suicide in adolescence.

Warning signs. Adolescents signal their distress in identifiable ways. The Center for Early Adolescence (82) identifies twelve early warning signs (Table 12.3).

Prevention and treatment. Prevention and treatment of adolescent suicide is a multifaceted activity, with attention being paid to the immediate precipitating condition as well as the underlying problems of the potential victim and the attempter. Attention must also be given to the survivors of those who are successful. The family, friends, and classmates of the suicide victim or attempter need help to deal with the event and to prevent further attempts (Schrut, 68; Curran, 79; D.F. Smith, 80).

Prevention is most often based in crisis intervention, especially through the use of telephone hotlines, where trained crisis counselors offer an empathetic ear to those in crisis. Obviously, crisis intervention deals only with the precipitating event

Table 12.4
What to Do, What Not to Do When You Suspect the Danger of Suicide

What to Do	*What Not to Do*
1. Ask direct, straightforward questions in a calm manner. "Are you thinking about hurting yourself?"	1. Do not ignore warning signs.
2. Assess the seriousness of the suicidal intent by asking questions about feelings, important relationships, who else the person has talked with, and the amount of thought given to the means to be employed. If a gun, pills, rope, or other means has been procured and a specific plan has been developed, the situation is very dangerous. Stay with the person until help arrives.	2. Do not refuse to talk about suicide if a young person approaches you.
	3. Do not react with horror, disapproval, or repulsion.
	4. Do not offer false reassurances ("Everything will be all right.") or platitudes and simple answers ("You should be thankful for . . .").
3. Listen and be supportive, without giving false reassurance.	5. Do not abandon the young person after the crisis has passed or after professional counseling has begun.
4. Encourage the young person to get professional help and assist the person in doing so.	

From: "Living with 10- to 15-Year-Olds," A Planning Guide for a One-Day Conference. © 1982, The Center for Early Adolescence, Suite 223, Carr Mill Mall, Carrboro, NC 27510.

and the potential victim's despair over it. The crisis counselor listens and refers. If the potential victim follows up on the referral, a therapist then deals with both the precipitating event and the underlying developmental problems and frequently includes the parents to help the adolescent resolve the chronic problems that cause vulnerability. These young people must be helped, for those who have already considered suicide are at the greatest risk of repeated attempts.

But intervention with those who are in immediate danger of attempting suicide is not sufficient. Schools, argues D.F. Smith (80), should provide opportunities for open discussion in order to dispel the myths surrounding suicide, and teachers should be trained to recognize warning signs, listen and refer, and lead class discussions on the topic of suicide.

If it is suspected that an adolescent is in danger of attempting suicide, the Center for Early Adolescence (82) has suggested that direct interaction techniques be employed. These are presented in Table 12.4.

Schizophrenia

Schizophrenia is characterized by bizarre behavior and an inability to relate to people or to cope with life's everyday stresses. Although most authors identify schizophrenia as the most significant adolescent psychotic disorder, Quay (79) argues that full-blown schizophrenia is not yet well enough developed in adolescence to permit specific diagnosis and that adolescents should be granted a more general psychotic diagnosis when behavior like that described by Ekstein (66, pp. 21–22) is evidenced:

It took but a moment's glance to determine that Rena was a severely psychotic adolescent girl. Her bizarre appearance was caused by her jet black hair streaming in disarray down her neck and face, the vacant depth of her eyes, and the vapid, flattened mood imprinted on her blotched, irritated face, atop a sturdy-framed body that drooped at the shoulders and seemed to slump and sag at the hips and knees. . .

Squinting through her still closed, fluttering eyelids, her fleeting expressions seemed to disclose the conflict between her desperate attempt to make some contact with a representative of external reality and her opposing drive to shut her eyes to the world. At best, she could permit only the faintest images to filter through the curtain drawn against her inner world by the fluttering eyelids.

Rena is a victim of schizophrenia, a condition that often begins in adolescence and peaks during late adolescence and early adulthood, with 17 being the age of highest risk (Weiner, 70; Holzman, 74; Reynolds, 76; Feinstein, 79; Cancro, 80). More adolescent males than females are affected (Feinstein, 79). About one percent of the adult population is affected, with most of these experiencing the first signs in late adolescence, when the individual experiences social and psychological pressures to behave in an adult fashion. When schizophrenia has its onset in adolescence, prognosis is poor. About one-quarter recover, one-quarter improve but have relapses, and half become permanently hospitalized. Later onset has a somewhat better prognosis (Weiner, 80).

Characteristics. Schizophrenia, as we can see in the case of Rena, is characterized by bizarre thinking, bizarre behavior, withdrawal, detachment, and poor emotional control (Reynolds, 76). Most importantly, schizophrenics have disordered thinking patterns; distort reality; can't express a simple train of thought; speak nonsequentially; grimace; fail to care for themselves; cannot maintain social or personal relationships; withdraw by staring, babbling, and shutting out the world; are flat and distant; and often express emotions inappropriately (Weiner, 70, 80; Reynolds, 76; Erickson, 78; Feinstein, 79; Zimbardo, 79; American Psychiatric Association, 80; Cancro, 80).

Early warning signs. Short of a full-blown psychosis that prevents the adolescent from functioning in daily life, early warning signs are detectable and should be heeded. Early childhood symptoms frequently associated with adolescent schizophrenia include shyness, withdrawal, poor social relationships, peculiar behavior, extreme sensitivity, lack of humor, inability to concentrate, fear, and a pattern of living from one crisis to another (Weiner, 70; Holzman, 74). The child who is a loner may be crying for help. In adolescence, schizophrenia is usually preceded by the onset of adult demands, the death of a significant person, or the stress of a heterosexual relationship (Feinstein, 79).

Masked schizophrenia. In adolescence, the withdrawal, poor control, and perceptual and thought distortions of schizophrenia may also be masked, as is the case with depression, so that the young person, instead of appearing schizophrenic, appears severely depressed and hopeless (most often the case with females) or acts aggressively, fighting, stealing, and lying (most often the case with males) (Weiner, 80). Furthermore, instead of a full-blown psychosis, less severe schizophrenia is seen in adolescents who experience: (1) difficulty organizing their thoughts; (2) no pleasures; (3) excessive dependency on adults; (4) failure in school and social situations; and (5) stress precipitating a breakdown (Holzman, 74). Siomopoulos (80) notes that the primary characteristic of milder adolescent schizophrenia is a disturbance of affectivity. The less severely schizophrenic adolescent is capable of daily living, but has relationships that are superficial, almost receptionistlike, devoid of feelings. This lack of emotion in relationships may develop into a psychosis, may be dealt with and disappear, or may remain essentially the same, leading to what is known as schizoid personality in adulthood.

Causes. As with all other disorders, schizophrenia is the result of the interaction of biological, psychological, and environmental factors. There may be a genetic predisposition to schizophrenia, as there is clearly a higher incidence of schizophrenia in identical twins than in fraternal twins (Gottesman, 65), as well as a higher incidence among biological relatives than among adoptive relatives (Kessler, 75).

Sex-role learning may also play a part. Boys are more prone to schizophrenia in their adolescent years, women in later life. Al-Issa (83) argues that this may be due to the fact that young boys are under great pressure to achieve, while women are under greater stress when their roles as mothers are ending.

Regardless of biological vulnerability and society's stresses, the role of the family in schizophrenia is well documented. Bateson (56) cites the classic double-bind behavior of the mother as the most significant factor in the development of schizophrenic-like behavior in the child. The mother sends contradictory messages about how close the child should come to her. For example, the mother may simultaneously say "Come here and give mommy a kiss" while holding herself rigid and cold, and perhaps even turning her face away from the child. The child is stuck, not knowing whether to respond to the verbal or the nonverbal message. In addition, Bender (74) found that 75 of 100 families with a schizophrenic youth were rated as severely pathological themselves. Either the mother, the father, or both were disturbed. In discussing the case of Rena, whom we described earlier, Ekstein (66) described Rena as caught in a tremendous fear of her mother combined with a desperate need for her. Her dilemma became hopeless. Rena had had a history of shyness in combination with an inconsistent mother who alternated between overprotection and neglect. Her mother was dependent on Rena for filling her parasitic ego needs, and when Rena couldn't fulfill them, Rena retreated from the stress of the conflict into psychosis.

The interaction of mother and child is fraught with complexity. The earlier and more severe the impairment of the mother-child relationship, the more severe will be the deficits in the child (Feinstein, 79).

EATING DISORDERS

Serious disturbances in eating habits result in obesity (fat), anorexia (self-starvation), and bulimia (binging and purging), disorders that affect as many as 25 percent of the adolescent population. Many more females than males are affected, probably because adolescent self-esteem is more closely tied to body image in females than in males (Bruch, 77; Maloney, 83). With the increased physical awareness of adolescence comes concern with weight, especially for girls, and when intense emotional issues combine with equally intense social and physical issues, eating disorders may result (Maloney, 83). We will look at each of the three disorders separately before summarizing the psychological and social factors that appear common to eating disorders in general.

Obesity

As we discussed in Chapter 6, obesity is the most prevalent eating disorder, affecting 15 percent of adolescents and 30 percent of adults in America, with the chronic nature of obesity attested to by the estimate that 60 to 80 percent of obese adolescents will *remain* obese as adults (Paulsen, 72; Maloney, 83). Because it is such a widespread disorder, a reminder of its characteristics is in order.

Obesity is commonly defined as weight that is 20 percent above ideal weight, when the additional weight is due to fat rather than muscle (Katchadourian, 77). Thus, if an adolescent who should weigh 150 pounds actually weighs 180, she would be considered obese *unless* the additional 30 pounds were composed of muscle, as in the case of a weight lifter or body builder.

Causes. Maloney (83) identifies six causes of obesity:

1. Emotional: Some adolescents overeat in order to fill loneliness; avoid social interaction; compensate for a lack of self-direction, a sense of competence, and the ability to define their needs; or even to punish themselves for perceived transgressions (Bruch, 74; Stunkard, 80).

2. Socioeconomic: There are significantly more obese people among those in the lower socioeconomic status, probably because of a diet that is high in carbohydrates.

3. Genetic: Fat people are often found to have metabolisms and an endocrine balance that differ from those of others of average weight. They also have a

larger number of fat cells, which make weight maintenance more difficult for them (Bruch, 74).

4. Developmental: Fat adolescents are frequently found to have been overfed as children, perhaps as a result of a mother who equates caring and love with food or who uses food as a reward (Schowalter, 83). As a result, the overfed adolescents lose their ability to read signs of hunger accurately. Schacter (71) found that when normal and obese adolescents who had just eaten were given the task of tasting crackers for comparison purposes, the obese adolescents ate many more crackers than did adolescents of normal weight. In fact, the obese adolescents ate as many or more crackers when their stomachs were full as they did when their stomachs were empty. Obese people apparently do not regulate their eating based on hunger cues.

5. Too little activity: Obese people, adolescents especially, generally get considerably less physical exercise than their peers of more average weight.

6. Neurological: Brain damage can interfere with the regulation of food intake.

Obesity has devastating results. Because they see themselves as unattractive, obese people *expect* hostility from others (Katchadourian, 77). They therefore accept social criticism as valid, become passive and withdrawn, tolerate the expected abuse, and may become overly eager to please others. Their self-deprecation contributes to an ever-decreasing sense of competence and self-esteem (Bruch, 74).

Treatment. Since 60 to 80 percent of obese adolescents will remain obese as adults, treatment has not been particularly effective, probably because most treatment programs offer only one approach. But because obesity results from a combination of medical, social, and psychological causes, treatment is effective only if intervention occurs on all dimensions.

On the behavioral level, eating habits and awareness need to be addressed in an effort to effect long-term changes in dietary habits. But changing eating habits is not sufficient in and of itself. Obese adolescents must also be helped to develop a sense of autonomy and control, take responsibility for their own actions, define needs, and set goals. They must, in other words, be helped to deal effectively with the complete tasks of growing to maturity. The inability to manage the tasks both contributes to and results from their obesity.

Anorexia

Just as obesity may signal a problem in the development of autonomy, independence, and maturity, so too does **anorexia nervosa** (nervous loss of appetite; no real loss of appetite), a condition marked by severe undereating, malnutrition, and weight loss. Between one and four percent of the adolescent population suffer from anorexia, with 90 to 95 percent of its victims being female (Gilbert 84).

Characteristics. Mogul (80) characterizes the highly destructive, highly irrational anorectic as one who displays:

1. A relentless pursuit of thinness: She restricts her diet, often to as little as 80 to 100 calories per day, loses between 25 and 50 percent of her original body weight, exercises to excess to lose more (Bruch, 73; Vigersky, 77), and may resort to vomiting or using laxatives and diuretics to purge what she has eaten.

2. Impaired cognitive functioning: Her body image is grossly distorted, and she sees fat where there is none, even to the point of perceiving the skin covering her emaciated frame as fat. She denies hunger, denies being ill, claims well-being, and has a distorted sensitivity to light and sound. She also is unable to read body cues and therefore doesn't recognize either hunger or fatigue (Bruch, 77). Although Casper (79) found that normal as well as anorectic adolescents overestimated their body widths, the anorectics' overestimations were significantly greater than those of the normals.

3. Hyperactivity: In addition to exercising excessively, she is alert, restless, and has difficulty relaxing and sleeping.

4. Other medical problems: Although there are no medical problems prior to the onset of anorexia, the weight loss and malnutrition cause amenorrhea (stopping of menstrual flow), altered endocrine balance, fine hair, hypothermia (lowered body temperature), and an intolerance for cold (Maloney, 83). Vomiting and inadequate diet also lead to dental problems. In extreme cases, the metabolism of muscle tissue leads to organ failure and heart attack, with 3 to 20 percent of anorectics literally starving themselves to death (Katchadourian, 77; Vigersky, 77; Maloney, 83).

5. A preoccupation with weight and food to the exclusion of other interests: The anorectic develops peculiar patterns of handling food — especially obsessional behavior such as hoarding food, collecting recipes, and cooking elaborately for others (Vigersky, 77).

The Diagnostic and Statistical Manual of the American Psychiatric Association identifies five diagnostic criteria of anorexia nervosa: (1) intense fear of obesity; (2) disturbance of body image; (3) weight loss of at least 25 percent; (4) refusal to maintain body weight over minimal normal weight; and (5) no known physical illness to account for weight loss.

The anorectic *feels* ineffective, out of control, unable to lead her own life, and required to be perfect for others. She comes from a family who encourages perfection, dependence, and control over pleasure, and her anorexia may be seen as an obsessive need to regain personal control over *something* (Bruch, 77; Sours, 79; Hood, 82). She usually has a history of being a very good girl and a very good student.

Family characteristics. Liebman (83), in an extensive review of the literature pertaining to anorexia, identifies five characteristics of the families of anorectics:

1. Enmeshment: Family members are extremely sensitive and responsive to one another. They follow unspoken rules of agreement, rarely criticize or disagree, and intuit one another's needs.

2. Overprotectiveness: Parents discourage autonomy and independence and frequently engage in highly intrusive interactions. Children have little or no privacy.

3. Rigidity: The family engages in interaction patterns that are more appropriate for younger children.

4. Lack of conflict resolution: The family denies conflict but carries a high degree of submerged tension, often thinly veiled.

5. Involvement of symptomatic child in unresolved marital and family conflicts. The symptoms of the patient frequently become the preoccupation of the entire family, thereby allowing them to avoid important family conflicts.

The patterns found in the families of anorectic adolescents are disturbed, often in ways that are much like those of the families of psychotic or delinquent adolescents. In all cases, it appears, dysfunction in the family is associated with dysfunction in the child, but the manifestation of that dysfunction can differ from child to child.

The family of the anorectic is highly demanding, and we might expect rebelliousness to be the result. But the anorectic has a history of meeting parental expectations and, rather than outwardly rebelling, attempts to gain some control over her life by exaggerating the self-discipline that healthy adolescents develop. That anorectics are overwhelmingly female is probably due both to the increased pressure of the media and the feminine stereotype (thin is in) of females and to the likelihood that girls are more tightly bound by their families than are boys. Anorexia often appears following a major, successful acceptance of independence. Having become more independent, the potential anorectic becomes terrified and retreats into a clearly defined area in which mastery seems achievable (Bruch, 77). Instead of becoming increasingly independent in a frightening world, the anorectic tests her will over her weight. Mogul (80) sees anorexia as an exaggeration of asceticism, the testing of the will to counter pleasure seeking. Anorexia becomes a defense against drives, a defense against powerlessness, and an expression of moral transcendence. The adolescent may become exhilarated by her discovery of her power to skip meals, live on few calories, and withstand the discomfort of hunger and exhaustion. She finds an inner strength and autonomy that her overprotective parents cannot control.

Fear of growing up. A final possibility contributing to anorexia is the fear of growing up. The anorectic, terrified of adulthood and sexuality, attempts to stop growing. Her body remains prepubertal, her menses stop, and she does not develop the roundness of womanhood. She attempts to remain a child (Bruch, 77) and therefore, in her eyes, escapes the conflicts of adulthood, especially in regard to sexuality.

Prognosis. The prognosis for anorexia is not much different from that for obesity. Anorectics typically resist attempts to change them. Maloney (83), in reviewing the literature, found that after five years, only 35 percent of anorectics are eating normally and are free of a fixation on weight. Most, however, eventually regain their menses and manage economically and socially, even though eating problems and exaggerated weight concerns continue.

And anorexia, as we have already noted, is potentially fatal, with between 3 and 20 percent dying from the effects of the condition (Maloney, 83).

Treatment. As with obesity, treatment of anorexia must be complex. Correction of the weight problem alone is insufficient, for the psychological aspects of the condition must be addressed if the patient is to regain accurate perceptions and control over her obsessive thinking. She needs to learn to see herself as having a separate identity and a right to self-respect (Bruch, 77), and this is most often done through a combination of operant conditioning to change the eating habits, individual therapy to foster self-awareness and understanding, and family therapy to change the dynamics that gave rise to the problems in the first place (Minuchin, 78).

Therapy is both intense and extensive, and may require hospitalization, especially when medical intervention is imperative. Once the patient is out of medical danger, long-term individual and family therapy becomes the treatment of choice. The family therapy usually includes at least one family lunch session, in which the therapist literally accompanies the family to lunch, the goal being to enable the patient to eat with her family without the inevitable power struggle. At the session, the struggle invariably erupts, allowing the therapist to intervene to redefine the problem as a family problem, thus eliminating the myths that all family members are fine except the patient and that there are no interpersonal conflicts in the family (Liebman, 83).

Bulimia

Bulimia, which literally translates as "ox hunger," is an eating disorder with characteristics of both obesity and anorexia. Bulimics are binge eaters, who consume thousands of calories on a binge. They do not, however, gain excessively because following a binge, the bulimic purges — through vomiting or fasting, or laxative, diuretic, or amphetamine (diet pill) abuse (American Psychiatric Association, 80; Johnson, 82; Maloney, 83). Most are slightly overweight or in the upper portion of their weight range (Halmi, 81).

Characteristics. Although 40 to 50 percent of anorectics also develop binge-purge behaviors, bulimics tend to be older, more aware of a strong appetite, more anxious, more depressed, more guilty, and more concerned with body functions than anorectics (Maloney, 83). They have usually left their original families for college or work and are frequently vulnerable to depression (Crisp, 82). They usually learn bulimic behavior in an attempt to maintain weight, and although they are extremely self-critical following a binge, they are afraid of not being able to stop eating and purging (American Psychiatric Association, 80; Johnson, 82). ''Refrigerator Raider'' describes characteristic features of bulimia:

> Alice is a single 17-year-old who lives with her parents, who insisted that she be seen because of binge eating and vomiting. She achieved her greatest weight of 180 pounds at 16 years of age. Her lowest weight since she reached her present height of 5'9'' has been 150 pounds, and her present weight is about 160 pounds.
>
> Alice states she has been dieting since age ten and says she has always been very tall and slightly chubby. At age 12 she started binge eating and vomiting. She was a serious competetive swimmer at that time, and it was necessary for her to keep her weight down. She would deprive herself of all food for a few days and then get an urge to eat. She could not control this urge, and would raid the refrigerator and cupboards for ice cream, pastries, and other desserts. She would often do this at night, when nobody was looking, and would eat, for example, a quart of ice cream, an entire pie, and any other desserts she could find. She would eat until she felt physical discomfort and then would become depressed and fearful of gaining weight, following which she would self-induce vomiting. When she was 15 she was having eating binges and vomiting four days a week. Since age 13 she has gone through only one period of six weeks without gaining weight or eating binges or vomiting. She quit school this year (at age 17) for a period of five months, during which she just stayed home, overeating and vomiting. She then went back to school and tried to do better in her schoolwork. She has obtained average or below-average grades in junior high and high school. (Spitzer, 81, p. 146)

Extent. Authorities on college campuses have become alarmed at the large numbers of normal-appearing young women who are reporting bulimic behavior, perhaps as many as 10 percent (Maloney, 83) or more, some of whom report that groups of young women engage in the behavior together. Halmi (81) found that 13 percent of college students displayed all the major symptoms of bulimia: 19 percent of college women and 5 percent of college men. This is an apparent change from earlier information about bulimia, when young women reported feeling very alone and secretive about their binging and purging. That the disorder has been addressed in the popular media and admitted to by celebrities like Jane Fonda may be allowing others to admit to it and may even be putting the idea into the heads of diet and figure-conscious young women.

Johnson (82) put notices in magazines expressing interest in people who binge and purge. He received responses from 509 people. Of these, 99 percent were women; 94 percent binged; and 74 percent met the criteria for a diagnosis of bulimia. Ninety-seven percent were white, and 84 percent had had some college education. The average respondent reported a weight problem at age 15, with binging beginning at age 18. And half of these bulimics binged *daily*, a binge comprising close to 5000 calories, the majority of them from sweets. Of the 95 percent who vomited to purge, 58 percent did so *daily*. We see, then, a picture of young women, many of whom engage in bulimic behavior every day.

The consequences of bulimia are both psychological and medical. In addition to the guilt, self-criticism, and depression, medical consequences include metabolic changes, electrolyte imbalance, hernia, ulcers, bowel problems, and tooth decay.

Treatment. Because bulimia is a relatively new disorder (that is, it has been discussed in the literature only recently), specific treatment modalities have not yet been developed. Unlike anorexia, bulimia is not considered a family problem, primarily because most of these young people have already left home. Issues of autonomy, independence, and control may well be at the root of the problem, but so is the immense social pressure to remain thin. These pressures are frequently felt to be best addressed in group therapy, where bulimics can learn that they are not alone, and where they can give and receive support for overcoming their difficulties.

In summary, eating disorders are a major disturbance of adolescents, with 25 percent or more being affected. In all cases, eating disorders are the result of a complex web of factors that include genetic predisposition, reaction to family interaction patterns, individual psychological factors, and social pressure. Eating disorders, like other emotional disturbances, are therefore difficult to treat, for they have developed over a lifetime and are usually deeply ingrained. Treatment is therefore effective only when it addresses all the contributing factors. Quick solutions virtually never work.

THERAPY

Considerations for therapy with adolescents emerge from the preceding discussions of behavior disorders. Maladjustment in adolescence is the result of a complex of factors: genetic, familial, psychological, and social. Adolescents experience new developmental tasks and changes, and when these combine with life stresses and less than ideal family support and dynamics, young people may feel overwhelmed and retreat into one or another form of maladjustment. Therapy must address all the underlying causes of disturbance, not just the precipitating event, and must therefore also include attention to the deficits of previous periods of adjustment.

It is both difficult and rewarding to work with adolescents. The developmental tasks and new cognitive and psychological characteristics make them somewhat unpredictable, but they also are less rigid and therefore more flexible than older people. In addition, they are dealing with basic autonomy and independence issues, and these issues are likely to surface in the relationship between the therapist and the adolescent, just as they do with parents and other figures of authority (Anthony, 74; Chapman, 74; Tramontana, 80). A sensitive therapist who is able to engender trust has the opportunity to witness exciting growth toward maturity. Reynolds (76, p. 336) describes the requirements for working with adolescents:

It is both difficult and rewarding to work with adolescents.

Working with adolescents, particularly maladjusted ones, requires a delicate but precise touch. An authoritarian approach, with its strict rules and harsh punishments, may produce either rebellious runaways or anxious neurotics. A too-permissive approach, often based on an idea that the maladjusted adolescent will ''outgrow'' his difficulty, offers too little stimulation and supportive structure and may lead to alienation, drug experimentation, or other difficulties. The *ideal* approach provides enough external control through parents, teachers, and others to prevent the adolescent from making too many serious mistakes for too long a time and places major responsibility on the adolescent for his own growth and developmental learning. It also provides an encouraging, instructive environment in which the adolescent can learn the behaviors or attitudes that he needs.

With the proper attitude and approach on the part of a therapist, treatment is effective. Disturbed adolescents need to develop the capacity for realistic self-appraisal and acceptance, success in the real world, and confidence in themselves and their environments. There is no single method of treatment, but a supportive and trusting therapist and environment are essential (Feinstein, 79). Crisis intervention is often necessary, as is hospitalization, but once the crisis is past, longer-term individual and family therapy is in order.

SUMMARY

Behavior disorders result when normal defense mechanisms are used in an exaggerated fashion, resulting in disturbed thinking, feelings, and behavior. The developmental tasks of adolescence, combined with new cognitive capacities, and the new stresses and expectations placed on adolescents make them vulnerable to disturbance, with about 20 percent experiencing severe enough reactions to warrant our attention.

All adolescents experience stress, sadness, loneliness, anxiety, self-consciousness, and self-doubt. Most take risks, engage in pranks, and find themselves somewhat unpredictable. Only when these normal reactions become excessive does disturbance result, and there are as many varieties and degrees of disturbance as there are individuals.

Genetics, individual psychology, family dynamics, and social expectations all contribute to an individual's vulnerability to stress, yet virtually all disturbed individuals are found to feel alienated from others. The alienation is most often traceable to faulty family dynamics, where the adolescent's struggle for autonomy is centered. Disturbed adolescents are unable to achieve a gradual and effective separation from their families, usually because the family messages are confused and confusing.

For our purposes in this book, we addressed milder disturbances (anxiety, psychosomatic disorders, hypochondria, and school phobia), more severe disturbances (depression, suicide, and psychoses), and eating disorders (obesity, anorexia, and bulimia), while realizing that the division between mild and more severe is truly arbitrary. Anxiety, for example, may range from the adaptive variety that facilitates achievement to completely debilitating irrational anxiety. Severe and chronic anxiety increases between puberty and early adulthood, probably because it is only with formal operational thinking skills that the introspection necessary for anxiety is possible. Extremely high anxiety may even result in obsessive-compulsive behavior, which can no longer be included in the classification of mild disorder. Anxiety may be considered to be associated with all other disorders.

Psychosomatic disorders in any vulnerable system of the body may result from reactions to stress and are fueled by lifestyles and family interaction patterns.

Whereas psychosomatic disorders involve real somatic problems, hypochondria, which also may be viewed as a reaction to stress as well as a learned pattern, involves no real somatic involvement.

Although not as common in adolescence as in childhood, some adolescents are plagued by an irrational fear of school known as school phobia. School-phobic adolescents are likely to have a long history of dependence problems and need help in dealing with issues of autonomy and separation from family.

No more than about 20 percent of the adolescent population is affected by the more severe emotional disturbances: depression, suicide, and psychoses.

Depression, though normal and adaptive at times of loss, can become severe and chronic in adolescence. Those who suffer from severe depression have unrealistically negative impressions of themselves and their potential for success and happiness, and tend to isolate themselves in their own private hells, where the downward spiral of depression gains even more momentum. Depressed adolescents need to experience success in the real world, on which to base more realistic and positive self-perceptions.

When the adolescent feels truly hopeless, suicide attempts may ensue. Suicide is the second leading cause of death among adolescents, and the suicide rate for adolescents has tripled in recent years. Whereas more girls than boys attempt suicide, more boys are successful in their attempts. Both, however, tend to signal their distress in identifiable ways: expressing suicidal thoughts, preoccupation with death, declining school and social performance, withdrawal, pervasive moodiness, and behavioral disturbances. All signs should be taken seriously, and discussion with the adolescent initiated to determine the likelihood of a suicide attempt.

The most easily identified psychosis of adolescence is schizophrenia, which is characterized by bizarre behavior and cognitive processing. Less severe forms may be manifested in milder behavioral and thought disturbances and an apparent lack of appropriate emotion. As with all other disorders, schizophrenia results from a complex interaction of biological, psychological, and environmental factors, with the family again playing a significant role.

In adolescence, a new awareness of and concern with the body develops, especially for girls, and this concern may lead in extreme cases to disturbances in eating; obesity, anorexia, and bulimia may result. Obesity affects 15 percent of adolescents, and obese adolescents are likely to become obese adults, with significant problems in self-image throughout life.

Anorexia (self-starvation) affects one to four percent of the population and is considered to be an expression of an adolescent's desire to control her body when, in fact, she feels that she has little control over the rest of her life. She also has great difficulty with the development of autonomy, independence, and maturity, and may be attempting to remain childlike. Her family has both protected her and made great demands on her, and her symptom has become the focal point of the family's concern.

Bulimia is an eating disorder that has features of both obesity and anorexia. The bulimic, who is older and more independent than the anorectic, alternately binges to satisfy her cravings and purges to maintain normal weight, and then feels extremely guilty for this unnatural behavior. Societal stereotypes may have considerable influence on the development of bulimia.

Therapy for adolescents must address all the causes of disturbance: precipitating events, social expectations, and family dynamics, as well as individual perceptions and the developmental demands of adolescence itself. This is done through crisis intervention, hospitalization, and individual and family therapy.

13

Juvenile Delinquency and the Courts

Bobby was 9 when he was arrested for shoplifting. As they always do with first offenders, Los Angeles police spoke sternly to him and released him. Three months later, Bobby had graduated to burglary, and was released with a warning. Bobby's sixteenth arrest — he was 12 years old by then — earned him his first jail term, two years at a California Youth Authority Camp, from which he escaped four times. A few days after his release, at age 14, he killed a man. He has been charged with 26 crimes, including murder. But now that he has turned 18, he is, so far as the law is concerned, no longer a juvenile. He is a free man.

Mark's mother was a junkie and he was born . . . with heroin withdrawal symptoms. He spent his first six years in a foster home before being returned to his mother, whom he did not know. When she went to work, she regularly tied Mark to a bed. A year later, she told New York juvenile authorities that he was disruptive and uncontrollable, and Mark was institutionalized. Last year he was in court, charged with fighting with his peers and being difficult to control. He is 10 years old.

Bobby and Mark are both products of the American system of juvenile justice. One has compiled an awesome criminal record; the other has never committed a crime. Yet they both have juvenile records and they have been confined in institutions for about the same time. (Footlick, 77, p. 279)

Bobby and Mark represent only the group of delinquents who are processed through the juvenile justice system, a group that represents only a fraction of all youth involved in delinquent acts of one kind or another.

In this chapter we will examine the maladaptive behavior labeled **delinquency,** both the recorded delinquency of the courts and the hidden delinquency that goes undetected or at least unreported. We will examine the extent of delinquency in adolescence, current legal and social responses to delinquency, the characteristics of delinquent youth, the causes of delinquency, the juvenile court, and current treatment and prevention approaches. As with emotional disturbances and drug and alcohol abuse, we consider delinquency to be a problem behavior that most often can be traced to disturbed relationships in the life of the adolescent and therefore must be understood, treated, and prevented within the context of the adolescent's physical, social, and emotional experiences.

THE EXTENT AND KINDS OF DELINQUENCY

What Is Delinquency?

Unfortunately, the term juvenile delinquency may mean almost anything, from truancy and misbehavior to rape and murder, depending only on who is using the term. From a psychological point of view, delinquency refers to maladaptive behavior in which young people act destructively toward themselves and others; from a legal point of view it is defined by arrest records of those under the age of eighteen. These arrest records, of course, are biased. They are biased not only by recording only those young people actually caught, but also by the enforcement and recording practices of the police. We know, for example, that black youth appear proportionately more frequently than whites on police rolls, but whether they actually commit more delinquent acts than their white counterparts is open to question. It may be that the police are more vigilant in black neighborhoods and more likely to arrest and prosecute black youth.

Statistics on child crime are frightening. Official (that is, reported) juvenile crime rose by 1600 percent between 1955 and 1975, though there is some evidence that the rate has tapered off since then (Footlick, 77; U.S. Bureau of the Census, 81); more crimes are committed by children and adolescents than by those over 25; and over half of all crimes in the United States are committed by juveniles (*Uniform Crime Reports*, 76; Footlick, 77).

But the actual crimes are only part of the story. Most juvenile crime, like most adult crime, goes unreported. Thus, in addition to official delinquency, there is substantial hidden delinquency, which we know about primarily through self-report mechanisms. And in the area of the juvenile court, a third of the cases involve **status offenders**, youngsters who are in court on charges that would not be crimes if they were eighteen years old (truancy, running away, incorrigibility, and sexual promiscuity).

Further complicating the scene is the consideration that a certain amount of delinquent experience in adolescence may be perfectly normal. Not only are most delinquent acts committed in groups, where the sense of an audience, the excitement of risk, and peer approval are very high, but some delinquent acts, especially status offenses, may be inherently attractive because they seem adultlike (P.Y. Miller,

Legally, delinquency is defined by the arrest records of those under eighteen.

79). To verify the normalcy of a certain amount of delinquent behavior, you might ask a number of your friends if they, during their adolescence, did anything for which they could have been arrested. Chances are that about 80 percent of them did.

Hidden delinquency. To determine the extent of hidden delinquency, researchers generally use anonymous self-report questionnaires. In general, this research indicates that there is a high incidence of unreported delinquent behavior among adolescents, with boys reporting both more frequent and more serious delinquency than girls (Rutter, 83). Haney (73) found that of 522 adolescents surveyed, 433 admitted to committing delinquent acts, but that only 47 of them made it into the police records. (These 47 had committed a total of 80 official offenses.) This hidden

Status offenders are in court on charges that would not be crimes if they were eighteen.

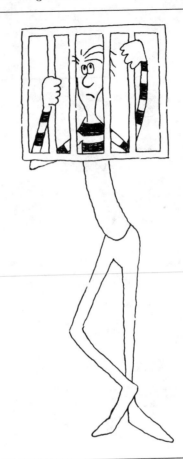

delinquency usually involves less serious crime than that which is officially charged (Hindelang, 79). Translating these figures into percentages, it was seen that 80 percent of the adolescents reported delinquent acts, but only 10 percent were arrested for 3 percent of the total delinquent acts. Haney noted that all adolescents estimate their chances of getting caught to be about 50-50, an estimate that is much higher than reality and indicates the moralistic expectations of adolescents.

Bachman (78), in the extensive longitudinal study of 2277 young men between 1966 and 1974 known as the Youth in Transition Project, interviewed the youth through their high-school years and five years beyond. He found that delinquent behavior decreases with age and maturity, with the greatest amount of delinquent behavior occurring at age 14 and 15. (Recall from Chapter 5 that the greatest discipline problems in school occur at this same time.)

Official delinquency. Although the incidence of hidden delinquency is obviously high, official delinquents differ from those who go undetected in significant ways. The official delinquents engage in more delinquent behavior and more serious delinquent behavior than do others (Kulik, 68). Table 13.1 details the number of arrests by type of crime, sex, and age in 1979.

These figures detail only juvenile arrests, which need also to be seen in the context of all crimes. Juveniles commit approximately one-half of all thefts and cases of arson and vandalism, one-third of all robberies, one-sixth of all aggravated assaults, one-seventh of all rapes, and one-tenth of all murders (U.S. Bureau of the Census, 80c; Isralowitz, 82).

That a disproportionate number of these delinquent acts are committed by relatively few serious and repeat offenders has been documented by numerous observers. One-third of those arrested for violent crimes have previous delinquent arrests, and the probability of adult arrest is $3^{1}/_{2}$ times greater for a person who has been arrested prior to the age of 18. Repeaters start earlier and commit a greater number of offenses than those not apprehended or apprehended only once. It seems clear that the earlier adolescents appear on the police rolls, the more likely they are to reappear, usually with increasingly severe offenses (Wolfgang, 78; Isralowitz, 82).

Status offenses. As noted earlier, status offenses are behaviors that would not be apprehendable if the individual involved were an adult. Juvenile law now demands that status offenders be separated from delinquents (though how effectively this is done is open to serious question), and status offenders are labeled, in different states, as PINS, CHINS, JINS, or MINS, standing for people, children, juveniles, or minors "in need of supervision." These young people, like Mark in the introduction to this chapter, are most often the victims of severely maladjusted home and family environments and truly need alternative arrangements. All too frequently, however, status offenders become more serious delinquents. The case of Christopher Devlin (Table 13.2) details the complex relationship between family problems, status offences, delinquency, and even tested intelligence and achievement.

Age differences in delinquency. Not only does the extent of all delinquency decrease with age and maturity (Bachman, 78), but the type of delinquency committed by adolescents of various ages differs as well. Over all, minor delinquency, which includes such nuisance offenses as violation of curfew, running away, minor vandalism, drinking, smoking marijuana, and petty theft, is fairly common in early adolescence, rises through mid- and late adolescence, and subsides in early adulthood. More serious delinquency, including breaking and entering, robbery, assault and threatened assault, peaks in midadolescence (15 years) and then declines. Violent crimes, including aggravated assault, rape, and murder, appear somewhat later, peaking in the 18- to 24-year-old group (Gold, 80).

The trend toward increasingly violent crime as youth get older is apparent in both the United States and Britain. West (77) conducted an extensive longitudinal

Table 13.1
Number of Arrests by Type of Crime, Sex, and Age: 1979

Offense	Males Under 18	Females Under 18
Serious Crimes		
Larceny (theft)	285,600	107,700
Burglary (breaking or entering)	187,400	13,100
Motor-vehicle theft	56,300	6,400
Robbery	34,100	2,600
Aggravated assault	31,100	5,400
Forcible rape	4,200	100
Murder[a]	1,300	200
Arson	7,200	800
Subtotal — serious crimes[b]	607,200	136,300
All Other Crimes		
Drug-abuse violations	82,900	16,600
Disorderly conduct	82,900	17,900
Liquor-law violations	97,600	27,200
Other assaults	57,400	14,900
Drunkenness	33,700	5,400
Stolen property[c]	28,800	2,800
Weapons (carrying, possessing)	20,200	1,300
Driving while intoxicated	23,200	2,600
Sex offenses[d]	9,400	700
Forgery and counterfeiting	6,300	2,600
Vagrancy	3,700	900
Fraud	5,200	1,900
Offenses against family, children	1,400	900
Gambling	1,300	100
Prostitution and commercial vice	1,100	1,900
Embezzlement	700	200
All other offenses, except traffic	208,000	50,500
Subtotal for all other crimes[e]	875,600	245,600
Total All Crimes	1,482,800	381,900

Source: Federal Bureau of Investigation, ''Uniform Crime Reports for the United States,'' *Statistical Abstract of the United States, 1980* (Washington, D.C.: Government Printing Office, 1980), p. 190.

[a] *Includes nonnegligent manslaughter.*
[b] *Includes arson arrests, a newly established index offense in 1979.*
[c] *Buying, receiving, possessing.*
[d] *Excludes forcible rape and prostitution, shown separately.*
[e] *Includes curfew violators and runaways.*

Table 13.2
Christopher Devlin (Prescott, 81, 200–201)

Age (Approximate)	Curriculum Vitae
Before birth	Father deserts mother after "casual affair" — father was pusher and addict.
3 months	Mother gives child to grandmother.
3 years	Neglect case in Brooklyn; Christopher given to mother on trial basis.
4 years	Mother turns herself into Bellevue. Feels guilty about severe beatings she is giving to Christopher and is afraid of what she may do — mother has been jailed previously for prostitution. Christopher returns to grandmother.
6 years	Grandmother stabbed to death by uncle. Christopher watches from next room. Christopher sits with body all day. Uncle returns, pretends to find body, calls cops. Christopher says nothing. Great-grandmother comes. Christopher tells her — cops arrest and jail uncle. Christopher goes to great-grandmother.
1 month later	Great-grandmother dies of stroke. Christopher goes to aunt and uncle.
7 years	Child runs away, winds up in Children's Center. Says aunt and uncle beat him badly. (Later, aunt abandons all of her own children and uncle drinks himself to death.) Christopher termed "depressed."
9 years	After several spells in Children's Center, Christopher goes to foster home.
12 years	Back to Children's Center. Foster parents "deny his problems."
13 years	To Geller House.
1 month later	To Bellevue, not psychotic. Doctors feel he could be worked with. Has "depressive neurosis."
Later	To Mount Loretto, back to Bellevue.
14 years	Phoenix House. Stays a year or so and leaves.
15 years	Juvenile Detention Center (Spofford).
A couple of months later	To St. Agnes. Inappropriate. Back to Juvenile Center.
16 years	After 8 months of Juvenile Center, to Holy Cross. After 1½ months, sent back to Juvenile Center.

Record	
1973 PINS	Children's Center PINS — absconding and truancy. Dismissed. (Note: case brought by center, not parent.)
1973 Delinquency	Petty larceny. Dismissed.
1973 Delinquency	Some sort of robbery. Adjusted.
1974 Delinquency	Taking penis out in subway station. Dismissed. (Christopher says he was urinating.)
1975 Delinquency	Stealing wallet. Dismissed.
1975 Delinquency	Stealing watch at knifepoint. Finding: Robbery 3.

(continued)

Table 13.2 (continued)

I.Q.

Has been as high as 107 Full Scale and 110 Verbal with higher range possible.

Latest testing was 95 performing, 97 verbal, and 90 Full Scale. But, qualified by stating that considering lack of motivation and background, this is a very good achievement and indicates a *much better* potential.

Bright enough to go beyond high school if he receives proper academic tutoring.

study of 400 males from a working-class, urban area of London. He found that by age 21, 30 percent of these admittedly high-risk boys had been arrested, that the peak age for conviction was 18, and that the type of crime changed as youths got older. As they got older, they become more likely to be involved in aggressive crimes, drug offenses, and fraud, and were also more likely to engage in solitary rather than group delinquency. Most importantly, he found, as has been observed in the United States (Conger, 66; Gold, 80; Osborn, 80), that the younger a boy was when first arrested and processed through the court, the more likely he was to sustain conviction as an adult. Of those who were first apprehended under the age of thirteen, half were convicted of serious offenses as young adults.

Although most adolescents who commit delinquent acts do not become adult criminals, adult crime clearly begins in adolescence, often very early adolescence. We are thus faced with a dilemma: it is clearly unwise to expect future delinquent behavior from those who commit minor offenses in early adolescence, yet it is also clear that some who commit minor offenses early are in need of intervention to prevent the development of more serious delinquency. Just what kind of intervention is appropriate depends on a thorough understanding of the causes of delinquency, the dynamics involved in any individual case, and an awareness of the relative effectiveness of various approaches, all of which we will discuss later in this chapter. First, we will look at social class, race, and sex differences in delinquency, and will examine current societal responses to juvenile delinquency.

Social class and race differences in delinquency. The arrest rates of lower-class and black youth are proportionately greater than those for middle-class and non-minority youth (Piliavin, 64; Haskell, 82). Of the 125,000 adolescents in jails, detention centers, and training schools in 1978, one-half were black and the vast majority were lower class (U.S. Bureau of the Census, 78). The question remains, however, as to whether black and lower-class youth are actually more involved in delinquency or whether they are the victims of discrimination and inaccurate reporting (Hindelang, 81; Rutter, 83). It is possible, for example, that both potential victims and police are suspicious of black and lower-class youth and therefore apprehend them more frequently. In addition, upper- and middle-class youth, who have parental and financial resources on which to rely, may be more likely to be given a warning rather than being apprehended, and if they are apprehended, may be more likely to be diverted from the official records. They then remain outside the realm of official delinquency, where lower-class and black youth predominate (Braithwaite, 81). During the 1960s and 1970s, middle-class suburban delinquency increased faster than the national average (*Uniform Crime Reports*, 77). Boodman (80) identified the typical suburban delinquent as being a fifteen-year-old white male who burglarizes a home in his own neighborhood during summer daylight hours.

Numerous researchers have documented that there are far fewer social-class differences in self-reported delinquency than in official delinquency reports (Haskell, 82; Rutter, 83), and that the higher the level of delinquency, the greater the social-class differences. Black and lower-class youth appear to commit the more serious offenses, but middle-class delinquency, especially that involving the lesser offenses, is also on the rise (Braithwaite, 81). Elliott (80), for example, conducted detailed interviews with a representative national sample of 1726 11- to 17-year-olds and found significant social class differences only in certain kinds of crime. "Predatory crimes against persons" (sexual assault, aggravated assault, and robbery) were three times more frequent among lower-class youth; and "predatory crimes against property" (burglary, auto theft, and vandalism) were twice as frequent among lower-class youth; but there were no significant social class differences in the "victimless crimes" (public disorder including drunkenness, disorderly conduct, marijuana use, and hitchhiking; status offenses; and serious drug use). It seems clear, then, that although more middle-class delinquency than lower-class delinquency remains hidden, lower-class youth are in fact involved in more violent and serious delinquency than are their middle-class counterparts. The reasons for this discrepancy will be explored later.

Sex differences in delinquency. A debate over the differences in delinquency between males and females has been raging for the past decade or so. Prior to the middle of the 1970s, it was assumed not only that girls commit far fewer crimes than boys, but that their crimes were primarily the status offenses of running away, incorrigibility, truancy, curfew violations, and sexual promiscuity. Underlying all these offenses was sexual misconduct, with the result being the labeling of sexually active girls as delinquent (Vedder, 70; Benedeck, 79). It was also assumed that girls were more likely to play accomplice roles than to commit delinquent acts themselves (P.Y. Miller, 79).

Although it is true that boys are almost never detained for sexual misconduct and that more girls than boys are referred to the courts by mothers who complain of their bad behavior, the last twenty-five years have seen an increase in the number of girls and women arrested, an increase in the percentage of women involved in all arrests, and a widening of the range of offenses with which girls and young women are being charged (P.Y. Miller, 79; Rutter, 83).

Boys still commit significantly more crimes than do girls, but female participation in delinquency has risen three times faster than that of males. Among those arrested, female participation in larceny, embezzlement, forgery and counterfeiting, theft, auto offense, fighting, carrying a weapon, and property damage has risen considerably. Whereas the ratio of official male delinquents to female delinquents used to be four or five to one, it is now nearer three to one (U.S. Census, 80c). Nevertheless, males still commit twice as many violent offenses as do females, and seven males are involved in property offenses for every five females so involved (Gold, 80). It is among the status offenses that there is now little difference between boys and girls (P.Y. Miller, 79; Hindelang, 81). As societal expectations for different behavior on the part of males and females lessens, so too may the differences in their involvement in delinquent behavior.

Although the behavior of girls is coming closer to that of boys, their treatment in the juvenile justice system remains quite different. Boys are more likely to be arrested than girls, but girls are more likely to be referred to court by their families, be recommended for institutionalization, receive severe dispositions, and serve longer terms once institutionalized. "Girls are less likely to get caught than boys, but once caught, they apparently fare worse at the hands of the criminal justice system" (Benedeck, 79, p. 100). Our society apparently feels that transgression by girls is a more significant problem than transgression by boys and therefore deals more harshly with female offenders. Perhaps we are more lenient with boys because we believe the stereotype that expects that "boys will be boys."

Responses to Delinquency

McMicking (82, p. 51) notes the severe treatment delinquents were historically subjected to:

> Juvenile delinquency can be traced back at least 4,000 years, when the Code Of Hammurabi (2270 B.C.) stated that "If a son strikes a father, one shall cut off his hands." In the Roman Empire, the father had supreme authority over his own family with the right to sell his own children into slavery if he so desired. Old English Law permitted the execution of any person over 12 who was responsible for the theft of over 12-pence. Sir William Blackstone in his "Commentaries on the Laws of England" in 1899 noted that two ten-year-old boys were executed for murder, one 8-year-old boy was hung for arson and a 13-year-old girl was burned to death for killing her mistress.

In more recent times, the response to juvenile delinquency has been a more humanitarian, one, as attested to by the development of the juvenile justice system. Especially during the last generation, juvenile delinquents have been considered misguided rather than criminal and therefore not necessarily responsible for their behavior. But juvenile crime is on the increase, and there is a general recognition that the varieties of treatment attempted recently have been less than successful in curbing the increase. As a result, there are currently two conflicting perspectives on dealing with juvenile delinquency, the "get-tough" or punitive approach and the community-based approach (Stott, 82; Armstrong, 82). Although a detailed discussion of prevention of delinquency will follow the discussion of the characteristics of delinquents and the causes of delinquency, these two conflicting community responses bear brief mention here.

Get-tough approach. Those who favor a get-tough approach blame the increase in juvenile crime on the humanitarian philosophy. In order to protect the public and reduce the crime rate, they support emphasizing punishment for offenses by: (1) waiving the juvenile court authority in all serious cases and sending the offenders through the punitive adult system; (2) lowering the age at which all young offenders come under the jurisdiction of the adult criminal court; and (3) imposing mandatory periods of incarceration for specific offenses.

Community-based approach. In conflict with the proponents of increased punitiveness are those who believe that the humanitarian ideal should not be discarded but should be strengthened by linking it closely to individual accountability and social responsibility. These characteristics, say the supporters of a community-based approach, are more likely to be learned by youthful offenders outside of institutional placement. They therefore support the development of many varieties of community-based programs to teach young people the meaning of individual and social responsibility. Some even support the notion of prohibiting the jailing of juveniles (Keve, 84).

Consider these alternative approaches to the problem of delinquency as you read the remainder of this chapter. Which seems to you to be better supported by an understanding of the characteristics and casues of delinquency? Which do you think is more likely to stem the tide of juvenile delinquency? And which individual offenders are more likely to be rehabilitated by each of the approaches?

CHARACTERISTICS OF DELINQUENTS

Adolescents Seen in Court

Although the vast majority of delinquent acts remain unreported, the young people that do appear before the court represent the population of adolescents who either need support services or display delinquent characteristics. The police exercise considerable discretion in deciding who will appear on the rolls of the juvenile justice system. They may, for example, let the offender go, call the adolescent's parents, refer the adolescent to a social agency, hold the adolescent in temporary custody, or petition for a court hearing; the police actually dispose of about one-half of all juveniles apprehended without sending them to court (*Uniform Crime Reports*, 77).

The juvenile court deals with three separate categories of cases: neglect and abuse cases, in which the parent or guardian has either failed to provide minimal care or has mentally or physically abused the child; status offenses, which constitute between 25 and 40 percent of the adolescents processed by the court (Law Enforcement Assistance Administration, 74; Haskell, 82); and cases of delinquency, in which the act committed would be a crime or misdemeanor even if committed by an adult (Guernsey, 83). In looking at the characteristics of delinquents, we will be considering only this latter group, who have committed either crimes against persons (such as assault, rape, or murder), or crimes against property (such as robbery, theft, or larceny).

Types of Delinquents

Delinquent behavior has been classified in various ways. We will discuss two classifications, both based on the personality characteristics of the delinquent.

Ross's classification. Ross (79) identifies: (1) impulsive delinquents; (2) unsocialized delinquents; and (3) social delinquents. The **impulsive delinquent** is the normal adolescent who engages in delinquent behavior once or a few times, but who refrains from further involvement out of guilt or fear of getting caught. The **social delinquent** gives in to the norms of the group and engages in delinquent behavior because it is expected by peers in the delinquent environment. The **unsocialized delinquent** has no internal controls. Poor family dynamics in the form of inconsistency, force, aggressiveness, and hostility are associated with maladjusted adolescents who act out their disturbances in delinquent behavior.

Stott's classification. Stott (82) did an intensive study of 102 delinquent youths and concluded that maladjustment resulting from disturbed family relationships is at the root of all delinquency. He identified five delinquent states of mind:

1. Avoidance-excitement: Adolescents seek excitement as a means of banishing the memory of distressing family situations.
2. Getting removed from home: Home is so distressing that adolescents commit repeated offenses in an effort to be committed to an institution.
3. Hostility: Adolescents feel rejected from the family and therefore become delinquent as a means of self-banishment.
4. Delinquent loyalty testing: Adolescents test their parents' threats of putting them out.
5. Bravado: Acting tough is a means of compensating for doubts about being valued and wanted at home.

Regardless of the classification system used, it is clear that except for the minor delinquent acts committed by normal adolescents and perhaps for the acts committed as the result of social pressure, the vast majority of delinquent acts are committed by the same group of adolescents that we have already described as emotionally disturbed or maladjusted. That serious delinquents are in fact disturbed is documented by their characteristics.

Common Characteristics of Delinquents

Serious delinquents are maladjusted both in school and in their home environments. Serious delinquents deal poorly with adults, peers, and the society as a whole, and although they may appear quite normal during a court appearance, for example, their disturbance is likely to erupt at any time that they find themselves under stress. Their disturbance is triggered by events beyond their control (such as a parental fight or threat or fear of desertion), and they react with inappropriate behavior. Maladjustment and delinquency are seen in their inability to control their behavior in their own best interest (Stott, 82).

Several general factors appear time and time again in the literature on the characteristics of delinquents. These include poor home conditions, poor school adjustment, antisocial tendencies, aggression, poor self-control, and low self-esteem. Although these characteristics are highly interrelated, we will look at each separately.

Poor home adjustment. Delinquents generally come from dysfunctional families. A disproportionate number of them suffer from one or more of the following circumstances: large families, poor parental supervision, poor parental behavior, low income, separation from parents, broken homes, and parental conflict (West, 77). Parents of delinquents have less positive involvement, more hostile detachment, and less rule enforcement than parents of nondelinquents (Robinson, 78), resulting in delinquents having significantly more negative attitudes toward their parents than nondelinquents (Duncan, 78). The strained family relationships create fear in the children that they will be abandoned; the children act out in response to the strained family system; the acting out creates even more strain; and the family is in a downward spiral of delinquency (Stott, 82).

Poor school adjustment. Delinquents adjust poorly to school, with their school adjustment problems generally recorded as early as the third grade. They often score below their peers on intelligence and achievement tests, display the attentional problems associated with learning disabilities, and experience failure early in their school careers. For most of them, school becomes a battleground with achievement and behavior becoming increasingly worse as they progress through the grades (Conger, 66; Hirschi, 77; Bachman, 78). By the end of the ninth grade, delinquents display differences from their nondelinquent peers in all areas of functioning, both tested and observed; their poor performance and adjustment often result in underachievement, failure, and dropping out.

Antisocial tendencies. The antisocial nature of delinquents is displayed early, with significant differences from nondelinquent peers showing clearly by age 10 (Conger, 66; Farrington, 82). They are less honest, less restrained, more hedonistic, more sexually preoccupied, and more prone to aggression and violence; they smoke, drink, and gamble more, spend more and save less. West (77) compared 101 delinquent 18-year-olds with 62 nondelinquent 18-year-olds, and found that the delinquents were less conforming and less socially restrained than nondelinquents in all aspects of their lives.

Aggression. The single most distinctive antisocial behavior and attitude associated with delinquency is aggression (West, 77; Goldstein, 80). Delinquent adolescents express attitudes that value doing whatever they please, settling arguments by fight-

An impulsive delinquent engages in delinquent behavior once or a few times.

ing, stealing to obtain desired goods, being tough, and not trusting others (Goldstein, 80). They admit aggressive behavior, express aggressive attitudes, commit violent offenses, and engage in destructive vandalism.

Poor self-control. Delinquent adolescents lack self-control and therefore score high on measures of impulsiveness and external locus of control and low on measures of the development of conscience and moral development (Conger, 66; Gold, 80). They tend, therefore, to blame others and external events for their problems, display immature levels of moral reasoning, and express little or no guilt over their delinquent behaviors. Some of them may even believe that they are punished, not for their delinquent acts, but for getting caught. (Parents and teachers may inadvertently foster such a belief with admonitions like ''Don't let me catch you . . .'')

Low esteem. The entire constellation of delinquent characteristics results in these young people feeling inadequate and undesirable and therefore having poor self-images and low self-esteem (Rosenberg, 78; Rutter, 83). They frequently engage in delinquent behavior in an attempt to bolster their self-esteem, and such behavior may serve to protect them from conscious feelings of inferiority, but it does not increase their more pervasive unconscious lack of esteem (Rutter, 83). Delinquents often act as if they were strong, tough, and invincible. Those who have studied them, however, are acutely aware that the bravado and swagger are merely a facade.

The characteristics described above should not be isolated and used as individual predictors of delinquency. Nearly all children engage in some of the behaviors described at some time in their lives. But when several of the patterns persist in one child over time, future delinquent behavior can be considered as a serious possibility. Obviously, the earlier intervention alters the destructive pattern, the better.

Delinquency in Gangs

Mistaken perceptions. Of special note is the delinquency that occurs in gangs. The popular musical *West Side Story* portrayed adolescent gang behavior as romantic: the teenagers involved were tough, and they fought one another, but underneath the bravado they were likeable, well-socialized, and caring young people. What little research there is into the reality of gang activity belies the romantic picture painted in the musical. Adolescent gangs, as we noted in Chapter 4, are larger than cliques, well-organized, determine the status of their members through their fighting ability, and engage in illegal behavior, often directed against the socially sanctioned institutions — the family, church, school, and legal system (Dunphy, 80). Although gang members tend to interact with one another in more socially acceptable ways than solitary delinquents, it is simply not true that they are basically well-adjusted young people who just happen to engage in fights in order to protect their turf. They do display loyalty to the group, and the gangs do have identifiable leaders, lines of authority, and continuing interaction, but the members also display the symptoms of disturbance discussed in the previous section of this chapter (W. B. Miller, 76b; 77). The bravado, swagger, emphasis on being tough, and vulnerability to peer pressure that are common to gang members are most likely to be symptoms of the struggle these young people are having with issues of personal identity and self-esteem.

Change from the 1950s. W. B. Miller (76b, 77) and his colleagues surveyed the country's largest cities and interviewed 150 representatives of more than sixty agencies to determine the type and extent of gang activity in the United States in the mid-1970s. Contrary to popular opinion, they found that the gangs that were so well known in the 1950s had not, in fact, disappeared in the 1960s and 1970s, but that their nature had changed. They centered their investigations on the six U.S. cities with the greatest amount of gang activity: New York, Los Angeles, Chicago, Philadelphia, Detroit, and San Francisco. In general, they found that gang activity is extensive. Gangs today are smaller (average size: twelve members), less highly structured, and concerned with money as well as with turf and prestige. Instead of large rumbles between rival gangs, modern gangs develop guerilla forays, create extensive property damage, carry and use sophisticated weapons, and victimize those who are not gang members, including ordinary citizens and students and teachers in schools. Crimes against both property and persons are common, with a great deal of personal violence committed during robbery and extortion activities. Over 525 recorded gang-related murders were recorded in the six cities in one two-year period.

Characteristics of members. Gangs remain predominately male (girls serve in auxiliary roles but are not members), of low-income and socioeconomic status, urban, and composed of members 17 and 18 years old. The racial and ethnic composition reflects the minority population of the city. In New York, for example, a majority of gangs are Hispanic, while in Philadelphia they are black, and in San Francisco they are Asian. Gangs are made up primarily of those most outside the mainstream of middle-class America, with recent immigrants and migrants being overwhelmingly represented. While only about 10 percent of all adolescents ever engage in gang-related behavior, that statistic rises sharply in urban ghettos, with estimates ranging from 25 to 75 percent (W.B. Miller, 76b, 77).

THE CAUSES OF DELINQUENCY

> When any new disease, especially of childhood, is identified, it immediately becomes the subject of public interest and of expert and expensive research. Delinquency and its companion, maladjustment, are among the most prevalent disorders of childhood. The youngsters in question do not get the same facilities as those with physical disorders; they are processed through a perfunctory legal machinery and given a pretense of treatment which leaves the majority unaffected, and some in a worse state than before. (Stott, 82, p. 297)

Stott (82) argues that the reason so little attention is given to the prevention and treatment of delinquency is that, unlike diseases like leukemia and cerebral palsy, the causes of delinquency have been poorly understood and little investigated, and what explanations have been offered often conflict with one another.

Several distinct but overlapping trends into the study of the causes of delinquency can be identified: the physiological viewpoint focuses on physiologic factors like mental deficiency; the sociological viewpoint focuses on environmental factors like low income and peer pressure; the family-learning viewpoint focuses on discipline measures and parental modeling; and the family-deprivation viewpoint focuses on disturbed relationships within the family that render the young person unable to cope with personal and societal demands. As has been emphasized throughout this book, both genetic and environmental factors are most likely to interact in complex ways to cause delinquency; it is nevertheless instructive to examine each of the viewpoints in relative isolation from the others.

Physiological Viewpoint

Genetic traits. Some theorists believe that inherited characteristics, including inadequate mental abilities, genetically determined personality characteristics, and learning disabilities contribute to delinquency. Schwarz (79), for example, suggests that a child's genetic tendencies (such as the extent of need for activity) must match the parent's style of child rearing, and when there is a mismatch, the problems that develop may lead to delinquency.

Mednick (77) studied the autonomic nervous system's functioning in criminals and noncriminals, and found that criminals have a slow autonomic recovery time. This was manifested in their slow reaction to punishment and caused them not to develop the fear normally associated with punishment. With no fear of punishment, the consequences of criminal behavior were simply not considered.

It is now common knowledge among juvenile authorities that many unincarcerated adolescent offenders are learning disabled, especially in terms of auditory attention deficits, and that the large majority of the incarcerated adolescent population is probably learning disabled. Young people with perceptual learning disabilities are slow to develop language skills; as a result they experience early and repeated school failure, which creates a diminished self-esteem that may lead to delinquency as a means of compensating.

Nutrition. Another physiological explanation of delinquency is represented by the newly emerging field of investigation known as **nutriophysiologic criminology**, which focuses on the role of nutrition in criminal behavior. Substances such as lead, mercury, cadmium, and sugar have all been proven to affect behavior. (Recall our discussion in Chapter 6 of the role that sugar plays in hyperactivity and behavior problems in children and adolescents.) With over 4000 chemical additives used regularly in our foods, it is possible that some foods and chemicals may work adversely on the brain and be a direct cause of violence and other criminal behavior. Geary (83, p. 12) views nutriophysiologic criminology as ''one of the most exciting possibilities to emerge in decades of trying to explain and prevent crime.''

Sociological Viewpoint

Although genetics and physiological circumstances may play a part in the development of some delinquency, they certainly cannot be considered the only, or even the single most important, cause of delinquency. Physiologic theories don't account either for delinquent adolescents who have no physiological dysfunctions or for the large numbers of retarded, disabled, and otherwise physiologically dysfunctional adolescents who do not become delinquent. A second approach to the study of the causes of delinquency places the blame on circumstances of society: the poverty of the lower class, peer-group influence, schools, sex-role stereotyping, and the influence of high technology and rapid change.

Poverty and peer group. Poverty, especially the poverty of the inner city, is linked with negative peer-group associations, lack of formal education, lack of appropriate role models, broken homes, lack of coping skills, irresponsible parenting, and lack of the opportunity to move into successful social roles (Smith, 83). In areas of poverty, there is little community support for young people (Conger, 71), and the poverty itself creates bitter awareness of the unequal distribution of resources. People feel helpless, outside of the mainstream of society, and may turn to crime to achieve access to the material wealth they are denied (Datesman, 75; Braithwaite, 81). Furthermore, say those who support a sociological explanation of delinquency, in areas of economic deprivation, delinquency is an approved way of life and a socially acceptable means of survival (Datesman, 75; Braithwaite, 81; Rutter, 83). Both the peer group and the society condone delinquent behavior as a means of achieving desired ends.

School. For young people of the lower class, school contributes to delinquency, say the sociological theorists, by demanding attendance in an alien, depressing, and oppressive environment that emphasizes academic achievement and middle-class values that are not understood by the lower class. Schools develop negative self-images in those of the lower class by labeling them as failures, subjecting them to teachers who demean them, and failing to provide programs in which they can succeed (Griffin, 78). Their low esteem creates a direct link to delinquent behavior.

Sex-role stereotyping. Until recently, as we discussed previously, sex-role socialization influenced boys and girls differently in the development of delinquent behavior. Boys were expected, for example, to take more risks and engage in more and different kinds of delinquency. Bad boys might be expected to steal cars; bad girls to be sexually promiscuous. But female delinquency is becoming increasingly similar to male delinquency, perhaps as a result of the modification of sex-role socialization that has been occurring over the past several decades. P.Y. Miller (79) discusses the women's movement and concludes that it cannot alone account for the increase in female delinquency. Rather, *both* the women's movement and the increase in female delinquency are the result of the massive social changes of the twentieth century.

They may be two separate responses to the larger changes in society and the resulting stresses placed on women.

Technology and social change. That technology and social change have created new pressures on adolescents was thoroughly discussed in Chapter 2. Urbanization, affluence, mass communication, the threat of nuclear war — all the pressures on young people to grow up fast and assume adult responsibilities before they are mature enough to handle them, says Elkind (81), have resulted in increased delinquency as well as increased sexuality, stress disease, drug and alcohol abuse, and suicide. Furthermore, the media portray the good life of affluence and comfort, making young people of the lower class especially vulnerable to delinquent behavior in an attempt to attain what they see on television and in the movies.

Although it cannot be denied that cultural influences are highly important in the development of delinquency, they, like genetic and physical influences, do not explain why the majority of deprived youth do not become delinquent, why people in other cultures who are even more deprived do not become delinquent, or why some youngsters in highly privileged environments do become delinquent (West, 77; Stott, 82). Investigators have therefore turned to exploring the roles and dynamics of the family as possible clues to understanding the development of delinquency.

Family-Learning Viewpoint

Attempts to link delinquency with the family date from the 1920s (P.Y. Miller, 79), with two somewhat different emphases. What we are calling the family-learning viewpoint emphasizes modeling within the family, child-rearing practices, and the stress resulting from the inability of the family to provide for basic needs. What we are calling the family-deprivation viewpoint focuses not so much on family circumstances and child-rearing practices but on relationships within the family, especially the affectional bond between parent and child. The two viewpoints are obviously highly interrelated, but we will separate them for purposes of discussion.

The following case (West, 77, pp. 111–112) illustrates some of the conditions that the family-learning viewpoint emphasizes.

Case 181: Both parents had a criminal record, but, whereas the father had only one conviction, the mother had 12, mostly for obtaining money by false pretences. The family was well known to the local police who noted that they were "hostile and obstructive." Three of their 8 children acquired a criminal record.

When the Study youth was nine, a psychiatric social worker from the Study visited his home and found "an indescribable state of filth and disorder." The family, chronically in arrears with rent, were frequently moved from one sub-standard house to another. The father, who was in poor health, left the running of the home to his wife. He had long periods without work, and the family was receiving support from a variety of social agencies. The social worker considered that the mother imposed harsh and punitive discipline upon the children.

When the Study youth was fourteen, a probation officer visiting his house noted a continuing state of chaos. "There is no regularity over meals, and mother's demands upon the children to go to work or school alternate with requests that they should stay at home to help her." When the Study youth was fifteen, a social workers' conference reported a complete breakdown of family functioning. The father had become an invalid, they were faced with eviction, one of the daughters was pregnant and the Study youth's persistent delinquency was bringing the mother "to the end of her tether." Interviewed at eighteen, the Study youth admitted numerous burglaries, explaining "We needed the money, you know, to help mother pay the rent." At that time he and his siblings were living in the parental house on their own, because his father had died and his mother moved out.

Modeling. The family described above displays several of the characteristics common to a poor family-learning environment. Both parents in this case had criminal records and were perpetuating criminality in their children. As West (77, p. 125) found, "The conviction of any one member of a family significantly increased the likelihood of other members being convicted." Criminal parents tend to have criminal children, regardless of the quality of the housing, the extent of overcrowding in the house, or the child's scholastic record (West, 77). Parental modeling, as we discussed in Chapter 3, is extremely important to the development of attitudes and behavior.

Child rearing. Most criminal parents display other difficulties as well, which are also seen in the case study above. They are poor, depend on social welfare, experience multiple family problems, and demonstrate poor child-rearing practices. The mother in the example above was inconsistent and harsh, and numerous researchers have documented that parents of delinquents are more harsh, more lenient, or more inconsistent than parents of nondelinquents. They rely on physical punishment, do not engage in moral reasoning, model aggression themselves, and fail to supervise their children (Glueck, 50; Conger, 66; Martin, 75; Rutter, 83). As a result, their children fail to develop internal controls. Cultures and families that emphasize and model self-control and restraint, regardless of environmental circumstances, have lower delinquency rates than those that do not (Stott, 82).

More specifically, Patterson (81) found four aspects of child rearing that were associated with delinquency:

1. Lack of house rules: The family has developed no patterns and has no specific expectations for the behavior of their children.

2. Lack of parental monitoring of behavior: Parents do not know what their children are doing or how they are feeling, and they neither see nor respond to deviant behavior.

3. Lack of effective contingencies: Parents shout and nag but do not follow through.

4. Lack of ways of dealing with crises and problems: When problems arise, conflict leads to tension, but the family has no way of resolving either the tension or the problem.

But modeling and child-rearing practices are not sufficient in themselves to explain delinquency. In the case study, for example, five of the eight children did not acquire criminal records. The important factor ignored in the family-learning viewpoint is the quality of the relationships between parent and child.

Family-Deprivation Viewpoint

Poor parent-child relationships are a frequent theme within the literature on the causes of delinquency (Glueck, 50; Ausubel, 70; Bachman, 72; Balswick, 75; McKissack, 75; Lang, 76; P.Y. Miller, 79; Gold, 80; Anolik, 83). Troubled family relationships seem to be endemic to children who are processed by the juvenile justice system, just as they are to children who display emotional disorders. Delinquents have few close ties to their parents, especially boys to their fathers, with a resulting lack of affection that leads the adolescents to feel unwanted. Anolik (83, p. 493) explains:

. . . when adolescents enjoy little prestige at home, they are motivated to find personal recognition elsewhere and are less concerned about the consequences of their conduct on their parents.

Rejection. The weak attachment between parent and child leads to low self-esteem, failure to instill in the children a concern for consequences, the child's rejection of the parents, impulsive behavior, and no capacity to learn from experience (McKissack, 75). Although the lack of affection between parent and child often holds true for all the children in the family, it is quite possible that a parent or parents may succeed in creating a bond with one child while simultaneously failing with another. This explains why only one or several children in a family, rather than all of them, may turn to delinquency.

As was discussed in Chapters 3 and 12, family-therapy theory suggests that one child in the family may also become the symptom-bearer or scapegoat for trouble in the family. This child may act out in delinquent ways while the other children remain relatively stable. If the delinquent is removed from the family, however, it is likely that another child will develop symptoms — maladjustment, delinquency, drug abuse — that continue to take the focus off the more pervasive family issues.

In an extremely extensive investigation into the causes of delinquency, Stott (82) conducted a five-year longitudinal study of 102 delinquent youths. He actually lived with the delinquents and their families, became intimately acquainted with the parents, the locality, the boys' associates, hangouts, and job history. He studied in detail the delinquent act and pieced together the states of mind of a delinquent that we discussed earlier (avoidance-excitement, getting removed from the home, hostility, delinquent loyalty testing, and bravado). Added to this was a series of controlled studies and a ten-year followup of 700 juvenile delinquents. He found that 93 percent of the delinquent acts stemmed from a "breach of affectional bond between parent and child" (p. 318). The delinquent adolescent had been deprived of a secure attachment to a caring adult in one of four ways:

1. The adolescent had been threatened with rejection from the family.
2. The adolescent had lost the only or preferred parent, and there was no satisfactory substitute.
3. The mother was not a dependable source of affection or care.
4. The adolescent feared the loss of the preferred parent.

Of particular interest to Stott was the relationship between parental disciplinary measures and delinquency. He found that it was not the failure of parental control that caused delinquency, but rather that both failure of control and delinquency were the byproducts of the breach in the affectional bond or the feared loss of the parent. Stott concluded that the delinquent adolescent who feels rejected has no incentive to avoid parental displeasure. If the child has given up on the expectation of parental affection, the parent has lost all hope of exercising control.

Stress. The breakdown of family relationships can happen as the result of parental tension, illness, death, or unemployment; inadequate parental coping; separation; poverty; and other stresses of daily living. According to the family-deprivation viewpoint, these stresses create discord that threaten the continued existence of the family, and the children are deprived of what they need most — the parents' affection and security. They react with maladaptive emergency responses, including delinquency.

Fernall Hoover, a serious delinquent in early adolescence, talks about his relationship with his father (Cottle, 77, p. 29):

> Most kids learn a lot from their folks, but we learned you don't learn anything from them. I wanted to talk to my father, but either he was never around, or when I'd go and see him he'd be drunk or too busy to talk to me. Or sometimes he'd want to tell me about what was going on in *his* life. He thought he was doing me some kind of favor telling me all these things, but I didn't go to his place to talk about *him*; I went there to talk about *me!* He never seemed to catch on to that. He was too busy being interested in himself. It was like he'd forgot I was his son. He'd act a lot like I was his brother or his business partner or something.

In summary, then, all four viewpoints on the causes of delinquency have merit and deserve our consideraton. Biological, intellectual, social, and familial factors work together to create the unfortunate lack of esteem and lack of concern with consequences that are so common among serious delinquents. Some children may be more genetically predisposed to delinquency either through temperament or disability; diet may effect the acting out of some, but not other children; poor environmental conditions certainly contribute to the expression of hostility; parental role-modeling and child-rearing practices play a significant role, and there seems to be no doubt that the relationships within the family are vitally important in the development of children.

Like disturbed adolescents, delinquent adolescents are reacting to stress; they are alienated and lack the emotional support necessary for healthy development; they usually have experienced repeated failures and have low self-esteem often disguised as bravado; and they have not developed moral reasoning and an appreciation for the consequences of their actions. Like disturbed adolescents their needs are great, and our approaches to prevention and treatment ought to be predicated on those needs.

THE JUVENILE COURT

History of the Juvenile Court

Punishment. As mentioned in Chapter 1 and earlier in this chapter, until the end of the nineteenth century, children who were difficult to handle were treated in harsh and punitive ways; the prevailing philosophy was one of protecting the interests and rights of society, and children who violated those rights were dealt with severely. Recall that up until the thirteenth century children who were bothersome to their parents were given away or sold into servitude. And the harsh treatment continued, as Footlick (77, p. 280) points out:

> In 1646, the Puritans of the Massachusetts Bay Colony decreed the death penalty for "a stubborn or rebellious son," and for more than two centuries afterward children were treated by the law more as possessions than as persons.

Rehabilitation. But in the nineteenth century, reformers began to look at criminal behavior as a treatable defect, not unlike disease or a correctable physical condition. Instead of punishment, rehabilitation became the aim of the criminal justice system, and children, in particular, were considered primary candidates for rehabilitative efforts. But in order to be properly treated, children needed also to be separated from adult offenders and protected from the potential damage of mingling with adult criminals. Thus was born the idea of a civil rather than criminal juvenile justice system. In 1899, the first juvenile court was established in Cook County, Illinois, where children were not only separated from adult offenders but were to be treated in a friendly, caring way under civil rather than criminal procedures (Prescott, 81; Armstrong, 82). The juvenile justice reform movement spread rapidly, as it become popular to view juvenile offenders not as criminals but as wayward children in need of protection and guidance. The juvenile court was viewed as *parens patriae* (in place of parents) and sought to treat children as a wise parent would. The juvenile court was to pay greater attention to the circumstances of the bothersome behavior than to the behavior itself and to act so as to treat and rehabilitate rather than to punish (Prescott, 81; Armstrong, 82; Guernsey, 83). By 1925, 46 states had enacted legislation to create juvenile courts (Footlick, 77).

New procedures. As a result of the emphasis on treatment (and eventually on prevention), the procedures commonly associated with criminal proceedings were discarded. Constitutional restraints, due process, criminal records, rules of evidence, and even the right to an attorney were all considered inappropriate. The court was relatively informal, hearsay evidence was admissable, and the proceedings were protected from the press and the public. Because it was considered wise in the ways of childhood, the court (in the form of the judge) was granted complete authority to determine what would be done with a child, regardless of whether anyone had proved anything against him. Even the language of the court is different from that of the criminal court: instead of a complaint, a child is issued a petition; instead of a warrant, there is a summons; instead of a crime there is a delinquent act; instead of a criminal there is a juvenile offender, wayward youth, PINS, client, patient, or resident; instead of a trial there is an adjudication; instead of police there are juvenile officers; instead of a finding of guilty there is a finding of not innocent; instead of a sentence there is a disposition; instead of prison there are reformatories, training schools, learning centers, treatment centers, or group homes; instead of guards there are correctional treatment officers; instead of parole officers there are aftercare workers (Czajkoski, 82).

Unintended outcomes. The unintended result of all these reforms, as Prescott (81, p. 57) points out, is that:

> . . . no one knew what was going on in these courts. Because lawyers were not permitted to make appeals, the appellate courts didn't know what was going on. Because the definition of delinquency was so vague, young people were being adjudged delinquents pretty much according to whether their behavior differed markedly from the judge's experience of what a child's orderly demeanor should be. Because the court's mandate was to assume jurisdiction over any child who needed help, any child who was picked up off the street could be charged with something in court. But then, the court was the child's *friend*. It acted in his "best interests." Could anyone disapprove of that?

Effects of contact with the court. For seventy-five years after its invention, juvenile courts across the country operated as they were designed with little outside intervention or cirticism. Without a doubt, they provided treatment and rehabilitation for hundreds of thousands of children and adolescents, but the problems associated with them went largely without response.

One of the most obvious difficulties the court faces is its mandate to treat not only legal offenders, but status offenders and victims of neglect and abuse as well. Prescott (81, p. 199) describes the problem, one that was all too vivid in the case of Christopher Devlin (See Table 13.2):

> Those familiar with Family Court are well aware that a child who appears on one kind of petition will presently be brought in on another. The line between a neglected child and a PINS is so tenuous that a child alleged to be a PINS by his parent may in fact be a neglect in disguise: the easiest way to dump a child you can't or won't care for is to insist that he is ungovernable. The line between a PINS and a delinquent is equally vague and was once defined as the difference between a child brought into court by a parent and one brought in by the police. What is certain is that one kind of appearance tends to lead to another.

In addition to the tendency of status offenders to become increasingly delinquent after their being recorded in the rolls of the court, court appearances may be harmful in other ways. Children who appear in court come from homes in which there is usually a great deal of tension, but the court appearance may only aggravate the tense family situation and thus add to the stress in the family. Furthermore, once young people have been labeled by the court, teachers and employers may become further alienated from them, as might the more ''respectable'' youths, who may choose not to associate with them. An adolescent who is identified delinquent by the court may well accept the label and confirm a negative identity (West, 77). All these potentialities may explain why court appearances have been found to be linked with subsequent delinquency. West (77), for example, compared youths who were convicted of a delinquent offense with equally badly behaving youth who escaped conviction and found that there was a significant trend toward perpetuation and increase in delinquent behavior following conviction that did not occur in nonconvicted but delinquent-prone youth. And beyond these problems, the juvenile court has been severely criticized on other grounds, with some of these criticisms leading to significant reform of the system within the last ten years. We will examine these criticisms in the next section.

Criticisms of the Juvenile Court

Lack of separation. The lack of separation of serious delinquents from PINS and victims of abuse and neglect, general ineffectiveness, and the curtailment of basic human rights have constituted the major criticisms of the juvenile justice system. We have already discussed the difficulty the court faces in having to deal with both delinquents and children who need protection; here we will explore the other two major issues.

Ineffectiveness. Critics of the juvenile justice system claim that it is ineffective because delinquents are committing repeated offenses. Because the majority of youth appearing before many juvenile courts have prior arrest records, the system can be said not to be working. It clearly is not deterring first offenders from subsequent delinquency. Two major reasons for its lack of effectiveness are its lack of appropriate correctional and treatment facilities and the incredible lag of time between arrest and court appearance and disposition. It has been demonstrated repeatedly that incarceration in juvenile facilities does not rehabilitate; the rates of recidivism from these "jails" (even though they may be euphemistically referred to as "learning centers") are extremely high. Furthermore, because there is so much time before a case comes to court, kids learn that nothing happens to them as a result of their delinquency (Prescott, 81). Inefficiency is also seen in what Scott (82) refers to as "money-gobblers" in the system. the commital institutions are extremely expensive to maintain; there is a tremendous amount of wasted court time; and the repair of vandalism caused by juveniles is high. The inefficiency and ineffectiveness of juvenile justice may well be attributed, say Stott (82) and others, to our generally inadequate understanding of both the causes and the appropriate treatments for delinquency. (We will discuss treatment issues in the next section.)

Denial of human rights. The other major focus of criticism of the juvenile justice system is the denial to children of fundamental human rights. A case that went all the way to the Supreme Court illustrated and publicized the problem. In 1964, fifteen-year-old Gerald Francis Gault was arrested for making an indecent phone call to a neighbor. Had young Gault been 18 years old, the maximum sentence he could have received would have been a $50 fine and a two-month jail sentence. However, because the juvenile court did not operate as a criminal court would, Gerald Gault was sentenced to an institution *until he reached the age of 21.* In addition, his parents were not notified of the charges, the petition made no mention of the facts, the complainant did not appear, there was no sworn testimony nor any record of the proceedings, and the judge never spoke to the complainant. At the state level, Gault's appeal failed, but his attorneys took the case to the Supreme Court, which literally changed the nature of juvenile law. In their decision, children were granted important civil rights: the right to notice of charges against them, the right to counsel, the right to confront and cross-examine sworn witnesses, the privilege against self-incrimination, the right to a transcript of the proceedings, and the right to an appellate review. Even with the incredible injustice that was delivered to Gault at the state level, the Supreme Court decision in his favor was made on a vote of 5–4, with the dissenters concerned that the decision would destroy the humanitarian quality of the juvenile court (*In re* Gault, 67; Prescott, 81). Justice Abe Fortas, in an often-quoted statement, summed up the problem (Prescott, 81, pp. 63–64):

> There is evidence, in fact, that there may be grounds for concern that the child receives the worst of both worlds: that he gets neither the protections accorded to adults nor the solicitous care and regenerative treatment postulated for children.

Reforms. The Supreme Court decision, as well as other criticisms of the system, led to a reexamination and overhaul during the 1970s. Armstrong (82) summarizes the reforms as the four *D*'s: decriminalization, which simply reinforces the concept of the treatment potential of young offenders; due process, by which basic human rights like those listed above are restored and which ensures that a young person who comes before the court will be treated fairly and will not be forgotten; deinstitutionalization, which demands the provision of alternatives to ineffective correctional facilities; and diversion, which attempts to place children in alternative services instead of facing the juvenile court.

CURRENT APPROACHES TO TREATMENT AND PREVENTION

Institutionalization and Probation

Once a young person has been determined by the court to need services, either as a result of demonstrated delinquency or by the lack of appropriate care in the home, the court must determine the best possible treatment for that child. Most abused or neglected children, as well as some status offenders, are referred to foster care if it is determined that they cannot remain in the family home. Although there is little documented consensus on the effectiveness of any kind of treatment for delinquents (Gold, 80; Singer, 83), the vast majority of young people adjudicated by the court are either institutionalized or placed on probation.

Institutionalization. Traditional juvenile institutions, as we have noted, are notoriously ineffective in dealing with delinquents (Gold, 80; Stott, 82; McPherson, 83; Rutter, 83). Juvenile institutions seldom rehabilitate; they tend to rely on external control rather than focusing on the needs of the offenders; they are poorly financed; and they tend to make matters worse for young offenders, who learn new delinquency and have their own bad behavior reinforced by others. All too often, says Stott (82), institutional commitment is used as a punishment for the number, rather than the nature, of the offenses committed. For some adolescents, home life is so unbearable that they commit offenses primarily as a means of getting out. Regardless of the documentation of the ineffectiveness of these institutions, over 900,000 adolescents are placed in them every year (Cottle, 77), and many who leave eventually return. All too often, the first institutionalization is only the beginning of a lifetime of commitments.

Probation. By far the most widely used method of dealing with delinquents is probation (*probare* is Latin for "to test" or "to prove"), which allows youths to remain in their home community under supervision of the court. Probation requires: (1) that the court find the child in need of probation; (2) that conditions be imposed upon the continued freedom (such as curfew hours, work requirement, and school attendance); and that (3) the court provide a means for helping the child meet those conditions (usually in the form of a regular meeting with a probation officer). There may be as many as four adolescents on probation for every one institutionalized, and 75 percent of these are demonstrated delinquents (Singer, 83). Probation is far less expensive than committal, and considerably more effective, although the increased effectiveness may be due to less serious offenders being put on probation.

Calls for reform. As a result of the ineffectiveness of these traditional methods of treating delinquents, both demand for and development of alternatives have increased in recent years. Stott (82) summarizes the calls for reform as those which emphasize professional training and retraining programs, demonstration projects in representative neighborhoods, community projects for the control of local vandalism and other bad behavior, the establishment of police social-work facilities, experiments in new forms of dispositon of the young offenders, a national advisory center, and a computer center for the storage and analysis of casework data for the improvement of diagnostic and counseling skills.

Clearly, the focus of such recommendations is on rehabilitation and the teaching of personal responsibility, rather than increased punitive measures. Early in this chapter, we discussed the two prevailing philosophies of rehabilitation — the get-tough approach and the community-based approach. Although the most serious delinquents may well need to be referred to criminal court and dealt with severely, as the American Bar Association contends, more adolescent delinquency needs to be dealt with in an individualized approach that teaches young people to be responsible for their behavior. A number of alternatives, most based on this philosophy, are currently in use in localities all over the country.

Alternatives

Among the most popular alternatives to traditional institutionalization and probation are family counseling, diversion programs, community-service projects, restitution, wilderness programs, and nontraditional residential programs. In many juvenile courts several of these experimental alternatives may be used together for a particular adolescent. For example, first-time offenders and their families might be offered the opportunity to stay out of court (diversion) if they agree to a specified number of family-counseling sessions along with the adolescents performing a specified number of hours engaged in service work in the community.

Family counseling. As we discussed in Chapters 3 and 12, family counseling is an increasingly popular method of intervention with troubled families. Troubled families produce disturbed and/or delinquent youth, and the most effective treatment frequently must involve the entire family. When the family learns to interact in positive ways and to develop secure and meaningful relationships with one another, delinquency tends to disappear (Alexander, 76; West, 77; Patterson, 81; Stott, 82). Families can learn to develop contracts for expected behaviors, learn noncoercive methods of control, develop skills of listening to and negotiating with one another, understand the stresses that create tension among them, and develop a sense of individual and collective responsibility. Family counseling or education has become a vital part of many successful treatment programs.

Diversion programs. Diversion programs are based on the recognition that court contact all too often predicts future court contact. The less serious offenders, especially those who have committed relatively minor offenses for the first time, are diverted from the court into programs designed to teach positive interaction skills and individual responsibility. Henrico County, Virginia, for example, has two diversion programs. In one of them, adolescents picked up for first-time minor offenses (most often possession of alcohol, drinking, or possession of marijuana) and their families are screened for possible inclusion in the CAP (Court Alternative Program). Those who meet the criteria for admission (they must be a reasonably well-functioning family with no overt pathology) are offered a fifteen-hour family-education group experience that focuses primarily on family communication and drug and alcohol information. If the family (other adolescents in the family are also encouraged to attend) successfully completes the program, the offender's record is destroyed. In a similar program for very young offenders (7- to 10-year-olds who have been picked up for such things as shoplifting or setting fires), the parents meet in a parent-education group while their children meet in a group that focuses on personal responsibility. Both programs have been demonstrated to be highly effective in preventing repeat appearances in court by the youngsters involved (Conner, 84).

Community service. Whether part of a diversion program or a condition of probation, community service is an increasingly popular method of teaching personal responsibility. Young offenders are required to work in community beautification projects, hospitals, and other places where their labor contributes to the well-being of the community. Youngsters involved in these projects frequently report a new sense of community pride and belonging as a result of their labors.

Restitution. Restitution, the paying back by an offender to a victim (usually in a case of a crime against property), is used as a means of instilling an appreciation for the effect on others of the offense. In some programs, the offender is even required to meet face-to-face with the victim:

> A recent innovation is to bring the offender face to face with his victim. This is done with the formal purpose of deciding upon the amount and form of the restitution. More important, however, are its social objectives. Being confronted by the victim, usually in the latter's own home, is calculated to make all except the most hardened psychopath appreciate that the personal harm for which he is thoughtlessly responsible far outweighs the satisfactions he gets from his delinquencies. The effect on the victim is to mellow feelings of hostility and punitiveness insofar as he sees the offender as a misguided, likeable, or unhappy youth. (Stott, 82, pp. 312–313)

Each member of the wilderness-training group must take responsibility for group survival.

Wilderness training. Finally, the generally low self-esteem and self-confidence of delinquents is bolstered by wilderness and survival training. Led by experienced wilderness counselors, groups are faced with challenging environments and problems that they must solve by working together and depending on one another. Each member of the group becomes vitally important to the success of the entire group, and each must take full responsibility for a share of the basic needs for group survival. Wilderness programs are offered to a wide variety of adolescents who have come into contact with the court and provide a basic structure for many nontraditional residential programs.

Nontraditional residential treatment. The alternatives described above are most often used with youth who remain in their home communities. But for some youth, remaining at home is impossible or at least highly unwise. The alternative to traditional institutionalization is referral to a nontraditional residential treatment program. These programs usually incorporate individual and group therapy, individualized instruction with teachers trained in learning disabilities, outdoor education or wilderness programs, and extensive recreation and training in social skills. Many also require regular family counseling. Jesse Mayo, a newspaper reporter, describes the program and outcomes of one such alternative: Elk Hill Farm (Figure 13.1).

Regardless of the form of the alternative, each is designed to promote the development of individual responsibility and self-esteem. Although many individual programs report high rates of success, there is little documentation of the effectiveness of alternatives overall. Such research, obviously, is extremely difficult to conduct when the programs vary to the extent that they do.

Figure 13.1

Elk Hill gives boys a last chance

By Jesse Mayo

Tonight's meeting inside the big house on the hill has begun. Ten boys, all teenagers, sit in a circle and attend to serious business. One of them wants to visit his family over the weekend and the others must decide with him if he should go. His attitude is the crucial factor. Another boy speaks to him: "Sit up straight, man. And *look* at us."

This is Elk Hill Farm, just west of George's Tavern. It is a privately owned school for boys with problems. For most of these boys it is their last chance to stay out of jail. They all share one condition: for one reason or another they have been unable to cope with the demands of school and society.

Classified as learning-disabled or perhaps emotionally disturbed, they have been shuffled from one agency to another with little or no effect until all resources have been exhausted. Elk Hill offers them an alternative. Here boys learn to be young men. They learn from each other.

Earlier I had listened to executive director Bob Fleischman explain the Elk Hill concept of "positive peer culture." Problems are good, he said. They provide the boy a chance to show his strengths or reveal his weaknesses. For example, when frustrated he might resort to verbal or physical aggression, shirking of responsibilities or the denial of his true feelings. Only someone who is familiar with such devices can help him overcome them. That "someone" is another boy his age.

Under the watchful eye of a staff counselor, the boys conduct group meetings each day after school and one night a week to discuss any problems that an individual may be having. There is no "hot seat," however, in which a boy is subjected to harsh criticism from the group. Instead, they concentrate on his strong points and strive to make him feel good about himself.

Because of this approach, Fleishman said, Elk Hill has aroused great interest in those who run other treatment programs. People from places like St. Joseph's Villa, the United Methodist Home and the Pennsylvania Association of Child Care Workers have come to see the methods used at Elk Hill.

But the system is not for everyone. When a boy has been referred to Elk Hill by the court or school system (which pays a fee for the service), he must first make a five-day "pre-placement" visit to the farm. This serves to introduce him to the other boys and the staff. They, in turn, will meet and appraise him to determine if he is ready and willing to enter the program.

If he is accepted, he must then present the group his "life story." That is, he must give an account of his problems with his family, friends, school, community and the courts with an emphasis on why he chose the actions that led him into trouble.

The new boy also has five weeks in which to develop "program goals" (both short- and long-term) which are linked to his specific problems and designed to correct

Figure 13.1 (continued)

them. These goals indicate the direction in which his peers will encourage him to move.

When these program goals have been reached, the boy is eligible for re-entry into his community. On the other hand, failure by the boy to demonstrate a genuine desire to change means immediate expulsion from the program and a transfer back to his original collision course with the authorities. All such decisions are made by the boys in concert with the staff. This responsibility is part of what associate director Jim Christopher calls "treatment as opposed to maintenance."

A boy at Elk Hill is never alone, never left entirely to his own devices or judgment. No matter what he does or where he goes, at least one other resident is there, watching and listening.

This intense, never-ending scrutiny is central to life at Elk Hill. Each boy watches out for the others. An intense group conscience is cultivated to generate strong pressure on each boy to conform to the home's standards.

New residents quickly learn the vocabulary that comes to shape their lives. A few phrases constantly recur in their speech to describe the kinds of behavior the program is designed to curb: authority problem, aggression, shirking, fronting (masking one's true feelngs). Using this behavioral shorthand, the residents can quickly and effectively bring their companions up short whenever they deviate from the norms encouraged at Elk Hill.

At tonight's meeting they decide that their friend has earned a home visit, but that he should not go alone. Another boy will go with him to lend support during what may be a difficult time. (A disruptive or indifferent home life is another common experience among these boys.) The next item for group discussion involves the buddy system that prevails at the farm. Are three boys together too many? Are two enough? As talk begins, I think back on my afternoon tour of the estate.

I was introduced to my initial guide, Tom (all names have been changed), in the first-floor room of the James M. Ball Memorial Cottage which functions as both cafeteria area and classroom. (Elk Hill established the Alfred L. Blake, Jr. School for its residents in 1978). A soft-spoken 17-year-old, Tom had serious problems with his family. He had been at Elk Hill for eight months. We were quickly joined by Ronnie and Rick. Ronnie, 16, was quite large

for his age. The scars on his brow and hands have evidence of his self-admitted "aggression problem." He claimed to have made great progress during his five months on the farm.

Rick was young (15) and too small to be a physical threat. In fact, it was hard to determine what his problems were. He obviously looked up to Tom and Ronnie as "big Brothers," although this is a tendency that the group and staffers try to moderate. Rick had been on the farm for only one month.

As we wandered over the grounds, past the horse barn where each boy has an assigned horse and duty, the woodworking shop, the basketball court, and out onto the sloping front lawn to see "Cornwallis' tree" (under which the general is reputed to have slept), I listened to a steady stream of enthusiasm from the three boys.

I began to notice that their differences in age, looks, mannerisms and time spent on the farm diminished as they spoke of the Elk Hill experience. Their faces became more serious and their conversation more formal when they recounted their first days on the farm and the not-quite-understandable feeling of "care" and "respect" (two words heard often at Elk Hill) which greeted them. They seemed to indicate that self-restraint was new to them.

Later, as we sat in one of their rooms in the "Old Cottage" (filled with books, posters, albums, barbells and the rest of a typical teenager's treasure), I asked them if they wouldn't be embarrassed to have one of their old hometown buddies hear them speak of "love" and "responsibility." As usual, they deferred politely to each other until Ronnie spoke up. "No," he smiled.

Tonight's meeting is over. It has been decided that two boys together are sufficient to provide mutual support, but that care should be taken to insure that it is not always the same two. Care and respect are owed to everyone.

Driving down the gravel road away from Elk Hill, I feel strangely dazed. It may be the uneasiness of hearing others speak of their inner feelings (or, at least, what they take to be inner feelings) only minutes after meeting them. It may be the result of the bombardment of my uninitiated mind with new terms and concepts. Or, more likely, it may be the realization that coming to terms with yourself and renouncing a lifetime of bad habits is an unsettling experience, no matter what your age.

Prevention: The Role of the Schools

Although it seems clear that the most important preventer of delinquency is the adolescent's self-esteem, which is developed primarily in the family, the school can also play an important role (Goldstein, 80; Stott 82). Rather than relying on external forms of control that teach only very low-level moral reasoning skill, schools might adopt discipline measures that require student input and responsibility (Curwin, 80). Breaking schools into smaller units in which students feel a greater sense of belonging and importance, better screening to identify the maladjusted, early intervention with children who display aggressive tendencies in elementary school, parent education and counseling, and more effective intervention with disruptive secondary students all could contribute to a decrease in the delinquency rate.

Goldstein (80) proposes systematic training in personal, social, and cognitive skills in order to build up the strengths of delinquency-prone adolescents. The skills

Table 13.3
Skills for Adolescents

Group I. Beginning Social Skills	25. Negotiation
1. Listening	26. Using Self-Control
2. Starting a Conversation	27. Standing Up for Your Rights
3. Having a Conversation	28. Responding to Teasing
4. Asking a Question	29. Avoiding Trouble with Others
5. Saying Thank You	30. Keeping Out of Fights
6. Introducing Yourself	**Group V. Skills for Dealing with Stress**
7. Introducing Other People	31. Making a Complaint
8. Giving a Compliment	32. Answering a Complaint
Group II. Advanced Social Skills	33. Sportsmanship After the Game
9. Asking for Help	34. Dealing with Embarrassment
10. Joining In	35. Dealing with Being Left Out
11. Giving Instructions	36. Standing Up for a Friend
12. Following Instructions	37. Responding to Persuasion
13. Apologizing	38. Responding to Failure
14. Convincing Others	39. Dealing with Contradictory Messages
Group III. Skills for Dealing with Feelings	40. Dealing with an Accusation
15. Knowing Your Feelings	41. Getting Ready for a Difficult Conversation
16. Expressing Your Feelings	42. Dealing with Group Pressure
17. Understanding the Feelings of Others	**Group VI. Planning Skills**
18. Dealing with Someone Else's Anger	43. Deciding on Something to Do
19. Expressing Affection	44. Deciding What Caused a Problem
20. Dealing with Fear	45. Setting a Goal
21. Rewarding Yourself	46. Deciding on Your Abilities
Group IV. Skill Alternatives to Aggression	47. Gathering Information
22. Asking Permission	48. Arranging Problems by Importance
23. Sharing Something	49. Making a Decision
24. Helping Others	50. Concentrating on a Task

are taught in a specific sequence consisting of demonstration, rehearsal, feedback, and transfer to external environments. A series of 50 skills (Table 13.3) is designed to provide adolescents with the strengths to deal with society's expectations of them.

SUMMARY

Juvenile delinquency, both reported and hidden, is a major problem of adolescence. Furthermore, a certain amount of delinquent behavior may be perfectly normal adolescent risk taking. The subject is a complicated one.

Official delinquency, that processed through the juvenile court, is more serious than hidden delinquency, and is often committed by a relatively few serious delinquents who repeat their offenses. A child who appears earlier on the court rolls is more likely to continue delinquency through adolescence and into adulthood.

Status offenders are young people who commit acts that would not be crimes were they adults. These children are most often the victims of oppressively maladjusted homes and are in need of stable environments and expectations. All too often, their contact with the court leads to involvement in more serious delinquency.

As adolescents get older, they commit more serious and more violent crimes than they did as younger children. A disproportionate number of delinquents come from poverty and from minorities that are discriminated against in mainstream society. Although the gap is narrowing, boys still commit significantly more and significantly more violent offenses than girls.

Society has responded to juvenile delinquency in one of two ways. The punitive get-tough approach was common until the turn of the twentieth century, but since then a more humanitarian approach, one that seeks to treat and rehabilitate, has been in vogue. It would seem reasonable to respond to delinquency based on a thorough understanding of the characteristics of delinquents and the causes of delinquency.

The juvenile court deals with three distinct kinds of adolescents: the victims of abuse and/or neglect; status offenders; and delinquents. Delinquents have been classified in a number of ways, all of which point out that serious delinquents are indeed disturbed young people. Their emotional problems cry out for understanding and treatment, just as do the disturbances discussed in Chapter 12.

Serious delinquents generally share with one another poor home conditions, poor school adjustment and achievement, antisocial tendencies, aggression, poor self-control, and low self-esteem. They feel inadequate and undesirable, though they usually mask these feelings with a facade of bravado.

Some adolescents commit their delinquent acts in gangs, which are becoming increasingly violent and destructive, especially in the largest urban ghettos in this country. Gangs are typically composed of poor minority youth who exist on the fringes of society.

Four trends in the study of the causes of delinquency can be identified. The genetic viewpoint focuses on physical and physiological factors like learning disabilities and a genetic predisposition to delinquency. The sociological viewpoint focuses on environmental factors like low income and peer pressure. The family-learning viewpoint focuses on family circumstances and child-rearing practices, and the family-deprivation viewpoint focuses on disturbed relationships within the family. All four viewpoints have merit. Biological, intellectual, social, and familial factors most likely work together to cause delinquency.

The juvenile court, designed to protect children from the punitive nature of criminal court, emphasizes understanding and treatment rather than punishment. Unfortunately, in its humanitarian intentions, it also served for many years to deny basic human rights to children and adolescents and thereby came under substantial criticism and reform. The court is faced with the dilemma of having to deal with all the young people that come before it and is hampered by inadequate resources and facilities as well as by inadequate understanding of the causes of disturbed and delinquent behavior. For the most part, it has been ineffective in dealing with delinquents.

Because the traditional methods of rehabilitating juvenile delinquents, incarceration and probation, have proved relatively ineffective, new alternatives to treatment and prevention are currently being experimented with throughout the country. These alternatives focus primarily on community-based approaches while acknowledging that the most serious delinquent offenders may not be capable of rehabilitation. For them, the more punitive adult criminal proceedings may be the only way of protecting society. Alternatives include, singly or in combination, family counseling, diversion, community service, restitution, wilderness training, nontraditional residential programs, and emphasis on early intervention in the schools.

14

Drug Use and Abuse

The Greeks had a word for it—**ataraxia:** a state in which mental serenity is combined with physical well-being. How to achieve it has been the quest of religion and philosophy for thousands of years. But because these paths call for long and arduous self-discipline, men have also sought a short cut to happiness through herbs and chemists' concoctions.

In one year alone, the sale of tranquilizers in America soared to $150,000,000. Millions more are spent on alcohol. Can we dispense happiness in pills? For thousands of years, man has tried to ''squirm his way out of himself'' with the help of strange brews and weird concoctions. Can we banish the specter of care, the burden of anxiety and guilt, with a pill after every meal? (DeRopp, 57, book jacket)

Short cuts to happiness are the subject of this chapter. We will comment on the extent of drug use and abuse in the United States before detailing the extent of use by adolescents of the most common drugs: the legal drugs of nicotine and alcohol and the illegal ones, including central nervous system depressants (inhalants, tranquilizers, PCP, Quaaludes, barbiturates), central nervous system stimulants (amphetamines, cocaine), hallucinogens (marijuana, LSD), and narcotics (opium, heroin, methadone). We will explore how adolescents begin experimenting with drugs and how some of them move into the abuse of drugs, and we will examine the causal factors leading to both use and abuse. Finally, we will look at treatments for drug abusers and current approaches to the prevention of drug abuse and dependency.

THE EXTENT OF DRUG USE IN THE UNITED STATES

A Drug-Oriented Society

Shortcuts to happiness and pain relief have been sought throughout history. Drugs, both natural and synthetic, have been used to dull both physical and emotional pain, stimulate the central nervous system and thereby produce energy and endurance, and create a pleasurable state of being. Contrary to the cries of many, drug use and abuse are not products of the latter half of the twentieth century.

Drug use in modern society. Ours is a drug-oriented society. To verify this, we need only list the contents of our medicine cabinets: analgesics to relieve pain, antacids to counteract stomach upset (often caused by overindulgence in food and alcohol), tranquilizers to calm us down, sleeping pills to wipe away the thoughts that intrude on our rest, antihistamines to clear our allergies. In addition, most homes contain liquor cabinets and most refrigerators chill beer and wine regularly. Although the Surgeon General has declared that cigarettes are indeed hazardous to our health, the tobacco industry is booming. And how many of us are virtually unable to function until we have a dose or two of caffeine to start the day? Yet these are merely the drugs that are available to all of us without prescription. Amphetamines and barbiturates, which have proven medical value, are produced in far greater quantity than the medical profession requires (400 tons of barbiturates, enough for 3.6 billion doses, are produced in the United States each year); the excess winds up on the street (*Drugs*, 78; Goyan, 80; Johnston, 83).

Adolescent exposure. Because drugs are an accepted part of society and because their use cuts across all social and economic lines (E.J. Smith, 81), every adolescent is faced with the decision of whether or not to smoke, drink, and indulge in one or more of the illegal drugs. The vast majority of them will experiment, at least with tobacco and alcohol, but only a very small minority will become abusers. Drug use today is no longer part and parcel of the attitude of protest that surrounded drug use in the 1960s, and the epidemic use of hard drugs that was predicted then has not materialized. Tobacco, alcohol, marijuana, cocaine, and PCP use has increased in the last fifteen years, but no more than one in five adolescents has tried LSD, inhalants, stimulants, sedatives, heroin, cocaine, PCP, or Quaaludes (Johnston, 79, 81).

Adolescents are experimenting and using drugs, especially tobacco, alcohol, and marijuana, but only a very few become abusers. Like the emotionally disturbed and the delinquent, the drug abusers belong to the 20 percent of the adolescent population that we have already identified as troubled, and there are complex relationships between disturbance, delinquency, and drug abuse. Abusers become delinquent to buy drugs; alcohol crimes are frequently violent; and about 20 percent of all juvenile crime stems from substance abuse (E.J. Smith, 81).

Kinds of Drugs

Drugs can be classified in a variety of ways, the most useful of which is the type of effect they have on the human body. When classified in this way, four major types of drugs can be distinguished: central nervous system depressants, central nervous system stimulants, hallucinogens, and narcotics.

CNS depressants. Central nervous system depressants depress or slow down the activity of the nervous system. People who use depressants may become physically dependent on them, and they usually develop a tolerance for the drug over time, thereby requiring ever-increasing doses. When dependence develops, they are unable to stop taking the drug without physical withdrawal symptoms. Depressants include alcohol; the inhalants (anesthetics and solvents), including glue, nail polish remover, cleaning fluid, lighter fluid, antifreeze, gasoline, and ethanol and other alcohols; the minor tranquilizers (Miltown, Librium, and Valium); and sedatives (barbiturates, Quaaludes, and PCP). PCP is frequently classified as a hallucinogen because of its sometimes bizarre effects, but it was developed as a CNS depressant for animals. All depressants except PCP can be obtained legally, but many of the legally produced pills (barbiturates and tranquilizers) find their way into the illegal market.

CNS stimulants. Central nervous system stimulants are used to stimulate activity, suppress the appetite, and ameliorate emotional depression. Overuse can result in increased tolerance, dependence, and withdrawal symptoms when the drug is curtailed. The stimulants include the legal drugs caffeine and nicotine as well as the legal and illegal amphetamines and the illegal methadrine and cocaine.

Hallucinogens. Hallucinogens are mind-distorters. They create altered perceptions and have no medical uses. Tolerance may develop, but there are generally no physical dependence and no physical symptoms of withdrawal when the drug is no longer used. Marijuana, mescaline, and LSD are the most commonly used hallucinogens; all hallucinogens are illegal.

Narcotics. Narcotics have an analgesic effect. They are used to relieve physical and mental pain, reduce frequency of coughing, stop diarrhea, and induce sleep or stupor. The narcotics have made surgery possible and are required in many medical circumstances. They are also highly addictive; tolerance develops quickly, and cessation of the drug may produce violent withdrawal symptoms. Most narcotics are derived from the opium poppy (morphine, codeine, heroin), but can also be produced synthetically (methadone). Legitimate use of narcotics is restricted to appropriate medical situations.

Use to Abuse

All of us use drugs (especially the legal ones), but only a few abuse them. Figure 14.1 outlines the stages of drug use, from early experimental use, in which the majority of adolescents engage, at least with alcohol, tobacco, and marijuana; through regular use

Figure 14.1
Stages of Drug Use

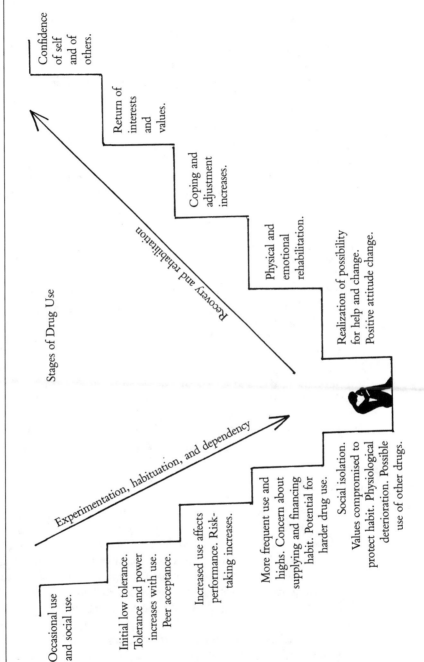

Stages of Drug Use

Experimentation, habituation, and dependency

Recovery and rehabilitation

Occasional use and social use.

Initial low tolerance. Tolerance and power increases with use. Peer acceptance.

Increased use affects performance. Risk-taking increases.

More frequent use and highs. Concern about supplying and financing habit. Potential for harder drug use.

Social isolation. Values compromised to protect habit. Physiological deterioration. Possible use of other drugs.

Realization of possibility for help and change. Positive attitude change.

Physical and emotional rehabilitation.

Coping and adjustment increases.

Return of interests and values.

Confidence of self and of others.

and preoccupation with drug use; to dependency, which may be psychological, physical, or both. **Substance use**, the social, even regular use of drugs without dependency, is widespread. **Abuse** occurs when there is impairment in functioning; the individual's daily living is affected adversely. For adolescents, academics, work, or social life may suffer. Individuals are **drug-dependent** either when they turn to the drug to alleviate psychological pain or when they need the drug to maintain themselves physically. They are **addicted** when the absence of the drug creates physiological withdrawal symptoms (E.J. Smith, 81).

In the early, experimental stage of drug use, adolescents use drugs only occasionally and always with a group of peers. They have a low tolerance and therefore get high fairly easily.

If they progress beyond the early stage, they begin to change their peer group (having fewer nonusing friends); increase their tolerance for drugs and therefore use more for the same effect; begin to become preoccupied with the next high; may begin to lie, feel guilty, hide and protect their supply; decrease their efforts in school; spend increasing amounts of money on drugs; lose interest in their physical appearance; drop all nonusing friends; appear depressed; and display increasingly low self-esteem. Such an adolescent may try unsuccessfully to quit and may begin to use drugs while alone. It is generally believed that the most successful intervention and treatment occurs in this middle stage of drug use, for an individual who has progressed to the late stage has less chance of rehabilitation.

In the latest stage, the drug user is continually preoccupied with the next high, drops out of school, is unable to maintain a job, experiences frequent blackouts (memory loss), loses friends, loses weight and is frequently sick, needs drugs to make it through the day, and accepts all excuses and alibis for dependence.

If the individual progresses to the later stages of drug dependence, the only potentially effective treatment is within an inpatient setting, where the individual can dry out both physically and mentally before therapy begins. More specific information about treatment will be discussed later in this chaper.

Adolescent Drug Use and Attitudes

Although it is difficult to obtain accurate statistics concerning adolescents' use of drugs, survey data reveal at least an approximation of drug use among students. Johnston (79, 81, 83) surveyed large numbers of students in the high school senior classes from 1975 to the present concerning their use of a variety of drugs. His questionnaire asked students to indicate if they had ever used the drug, if they had used the drug within the past thirty days, and if they used the drug daily. Tables 14.1 and 14.2 and Figures 14.2 and 14.3 demonstrate some of his findings.

Use by seniors within previous thirty days. Table 14.1 shows the trends in the use of the drugs within the previous thirty days by senior classes of 1975 through 1984. Note that alcohol is consistently the most used drug, at least when the past thirty days is the time period under question. (For daily use, cigarettes are clearly the most used, as

Table 14.1
Trends in Thirty-Day Prevalence of Sixteen Types of Drugs among High School Seniors

Percent Who Used in Last Thirty Days

	Class of 1975	Class of 1976	Class of 1977	Class of 1978	Class of 1979	Class of 1980	Class of 1981	Class of 1982	Class of 1983	Class of 1984
Approx. N =	(9400)	(15,400)	(17,100)	(17,800)	(15,500)	(15,900)	(17,500)	(17,700)	(16,300)	(15,900)
Marijuana/Hashish	27.1	32.2	35.4	37.1	36.5	33.7	31.6	28.5	27.0	25.2
Inhalants[a]	NA	0.9	1.3	1.5	1.7	1.4	1.5	1.5	1.7	1.9
Inhalants Adjusted[b]	NA	NA	NA	NA	3.1	2.7	2.3	2.5	2.7	2.7
Amyl & Butyl Nitrites[c]	NA	NA	NA	NA	2.4	1.8	1.4	1.1	1.4	1.4
Hallucinogens	4.7	3.4	4.1	3.9	4.0	3.7	3.7	3.4	2.8	2.6
Hallucinogens Adjusted[d]	NA	NA	NA	NA	5.5	4.4	4.4	4.3	3.8	3.6
LSD	2.3	1.9	2.1	2.1	2.4	2.3	2.5	2.4	1.9	1.5
PCP[c]	NA	NA	NA	NA	2.4	1.4	1.4	1.0	1.3	1.6
Cocaine	1.9	2.0	2.9	3.9	5.7	5.2	5.8	5.0	4.9	5.8
Heroin	0.4	0.2	0.3	0.3	0.2	0.2	0.2	0.2	0.2	0.3
Other opiates[e]	2.1	2.0	2.8	2.1	2.4	2.4	2.1	1.8	1.8	1.8
Stimulants[e]	8.5	7.7	8.8	8.7	9.9	12.1	15.8	13.7	12.4	NA
Stimulants Adjusted[ef]	NA	NA	NA	NA	NA	NA	NA	10.7	8.9	8.3
Sedatives[e]	5.4	4.5	5.1	4.2	4.4	4.8	4.6	3.4	3.0	2.3
Barbiturates[e]	4.7	3.9	4.3	3.2	3.2	2.9	2.6	2.0	2.1	1.7
Methaqualone[e]	2.1	1.6	2.3	1.9	2.3	3.3	3.1	2.4	1.8	1.1
Tranquilizers[e]	4.1	4.0	4.6	3.4	3.7	3.1	2.7	2.4	2.5	2.1
Alcohol	68.2	68.3	71.2	72.1	71.8	72.0	70.7	69.7	69.4	67.2
Cigarettes	36.7	38.8	38.4	36.7	34.4	30.5	29.4	30.0	30.3	29.3

Notes: Level of significance of difference between the two most recent classes: s = .05, ss = .01, sss = .001. NA indicates data not available.

[a] Data based on four questionnaire forms. N is four-fifths of N indicated.

[b] Adjusted for underreporting of amyl and butyl nitrites.

[c] Data based on a single questionnaire form. N is one-fifth of N indicated.

[d] Adjusted for underreporting of PCP.

[e] Only drug use which was not under a doctor's orders is included here.

[f] Adjusted for overreporting of the non-prescription stimulants. Data based on three questionnaire forms. N is three-fifths of N indicated.

Source: NIDA, Monitoring the Future Study, 1984.

471

Figure 14.2
Prevalence and Recency of Use of Eleven Types of Drugs, Class of 1983. *Note:*
The brace near the top of a bar indicates the lower and upper limits of the 95%
confidence interval.

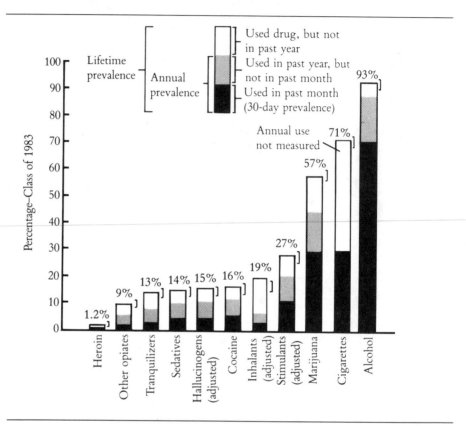

From L. D. Johnston, J. G. Bachman, and P. M. O'Malley. *Student Drug Use in America, 1975–1983.* U.S.
Department of Health and Human Services, Washington, D.C.: National Institute on Drug Abuse, 1983.

Figure 14.3 demonstrates.) From 1975 through 1978 cigarettes were second, but from
1979 through 1981 marijuana was used more than tobacco. Alcohol, cigarettes, and
marijuana are consistently the only drugs used regularly by more than 25 percent of
seniors in high school. Note the trends identified in Table 14.1: the use of marijuana
increased through 1978 and then began to decline; the use of inhalants increased
through 1979 and then began to decline; the use of hallucinogens has fluctuated very
slightly; the use of cocaine has increased slightly; the use of heroine has remained
steady but very slight, with the use of other opiates declining very slightly; the use of
stimulants has increased; the use of all sedatives and tranquilizers has decreased slightly;
the use of alcohol has fluctuated slightly; and the use of cigarettes increased through
1977 and then began to decline.

Figure 14.3
Thirty-Day Prevalence of Daily Use of Eleven Types of Drugs, Class of 1983.

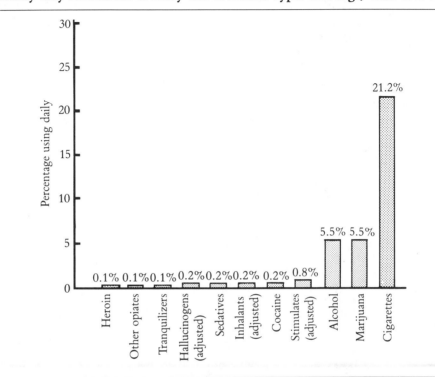

From L. D. Johnston, J. G. Bachman, and P. M. O'Malley. *Student Drug Use in America, 1975–1983.* U.S. Department of Health and Human Services, Washington, D.C.: National Institute on Drug Abuse, 1983.

Figure 14.2 demonstrates the use of drugs by seniors in the class of 1983. The top of each bar indicates the percentage of those who have ever used the drug but not within the past year. These are clearly the experimenters. The second bar indicates the percentage of those who have used the drug in the past year but not in the past month. These too can be called experimenters. Only the bottom bar includes those who have used the drug in the past month, a group that may include both experimenters and regular users.

Daily use. Figure 14.3 demonstrates the daily use by high-school seniors in 1984 of eleven types of drugs. Note that except for cigarettes, marijuana, and alcohol, only one out of a hundred or fewer are involved in daily drug use. The vast majority of high-school students are clearly not abusing drugs, yet the few who are need our careful attention, just as do the other disturbed adolescents we have been discussing in this section.

Table 14.2
Trends in Proportions Disapproving of Drug Use

Q. Do you disapprove of people (who are 18 or older) doing each of the following?[b]	Percent "Disapproving"[a]									
	Class of 1975	Class of 1976	Class of 1977	Class of 1978	Class of 1979	Class of 1980	Class of 1981	Class of 1982	Class of 1983	'82-'83 Change
Try marijuana once or twice	47.0	38.4	33.4	33.4	34.2	39.0	40.0	45.5	46.3	+0.8
Smoke marijuana occasionally	54.8	47.8	44.3	43.5	45.3	49.7	52.6	59.1	60.7	+1.6
Smoke marijuana regularly	71.9	69.5	65.5	67.5	69.2	74.6	77.4	80.6	82.5	+1.9
Try LSD once or twice	82.8	84.6	83.9	85.4	86.6	87.3	86.4	88.8	89.1	+0.3
Take LSD regularly	94.1	95.3	95.8	96.4	96.9	96.7	96.8	96.7	97.0	+0.3
Try cocaine once or twice	81.3	82.4	79.1	77.0	74.7	76.3	74.6	76.6	77.0	+0.4
Take cocaine regularly	93.3	93.9	92.1	91.9	90.8	91.1	90.7	91.5	93.2	+1.7s
Try heroin once or twice	91.5	92.6	92.5	92.0	93.4	93.5	93.5	94.6	94.3	−0.3
Take heroin occasionally	94.8	96.0	96.0	96.4	96.8	96.7	97.2	96.9	96.9	0.0
Take heroin regularly	96.7	97.5	97.2	97.8	97.9	97.6	97.8	97.5	97.7	+0.2
Try amphetamines once or twice	74.8	75.1	74.2	74.8	75.1	75.4	71.1	72.6	72.3	−0.3
Take amphetamines regularly	92.1	92.8	92.5	93.5	94.4	93.0	91.7	92.0	92.6	+0.6
Try barbiturates once or twice	77.7	81.3	81.1	82.4	84.0	83.9	82.4	84.4	83.1	−1.3
Take barbiturates regularly	93.3	93.6	93.0	94.3	95.2	94.4	95.2	94.4	95.1	+0.7
Try one or two drinks of an alcoholic beverage (beer, wine, liquor)	21.6	18.2	15.6	15.6	15.8	16.0	17.2	18.2	18.4	+0.2
Take one or two drinks nearly every day	67.6	68.9	66.8	67.7	68.3	69.0	69.1	69.9	68.9	−1.0
Take four or five drinks nearly every day	88.7	90.7	88.4	90.2	91.7	90.8	91.8	90.9	90.0	−0.9
Have five or more drinks once or twice each weekend	60.3	58.6	57.4	56.2	56.7	55.6	55.5	58.8	56.6	−2.2
Smoke one or more packs of cigarettes per day	67.5	65.9	66.4	67.0	70.3	70.8	69.9	69.4	70.8	+1.4
Approx. N =	(2677)	(3234)	(3582)	(3686)	(3221)	(3261)	(3610)	(3651)	(3341)	

Note: Level of significance of difference between the two most recent classes: s = .05, ss = .01, sss = .001.
[a] Answer alternatives were: (1) Don't disapprove, (2) Disapprove, and (3) Strongly disapprove. Percentages are shown for categories (2) and (3) combined.
[b] The 1975 question asked about people who are "20 or older."

474

Attitudes toward illicit drugs. Although the majority of high-school seniors drink and more than one-quarter use marijuana or cigarettes regularly, the majority disapprove of even trying the more serious illicit drugs and of regular use of all nonprescription drugs, including marijuana, alcohol, and cigarettes (Table 14.2). This leads to the conclusion that the small numbers of adolescents who do use the more serious drugs are probably not doing so out of peer pressure but rather are likely to be using to escape from relatively serious disturbances in their lives.

Alcohol and marijuana. Norman (81), in his extensive survey of adolescents of all ages, found that one out of four teenagers drinks more than once a week, that 40 percent smoke marijuana regularly, and that 70 percent have tried marijuana at least once. Most of them believe that their parents know they drink, but only 29 percent report that their parents know about the marijuana use. Fifty percent of them lie to their parents about marijuana, but not about alcohol, most likely because alcohol is a more acceptable drug to the adult generation than is marijuana. The majority (better than 60 percent) report believing that alcohol and marijuana are bad for health, but significant numbers of them use them anyway.

THE LEGAL DRUGS

Nicotine

Dangers. Despite overwhelming evidence of the harmful effects of nicotine, millions of adults and adolescents smoke cigarettes regularly. In the short run, nicotine is both a central nervous system stimulant and a sedative, used for increased sociability and calm. Smoking increases the risk of heart disease, lung cancer, chronic bronchitis, emphysema, and all other respiratory diseases and is implicated in a shortened life span. Smoking contributes to 300,000 deaths in the United States each year, and pregnant women endanger their babies by smoking (J.D. Miller, 79; *Smoking and Health,* 79; *Women and Smoking,* 80).

Extent of use. Despite the known dangers of smoking, 83 percent of the population at least try it by the age of 25 (J.D. Miller, 79), and 27 percent of high-school students and 16 percent of junior-high-school students smoke seven or more cigarettes per day (G.M. Smith, 80; Johnston, 81). Between 1975 and 1984 the overall incidence of cigarette smoking among high-school seniors dropped (Table 14.1), with boys smoking significantly less and girls smoking significantly more. More specifically, between 1968 and 1979, the percentage of boys smoking regularly dropped from 31 percent to 19 percent, while the percentage of girls smoking rose from 19 percent to 26 percent. And not only is the incidence of smoking rising among girls, but girls tend to smoke more heavily than boys (Johnston, 81). Although the reasons for the increase in smoking by girls have not been documented, it is hypothesized that changing sex-roles may be influencing girls to demonstrate their increasing autonomy, and smoking is seen as one way to do so (Urberg, 81).

Smoking is seen as one way to demonstrate increasing autonomy.

Adolescents, like adults, do not smoke out of ignorance of the dangers. Johnston (81) found that about 70 percent of high school seniors disapprove of smoking a pack or more of cigarettes per day (Table 14.2). Of teenagers who smoke, 78 percent believe that smoking can cause cancer and heart disease, 77 percent believe it is better not to start smoking than to have to quit, and 84 percent believe that smoking is habit forming. They smoke anyway.

Characteristics of smokers. Numerous researchers have investigated the personality characteristics of smokers with generally consistent results from both adult and adolescent populations. Smokers tend to score higher on measures of extraversion and lower on measures of agreeableness and strength of character than nonsmokers (G.M. Smith, 80). Smokers are more tense, aggressive, rebellious, frank, crude, and happy-go-lucky than nonsmokers. They are less obedient and conventional and have poorer impulse control (G.M. Smith, 80; Brook, 81).

Reasons for smoking.   Adolescents begin smoking for a variety of reasons. Perhaps the personal fable we discussed earlier makes the adolescent vulnerable to ignoring the danger signs and trying smoking as one way of expressing emerging adulthood. Urberg (81) studied 155 middle-class adolescents and found that boys were smoking as a means of social coping while girls were smoking as a sign of rebellion and autonomy. Parental behavior and attitude toward smoking are especially important. Parents who smoke or condone smoking are more likely to have children who smoke than are parents who themselves do not smoke and who clearly express their negative attitudes toward smoking. Chassin (81) found that smoking is related to self-concept. In this study, 175 adolescent subjects rated themselves, their ideal dates, and their perceptions of smokers. Those whose self-concepts and concepts of their ideal dates matched their perceptions of smokers were most likely to be smokers themselves, and nonsmokers who had self-concepts and ideal dates that matched their perceptions of smokers were most likely to start smoking. Chassin concluded that smoking is adopted because it fits with self-perceptions of being tough, group-oriented, and disobedient.

Regardless of the reasons adolescents smoke, the fact that so many of them do despite their knowledge of the dangers clearly indicates that smoking prevention must entail more than the information about the harmful effects that too often comprise the only content of smoking prevention programs. Smoking prevention, like the prevention of other drug abuse, must include the development of a positive nonsmoking self-concept and prosocial skills that preclude the image of smoking as being cool or grown up. We will look at approaches to prevention in more detail later in this chapter.

Alcohol

Approximately 70 percent of high school seniors have used alcohol within the last thirty days (Table 14.1; Figure 14.1), making alcohol the most used drug by adolescents.

A drinking society.   Ours is a drinking society; we drink to celebrate, socialize, relax, honor one another, and escape; and children are exposed early to alcohol in its various forms. Although antismoking campaigns succeeded in removing cigarette advertising from television, alcohol advertising remains. On television, hard-working men enjoy a beer after a day's work or sport, and wine is a natural part of a romantic evening. Alcohol is also a part of our history: beer and wine were used some 8400 years ago, and our written history contains reports of drunken behavior as early as 2500 B.C. (Blum, 69).

Drinking has been, for as long as history records, a familiar, socially acceptable behavior, with today's consumption the highest ever. It is a part of growing up, with age limits determining maturity (O'Gorman, 76). Adolescents and adults use the drinking age as the single most important hallmark of having achieved adult status.

We drink to celebrate, socialize, relax, honor one another, and escape.

Parents tend to condone drinking when they strongly disapprove of the use of marijuana, even though the dangers of alcohol are more clearly established than are the dangers of marijuana (DeLuca, 81).

Effects of alcohol. Although alcohol appears to affect different people differently, it is basically a central nervous system depressant, the effects of which increase in direct proportion to the amount of alcohol in the blood. An initial euphoria is produced as a result of the depressing of inhibitions; this is followed by poor motor coordination, dulling of the senses, impairment of the perceptions, time distortions, inability to reason, and memory loss. Abusers may experience blackouts (complete memory loss), and continual abuse causes impairment of brain function, cirrhosis of the liver, malnutrition, coma, and death. Alcohol is addictive, both mentally and physically, and withdrawal can be painful.

The price of alcohol misuse is high. Cirrhosis of the liver is the sixth most common cause of death in the United States, and 95 percent of these deaths are alcohol related. Estimates of all alcohol-related deaths range to 205,000 per year (Noble, 78; De Luca, 81). It is estimated that 60 percent or more of fatal auto crashes are alcohol related and that $50 billion are lost every year in lost production, medical costs, motor-vehicle accidents, violent crime, social responses to alcohol problems, and fire losses associated with problem drinking (De Luca, 81). The costs and long-term problems are enormous, yet adults and adolescents continue to drink, apparently because the immediate reward of feeling good is more important than the long-term negative consequences.

Adolescent alcohol use. Virtually all adolescents have at least tried alcohol by the end of adolescence. In the seventh grade, 60 percent of the boys and 47 percent of the girls have tried drinking, and by the twelfth grade 95 percent of the boys and 92 percent of the girls have indulged (Donovan, 78; Johnston, 81). Students not planning to go to college drink more than the college-bound; urban students drink more than those in rural areas; and students in the northeast and north-central states drink more than those in the south and west; but the differences are relatively minor (*Alcohol and Health*, 74; Rachal, 75; Johnston, 81).

Fortunately, most adolescents drink temperately, either in order to induce a pleasant relaxation or because alcohol is a part of a congenial social activity (Forslund, 78), and do not become problem drinkers. Problem drinkers drink heavily and frequently and are prone to having difficulty with adults or peers as a result of their drinking. An unfortunate number of adolescents display such problem-drinking behavior. Donovan (78) found that 23 percent of the boys and 15 percent of the girls in grades 7 through 12 drank heavily; Johnston (81) found that 17.5 percent of high-school seniors could be so classified; and Rachal (83) found 21 percent of boys and 8.9 percent of girls in grades 10 through 12 could be so classified. It seems clear that about 20 percent of high school students drink often enough and heavily enough to be classified as problem drinkers, and the number of adolescent problem drinkers may be even higher. All studies report on students in schools, yet the drinking rate for dropouts is even higher (*Alcohol and Health*, 74).

Heavy adolescent drinkers have been found to have distinct personality characteristics. They seem to value independence and heavy social activity, are impulsive, do poorly in school, are involved in other deviant behavior (cutting classes, cheating, driving too fast, being sexually active, using other drugs), and are vulnerable to peer pressure. They often seem exuberant and outgoing but are, beneath the bravado, pessimistic, irresponsible, and cynical. They have problems getting along with their parents, who are likely to be problem drinkers themselves, and with other adults and their peers (Moos, 76; Jessor, 77; Margulies, 77; Donovan, 78; Eisterhold, 79; Braucht, 83; Rachal, 83). For problem drinkers, alcohol provides a readily accessible means of escaping from a troubled existence.

Drinking usually begins at home, under adult supervision, but gradually moves out of the home to places where adults are not present (*Alcohol and Health*, 74).

Adolescents begin drinking out of curiosity, in the context of a condoning peer group, as a means of testing the waters of the adult world (Kandel, 80b). Drinking can be viewed as an integral aspect of growing up, as ". . . part of adolescent development as a whole, that is, as an integral aspect of personality, social and behavioral change during adolescence" (Jessor, 80). For those who drink in moderation, drinking can be seen as a transitional behavior, but for those who become abusers, drinking is clearly more than a symbol of approaching adulthood.

Because alcohol is such an integral part of modern American society, prevention efforts are currently being directed toward helping adolescents develop responsible drinking habits. Since virtually all will at least experiment with alcohol, abstinence is an unrealistic goal, but temperence and responsibility are not. For example, some alcohol education programs encourage young people who will be out drinking together to name one individual who agrees not to drink that particular evening; this person becomes the driver for the evening.

THE ILLEGAL DRUGS

Although some of the substances included in the following discussion are produced legally, their use by the general public without a medical prescription is illegal; therefore, they are included here rather than in the preceding discussion of the legal drugs nicotine and alcohol.

CNS Depressants

Substances that slow down the activity of the central nervous system include the inhalants, the tranquilizers, and the sedatives.

Inhalants. A number of substances manufactured for legitimate use produce a mild intoxication when inhaled. Although fewer than 2 percent of graduating seniors have used inhalants in the past month (Table 14.1) and only 12 percent have ever sniffed, the inhalants pose a serious threat to physical health. The solvents most often inhaled include glue, nail polish remover, gasoline, cleaning fluid, lighter fluid, antifreeze, and ethanol and other alcohols, all of which contain hydrocarbons. The immediate effect is one of euphoria and dizziness, often followed by headaches and vomiting. Long-term use can result in damage to the internal organs and perhaps even brain damage. The solvents are readily available to anyone, which probably accounts for the fact that users of the inhalants tend to be young, sometimes as young as 8 or 9. The typical abuser is male, a poor student, depressed, anxious, alienated, vulnerable to peer pressure, and the product of a dysfunctional family and poor parent-child relationships (Barnes, 79; Cohen, 79; Johnston, 79, 81; *Committee,* 82).

Tranquilizers. The mild tranquilizers (Librium, Miltown, and Valium) are prescribed as much or more than any other drug, and their popularity has led to the overmanufacture of them. Those not prescribed legitimately find their way into the streets. About 3 percent of high-school seniors used the tranquilizers within the past month (Table 14.1), and very few adolescents abuse them. Their misuse and abuse are far greater in the adult population.

Sedatives.   The sedatives produce effects that range from mild sedation to depression, impaired motor functioning, unconsciousness, and even death. **PCP** (phencyclide), commonly known as angel dust, is a highly dangerous and unpredictable drug. Because of its unpredictability it is often classified as a hallucinogen, but it was developed as an animal tranquilizer; in humans it produces everything from a pleasant dreamlike state to paranoia and psychosis. Those who take it often become aggressive and may lose body control and the ability to sense danger. It can, especially when combined with other drugs, produce coma and death. Although there is not a lot of research concerning its use, users tend to be young and already somewhat aggressive; only a small number of high-school seniors have ever used the drug (Pittel, 79; Simonds, 79; Johnston, 83).

Methaqualone (commonly known as Quaaludes or Ludes) is a nonbarbiturate sedative that produces a sedative high. Because it is not a barbiturate, adolescents often mistakenly think that it is not addictive; they couldn't be more wrong. Its use among high school students was on the rise from 1975 (5.1 percent) to 1981 (7.6 percent), making it one of the few drugs that has seemed to gain in popularity (Smith, 79; Johnston, 81).

Barbiturates.   Over 2500 different barbiturates can be divided into two categories: long-acting barbiturates are those sleeping pills and sedatives that are prescribed for nighttime use. They are mildly addictive but not nearly so dangerous as the powerfully addictive short-acting barbiturates, which produce the most severe withdrawal symptoms of all the drugs, including heroin (Smith, 79). Barbiturates produce everything from mild euphorias to coma and death. Tolerance builds rapidly, and the potential for physical and psychological addiction is extremely high. The barbiturates are most dangerous when used in combination with alcohol; in this combination, blood pressure and respiration may lower to the point of death—more than 5000 people die this way annually. Although 15 percent of high-school seniors have tried barbiturates, daily use and abuse in the adolescent population remain low (Smith, 79; Johnston, 79, 81).

CNS Stimulants

A second major category of drugs are those that stimulate, or speed up, the central nervous system. The two most common stimulants in use today are caffeine and nicotine, and both, of course, are readily available to everyone, including children. Stimulants comprise the only category of drug that is used more by females than by males (Johnston, 81). The amphetamines (synthetically produced stimulants) and cocaine (a natural stimulant) are the most widely used after caffeine and nicotine.

Amphetamines.   The amphetamines are produced in many varieties, the most common of which are Benzedrine (''bennies''), Dexedrine (''dex''), and Methedrine (''meth''). Street references to amphetamines include ''speed,'' ''copilot,'' and ''pep pills.'' Although the amphetamines can be injected, they are most often ingested in the form of pills. They are legally prescribed to suppress appetite, restore and maintain high levels of energy, and elevate mood. When taken in greater doses, they may produce restlessness, dizziness, insomnia, headache, nausea, diarrhea, vomiting, and even convulsions, coma, cerebral hemorrhage, and death. Although physical dependence is unlikely, psychological dependence develops rather quickly, and there is considerable physical danger. Abusers are likely to be multiple drug users, often alternating amphetamines and barbiturates (''runs and crashes''). Continual abusers (''speed freaks'') frequently display poor judgment, intellectual impairment, aggressive behavior, lack of coordination, hallucinations, irritability, and paranoia (Brook, 74; *Drugs*, 78; Ellinwood, 79). Use of stimulants other than cocaine by high-school seniors rose between 1975 and 1981, with 15.8 percent of the seniors class of 1981 reporting use within the previous thirty days (Table 14.1). That figure has since dropped to 12.4 percent.

Cocaine.   Cocaine (''coke,'' ''C'', ''snow,'' ''uptown lady'') was isolated from the coca shrub *(Erythroxylon coca)* in Germany about two hundred years ago. Prior to that time, an alkaloid derived from the plant was used in aristocratic tribal ceremonies by the Incas in Peru and Bolivia. When German scientists isolated it, it was used medically as an anesthetic and antidepressant, and Sigmund Freud at one time believed it to have magical medical effects. He became disenchanted with it, however, when a close friend of his suffered hallucinations and paranoia (Grinspoon, 76, 79; Johnston, 81).

Cocaine, which can be injected but is more often inhaled, stimulates the central nervous system, producing effects like those of the amphetamines. Euphoria and confidence reduce pain and fatigue, with excitement and alertness leading to hallucinations, convulsions, and, in large doses, death. Tolerance builds quickly, and the potential for psychological dependence is high. Cocaine has been increasing in popularity since the early 1970s, especially among upper-middle-class youth and young adults. A particularly popular method of use is freebasing, in which ether is used to cut out additives. The purified cocaine is then inhaled but has the more dramatic effects of injection (Dye, 83). The drug is extremely expensive; therefore few adolescents have become abusers (Connell, 77), but a significant number of high-school seniors (16.5 percent in 1981) have experimented with it (Grinspoon, 79; Johnston, 81).

Hallucinogens

The hallucinogens produce distortions of perception. Although marijuana is thought to have some nausea- and pain-reducing effects in cancer patients on chemotherapy, hallucinogens have no known medical uses; their use is therefore strictly recreational. Marijuana, a relatively mild drug; mescaline, a slightly more potent drug; and LSD, a far more potent one, are the most popular of the hallucinogens.

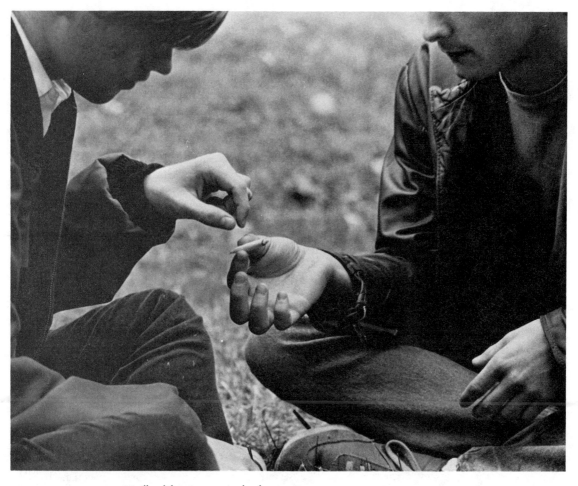

No illegal drug is more popular than marijuana.

Marijuana. No drug has created more controversy than marijuana, and no other illegal drug is so popular and widely used. One-fourth of all adults and 40 percent of all teenagers have at least tried marijuana, and although regular use may be beginning to decline slightly, first experimentation is beginning at earlier and earlier ages (Petersen, 79; Johnston, 81; *Committee,* 82). In 1981, 59 percent of the senior class had at least tried marijuana, and about 7 percent were using it daily (Johnston, 81). The popularity, widespread use, and failure to identify long-term negative effects of marijuana have even led to a movement to legalize its use in small quantities: President Carter, for example, in a 1977 address, suggested decriminalization of possession of up to one ounce.

Marijuana is derived from the Indian hemp plant *Cannabis sativa,* the use of which has been controversial since ancient times. The strength of marijuana can vary considerably, depending on the concentration of THC (tetrahydrocannabinol), which is affected by climate, types of cultivation, and manner of preparation. The most potent form of marijuana is known as hashish or hash. In mild doses, marijuana produces a pleasant relaxation, some relaxing of inhibitions, increased self-confidence, and an illusion of enhanced awareness, effects not unlike those of mild doses of alcohol. In fact, many adolescents consider the use of marijuana to be a safe alternative to the use of alcohol; their parents generally disagree, probably because they are familiar with alcohol but not with marijuana. In more potent doses, perceptual distortions occur, including a heightened awareness of color and sound and a distortion of time. Physical effects include an increased heart rate, reddening of the eyes, and dry mouth. In especially high doses, delusions and hallucinations may occur. In addition, the expectation of the user seems to alter the effect. A user who expects to experience altered perceptions is more likely to do so than one who expects no changes. Marijuana is not physically addictive, nor does it produce aggressive behavior or lead to the use of harder drugs. Although it has some potential for psychological dependence, we simply do not yet know if there are any dangerous long-term effects from its use. There may be some possible effects on lung function, and genetic and reproductive functions, but research has so far failed to find conclusive evidence (*Committee*, 82).

The greatest dangers in the use of marijuana may be in the false sense of well-being and awareness that its users perceive and in the potential for adolescents to use it as an escape from the tasks of living. Users are not, in fact, more aware of their surroundings, as they may falsely believe, and a cavalier attitude toward driving may result. Marijuana and driving do not mix any better than drinking and driving do (R. Jones, 77; Pace, 81). Furthermore, the use of any drug, including marijuana, to escape life's problems is counterproductive in that the problems multiply while the user fails to learn to cope with them (Pollin, 80). A further danger comes not from the marijuana itself, but from other chemicals that may be mixed with it. In an effort to destroy marijuana fields, for example, many of them have been sprayed with a poisonous weed killer. But the fields that were sprayed may have been harvested anyway, with the processed marijuana posing a serious danger to the user. Other marijuana has been found to be laced with other poisons (strychnine, for example, which is a deadly killer).

In studying the personality characteristics of marijuana users, we must separate experimenters and occasional users from chronic, heavy users. All the research indicates that experimenters and occasional social users are no different from nonusers and are not maladjusted (Smith, 78; Jessor, 79; Petersen, 79; Kandel, 80a,b). It is only the heavy (that is, daily) users who display disturbed characteristics: poor adjustment, hostility, impulsiveness, irresponsibility, pessimism, poor academic achievement, alienation, and avoidance of problems, characteristics that are common to abusers of alcohol and other drugs as well. Heavy marijuana use is also associated with multiple drug use and abuse, but it is clear that experimentation and occasional use do not lead to heavy use. Adolescents who become abusers display negative personality characteristics before they begin using marijuana, alcohol, and any other substance that alters their psychological world.

Mescaline. Mescaline, the active ingredient of the mescal bud of the peyote cactus, is more potent than marijuana and less so than LSD. It has long been a part of some Native American rituals, and it creates a mild euphoria, an intensification and distortion of perception, and occasional sadness and detachment. It is used by only a very few adolescents (*Drugs*, 78; *Committee*, 82).

LSD. The strongest of the popular hallucinogens (unless PCP is classified here) is LSD (lysergic acid diethylamide), an odorless, tasteless, white crystalline powder that is soluble in water and highly potent. LSD is ingested as tablets or licked from impregnated paper. Children and young adolescents have inadvertently taken LSD disguised as candy on stickers of cartoon characters. LSD causes chemical disturbances in brain functioning resulting in time distortions, visual hallucinations, an inaccurate sense of achieving new insights, and a sense of unity with others—people, animals, and inanimate objects. The experience may range from a general euphoria to a seemingly mystical experience, and high doses may produce bizarre and frightening illusions and some psychoses. LSD is neither physically nor psychologically addictive, but users may experience flashbacks (recurrences of the LSD experience in the absence of the drug). The long-term effects of LSD are still unknown, and whereas chronic users report feeling more relaxed and open to experience, observers report them to be very passive and lacking in good judgment (''blown mind'') (Blum, 79; Jacobs, 79; *Committee*, 82).

The use of LSD grew in the late 1960s and early 1970s, probably in reaction to the social upheaval of the time, but has been declining ever since. In 1981 13 percent of seniors in high school had tried LSD, but there were almost no regular users (Johnston, 81).

Narcotics

The final category of drugs, the narcotics, includes the natural narcotics morphine, codeine, and heroin, which are derived from opium, and the synthetic narcotic methadone.

Opium comes from the fluid in the seed pod of the opium poppy *(Papaver Somniferum)*. From it is derived **morphine**, which is used medically as a highly potent and effective, but highly addictive, pain killer. **Heroin**, which has no legitimate use, is synthesized from morphine. Although heroin can be sniffed or injected under the skin, the effects are not as strong as when it is injected directly into the bloodstream (''mainlined''); addicts therefore prefer to mainline heroin.

Heroin Heroin diminishes physical and mental pain without creating excessive drowsiness. A warm rush is followed by lethargy, relief from tension, euphoria, and dulling of sensibilities. The user feels peaceful and confident. These effects make heroin especially appealing to people who face unpleasant and highly tense personal problems, for it effectively shuts out pain and makes life more tolerable (Johnston, 81; *Committee*, 82). An exjunkie (former heroin addict) noted that heroin helped him to survive the ghetto by dulling his senses so that he didn't notice the putrid smells and the ever-present sirens.

In too great a dosage, however, heroin slows respiration and thereby starves the brain of oxygen. Sleep, coma, even death can result. Heroin tolerance builds rapidly, and the drug is highly addictive both physically and psychologically. The pleasant effects begin to wear off after about four hours, and users become irritable as the pain they were escaping begins to return. Once individuals are addicted, physical withdrawal symptoms begin about twelve hours after an injection. At this point, users begin yawning, sweating, and sniffling, and their eyes begin to water. After about twenty-four hours, they begin to twitch and shake, feel cold, get muscle cramps, vomit, and convulse (Johnston, 81; *Committee*, 82).

Although not all users become addicts, the addictive potential of heroin is extremely high, and a $200-per-day habit is quite common. Obtaining the drug becomes a preoccupation, and addicts frequently turn to crime to support their habits (Johnston, 81; *Committee*, 82).

Although adolescent experimentation with heroin spread in the late 1960s, use by 12- through 17-year-olds has been declining from a high of 6 percent in 1972 to 1 percent or less in 1979 to 1981; most of the few who do try it do so only once or twice, and addiction is a problem for only a very small number (Johnston, 79, 81).

Like abusers of other dangerous drugs, heroin addicts are usually depressed, unable to cope, and self-destructive, with low self-esteem. They come from dysfunctional families where they have experienced parental rejection and little supervision, and their parents also are likely to abuse alcohol and other drugs (Austin, 78; Woody, 79; Zinberg, 79).

Codeine.   Codeine is a pain reliever and cough suppressant that is legally prescribed in both liquid and pill form. It can be abused and is therefore controlled through pharmacies. It is not usually included in studies of drug abuse.

Methadone.   Methadone is a synthetic substitute for heroin that is dispensed legally through drug-abuse clinics. Although it satisfies the heroin addict, there is a great deal of controversy surrounding its use. Critics of methadone treatment argue that it does not rehabilitate the addict but merely provides a new, legal addiction in place of the illegal one. Supporters of methadone treatment argue that the drug is not as dangerous as heroin and, because it is obtained legally, does not create the potential for criminal behavior that heroin does. It is not available on the street, and few adolescents are likely to have experience with it.

THE DEVELOPMENT OF DRUG USE

Sequence in Drug Use

Many adults believe, inaccurately, that the use of marijuana leads to the use of harder, more dangerous drugs. That the majority of marijuana users do not progress to harder drugs has been amply demonstrated (*Report*, 72; Single, 74; Petersen, 79; Johnston,

81; *Committee,* 82). Furthermore, Kandel and her associates (80a,b) have done extensive longitudinal studies of over 6000 high-school students to determine, firstly, whether or not there is a sequence in adolescent drug use and, secondly, if use of one drug leads to the use of others. They found that there is a clear sequence in adolescent drug use, but that although use of hard drugs is *preceded* by use of alcohol, nicotine, and marijuana, it is not *caused* by their use.

The legal drugs first.   Kandel found that adolescents generally begin experimenting with the legal drugs alcohol and nicotine, and that most first try beer and wine. Smoking is frequently associated with drinking, and smoking is almost always followed by drinking, but drinking without smoking is not necessarily followed by smoking. After beer, wine, and cigarettes, some adolescents progress to hard liquor. The combined use of cigarettes and hard liquor is most predictive of use of the illicit drugs. Marijuana is the first (and usually the last) illicit drug tried. The few who go on to harder drugs usually follow a sequence in their use as well: first come stimulants, then hallucinogens, then depressants, then cocaine, and finally heroin.

> Although the data show a clear sequence in drug use, a particular drug does not invariably lead to other drugs higher up in the sequence. Many youths stop at a particular stage and do not progress further; many regress to lower drugs. (Kandel, 80b, p. 444)

This finding is supported by the percentages of adolescents who have ever tried any of the substances (Figure 14.2). Although 92.6 percent of seniors in 1984 had tried alcohol, 69.7 percent had tried cigarettes, and 54.9 percent had tried marijuana, only 27.9 percent went on to stimulants, and only 1.3 percent progressed so far as to experiment with heroin. Drug users begin with beer and wine, progress to tobacco and hard liquor, and then go to other drugs, but the connection is not a casual one. By far the greatest use of substances by adolescents is of alcohol, cigarettes, and marijuana.

Beyond marijuana.   Those who progress beyond these are in the minority and are likely to be predisposed to deviance not only in their use of substances but in other areas of their behavior as well (Stumphauzer, 80; Biddle, 80; Kandel, 80a, 80b; *Committee,* 82). Hundleby (82) investigated drug use across the full domain of adolescent behavior and found that seven behaviors correlated positively with drug use. These were sexual behavior, general delinquency, school misbehavior, poor social behavior, poor study and reading habits, poor school achievement, and poor domestic behavior.

Causes of Drug Use

As we have seen, the vast majority of adolescents will experiment with drugs, at least with alcohol, tobacco, and marijuana. These experimenters must not be considered in the same category as those who regularly use drugs and who may occasionally or regularly abuse them. We live in a drug culture, and with drugs readily available, it is not surprising that adolescents, who we know are curious, egocentric, testing adult limits, and looking for fun with friends, will experiment with them. What we are concerned with here are the causes of regular drug use and abuse among adolescents. The literature on this subject is vast and very confusing, with different studies attributing adolescent drug use to a variety of causal agents.

In an extensive review of the literature, Capuzzi (83) identified **social determinants** of alcohol and marijuana use (including parental influence, religious affiliation, peer influence, and school influence) and **personal determinants** (including low esteem, rebelliousness, adventuresomeness, impulsivity, independence, and low trust). He further identified the differences in causation for males and females. We will explore each of the determinants Capuzzi found in the literature and add additional research findings that support each one.

Family influence. The literature is replete with studies that attribute drug use and abuse to family factors. Goodwin (76, 79) investigated the possibility that the connection between alcoholic parents and an alcoholic child is a genetic one, and although it was demonstrated that children of alcoholic parents who are adopted into nonalcoholic families still have a 25 percent chance of becoming alcoholic, the findings were considered inconclusive. Much more of the literature investigating family factors concerns such things as parental alcohol and drug use, parental warmth and closeness to their children, and parental child-rearing practices (that is, democratic, autocratic, or *laissez-faire*). Capuzzi (83) noted that parental alcohol use is related to adolescent alcohol use, that adolescent drug users feel rejected and distant from their parents, and that *laissez-faire* and autocratic families have a higher incidence of drug use than democratic families.

Other researchers who have found the relationship between the parent and the adolescent to be the primary factor in adolescent drug use include Barnes (77), Evans (79), Mitchell (79), Mercer (80), Tudor (80), Brook (81), Dembo (81), Glynn (81), Svobodny (82), Rees (83), Johnson (84), and McDermott (84). It appears that the family influence is greatest on the use of alcohol and tobacco, and less on the use of marijuana, although strong opposition to the use of marijuana by parents tends to lead to less use by children. Parents who themselves use alcohol and tobacco as well as prescription drugs (especially amphetamines, barbiturates, and tranquilizers) are more likely to have children who use drugs. Parental warmth and positive control are positively correlated with absence of abuse, as they have been shown to be with absence of disturbance and delinquency.

Peer influence. The second most strongly supported causative factor in adolescent drug use appears to be relationships with peers. Peer influence has been found to be clearly influential in establishing and maintaining substance involvement. It has been found responsible for initial marijuana use (Brook, 80; Kandel, 80a,b; Glynn, 81), as predictive of smoking behavior (Evans, 79; McCaul, 82), as reinforcing of drinking, as support for continued use of drugs and alcohol (users tend to associate with other users) (Huba, 79; Dembo, 81), and as responsible for the introduction to multiple drug use (Capuzzi, 83). Brook (80) found that peers are *not* the cause of initiation into marijuana use once personality, family, and demographic factors are controlled. Peers *correlate* with drug use because both peers and drugs are heavily influenced by personality and family attributes.

School influence.   Although the school has not been found to cause drug use, it also has not been effective in preventing or stopping it. Schools are all too often either autocratic or *laissez-faire*, and, as with parenting, neither is effective in promoting the healthy problem solving and social characteristics that adolescents need to resist use. Drug education, furthermore, has consisted primarily of facts and scare tactics that not only are ineffective in themselves, but also contribute to the school's lack of credibility in the adolescents' eyes (Capuzzi, 83).

Socioeconomic status.   One final social characteristic bears mention. Adolescents from the lower socioeconomic class are more often alcohol and drug users and abusers than are adolescents from the more affluent groups (Goodman, 83). However, as we have noted previously, socioeconomic status cannot be isolated from family and other characteristics, and the fact that most economically disadvantaged students do not become abusers effectively rules out socioeconomic status as a primary causal factor in drug use.

Personality factors.   Personality factors have been associated with drug use. Adolescdents use drugs: (1) because they believe that drug use is pleasurable and that it will reduce emotional pain and boredom; (2) as a result of low self-esteem and low expectation of achievement; (3) because they lack impulse control and are highly adventuresome and independent; and (4) as a way to achieve inclusion (Capuzzi, 83).

> The problems of adolescent drug abusers emerge because of the inadequacy of their inner resources to master the normal difficulties of adolescence. Drugs, then, provide a way of avoiding the dilemmas of adolescence, making unbearable feelings bearable. (E.J. Smith, 81, p. 322)

These characteristics bear considerable similarity to those of disturbed and delinquent adolescents. What is not clear is the extent to which these characteristics are influenced by heredity, family interactions, and social circumstances outside the family.

Sex differences.   Finally, there appears to be some difference in the causative factors associated with male versus female drug use. In his review of the literature, Capuzzi (83) found that males use and abuse drugs (except for tobacco) more than females, with twice as many being problem drinkers and daily marijuana users. These males exhibited uncontrolled impulsivity and extraversion, sensitivity to criticism, an inability to maintain personal relationships, and an overemphasis on masculinity, including a need to accentuate feelings of power. Females apparently are socialized toward responsible use, but female users were found to be submissive, rebellious, sensitive to criticism, hostile, unpredictable, impulsive, depressed, self-negating, and distrustful. Holroyd (80) concluded that male heavy users who are impulsive and curious and female heavy users who display achievement needs have rejected their cultural stereotypes; while male nonusers concerned with conventional achievement and female nonusers who are nurturant typify the stereotypes. Probably due to recent changes in sex-role expectations, it is unlikely that consensus will be found when male and female drug use are compared.

Making sense of contradictory findings. Because of the contradictory findings in the literature concerning the causes of drug abuse, Bry (82) hypothesized that drug use is in fact the result of the number of causative factors present rather than one alone, that the "extent of drug use is an increasing function of the number of diverse etiological variables instead of any particular set of them" (p. 274). The factors chosen for study with almost 2000 adolescent subjects were grades, affiliation with religion, age of first independent use of alcohol, psychological distress, and perception of parental love. As the number of risk factors increased, the extent of drug use, as measured by a Substance Use Index, increased as well. This study makes the findings reported in the literature complementary rather than contradictory. In other words, an adolescent who comes from an unsupportive and dysfunctional family, in which one or both parents abuse drugs, and who is an underachiever, hangs around with drug users, is not affiliated religiously, is from the lower socioeconomic class, and is likely to be impulsive and have low self-esteem, is at considerable risk of drug abuse. An adolescent with a democratic, non-drug-abusing family of the upper socioeconomic class, who is doing well in school, has non-drug-using friends, and is confident and self-assured is at very low risk. The large numbers of adolescents who fall between these two extremes vary in their risk of drug use and abuse depending on the number of risk factors in their lives.

TREATMENT AND PREVENTION OF DRUG DEPENDENCY

The discussions of treatment and prevention of emotional disorders and of delinquency in the previous two chapters apply to the treatment and prevention of drug dependency as well, just as the causative factors leading to each kind of problem are remarkably similar. In addition, we will look specifically at treatment and prevention of drug abuse.

Treatment

A person who has become dependent on drugs is unlikely to get free of that dependence without help. E.J. Smith (81) delineates six different approaches to treatment: the punitive, the medical-psychiatric, the communal, the religious, the chemotherapeutic, and the community-based.

Punitive. In the punitive approach, the individual is imprisoned. While it is true that such people may be kept drug-free while in prison, it is also overwhelmingly clear that they are unlikely to be rehabilitated and that when they return to society they will return to drug abuse as well.

Medical-psychiatric. In the medical-psychiatric approach the individual is first detoxified, or given medical care during physical and psychological withdrawal, and then is treated through either individual or family therapy. Individual therapy has been demonstrated to be effective only when used in conjunction with other treatment (for example, methadone, self-help, or job training) (Wesson, 79). The drug-dependent person apparently needs considerably more than psychotherapy alone. Family therapy is used for the same reasons that it is used with emotional disturbances and delinquency: the problem is a family rather than an individual issue. In the case of the drug-dependent adolescent, the young person may be distracting energy and attention from other family problems and may therefore be unknowingly encouraged by the family to continue the distracting behavior. Only in family therapy can these mitigating problems surface and be dealt with. In adolescent-treatment units in hospitals, drug and alcohol dependency are treated through individual, group, and family therapy combined with a strong recreational and educational program.

Communal. Communal treatment refers to structured residential therapeutic communities. In these communities, recovering users live with exusers in a group home; they are under group pressure and support to remain drug free and to change their destructive patterns of behavior; and they receive educational and employment opportunities by which to develop positive behaviors in the community and when they return to society. The treatment is intense, so much so that only about 10 to 15 percent of all who are admitted complete the program. Those who do tend to remain clean and out of trouble five years later (De Leon, 79).

Religious. Religious treatment stresses the sin of abuse and focuses on religious training. Very little research or emphasis in current treatment programs is on religious treatment.

Chemotherapeutic. Chemotherapeutic treatment is the administering of a medically controlled substitute for the dependent drug. Methadone is the medically controlled alternative to heroin, but its use is debatable. Although it blocks the withdrawal effect of heroin and allows the addict to resume life, it is itself a narcotic, and abuse is possible. It is nevertheless a popular and widely used treatment for heroin addicts.

Community-based. Community-based treatment programs keep the abuser in the community and stress family, school, and community resources for learning new, more adaptive responses to stress. Alcoholics Anonymous and other self-help groups are included here. They use exabusers as helpers and change agents, stress changing behavior and abstinence, and use a buddy system and peer support. Alcoholics Anonymous and its affiliates, Al-Anon and Ala-Teen (for the family members of the alcoholics), have been demonstrated to be highly effective, provided the alcoholic truly wants to be helped and is willing to admit to alcoholism (Brown, 79).

Certainly, any of the above approaches can be used in conjunction with any of the others. The most effective treatments generally combine several of them (excluding imprisonment). Their selection might be guided by the implications for intervention that Capuzzi (83) gleaned from his extensive review of the literature:

1. Understand the expectations of the individual's religion.
2. Use parent education and family counseling.
3. Use peers in group counseling.
4. Individual and group counseling are more promising than traditional drug education.
5. Help adolescents to examine the perceptions that drugs enhance pleasure and alleviate pain.
6. Develop programs to build self-esteem.
7. Don't assume that every user is a rebellious underachiever.
8. Channel adventuresomeness into productive activity.
9. Help adolescents learn to exert personal control and to postpone gratification.
10. Help adolescents develop other means of feeling independent.
11. Help adolescents to develop interpersonal trust.
12. Be sensitive to sex-role stereotypes and help adolescents to learn adaptive roles.
13. Evaluate the effectiveness of treatment programs.

Prevention

Because our society is clearly oriented to the use of alcohol and drugs, prevention efforts are generally not focused on prevention of all use, but rather on prevention of dependency and abuse. Efforts are of three kinds: legislative, educational, and personal. Legislative efforts are directed at controlling the source of drugs; educational efforts provide information concerning drugs and their effects; personal efforts focus on developing the personal and social competence that provides young people with the armor to resist drug abuse.

Legislative efforts. Legislative efforts to restrict production of drugs may be effective for amphetamines, barbiturates, and solvents because their manufacture can be controlled, but they have not proven effective in the reduction of tobacco, alcohol, or marijuana use, the use that most affects adolescents. In these cases, prevention efforts must be directed at the potential consumers, for it is they who determine whether or not the substances are used. Both educational and personal efforts are directed at young people themselves. The current emphasis on cracking down on drunk drivers is an example of legislative efforts designed to have educational and personal impact.

Educational and personal efforts. It is clear that information alone is insufficient to curb adolescent drug abuse. Young people need accurate information concerning the various drugs and their effects, but they need considerably more if they are to avoid regular use and abuse. What they need is assistance in developing personal and social competence, a positive self-esteem, achievement motivation, and self- understanding. Communication skills, peer counseling, assertiveness training (learning to say ''no''), wilderness training, problem solving, community service, athletics, and recreation all help adolescents to cope with the problems and issues of growing up, including peer pressure, family problems, and personal disappointments. Personally and socially competent people do not abuse drugs (McAlister, 79; Engs, 81; McCaul, 82; Oster, 83).

SUMMARY

The promise of drugs to provide pleasure and release from physical and psychic pain continue to lure both adolescents and adults to their use, and ours is a drug-oriented society. Adolescents, who are naturally curious, as well as testing adult limits and trying on adultlike behaviors, find drugs, especially tobacco, alcohol and marijuana, a ripe field for experimentation. Most of them will try these three drugs at least once before they graduate from high school, but most do so without serious harm. Of greater concern are the approximately 20 percent (essentially the same 20 percent who display disturbances and who engage in delinquent behavior) who use drugs regularly and abusively to escape the problems of growing up.

One common way to classify drugs is by their effect on the body. Central nervous system depressants slow down body reactions: they are dangerous in that they are likely to cause physical and psychological dependence. The depressants include alcohol, the inhalants, the tranquilizers, and the sedatives. Central nervous system stimulants stimulate activity, suppress appetite, and ameliorate depression. They can cause dependence. Caffeine, nicotine, amphetamines, methadrine, and cocaine are stimulants. Hallucinogens cause distorted perceptions. They are not usually addictive. Marijuana, mescaline, and LSD are the most common hallucinogens. Narcotics, which have an analgesic effect, are highly addictive. Morphine, codeine, heroin, and methadone are the most commonly used narcotics.

All of us use drugs; only a few of us abuse them. Abuse is defined by impaired functioning. People who are drug-dependent need the drug to alleviate pain or to sustain themselves; they are addicted when the absence of the drug creates physiological withdrawal symptoms.

For daily use, cigarettes are clearly the drug of choice for adolescents, but overall, more adolescents drink regularly than smoke daily. And many have used marijuana at least occasionally. By the time they graduate from high school, 93 percent will have tried alcohol, 71 percent will have tried cigarettes, and 60 percent will have tried marijuana. Only a very small minority have tried other drugs, with even fewer abusing them. Clearly, when adolescent drug use is discussed, alcohol, tobacco, and marijuana are the drugs being discussed.

Adolescents who smoke tobacco know the health dangers of smoking. They are influenced in their smoking behavior by their parents, peers, and older siblings.

Apparently, adolescent smokers see themselves as they see smokers: tough, group-oriented, and disobedient. Prevention efforts ought to focus on developing non-smoking self-concepts.

Adolescents drink for the same reasons as adults, and in our society drinking may be considered an essentially normal aspect of growing up. We even define maturity as the acquisition of the drinking age. Parents tend to condone drinking, at least in moderation, but the price of adolescent drinking is high—in accidental deaths involving alcohol, in crime, and in long-term health problems resulting from alcohol abuse. Alcohol education efforts ought to be focused on responsible and temperate drinking.

The depressants, stimulants, hallucinogens other than marijuana, and narcotics are used by few adolescents. Education focusing on their dangerous effects is probably sufficient to keep psychologically healthy adolescents from abusing them.

Marijuana, the only illegal drug that is experimented with by a majority of adolescents, holds a unique place in the world of the adolescent. It is feared by most adults, probably as a result of their unfamiliarity with it, but is seen by many adolescents as a safer alternative to alcohol. Thus marijuana has become a point of contention between adolescents and their parents. Although marijuana poses some dangers, especially in the false sense of increased awareness it tends to produce, the long-term effects of marijuana have not been conclusively demonstrated. It remains the center of considerable controversy. Prevention efforts ought to be similar to those for alcohol.

Although there is a clear sequence in drug use, the use of one drug does not cause or necessarily lead to the use of other drugs. Poly-drug users are more likely to be vulnerable to drug use and abuse as a result of other causal factors in their lives. Social determinants (parental influence, religious affiliation, peer influence, school influence) and personal determinants (low self-esteem, rebelliousness, adventuresomeness, impulsivity, independence, low trust) combine in complex ways to creat vulnerability to drug abuse. As the number of risk factors in an adolescent's life increase, that adolescent becomes more likely to use and/or abuse drugs.

Treatment of drug dependence may be punitive, medical-psychiatric, communal, religious, chemotherapeutic, community-based, or any combination thereof. Effective treatment generally includes the adolescent, the family, and the community, and is effective because it helps an abuser to gain a positive self-image and a responsible attitude toward self and others.

Prevention of dependency and abuse must include both education and personal development. Prevention programs generally focus on developing personal and social skills and attitudes that equip adolescents to deal effectively with the tasks of growing up. Personally and socially competent people to not abuse drugs.

References

A double suicide adds to the tragedy of teenagers who take their own lives. *People Magazine,* June 27, 1982, 32–34.

Achenbach, T.M., and Edelbrock, C. S. (1981). Behavioral problems and competencies reported by parents of normal and disturbed children aged four through sixteen. *Monographs of the Society for Research in Child Development* **46**:1–82.

Adams, C. H., and Sherer, M. (1982). Sex-role orientation and psychological adjustment: Comparisons of MMPI profiles among college women and housewives. *Journal of Personality Assessment* **46**(6):607–613.

Adams, G. R., and Gullotta, T. (1983). *Adolescent life experiences.* Monterey, CA: Brooks-Cole.

Adams, G. R., and Jones, R. M. (1982a). Adolescent egocentrism: Exploration into possible contributions of parent-child relations. *Journal of Youth and Adolescence* **11**(1):25–31.

Adams, G. R., and Jones, R. M. (1982b). Female adolescents' identity development: Age comparisons and perceived child-rearing experience. *Developmental Psychology* **19**(2):249–256.

Adams, J. F. (1981). Earlier menarche, greater height and weight: A stimulation-stress factor hypothesis. *Genetic Psychology Monographs* **104**(1):3–22.

Adams, V. (1981). The sibling bond. *Psychology Today,* June, 32–47.

Adelson, J. (1971). The political imagination of the young adolescent. *Daedalus* **100**(4):1013–1050.

Adelson, J. and O'Neil, R. P. (1966). Growth of political ideas in adolescence: The sense of community. *Journal of Personality and Social Psychology* **4**(3):295–306.

Adler, A. (1932). *What life should mean to you.* London: Allen & Unwin.

Adler, A. (1963). *The practice and theory of individual psychology.* Patterson, NJ: Littlefield, Adams.

Adler, N. E. (1981). Sex roles and unwanted pregnancy in adolescent and adult women. *Professional Psychology* **12**(1):56–66.

Ahrons, C. R. (1976). Counselors' perceptions of career images of women. *Journal of Vocational Behavior* **8**:197–207.

Albert, N., and Bec, A. T. (1975). Incidence of depression in early adolescence. *Journal of Youth and Adolescence* **4**:301–307.

Alcohol and Health: New Knowledge (1974). Second special report to the U.S. Congress, National Institute of Alcohol Abuse and Alcoholism, Department of Health, Education and Welfare. Washington, DC: Superintendent of Documents, U. S. Government Printing Office.

Alexander J., and Parsons, B. V. (1982). *Functional family therapy.* Monterey, CA: Brooks-Cole.

Alexander, J.F. (1973). Defensive and supportive communications in normal and deviant families. *Journal of Consulting and Clinical Psychology* **40**:223–231.

Alexander, J. F.; Barton, C.; Shiaro, R. S.; and Parsons, B. V. (1976). Systems-behavioral intervention with families of delinquents: Therapist characteristics, family behavior, and outcome. *Journal of Consulting and Clinical Psychology* **44**:656–664.

Alexander, K. L., and Eckland, B. K. (1975). School experience and status attainment. In S. E. Dragastin and G. H. Elder, Jr. (eds.), *Adolescence in the life cycle.* New York: Wiley.

Al-Issa, I. (1983). Gender and schizophrenia. In I. Al-Issa (ed.), *Gender and psychopathology.* New York: Academic Press.

Allen, V. L., and Feldman, R. S. (1976). Studies on the role of the tutor. In V. L. Allen (ed.), *Children as teachers: Theory and research on tutoring.* New York: Academic Press.

Allport, G. W. (1963). Values and our youth. In R. E. Grinder (ed.), *Studies in adolescence.* New York: Macmillan.

Alschuler, A. S. (1973). *Developing achievement motivation in adolescence.* Englewood Cliffs, NJ: Educational Technology Publications.

Ambrosino, L. (1971). *Runaways.* Boston: Beacon Press.

American Psychiatric Association (1980). *Diagnostic and statistical manual of mental disorders* (3rd ed.). Washington, DC: APA.

American School Counselor Association (1978). *Position statement on peer counseling.* (November; mimeo).

Anderson, F. J. (1979). Adjustment of adolescents to chronic disability. *Rehabilitation Psychology* **26**(4):177–185.

Aneshensel, C. S. and Rosen, B. C. (1980). Domestic roles and sex differences in occupational expectations. *Journal of Marriage and the Family* **42**(1):121–131.

Anolik, S. A. (1981). Imaginary audience behavior and perceptions of parents among delinquent and nondelinquent adolescents. *Journal of Youth and Adolescence* **10**(6):443–454.

Anolik, S. A. (1983). Family influences upon delinquency: Bisocial and psychosocial perspectives. *Adolescence* **18**(71):489–498.

Ansbacher, H. L., and Ansbacher, R. R. (eds.) (1956). *The individual psychology of Alfred Adler.* New York: Basic Books.

Anthony E. J. (1970). The behavior disorders of children. *Carmichael's Manual of Child Psychology* **2**:667–764.

Anthony E. J. (1974). Psychotherapy of adolescence. *American Handbook of Psychiatry: Child and Adolescent Psychiatry, Sociocultural and Community Psychiatry* **2**:234–249.

Aptekar, L. (1983). Mexican-American high school students' perception of school. *Adolescence* **18**(70):345–357.

Aries, P. (1962). *Centuries of childhood.* New York: Knopf.

Armstrong, T. L., and Altschuler, D. M. (1982). Conflicting trends in juvenile justice sanctioning: Divergent strategies in the handling of the serious juvenile offender. *Juvenile and Family Court Journal* **33**(4):15–30.

Arnold, J. (1982). Rhetoric and reform in middle schools. *Phi Delta Kappan* **63**(7):453–456.

Atwater, E. (1983). *Adolescence.* Englewood Cliffs, NJ: Prentice-Hall.

Austin, G. A.; Macari, M. A.; and Lettieri, D. J. (1978). *Research issues update.* Rockville, MD: National Institute on Drug Abuse.

Ausubel, D. P.; Montemayor, R.; and Svajian, P. (1977). *Theories and problems of adolescent development.* New York: Greene & Stratton.

Ausubel, D. P., and Sullivan, E. V. (1970). *Theory and problems of child development* (2nd ed.). New York: Greene & Stratton.

Avery, R. K. (1979). Adolescents' use of the mass media. *American Behavioral Scientist* **23**:53–70.

Azcarate, E. (1971). Identity formation as a function of physical maturation and physique in early adolescent boys. *Dissertation Abstracts International* **32**:2974B.

Bachman, J. G. (1972). *Young men in high school and beyond: A summary of findings from the youth in transition project.* Ann Arbor, MI: Institute for Social Research.

Bachman, J. G.; Green, S.; and Wirtanen, I. D. (1971). *Youth in transition: Dropping out—problem or symptom?* (Vol. 3). Ann Arbor: University of Michigan Press.

Bachman, J. G.; O'Malley, P. M.; and Johnston, J. (1978). *Youth in transition: Adolescence to adulthood: Change and stability in the lives of young men* (Vol. 6). Ann Arbor, MI: Institute for Social Research.

Bakan, D. (1971). Adolescence in America: From idea to social fact. *Daedalus* **100**(4):979–995.

Balswick, J. (1974). The Jesus people movement: A generational interpretation. *Journal of Social Issues* **30**:23–42.

Balswick, J. D., and Macrides, C. (1975). Parental stimulus for adolescent rebellion. *Adolescence* **10**:253–266.

Bandura, A. (1964). The stormy decade: Fact or fiction? *Psychology in the Schools* **1**:224–231.

Bandura, A. (1974). Behavior theory and the models of man. *American Psychologist* **29**:859–869.

Barak, A. (1981). Vocational interests: A cognitive view. *Journal of Vocational Behavior* **19**(1):1–14.

Bardwick, J. (1979). *In transition.* New York: Holt, Rinehart & Winston.

Barenboim, D. (1977). Developmental changes in the interpersonal cognitive system from middle childhood to adolescence. *Child Development* **48**:1467–1474.

Barenboim, D. (1981). The development of person perception in childhood and adolescence: From behavioral comparisons to psychological constructs to psychological comparison. *Child Development* **52**:129–144.

Barker, R. G., and Gump, P. V. (1964). *Big school, small school: High school size and student behavior.* Stanford, CA: Stanford University Press.

Barnes, G. E. (1979). Solvent abuse: A review. *International Journal of the Addictions* **14**:1–26.

Barnes, G. M. (1977). The development of adolescent drinking behavior: An evaluative review of the impact of the socialization process within the family. *Adolescence* **12**:571–591.

Barnett, R. C. (1975). Sex differences and age trends in occupational preference and occupational prestige. *Journal of Counseling Psychology* **22**:35–38.

Bateson, G. (1956). Toward a theory of schizophrenia. *Behavioral Science* **1**:251–264.

Baumrind, D. (1971). Current patterns of parental authority. *Developmental Psychology Monographs* **4**:(1, Pt. 2).

Baumrind, D. (1972). From each according to her ability. *School Review* **80**:161–197.

Baumrind, D. (1975). Early socialization and adolescent competence. In S. E. Dragastin and G. D. Elder, Jr. (eds.), *Adolescence in the life cycle: Psychological change and social context.* Washington, DC: Hemisphere Publishing.

Baumrind, D. (1978). Parental disciplinary patterns and social competence in children. *Youth and Society* **9**:239–276.

Baumrind, D. (1982). Are androgynous individuals more effective persons and parents? *Child Development* **53**:44–75.

Beane, A., and Zachmanoglou, M. A. (1979). Career education for the handicapped: A psychosocial impact. *The Vocational Guidance Quarterly* **28**:44–47.

Beck, A. T. (1967). *Depression.* New York: Harper & Row.

Becker, W. C. (1964). Consequences of different kinds of parental discipline. In M. L. Hoffman and L. W. Hoffman (eds.), *Review of child development research* (Vol. I). New York: Russell Sage Foundation.

Bedein, A. G., and Touliatos, J. (1979). Work-related motives and self-esteem in American women. *Journal of Psychology* **99**:63–70.

Bell, D. (1973). *The coming of post-industrial society: A venture in social forecasting.* New York: Basic Books.

Bell, R. R., and Chaskes, J. B. (1970). Premarital sexual experience among coeds, 1958 and 1968. *Journal of Marriage and the Family* **32**:81–84.

Bellak, L. (1975). *Overload: The new human condition.* New York: Human Services Press.

Beller, E. K. (1968). Theories of adolescent development. In J. F. Adams (ed.), *Understanding adolescence* (pp. 70–100). Boston: Allyn and Bacon.

Belmont, L., and Marolla, F. (1973). Birth order, family size, and intelligence. *Science* **182**:1096–1101.

Bem, S. (1975a). Androgyny vs. the tight little lives of fluffy women and chesty men. *Psychology Today*, September, pp. 58–62.

Bem, S. L. (1975b). Sex role adaptability: One consequence of psychological androgyny. *Journal of Personal Social Psychology* **31**:634–643.

Bender, L. (1974). The family patterns of 100 schizophrenic children observed at Bellevue, 1935–1952. *Journal of Autism and Childhood Schizophrenia* **4**:279–292.

Benedeck, E. P. (1979). Female adolescents and the law in the United States. In M. Sugar (ed.), *Female adolescent development.* New York: Brunner-Mazel.

Benedict, R. (1954). Continuities and discontinuities in cultural conditioning. In W. Martin and C. Stendler (eds.), *Readings in child development.* New York: Harcourt Brace.

Berger, B. (1963). Adolescence and beyond. *Social Problems* **10**:395.

Berkovitz, I. H. (1979). Effects of secondary experience on adolescent female development. In M. Sugar (ed.), *Female adolescent development.* New York: Brunner-Mazel.

Berlin, I. (1980). Opportunities in adolescence to rectify developmental failures. *Adolescent Psychiatry* **8**:231–243.

Berlin, I. N. (1979). Some implications of the development processes for treatment of depression in adolescence. In A. French and I. Berlin (eds.), *Depression in children and adolescents* (pp. 87–108). New York: Human Sciences Press.

Berndt, T. J. (1979). Developmental changes in conformity to peers and parents. *Developmental Psychology* **15**:608–616.

Bernhard, Y. (1975). *How to be somebody: Open the door to personal growth.* Milbrae, CA: Celestial Arts.

Bernstein, R. M. (1980). The development of the self-system during adolescence. *Journal of Genetic Psychology* **136**(2):231–245.

Berscheid, E.; Dion, D.; Walster, E.; and Walster, G. (1971). Physical attractiveness and dating choice: A test of the matching hypothesis. *Journal of Personality and Social Psychology* **7**:173–189.

Biddle, B. J.; Bank, B.; and Marim, M. M. (1980). Social determinants of adolescent drinking. *Journal of Studies on Alcohol* **41**:215–241.

Bigelow, B. J., and La Gaipa, J. J. (1975). Children's written descriptions of friendship. *Developmental Psychology* **11**:857–858.

Biller, H. B., and Bahm, R. M. (1971). Father-absence, perceived maternal behavior, and masculinity of self-concept among junior high school boys. *Developmental Psychology* **4**:178–181.

Blackburne-Stover, G.; Belenky, M. F.; and Gilligan, C. (1982). Moral development and reconstructive memory: Recalling a decision to terminate an unplanned pregnancy. *Developmental Psychology* **18**(6):862–870.

Bloch, D. (1978). Sex education practices of mothers. *Journal of Sex Education and Therapy* **4**:7–12.

Block, R., and Langman, L. (1974). Youth and work: The diffusion of ''countercultural'' values. *Youth and Society* **5**:411–432.

Blos, P. (1962). *On adolescence: A psychoanalytic interpretation.* New York: The Free Press.

Blos, P. (1967). The second individuation process of adolescence. *Psychoanalytic Study of the Child* (Vol. 22), 162–187.

Blum, R. H. (1969). *Society and drugs.* San Francisco: Jossey-Bass.

Blum, R. H. (1979). Youthful drug use. In R. I. Dupont, A. Goldstein, and J. O'Donnell (eds.), *Handbook on drug abuse.* Washington, DC: U.S. Government Printing Office.

Blyth, D. A.; Hill, J. P.; and Smyth, C. K. (1981). The influence of older adolescents on younger adolescents: Do grade-level arrangements make a difference in behavior, attitudes and experiences? *Journal of Early Adolescence* **1**:85–110.

Blyth, D. A.; Hill, J. P.; and Thiel, K. S. (1982). Early adolescents' significant others: Grade and gender differences in perceived relationships with familial and nonfamilial adults and young people. *Journal of Youth and Adolescence* **11**(6):425–450.

Blyth, D. A.; Simmons, R. G.; and Bush, D. M. (1978). The transition into early adolescence: A longitudinal comparison of youth in two educational contexts. *Sociology of Education* **51**:149–162.

Boocock, S. S. (1974). Youth in three cultures. *School Review* **83**:93–111.

Boodman, S. G. (1980). What makes Johnny steal in suburbia? *The Washington Post,* May 31, pp. 1, 7.

Booker, B. (1983). Strength, values defy formulas, Coles finds. *Richmond Times-Dispatch.*, April 3.

Bordin, E. S., and Kopplin, D. A. (1973). Motivational conflict and vocational development. *Journal of Counseling Psychology* **10**:107–116.

Bowen, M. (1966). The use of family therapy in clinical practice. *Comprehensive Psychiatry* **7**:345–374.

Bowerman, C. E., and Dobash, R. M. (1974). Structural variations in intersibling affect. *Journal of Marriage and the Family* **36**:48–54.

Boyle, R. P. (1966). The effect of the high school on students' aspirations. *American Journal of Sociology* **71**:628–639.

Braithwaite, J. (1981). The myth of social class and criminality reconsidered. *American Sociological Review* **46**:36–57.

Brandt, G.; Maschhoff, T.; and Chandler, N. (1980). A residential camp experience as an approach to adolescent weight management. *Adolescence* **15**(60):807–822.

Brandwein, R. A.; Brown, C. A.; and Fox, E. M. (1974). Women and children last: The social situation of divorced mothers and their families. *Journal of Marriage and the Family* **36**(3):498–514.

Braucht, G. N. (1983). *Problem drinking among adolescents: A review and analysis of psychosocial research* (Alcohol and Health Monograph No. 4). Rockville, MD: The National Institute on Alcohol Abuse and Alcoholism.

Brazee, E., and Smalley, B. (1982). What are middle schools good for? *Instructor* **92**(4):30–33.

Breland, H. M. (1978). Birth order, family configuration, and verbal achievement. In M. S. Smart and R. C. Smart (eds.), *Adolescents* (2nd ed.). New York: Macmillan.

Bremer, T. H., and Wittig, M. A. (1980). Fear of success: A personality trait or a response to occupational deviance and role overload? *Sex Roles* **6**:27–47.

Brenner, D., and Hinsdale, G. (1978). Body build stereotypes and self-identification in three age groups of females. *Adolescence* **13**:551–561.

Brenner, M. H. (1980). Estimating the social costs of youth employment problems. *A review of youth employment problems, programs, and policies* (Vol. 1). Washington, DC: The Vice President's Task Force on Youth Employment, U.S. Department of Labor.

Brill, A. A. (1949). *Basic principles of psychoanalysis.* Garden City, NY: Doubleday.

Brittain, C. V. (1963). Adolescent choices and parent-peer cross pressures. *American Sociological Review* **28**:385–391.

Bronfenbrenner, U. (1967). The psychological costs of quality and equality in education. *Child Development* **38**:909–925.

Bronfenbrenner, U. (1970). *Two worlds of childhood: U.S. and U.S.S.R.* New York: Russell Sage Foundation.

Bronfenbrenner, U. (1977). Toward an experimental ecology of human development. *American Psychologist* **32**:513–531.

Brook, J. S.; Lukoff, I. F.; and Whiteman, M. (1980). Initiation into adolescent marijuana use. *The Journal of Genetic Psychology* **137**:133–142.

Brook, J. S.; Whiteman, M.; and Gordon, A. S. (1981). Maternal and personality determinants of adolescent smoking behavior. *The Journal of Genetic Psychology* **139**:185–193.

Brook, R.; Kaplum, J.; and Whitehead, P. C. (1974). Personality characteristics of adolescent amphetamine users as measured by the MMPI. *British Journal of the Addictions* **69**:61–66.

Brophy, J. (1979). Teacher behavior and its effects. *Journal of Educational Psychology* **71**:733–750.

Brown, B. B. (1982). The extent and effects of peer pressure among high school students: A retrospective analysis. *Journal of Youth and Adolescence* **11**(2):121–133.

Brown, B. S., and Ashery, R. S. (1979). Aftercare in drug abuse programming. In R. I. Dupont, A. Goldstein, and J. O'Donnell (eds.), *Handbook on drug abuse.* Washington, DC: U.S. Government Printing Office.

Brown, B. W. (1982). Family intimacy in magazine advertising, 1920–1977. *Journal of Communication* **32**(3):173–183.

Brown, F. (1980). *Transition of youth to adulthood: A bridge too far.* Boulder, CO: Westview Press.

Bruch, H. (1973). *Eating disorders: Obesity, anorexia nervosa and the person within.* New York: Basic Books.

Bruch, H. (1974). Eating disturbances in adolescence. In G. Caplan (ed.), *American handbook of psychiatry* (pp. 275–286). New York: Basic Books.

Bruch, H. (1977). Psychological antecedents of anorexia nervosa. In R. A. Vigersky (ed.), *Anorexia nervosa.* New York: Raven Press.

Brutten, M.; Richardson, S.; and Mangel, C. (1973). *Something's wrong with my child.* New York: Harcourt Brace Jovanovich.

Bry, B. H.; McKeon, P.; and Pandina, R. J. (1982). Extent of drug use as a function of number of risk factors. *Journal of Abnormal Psychology* **91**(4):273–279.

Bryan, D. P., and Herjanic, B. (1980). Depression and suicide among adolescents and young adults with selective handicapping conditions. *Exceptional Education Quarterly* **1**(2):57–65.

Bryan, J. W., and Freed, F. W. (1982). Corporal punishment: Normative data and sociological and psychological correlates in a community college population. *Journal of Youth and Adolescence* **11**(2):77–85.

Buerkel-Rothfuss, N. L.; Greenberg, B. S.; Atkin, C. K.,; and Neuendorf, K. (1982). Learning about the family from television. *Journal of Communication* **32**(3):191–201.

Bumpass, L. L., and Sweet, J. A. (1972). Differentials in marital instability: 1970. *American Sociological Review* **37**:754–766.

Burlin, F. (1976). Locus of control and female occupational aspiration. *Journal of Counseling Psychology* **23**:126–129.

Burton, N. W., and Jones, L. V. (1982). Recent trends in achievement levels of black and white youth. *Educational Researcher* **11**:10–17.

Caine, D. (1979). Two contemporary tragedies: Adolescent suicide/adolescent alcoholism. *Journal of the National Association of Private Psychiatrists* **9**:4–11.

Campbell, D. (1974). *If you don't know where you're going, you'll probably end up somewhere else.* Allen, TX: Argus Communications.

Campbell, P. B. (1976). Adolescent intellectual decline. *Adolescence* **11**:629–635.

Cancro, R. (1980). Overview of schizophrenia. In H. I. Kaplan, A. M. Freedman, and B. J. Sadock (eds.), *Comprehensive textbook of psychiatry* (pp. 1093–1104). Baltimore: Williams & Wilkins.

Canino, F. J. (1981). Learned-helplessness theory: Implications for research in learning disabilities. *Journal of Special Education* **15**(4):471–484.

Capuzzi, D., and Lecoq, L. L. (1983). Social and personal determinants of adolescent use and abuse of alcohol and marijuana. *The Personnel and Guidance Journal* **62**(4):199–205.

Card, J. J.; Steel, L.; and Abeles, R. P. (1980). Sex differences in realization of individual potential for achievement. *Journal of Vocational Behavior* **17**(1):1– 21.

Carter, R. C. (1984). *Dimensions of moral education.* Toronto: University of Toronto Press.

Casper, R. C.; Halmi, K. A.; Goldber, S. C.; Eckert, E. D.; and Davis, J. M. (1979). Disturbances in body image estimation as related to other characteristics and outcome in anorexia nervosa. *British Journal of Psychiatry* **134**:60–66.

Cavior, N., and Dokecki, P. R. (1975). Physical attractiveness, perceived attitude similarity, and academic achievement as contributors to interpersonal attraction among adolescents. In R. E. Grinder (ed.), *Studies in adolescence* (3rd ed.). New York: Macmillan.

Center for Early Adolescence. (1982). Living with 10- to 15-year-olds. *A planning guide for a one-day conference.* Carrboro, NC.

Chand, I. P.; Crider, D. M.; and Willets, F. K. (1975). Parent-youth disagreement as perceived by youth: A longitudinal study. *Youth and Society* **6**:365–375.

Chandler, M. J. (1975). Egocentrism and anti-social behavior: The assessment and training of social perspective-taking skills. *Developmental Psychology* **9**:326–332.

Changes in mathematical achievement, 1973–1978 (1979). Denver, CO: National Assessment of Educational Progress.

Chapman, A. H. (1974). *Management of emotional problems in children and adolescents.* Philadelphia: Lippincott.

Charlesworth, R., and Hartup, W. W. (1973). Positive social reinforcement in the nursery school peer group. *Child Development* **38**:993–1002.

Charlton-Seifert, J.; Stratton, B. D.; and Williams, M. G. (1980). Sweet and slow:

Diet can affect learning. *Academic Therapy* **16**(2):211–217.

Chassin, L., *et al.* (1981). Self-images and cigarette smoking in adolescence. *Personality and Social Psychology Bulletin* **7**(4):670–676.

Cherlin, A. (1980). Postponing marriages: The influence of young women's work expectations. *Journal of Marriage and the Family* **43**:355–365.

Cherry, F., and Deaux, K. (1978). Fear of success versus fear of gender-inappropriate behavior. *Sex Roles* **4**:97–101.

Chesler, B. M. (1980). *A talking mouth speaks: About learning-disabled college students.* Sacramento: B. Chesler.

Chilman, C. S. (1978). *Adolescent sexuality in a changing American society: Social and psychological perspectives.* Bethesda, MD: U.S. Dept. of Health, Education and Welfare.

Cronbach, L. S., and Snow, R. E. (1977). *Aptitudes and instructional methods.* New York: Irvington.

Cicirelli, V. G. (1977). Family structures and interaction: Sibling effrects on socialization. In M. McMillan and M. Segio (eds.), *Child psychiatry: Treatment and research.* New York: Brunner-Mazel.

Clark, K. (1965). *Dark ghetto.* New York: Harper.

Clayton, R. R., and Bokemeier, J. L. (1980). Premarital sex in the seventies. *Journal of Marriage and the Family* **42**(4):759–775.

Clemens, P. W., and Rust, J. O. (1979). Factors in adolescent rebellious feelings. *Adolescence* **14**(53):159–173.

Clifford, E. (1980). Body satisfaction in adolescence. In R. E. Muuss (ed.), *Adolescent behavior and society, a book of readings* (pp. 53–59). New York: Random House.

Coakley, M. (1981). Robert, a robber at age 9, and just one of thousands. *Chicago Tribune*, March 8.

Cogle, F. L.; Tasker, G. E.; and Morton, D. G. (1982). Adolescent time use in household work. *Adolescence* **17**(66):451–455.

Cohen, S. (1979). Inhalants. In R. I. Dupont, A Goldstein, and J. O'Donnell (eds.), *Handbook on drug abuse.* Washington, DC: U.S. Government Printing Office.

Cohen, Y. A. (1964). *The transition from childhood to adolescence: Cross-cultural studies of initiation ceremonies, legal systems, and incest taboos.* Chicago: Aldine.

Cole, S. (1980). Send our children to work? *Psychology Today*, June, pp. 44–68.

Coleman, E. (1981). Counseling adolescent males. *The Personnel and Guidance Journal* **60**(4):215–218.

Coleman, J. C. (1980a). Friendship and the peer group in adolescence. In J. Adelson (ed.), *Handbook of adolescent psychology.* New York: Wiley.

Coleman, J. C.; Butcher, J. N.; and Carson, R. C. (1980b). *Abnormal psychology and modern life* (6th ed.). Glenview, IL: Scott, Foresman.

Coleman, J. S. (1961). *The adolescent society.* New York: Macmillan.

Coleman, J. S. (1974). *Youth: Transition to adulthood.* Chicago: University of Chicago.

Coleman, J. S. (1975). How do the young become adults? In R. E. Grinder (ed.), *Studies in adolescence* (3rd ed.). New York: Macmillan.

Combs, A. W.; Avila, D. L.; and Parkey, W. W. (1971). *Helping relationships, basic concepts for the helping professions.* Boston: Allyn and Bacon.

Combs, J., and Cooley, W. W. (1968). Dropouts: In high school and after school. *American Educational Research Journal* **5**:343–363.

Comeau, H. (1980). Changes in reported self-values among students in grades 9–12. *Adolescence* **15**(57):143–148.

Committee to study the health-related effects of cannabis and its derivatives (1982). National Academy of Sciences, Institute of Medicine. Washington, DC: National Academy Press.

Conant, J. B. (1959). *The American high school today.* New York: McGraw-Hill.

Condry, J. C., and Siman, M. L. (1974). Characteristics of peer- and adult-oriented children. *Journal of Marriage and the Family* **36**:543–554.

Conger, J. J. (1971). A world they never knew: The family and social change. *Daedalus* **100**(4):1105–1138.

Conger, J. J. (1977). *Adolescence and youth* (3rd ed.). New York: Harper & Row.

Conger, J. J., and Miller, W. C. (1966). *Personality, social class, and delinquency.* New York: Wiley.

Connell, P. (1977). Drug-taking in Great Britain: A growing problem. *Research issues 15: Cocaine—summaries of psychological research.* Washington, DC: U.S. Government Printing Office.

Conner, D. G. (1984). Multifamily educational groups in juvenile court settings with drug/alcohol offenders. *The Journal for Specialists in Group Work* **9**(1):21–25.

Cooper, J. E.; Holman, J.; and Braithwaite, V. A. (1983). Self-esteem and family cohesion: The child's perspective and adjustment. *Journal of Marriage and the Family* **45**(1):153–159.

Coopersmith, S. (1967). *The antecedents of self-esteem.* San Francisco: W. H. Freeman.

Corey, G. (1982). *Theory and practice of counseling and psychotherapy* (2nd ed.). Monterey, CA: Brooks-Cole.

Costanzo, P. R. (1970). Conformity development as a function of self-blame. *Journal of Personality and Social Psychology* **14**:366–374.

Cottle, T. (1971). *Time's children.* Boston: Little, Brown.

Cottle, T. J. (1977). *Children in jail.* Boston: Beacon.

Cottle, T. J. (1979). Adolescent voices. *Psychology Today*, February, pp. 40–44.

Cretkovich, G. (1978). Sex role development and teenage fertility-related behavior. *Adolescence* **13**(50):231–236.

Crino, M. D., and White, M. C. (1983). Female participation rates and the occupational prestige of the professions: Are they inversely related? *Journal of Vocational Behavior* **22**(2):243–255.

Crisp, A. H. (1982). Anorexia nervosa at normal body weight: The abnormal weight syndrome. *International Journal of Psychiatric Medicine* **11**:203–233.

Cross, K. P. (1984). The rising tide of school reform reports. *Phi Delta Kappan* **66**(3):167–172.

Curran, B. E. (1979). Understanding suicide. *Pediatric Clinics of North America* **26**:737–746.

Curtis, R. L. (1975). Adolescent orientation toward parents and peers: Variations by sex, age, and socioeconomic status. *Adolescence* **10**:483–494.

Curwin, R. L., and Mendler, A. N. (1980). *The discipline book: A complete guide to school and classroom management.* Reston, VA: Reston.

Czajkoski, E. H. (1982). Why confidentiality in juvenile justice? *Juvenile and Family Court Journal* **33**(4):49–53.

Czikszentmikalyi, M.; Larson, R.; and Prescott, S. (1977). The ecology of adolescent activity and experience. *Journal of Youth and Adolescence* **6**:281–294.

Danner, F. W., and Day, M. C. (1977). Elicting formal operations. *Child Development* **48**:1600–1606.

da Nobrega, J. C. (1980). *The perils of cultism.* Hauppauge, NY: Exposition Press.

Darabi, K. F.; Jones, J.; Varga, P.; and House, M. (1982). Evaluation of sex education outreach. *Adolescence* **17**(65):57–64.

Darling, C.A., and Hicks, M. W. (1982). Parental influence on adolescent sexuality: Implications for parents as educators. *Journal of Youth and Adolescence* **11**(3):231–245.

Datesman, S. K.; Scarpitto, F. R.; and Stephenson, R. M. (1975). Female delinquency: An application of self and opportunity theories. *Journal of Research in Crime and Delinquency* **12**:107–123.

Davids, L. (1982). Ethnic identity, religiosity, and youthful deviance: The Toronto computer dating project, 1979. *Adolescence* **17**(68):673–684.

Davies, M., and Kandel, D. B. (1981). Parental and peer influences on adolescents' educational plans: Some further evidence. *American Journal of Sociology* **87**:363–387.

Dean, R. A. (1982). Youth: Moonies' target population. *Adolescence* **17**(67):567–574.

Dearman, N. B., and Plisko, V. W. (eds.) (1979). *The condition of education: 1979 edition.* Washington, DC: U.S. Department of Health, Education, and Welfare, National Center for Educational Statistics.

de Fonseca, A. C.; de Hernandez, C.; Ingianna, Y.; and de Thomas, Z. (1980). Level of operational thinking in Costa Rican youths. *Revista Latinoamericana de Psicologia* **12**(3):471–486.

DeLeon, G., and Rosenthal, M. S. (1979). Therapeutic communities. In R. I. Dupont, A. Goldstein, and J. O'Donnell (eds.), *Handbook on drug abuse.* Washington, DC: U.S. Government Printing Office.

DeLissovoy, V. (1973). High school marriages: A longitudinal study. *Journal of Marriage and the Family* **35**(2):245–255.

Dellas, M., and Gaier, E. L. (1975). The self and adolescent identity in women: Options and implications. *Adolescence* **10**:399–407.

Delp, J. L., and Martinson, R. A. (1977). *A handbook for parents of gifted and talented.* Ventura, CA: Ventura County Superintendent of Schools.

De Luca, J. R. (1981). *Fourth special report to the U.S. Congress on alcohol and health.* Washington, DC: U.S. Government Printing Office.

de Mause, L. (1974). *The history of childhood.* New York: Atcom.

Dembo, R.; Farrow, D.; Des Jarlais, D.; Burgos, W.; and Schmeidler, J. (1981). Examining a causal model of early drug involvement among inner-city junior high school youths. *Human Relations* **34**(3):169–193.

Demos, J. P. (1976). The American family in past time. In H. Grunebaum and J. Christ (eds.), *Contemporary marriage: Structure, dynamics and therapy.* Boston: Little, Brown.

Denmark, F. L. (1977). Growing up male. In C. G. Carney and S. L. McMahan (eds.), *Exploring contemporary male and female roles.* La Jolla, CA: University Associates.

Denno, D. (1982). Sex differences in cognition: A review and critique of the longitudinal evidence. *Adolescence* **17**(68):779–788.

DeRopp, R. S. (1957). *Drugs and the mind.* New York: Grove Press.

de Vaus, D. A. (1983). The relative importance of parents and peers for adolescent religious orientation: An Australian study. *Adolescence* **18**(69):147–158.

Devereux, E. C. (1970). The role of peer group experience in moral development. In J. P. Hill (ed.), *Minnesota Symposia on Child Psychology: Vol. 4* (pp. 94–140). Minneapolis: University of Minnesota Press.

Dewey, J. (1966). *Democracy and education.* New York: Free Press.

Dickinson, G. E. (1975). Dating behavior of black and white adolescents before and after desegregation. *Journal of Marriage and the Family* **37**:602–608.

Dodson, F. (1974). *How to father.* New York: Signet Books.

Dodson, L. S., and Kurpius, D. J. (1977). *Family counseling: A systems approach.* Muncie, IN: Accelerated Development.

Dole, A. A., and Passons, W. R. (1972). Life goals and plan determinants reported by black and white high school seniors. *Journal of Vocational Behavior* **2**:209–222.

Donahue, T. J., and Costar, J. W. (1977). Counselor discrimination against young women in career selection. *Journal of Counseling Psychology* **24**:481–486.

Donohue, K. C., and Gullotta, T. P. (1983). The coping behavior of adolescents following a move. *Adolescence* **18**(70):391–401.

Donovan, J. E., and Jessor, R. (1978). Adolescent problem drinking: Psychosocial correlates in a national study sample. *Quarterly Journal of Studies in Alcohol* **39**:1506–1524.

Donovan, J. M. (1975). Identity status and interpersonal style. *Journal of Youth and Adolescence* **41**:37–55.

Dornbush, S. M.; Carlsmith, L.; Gross, R. T.; Martin, J. A.; Jenning, D.; Rosenberg, A.; and Duke, D. (1981). Sexual development, age, and dating: A comparison of biological and sociological influences upon the set of behaviors. *Child Development* **52**:179–185.

Douvan, E. A., and Adelson, J. (1966). *The adolescent experience.* New York: Wiley.

Douvan, E. A., and Kaye, C. (1957). *Adolescent girls.* Ann Arbor: University of Michigan.

Downing, C. (1984). *The Cinderella syndrome.* New York: Crossroad.

Downton, J. W. (1979). *Sacred journeys: The conversion of young Americans to divine light mission.* New York: Columbia University.

Dreyer, P. H. (1975). Changes in the meaning of marriage among youth: The impact of the "revolution" in sex and sex role behavior. In R. Grinder (ed.), *Studies in adolescence* (3rd ed.). New York: Macmillan.

Dreyfus, E. A. (1976). *Adolescence: Theory and experience.* Columbus, OH: Charles E. Merrill.

Drugs, '78: The great American roller coaster (1978). *Playboy*, September, pp.157 ff.

Duberman, L. (1973). Step-kin relationships. *Journal of Marriage and the Family* **35**(2):283–292.

Duck, S. W. (1975). Personality similarity and friendship choices by adolescents. *European Journal of Social Psychology* **5**:351–365.

Dufty, W. (1975). *Sugar blues.* New York: Warner Books.

Duncan, D. F. (1978). Attitudes toward parents and delinquency in suburban adolescent males. *Adolescence* **13**:365–369.

Dunn, R., and Dunn, K. (1979). *Student learning styles: Diagnosing and prescribing programs.* Reston, VA: National Association of Secondary School Principals.

Dunne, F.; Elliot, R.; and Carlsen, W. S. (1981). Sex differences in the educational and occupational aspirations of rural youth. *Journal of Vocational Behavior* **18**(1):56–66.

Dunphy, D. C. (1963). The social structure of urban adolescent peer groups. *Sociometry* **26**:230–246.

Dunphy, D. C. (1972). Peer group socialization. In R. J. Hunt (ed.), *Socialization in Australia.* Sydney: Angus & Robertson.

Dunphy, D. C. (1980). Peer group socialization. In R. Muuss (ed.), *Adolescent behavior and society* (3rd ed.). New York: Random House.

Dye, C. (1983). *Cocaine papers: From Freud to freebase.* Phoenix: Do It Now Foundation.

Easson, W. M. (1977). Depression in adolescents. In S. Feinstein and P. Giovacchini (eds.), *Adolescent psychiatry* (Vol. 5). New York: Aronson.

Easterlin, R. A. (1982). The changing circumstances of child-rearing. *Journal of Communication* **32**(3):86–98.

Eberly, D. J. (1978). Patterns of volunteer service by young people, 1965 and 1974. In R. E. Grinder (ed.), *Adolescence* (2nd ed.). New York: Wiley.

Edelman, M. (1980). *Portrait of inequality: Black and white children in America.* Washington, DC: Children's Defense Fund.

Edwards, B. (1979). *Drawing on the right side of the brain.* Los Angeles: J. P. Tarcher.

Edwards, C. P. (1981). The comparative study of moral judgement and reasoning. In R. H. Munroe, R. L. Monroe, and B. Whiting (eds.), *Handbook of cross-cultural human development* (pp. 510–528). New York: Garland Press.

Eisikovits, Z., and Sagi, A. (1982). Moral development and discipline encounter in delinquent and non-delinquent adolescents. *Journal of Youth and Adolescence* **11**(3):217–230.

Eisterhold, M. J.; Murphy, P.; Beneke, W.; and Scott, G. (1979). Multiple drug use among high school students. *Psychological Reports* **44**:1099–1106.

Eitzen, D. S. (1975). Athletics in the status systems of male adolescents: A replication of Coleman's *The adolescent society. Adolescence* **10**:267–276.

Ekstein, R. (1966). *Children of time and space, of action and impulse.* New York: Appelton-Century-Crofts.

Elder, G. H. (1980). Adolescence in historical perspective. In J. Adelson (ed.), *Handbook of adolescent psychology* (pp. 3–46). New York: Wiley.

Elder, G. H., Jr. (1962). Structural variations in the child rearing relationship. *Sociometry* **25**:241–262.

Elkind, D. (1961). The child's conception of his religious denomination. I: The Jewish child. *Journal of Genetic Psychology* **99**:209–225.

Elkind, D. (1962). The child's conception of his religious denomination. II: The Catholic child. *Journal of Genetic Psychology* **101**:185–193.

Elkind, D. (1963). The child's conception of his religious denomination. III: The Protestant child. *Journal of Genetic Psychology* **103**:291–304.

Elkind, D. (1974). *Children and adolescents: Interpretive essays on Jean Piaget* (2nd ed.). New York: Oxford.

Elkind, D. (1981). *The hurried child: Growing up too fast too soon.* Reading, MA: Addison-Wesley.

Elkind, D., and Bowen, R. (1979). Imaginary audience behavior in children and adolescents. *Developmental Psychology* **15**:38–44.

Ellinwood, E. H. (1979). Amphetamines/anorectics. In R. I. Dupont, A. Goldstein, and J. O'Donnell (eds.), *Handbook on drug abuse.* Washington, DC: U.S. Government Printing Office.

Elliot, G. C. (1982). Self-esteem and self-presentation among the young as a function of age and gender. *Journal of Youth and Adolescence* **11**(2):135–153.

Elliott, D. S., and Ageton, S. S. (1980). Reconciling race and class differences in self-reported and official estimates of delinquency. *American Sociological Review* **45**:95–110.

Ellis, A. (1973). *Humanistic psychotherapy: The rational-emotive approach.* New York: Julian Press.

Ellis, A. (1979). *New developments in rational- emotive therapy.* Monterey, CA: Brooks-Cole.

Ellwood, R. S. (1973). *Religious and spiritual groups in modern America.* Englewood Cliffs, NJ: Prentice-Hall.

Emery, P. E. (1983). Adolescent depression and suicide. *Adolescence* **18**(70):245–258.

Emmerich, W., and Shepard, K. (1982). Development of sex-differentiated preferences during late childhood and adolescence. *Developmental Psychology* **18**(3):406–417.

Endsley, W. R. (1980). *Peer tutorial instruction.* Englewood Cliffs, NJ: Educational Technology Publications.

Engs, R. C. (1981). Responsibility and alcohol. *Health Education* **12**:20–22.

Enright, R. D.; Lapsley, D. K.; Drivas, A. E.; and Fehr, L. A. (1980a). Parental influences on the development of adolescent autonomy and identity. *Journal of Youth and Adolescence* **9**:529–546.

Enright, R. D.; Lapsley, D. K.; and Shukla, D. G. (1979). Adolescent egocentrism in early and late adolescence. *Adolescence* **14**:687–695.

Enright, R. D.; Shukla, D. G.; and Lapsey, D. K. (1980b). Adolescent egocentrism-sociocentrism and self-consciousness. *Journal of Youth and Adolescence* **9**:101–116.

Epstein, H. T. (1978). Growth spurts during brain development: Implications for educational policy. *Yearbook of the National Society for the Study of Education.* Chicago: University of Chicago.

Epstein, J. L. (1981). *Secondary school environments and student outcomes: A review and annotated bibliography.* Baltimore: The Johns Hopkins University Center for Social Organization of Schools.

Erdwins, C.; Small, A.; and Gross, R. (1980). The relationship of sex role to self concept. *Journal of Clinical Psychology* **36**:111–115.

Erickson, M. T. (1978). *Child psychopathology.* Englewood Cliffs, NJ: Prentice-Hall.

Erickson, V. L. (1977). Beyond Cinderella: Ego maturity and attitudes toward the rights and roles of women. *Counseling Psychologist* **7**:83–88.

Erikson, E. H. (1959). *Identity and the life-cycle: Selected papers.* New York: International Universities.

Erikson, E. H. (1963). *Childhood and society* (2nd ed.). New York: Norton.

Erikson, E. H. (1964). *Insight and Responsibility: Lectures on the ethical implications of psychoanalytic insight.* New York: Norton.

Erikson, E. H. (1968). *Identity, youth and crisis.* New York: Norton.

Erikson, E. H. (1974). *Dimensions of a new identity: The 1973 Jefferson lectures in the humanities.* New York: Norton.

Erikson, E. H. (1980). Youth and the life cycle. In R. E. Muuss (ed.), *Adolescent behavior and society: A book of readings* (3rd ed., pp. 226–237). New York: Random House.

Esposito, R. P. (1977). Relationship between motive to avoid success and vocational choice. *Journal of Vocational Behavior* **10**:347–357.

Evans, R.; Henderson, A.; Hill, P.; and Raines, B. (1979). Smoking in children and adolescents: Psychosocial determinants and prevention strategies. *Smoking and health: A report of the Surgeon General.* Washington, DC; U.S. Government Printing Office.

Eysenck, H. J. (1953). *Uses and abuses of psychology.* London: Pelican Books.

Eysenck, H. J. (1979). *The structure and measurement of intelligence.* Berlin: Springer-Verlag.

Eysenck, H. J., and Kamin, L. (1981). *Intelligence: The battle for the mind.* London: Macmillan.

Facts about women in education (1971). Cleveland, OH: Women's Equity Action.

Falkowski, C. K., and Falk, W. W. (1983). Homemaking as an occupational plan: Evidence from a national longitudinal study. *Journal of Vocational Behavior* **22**:227–242.

Fannin, P. M. (1979). The relation between ego identity status and sex role attitude, work role salience, atypicality of major, and self-esteem in college women. *Journal of Vocational Behavior* **14**:12–22.

Farel, A. M. (1982). *Early adolescence and religion: A status study.* Carrboro, NC: Center for Early Adolescence.

Farmer, H. S. (1980). Environmental, background, and psychological variables related to optimizing achievement and career motivation for high school girls. *Journal of Vocational Behavior* **17**(1):58–70.

Farrington, D. P.; Biron, L.; and Le Blanc, M. (1982). Personality and delinquency in London and Montreal. In J. C. Gunn and D. P. Farrington (eds.), *Abnormal offenders: Delinquency and the criminal justice system.* New York: Wiley.

Feather, N. T., and Hutton, M. A. (1974). Value systems of students in Papua, New Guinea and Australia. *International Journal of Psychology* **9**(2):91–104.

Federbush, M. (1974). The sex problem in school math books. In J. Stacey and B. J. Daniels (eds.), *And Jill came tumbling after: Sexism in American education.* New York: Dell.

Feeney, S. (1980). *Schools for young adolescents: Adapting the early childhood model.* Carrboro: University of North Carolina.

Feinstein, S.C., and Miller, D. (1979). Psychoses of adolescence. In J. D. Noshpitz (ed.), *Basic handbook of child psychiatry* (pp. 708–721). New York: Basic Books.

Ferrell, M. Z.; Tolone, W. L.; and Walsh, R. H. (1977). Maturational and societal changes in the sexual double-standard: A panel analysis (1967–71; 1970–74). *Journal of Marriage and the Family* **39**:255–271.

Festinger, L. (1962). Cognitive dissonance. In G. Aronson (ed.), *Readings about the social animal.* San Francisco: W. H. Freeman & Company.

Fetters, W. B. (1976). *National longitudinal study of the high school class of 1972* (DHEW Pub. No. 76-235). Washington, DC: National Center for Educational Statistics.

Feuer, L. S. (1969). Conflict of generations. *Saturday Review of Literature* (January 18), pp. 53–55, 66–68.

Finch, S. M. (1980). Psychological factors affecting physical conditions (psychosomatic disorders). In H. I. Kaplan, A. M. Freedman, and B. J. Sadock (eds.), *Comprehensive textbook of psychiatry: Vol. 2* (pp. 2605–2612). Baltimore: Williams & Wilkins.

Finkelstein, M. J., and Gaier, E. L. (1983). The impact of prolonged student status on late adolescent development. *Adolescence* **18**(69):115–129.

Fiske, E. B. (1975). College entry test scores drop sharply. *The New York Times,* September 7, p. 1.

Fitzgerald, L. F., and Crites, J. O. (1980). Toward a career psychology of women: What do we know? What do we need to know? *Journal of Counseling Psychology* **27**:44–62.

Flavell, J. H. (1977). *Cognitive development.* Englewood Cliffs, NJ: Prentice-Hall.

Flexer, B. K., and Roberge, J. (1980). I.Q., field dependence-independence, and the development of formal operational thought. *Journal of General Psychology* **103**(2):191–201.

Folkins, C. H., and Sims, W. E. (1981). Physical fitness training and mental health. *American Psychologist* **36**(4):373–489.

Footlick, J. K. (1977). Children and the law. In T. J. Cottle (ed.), *Readings in adolescent psychology: Contemporary perspectives* (pp. 279–281). New York: Harper & Row.

Forslund, M. A. (1978). Functions of drinking of Native American and white youth. *Journal of Youth and Adolescence* **7**:327–332.

Foster, H. (1974). *A bill of rights for children.* Springfield, MA: Charles C. Thomas.

Fottler, M. D., and Bain, T. (1980). Managerial aspirations of high school seniors: A comparison of males and females. *Journal of Vocational Behavior* **16**(1):83–95.

Fowler, J. W. (1976). Stages in faith: The structural-developmental approach. In T. Hennessey (ed.), *Values and development.* New York: Paulist Press.

Fowler, J. W. (1980). *Trajectories in faith: Five live stories.* Nashville: Abingdon.

Fowler, J. W. (1981). *Stages of faith: The psychology of human development and the quest for meaning.* San Francisco: Harper & Row.

Frankl, V. E. (1962). *Man's search for meaning.* Boston: Beacon.

Frazier, D. J., and DeBlassie, R. R. (1982). A comparison of self-concept in Mexican American and Non-Mexican American late adolescents. *Adolescence* **17**(66):327–334.

Frazier, N., and Sadker, M. (1973). *Sexism in school and society.* New York: Harper & Row.

Frederick, C. J. (1978. Current trends in suicidal behavior in the United States. *American Journal of Psychotherapy* **32**:172–200.

Freeman, D. (1983). *Margaret Mead and Samoa: The making and unmaking of an anthropological myth.* Cambridge, MA: Harvard University.

Freud, A. (1946). *The ego and the mechanisms of defense.* New York: International University.

Freud, A. (1958). Adolescence. *Psychoanalytic Study of the Child* **13**:255–278.

Freud, S. (1943). *A general introduction to psychoanalysis.* New York: Doubleday.

Friedrich, W.; Reams, R.; and Jacobs, J. (1982). Depression and suicidal ideation in early adolescents. *Journal of Youth and Adolescence* **11**(5):403–407.

Frieri, F.; Bartal, D.; and Carrol, D. (eds.) (1980). *Attribution theory: Application to social problems.* San Francisco: Jossey-Bass.

Friesen, D. (1972). Value orientations of modern youth—a comparative study. *Adolescence* **7**(26):265–275.

Frith, G. H., and Edwards, R. (1981). Misconceptions of regular classroom teachers about physically handicapped students. *Exceptional Children* **48**(2):192–184.

Fuhrmann, B. S. (1975). Androgyny: Getting rid of sex role stereotypes. *VCU Magazine,* pp. 2–5.

Fuhrmann, B. S. (1983). Adolescents. In J. A. Brown and R. H. Pate (eds.), *Being a counselor: Directions and challenges* (pp. 207–229). Monterey, CA: Brooks-Cole.

Fuhrmann, B. S., and Grasha, A. (1983). *A practical handbook for college teachers.* Boston: Little, Brown.

Furth, H. G. (1974). *Piaget for teachers.* Englewood Cliffs, NJ: Prentice-Hall.

Furth, H. G., and Youniss, J. (1971). Formal operations and language: A comparison of deaf and hearing adolescents. *International Journal of Psychology* **6**:49–64.

Gagnon, J. H., and Greenblat, C. S. (1978). *Life designs.* Glenview, IL: Scott, Foresman.

Galanter, M.; Rabkin, R.; Rabkin, J.; and Deutsch, A. (1979). The Moonies: A psychological study of conversion and membership in a contemporary religious sect. *American Journal of Psychiatry* **136**:165–169.

Gallagher, J. M., and Noppe, I. C. (1976). Cognitive development and learning. In J. F. Adams (ed.), *Understanding adolescence* (3rd ed.). Boston: Allyn and Bacon.

Gallatin, J. (1976). Theories of adolescence. In J. F. Adams (ed.), *Understanding adolescence* (3rd ed.). Boston: Allyn and Bacon.

Gallatin, J. E. (1975). *Adolescence and individuality.* New York: Harper & Row.

Gallup, A. (1984). The Gallup poll of teachers' attitudes toward the public schools. *Phi Delta Kappan* **66**(2):97–107.

Gallup, G. H. (1978). *The Gallup poll: Public opinion survey, 1972–1977* (Vol. 1). Wilmington, DE: Scholarly Resources.

Gallup, G. H. (1979). *The Gallup poll: Public opinion survey, 1978* (Vol. 2). Wilmington, DE: Scholarly Resources.

Galton, F. (1896). *Hereditary genius: An inquiry into its laws and consequences.* London: Macmillan.

Ganong, L.; Coleman, M.; and Brown, G. (1981). Effect of family structures on marital attitudes of adolescents. *Adolescence* **16**(62):281–288.

Ganzer, V. J., and Sarason, I. G. (1975). Variables associated with recidivism among juvenile delinquents. In R. E. Grinder (ed.), *Studies in adolescence* (3rd ed.). New York: Macmillan.

Garbarino, J. (1980). Some thoughts on school size and its effects on adolescent development. *Journal of Youth and Adolescence* **9**:19–31.

Gardner, H. (1980). Cognition comes of age. In M. Piatelli-Palmarini (ed.), *Language and learning: The debate between Piaget and Noam Chomsky.* Cambridge, MA: Harvard University.

Garrison, K. C. (1976). Physiological development. In J. F. Adams (ed.), *Understanding adolescence* (3rd ed.), pp. 117–144. Boston: Allyn and Bacon.

Garrod, A. C., and Bramble, G. A. (1977). Moral development and literature. *Theory into practice* **16**(2):105–111.

Gawronski, D. A., and Mathis, C. (1965). Differences between over-achieving, normal achieving, and underachieving high school students. *Psychology in the schools* **2**:152–155.

Gaylin, J. (1978). What boys look for in girls. *Seventeen*, March, pp. 107–113.

Geary, D. P. (1983). Nutrition, chemicals and criminal behavior: Some physiological aspects of antisocial conduct. *Juvenile and Family Court Journal* **34**(1):9–13.

Gecas, V., and Nye, F. I. (1974). Sex and class differences in parent-child interaction: A test of Kohn's hypotheses. *Journal of Marriage and the Family* **36**:742–749.

Gerber, M., and Kauffman, J. M. (1981). Peer tutoring in academic settings. In P. S. Strain (ed.), *The utilization of classroom peers as behavior change agents.* New York: Plenum.

Gesell, A., and Ilg, F. L. (1949). *Child development, an introduction to the study of human growth.* New York: Harper.

Gibbs, J. C. (1977). Kohlberg's stages of moral judgment: A constructive critique. *Harvard Educational Review* **47**(1):43–61.

Gilbert, E. H.; and DeBlassie, R. R. (1984). Anorexia nervosa: Adolescent starvation by choice. *Adolescence* **19**(76):839–846.

Gilligan, C. (1977). In a different voice: Women's conceptions of the self and morality. *Harvard Educational Review* **47**:481–517.

Gilligan, C. (1982a). *In a different voice: Psychological theory and women's development.* Cambridge, MA: Harvard University.

Gilligan, C. (1982b). New maps of development: New visions of maturity. *American Journal of Orthopsychiatry* **52**(2):199–212.

Ginsberg, G., and Harrison, C. H. (1977). *How to help your gifted child.* New York: Simon & Schuster.

Ginsberg, H., and Opper, S. (1979). *Piaget's theory of intellectual development* (2nd ed.). Englewood Cliffs, NJ: Prentice-Hall.

Ginzberg, E. (1972). Toward a theory of occupational choice: A restatement. *The Vocational Guidance Quarterly* **20**:169–176.

Giovanni, J., and Bilingsley, A. (1970). Child neglect among the poor: A study of parental inadequacy in families of three ethnic groups. *Child Welfare* **49**:196–204.

Glasser, W. (1965). *Reality therapy.* New York: Harper & Row.

Glasser, W. (1969). *Schools without failure.* New York: Harper & Row.

Glenn, N. D., and Weaver, C. N. (1979). Attitudes toward premarital, extramarital, and homosexual relationships in the U.S. in the 70's. *Journal of Sex Research* **15**:108–118.

Glueck, S., and Glueck, E. T. (1950). *Understanding juvenile delinquency.* New York: Commonwealth Fund.

Glynn, T. J. (1981). From family to peer: A review of transitions of influence among drug-using youth. *Journal of Youth and Adolescence* **10**(5):363–383.

Gold, M., and Petroni, R. J. (1980). Delinquent behavior in adolescence. In J. Adelson (ed.), *Handbook of adolescent psychology.* New York: Wiley.

Goldberg, H. (1983). *The new male-female relationship.* New York: William Morrow.

Goldman, R. (1964). *Religious thinking from childhood to adolescence.* London: Routledge & Kegan Paul.

Goldman, R. (1965). *Readiness for religion.* London: Routledge & Kegan Paul.

Goldstein, A. P.; Sprafkin, R. P.; Gershaw, N. J.; and Klein, P. (1980). *Skillstreaming the adolescent.* Champaign, IL: Research Press.

Goodlad, J. I. (1983). A study of schooling: Some findings and hypotheses. *Phi Delta Kappan*, March, pp. 465–470.

Goodman, A. B.; Siegel, C.; Craig, T. J.; and Lin, S. P. (1983). The relationship between socioeconomic class and prevalence of schizophrenia, alcoholism, and affective disorders treated by inpatient care in a suburban area. *American Journal of Psychiatry* **140**(2):166–170.

Goodwin, D. (1976). *Is alcoholism hereditary?* New York: Oxford U.

Goodwin, D. (1979). Alcoholism and heredity: A review and hypothesis. *Archives of General Psychiatry* **36**(1):57–61.

Goranson, R. E. (1975). The impact of T.V. violence. *Contemporary Psychology* **20**:291–293.

Gordon, T. (1970). *Parent effectiveness training.* New York: Plenum Books.

Gormally, J., and Rardin, D. (1981). Weight loss and maintenance and changes in diet and exercise for behavioral counseling and nutrition education. *Journal of Counseling Psychology* **28**(4):295–304.

Goswick, R. A., and Jones, W. H. (1982). Components of loneliness during adolescence. *Journal of Youth and Adolescence* **11**(5):373–383.

Gottesman, I. I. (1965). Personality and natural selection. In S. G. Vandenberg (ed.), *Methods and goals in human behavior genetics.* New York: Academic Press.

Gottlieb, D. (1966). Teaching and students: The views of negro and white teachers. *Sociology of Education* **37**:345–353.

Gove, W. R., and Herb, T. R. (1974). Stress and mental illness among the young: A comparison of the sexes. *Social Forces* **53**:256–265.

Gowan, J. C. (1979). The production of creativity through right hemisphere imagery. *Journal of Creative Behavior* **13**(1):39–51.

Goyan, J. (1980). U.S. Food and Drug Administration, United Press International.

Grabe, M. (1981). School size and the importance of school activities. *Adolescence* **16**(61):21–31.

Gray-Little, B., and Applebaum, M. I. (1979). Instrumentality effects in the assessment of racial differences in self-esteem. *Journal of Personality and Social Psychology* **37**(7):1221–1229.

Greenberg, B. S., and Atkin, C. K. (1983). The portrayal of driving on television, 1975–1980. *Journal of Communication* **33**(2):44–55.

Greenberger, E., and Steinberg, L. (1980). Part-time employment in in-school youth: A preliminary assessment of costs and benefits. In R. Taggart and B. Linder (eds.), *A review of youth employment problems, programs, and policies: Vol. 1. The youth employment problem: Causes and dimensions.* Washington, DC: Vice President's Task Force on Youth Employment, U.S. Department of Labor.

Greuling, J. W., and DeBlassie, R. R. (1980). Adolescent suicide. *Adolescence* **15**(59):589–601.

Griffin, B. S., and Griffin, C. T. (1978). *Juvenile delinquency in perspective.* New York: Harper & Row.

Grinder, R. E. (ed.). (1975). *Studies in adolescence.* (3rd ed.). New York: Macmillan.

Grinspoon, L., and Bakalor, J. B. (1976). *Cocaine: A drug and its social evolution.* New York: Basic Books.

Grinspoon, L., and Bakalor, J. B. (1979). Cocaine. In R. I. Dupont, A. Goldstein, and J. O'Donnell (eds.), *Handbook on drug abuse.* Washington, DC: U.S. Government Printing Office.

Grotevant, H. D., and Cooper, C. R. (1985, in press). Individuation in family relationships: A perspective on individual differences in the development of identity and role-taking skill in adolescence. *Human Development.*

Grotevant, H. D., and Durrett, M. E. (1980). Occupational knowledge and career development in adolescence. *Journal of Vocational Behavior* 17(2):171–182.

Grotevant, H. D. and Thorbecke, W. L. (1982). Sex differences in styles of occupational identity formation in late adolescence. *Developmental Psychology* 18(3):396–405.

Grotevant, H. D.; Thorbecke, W.; and Meyer, M. (1982). An extension of Marcia's identity status interview into the interpersonal domain. *Journal of Youth and Adolescence* 11(1):33–47.

Guernsey, C. E. (1983). Accountability of the juvenile court. *Juvenile and Family Court Journal* 34(2):67–78.

Guidance Associates. (1976). *Teacher training in values education: A workshop.*

Guidepost (1984). **27**(6):6.

Guilford, J. P. (1967). *The nature of human intelligence.* New York: McGraw-Hill.

Gullotta, T. P.; Stevens, S. J.; Donohue, K. C.; and Clark, V. S. (1981). Adolescents in corporate families. *Adolescence* 16(63):621–628.

Gump, P. V. (1966). *Big schools, small schools.* Moravia, NY: Chronicle Guidance Publications.

Guyot, G. W.; Fairchild, L.; and Hill, M. (1981). Physical fitness, sport participation, body build, and self-concept of elementary school children. *International Journal of Sport Psychology* 12(2):105–116.

Haan, N. (1978). Two moralities in action contexts: Relationships to thought, ego regulation, and development. *Journal of Personality and Social Psychology* 36(3):286–305.

Haan, N.; Smith, M. B.; and Block, J. (1968). Moral reasoning of young adults: Political-social behavior, family background, and personality correlates. *Journal of Personality and Social Psychology* 10(3):183–201.

Haan, N.; Weiss, R., and Johnson, V. (1982). The role of logic in moral reasoning and development. *Developmental Psychology* 18(2):245–256.

Hackett, G., and Betz, N. E. (1981). A self-efficacy approach to the career development of women. *Journal of Vocational Behavior* **18**(3):326–339.

Haggstrom, G. W.; Blaschke, D. E.; Lisowski, W.; and Morrison, P. A. (1981). *Teenage parents: Their ambitions and attainments.* Santa Monica, CA: Rand.

Haley, J. (1976). *Problem-solving therapy.* San Francisco: Jossey-Bass.

Haley, J. (1980). *Leaving home: The therapy of disturbed young people.* New York: McGraw-Hill.

Hall, G. S. (1904). *Adolescence: Its psychology and its relations to physiology, anthropology, sociology, sex, crime, religion, and education.* New York: Appleton.

Halmi, K. A.; Falk, J. R.; and Schwartz, E. (1981). Binge-eating and vomiting: A survey of a college population. *Psychological Medicine* **11**:697–706.

Hamachek, D. (1978). *Encounters with the self.* New York: Holt, Rinehart & Winston.

Hamachek, D. E. (1976). Development and dynamics of the self. In J. F. Adams (ed.), *Understanding adolescence* (3rd ed.). Boston: Allyn and Bacon.

Handel, A. (1980). Perceived change of self among adolescents. *Journal of Youth and Adolescence* **9**(6):507–519.

Hansen, I. (1980). *Sex education for young children.* Lecture presented at Wayne State University, Health Care Institute, Detroit, MI.

Hansen, L. S. (1977). Counseling and career (self) development of women. In H. J. Peters and J. C. Hansen (eds.), *Vocational guidance and career development* (3rd ed.). New York: Macmillan.

Hansen, S. L. (1977). Dating choices of high school students. *Family Life Coordinator* **26**:133–138.

Hansen, S. L., and Hicks, M. W. (1980). Sex role attitudes and perceived dating-mating choices of youth. *Adolescence* **15**:83–90.

Haraguchi, R. (1976). Developing programs meeting the special needs of physically disabled adolescents. *Rehabilitation Literature* **42**(3–4):75–78.

Harmon, L. W. (1981). The life and career plans of young adult college women: A follow-up story. *Journal of Counseling Psychology* **28**:416–427.

Harren, V. A. (1979). A model of career decision making for college students. *Journal of Vocational Behavior* **14**:119–133.

Harris, R.; Nolte, D.; and Nolte, C. (1980). Effects of intervention on teenagers' physical and psychological identity. *Psychological Reports* **46**:505–506.

Hartup, W. W. (1970). Peer interaction and social organization. In P. H. Mussen (ed.), *Carmichael's manual of child psychology* (Vol. 2, 3rd ed.). New York: John Wiley.

Hartup, W. W. (1976). Peer interaction and the behavioral development of the individual child. In E. Schopler and R. J. Reichler (eds.), *Psychopathology and child development.* New York: Plenum.

Hartup, W. W. (1979a). Peer relations and the growth of social competence. In M. W. Kent and J. E. Rolf (eds.), *The primary prevention of psychopathology* (Vol. 3). Hanover, NH: University Press of New England.

Hartup, W. W. (1979b). Perspectives on child and family interaction: Past, present, and future. In R. M. Lerner and G. B. Spanier (eds.), *Child influences on marital and family interaction: A life-span perspective.* New York: Academic Press.

Haskell, M. R., and Yablonsky, L. (1982). *Juvenile delinquency* (3rd ed.). Boston: Houghton Mifflin.

Hass, A. (1979). *Teenage sexuality: A survey of teenage sexual behavior.* New York: Macmillan.

Havighurst, R. J. (1972). *Developmental tasks and education.* New York: David McKay.

Havighurst, R. J. (1976). A cross-cultural view. In J. F. Adams (ed.), *Understanding adolescence* (3rd ed.). Boston: Allyn and Bacon.

Hayes, R. L. (1982). A review of adolescent identity formation: Implications for education. *Adolescence* **17**(65):153–165.

Hays, W. C., and Mindel, C. H. (1973). Extended kinship relations in black and white families. *Journal of Marriage and the Family* **35**:51–57.

Healy, C. C. (1982). *Career development: Counseling through the life stages.* Boston: Allyn and Bacon.

Hechinger, F. M. (1981). About education: A warning on the decline of quality in teacher training. *New York Times*, June 16, p. 17.

Hechinger, F. M., and Hechinger, G. (1975). *Growing up in America.* New York: McGraw-Hill.

Henderson, B. B.; Gold, S. R.; and McCord, M. T. (1982). Daydreaming and curiosity in gifted and average children and adolescents. *Developmental Psychology* **18**(4):576–582.

Hendry, L. B., and Gullies, P. (1978). Body type, body esteem, school and leisure: A study of overweight, average, and underweight adolescents. *Journal of Youth and Adolescence* **7**:181–195.

Henggeler, S. W.; Borduin, C. H.; Rodlick, J. D.; and Tavormina, J. B. (1979). Importance of task content for family interaction research. *Developmental Psychology* **15**:660–661.

Henning, J. S. (ed.) (1982). *The rights of children: Legal and psychological perspectives.* Springfield, Ill.: Chas. C. Thomas.

Herold, E. S. (1974). Stages of date selection: A reconciliation of divergent findings on campus values in dating. *Adolescence* **9**:113–120.

Herold, E. S., and Goodwin, M. S. (1979). Self-esteem and sexual permissiveness.

Journal of Clinical Psychology **35**:908–912.

Herold, E. S., and Goodwin, M. S. (1981). Adamant virgins, potential nonvirgins, and nonvirgins. *The Journal of Sex Research* **17**(2):97–113.

Herr, E. L., and Cramer, S. H. (1979). *Career guidance through the life span: Systematic approaches.* Boston: Little, Brown.

Herr, E. L., and Enderlein, T. E. (1976). Vocational maturity: The effects of school, grade, curriculum and sex. *Journal of Vocational Behavior* **8**:227–238.

Herzberg, F. (1966). *Work and the nature of man.* Cleveland: World Publishing.

Hetherington, E. M. (1972). Effects of father absence on personality development in adolescent daughters. *Developmental Psychology* **7**:313–326.

Hetherington, E. M.; Cox, M.; and Cox, R. (1978). The aftermath of divorce. In J. H. Stephens, Jr., and M. Matthews (eds.), *Mother-child, father-child relations.* Washington, DC: NAEYC.

Hill, A., and Boone, B. (1982). *If Maslow taught writing: A way to look at motivation in the composition classroom.* Berkeley: University of California.

Hill, J. P. (1978). *Secondary schools, socialization, and social development during adolescence.* Position paper prepared for the National Institute of Education, U.S. Department of Health, Education and Welfare, June.

Hill, J. P. (1980a). The family: Transformations in family relations. *Toward adolescence: The middle-school years.* Chicago: University of Chicago.

Hill, J. P. (1980b). *Understanding early adolescence: A framework.* Carrboro, NC: Center for Early Adolescence.

Hill, J. P., and Steinberg, L. D. (1976). *The development of autonomy in adolescence.* Paper presented at the Symposium on Research on Youth Problems, April 26–30, Fundacion Orbegoza Elizaquirre, Madrid, Spain.

Himadi, W. G.; Arkowitz, H.; Hinton, R.; and Perl, J. (1980). Minimal dating and its relationship to other social problems and general adjustment. *Behavior Therapy* **11**:345–352.

Hindelang, M. J. (1981). Variations in sex-race-age-specific incidence of offending. *American Sociological Review* **46**:461–474.

Hindelang, M. J.; Hirschi, T.; and Weiss, J. G. (1979). Correlates of delinquency: The illusion of discrepancy between self-report and official measures. *American Sociological Review* **44**:995–1014.

Hirschi, T. (1969). *Causes of delinquency.* Berkeley: University of California.

Hirschi, T., and Hindelang, M. J. (1977). Intelligence and delinquency: A revisionist review. *American Sociological Review* **42**:571–587.

Hispanic youth employment needs (1981). *El Noticiero* **20**:4.

Hlavsa, J.; Balanova E.; and Kolaj, D. (1980). Effectiveness of group creativity training. *Ceskoslovenska Psychologie* **24**(6):503–508.

Hoffman, M. L. (1970). Moral development. In P. H. Mussen (ed.), *Carmichael's manual of child psychology* (Vol. 2, 3rd ed.). New York: John Wiley.

Hoffman, M. L. (1974). Moral internalization: Current theory and research. In L. Berkowitz (ed.), *Advances in experimental social psychology* (Vol. 10). New York: Academic Press.

Hoffman, M. L. (1980). Moral development in adolescence. In J. Adelson (ed.), *Handbook of adolescent psychology.* New York: John Wiley.

Hohmann, M.; Hawker, D.; and Hohmann, C. (1982). Group process and adolescent leadership development. *Adolescence* **18**(67):613–620.

Holinger, P. C. (1978). Adolescent suicide: An epidemiological study of recent trends. *American Journal of Psychiatry* **135**:754–756.

Holland, M. (1981). Relationships between vocational development and self concept in sixth-grade students. *Journal of Vocational Behavior* **18**(2):228–236.

Hollinger, C. L. (1983). Self-perception and the career aspirations of mathematically talented female adolescents. *Journal of Vocational Behavior* **22**:49–62.

Hollingshead, A. B. (1975). *Elmtown's youth and Elmtown revisited.* New York: John Wiley.

Holowinsky, I. Z. (1980). Qualitative assessment of cognitive skills. *Journal of Special Education* **14**(2):155–163.

Holroyd, K., and Kahn, M. (1980). Personality factors in student drug use. In R. E. Muuss (ed.), *Adolescent behavior and society: A book of readings.* New York: Random House.

Holtzman, W. H., and Moore, B. M. (1965). Family structures and youth attitudes. In M. Sherif and C. W. Sherif (eds.), *Problems of youth: Transition to adulthood in a changing world.* Chicago: Aldine.

Holzman, P. S., and Grinker, R. R. (1974). Schizophrenia in adolescence. *Journal of Youth and Adolescence* **3**:267–279.

Honig, R. G. (1982). Group meetings on an adolescent medical ward. *Adolescence* **17**(65):99–106.

Hood, J.; Moore, T. E.; and Garner, D. (1982). Locus of control as a measure of ineffectiveness in anorexia nervosa. *Journal of Consulting and Clinical Psychology* **50**:3–13.

Horner, M. S. (1972). Toward an understanding of achievement-related conflicts in women. *Journal of Social Issues* **28**:157–176.

Horrocks, J. E., and Benimoff, M. (1967). Isolation from the peer group during adolescence. *Adolescence* **2**:41–52.

Howard, M. P., and Anderson, R. J. (1978). Early identification of potential school dropouts: A literature review. *Child Welfare* **57**:221–231.

Howell, F. M., and Frese, W. (1982). Early transition into adult roles: Some antecedents and outcomes. *American Educational Research Journal* **19**:51–73.

Hoyt, K. B. (1974). *An introduction to career education.* Washington, DC: U.S. Office of Education Policy Paper.

Hoyt, K. B. (1975). Career education: Challenges for counselors. *The Vocational Guidance Quarterly* **23**:303–310.

Huba, G. J., Wingard, J. A., and Bentler, P. M. (1979). Beginning adolescent drug use and peer and adult interaction patterns. *Journal of Consulting and Clinical Psychology* **47**:265–276.

Humphrey, H., and Lenham, C. (1984). Adolescent fantasy and self-fulfillment: The problem of female passivity. *Journal of Adolescence* **1**:295–304.

Hundleby, J. D.; Carpenter, R. A.; Ross, R. A. J.; and Mercer, G. W. (1982). Adolescent drug use and other behaviors. *The Journal of Child Psychology and Psychiatry and Allied Disciplines* **23**(1):61–68.

Hung, Y. (1978). Internal-external locus of control in physically handicapped students. *Bulletin of Educational Psychology* **11**:113–122.

Iacovetta, R. G. (1975). Adolescent-adult interaction and peer-group involvement. *Adolescence* **10**:327–336.

In re Gault, 387 U.S. 1 (1967).

Isralowitz, R. E. (1982). Juvenile violence in the school: An examination of the problem. *Juvenile and Family Court Journal* **33**(4):31–36.

Jackson, J. (1978). In pursuit of equity, ethics, and excellence. *Phi Delta Kappan,* November, p. 92.

Jackson, P. (1968). *Life in the classrooms.* New York: Holt, Rinehart & Winston.

Jacob, T. (1974). Patterns of family conflict and dominance as a function of child age and social class. *Developmental Psychology* **10**:1–12.

Jacobs, B. L., and Trulson, M. E. (1979). Mechanisms of action of LSD. *American Scientist* **67**:396–404.

Jacobs, J. (1971). *Adolescent suicide.* New York: Wiley.

James, T., and Tyack, D. (1983). Learning from past efforts to reform the high school. *Phi Delta Kappan,* February, 400–406.

Jariel, G. S. and Sharma, A. K. (1980). Creativity and its components as affected by intelligence, personality and their interaction. *Asian Journal of Psychology and Education* **6**(2):26–32.

Jasnoski, M. L. (1981). Exercise, changes in aerobic capacity, and changes in self-perceptions. *Journal of Research in Personality* **15**:460–466.

Jencks, C. S., and Brown, M. D. (1975). Effects of high schools on their students. *Harvard Educational Review* **45**:273–324.

Jensen, A. R. (1973). *Educability and group differences.* London: Methuen.

Jepsen, D. A. (1975). Occupational decision development over the high school years. *Journal of Vocational Behavior* **7**:225–237.

Jersild, A. T.; Brook, J. S.; and Brook. D. W. (1978). *The psychology of adolescence* (3rd ed.). New York: Macmillan.

Jessop, D. J. (1981). Family relationships as viewed by parents and adolescents: A specification. *Journal of Marriage and the Family* **43**:95–108.

Jessor, R. (1979). Marijuana: A review of recent psychological research. In R. I. Dupont, A. Goldstein, and J. O'Donnell (eds.), *Handbook on drug abuse.* Washington, DC: U.S. Government Printing Office.

Jessor, R.; Chase, J. A.; and Donovan, J. E. (1980). Psychological correlates of marijuana use and drinking in a national sample of adolescents. *American Journal of Public Health* **70**:604–612.

Jessor, R., and Jessor, S. L. (1977). *Problem behavior and psychosocial development: A longitudinal study of youth.* New York: Academic Press.

Jessor, S. L., and Jessor, R. (1975). Transition from virginity to nonvirginity among youth: A social-psychological study over time. *Developmental Psychology* **11**:473–484.

Johnson, C. (1982). Anorexia nervosa and bulimia. In T. J. Coates, A. C. Peterson, and C. Perry (eds.) *Adolescent health: Crossing the barriers.* New York: Academic Press.

Johnson, G. M.; Franklin, C. S.; and Locke, T. P. (1984). Relationships between adolescent drug use and parental drug behaviors. *Adolescence* **19**(74):295–300.

Johnson, S. S. (1975). *Update on education: A digest of the national assessment of educational progress.* Denver: The Education Commission of the States.

Johnston, J. A. (1948). Nutritional problems of adolescence. *American Medical Association Journal* **137**:1587–1588.

Johnston, L. D., and Bachman, J. G. (1976). Educational institutions. In J. F. Adams (ed.), *Understanding adolescence* (3rd ed.). Boston: Allyn and Bacon.

Johnston, L. D.; Bachman, J. G.; and O'Malley, P. M. (1979). *1979 Highlights, drugs and the nation's high school students: Five year national trends.* Rockville, MD: National Institute on Drug Abuse.

Johnston, L. D.; Bachman, J. G.; and O'Malley, P. M. (1981). *Highlights from student drug use in America, 1975–1981.* Rockville, MD: National Institute on Drug Abuse.

Johnston, L. D.; Bachman, J. G.; and O'Malley, P. M. (1983). *Highlights from student drug use in America, 1975–1983.* Rockville, MD: National Institute on Drug Abuse.

Jones, M. C. (1965). Psychological correlates of somatic development. *Child Development* **36**:899–991.

Jones, M. C., and Bayley, N. (1950). Physical maturing among boys as related to behavior. *Journal of Educational Psychology* **41**:129–148.

Jones, R. (1977). Human effects. In R. Peterson (ed.), *Marijuana research findings:*

1976 NIDA Research Monograph 14. Washington, DC: U.S. Government Printing Office.

Jones, W. M. (1977). The impact on society of youth who drop out or are under-educated. *Educational Leadership* **34**:411–416.

Jordaan, J. P., and Heyde, M. B. (1979). *Vocational maturity during high school years.* New York: Teachers College Press.

Josselyn, I. M. (1971). *Adolescence.* New York: Harper & Row.

Jucha, Z.; Rendecka, A.; and Zuraw, J. (1976). Self-acceptance and its relation to acceptance of others. *Psychologia Wychowawcza* **22**(1):14–38.

Juhasz, A. M. (1975). Sexual decision-making, the crux of the adolescent problem. In R. E. Grinder (ed.), *Studies in adolescence* (3rd ed.). New York: Macmillan.

Juhasz, A. M. (1976). A cognitive approach to sex education. In J. F. Adams (ed.), *Understanding adolescence* (3rd ed.). Boston: Allyn and Bacon.

Juhasz, A. M. (1982). Youth, identity and values: Erikson's historical perspective. *Adolescence* **18**:443–450.

Kahana, B., and Kahana, E. (1970). Grandparenthood from the perspective of the developing grandchild. *Developmental Psychology* **3**:98–105.

Kahn, J. H., and Nursten, J. P. (1962). School phobias: Refusal, a comprehensive view of school phobia, and other failures of school attendance. *American Journal of Orthopsychiatry* **32**:707–718.

Kalter, N. (1977). Children of divorce in an outpatient psychiatric population. *American Journal of Orthopsychiatry* **47**:40–51.

Kandel, D. B. (1978). Similarity in real-life adolescent friendship pairs. *Journal of Personality and Social Psychology* **36**:306–312.

Kandel, D. B. (1980a). Drug and drinking behavior among youth. *Annual Review of Sociology* **6**:235–285.

Kandel, D. B. (1980b). Stages in adolescent involvement in drug use. In R. E. Muuss (ed.), *Adolescent behavior and society: A book of readings.* New York: Random House.

Kandel, D. B., and Lesser, G. S. (1969). Parent-adolescent relationships and adolescent independence in the United States and Denmark. *Journal of Marriage and the Family* **31**:348–358.

Kandel, D. B., and Lesser, G. S. (1972). *Youth in two worlds: United States and Denmark.* San Francisco: Jossey-Bass.

Kaplan, S. L. (1980). Health habits and depression in adolescence. *Journal of Youth and Adolescence.* **9**(4):299–304.

Kaslow, F., and Sussman, M. B. (eds.) (1982). *Cults and the family.* New York: The Haworth Press.

Kassner, M.W. (1981). Will both spouses have careers? Predictions of preferred traditional or egalitarian marriages among university students. *Journal of Vocational Behavior* **18**(3):340–355.

Katchadourian, H. A. (1977). *The biology of adolescence.* San Francisco: Freeman.

Katchadourian, H. A., and Lunde, D. T. (1975). *Fundamentals of human sexuality* (2nd ed.). New York: Holt, Rinehart & Winston.

Katz, J. (1968). *No time for youth: Growth and constraint in college.* San Francisco: Jossey–Bass.

Kaufman, F. (1976). *Your gifted child and you.* Reston, VA: The Council for Exceptional Children.

Kaye, E. (1974). *The family guide to children's television.* New York: Pantheon Books.

Kazdin, A. E. (1983). Hopelessness, depression, and suicidal intent among psychiatrically disturbed inpatient children. *Journal for Consulting and Clinical Psychology* **514**(4):504–510.

Keating, D. P., and Clark, L. V. (1980). Development of physical and social reasoning in adolescence. *Developmental Psychology* **16**:23–30.

Kelley, R. K. (1972). The premarital sexual revolution: Comments on research. *Family Coordinator* **21**:334–336.

Keniston, K. (1965). *The uncommitted: Alienated youth in American society.* New York: Harcourt Brace & World.

Keniston, K. (1977). *All our children: The American family under pressure.* New York: Harcourt Brace Jovanovich.

Kephart, W. M. (1977). *The family, society and the individual* (4th ed.). Boston: Houghton Mifflin.

Kessler, S. (1975). Psychiatric genetics. In D. A. Hamburg and K. Brodie (eds.), *American handbook of psychiatry, Vol. VI: New psychiatric frontiers* (pp. 352–384). New York: Basic Books.

Kessler-Harris, A. (1982). *Out to work: A history of wage-earning women in the United States.* New York: Oxford University Press.

Kett, J. F. (1977). *Rites of passage: Adolescence in America 1790 to the present.* New York: Basic Books.

Keve, P. W. (1984). The consequences of prohibiting the jailing of juveniles. *VCU Department of Administration of Justice and Public Safety* **2**(5):3–29.

Khatena, J. (1978). *The creatively gifted child.* New York: Vantage.

Kidwell, J. S. (1981). Number of siblings, sibling spacing, sex, and birth order: Their effects on perceived parent-adolescent relationships. *Journal of Marriage and the Family* **43**(2):315–332.

Kimble, C., and Helmreich, R. (1972). Self-esteem and the need for social approval. *Psychonomic Science* **26**:339–342.

Kimmel, D. C. (1980). *Adulthood and aging* (2nd ed.). New York: John Wiley.

Klapp, O. E. (1982). Meaning lag in the information society. *Journal of Communication* **32**(2):56–66.

Klausmeier, H. J., and Allen, P. S. (1978). *Cognitive development in children and youth: A longitudinal study.* New York: Academic Press.

Klein, D.; Belcastro, P.; Gold, R. (1984). Achieving sex education program outcomes: Points of view from students and alumni. *Adolescence* **19**(76):805–816.

Klemer, R. H. (1971). Self-esteem and college dating experience as factors in mate selection and marital happiness: A longitudinal study. *Journal of Marriage and the Family* **33**:183–187.

Koff, E.; Rierdon, J.; and Sheingold, K. (1982). Memories of menarche: Age, preparation, and prior knowledge as determinants of initial menstrual experience. *Journal of Youth and Adolescence* **11**(1):1–9.

Kohlberg, L. (1971a). Stages of moral development as a basis for moral education. In C. M. Beck, B. S. Crittenden, and E. Sullivan (eds.), *Moral education: Interdisciplinary approaches.* Toronto: University of Toronto.

Kohlberg, L. (1975). The cognitive developmental approach to moral education. *Phi Delta Kappan*, June. **56**(10):670–677.

Kohlberg, L., and Hersh, R. H. (1977). Moral development: A review of the theory. *Theory into Practice* **16**(2):53–59.

Kohlberg L., and Kramer, R. B. (1969). Continuities and discontinuities in childhood and adult moral development. *Human Development* **12**:93–120.

Kohlberg, L., and Turiel, E. (1971b). Moral development and moral education. In Lesser, G. (ed.), *Psychology and the educational process.* Chicago: Scott, Foresman.

Kohn, M. L. (1977). *Class and conformity* (2nd ed.). Chicago: University of Chicago.

Krebs, D., and Rosenwald, A. (1977). Moral reasoning and moral behavior in conventional adults. *Merrill-Palmer Quarterly* **23**(2):77–87.

Kuhn, D. (1976). Short-term longitudinal evidence for the sequentiality of Kohlberg's early stages of moral judgment. *Developmental Psychology* **12**(2):162–166.

Kulik, J. A.; Stein, K. B.; and Sarbin, T. R. (1968). Disclosure of delinquent behavior under conditions of anonymity and nonanonymity. *Journal of Counseling and Clinical Psychology* **32**:506–509.

Kurdek, L. A. (1978). Perspective taking as the cognitive basis of children's moral development: A review of the literature. *Merrill-Palmer Quarterly* **24**(1):3–28.

Ladame, F., and Jeanneret, O. (1982). Suicide in adolescence: Some comments on epidemiology and prevention. *Journal of Adolescence* **5**:355–366.

Ladenburg, M., and Ladenburg, T. (1977). Moral reasoning and social studies. *Theory into Practice* **16**(2):112–117.

Lambie, R. (1983). Personal discussion (October). Richmond, VA.

Lamke, L. K. (1982). Adjustment and sex-role orientation in adolescence. *Journal of Youth and Adolescence* **11**(3):247–259.

Langdell, J. (1973). Depressive reactions in childhood and adolescence. In S. A. Szurek and I. N. Berlin (eds.), *Clinical studies in childhood psychoses* (pp. 128–148). New York: Brunner/Mazel.

Larkin, R. W. (1979). *Suburban youth in cultural crisis.* New York: Oxford University.

Larson, D. L.; Spreitzer, E. A.; and Snyder, E. E. (1976). Social factors in the frequency of romantic involvement among adolescents. *Adolescence* **11**:7–12.

Larson, L. E. (1980). The influence of parents and peers during adolescence: The situation hypothesis revisited. In R. E. Muuss (ed.), *Adolescent behavior and society* (3rd ed.). New York: Random House.

Larson, R., and Csikszentmihalyi, M. (1978). Experiential correlates of time alone in adolescence. *Journal of Personality* **46**(4):677–693.

Law Enforcement Assistance Administration (1974). *Sixth annual report of LEAA.* Washington, DC: U.S. Government Printing Office.

Lazarus, R. S. and Monat, A. (1979). *Personality* (3rd ed.). Englewood Cliffs, NJ: Prentice-Hall.

Leadbetter, B. J., and Droune, J. P. (1981). The adolescent's use of formal operational thinking in solving problems related to identity resolution. *Adolescence* **16**(1):111–121.

Lee, L. C. (1971). The concomitant development of cognitive and moral modes of thought: A test of selected deductions from Piaget's theory. *Genetic Psychology Monographs* **83**:93–146.

Lefkowitz, M. M.; Eron, L. D.; Walder, L. O.; and Huesman, L. R. (1972). Television violence and children's aggression: A follow-up study. In G. A. Comstock and E. A. Rubenstein (eds.), *Television and social behavior: Television and adolescent aggressiveness* (Vol. 3). Washington, DC: U.S. Government Printing Office.

Lehtinen-Rogan, L. E. (1971). How do we teach him? In E. Schloss (ed.), *The educator's enigma.* San Rafael, CA: Academic Therapy.

Lenney, E. (1979). Androgyny: Some audacious assertions toward its coming of age. *Sex Roles* **5**:703–719.

Leona, M. H. (1978). An examination of adolescent clique language in a suburban secondary school. *Adolescence* **13**(51):496–502.

Lerner, R. M. (1976). Physical attractiveness, physical effectiveness, and self-concept in late adolescents. *Adolescence* **11**:313–326.

Lerner, R. M. and Spanier, G. B. (1980). *Adolescent development, a life-span perspective.* New York: McGraw-Hill.

Levinson, D. J. (1978). *The seasons of a man's life.* New York: A. A. Knopf.

Levy, B. (1972). Do teachers sell girls short? *Today's Education* **61**:27–29.

Levy, B. (1974). Do schools sell girls short? In J. Stacey and B. J. Daniels (eds.), *And Jill came tumbling after: Sexism in American education.* New York: Dell.

Lewin, K. (1939). Field theory and experiment in social psychology: Concepts and methods. *American Journal of Sociology* **44**:868–897.

Liben, L. S. (ed.) (1978). *Deaf children: Developmental perspectives.* New York: Academic Press.

Lickona, T. (1977). Creating a just community with children. *Theory into Practice* **16**(2):97–104.

Lidz, T. (1968). *The person: His development throughout the life cycle.* New York: Basic Books.

Lidz, T. (1976). *The person.* New York: Basic Books.

Liebert, R. M.; Neale, J. M.; and Davidson, E. S. (1973). *The early window: Effects of television on children and youth.* Elmsford, NY: Pergamon Press.

Liebman, R.; Sargent, J.; and Silver, M. (1983). A family systems orientation to the treatment of anorexia nervosa. *Journal of the American Academy of Child Psychiatry* **22**(2):128–133.

Lincoln, B. (1981). *Emerging from the chrysalis: Studies in rituals of women's initiation.* Cambridge, MA: Harvard University.

Linn, M. C., and Swiney, J.F. (1981). Individual differences in formal thought: Role of expectations and aptitudes. *Journal of Educational Psychology* **73**(2):274–286.

Lipsitz, J. S. (1979). Adolescent development: Myths and realities. *Children Today* (September-October), pp. 2–7.

Lipsitz, J. S. (1980). *Growing up forgotten: A review of research and programs concerning early adolescence.* New Brunswick, NJ: Transaction.

Lipsitz, J. S. (1983). *Successful schools of young adolescents.* Chapel Hill, NC: The Center for Early Adolescence.

Lipton, D. N., and Nelson, R. O. (1980). The contribution of initiation behaviors to dating frequency. *Behavior Therapy* **11**:59–67.

Lloyd, D. N. (1978). Prediction of school failure from third grade data. *Educational and Psychological Measurement* **38**(4):1193–1200.

Lockheed, M. E. (1978). *American Educational Research Journal* (book review) **15**:586–589.

Lockwood, A. L. (1978). The effects of values clarification and moral development curricula on school-age subjects: A critical reveiew of recent research. *Review of Educational Research* **48**(3):325–364.

Long, N. J.; Morse, W. C.; and Newman, R. G. (eds.) (1971). *Conflict in the classroom: The education of children with problems* (2nd ed.). Belmont, CA: Wadsworth.

Long-Laws, J., and Schwartz, P. (1977). *Sexual scripts: The social construction of female sexuality.* Hinsdale, IL: Dryden.

Louden, D. M. (1980). A comparative study of self-esteem among minority group adolescents in Britain. *Journal of Adolescence* **3**:17–33.

Luepnitz, D. A. (1979). Which aspects of divorce affect children? *Family Coordinator* **28**:79–85.

Lueptow, L. B. (1980a). Social change and sex-role change in adolescent orientations toward life, word, and achievement: 1964–1975. *Social Psychology Quarterly* **43**:48–58.

Lueptow, L. B. (1980b). Social structure, social change and parental influence in adolescent sex-role socialization: 1964–1975. *Journal of Marriage and the Family* **42**(1):93–103.

Lull, J. (1982). Popular music: Resistance to new wave. *Journal of Communication* **32**(1):121–131.

Lunneborg, P. W. (1975). Interest differentiation in high school and vocational indecision in college. *Journal of Vocational Behavior* **7**:297–303.

Lutwak, N. (1984). The interrelationship of ego, moral, and conceptual development in a college group. *Adolescence* **19**(75):675–688.

Lyle, J., and Hoffman, H. R. (1972). Children's use of television and other media. In E. A. Ruberstein, G. A. Comstock, and J. P. Murray (eds.), *Television and social behavior* (Vol. 4). Washington, DC: U.S. Government Printing Office.

Lynn, D. B. (1959). A note on sex differences in the development of masculine and feminine identification. *Psychological Review* **46**:126–135.

Maccoby, E., and Jacklin, C. (1974). *The psychology of sex differences.* Stanford, CA: Stanford University Press.

Mackey, J. (1977). Strategies for reducing adolescent alienation. *Educational Leaderhsip* **34**:449–452.

Madigan, C., and Neikirk, B. (1982). A technological age: The dawning of a new way of life finds Americans largely unprepared. *The Charlotte Observer,* December 12.

Maeroff, G. L. (1981). Discipline leads concern in poll on school. *The New York Times,* August 23, p. 32.

Maloney, M. J., and Klykylo, W. M. (1983). An overview of anorexia nervosa, bulimia, and obesity in children and adolescents. *Journal of the American Academy of Child Psychiatry* **22**(2):99–107.

Marcia, J. E. (1966). Development and validation of ego-identity status. *Journal of Personality and Social Psychology* **3**:551–558.

Marcia, J. E. (1967). Ego identity status: Relationship to change in self-esteem, "general maladjustment," and authoritarianism. *Journal of Personality* **35**:118–133.

Marcia, J. E. (1976). Identity six years after: A follow up study. *Journal of Youth and Adolescence* **5**(4):145–160.

Marcia, J. E. (1980). Identity in adolescence. In J. Adelson (ed.), *Handbook of adolescent psychology.* New York: John Wiley.

Margulies, R. Z.; Kessler, R. C.; and Kandel, D. B. (1977). A longitudinal study of onset of drinking among high school students. *Journal of Studies on Alcohol* **35**:897–911.

Marland, S. P. (1974). *Career education: A proposal for reform.* New York: McGraw-Hill.

Marsh, G. E., and Price, J. (1980). *Methods for teaching the mildly handicapped adolescent.* St. Louis: C. V. Mosby.

Marshall, S. J., and Wijting, J. P. (1980). Relationships of achievement motivation and sex-role identity to college women's career orientation. *Journal of Vocational Behavior* **16**(3):299–311.

Martin, B. (1975). Parent-child relations. In F. D. Horowitz (ed.), *Review of child development research* (Vol. 4). Chicago: University of Chicago Press.

Martin, B. (1977). *Abnormal psychology.* New York: Holt, Rinehart & Winston.

Maruyama, G.; Rubin, R.; and Kinsbury, G. (1981). Self esteem and educational achievement: Independent constructs with a common cause? *Journal of Personality and Social Psychology* **40**(5):962–975.

Marvin, D., and Winther, M. (1983). Computer-ease: A twentieth-century literacy emergent. *Journal of Communication* **33**(1):92–108.

Maslow, A. H. (1954). *Motivation and personality.* New York: Harper & Row.

Maslow, A. H. (1971). *The farther reaches of human nature.* New York: Viking.

Matteson, R. (1974). Adolescent self-esteem, family communication, and marital satisfaction. *The Journal of Psychology* **86**:35–47.

Matthews, E., and Tiedeman, D. V. (1964). Attitudes toward career and marriage and the development of life style in young women. *Journal of Counseling Psychology* **11**:375–384.

Matthews, M., and McCune, S. (1977). *Complying with Title IX: Implementing institutional self-evaluation.* Washington, DC: U.S. Department of Health, Education and Welfare.

Mayle, P. (1975). *What's happening to me?* Secaucus, NJ: Lyle.

McAlister, A. L.; Perry, C.; and Maccoby, N. (1979). Adolescent smoking: Onset and prevention. *Pediatrics* **63**:650–658.

McAnarney, E. R. (1979). Adolescent and young adult suicide in the United States: A reflection of social unrest. *Adolescence* **14**:765–774.

McCabe, A. E., and Moriarity, R. J. (1977). *A laboratory/field study of television violence and aggression in children's sports.* Paper presented at the Biennial Meeting of the Society for Research in Child Development, New Orleans, March.

McCallum, R. S., and Glynn, S. M. (1979). Hemispheric specialization and creative behavior. *Journal of Creative Behavior* **13**(4):263–273.

McCandless, B. R., and Coop, R. H. (1979). *Adolescents: Behavior and development* (2nd ed.). New York: Holt, Rinehart & Winston.

McCandless, B. R., and Evans, E. D. (1973). *Children and youth.* Hinsdale, IL: Dryden.

McCandless, B. R.; Roberts, A.; and Starnes, T. (1972). Teachers' marks, achievement test scores, and aptitude relations with respect to social class, race, and sex. *Journal of Educational Psychology* **63**:153–159.

McCaul, K. D.; Glascow, R.; O'Neil, N. K.; Freeborn, V.; and Rump, B. S. (1982). Predicting adolescent smoking. *The Journal of School Health* **8**:342–346.

McDaniel, T. R. (1982). What's your P.Q.? *Phi Delta Kappan* **63**(7):464–468.

McDermott, D. (1984). The relationship of parental drug use and parents' attitude concerning adolescent drug use to adolescent drug use. *Adolescence* **19**(73):89–98.

McDonald, G. W. (1977). Parental identification by the adolescent: A social power approach. *Journal of Marriage and the Family* **39**:705–720.

McDonald, G. W. (1980). Parental power and adolescents' parental identification. *Journal of Marriage and the Family* **42**:289–296.

McGovern, K. B.; Arkowitz, H.; and Gilmore, S. K. (1975). Evaluation of social skill training programs for college dating inhibitions. *Journal of Counseling Psychology* **22**:505–512.

McKissack, I. J. (1975). Early socialization: The baseline in delinquency research. *International Journal of Criminology and Psychology* **3**:43–51.

McLaughlin, D., and Whitfield, R. (1984). Adolescents and their experience of parental divorce. *Journal of Adolescence* **1**:155–170.

McMicking, L. (1982). Proposed radical changes in our juvenile justice system. *Juvenile and Family Court Journal* **33**(1):51–53.

McMillan, D. W., and Hiltonsmith, R. W. (1982). Adolescents at home: An exploratory study of the relationship between perception of family social climate, general well-being, and actual behavior in the home setting. *Journal of Youth and Adolescence* **11**(4):301–315.

McMillan, E. (1984). *Recollections of a sex-educator's experiment.* Unpublished paper.

McPherson, S. J.; McDonald, L. E.; and Ryer, C. W. (1983). Intensive counseling with families of juvenile offenders. *Juvenile and Family Court Journal* **34**(1):27–33.

Mead, M. (1928). *Coming of age in Samoa.* New York: William Morrow.

Mead, M. (1935). *Sex and temperament in three primitive societies.* New York: Dell.

Mead, M. (1970). *Culture and commitment: A study of the generation gap.* Garden City, NY: Doubleday.

Meadow, K. P. (1975). The development of deaf children. In E. M. Hetherington (ed.), *Review of child development research* (Vol. 5). Chicago: University of Chicago.

Mednick, S. S., and Christiansen, K. O. (1977). *Biosocial bases of criminal behavior.* New York: Garden Press.

Mehl, L.; Brendsel, C.; and Peterson, G. (1977). Children at birth: Effects and implications. *Journal of Sex and Marital Therapy* **3**(4):274–279.

Menge, C. P. (1982). Dream and reality: Constructive change partners. *Adolescence* **17**(66):419–442.

Mercer, G. W., and Kohn, P. M. (1980). Child-rearing factors, authoritarianism, drug use attitudes, and adolescent drug use: A model. *The Journal of Genetic Psychology* **136**:159–171.

Merritt, R. (1983). Comparison of tolerance of white graduates of racially integrated and racially segregated schools. *Adolescence* **18**(69):67–70.

Mickelson, R. A. (1980). Social stratification processes in secondary schools: A comparison of Beverly Hills High School and Morningside High School. *Journal of Education,* **162**:83–112.

Milgram, S. (1962). Behavioral study of obedience. In E. Aronson (ed.), *Readings about the social animal.* San Francisco: W. H. Freeman.

Milgram, S. (1963). Behavioral study of obedience. *Journal of Abnormal Social Psychology* **67**(4):371–378.

Milgram, S. (1974). *Studies on obedience.* New York: Harper & Row.

Miller, C. J. (1981). Sex roles, personality, and intellectual abilities in adolescents. *Journal of Youth and Adolescence* **10**(2):85–112.

Miller, J. D., and Cisin, I. H. (1979). *Highlights from the national survey on drug abuse: 1979.* Washington, DC: National Institute on Drug Abuse.

Miller, N. B., and Cantwell, D. P. (1976). Siblings as therapists. *American Journal of Psychiatry* **133**:447–450.

Miller, P. Y. (1979). Female delinquency: Fact and fiction. In M. Sugar (ed.), *Female adolescent development.* New York: Brunner/Mazel.

Miller, W. B. (1976a). Sexual and contraceptive behavior in young unmarried women. *Primary Care* **3**:427–453.

Miller, W. B. (1976b). Youth gangs in the urban crisis era. In J. F. Short, Jr. (ed.), *Delinquency, crime and society.* Chicago: University of Chicago.

Miller, W. B. (1977). The rumble this time. *Psychology Today*, May, pp. 52–55.

Minahan, N. M. (1971). Relationships among self-perceived physical attractiveness, body shape, and personality of teen-aged girls. *Dissertation Abstracts International* **32**:1249–1250.

Minuchin, S. (1974). *Families and family therapy.* Cambridge, MA: Harvard University.

Minuchin, S., and Fishman, H. C. (1981). *Family therapy techniques.* Cambridge, MA: Harvard University.

Minuchin, S.; Rosman, B. L.; and Baker, L. (1978). *Psychosomatic families: Anorexia nervosa in context.* Cambridge, MA: Harvard University Press.

Mischel, W. (1976a). *Introduction to personality.* New York: Holt, Rinehart & Winston.

Mischel, W., and Mischel, H. N. (1976b). A cognitive social-learning approach to morality and self-regulation. In T. Lickona (ed.), *Moral development and behavior: Theory, research, and social issues* (pp. 84–107). New York: Holt, Rinehart & Winston.

Mitchell, J. E.; Hong, M. K.; and Corman, C. (1979). Childhood onset of alcohol abuse. *American Journal of Orthopsychiatry* **51**:511–513.

Mogul, S. L. (1980). Asceticism in adolescence and anorexia nervosa. *Psychoanalytic Study of the Child* **35**:155–175.

Mokros, J.; Taylor, R.; and O'Neill, M. (1977). Adolescents' perceptions of the causes and consequences of success in sex-linked occupations. *Sex Roles* **3**:353–364.

Money, J., and Ehrhardt, A. A. (1972). *Man and woman, boy and girl: The differentiation and dimorphism of gender identity from conception to maturity.* Baltimore: Johns Hopkins University.

Montemayor, R., and Eisen, M. (1977). The development of self-conceptions from childhood to adolescence. *Developmental Psychology* **13**(4):314–319.

Moore, D., and Schultz, N. R. (1983a). Loneliness at adolescence: Correlates, attributions, and coping. *Journal of Youth and Adolescence* **12**:95–100.

Moore, D. W., and Hotch, D. F. (1982). Parent-adolescent separations: The role of parental divorce. *Journal of Youth and Adolescence* **11**(2):115–119.

Moore, D. W., and Hotch, D. F. (1983b). The importance of different home-leaving strategies to late adolescents. *Adolescence* **18**(70):413–416.

Moos, R. H.; Moos, B. S.; and Kulik, J. A. (1976). College-student abstainers, moderate drinkers, and heavy drinkers: A comparative analysis. *Journal of Youth and Adolescence* **5**:349–360.

Morash, M. A. (1980). Working class membership and the adolescent identity crisis. *Adolescence* **15**(58):313–320.

More women chiefs (1983). *Parade Magazine,* February 6.

Morgan, E., and Farber, B. A. (1982). Toward a reformulation of the Eriksonian model of female identity development. *Adolescence* **17**(65):199–211.

Morrison, E.; Starks, K.; Hyndman, C.; and Ronzio, N. (1980). *Growing up sexual.* New York: D. Van Nostrand.

Morrison, J. R. (1974). Parental divorce as a factor in childhood psychiatric illness. *Comprehensive Psychiatry* **15**(2):95–102.

Mosher, R. (1977). Theory and practice: A new e.r.a.? *Theory into Practice* **16**(2):81–88.

Mosley, M. H., and Smith, P. J. (1982). What works in learning? Students provide the answers. *Phi Delta Kappan* **64**(4):273.

Mosteller, F., and Moynihan, D. P. (1972). *An equality of educational opportunity.* New York: Vintage.

Munley, P. H. (1975). Erik Erikson's theory of psychosocial development and vocational behavior. *Journal of Counseling Psychology* **22**:314–319.

Munley, P. H. (1977). Erikson's theory of psychosocial development and career development. *Journal of Vocational Behavior* **10**:261–269.

Murray, F. D., and Armstrong, S. L. (1978). Adult nonconversation of numerical equivalence. *Merril-Palmer Quarterly* **24**:255–263.

Murray, J. P. (1980). *Television and youth: 25 years of research and controversy.* Boys Town, NE: Boys Town Center for the Study of Youth Development.

Mussen, P. H.; Conger, J. J.; and Kagan, J. (1974). *Child development and personality* (4th ed.). New York: Harper & Row.

Muuss, R. E. (1980). Identity in adolescence. In J. Adelson (ed.), *Handbook of adolescent psychology.* New York: Wiley.

Muuss, R. E. (1982a). Social cognition: David Elkind's theory of adolescent egocentrism. *Adolescence* **17**(66):249–265.

Muuss, R. E. (1982b). Social cognition: Robert Selman's theory of role taking. *Adolescence* **17**(67):499–525.

Nasaw, D. (1979). *Schooled to order: A social history of public schooling in the United States.* New York: Oxford University.

Nash, S. C. (1978). Sex roles as a mediator of intellectual functioning. In M. A. Wittig and A. C. Peterson (eds.), *Sex-related differences in cognitive functioning: Developmental issues.* New York: Academic Press.

National Assessment of Educational Progress (1979). *Changes in mathematical achievement 1973–78.* Washington, DC: National Institute of Education.

National Assessment of Educational Progress. (1981). *Reading, thinking and writing: Results from the 1979–80 national assessment of reading and literature.* Denver, CO: Education Commission of the States.

National college bound seniors, 1981 (1982). New York: College Entrance Examination Board.

National Commission on Excellence in Education (1983). *A Nation at risk: The imperative for educational reform.* Washington, DC: U.S. Department of Education.

National Institute of Mental Health (1978). *Yours, mine, and ours: Tips for stepparents* (U.S. Department of HEW, #ADM 78-676). Washington, DC: U.S. Government Printing Office.

National Panel on High School and Adolescent Education (1976). *The education of adolescents.* Washington, DC: U.S. Government Printing Office.

Neapolitan, J. (1981). Parental influences on aggressive behavior: A social learning approach. *Adolescence* **16**(64):831–840.

Neimark, E.D. (1975). Intellectual development during adolescence. In F. D. Horowitz (ed.), *Review of child development research* (Vol. 4). Chicago: University of Chicago Press.

Nelson, E. A., and Rosenbaum, E. (1975). Language patterns within the youth subculture: Development of slang vocabularies. In R. E. Grinder (ed.), *Studies in adolescence* (3rd ed.). New York: Macmillan.

Nelson, J. L. (1980). The uncomfortable relationship between moral education and citizenship instruction. In R. W. Wilson and G. J. Schochet (eds.), *Moral development and politics* (pp. 256–285). New York: Praeger.

Newland, G. A. (1981). Differences between left- and right-handers on a measure of creativity. *Perceptual and Motor Skills* **53**(3):787–792.

Newman, B. M., and Newman, P. R. (1978). The concept of identity: Research and theory. *Adolescence* **13**:157–166.

Newsweek magazine (1969).

Nicholson, S. I., and Antill, J. K. (1981). Personal problems of adolescents and their relationship to peer acceptance and sex-role identity. *Journal of Youth and Adolescence* **10**(4):309–325.

Nielsen, L. (1982). *How to motivate adolescents.* Englewood Cliffs, NJ: Prentice-Hall.

Noble, E. (1978). *Third special report to the U.S. Congress on alcohol and health.* Washington, DC: U.S. Government Printing Office.

Noeth, R. J., and Prediger, D. J. (1978). Career development over the high school years. *Vocational Development Quarterly* **26**:244–254.

Norman, J., and Harris, M. W. (1981). *The private life of the American teenager.* New York: Rawson, Wade.

Oberlander, M. I.; Frauenfelder, K. J.; and Heath, H. (1970). Ordinal position, sex of sibling, sex, and personal preferences in a group of eighteen-year-olds. *Journal of Consulting and Clinical Psychology* **35**:122–125.

O'Connell, A. N. (1976). The relationship between life style and identity synthesis and resynthesis in traditional, neotraditional, and nontraditional women. *Journal of Personality* **44**:675–688.

Oetting, E., and Miller, C. D. (1977). Work and the disadvantages: The work adjustment hierarchy. *Personnel and Guidance Journal* **56**:29–35.

Offer, D., and Offer, J. B. (1975). *From teenage to young manhood: A psychological study.* New York: Basic Books.

Offer, D.; Ostrov, E.; and Howard, K. I. (1977). The self-image of adolescents: A study of four cultures. *Journal of Youth and Adolescence* **6**(3):265–280.

Offer, D.; Ostrov, E.; and Howard, K. I. (1981). *The adolescent: A psychological self-portrait.* New York: Basic Books.

Offer, D.; Ostrov, E.; and Howard, K. I. (1982). Family perceptions of adolescent self-image. *Journal of Youth and Adolescence* **11**(4):281–291.

Offord, D. R.; Abrams, N.; Allen, N.; and Poushinsky, M. (1979). Broken homes, parental psychiatric illness, and female delinquency. *American Journal of Orthopsychiatry* **49**:252–263.

O'Gorman, P. A.; Stringfield, S.; and Smith, I. (eds.). (1976). *Defining adolescent alcohol use: Implications toward and definition of adolescent alcoholism.* Washington, DC: National Council on Alcoholism.

Olson, D. H.; Russell, C. S.; and Sprenkle, D. H. (1980). Marital and family therapy: A decade review. *Journal of Marriage and the Family* **42**:973–994.

O'Malley, P. M., and Bachman, J. G. (1983). Self-esteem: Change and stability between ages 13 and 23. *Developmental Psychology* **19**(2):257–268.

O'Malley, P. M.; Bachman, J. G.; and Johnston, J. (1977). *Youth in transition, final report: Five years beyond high school: Causes and consequences of educational attainment.* Ann Arbor, MI: Institute for Social Research.

O'Moore, M. (1980). Social acceptance of the physically handicapped child in the ordinary school. *Child Care, Health and Development* **6**(6):317–338.

Orbel, S. F. (1981). Formal operational thinking among African adolescents. *Journal of Instructional Psychology* **8**(1):10–14.

Osborn, S. G., and West, D. J. (1980). Do young delinquents really reform? *Journal of Adolescence* **3**:99–114.

Osipow, S. H. (1983). *Theories of career development.* Englewood Cliffs, NJ: Prentice-Hall.

Oster, R. A. (1983). Peer counseling: Drug and alcohol abuse prevention. *Journal of Primary Prevention* **3**(3):188–199.

Owuamanam, D. O. (1983). Peer and parental influence on sexual activities of school-going adolescents in Nigeria. *Adolescence* **18**(64):169–179.

Pace, N. A. (1981). Driving on pot. In L. H. Gross (ed.), *The parent's guide to teenagers.* New York: Macmillan.

Page, E. B., and Grandon, G. M. (1979). Family configuration and mental ability: Two theories contrasted with U.S. data. *American Educational Research Journal* **16**(3):257–272.

Palmer, A. B., and Wohl, J. (1972). Some personality characteristics of honors students. *College Student Journal* **6**:106–111.

Paolitto, D. R. (1977). The role of the teacher in moral education. *Theory into Practice* **16**(2):73–80.

Parikh, B. (1980). Development of moral judgment and its relation to family environmental factors in Indian and American families. *Child Development* **51**:1030–1039.

Parish, T. S. (1980a). The relationship between factors associated with father loss and individuals' level of moral judgment. *Adolescence* **13**(59):535–541.

Parish, T. S., and Dostal, J. W. (1980b). Evaluations of self and parent figures by children from intact, divorced and reconstituted families. *Journal of Youth and Adolescence* **9**:347–351.

Parish, T. S., and Taylor, J. (1979). The impact of divorce and subsequent father absence on children's and adolescents' self-concepts. *Journal of Youth and Adolescence* **8**:427–432.

Parker, M., and Gaier, E. L. (1980). Religion, religious beliefs, and religious practices among conservative Jewish adolescents. *Adolescence* **15**(58):361–374.

Parlee, M. B. (1979). The friendship bond. *Psychology Today,* October, pp. 43–45.

Parsons, J. E.; Kaczala, C. M.; and Meece, J. L. (1982). Socialization of achievement attitudes and beliefs: Classroom influences. *Child Development* **53**:322–339.

Passmore, D. L., and Welch, F. G. (1983). Relationship between preferences for part-time work and characteristics of unemployed youths. *Adolescence* **18**(69):181–192.

Patterson, G. R. (1981). *Cooercive family processes.* Eugene, OR: Castala Publishing.

Paul, M. J., and Fischer, J. L. (1980). Correlates of self-concept among black early adolescents. *Journal of Youth and Adolescence* **9**(2):163–173.

Paulsen, E. P. (1972). Obesity in children and adolescents. In H. L. Barnett and A. H. Einhorn (eds.), *Pediatrics.* New York: Appleton-Century-Crofts.

Paulson, M. J.; Lin, T. T.; and Hanssen, C. (1980). Family harmony: An etiologic factor in alienation. In R. E. Muuss (ed.), *Adolescent behavior and society* (3rd ed.). New York: Random House.

Pearl, D. (1978). *TV and social behavior* (National Institute of Mental Health, DHEW Publication #ADM 77–469). Washington, DC: U.S. Government Printing Office.

Perry, W. G., Jr. (1970). *Forms of intellectual and ethical development in the college years.* New York: Holt, Rinehart & Winston.

Peskin, H. (1972). Pubertal onset and ego functioning. In J. Kestenberg (ed.), *The adolescent: Physical development, sexuality and pregnancy.* New York: MSS Information.

Petersen, R. C. (1979). *Marijuana and health: Seventh annual report to the U.S. Congress from the Secretary of Health, Education, and Welfare.* Rockville, MD: National Institute on Drug Abuse.

Peterson, A. C., and Wittig, M. A. (1979). Differential cognitive development in adolescent girls. In M. Sugar (ed.), *Female adolescent development.* New York: Brunner/Mazel.

Peterson, C. (1982). The imaginary audience and age, cognition, and dating. *The Journal of Genetic Psychology* **140**:317–318.

Peterson, E. T., and Kunz, P. R. (1975). Parental control over adolescents according to family size. *Adolescence* **10**:419–427.

Peterson, N. (1982). Is the rebellion over? *Parade*, January 31.

Petroni, F. A. (1972). Adolescent liberalism: The myth of a generation gap. *Adolescence,* **7**(26):221–232.

Phares, J. (1976). *Locus of control in personality.* Morristown, NJ: General Learning Press.

Philliber, S. G., and Tatum, M. L. (1982). Sex education and the double standard in high school. *Adolescence* **17**(66):273–283.

Piaget, J. (1932). *The moral development of the child.* London: Kegan Paul.

Piaget, J. (1970). *Science of education and the psychology of the child.* New York: Orion.

Piaget, J., and Inhelder, B. (1969). *The psychology of the child.* New York: Basic Books.

Piazza, E.; Rollins, N.; and Lewis, F. S. (1983). Measuring severity and change in anorexia nervosa. *Adolescence* **18**(70):293–305.

Piliavin, I., and Briar, S. (1964). Police encounters with juveniles. *American Journal of Sociology* **70**:206–214.

Pittel, S. M., and Oppedahl, M. C. (eds.) (1979). The enigma of PCP. In R. I. Dupont, A. Goldstein, and J. O'Donnell (eds.), *Handbook on drug abuse.* Washington, DC: U.S. Government Printing Office.

Place, D. M. (1975). The dating experience for adolescent girls. *Adolescence* **10**:157–174.

Plato (1968). *Plato's republic* (B. Josett, Trans.). Bridgeport, CT: Airmont.

Podd, M. H. (1972). Ego-identity status and morality: The relationship between two developmental constructs. *Developmental Psychology* **6**(3):497–507.

Pollin, W. (1980). Health consequences of marijuana use. Statement before the Subcommittee on Criminal Justice, Committee on the Judiciary, U.S. Senate, January 16. Rockville, MD: National Institute on Drug Abuse.

Polovy, P. (1980). A study of moral development and personality relationships in adolescents and young adult Catholic students. *Journal of Clinical Psychology* **36**(3):752–757.

Pomerantz, S. C. (1979). Sex differences in relative importance of self-esteem, physical self-satisfaction, and identity in predicting adolescent satisfaction. *Journal of Youth and Adolescence* **8**:51–61.

Pond, M. (1982). *The valley girls' guide to life.* New York: Dell.

Poole, M. E. (1984). The schools adolescents would like. *Adolescence* **19**(74):447–458.

Porter, H., and Taylor, N. (1972). *How to assess the moral reasoning of students.* Toronto: Ontario Institute for Studies in Education.

Postman, N. (1982). *The disappearance of childhood.* New York: Delacorte.

Prerost, F. J. (1980). Developmental aspects of adolescent sexuality as reflected in reactions to sexually explicit humor. *Psychological Reports* **46**(2):543–548.

Prescott, P. (1981). *The child savers.* New York: Alfred A. Knopf.

President Carter's address to the U.S. Congress on drug use (1977). *Drug Survival News,* September–October, p. 6.

Princeton Religious Research Center (1980). *Religion in America, 1979–1980.* Princeton, NJ.

Protinsky, H. O., and Farrier, S. (1980). Self-image changes in preadolescents and adolescents. *Adolescence* **15**(60):887–893.

Psathas, G. (1969). Toward a theory of occupational choice for women. *Sociology and Social Research* **52**:252–268.

Public Law 91–230 (1970). *United States Statutes at Large,* Vol. 84, p. 177.

Purcell, K., and Weiss, J. H. (1971). Emotions and asthma: Assessment and treatment. In C. G. Costello (ed.), *Symptoms of psychopathology.* New York: Wiley.

Quay, H. C.. and Werry, J. S. (1979). *Psychopathological disorders of childhood* (2nd ed.). New York: Wiley.

Rachal, J.V. (1975). *A national study of adolescent drinking behavior, attitudes, and correlates.* Research Triangle Park, NC: Research Triangle Institute.

Rachal, J. V.; Maisto, S. A.; Guess, L. L., and Hubbard, R. L. (1983). Alcohol use among adolescents. *Alcohol consumption and related problems.* Rockville, MD: National Institute on Drug Abuse.

Raphael, D., and Xelowski, H. G. (1980). Identity status in high school students: Critique and a revised paradigm. *Journal of Youth and Adolescence* **9**(5):383–389.

Raschke, H. J., and Raschke, V. J. (1979). Family conflict and children's self concepts: A comparison of intact and single-parent families. *Journal of Marriage and the Family* **41**:367–374.

Raths, L. E.; Harmin, M.; and Simon, S. B. (1966). *Values and teaching.* Columbus, OH: Charles E. Merrill.

Real, M. R. (1977). *Mass mediated culture.* Englewood Cliffs, NJ: Prentice-Hall.

Redfering, D. L., and Cook, D. (1980). Relationship among vocational training, income, and job complexity of high school dropouts and high school graduates. *Journal of Vocational Behavior* **16**:158–162.

Rees, C. D., and Wilborn, B. L. (1983). Correlates of drug abuse in adolescents: A comparison of families of drug abusers with families of nondrug abusers. *Journal of Youth and Adolescence,* **12**(1):55–63.

Reimer, J. (1977). A structural theory of moral development. *Theory into Practice* **16**(2):60–66.

Reimer, J.; Paolitto, D. P.; and Hersh, R. H. (1983). *Promoting moral growth from Piaget to Kohlberg.* New York: Longman.

Reinhard, D. W. (1977). The reaction of adolescent boys and girls to the divorce of their parents. *Journal of Clinical Child Psychology* **6**(2):21–23.

Reinhart, T., and Tate, S. (1983). Class of 83: What your kids won't tell you about high school today. *Ladies' Home Journal,* June, pp. 98–99, 136–140.

Renwick, P. A., and Lawler, E. E. (1978). What you really want from your job. *Psychology Today,* May, 53–65.

Report of the National Commission on Marijuana and Drug Abuse (1972). Washington, DC: U.S. Government Printing Office.

Resnick, H. L. P. (1980). Suicide. In H. I. Kaplan, A. M. Freedman, and B. J. Sadock (eds.), *Comprehensive textbook of psychiatry* (Vol. 2, pp. 2085–2097). Baltimore: Williams & Wilkins.

Rest, J. R. (1976). New approaches in the assessment of moral judgment. In T. Lickona (ed.), *Moral development and behavior.* New York: Holt, Rinehart & Winston.

Rest, J. R.; Davison, M. L.; and Robbins, S. (1978). Age trends in judging moral issues: A review of cross-sectional, longitudinal, and sequential studies of the Defining Issues Test. *Child Development* **49**:263–279.

Reyes, F., and Meyer, S. (1981). *Peer counseling: New directions — program and evaluation, the Medgar Evers College Experience.* Paper presented at the Annual Meeting of the American Personnel and Guidance Association, April 13, St. Louis, MO.

Reynolds, C. R., and Torrance, E. P. (1978). Perceived change in styles of learning and thinking (hemisphericity) through direct and indirect training. *Journal of Creative Behavior* **12**(4):247–252.

Reynolds, D. J. (1976). Adjustment and maladjustment. In J. F. Adams (ed.), *Understanding adolescence* (3rd ed.). Boston: Allyn and Bacon.

Reynolds, J. (1977). Two hundred years of children's recreation. In E. H. Grotberg (ed.), *200 years of children* (DHEW Publication No. OHD 77–30103). Washington, DC: U.S. Government Printing Office.

Rice, B. (1976). Honor thy father Moon. *Psychology Today* **10** (June), p. 36.

Rice, F. P. (1981). *The adolescent: Development, relationships and culture* (3rd ed.). Boston: Allyn and Bacon.

Richardson, M. S. (1975). Self-concept and role concepts in the career orientation of college women. *Journal of Counseling Psychology* **22**:122–126.

Riegel, K. F. (1973). Dialectical operations: The final period of cognitive development. *Human Development* **16**:346–370.

Riegel, K. F. (1976). The dialectics of human development. *American Psychologist* **31**:689–700.

Riesman, D. (1961). *The Lonely Crowd.* New Haven, CT: Yale University.

Rigsby, L. C., and McDill, E. L. (1972). Adolescent peer influence processes: Conceptualization and measurement. *Social Science Research* **1**:305–321.

Ritvo, S. (1976). Adolescent to woman. *Journal of the American Psychoanalytic Association* **24**:127–138.

Roberge, J. J., and Flexer, B. K. (1982). The formal operational reasoning test. *The Journal of General Psychology* **106**(1):61–67.

Robertson, J. F. (1976). Significance of grandparents: Perceptions of young adult children. *Gerontologist* **16**:137–140.

Robinson, P. A. (1978). Parents of "beyond control" adolescents. *Adolescence* **13**:109–119.

Roff, M.; Sells, S. B.; and Golden, M. M. (1972). *Social adjustment and personality development in children.* Minneapolis: University of Minnesota.

Rogers, C. R. (1961). *On becoming a person: A therapist's view of psychotherapy.* Boston: Houghton Mifflin.

Roll, S., and Millen, L. (1979). The friend as represented in the dreams of late adolescents: Friendship without rose colored glasses. *Adolescence* **14**(54):255–275.

Roosa, M. W.; Fitzgerald, H. E.; and Carson, N. A. (1982). Teenage and older mothers and their infants: A descriptive comparison. *Adolescence* **17**(65):1–17.

Rosenberg, B. G., and Sutton-Smith, B. (1964). Ordinal position and sex-role identification. *Genetic Psychology Monographs* **70**:297–328.

Rosenberg, F. R., and Rosenberg, M. (1978). Self-esteem and delinquency. *Journal of Youth and Adolescence* **7**:279–291.

Rosenberg, M. (1965). *Society and the adolescent self-image.* Princeton, NJ: Princeton University Press.

Rosenthal, D. A., and Conway, M. (1980). Adolescents' creativity and non-conformity in school. *Psychological Reports* **47**(2):668.

Rosenthal, D. A.; Gurney, R. M.; and Moore, S. M. (1981). From trust to intimacy: A new inventory for examining Erikson's stages of psychosocial development. *Journal of Youth and Adolescence* **10**(6):525–537.

Rosenthal, R., and Jacobson, L. (1968). *Pygmalion in the classroom: Teacher expectation and pupils' intellectual development.* New York: Holt, Rinehart & Winston.

Ross, A. O. (1979). *Psychological disorders of children: A behavioral approach to theory, research, and therapy* (2nd ed.). New York: McGraw-Hill.

Ross, D. (1972). *G. Stanley Hall: The psychologist as prophet.* Chicago: The University of Chicago.

Rotter, J. B. (1971). Who rules you? External control and internal control. *Psychology Today* **5**:37–42.

Rowe, I., and Marcia, J. E. (1980). Ego identity status, formal operations, and moral development. *Journal of Youth and Adolescence* **9**(2):87–99.

Rubin, A. M. (1977). Television usage, attitudes, and viewing behaviors of children and adolescents. *Journal of Communication* **21**:355–369.

Ruby, T., and Law, R. (1982). School dropouts — they are not what they seem to be. *Children and Youth Services Review* **4**(3):279–291.

Runyan, W. M. (1980). The life-satisfaction chart: Perceptions of the course of subjective experience. *International Journal of Aging and Human Development* **11**(1):45–64.

Rust, J. O., and Lloyd, M. W. (1982). Sex-role attitudes and preferences of junior high school age adolescents. *Adolescence* **17**(65):37–43.

Rutter, M., & Giller, H. (1983). *Juvenile delinquency: Trends and prospects.* Baltimore: Penguin Books.

Rutter, M.; Graham, P.; Chadwick, O.; and Yule, W. (1976). Adolescent turmoil: Fact or fiction? *Journal of Child Psychology and Psychiatry* **17**:35–56.

Rutter, M.; Maughan, B.; Mortimore, P.; and Ouston, J. (1979). *Fifteen thousand hours: Secondary schools and their effects on children.* Cambridge, MA: Harvard University Press.

Ryan, K. (1980). *Biting the apple: Accounts of first year teachers.* New York: Longman.

Saltzstein, H. D. (1978). Social influence and moral development: A perspective on the role of parents and peers. In T. Lickona (ed.), *Moral development and behavior: Theory, research, and social issues.* New York: Holt, Rinehart & Winston.

Santrock, J. W., and Tracy, R. L. (1978). The effects of children's family-structure status on the development of stereotypes by teachers. *Journal of Educational Psychology* **70**:754–757.

Sarason, I. G., and Spielberger, C. D. (eds.) (1975). *Stress and anxiety.* Washington, DC: Hemisphere Publishing.

Sarri, R. (1976). Juvenile law: How it penalizes females. In L. Crites (ed.), *The female offender: An anthology.* Lexington, MA: Lexington Books.

Satir, V. M. (1972). *Peoplemaking.* Palo Alto, CA: Science & Behavior Books.

Satir, V. M. (1983). *Conjoint family therapy* (3rd ed.). Palo Alto, CA: Science & Behavior Books.

Saucier, J. F., and Ambert, A. M. (1983). Parental marital status and adolescents' health-risk behavior. *Adolescence* **18**(70):403–411.

Scanzoni, J., and Fox, G. L. (1980). Sex roles, family and society: The seventies and beyond. *Journal of Marriage and the Family* **42**(4):743–756.

Schab, F. (1980). Cheating in high school: Differences between the sexes (revisited). *Adolescence* **15**(60):959–965.

Schachter, R. J.; Pantel, E. S.; Glassman, G. M.; and Zweibelson, I. (1971). Acne vulgaris and psychological impact on high school students. *New York State Journal of Medicine* **71**:2886–2890.

Schacter, S. (1971). *Emotion, obesity, and crime.* New York: Academic Press.

Schafer, W. E.; Olexa, C.; and Park, K. (1972). Programmed for social class:

Tracking in high school. In K. Park and W. E. Schafer (eds.), *Schools and delinquency.* Englewood Cliffs, NJ: Prentice-Hall.

Scharf, P. (1977). Moral development and democratic schooling. *Theory into Practice* **16**(2):89–96.

Schlesinger, B., and Stasiuk, E. (1972). Children of divorced parents in second marriages. In I. R. Stuart and L. E. Abt (eds.), *Children of separation and divorce.* New York: Grossman.

Schmiedeck, R. A. (1979). Adolescent identity formation and the organizational structure of high schools. *Adolescence* **14**:191–196.

Schmitt, N., and Mellon, P. M. (1980). Life and job satisfaction: Is the job central? *Journal of Vocational Behavior* **16**(1):51–58.

Schneider, S. (1982). Helping adolescents deal with pregnancy: A psychiatric approach. *Adolescence* **17**(66):286–292.

Schoo, P. H. (1970. *Students' self-concept, social behavior, and attitudes toward school in middle and junior high schools.* Unpublished doctoral dissertation, University of Michigan.

Schowalter, J. E. (1983).Eating disorders: Introduction. *Journal of the American Academy of Child Psychiatry* **22**(2):97–98.

Schrut, A. (1968). Some typical patterns in the behavior and background of adolescent girls who attempt suicide. *American Journal of Psychiatry* **125**:69–74.

Schwarz, J. C. (1979). Childhood origins of psychopathology. *American Psychologist* **34**:879–885.

Sears, P. S., and Sherman, V. (1964). *In pursuit of self-esteem.* Belmont, CA: Wadsworth.

Sebald, H. (1981). Adolescents' concept of popularity and unpopularity, comparing 1960 and 1976. *Adolescence* **16**(61):187–193.

Seligman, M. (1975). *Helplessness.* New York: N. H. Freeman.

Sewall, G. T. (1982). Against anomie and amnesia: What basic education means in the eighties. *Phi Delta Kappan* **63**(9):603–607.

Shapiro, B. Z. (1977). Friends and helpers: When ties dissolve. *Small Group Behavior* **8**(4):469–478.

Shatin, L. (1981). Psychopathogenic abuses of music in hospitals. *Interaction* **4**(1 and 2):61–68.

Shavelson, R. J.; Hubner, J. J.; and Stanton, G. C. (1976). Self-concept: Validation of construct interpretations. *Review of Educational Research* **46**(3):407–441.

Shaw, M. E., and White, D. L. (1965). The relationship between child-parent identification and academic achievement. *Journal of Clinical Psychology* **21**:10–13.

Sheehy, G. (1976). *Passages: Predictable crises of adult life.* New York: E. P. Dutton.

Shephard, R. (1975). Juvenile delinquency and the juvenile court after 75 years. Unpublished paper.

Sherif, M. (1951). Experimental study of intergroup relations. In J. H. Rohrer and M. Sherif (eds.), *Social psychology at the crossroads* (pp. 388–426). New York: Harper & Row.

Sherif, M. (1966). *In common predicament: Social psychology of intergroup conflict and cooperation.* Boston: Houghton Mifflin.

Sherif, M.; Harvey, O. J.; White, B. J.; Hood, W. R.; and Sherif, C. W. (1961). *Intergroup conflict and cooperation: The robbers cave experiment.* Norman, OK: Institute of Group Relations, University of Oklahoma.

Sherif, M., and Sherif, C. W. (1964). *Reference groups: Exploration into conformity and deviation of adolescents.* New York: Harper.

Shlechter, T. M., and Gump, P. V. (1983). Car availability and the daily life of the teenage male. *Adolescence* **18**(69):101–113.

Showalter, E. (1974). Women and the literary curriculum. In J. Stacey and B. J. Daniels (eds.), *And Jill came tumbling after: Sexism in American education.* New York: Dell.

Shulman, S., and Klein, M. M. (1982). The family and adolescence: A conceptual and experimental approach. *Journal of Adolescence* **5**:219–234.

Siegfried, W. D.; Macfarlane, I.; Graham, D. B.; Moore, N. A.; and Young, P. L. (1981). A reexamination of sex differences in job preferences. *Journal of Vocational Behavior* **18**(1):30–42.

Silberman, C. (1970). *Crisis in the classroom.* New York: Random House.

Silverstein, C. (1977). *A family matter.* New York: McGraw-Hill.

Simkins, L. (1984). Consequences of teenage pregnancy and motherhood. *Adolescence* **19**(73):39–54.

Simmons, R.; Rosenberg, F.; and Rosenberg, M. (1973). Disturbance in the self-image at adolescence. *American Sociological Review* **38**:553–568.

Simon, S. B.; Howe, L. W.; and Kirschenbaum, H. (1972). *Values clarification.* New York: Hart.

Simon, W.; Gagnon, J. H.; and Buff, S. A. (1972). Son of Joe: Continuity and change among white working class adolescents. *Journal of Youth and Adolescence* **1**(1):13–34.

Simonds, J. F., and Kashani, J. (1979). Phencyclidine use in delinquent males committed to a training school. *Adolescence* **14**:721–725.

Simpson, R. L. (1962). Parental influence, anticipatory socialization, and social mobility. *American Sociological Review* **27**:517–522.

Singer, M., and Isralowitz, R. (1983). Probation: A model for coordinating youth services. *Juvenile and Family Court Journal* **34**(1):35–41.

Singh, B. K. (1980). Trends in attitudes toward premarital sexual relations. *Journal of Marriage and the Family* **42**(2):387–393.

Singh, R. P. (1981). Creativity in relation to adjustment. *Psychological Studies* **26**(2):84–85.

Single, E.; Kandel, D., and Faust, R. (1974). Patterns of multiple drug use in high school. *Journal of Health and Social Behavior* **15**:344–357.

Siomopoulos, G. (1980). On a disturbance of affectivity in schizophrenic adolescents: Implications for affect theory. *Adolescence* **15**(57):123–142.

Sistrunk, F., and McDavid, J. W. (1971). Sex variable in conforming behavior. *Journal of Personality and Social Psychology* **17**:200–207.

Sizer, T. R. (1983). High school reform: The need for engineering. *Phi Delta Kappan,* **64**(7):679–683.

Sjoberg, H.; Ohlsson, M., and Dornic, S. (1975). *Physical fitness, work load and mental performance* (April, Report No. 444). Stockholm: Department of Psychology, University of Stockholm.

Skinner, B. F. (1971). *Beyond freedom and dignity.* New York: Knopf.

Skipper, J. K., and Nass, G. (1966). Dating behavior: A framework for analysis and an illustration. *Journal of Marriage and the Family* **28**:412–420.

Skolnick, A. (1978). *The intimate environment: Exploring marriage and family* (2nd ed.). Boston: Little, Brown.

Small, A.; Teagno, L.; and Selz, K. (1980). The relationship of sex role to physical and psychological health. *Journal of Youth and Adolescence* **9**(4):305–314.

Smart, M. S., and Smart, R. C. (1973). *Adolescents, development and relationships.* New York: Macmillan.

Smith, B. (1976). Adolescent and parent: Interaction between developmental stages. *The Center Quarterly Focus,* Fall. St. Paul: University of Minnesota.

Smith, D. E.; Wesson, D. R.; and Seymour, R. B. (1979). The abuse of barbiturates and other sedative-hypnotics. In R. I. Dupont, A. Goldstein, and J. O'Donnell (eds.), *Handbook on drug abuse.* Washington, DC: U.S. Government Printing Office.

Smith, D. F. (1980). Adolescent suicide. In R. E. Muuss (ed.), *Adolescent behavior and society* (3rd ed.). New York: Random House.

Smith, E. J. (1981). Adolescent drug abuse and alocholism: Directions for the school and family. *Urban Education* **16**(3):311–332.

Smith, G. M. (1980). Relations between personality and smoking behavior in preadult subjects. In R. E. Muuss (ed.), *Adolescent behavior and society: A book of readings.* New York: Random House.

Smith, G. M., and Fogg, C. P. (1978). Psychological predictors of early use, late use, and nonuse of marijuana among teenage students. In D. B. Kandel (ed.), *Longitudinal research on drug use: Empirical findings and methodological issues.* Washington, DC: Hemisphere.

Smith, P. B.; Nenney, S. W.; Weinman, M. L.; and Mumford, D. M. (1982). Factors affecting perception of pregnancy risk in the adolescent. *Journal of Youth and Adolescence* **11**(3):207–214.

Smith, S. L. (1981). *No easy answers: The learning disabled child at home and school.* Cambridge, MA: Winthrop.

Smith, T. E. (1976). Push versus pull: Intra-family versus peer-group variables on possible determinants of adolescent orientations towards parents. *Youth and Society* **8**:5–26.

Smith, W. C. (1983). Contemporary child saving: A study of juvenile justice decision-making. *Juvenile and Family Court Journal* **34**(1):63–74.

Smoking and health: A report of the Surgeon General (1979). Washington, DC: U.S. Government Printing Office.

Snarey, J. (1982). *The moral development of Kibbutz founders and Sabras: A cross-cultural study* (Doctoral dissertation, Howard University).

Snyder, E. E. (1972). High school student perceptions of prestige criteria. *Adolescence* **7**:129–136.

Solomon, R. W., and Whalen, R. G. (1973). Peer reinforcement control of classroom problem behavior. *Journal of Applied Behavior Analysis* **6**:49–56.

Sours, J. (1979). The primary anorexia nervosa syndrome. In J. Noshpitz (ed.), *Basic handbook of child psychiatry.* New York: Basic Books.

Spacks, P. M. (1981). *The adolescent idea: Myths of youth and the adult imagination.* New York: Basic Books.

Spence, J. T., and Helmreich, R. L. (1978). *Masculinity and femininity: Their psychological dimensions, correlates and antecedents.* Austin: University of Texas.

Sperry, R. W. (1973). Lateral specialization of cerebral function in the surgically separated hemispheres. In F. J. McGuigan and R. A. Schoonover (eds.), *The psychophysiology of thinking,* pp. 209–229). New York: Academic Press.

Spitzer, R. L.; Skodol, A. E.; Gibbon, M.; and Williams, J. B. W. (1981). *DSM-III case book.* New York: American Psychiatric Association.

Spranger, E. (1955). *Psychologie dus iugendalters* (24th ed.). Heidelberg: Quelle & Meyer.

Sprinthall, N. A. (1976). Learning psychology by doing psychology. In G. D. Miller (ed.), *Developmental education.* St. Paul: Minnesota Department of Education.

Srebalus, D. J.; Marinelli, R. P.; and Messing, J. K. (1982). *Career development: Concepts and procedures.* Monterey, CA: Brooks-Cole.

Staffieri, J. R. (1972). Body build and behavioral expectancies in young females. *Developmental Psychology* **6**:125–227.

Stahmann, R. F.; Hanson, G. R.; and Whittlesey, R. R. (1973). Parent and student perceptions of influences on college choices. *National Association of College Admissions Counselors Journal* **16**(2):21–22.

Stanton, M. (1975). Pupil's assessments of social action; A cross-cultural study. *Educational Review* **27**(2):126–137.

Stanton, M. (1980). Moral judgments among students: a cross-cultural study. *Adolescence* **15**(57):231–241.

Steele, C. I. (1974). Obese adolescent girls: Some diagnostic and treatment considerations. *Adolescence* **9**:81–96.

Stein, S. L., and Weston, L. C. (1982). College women's attitudes toward women and identity achievement. *Adolescence* **17**(68):895–899.

Steinberg, L. D.; Greenberger, E.; Garduque, L.; Ruggiero M.; and Vaux, A. (1982). Effects of working on adolescent development. *Developmental Psychology* **18**(3):385–395.

Steinberg, L. D., and Hill, J. P. (1978). Patterns of family interaction as a function of age, the onset of puberty, and formal thinking. *Developmental Psychology* **14**:683–684.

Steinhausen, H. C. (1981). Chronically ill and handicapped children and adolescents: Personality studies in relation to disease. *Journal of Abnormal Child Psychology* **9**(2):291–297.

Stevens, S. H. (1980). *The learning disabled child: Ways that parents can help.* Winston-Salem, NC: John F. Blair.

Stickle, G. (1975). Pregnancy in adolescence: Scope of the problem. *Contemporary OB/GYN* **5**:85–91.

Stinchcombe, A.L. (1964). *Rebellion in a high school.* Chicago: Quadrangle Books.

Stipek, D. (1981). Adolescents — too young to earn, too old to learn? Compulsory school attendance and intellectual development. *Journal of Youth and Adolescence* **10**(2):113–139.

Stoner, C., and Parke, J. (1977). *All God's children.* Radnor, PA: Chilton.

Story, M. (1982). A comparison of university student experience with various sexual outlets in 1974 and 1980. *Adolescence* **17**(68):737–747.

Stott, D. (1982). *Delinquency: The problem and its prevention.* New York: SP Medical and Scientific Books.

Strain, P. S. (ed.) (1981). *The utilization of classroom peers as behavior change agents.* New York: Plenum.

Strommen, M. P. (1974). *Five cries of youth.* New York: Harper & Row.

Strother, S. G. (1983). Survey points up sexually active females. *The Commonwealth Times* **15**(15):1.

Stumphauzer, J. S. (1980). Learning to drink: Adolescents and alcohol. *Addictive Behaviors* **5**:277–283.

Stunkard, A. J. (1980). Obesity. In H. I. Kaplan, A. M. Freedman, and B. J. Sadock (eds.), *Comprehensive textbook of psychiatry* (Vol. 3, pp. 1872–1882). Baltimore: Williams & Wilkins.

Suchner, R. (1979). Sex ratios and occupational prestige: Three failures to replicate a sexist bias. *Personality and Social Psychology Bulletin* **5**:236–239.

Suedfeld, P. (1967). Paternal absence and overseas success of Peace Corps volunteers. *Journal of Consulting Psychology* **31**:424–425.

Sullivan, H. S. (1953a). *Conceptions of modern psychiatry.* New York: Norton.

Sullivan, H. S. (1953b). *The interpersonal theory of psychiatry.* New York: Norton.

Sullivan, K. and Sullivan, A. (1980) Adolescent-parent separation. *Developmental Psychology* **16**:93–99.

Sundberg, N. D.; Sharma, V.; Wodtli, T.; and Rohila, P. (1969). Family cohesiveness and autonomy of adolescents in India and the United States. *Journal of Marriage and the Family* **31**:403–407.

Super, D. E. (1957). *The psychology of careers.* New York: Harper & Row.

Super, D. E. (1974). *Measuring vocational maturity for counseling and evaluation.* Washington, DC: National Vocational Guidance Association.

Super, D. E. (1980). A life-span life-space approach to career development. *Journal of Vocational Behavior* **16**(3):282–298.

Sussman, M. (1977). Family life of old people. In R. H. Binstock and E. Shanas (eds.), *Handbook of aging and the social sciences.* New York: Van Nostrand/Reinhold.

Sutherland, J. C., and Siniawsky, S. J. (1982). The treatment and resolution of moral violations on soap operas. *Journal of Communication* **32**(2):67–74.

Sutton-Smith, B.; Roberts, J. M.; and Rosenberg, B. G. (1964). Sibling associations and role involvement. *Merrill-Palmer Quarterly on Behavioral Development* **10**:25–38.

Sutton-Smith, B., and Rosenberg, B. G. (1970). *The sibling.* New York: Holt, Rinehart & Winston.

Svobodny, L. A. (1982). Biographical, self-concept and educational factors among chemically dependent adolescents. *Adolescence* **17**(68):847–853.

Swanson, R. B.; Massey, R. H.; and Payne, I. R. (1972). Ordinal position, family size, and personal adjustment. *Journal of Psychology* **81**:53–58.

Tanner, J. M. (1961). *Education and physical growth: Implications of the study of children's growth for educational theory and practice.* London: University Press.

Tanner, J. M. (1975). Sequence, tempo and individual variation in the growth and development of boys and girls aged twelve to sixteen. In R. E. Grinder (ed.), *Studies in adolescence* (pp. 502–522). New York: Macmillan.

Tara, S. N. (1981). Sex differences in creativity among early adolescents in India. *Perceptual an Motor Skills* **52**(3):959–962.

Terkel, S. (1974). *Working.* New York: Random House.

Thomas, S., and Callahan, B. P. (1982). Allocating happiness: TV families and social class. *Journal of Communication* **32**(3):184–190.

Thompson, T. (1981). The development of communication skills in physically handicapped children. *Human Communication Research* **7**:312–324.

Three national assessments of reading: Changes in performance 1970–1980 (1981). Denver, CO: National Assessment of Educational Progress.

Tiedeman, D. V., and O'Hara, R. P. (1963). *Career development: Choice and adjustment.* Princeton, NJ: College Entrance Examination Board.

Time (1980). June 16, pp. 54–63.

Tobias, S. (1976). Math anxiety. *Ms.* **5**:56–59.

Toepfer, C. F. (1980) Brain growth periodization data: Some suggestions for rethinking middle grades education. *High School Journal* **63**(6):222–227.

Toffler, A. (1980). *The third wave.* New York: William Morrow.

Tolbert, E. L. (1980). *Counseling for career development* (2nd ed.). Boston: Houghton Mifflin.

Toman, W. (1970). Birth order rules all. *Psychology Toay,* December, pp. 45–49, 68–69.

Torrance, E. P., and Horng, R. (1980). Creativity and style of learning and thinking characteristics of adaptors and innovators. *Creative Child and Adult Quarterly* **5**(2):80–85.

Torrance, E. P., and Myers, R. F. (1970). *Creative learning and teaching.* New York: Harper & Row.

Torres, A. (1978). Does your mother know? *Family Planning Perspectives* **10**:280–282.

Tramontana, M. G. (1980). Critical review of research on psychotherapy outcome with adolescents: 1967–1977. *Psychological Bulletin* **88**:429–450.

Travis, G. (1976). *Chronic illness in children: Its impact on child and family.* Stanford, CA: Stanford University.

Treagust, D. F. (1982). Development of Piagetian infralogical groupings in high school students. *The Journal of Genetic Psychology* **14**(1):119–130.

Trickett, E., and Moos, R. (1974). Personal correlates of contrasting environments: Student satisfaction in high school classrooms. *American Journal of Community Psychology* **2**:1–12.

Trotter, S. (1976). Zajonc defuses I.Q. debate: Birth order work wins prize. *APA Monitor* **7**(5):1, 10.

Tudor, C. G.; Petersen, D. M.; and Elifson, K. W. (1980). An examination of the relationship between peer and parental influence and adolescent drug use. *Adolescence* **16**(60):783–798.

Turiel, E. (1966). An experiment test of the sequentiality of developmental stages in the child's moral judgments. *Journal of Personality and Social Psychology* **3**:611–618.

Turner, R. (1972). some aspects of women's ambitions. In R. M. Pavalko (ed.), *Sociological perspectives on occupations* (pp. 295–316). Itasca, IL: Peacock.

Tyerman, A., and Humphrey, M. (1983). Life stress, family support and adolescent disturbance. *Journal of Adolescence* **6**:1–12.

Tyler, R. (1983). A place called school. *Phi Delta Kappa* **64**(7):462–464.

Uniform crime reports for the United States, 1975 (1976, 1977, 1980). Washington, DC: U.S. Government Printing Office.

U.S. Bureau of the Census (1978). *School enrollment — social and economic characteristics of students: October, 1976* (Current Population Reports, Series P–20, No. 319, February). Washington, DC: U.S. Government Printing Office.

U.S. Bureau of the Census (1980a). *Current population reports, 1980.* Washington, DC: U.S. Government Printing Office.

U.S. Bureau of the Census (1980b). *Social indicators.* Washington, DC: U.S. Government Printing Office.

U.S. Bureau of the Census (1980c). *Statistical abstract of the United States: 1980* (101st ed.). Washington, DC: U.S. Government Printing Office.

U.S. Bureau of the Census (1981). *Statistical abstract of the United States: 1981* (102nd ed.). Washington, DC: U.S. Government Printing Office.

Urberg, K. A. (1982). A theoretical framework for studying adolescent contraceptive use. *Adolescence* **17**(67):527–540.

Urberg, K., and Robbins, R. L. (1981). Adolescents' perceptions of the costs and benefits associated with cigarette smoking: Sex differences and peer influence. *Journal of Youth and Adolescence* **10**(5):353–361.

Vaillant, G. E. 1977). *Adaptation to life.* Boston: Little, Brown.

Vaillant, G. E., and Perry, J. C. (1980). Personality disorders. In H. I. Kaplan, A. M. Freedman, and B. J. Sadock (eds.), *Comprehensive textbook of psychiatry* (Vol. 2, pp. 1562–1590). Baltimore: Williams & Wilkins.

Vedder, C., and Sommerville, D. (1970). *The delinquent girl.* Springfield: Charles C. Thomas.

Verney, T., and Kelly, J. (1981). *The secret life of the unborn child.* New York: Dell.

Versluys, H. P. (1980). Physical rehabilitation and family dynamics. *Rehabilitation Literature* **41**(3–4):58–65.

Vigersky, R. A. (ed.). (1977). *Anorexia nervosa.* New York: Raven Press.

Vincenzi, H. (1977). Minimizing occupational stereotypes. *The Vocational Guidance Quarterly* **25**:165–268.

Violent schools — safe schools: The safe school study report to the Congress: Executive summary (1979). In R. Rubel (ed.), *Crime and disruption in schools.* Washington, DC: U.S. Department of Justice, National Institute of Law Enforcement and Criminal Justice, U.S. Superintendent of Documents.

Vockell, E. L., and Asher, J. W. (1972). Dating frequency among high school seniors. *Psychological Reports* **31**:381–382.

Voss, H. L.; Wendling, A.; and Elliot, D. S. (1966). Some types of high-school dropouts. *Journal of Educational Research* **59**:363–368.

Walberg, H. J.; House, E.R.; and Steele, J. M. (1973). Grade level, cognition, and affect: A cross-section of classroom perceptions. *Journal of Educational Psychology* **64**:142–146.

Walker, L. J. (1980). Cognitive and perspective-taking prerequisites for moral development. *Child Development* **51**:131–139.

Walker, L. J., and Richards, B. S. (1979). Stimulating transition in moral reasoning as a function of stage of cognitive development. *Developmental Psychology* **15**:95–103.

Wallerstein, J. S., and Kelly, J. B. (1974). The effects of parental divorce: The adolescent experience. In E. J. Anthony and C. Koupernik (eds.), *The child in his family: Children of psychiatric risk* (Vol. 3, pp. 479–505). New York: John Wiley.

Ware, M. (1980). Antecendents of educational/career preferences and choices. *Journal of Vocational Behavior* **16**(3):312–319.

Warren, M. (1982). *Youth in the future of the church*. New York: Seabury Press.

Washington Post (1980, October 5). Children and drugs (p. 1).

Waterman, A. S. (1982). Identity development from adolescence to adulthood: An extension of theory and a review of research. *Developmental Psychology* **18**(3):341–358.

Waterman, A. S., and Goldman, J. A. (1976). A longitudinal study of ego identity development at a liberal arts college. *Journal of Youth and Adolescence* **5**(4):361–369.

Waterman, C. K., and Nevid, J. S. (1977). Sex differences in the resolution of the identity crisis. *Journal of Youth and Adolescence* **6**:337–342.

Weatherford, R. R., and Horrocks, J. E. (1967). Peer acceptance and under- and over-achievement in school. *Journal of Psychology* **66**:215–220.

Weatherley, D. (1975). Self-perceived rate of physical maturation and personality in late adolescence. In R. E. Grinder (ed.), *Studies in adolescence* (pp. 522–536). New York: Macmillan.

Wechsler, D. (1958). *The measurement and appraisal of adult intelligence* (4th ed.). Baltimore: Williams & Wilkins.

Weeks, M. O.; Wise, G. W.; and Duncan, C. (1984). The relationship between sex-role attitudes and career orientations of high school females and their mothers. *Adolescence* **19**(75):595–608.

Wegner, D. M., and Vallacher, R. R. (1977). *Implicit psychology: An introduction to social cognition*. New York: Oxford University Press.

Weiner, I. B. (1970). *Psychological disturbance in adolescence.* New York: Wiley.

Weiner, I. B. (1980). Psychopathology in adolescence. In J. Adelson (ed.), *Handbook of the psychology of adolescence.* New York: Wiley.

Weiner, I. B., and Elkind, D. (1972). *Child development: A core approach.* New York: Wiley.

Weinrach, H. (1974). The structure of moral reason. *Journal of Youth and Adolescence* 3(2):135–143.

Weinstein, G., and Fantini, M. D. (eds.). (1970). *Toward humanistic education: A curriculum of affect.* New York: Praeger.

Weinstein, G.; Hardin, J.; and Weinstein, M. (1976). *Education of the self.* Amherst, MA: Mandala.

Weisfeld, G. E.; Bloch, S. A.; and Ivers, J. W. (1983). A factor analytic study of peer-perceived dominance in adolescent boys. *Adolescence* 18(70):229–243.

Weishaar, M. E.; Green, B. J.; and Craighead, L. W. (1981). Primary influences of initial vocational choices for college women. *Journal of Vocational Behavior* 18(1):67–78.

Weiss, R. J. (1982). Understanding moral thought: Effects on moral reasoning and decision-making. *Developmental Psychology* 18(6):852–861.

Weissman, M. M., and Klerman, G. L. (1977). Sex differences and the epidemiology of depression. *Archives of General Psychiatry* 34:98–111.

Weller, L. (1974). Birth order and marital bliss in Israel. *Journal of Marriage and the Family* 36:794–797.

Wells, K. (1980). Gender-role identity and psychological adjustment in adolescence. *Journal of Youth and Adolescence* 9(1):59–73.

Wesson, D. R., and Smith, D. E. (1979). Treatment of the poly-drug abuser, In R. I. Dupont, A. Goldstein, J. O'Donnell (eds.), *Handbook on drug abuse.* Washington, DC: U.S. Government Printing Office.

West, D. J., and Farrington, D. P. (1977). *The delinquent way of life.* London: Heinemann.

Westbrook, B. W., and Parry-Hill, J. W. (1973). The measurement of cognitive vocational maturity. *Journal of Vocational Behavior* 3:239–252.

Westley, W. A., and Elkin, F. (1969). The protective environment and adolescent socialization. In M. Gold and E. Douvan (eds.), *Adolescent development: Readings in research and theory* (pp. 158–164). Boston: Allyn and Bacon.

White, C. B.; Bushnell, N.; and Regnemer, J. L. (1978). Moral development in Bahamian school children: A 3-year examination of Kohlberg's stages of moral development. *Development Psychology* 14(1):58–65.

White, M.; Crino, M.; and De Sanctis, G. (1981). The effects of additional women on ratings of prestige and desirability. *Personality and Social Psychology Bulletin* 7:588–592.

Whiteside, M., and Merriman, G. (1976). Dropouts look at their teachers. *Phi Delta Kappan* **57**:700–702.

Whitley, B. E. (1983). Sex-role orientation and self-esteem: A critical meta-analytic review. *Journal of Personality and Social Psychology* **44**:765–778.

Wilcox, M. M. (1979). *Developmental journey.* Nashville: Abingdon Press.

Wiley, R. E., and Neustadt, R. M. (1982). U.S. communications policy in the new decade. *Journal of Communication* **32**(2):22–32.

Williams, D. A. (1981). Why public schools fail. *Newsweek.* April 20, 62–65.

Williams, E. P. (1967). Sense of obligation to high school activities as related to school size and marginality of student. *Child Development* **38**:1247–1260.

Williams, J. M., and White, K. A. (1983). Adolescent status systems for males and females at three age levels. *Adolescence* **18**(70):381–389.

Wilson, A. N. (1978). *The developmental psychology of the black child.* New York: Africana Research Publications.

Wilson, F. (1980). Psychometric views in the measurement of androgyny. Paper presented at the 1980 Annual Meeting of the American Research Association, Boston, MA, April 11.

Wilson, K.; Zurcher, L. A.; McAdams, D. C.; and Curtis, R. (1975). Stepfathers and stepchildren: An exploratory analysis from two national surveys. *Journal of Marriage and the Family* **37**(3):526–536.

Windmiller, M. (1976). Moral development. In J. F. Adams (ed.), *Understanding adolescence* (3rd ed.). Boston: Allyn and Bacon.

Witkin, H. A. (1954). *Personality through perception.* New York: Harper & Brothers.

Witkin, H. A. (1974). Social conformity and psychological differentiation. *International Journal of Psychology* **9**(1):11–29.

Witkin, H. A. (1977a). Cognitive styles in the educational setting. *New York University Education Quarterly* **8**:14–20.

Witkin, H. A.; Goodenough, D. R.; and Oltman, P. K. (1977b). Role of field-dependent and field-independent cognitive styles in academic evolution: A longitudinal study. *Journal of Educational Psychology* **69**:197–211.

Witkin, H.A., and Moore, C. A. (1975). *Field-dependent and field-independent cognitive styles and their educational implications.* Princeton, NJ: Educational Testing Service.

Wolf, F. M., and Larson, G. L. (1981). On why adolescent formal operators may not be creative thinkers. *Adolescence* **16**(62):345–348.

Wolfe, L. K., and Betz, N. E. (1981). Traditionality of choice and sex-role identification as moderators of the congruence of occupational choice in college women. *Journal of Vocational Behavior* **18**:43–55.

Wolfe, T. (1976). The ''me decade'' and the third great awakening. *New York,* August 23, pp. 26–40.

Wolfgang, M. E. (1978). from boy to man — from delinquency to crime. *Serious youth crime.* Washington, DC: U.S. Government Printing Office.

Women and smoking: Report of the Surgeon General (1980). Washington, DC: U.S. Public Health Service, Department of Health, Education & Welfare.

Wonderly, D. M., and Kupfersmid, J. H. (1980). Promoting postconventional morality: The adequacy of Kohberg's aim. *Adolescence* **15**(59):609–631.

Woodman, N. J., and Lenna, H. R. (1980). *Counseling with gay men and women.* San Francisco: Jossey-Bass.

Woody, G. E., and Blaine, J. (1979). Depression in narcotic addicts. In R. I. Dupont, A. Goldstein, and J. O'Donnell (eds.), *Handbook on drug abuse.* Washington, DC: U.S. Government Printing Office.

Wormack, L. (1980). Sex differences in factorial dimension of verbal, logical, mathematical and visio-spatial ability. *Perceptual and Motor Skills* **50**(2):445–446.

Wright, B. A. (1960). *Physical disability — A psychological approach.* New York: Harper & Row.

Wu, T. (1980). The nature of intelligence. *Acta Psychologica Sinica* **12**(3):259–266.

Wylie, L. (1965). Youth in France and the United States. In E. H. Erikson (ed.), *The challenge of youth.* New York: Doubleday.

Wynne, L. C., and Frader L. (1979). Female adolescence and the family: An historical view. In M. Sugar (ed.), *Female adolescent development.* New York: Brunner/Mazel.

Yongue, I. T.; Todd, R. M.; and Burton, J. K. (1981). The effects of didactic classroom instruction versus field exposure on career maturity. *Journal of Vocational Behavior* **19**(3):369–373.

York, P., and York, D. (1980). *Toughlove: A self-help manual for parents troubled by teenage behavior.* Sellersville, PA: Community Service Foundation.

Young, C. C. (1981). Children as instructional agents for handicapped peers. In P. S. Strain (ed.), *The utilization of classroom peers as behavior change agents.* New York: Plenum.

Young, J. W., and Ferguson, L. R. (1979). Developmental changes through adolescence in the spontaneous nomination of reference groups as a function of decision content. *Journal of Youth and Adolescence* **8**:239–252.

Yussen, S. R. (1977). Characteristics of moral dilemmas written by adolescents. *Developmental Psychology* **13**:162–163.

Zajonc, R. B., and Markus, G. B. (1975). Birth order and intellectual development. *Psychological Review* **82**(1):74–88.

Zakus, G. (1979). A group behavior modification approach to adolescent obesity. *Adolescence* **14**:481–490.

Zeller, W. (1951). Ueber de Entwicklungstypus. *Psychologische rundschau.*

Zeller, W. W. (1970). Adolescent attitudes and cutaneous health. *Journal of School Health* **40**:115–120.

Zelnick, M., and Kantner, J. F. (1972). Sexuality, contraception, and pregnancy among young unwed females in the United States. In F. Westoff and R. Parke (eds.), *Commission on population growth and the American future, research reports, Vol. 1: Demographic and social aspects of population growth* (pp. 355–374). Washington, DC: U.S. Government Printing Office.

Zelnick, M., and Kantner, J. F. (1977). Sexual and contraceptive experience of young unmarried women in the United States, 1976 and 1971. *Family Planning Perspectives* **9**:55–71.

Zelnick, M., and Kantner, J. F. (1979). Sexual activity, contraceptive use and pregnancy among metropolitan-area teenagers: 1971–1979. *Family Planning Perspectives* **12**(5):230–239.

Zeltzer, L. (1980). Psychologic effects of illness in adolescence II: Impact of illness in adolescence — crucial issues and coping styles. *The Journal of Pediatrics* **97**(1):132–138.

Zillmann, D., and Bryant, J. (1982). Pornography, sexual callousness, and the trivialization of rape. *Journal of Communication* **32**(4):10–21.

Zimbardo, P.; Pilkonis, P.; and Norwood, R. (1974). *The silent prison of shyness.* Glenview, IL: Scott, Foresman.

Zimbardo, P., and Ruch, F. L. (1979). *Psychology and life* (10th ed.). Glenview, IL: Scott, Foresman.

Zimring, F. E. (1982). *The changing legal world of adolescence.* New York: The Free Press.

Zinberg, N. E. (1979). Nonaddictive opiate use. In R. I. Dupont, A. Goldstein, and J. O'Donnell (eds.), *Handbook on drug abuse.* Washington, DC: U.S. Government Printing Office.

Zunker, V. G. (1981). *Career counseling: Applied concepts of life planning.* Monterey, CA: Brooks-Cole.

Zytowski, D. G. (1969). Toward a theory of career development for women. *Personnel and Guidance Journal* **47**:660–664.

Zytowski, D. G. (1972). Four hundred years before Parsons. *Personnel and Guidance Journal* **30**:443–450.

Data for diagram based on "Hierarchy of Needs" in *Motivation and Personality,* 2nd edition by Abraham H. Maslow. Copyright © 1970 by Abraham H. Maslow. Reprinted by permission of Harper & Row, Publishers, Inc.

Adapted from *Childhood and Society* by Erik H. Erikson, by permission of W. W. Norton & Company, Inc. and The Hogarth Press Ltd. Copyright © 1950, © 1963 by W. W. Norton & Company, Inc.

Reprinted from *Identity, Youth and Crisis* by Erik H. Erikson, by permission of W. W. Norton & Company, Inc. and Faber and Faber Limited. Copyright © 1968 by W. W. Norton & Company, Inc.

From D. A. Rosenthal, R. M. Gurney, and S. M. Moore, "From Trust to Intimacy: A New Inventory for Examining Erikson's States of Psychosocial Development," *Journal of Youth and Adolescence* 10, no. 6 (1981):535–537. © 1981 by Plenum Publishing Corporation. Reprinted by permission of the publisher and authors.

From Teacher Training in Values Education: A Workshop, © 1976, Guidance Associates, Inc. Reprinted by permission.

From *Working: People Talk about What They Do All Day and How They Feel about What They Do,* by Studs Terkel. Copyright © 1972, 1974 by Studs Terkel. Reprinted by permission of Pantheon Books, a division of Random House, Inc., and Wildwood House Ltd.

From Bureau of Labor Statistics.

From G. Hackett and N. E. Betz, "A Self-Efficacy Approach to the Career Development of Women," *Journal of Vocational Behavior* 18, no. 3 (1981):333. Reprinted by permission of Academic Press and the authors.

Prepared by the California Advisory Commission on the Status of Women, 1972. Reprinted by permission.

From A. J. Miller, "The Emerging School-Based Comprehensive Education Model," presented to the National Conference on Career Education for Deans of Colleges of Education, Columbus, Ohio, April 24–26, 1972. Reprinted by permission of the author.

Reprinted by permission of Richard L. Simpson, Professor of Special Education, University of Kansas.

From "Living with 10- to 15-Year-Olds," A Parent Education Curriculum. © 1984 Center for Early Adolescence, Suite 223, Carr Mill Mall, Carrboro, NC 27510. Reprinted by permission.

From R. L. Spitzer et al. (eds.), *DSM-III Casebook: A Learning Companion to the Diagnostic and Statistical Manual of Mental Disorders,* 3rd ed. (Washington, D.C.: American Psychiatric Association, 1981). Reprinted by permission of the publisher.

From "Children and the Law" by Jerrold K. Footlick. Copyright 1975, Newsweek, Inc. All Rights Reserved. Reprinted by Permission.

Reprinted by permission of the publisher from pages 297, 318, 322–323, 312–313 in *Delinquency: The Problem and Its Prevention* by Denis Stott. Copyright © 1982 Spectrum Publications, Inc., Jamaica, New York.

From D. J. West and D. P. Farrington, *The Delinquent Way of Life,* 1977. Reprinted by permission of Academic Books.

Reprinted courtesy of The Gazette of Goochland.

From A. P. Goldstein, R. P. Sprafkin, N. J. Gershaw, and P. Klein, *Skillstreaming the Adolescent* (Champaign, Ill.: Research Press, 1980). Reprinted by permission of the publisher.

Name Index

Subject Index